echoes

THE COMPLETE HISTORY OF PINK FLOYD

echoes

THE COMPLETE HISTORY OF PINK FLOYD

GLENN POVEY

CHICAGO
REVIEW
PRESS

An A Cappella Book

Echoes: The Complete History of Pink Floyd

Cover and interior design: Bradbury & Williams
Front cover and spine images: Collection of Glenn Povey
Back cover image: M J Kim/Getty Images Entertainment

This edition is reprinted by special arrangement with
Mind Head Publishing

This edition published in 2010 by
Chicago Review Press, Incorporated
814 North Franklin Street
Chicago, Illinois 60610

ISBN 978-1-56976-313-1

Printed in China

5 4 3 2 1

introduction

WHEN PINK FLOYD ANNOUNCED THEY WOULD REUNITE WITH FORMER BANDMATE ROGER WATERS TO PERFORM AT *LIVE 8* IN LONDON IN THE SUMMER OF 2005, THEIR APPEARANCE ALMOST ECLIPSED THE IMPORTANCE OF THE EVENT ITSELF. TO THAT POINT PINK FLOYD WERE STILL LARGELY PERCEIVED AS SOMETHING OF A CULT BAND, THEIR COMBINED PUBLIC ANONYMITY AND INACTIVITY FUELLING THAT PERCEPTION. LIKE THE VAST MAJORITY OF THE AUDIENCE IN ATTENDANCE AT *LIVE 8* I HAD BEEN TOO YOUNG TO SEE THE BAND PERFORM TOGETHER IN ITS 'CLASSIC' LINE-UP (THOUGH I HAD BEEN WRITING ABOUT AND RESEARCHING THE BAND'S HISTORY AND MUSIC FOR 20 YEARS). THIS LONE APPEARANCE DROVE HOME THE IMPACT THIS BAND HAS HAD ON POPULAR CULTURE.

Echoes aims to present a thorough and comprehensive illustrated look at Pink Floyd's professional career as a whole. The narrative sheds new light on their humble beginnings but also explains their enduring appeal whilst the compilation of appearances serves as a reminder of the relentless touring that Pink Floyd had to undertake in their early career in order to build a fan base in the pre-Internet era.

Many readers of this volume will be aware that Pink Floyd gleaned its first flush of real success in the early Seventies with the release of the album *The Dark Side of the Moon*. They had the fledgling American FM radio networks to thank for their meteoric rise to fame and consequently their first taste of stadium touring. From thereon, and in distinct contrast to their contemporaries (Led Zeppelin and The Who, for example), they didn't actually tour that much, but they did sell albums, in anonymous but well designed sleeves, in ridiculously vast quantities. It would be difficult to pick up an old edition of *Billboard* and not find Pink Floyd placed somewhere in the album chart.

A remarkable David Gilmour-led comeback in 1987, after a well documented split with founding member Roger Waters, secured their place among rock's new elite with commercial exploitation that went above and beyond anything previously known, and extravagant shows that literally redefined the standard. Gilmour had made his point and retired the band in 1994, leaving Waters to continue an erratic solo career that has ultimately seen a solid fan base develop. Unfortunately, after *Live 8*, Pink Floyd slipped out of the public consciousness as quickly as it had temporarily moved in, kept only partially alive by the solo works and tours of its chief protagonists Roger Waters and David Gilmour.

During the course of conducting additional research for this first U.S. edition (the first U.K. edition was published in 2007), the long and fraught career of one of rock music's most elusive, misunderstood and strangely successful bands finally reached the end of the road with the passing of its keyboard player Richard Wright in September 2008. For many fans it was a time to re-evaluate his contribution and to re-identify his place within Pink Floyd. I for one am grateful to have seen him perform so brilliantly, and for the last time, on David Gilmour's 2006 tour. For the remaining band members it was perhaps an occasion to reflect upon missed opportunities. *Live 8* ultimately proved to be their swansong.

Glenn Povey

GLENN POVEY, HERTFORDSHIRE, SUMMER 2009

THIS BOOK IS DEDICATED TO JANE, TO MY FATHER GEORGE AND TO THE MEMORY OF MY MOTHER, SYLVIA. THANK YOU FOR EVERYTHING.

Research Notes

Researching Pink Floyd's concert dates was the most time consuming aspect that forms the foundation of this work. I decided from a very early stage to absolutely verify each and every date rather than copy or take for granted that which has already appeared in print. As a result it soon became apparent that a lot of previously misleading and incorrect information had been previously printed on the band, and this in turn led to exploration down other avenues. The consequences of this meant that days and weeks were spent buried in various archives and libraries around the world poring over old newspapers, magazines and periodicals for advertisements, reviews and snippets of information. To say this could be mind numbing in the extreme would be an understatement – spending hours and sometimes days trying to glean even the tiniest morsel, and often without luck. Any normal, sane person would have given up long ago. Sometimes though, I would stumble upon something quite unexpected and enjoy a smug sense of achievement, knowing that this was an entirely exclusive finding.

With the amount of information being gleaned the book soon evolved into a wider archival work, which now covers the entire history of Pink Floyd and its individual members careers, including a comprehensive catalogue of their respective concert performances, recording sessions, TV and radio appearances as well as discographic information.

I have even, for the very first time in print, dedicated a lot of energy into researching the pre-Pink Floyd bands its members had participated in as an essential piece of the chronological jigsaw. Unfortunately many facts from the early days could not be completely corroborated, mainly due to fading memories and a lack of documentary evidence, but what I have attempted to present is as accurate as it can be.

Furthermore, much of the narrative information has been gleaned from contemporary press reports and interviews, which must be assumed to be accurate at the time. I have deliberately chosen not to interview individual members of the band as they now have the benefit of hindsight and have in some cases, as has been proven, invented convenient memories to suit their own version of events, especially as latter-day rifts have presented conflicting opinions. Therefore, and in general terms, I have attempted to present a balanced picture and have collated many important facts, straightened out previously printed inaccuracies and presented a whole host of information that has, until now, remained undocumented.

There are many wide and varied sources that have been used to research the contents of this book and the reader may find the following sources and information as a useful guide before plunging into its depths.

Like many fans of my generation, my introduction to Pink Floyd in print came from the picture-book diary *Pink Floyd* by Miles (Omnibus) and as a collector I was also very grateful for the use of Jon Rosenberg's indispensable tape collector's guide, *A Journey Thru Time & Space* which gave me some basis to work from. Needless to say the collectors market is rife with bootleg recordings and this also helped a great deal with set lists. As time went on, it became increasingly obvious how many gaps there were in the band's diary and so the quest began by searching through newspapers and magazines to search out new shows – many of which were chanced upon quite accidentally in the most unlikely of places and others by deduction or sheer guesswork. Nevertheless piecing it all together was as exciting as it was frustrating with as many fruitless hours of research as there was success; not forgetting of course that the majority of the research took place prior to the advent of the Internet. Therefore it cannot be underestimated how much time and effort went into chasing even the most tenuous of leads in order to locate a single fact or tour date - some of which required great detective work.

Most of the research was carried out at the British Newspaper Library, London, England and the Library of Congress, Washington DC, USA. Additional research was carried out at the Architects Association Library, London, England; City of London Library, London, England; British National Library, St. Pancras, London, England; Kensington Public Library, London, England; Koninklijke Bibliotheek, Brussels, Belgium; The National Sound Archive, London, England; The Public Library, San Franscico, USA; The Public Library, Los Angeles, USA; The Public Library, Toronto, Canada; University College of London, London, England and Westminster Public Library, London, England.

In the course of the research letters were sent to newspaper and magazine editors all over the world, requesting reader information on Pink Floyd concerts from which I received an overwhelming response from readers who were kind enough to impart valuable information. I would particularly like to thank the editors of the following publications who kindly responded to my request and in some cases even duplicated their archives: *Apeldoornse Courant, Arizona Daily Star, Bath Chronicle, Berkshire Observer, Bournemouth Evening Echo, Brighton Argus, Brighton & Hove Leader, Bristol Evening Post,*

Cambridge Evening News, Chichester & Bognor Observer, Cornish Times, Coventry Evening Telegraph, Derby Evening Telegraph, East Anglia Times, Edinburgh Evening News, Exeter Express & Echo, Financial Times, Gazet van Antwerpen, De Gelderlander, Glasgow Herald, Haagsche Courant, Ipswich Evening Star, Kent Today, Lancashire Evening Telegraph, Lancaster Guardian, Leicester Mercury, Malvern Gazette, Oxford Mail, Oxford Star, Oxford Times, Record Collector, St. Petersburg Times, South London Press, Swansea Herald, Wantage Herald, Western Evening Herald, Windsor Express and Worthing Herald.

There are also a great many extracts of concert reviews that have been reproduced from newspapers, magazines and periodicals and my grateful thanks go to the author's of those articles and reviews, the sources of which have all been credited. However, a special mention must be given to the UK music press, in particular Melody Maker, Mojo, Music Now, New Musical Express, Q Magazine, Record Mirror and Sounds for giving Pink Floyd such extensive coverage over the years.

In addition letters were sent to almost every surviving venue, establishment and university that hosted a performance by Pink Floyd and I am most grateful to the following for supplying me with valuable information: Amsterdam Concertgebouw, Arizona State University, Bristol City Council (on behalf of The Colston Hall), Bristol University, Case Western Reserve University, Clemson University, Edinburgh University, Empire Theatre Liverpool, Fairfield Halls Croydon, Hallenstadion Zurich, Keele University, Kent State University, Konzerthaus Vienna, Leicester University, Princeton University, Queens College Oxford, Royal Albert Hall, Royal Festival & Queen Elizabeth Halls, Royal Holloway College (University of London), Sussex University, Théâtre des Champs Elysées, University of Bradford, University of California Los Angeles, University of Denver, University of Essex, University of Montreal, University of Reading, University of Wales, University of Toledo and University of Westminster.

Concert and Appearance Listings

All of the entries are listed chronologically in date order. The locations are listed by the name of the event (in italics), followed by the name of the venue, followed by town/city and country. All venue names are written in the language of the country, although some place names have been Anglicised to avoid confusion. In the case of a performance commencing after midnight, as is the case with many of the all-night raves in their early years, I have listed the date the event as a whole commenced as advertised. Set lists are as accurate as possible and are taken from recordings, reviews or first hand accounts and to the best of my knowledge in the correct running order. An oblique (/) denotes song separation and a double oblique (//) where an intermission has occurred and encores are noted as such. Where no set list appears it is because I have been unable to completely and independently verify the content of that performance, although the reader would not have too much trouble best-guessing the set list on tours from the mid-Seventies onwards as they tended to be repetitive.

One other thing to remember when reading some of the reprinted reviews is the spelling (or rather mis-spelling) of the band members names, which I have retained purely for my own amusement rather than write '[sic]' every time, which I am sure you too would be sick of reading.

Recording Sessions

I have had to accept that this is an area I have been unable to thoroughly research to the same meticulous degree as the appearance listings as access to EMI Abbey Road recording studios to research this area has not been possible. However, the dates that are noted in the text come from a variety of sources and acknowledgement is given to Pink Floyd by Miles, and Random Precision by David Parker. Additional dates were gleaned from a limited edition booklet on Syd Barrett's recording career, The Making Of The Madcap Laughs by Malcolm Jones as well as a series of late 1960's fan-club newsletters and a variety of contemporary press reports. Please bear in mind that even these cannot always be taken as being completely reliable as very often the actual mixing and mastering process may have taken place without the band being present. However, in broad terms the dates listed do give some chronology and give context to the recording process.

It is also worth noting, in the case of the pre-recorded BBC radio sessions, that the times noted (as well as the programme details) are all taken from contractual paperwork and often include rehearsal time.

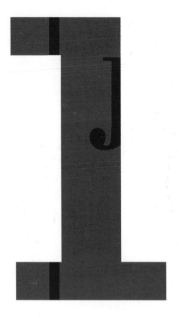

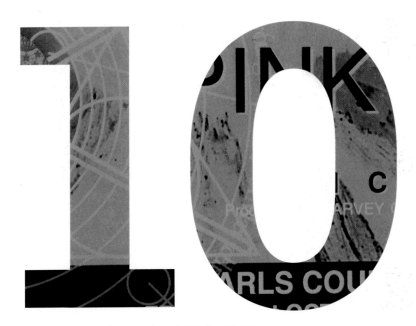

1Jokers

5-PIECE VOC

Bookings: D.

109 Grantchester M

remember when you

L HARMONY

s Wild

GILMOUR

adows, Cambridge

were young

1962 - 1967

ALTHOUGH PINK FLOYD DIDN'T ENJOY WIDESPREAD PUBLIC RECOGNITION UNTIL 1967, THEIR ROOTS CAN BE TRACED AS FAR BACK AS THE VERY EARLY SIXTIES AND AN EVER–GROWING CIRCLE OF INTERRELATED GROUPS AND MUSICIANS BASED IN AND AROUND THE COMPACT AND COSMOPOLITAN UNIVERSITY CITY OF CAMBRIDGE LOCATED IN THE EAST OF ENGLAND.

Two of the founder members grew up there: Syd Barrett (born Roger Keith Barrett in Cambridge on 6 January 1946; he acquired the nickname 'Syd' in his late teens after a local ageing trad-jazz band member named Sid Barrett) and Roger Waters (born George Roger Waters in Great Bookham, Surrey on 6 September 1943). It was also the hometown of late-Sixties addition David Gilmour (born David Jon Gilmour in Cambridge on 6 March 1946), although only Barrett and Gilmour, in their teens, became active musicians in the city.

Cambridge had an incredibly vibrant music scene in the early Sixties and many bands flourished on the university and town circuit, many of which interchanged members quite regularly. By the end of 1966, however, a very noticeable change had taken place, as more and more talented musicians were lured to London and the scene became a shadow of its former self as the Sixties drew to a close.

The first signs of any constructive activity from any of the future members of Pink Floyd can be pinpointed to early 1962, at the Barrett family home in Hills Road, Cambridge, which was the venue for a series of Sunday afternoon gatherings of Syd and his friends.

In a back room of this large house the youngsters, like so many of their age, listened avidly to Radio

Luxembourg and played along to their latest musical finds, mainly American rock 'n' roll singles indirectly acquired from the US forces personnel based in East Anglia, with makeshift instruments and, if they were lucky, their first acoustic guitars. Barrett, as well as being the youngest in the family, was the only child still at home, his two sisters and brother having long since moved away. His mother was tolerant and welcomed the company his friends gave him, not only because of this, but also because of his father's recent death.

These gatherings are believed to have become a local focus of activity for an ever-growing circle of teenagers. Among those in regular attendance were local boys Geoff Mott, Clive Welham – a would-be drummer, tapping out tunes on a biscuit tin with a knife and fork – and Tony Sainty. After one particular get-together the keen young musicians, including Barrett, decided to form a group and in doing so became the band that started the Pink Floyd family tree. They called themselves Geoff Mott and the Mottoes.

Mott had something of a reputation, having been expelled from school for his outlandish behaviour. His apparent arrogance and imposing stature made him the natural choice of front man for the new band, although they played to an audience only a handful of times. 'We did a lot of work at private parties,' Barrett later recalled. 'Some of our material was original but mostly we stuck to Shadows instrumentals and a few American songs. Eventually the group dissolved and I moved into the blues field, this time playing bass. It was a Hofner, and I played that for a couple of years.'[1]

School friend Albert 'Albie' Prior fondly remembers Barrett: 'I was at Cambridge High School in the Sixties and Syd was a year younger

KEN WATERSON   << This guy Barney came to me and said can we borrow your amp? And I said OK, so we went up to the Victoria Road Congregational Church and he said, right, as it's your amp, you're in the band! >>

than me at the school. He was artistic, creative and friendly. An incident that sticks in my mind for some reason is a group of us being in the school toilets, of all places, and Syd saying that he wanted to get into a group and asking [as I was already in The Ramblers] what it involved and in particular what sort of haircut was best.'[2]

One of the Mottoes first public concerts – if not their only one – was a dance at the Friends Meeting House following the culmination of a CND march through Cambridge on 11 March 1962 and as a member of the YCND Waters was involved in its organisation and designed the advertising poster. Although he had only been around the periphery of the band, significantly in this period, he had established a very close friendship with Barrett.

In September of that year Barrett won a scholarship for a two year course at Cambridge College of Arts and Technology. Waters left Cambridge altogether that summer, moving to London to gain experience in an architectural office before enrolling on a seven-year Architecture Studies course at The Regent Street Polytechnic in September. It was only here that any serious interest in becoming a musician began.

As it turned out the Mottoes' career was extremely brief. Geoff Mott went on to better things with The Boston Crabs, remembered by some as the first Cambridge band to get a record deal (with EMI) although, like so many young bands, they split up shortly afterwards.

It was not until the summer of 1964, after graduating from the Cambridge College of Arts and Technology, that Barrett joined another band, The Hollerin' Blues. Giving only a handful of shows, all in July, band member Ken Waterson recalled the band quite clearly: 'This guy Barney came to me and said "Can we borrow your amp?" And I said "OK," so we went up to the Victoria Road Congregational Church and he said, "Right, as it's your amp, you're in the band!" We had Stephen Pyle and this guy Pete Glass on harmonica; me singing and we were playing Bo Diddley. Hollerin' Blues used to play Bo Diddley and then started playing Jimmy Reed stuff. We got hold of this album, [Jimmy Reed] *Live at Carnegie Hall*, and started learning stuff off that. This one [gig] up at the Footlights Club went out on a blast of "La Bamba" which went on for about half an hour, with

me and Barney doing a conga with the audience, stoned out of our heads. That was a bit wild!'[3]

Impromptu sets and mad jam sessions like this went on regularly at the Union Society, a small University basement meeting hall-cum-venue that Waterson remembers fondly: 'Syd, Barney, Alan Sizer and John Gordon all went down and everyone did a spot and they would pat you on the back, they would all give you a boost. They were good old boys – if you fucked up they'd still say, Well done, mate." They said we've got this Yank coming down, this short, squatty geezer, and they said he's good, and he did five numbers, and it was Paul Simon, who was at the University. All the arty-farty lot used to hang out in the Criterion pub. Storm Thorgerson [later designer of Pink Floyd album sleeves] was one, and someone who later became an actor – they were the more studenty types – and Storm was quite involved

ROGER WATERS << We just sat around talking about how we would spend the money we would make. I invested some of my grant in a Spanish guitar and I went and had two lessons at the Spanish Guitar Centre. But I couldn't do with all that practice. >>

with Syd quite a bit then.'[4]

But Hollerin' Blues were inevitably short lived, Barrett having successfully applied to pursue a three–year degree course at the Camberwell School of Art in south London, starting in September 1964.

When Barrett arrived in London, Waters had already been away from Cambridge for over a year. He had joined a band formed by fellow students Clive Metcalf and Keith Noble in autumn 1963 called Sigma 6 (with 'Sigma' sometimes written as the Greek letter).

'I was doing architecture at Regent Street Polytechnic,' recalled Waters. 'I suppose we formed several groups there. It wasn't serious, we didn't play anywhere. We had lots of names, Meggadeaths was a great one. We just sat around talking about how we would spend the money we would make. I invested some of my grant in a Spanish guitar and I went and had two lessons at the Spanish Guitar Centre. But I couldn't do with all that practice. In college there's always a room where people seem to gravitate to with their instruments and bits of things.'[5]

FAR RIGHT: THE ABDABS AS THEY APPEARED IN *WEST ONE*, THE REGENT STREET POLYTECHNIC STUDENT NEWSPAPER, IN EARLY 1964. PICTURED FROM LEFT ARE NICK MASON, ROGER WATERS, KEITH NOBLE AND CLIVE METCALF.

The line-up included future Pink Floyd members Nick Mason (born Nicholas Berkeley Mason in Birmingham on 27 January 1944) and Richard Wright (born Richard William Wright in Hatch End, Middlesex on 28 July 1943). Mason had flirted with a post-school band called The Hotrods comprising of a group of local friends whose career never got beyond the bedroom rehearsal stage; Wright had graduated from an unknown trad jazz band as a saxophonist. All three eventually ended up living in a shared house in Highgate, north London, let by live-in landlord Mike Leonard and part-time lecturer at The Polytechnic.

The band even boasted its own manager, a former Poly student called Ken Chapman, who had cards made up

living in a bed-sit off Tottenham Court Road the pair moved into Leonard's house in Highgate, just as Mason and Wright had decided to vacate their rooms in order to move back to the more comfortable confines of their respective parents' houses.

When Metcalf and Noble decided to form a duo, Barrett and Klose were immediately recruited to The Abdabs. 'I had to buy another guitar,' explained Barrett, 'because Roger played bass – a Rickenbacker – and we didn't want a group with two bass players. So I changed guitars and we started doing the pub scene. During that period we kept changing the name of the group.' [7] Waters recalled that, 'With the advent of Bob Close [sic] we actually had someone who could play an instrument.

ROGER WATERS **<< With the advent of Bob Close [sic] we actually had someone who could play an instrument. It was really then we did the shuffle job of who played what. I was demoted from lead guitar to rhythm guitar and finally bass. There was always this frightful fear that I could land up as the drummer. >>**

of the 'Available for Weddings and Parties' variety. 'We used to learn his songs and then play them for Gerry Bron [later of the Bronze record label],' recalled Waters. 'They were fantastic songs, "Have You Seen A Morning Rose", to the tune of a Tchaikovsky prelude or something.' [6]

By the start of 1964 Sigma 6 became known as The Abdabs (or the Screaming Abdabs). They were the only one of these early London bands to receive any press coverage, in an early edition of *West One*, the Polytechnic's student newspaper. Contrary to popular belief, there never was an 'Architectural Abdabs' – this was just the headline under which the piece appeared. Regarded as the college house band they performed a fairly solid set that included 'I'm A Crawling King Snake', various Searchers numbers and with guest vocals from Richard Wright's girlfriend Juliette Gale on 'Summertime' and 'Careless Love', were often the opening act at the college dances.

Barrett had travelled down to London with another Cambridge musician, Rado 'Bob' Klose formerly of a Cambridge band called Blues Anonymous and was coincidentally also enrolled onto the same course, two years below, as Waters and Mason at The Polytechnic. Barrett remembered that Waters suggested they meet up when he got to London and after a couple of weeks

It was really then we did the shuffle job of who played what. I was demoted from lead guitar to rhythm guitar and finally bass. There was always this frightful fear that I could land up as the drummer.' [8]

Fortunately for Barrett, Klose and Waters, despite all living under the same roof as their live-in landlord, Leonard was a man of a musical inclination and apart from being a part time tutor at their Polytechnic was also a lecturer at the Hornsey College of Art. He firmly approved of his tenants' increased activities and allowed rehearsals in his front room.

Within a short time the band were calling themselves Leonard's Lodgers. As Wright was taking a sabbatical, having recognised further education was not best suited to him, he was enjoying an extended holiday in the Greek islands before enrolling at the Royal College of Music for the next term – Leonard was invited to stand in on organ for the occasional booking, mostly at local pubs. 'Mike thought of himself as one of the band. But we didn't, because he was too old basically. We used to leave the house to play gigs secretly without telling him,' [9] recalled Mason. Over time they started rehearsing away from the house, falling victim to an overwhelming spate of local objection to the volume of their rehearsals and operations swiftly moved to The Polytechnic.

OVERLEAF: THE ONLY KNOWN PHOTOGRAPHS OF THE TEA SET. TAKEN AT A PRIVATE PARTY IN OXSHOTT, SURREY IN OCTOBER 1964 THE LINE-UP FEATURES ROGER WATERS (GUITAR), RADO 'BOB' KLOSE (GUITAR, HARMONICA), ROGER 'SYD' BARRETT (GUITAR, VOCALS), CHRIS DENNIS (CENTRE STAGE LEAD VOCALS), NICK MASON (DRUMS) AND REMARKABLY, THE BAND'S LANDLORD, MIKE LEONARD (KEYBOARDS).

ARCHITECTURAL ABDABS

By BARBARA WALTERS

AN up-and-coming pop group here at the Poly call themselves "The Abdabs" and hope to establish themselves playing Rhythm and Blues. Most of them are architectural students.

Their names are Nick Mason (drums); Rick Wright (Rhythm guitar); Clive Metcalf (bass); Roger Walters (lead); and finally Keith Noble and Juliette Gale (singers).

Why is it that Rhythm and Blues has suddenly come into its own? Roger was the first to answer.

"It is easier to express yourself rhythmically in Blues-style. It doesn't need practice, just basic understanding."

"I prefer to play it because it is musically more interesting," said Clive. I suppose he was comparing it to Rock. Well, how does it compare? Roger was quite emphatic on this point: "Rock is just beat without expression, though admittedly Rhythm and Blues forms the basis of original rock."

It so happens that they are all modern Jazz enthusiasts.

Was there any similarity? I asked.

In Keith's opinion there was. "The Blues is just a primitive form of modern jazz.

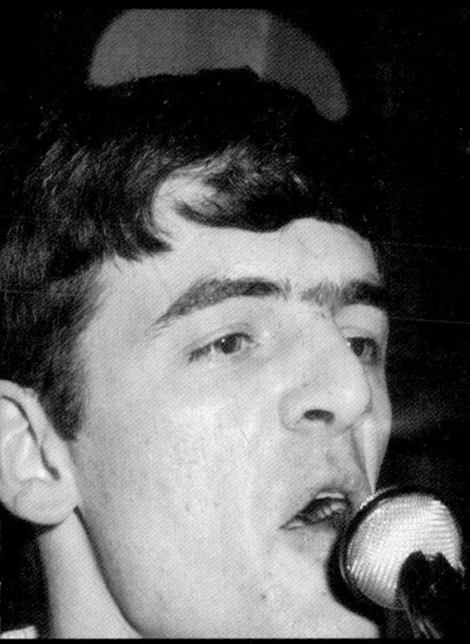

VOCAL HARM

rs W

g: D. J. GILMOU
ter Meadows, Car

17

Meanwhile the band continued to perform in the locality, notably The Woodman and The Winchester pubs on Archway Road, Highgate. Mason remembers at that time they learned their repertoire from a clutch of albums, 'Authentic R&B Volumes 1-3 and Syd's collection of Bo Diddley.'[10] (Note: There was only ever one Authentic R&B release – an LP in 1964 on Stateside. Mason is probably thinking of the Pye International R&B LP series.)

The band then apparently adopted the name Spectrum Five, although this appears to have been a very brief flirtation – and then maybe only for a single gig at Camberwell School of Art. Significantly, it soon became apparent that the band lacked a front man of any substance. Barrett and Klose fumbled through the vocals as best they could, but neither had the confidence or vocal range to carry it off effectively in the style that the band was aiming for. Therefore, during the autumn break of 1964, Barrett was dispatched to Cambridge to try to convince his former band mate Geoff Mott to join them in London. But there was hardly any incentive for Mott to join a group that had very few gigs, no agency, no manager and, on the face of it, no prospects.

Although he couldn't persuade Mott to join, by extreme good fortune, Waters and Klose bumped into a face they vaguely knew from Cambridge in a West End music store: Chris Dennis. At that time he was serving with the Royal Air Force at its Uxbridge base in west London and had, until recently, been the lead vocalist in a not long disbanded but quite successful Cambridge group called The Redcaps. He was looking for another band and accepted the offer immediately. 'At this stage we were like a lot of other bands, doing R&B stuff. Syd did a lot of

Bo Diddley numbers on his white Fender guitar. He'd do "No Money Down" and I would sing Jimmy Witherspoon, Muddy Waters and Chuck Berry stuff along with Lazy Lester's "I'm A Lover Not A Fighter" and "I Got Love If You Want It" by Slim Harpo.' [11]

It is also during this period that the band started to use the name The Tea Set - a pun on the technical drawing instrument. The name wasn't in constant use but was certainly adopted for many bookings in the coming months and indeed right through to early 1966 - even after they had found their new and more permanent name of "Pink Floyd". Accounts vary considerably but it has been said that the new name was adopted mid-way through a dance at RAF Uxbridge where, and it does seem highly unlikely that two bands would be booked, another band was also performing under the name The Tea Set. As improbable as this story may seem, there was indeed another north London based band with that name, and they went on to perform across the city throughout the coming year.

The name-change was all very spur-of-the-moment stuff and in the absence of any better ideas this suggestion was immediately adopted, although initially and according to Keith Noble, they called themselves "The Pink Floyd Blues Band". Far from coming to him in a blinding flash while in an LSD induced trance or being beamed to him by passing aliens from space, as some might have it, the name's true origins lay in Barrett's record collection. It is the amalgamation of the first names of two old Carolina bluesmen whose work was very familiar to him: Pink Anderson (1900-1974) and Floyd 'Dipper Boy' Council (1911-1976). As Waters once

BELOW: PINK FLOYD PHOTOGRAPHED IN HIGHGATE, LONDON IN EARLY 1965. PICTURED WITH ROGER 'SYD' BARRETT, NICK MASON, ROGER WATERS AND RICHARD WRIGHT IS RADO 'BOB' KLOSE SHORTLY BEFORE HE LEFT THE BAND.

put it, if they had opted for the other combination – Anderson Council – it would have sounded like a local authority.

By the end of January 1965, Dennis had received a posting to the Persian Gulf, leaving Barrett, as the most charismatic member, to take on what was for him the unnatural role of lead singer. Something of an introvert, he may have been a far more disciplined musician and indeed of greater ability, but he lacked Barrett's spontaneity and raw talent. As Gilmour reflected, 'The thing with Syd was that his guitar playing wasn't his strongest feature. His style was very stiff. I always thought I was the better guitar player. But he was very clever, very intelligent, an artist in every way. And he was a frightening talent when it came to words, and lyrics. They just used to pour out.'[12] These changes also gave the band their opportunity to finally nudge Leonard out in favour of Wright, who was invited back on board.

Confident that they now had a stable line-up the band attempted to record some of their repertoire including the tracks 'Butterfly' and 'Lucy Leave', both Barrett originals; 'I'm A King Bee', the Slim Harpo blues standard, and 'Double-O-Bo', a group composition. 'Lucy Leave' and 'I'm A King Bee' was then pressed as an acetate single to send out to clubs in order to obtain live bookings. Copies have since found their way onto the

bootleg market – a studio acetate having been unearthed in the late Eighties - albeit of poor quality, and whilst it is clearly Barrett on lead vocals, the R&B style performances are distinctly average. As Klose later recalled, 'We recorded a few numbers... I can't remember exactly where we did them... it was some place where a friend of Rick Wright's worked as an engineer. I think they were recorded on two-track. It was definitely a professional set-up. The songs themselves were mainly group compositions, although I think Syd wrote "Lucy Leave". "Double-O-Bo" was a Bo Diddley tribute of sorts - a pun on the James Bond 007 thing. The title was the main lyric! I think we had one verse written out, and then dreamt up a second whilst we were in the studio. I can't remember the title of the last number... it was a shuffle type thing in E as far as I can recall. Nick Mason played them to me during a visit a couple of years after they were recorded. Very embarrassing!'[13]

Although the band had picked up a short-lived residency at The Countdown Club in Kensington, in reality a private members club, where at least one show was

DAVID GILMOUR << The thing with Syd was that his guitar playing wasn't his strongest feature. His style was very stiff. I always thought I was the better guitar player. But he was very clever, very intelligent, an artist in every way. >>

ABOVE: THOSE WITHOUT, CAMBRIDGE, 1965. FROM LEFT: ROGER 'SYD' BARRETT, 'SMUDGE' AND STEVE PYLE. PINK FLOYD'S ERRATIC ENGAGEMENTS ALLOWED BARRETT TO RETURN TO HIS HOME TOWN AND PLAY WITH THE BAND OVER THE SPRING AND SUMMER MONTHS.

performed in an acoustic configuration and included the songs 'Long Tall Texan' and 'How High The Moon', their career was slow going.

Klose as it turned out didn't stay much longer and under pressure from both parents and college tutors – maybe even musical differences - he left the band in the early summer of 1965. Wright says of Klose's departure, 'Before him we used to play the R&B classics, because that's what all groups were supposed to do then. But I never liked R&B very much. I was actually more of a jazz fan. With Syd the direction changed, it became more improvised around the guitar and keyboards. Roger started playing bass as a lead instrument, and I started to introduce more of my classical feel.'[14]

From this point until the following year Pink Floyd remained a sideline for its members, all still pursuing their studies. Their only notable achievement was to compete in the seventh heat of the *Melody Maker* "National Beat Contest" in June, but after failing to gain a place in the subsequent heats the band slipped back into obscurity.

This lull in activity enabled Barrett to visit Cambridge from time to time and in the spring and summer term breaks of 1965 he played bass with a local band called Those Without, which featured Steve Pyle from his former band Hollerin' Blues. The band continued a patchy, short-lived career even when Barrett returned to London permanently.

In August he hooked up with Gilmour and a group of other Cambridge friends to take off on a brief summer holiday to the south of France, trundling around in a bashed–up Land Rover. Apart from devoting time in trying to search out the starlet Bridget Bardot, the only

remarkable event of their activities was while in St. Tropez the pair briefly wound up in police custody for busking.

In Cambridge in March 1962, The Mottoes drummer, Clive Welham, went on to form The Ramblers, who picked up from where the Mottoes had left off and enjoyed a successful couple of years together.

'In those days we basically played the music of The Shadows and similar groups,' recalls guitarist Albert Prior. 'It was a time when groups had one singer rather than everyone joining in. I recall early Fenders, Vox amps and drum kits that were very basic. I think that just about our first gig was a church hall on Cherry Hinton Road, Cambridge, not far from where Syd eventually lived for some time. This was the first time we publicly used the Watkins Copycat echo chamber, which allowed us to get The Shadows "Wonderful Land" just right. Other gigs that I remember were the University May Balls, the Guildhall and Corn Exchange at Cambridge, supporting major acts and also playing at the Town Hall in Newmarket, with jockey's fighting on the dance floor. We and our gear travelled in a little van, owned by our "manager", Mick Turner.'[15]

David Gilmour, in his first known band, was recruited as a member of The Ramblers towards the end of their first year, following Prior's departure in November 1962. Welham knew Gilmour already from their time at The Perse Preparatory School for Boys, despite being two years his senior. It was he who introduced Gilmour to Barrett at the Cambridge College of Art and Technology: Barrett had already been in a year of study in Art and Design; Gilmour enrolled in 1963 for one year in order to re-sit Modern Languages.

They became good friends in their year of study: 'We spent a lot of time together listening to the same music,' recalled Gilmour. 'Our influences are probably pretty much the same and I was a couple of streets ahead of him at the time and was teaching him to play Stones riffs.'[16]

It is surprising, though, that they never formed a band together. 'There was a bit of rivalry there,' Gilmour's future band mate Ken Waterson noted. 'They would always wind each other up, saying "Ah, you bastard, I'm better than you." Not offensive or anything, just a bit of a laugh.'[17]

The Ramblers performed very erratically through 1963, and this enabled Gilmour to perform simultaneously with Chris Ian & The Newcomers, where his ability soon earned him an excellent reputation on the local scene.

Chris Ian & The Newcomers had, under successive managers David Hurst and Nigel Smith, been enjoying moderate success on the Cambridge gig circuit, performing cover versions of Beatles and other Merseybeat numbers. Ken Waterson, the vocalist, recalled: 'We used to support a lot of Cambridge bands. We never got any money for it. This guy Chris Ian, any money we got he had, it went on equipment. Even with the crap equipment, old Dave [Gilmour] sounded pretty good, he had a poxy old Burns guitar and a crappy amp but you could see he'd got it even then. He was bloody good. He was having lessons from Chris Jones, who was in the Hi–Fi's. He was shy, pretty laid back, he didn't like the violence. We'd be up on stage and some bloody great ruck would start in the audience with these American servicemen punching the crap out of each other.'[18]

After Chris Ian's departure (where he became a regular fixture as a local disc jockey), the band, now renamed The Newcomers, had a patchy career, but did feature some future Pink Floyd associates, drummer John 'Willie' Wilson (of Johnny Phillips & The Hi-Fi's) and saxophonist Dick Parry (of Soul Committee). Even Gilmour signed up for a couple of shows but as 1963 drew to a close and after an altercation with Waterson, The Newcomers disbanded.

It was around this time that a little–known Cambridge outfit called The Four Posters emerged, with David Altham, Tony Sainty and Will Garfitt among its members. 'We had the advantage of having so many members doing different things,' remembers Garfitt. 'One would be at the Cambridge Tech and so we'd get gigs there, another at the Gas Works for their do's, one at the University where we would play at the Pit Club and so on. I just decided my talents lay in painting rather than struggling in a band. One thing I always remember was riding in Syd's car, a Ford Popular or something similar, and I remember asking him if we could go any faster because he was driving so slowly. But he came out with a very strange line, something like, "I'm too young to die, I've got too much to give to the world, so we'll have to

BELOW: THE RAMBLERS, PRE-DAVID GILMOUR, CAMBRIDGE, 1962. FROM LEFT: RICHARD BAKER, MERVYN MARRIOT, CHRIS 'JIM' MARRIOT, ALBERT 'ALBIE' PRIOR, CLIVE WELHAM, JOHN GORDON AND THEIR MANAGER, MICK TURNER.

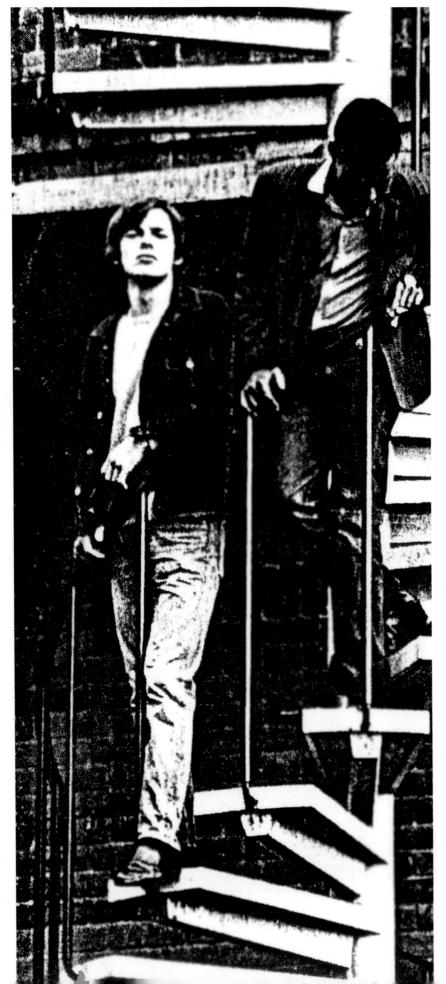

drive at my speed or not at all", which was an incredibly... well, I don't know, it was just a very strange thing to say... considering.'[19]

The Four Posters and The Newcomers split at almost the same time, creating a glut of musicians, and out of this came Jokers Wild. They are regarded as one of the Cambridge scene's most successful semi-pro groups, and one that Gilmour is most widely associated with. But in their own right they had a very strong following as a result of a series of residencies at the fashionable Dorothy and Victoria ballrooms in the centre of the city.

Drummer Clive Welham remembers his time with Jokers Wild very fondly: 'We did R&B, harmony pieces, Beach Boys, Four Seasons, which seemed to appeal to a wide audience. We didn't do any of our own material – no one did in those days. People used to write songs and then get bands to do them. We used to do Beatles numbers as well. We had a chap come down from Liverpool who saw us at the Victoria Ballroom, where we had a residency. He brought some people down to see us; one was Brian Sommerville, the ex–publicity agent for The Beatles. David Altham had been involved in some incident with his girlfriend – he was caught in a compromising position in his room at college with this girl and there was a big stink, and I don't think he was allowed to play at that gig with us. It was in the paper because he was the son of some Lord or whatever. Dave went off to do some recording stuff in London but I think they were after some things from him. While he was there he met Lionel Bart [the composer/lyricist who created the musical *Oliver!*]. The papers made reference to the fact that he may be leaving Jokers Wild but it came to nothing.'[20]

By autumn 1965 and gigging more than ever, Jokers Wild were hot property on the Cambridge scene and travelled to the Regent Sound Studios in London's Denmark Street, to record some of their repertoire. This material was eventually pressed on a five–track, 12-inch album and a 7-inch EP single and these were distributed among family and friends and both original and bootleg copies have found their way onto the collectors market in recent years. Among the tracks were covers of Frankie Lymon and The Teenagers' 1956 doo-wop classic 'Why Do Fools Fall In Love?' and Manfred Mann's 'Don't Ask Me

DAVID GILMOUR MODELLING
THE LATEST FASHIONS FOR AN
EDITION OF *VARSITY*, THE
CAMBRIDGE UNIVERSITY
STUDENT NEWSPAPER.

What I Say' (released in 1964 on their debut album *The Five Faces Of Manfred Mann*.)

Before the end of the year they were again back at the studio, this time recording for the Decca label under the guidance of an up–and–coming pop impresario and Cambridge graduate, Jonathan King. 'He went to see us at the Victoria Ballroom, but he went on the wrong night and saw Hedgehoppers Anonymous and got them to record a single,' recalled Welham. But they were soon back on track with King: 'A cover of Sam and Dave's 'You Don't Know Like I Know', with Dave singing the lead. It was much better than our first recording effort. Dave Altham and Dave Gilmour produced it; we got it right that time, we were properly prepared. Decca was very pleased with it but Sam and Dave released it here and that was it.'[21] (Sam And Dave recorded the original version at Stax in Memphis in October 1965).

This fact sealed their fate overnight and although they continued to perform it was a downhill ride. Tony Sainty left the band in early 1966 and was replaced by Peter Gilmour, one of David's two brothers.

Thereafter Welham remembers the band briefly progressing to the débutante scene, performing at London society parties and other high–profile gigs: 'We drove to London with two coach–loads of fans from Cambridge and did a gig with the Animals at an art college. It was a sizeable audience, about 800 crammed in. We did two fifteen–minute sets and they did about an hour. We did an Admiralty League at the Dorchester in London, all upper-crust types with Rolls Royce's and Bentley's everywhere.'[22]

But Welham's departure from the group wasn't far behind Sainty's: he suffered a nervous breakdown trying to hold down a full-time job at the same time as travelling to and from venues. John 'Willie' Wilson had been deputising for him on occasion since April, but with Welham's condition worsening he now took over full time.

By the late summer of 1966 Peter Gilmour and John Gordon, another defector to art college, also quit leaving David Gilmour, John 'Willie' Wilson and David Altham at the core with new recruit Rick Wills. Under the guidance of a newly appointed manager, John-Paul Salvatore (who happened to be the brother-in-law of Tony Secunda who managed the Move), the band reinvented themselves as Bullit, securing a residency at the Los Menteros Hotel in Marbella, Spain followed by the Jean-Jacques hotel in St. Etienne, after which Altham departed.

The trio of Gilmour, Wilson and Wills then re-invented themselves as Flowers, working around France including a residency at the Bilboquet club in Paris, before finally calling it a day in September 1967.

John 'Willie' Wilson went on to join Sutherland Brothers & Quiver and Rick Wills eventually joined Foreigner. Flowers was Gilmour's last band before joining Pink Floyd in early 1968.

Sources
1. *Beat Instrumental*, October. 1967
2. Letter from Albert Prior to the Author, 27 April 1998
3-4. Authors' interview with Ken Waterson, September 1996
5. *Voxpop*, by Michael Wale, George g. Harrap & Co. Ltd., 1972
6. *Zig Zag*, Issue 32, July 1973
7. *Beat Instrumental*, October 1967
8. *Zig Zag*, Issue 32, July 1973
9-10. *Mojo*, May 1994
11. *Crazy Diamond. Syd Barrett & The Dawn Of Pink Floyd*, Watkinson/Anderson, Omnibus 1991
12. *Zig Zag*, Issue 32, July 1973
13 -14. *Random Precision*, David Parker, Cherry Red 2001
15. Letter from Albert Prior to the Author, 27 April 1998
16. *Mojo*, May 1994
17-18. Authors' interview with Ken Waterson, September 1996
19. Authors' interview with Will Garfitt, 25 September 1996
20-22. Authors' interview with Clive Welham, October 1996

BELOW: JOKERS WILD, AS FEATURED IN THE CAMBRIDGE PRESS, FEBRUARY 1965. FROM LEFT TO RIGHT: DAVID GILMOUR, DAVID ALTHAM, JOHN GORDON, TONY SAINTY, CLIVE WELHAM.

RIGHT: JOKERS WILD, PERFORMING AT GREAT SHELFORD, CAMBRIDGE IN OCTOBER 1965. FROM LEFT: DAVID GILMOUR, JOHN GORDON, CLIVE WELHAM, TONY SAINTY.

CHRIS CHENEY

THE JOKERS WILD, one of the town groups, playing at the Victoria Ballroom last Wednesday evening.

CAMBRIDGE 1962 – 1967

Between spring 1962 and summer 1967 a series of bands containing members of the future Pink Floyd were formed in Cambridge, England. The dates listed in this section have been gleaned mainly through local newspaper advertisements, contemporary newspaper reports and items of memorabilia. It is certain that many more appearances by these bands remain undocumented.

GEOFF MOTT & THE MOTTOES

(Spring 1962)
Roger 'Syd' Barrett: Rhythm Guitar
Nobby Clarke: Guitar
Geoff Mott: Vocals
Tony Sainty: Bass Guitar
Clive Welham: Drums

Sunday 11 March 1962
CONCERT
Friends Meeting House, Cambridge, England
The Mottoes only known concert was at a dance held at the culmination of a CND rally through the city.

THE RAMBLERS

(March 1962 - October 1963. Shows prior to David Gilmour joining are not listed)
Richard Baker: Bass Guitar
David Gilmour: Guitar (from 13 November, replacing Albert 'Albie' Prior)
John Gordon: Rhythm Guitar
Chris 'Jim' Marriot: Vocals
Mervyn Marriot: Guitar
Clive Welham: Drums

Tuesday 13 November 1962
CONCERT
The King's Head public house, Fen Ditton, near Cambridge, England
The Ramblers were announced in the local press as performing every Tuesday night from this date , although it is uncertain when this residency ended.

Saturday 24 November 1962
CONCERT
Church Hall Youth Club, Free Church, Cambridge, England

Saturday 1 December 1962
CONCERT
Guildhall, Cambridge, England

Saturday 15 December 1962
CONCERT
Staff Social Club, Fulbourn Hospital, Fulbourn, near Cambridge, England

Saturday 16 February 1963
CONCERT
Memorial Hall, Great Shelford, near Cambridge, England

Thursday 7 March 1963
CONCERT
Victoria Ballroom, Cambridge, England
With the Sundowners

Monday 15 April 1963
CONCERT
Free Church Hall, Sawston, near Cambridge, England

Thursday 16 May 1963
CONCERT
Victoria Ballroom, Cambridge, England
Supporting The Worryin' Kind.

Friday 2 August 1963
CONCERT
Rex Ballroom, Cambridge, England
With Steve Francis and The London Strollers.

Saturday 17 August 1963
CONCERT
Rex Ballroom, Cambridge, England
With Rikki & The Caravelles.

Saturday 21 September 1963
CONCERT
Assembly Hall, Melbourn Primary School, Melbourn, near Royston, England

Saturday 12 October 1963
CONCERT
Village Hall, Harston, near Cambridge, England
Supporting the Hi-Fi's

Sunday 13 October 1963
CONCERT
ABC Regal Cinema, Cambridge, England
Opening act for Billy Fury, Joe Brown & The Bruvvers, Karl Denver Trio, The Tornados, Marty Wilde & His Wildcats, Daryl Quist, Dickie Pride and Larry Burns package tour.

CHRIS IAN & THE NEWCOMERS

(January – July 1963)
John 'Barney' Barnes: Rhythm Guitar
Roger Bibby: Bass Guitar
Chris Ian Culpin: Drums
David Gilmour: Guitar, Vocals
Ken Waterson: Vocals

Saturday 26 January 1963
CONCERT
Memorial Hall, Fulbourn, near Cambridge, England

Saturday 16 March 1963
CONCERT
Guildhall, Cambridge, England
Supporting Mark Arnold & The Dawnbreakers.

Saturday 23 March 1963
CONCERT
Village Hall, Dry Drayton, near Cambridge, England

Saturday 4 May 1963
CONCERT
Guildhall, Cambridge, England
Supporting Johnny Philips & The Swinging Hi-Fi's.

Saturday 25 May 1963
CONCERT
Village Hall, Trumpington, near Cambridge, England

Monday 27 May 1963
CONCERT
Lower Hall, St. Andrew's Street Baptist Church, Cambridge, England

Saturday 8 June 1963
CONCERT
Rex Ballroom, Cambridge, England
With The Roy Dennis Orchestra and Kenny Lennon.

THE NEWCOMERS

(July 1963 - October 1963)
John 'Barney' Barnes: Rhythm Guitar
Roger Bibby: Bass Guitar
David Gilmour: Guitar, Vocals
Kenny Lennon: Vocals
Johnny Philips: Vocals
Ken Waterson: Vocals
John 'Willie' Wilson: Drums

Saturday 3 August 1963
CONCERT
Rex Ballroom, Cambridge, England
With The Prowlers.

Saturday 24 August 1963
CONCERT
Rex Ballroom, Cambridge, England
With Rikki Elwin & The Kobalts.

Saturday 5 October 1963
CONCERT
Rex Ballroom, Cambridge, England
With The Johnny Quantrose 5.

THE HOLLERIN' BLUES

(July 1964)
John 'Barney' Barnes: Rhythm Guitar
Roger 'Syd' Barrett: Guitar
Pete Glass: Harmonica
Steve Pyle: Drums

Ken Waterson: Vocals, Maracas, Harmonica

July 1964
CONCERT
Masonic Hall, Cambridge, England

July 1964
CONCERT
Congregational Church Hall, Cambridge, England

July 1964
CONCERT
Blue Horizon Club, Guildhall, Cambridge, England

July 1964
CONCERT
Footlights Club, Arts Theatre Rehearsal Room, Cambridge, England

Saturday 25 July 1964
CONCERT
Beat Nite, Village Hall, Little Gransden, near Cambridge, England
Supported by The Huntsmen. A benefit concert for Church funds.

Alan Sizer: Guitar, Vocals
'Smudge': Guitar

Saturday 13 March 1965
CONCERT
Village Hall, Little Gransden, near Cambridge, England
Supporting The Wayfarers.

Saturday 8 May 1965
CONCERT
Village Hall, Trumpington, near Cambridge, England

Wednesday 16 June 1965
CONCERT
Youth Club, Congregational Church Hall, Cambridge, England

Sunday 20 June 1965
CONCERT
The Racehorse public house, Cambridge, England

Wednesday 30 June 1965
CONCERT
Dorothy Ballroom, Cambridge, England
With Bob Kidman & His Orchestra and The Washington DC's.

Thursday 15 July 1965
CONCERT
Victoria Ballroom, Cambridge, England

Saturday 17 July 1965
CONCERT
Dorothy Ballroom, Cambridge, England
With Bob Kidman & His Orchestra, The Hedgehoppers, The Seminoles and Bern Elliot & The Klan.

Saturday 7 August 1965
CONCERT
Gardiner Memorial Hall, Burwell, near Cambridge, England
With DJ Chris Ian. This was almost certainly Roger 'Syd' Barrett's last show with Those Without before turning his full attention to Pink Floyd.

THOSE WITHOUT

(March - August 1965)
Roger 'Syd' Barrett: Bass Guitar
Robert Smith: Bass Guitar (replacing Roger 'Syd' Barrett after August 1965)
Steve Pyle: Drums

JOKERS WILD

(October 1964 – May 1966)
David Altham: Guitar, Saxophone, Keyboards, Vocals
David Gilmour: Guitar, Vocals, Harmonica
Peter Gilmour: Bass Guitar, Vocals (replacing Tony

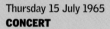

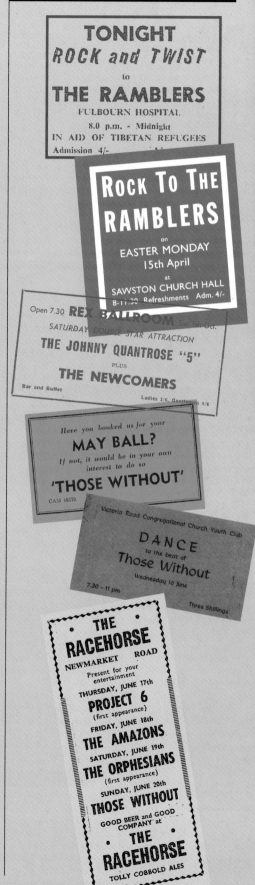

25

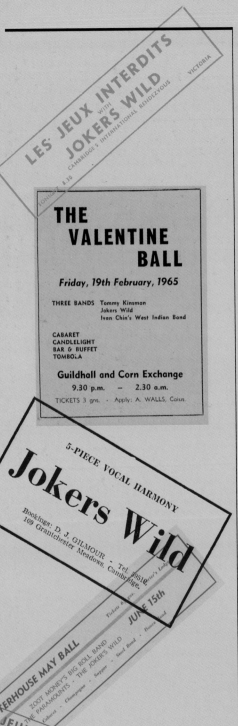

THE
VALENTINE
BALL

Friday, 19th February, 1965

THREE BANDS Tommy Kinsman
Jokers Wild
Ivan Chin's West Indian Band

CABARET
CANDLELIGHT
BAR & BUFFET
TOMBOLA

Guildhall and Corn Exchange

9.30 p.m. — 2.30 a.m.

TICKETS 3 gns. · Apply: A. WALLS, Caius.

5-PIECE VOCAL HARMONY

Jokers Wild

Bookings: D. J. GILMOUR – Tel. 50518,
109 Grantchester Meadows, Cambridge.

Sainty from early 1966)
John Gordon: Rhythm Guitar, Vocals (to late 1965)
Tony Sainty: Bass Guitar, Vocals (to early 1966)
Clive Welham: Drums, Vocals (to late 1965)
John 'Willie' Wilson: Drums (replacing Clive Welham from late 1965)

N.B: A popular eight-piece soul band from London performed under the name Jokers Wild across the south of England throughout 1967 and 1968, but are unrelated.

Saturday 5 September 1964
CONCERT
Dorothy Ballroom, Cambridge, England
With Bob Kidman & His Orchestra, Eric Squires & His Quartet, Squad 5, The Prestons and The Beat Syndicate.
Dances at the Dorothy Ballroom often made use of three spaces for different types of bands: The Ballroom was set aside for the more trad-jazz dance bands and both "The Beat Room" and "Jive Hive" for contemporary bands, the latter of which is where Jokers Wild usually performed.

Saturday 19 September 1964
CONCERT
Dorothy Ballroom, Cambridge, England
With Bob Kidman & His Orchestra, Eric Squires & His Quartet, Squad 5, Monica & The Vulcans and Andy & The Paliminos.

Wednesday 14 October 1964
CONCERT
Les Jeux Interdits, Victoria Ballroom, Cambridge, England

Wednesday 6 January 1965
CONCERT
Les Jeux Interdits, Victoria Ballroom, Cambridge, England

Wednesday 13 January 1965
CONCERT
Les Jeux Interdits, Victoria Ballroom, Cambridge, England

Saturday 16 January 1965
CONCERT
Dorothy Ballroom, Cambridge, England
With Bob Kidman & His Orchestra, Eric Squires & His Quartet, Larry Bond & The Trojans, Guitars Incorporated and Johnny Dean & The Deacons.

Wednesday 20 January 1965
CONCERT
Les Jeux Interdits, Victoria Ballroom, Cambridge, England

Wednesday 27 January 1965
CONCERT
Les Jeux Interdits, Victoria Ballroom, Cambridge, England

Saturday 30 January 1965
CONCERT
Dorothy Ballroom, Cambridge, England
With Bob Kidman & His Orchestra, Mark Arnold & The Dawnbreakers, The Worryin' Kind and The Blobs.

Wednesday 10 February 1965
CONCERT
Les Jeux Interdits, Victoria Ballroom, Cambridge, England

Saturday 13 February 1965
CONCERT
Dorothy Ballroom, Cambridge, England
With Bob Kidman & His Orchestra, Larry Bond & The Trojans, Guitars Incorporated and Johnny Dean & The Deacons.

Wednesday 17 February 1965
CONCERT
Les Jeux Interdits, Victoria Ballroom, Cambridge, England

Friday 19 February 1965
CONCERT
Caius College Valentine Ball, Guildhall and Corn Exchange, Cambridge, England
With Tommy Kinsman and Ivan Chin's West Indian Band, cabaret and tombola.

Monday 22 February 1965
CONCERT
The Old English Gentleman public house, Harston, near Cambridge, England

Wednesday 24 February 1965
CONCERT
Les Jeux Interdits, Victoria Ballroom, Cambridge, England

Saturday 27 February 1965
CONCERT
Dorothy Ballroom, Cambridge, England
With Bob Kidman & His Orchestra, Eric Squires & His Quartet and The Sonnets.

Wednesday 10 March 1965
CONCERT
Les Jeux Interdits, Victoria Ballroom, Cambridge, England

Wednesday 17 March 1965
CONCERT
Les Jeux Interdits, Victoria Ballroom, Cambridge, England

Wednesday 24 March 1965
CONCERT
Les Jeux Interdits, Victoria Ballroom, Cambridge,
England

Friday 26 March 1965
CONCERT
The Racehorse public house, Cambridge, England

Saturday 27 March 1965
CONCERT
Dorothy Ballroom, Cambridge, England
With The Prowlers.

Wednesday 7 April 1965
CONCERT
Les Jeux Interdits, Victoria Ballroom, Cambridge,
England

Saturday 10 April 1965
CONCERT
Dorothy Ballroom, Cambridge, England

Wednesday 14 April 1965
CONCERT
Les Jeux Interdits, Victoria Ballroom, Cambridge,
England

Wednesday 21 April 1965
CONCERT
Les Jeux Interdits, Victoria Ballroom, Cambridge,
England

Wednesday 28 April 1965
CONCERT
Les Jeux Interdits, Victoria Ballroom, Cambridge,
England

Wednesday 5 May 1965
CONCERT
Les Jeux Interdits, Victoria Ballroom, Cambridge,
England

Saturday 8 May 1965
CONCERT
Dorothy Ballroom, Cambridge, England
With Bob Kidman & His Orchestra, The Tykes, The
Mamas and Fernando & The Hideaways.

Wednesday 12 May 1965
CONCERT
Les Jeux Interdits, Victoria Ballroom, Cambridge,
England

Wednesday 19 May 1965
CONCERT
Les Jeux Interdits, Victoria Ballroom, Cambridge,
England

Wednesday 2 June 1965
CONCERT
Les Jeux Interdits, Victoria
Ballroom, Cambridge, England

Saturday 5 June 1965
CONCERT
Dorothy Ballroom, Cambridge,
England
With Bob Kidman & His Orchestra,
The Prowlers, Bryan & The Brunelles
and Fernando & The Hideaways.

Tuesday 15 June 1965
CONCERT
Peterhouse College May Ball,
Peterhouse College, Cambridge,
England
With Zoot Money's Big Roll Band, The
Paramounts (later known as Procol
Harum), steel band, dance band and
cabaret.

Wednesday 30 June 1965
CONCERT
Les Jeux Interdits, Victoria Ballroom, Cambridge,
England

Saturday 3 July 1965
CONCERT
Dorothy Ballroom, Cambridge, England
Tuesday 6 & Wednesday 7 July 1965
CONCERTS
Les Jeux Interdits, Victoria Ballroom, Cambridge,
England

Wednesday 1 September 1965
CONCERT
Les Jeux Interdits, Victoria Ballroom, Cambridge,
England

Wednesday 8 September 1965
CONCERT
Les Jeux Interdits, Victoria Ballroom, Cambridge,
England

October 1965
CONCERT
Great Shelford, near Cambridge, England
With The Tea Set and Paul Simon (see Pink Floyd
1965 for further information).

Friday 12 November 1965
CONCERT
Youth Club Dance, Main Hall, Bassingbourn Village
College, Bassingbourn, near Royston, England

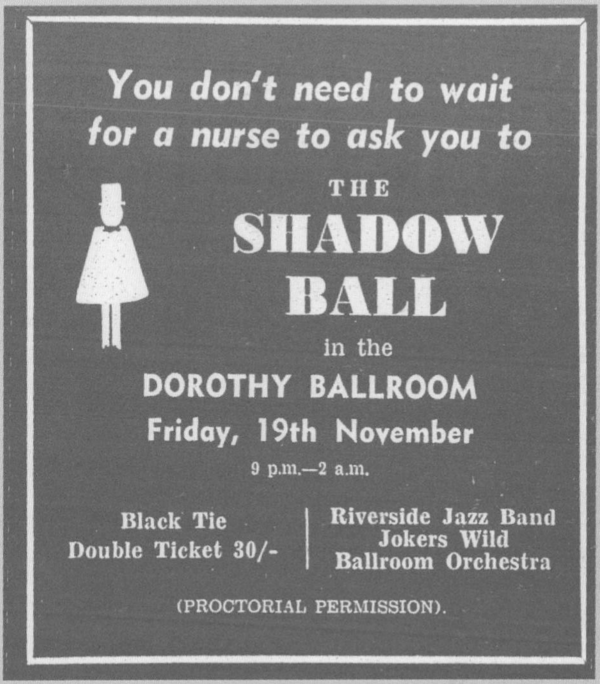

You don't need to wait
for a nurse to ask you to
THE
**SHADOW
BALL**
in the
DOROTHY BALLROOM
Friday, 19th November
9 p.m.—2 a.m.

Black Tie   Riverside Jazz Band
Double Ticket 30/-   Jokers Wild
               Ballroom Orchestra

(PROCTORIAL PERMISSION).

Friday 19 November 1965
CONCERT
Shadow Ball, Dorothy Ballroom, Cambridge,
England
With the Riverside Jazz Band and Ballroom
Orchestra.

Friday 26 November 1965
CONCERT
The Gymnasium, Comberton Village College,
Comberton, near Cambridge, England

Autumn 1965
CONCERT
The Pit Club, Cambridge University, Cambridge,
England
Supporting George Melly.

Autumn 1965
CONCERT
Byam Shaw School of Art, Kensington, London,
England
With Pink Floyd Sound (see: Pink Floyd 1965 for
further information).

Wednesday 12 January 1966
CONCERT
Les Jeux Interdits, Victoria Ballroom, Cambridge,
England
Wednesday 30 March 1966
CONCERT
Les Jeux Interdits, Victoria Ballroom, Cambridge,
England

> pre-pink floyd

Wednesday 20 April 1966
CONCERT
Les Jeux Interdits, Victoria Ballroom, Cambridge, England

Wednesday 18 May 1966
CONCERT
Les Jeux Interdits, Victoria Ballroom, Cambridge, England
This is the last advertised performance by Jokers Wild in the Cambridge area. In addition to the shows listed above, they are said to have performed at dances at the RAF and USAF bases around the Cambridge area including those at Mildenhall, Lakenheath, Alconbury and Chicksands. Additionally Clive Welham recalls, in his last few weeks with the band, performing at various society parties in London as well as an Admiralty League dance at the Dorchester Hotel in London and a support slot with The Animals at a London art college.

ABOVE: DAVID GILMOUR AND RICK WILLS PERFORMING AS FLOWERS AT LE BILBOQUET, PARIS, FRANCE IN 1967

JOKERS WILD / THE FLOWERS / BULLIT

(Summer 1966 – Summer 1967)
David Altham: Rhythm Guitar (to December 1966)
David Gilmour: Guitar, Vocals
Rick Wills: Bass Guitar (from January 1967)
John 'Willie' Wilson: Drums

Summer 1966 – Summer 1967
CONCERTS
Spain, France and The Netherlands

When Gilmour moved to London in the early summer of 1966, the original Jokers Wild effectively split. However, with former band mates John 'Willie' Wilson, David Altham and new recruit Rick Wills the name was briefly revived and under the guidance of a newly appointed manager, John-Paul Salvatore (who happened to be the brother-in-law of Tony Secunda who managed the Move), the band changed their name to Bullit and headed off for a three-month residency at the Los Monteros Hotel in Marbella, Spain. They also performed at a coming-out ball for a member of the Dutch royal family in The Netherlands, worked around the French Riviera as well as a residency at the Jean-Jacques Hotel in St. Etienne, France. When Altham quit the band at the end of 1966 the trio of Gilmour, Wilson and Wills changed their name to Flowers and toured France before securing a three-month residency at the Bilboquet club in Paris which ended in September 1967, whereupon the band folded and returned to the UK. Of the type of material the band performed in their latter period, Gilmour recalled in an interview with *Record Collector* that, 'We did a lot of soul: Wilson Pickett, the Four Tops and one or two Beach Boys type things. We had some mics stolen in France and I had to zoom back to London to buy some new ones. I went to a club called Blaises in South Kensington and saw Hendrix by chance, jamming with the Brian Auger Trinity [21 December 1966]. It was amazing. So we started to do Hendrix things as well. We did nearly all of *Are You Experienced*'.

LONDON 1963 - 1965

Between autumn 1963 and the end of 1965 a series of bands containing one or more members of the future Pink Floyd were formed in London, England.

THE TAILBOARD TWO

(Autumn 1963)
Keith Noble: Vocals
Roger Waters: Guitar

SIGMA 6 / THE MEGGADEATHS

(Autumn / Winter 1963)
Nick Mason: Drums
Clive Metcalf: Bass Guitar
Keith Noble: Vocals
Sheilagh Noble: Backing vocals
Chris Thomson: Rhythm Guitar
Roger Waters: Guitar
Richard Wright: Keyboards, Brass

THE ABDABS / THE SCREAMING ABDABS

(Spring / Summer 1964)
Juliette Gale: Vocals
Nick Mason: Drums
Clive Metcalf: Bass Guitar
Keith Noble: Vocals
Roger Waters: Guitar

Richard Wright: Rhythm Guitar, Keyboards, Brass

Spring 1964
CONCERT
The Marquee, Wardour Street, London, England
Billed as The Abdabs. The band's only appearance at a proper music venue, according to Keith Noble, was at the Marquee appearing as extras in an unknown film production.

LEONARD'S LODGERS

(Autumn 1964)
Roger 'Syd' Barrett: Rhythm Guitar, Vocals
Rado 'Bob' Klose: Guitar, Vocals
Mike Leonard: Keyboards
Nick Mason: Drums
Roger Waters: Bass Guitar, Vocals

Autumn 1964
CONCERTS
The Woodman public house, Highgate, London, England

Autumn 1964
CONCERTS
The Winchester public house, Highgate, London, England
Although no specific dates have been found it is known the above two pubs hosted regular performances by the band.

THE SPECTRUM FIVE

(Autumn 1964)
Roger 'Syd' Barrett: Rhythm Guitar, Vocals
Rado 'Bob' Klose: Guitar, Vocals
Nick Mason: Drums
Roger Waters: Bass Guitar
Mike Leonard: Keyboards

Autumn 1964
CONCERT
Camberwell School of Art, Camberwell, London, England
Dick Maunders, the promoter of the show, recalled that: 'I was attending Camberwell Art School during the mid Sixties at the time Syd Barrett was there [although I seem to remember he was called Roger]. He was a couple of years above me. I was the college social secretary and I recall that on one occasion we were stuck for a group to play at a dance. I was told that there was a sort of in-house group who might play on the night in question. This turned out to be Syd Barrett's band, who were called The Spectrum Five, most of whom went on to be Pink Floyd. They played a mixture of blues and rock; I think we paid them about £20 plus booze! We never booked them again as I think Syd left the college.'

THE TEA SET

(Autumn 1964)

Roger 'Syd' Barrett: Rhythm Guitar, Vocals
Rado 'Bob' Klose: Guitar, Vocals
Chris Dennis: Vocals
Nick Mason: Drums
Mike Leonard: Keyboards (on occasion)
Roger Waters: Bass Guitar

October 1964
CONCERT
High Pines, Oxshott, England
Billed as The Tea Set. The band were booked to appear at a private party at this manor house in Surrey.

October 1964
CONCERT
The Large Hall, Regent Street Polytechnic, London, England
Billed as The Tea Set. Supporting The Tridents (featuring 20-year old Jeff Beck on guitar).

THE TEA SET / PINK FLOYD
(Winter - Spring 1965)
Roger 'Syd' Barrett: Rhythm Guitar, Vocals
Rado 'Bob' Klose: Guitar, Vocals
Nick Mason: Drums
Roger Waters: Bass Guitar, Vocals
Richard Wright: Keyboards

January 1965
CONCERT
RAF Uxbridge, Uxbridge, England
Billed as The Tea Set. It has been reported that the band changed their name from The Tea Set to Pink Floyd halfway through a show at this west London RAF station. Although Chris Dennis was supposedly stationed at this base further research through the RAF archives has failed to reveal anything to corroborate this story.

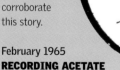

February 1965
RECORDING ACETATE
'Lucy Leave' / 'I'm A King Bee'
UK Pressing (7-inch acetate single).
A collector discovered this Emidisc acetate in the late Eighties. 'Lucy Leave' is a band composition and 'I'm A King Bee' a cover of the R&B standard by Slim Harpo. Whilst it clearly is a recording of the formative Pink Floyd - Barrett's distinctive lead vocal and guitar is particularly evident - it also shows a band performing a very straightforward R&B style.

February 1965
CONCERT
The Count Down Coffee and Wine Bar, Kensington, London, England
Billed as The Tea Set. According to Nick Mason, in his book *Inside Out, A Personal History of Pink Floyd*, the band performed here on at least two other occasions, with at least one being an acoustic set that included the songs 'How High The Moon' and 'Long Tall Texan'. Additionally, Roger Waters commented in *Vox Pop* that, 'We played from eight 'til one in the morning with a twenty minute break in the middle. We were paid £15 for that.'

March 1965
AUDITION
Beat City, Oxford Street, London
Billed as Pink Floyd. The band attended a live audition at this club but failed to secure any bookings.

PINK FLOYD / THE TEA SET
(Summer – Winter 1965)
Roger 'Syd' Barrett: Rhythm Guitar, Vocals
Nick Mason: Drums
Roger Waters: Bass Guitar, Vocals
Richard Wright: Keyboards, Saxophone, Vocals

Saturday 22 May 1965
CONCERT
Summer Dance, Homerton College, Cambridge, England
Billed as Pink Floyd. With Geoff Mott's Boston Crabs and Unit 4 + 2.

Sunday 27 June 1965
CONCERT
Melody Maker National Beat Contest, Wimbledon Palais, Wimbledon, London, England
Billed as Pink Floyd. The band entered into the ninth heat of this annual contest, organised by *Melody Maker*, but failed to gain a place in any successive heats. Also appearing were St. Louis Union (winners of this heat), Phil Hunter & The Jaguars, The Ravens and The Poachers.

Sunday 27 June 1965
CONCERT
Beat Contest, The Country Club, Belsize Park, London, England
Billed as Pink Floyd. In Pink Floyd's 1974-5 UK/US tour programme mention is made that the group lost

both this and the above contest on the same night. The band had already played at this venue on occasion but no further details could be found.

October 1965
CONCERT
Great Shelford, near Cambridge, England
Billed as The Tea Set. The band together with Jokers Wild and Paul Simon performed at a highbrow private party hosted by Mr. Douglas January on behalf of his daughter Libby's 21st birthday, who was being courted by Storm Thorgerson. Of Paul Simon, Clive Welham recalled that, 'He did a set with classics like "Where Have All The Flowers Gone?" in front of all these rich businessmen. Some songs were quite critical of them, but they had no idea and were applauding wildly. It was in a marquee at the back of this large country house. I sat on and off the drum kit because of my wrist problems. Willie Wilson sat in on drums and I came to the front on tambourine.' Four years later the house was used as the location for the front cover of Pink Floyd's *Ummagumma* album sleeve.

October 1965
CONCERT
Byam Shaw School of Art, Kensington, London, England
Billed as Pink Floyd. Will Garfitt, the promoter of the show, recalled that, 'There was a big end of term party that had a birdcage theme and we had both Pink Floyd and Jokers Wild play inside this enormous birdcage we had built with bird mobiles hanging up everywhere and all that psychedelic lighting. I think they got paid £10 each for that gig.'

October 1965
CONCERT
Cambridge, England
Billed as Pink Floyd. Supporting Humphrey Lyttelton at an unknown Cambridge University ball.

December 1965
CONCERT
Goings On Club, Archer Street, London, England
Billed as Pink Floyd.

Saturday 18 December 1965
CONCERT
Village Hall, Old Weston, near Huntingdon, England
Billed as The Tea Set.

Friday 31 December 1965
CONCERT
New Years Dance, Youth Centre, Kimbolton, near Huntingdon, England
Billed as The Tea Set.

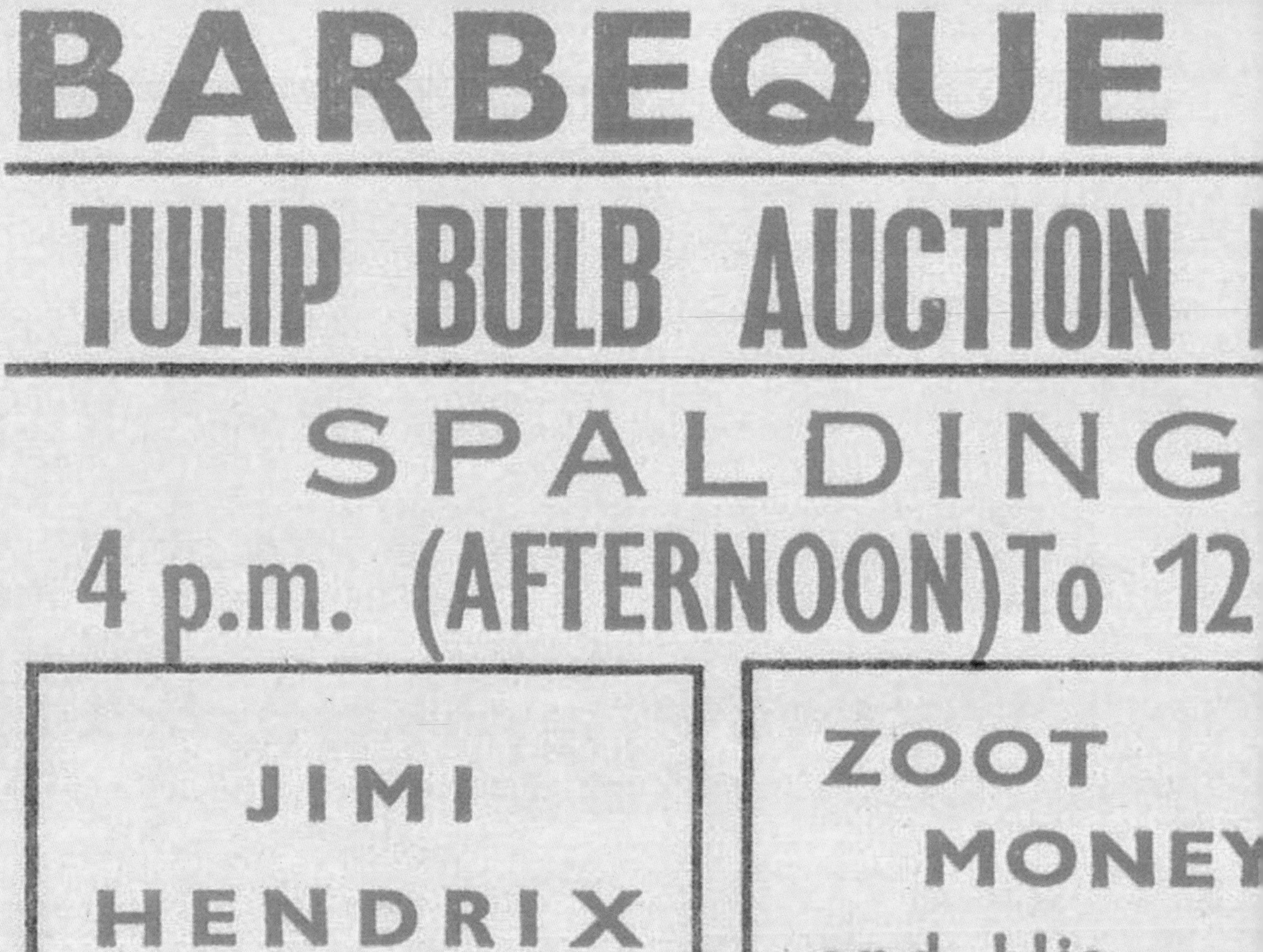

BARBEQUE

TULIP BULB AUCTION

SPALDING

4 p.m. (AFTERNOON) To 12

JIMI HENDRIX EXPERIENCE

ZOOT MONEY and His Big Roll Ba

CREAM

PINK FLO

ADVANCE TICKETS £1 (OR

streaming through the starlit skies

67

ALL

MON.
29th
MAY

.m.   (AT NIGHT)

GENO
Washington
and the RAM
JAM BAND

d

MOVE

Y AT THE DOOR)

Nº

7380

2

b

BY EARLY 1966 PINK FLOYD'S FORTUNES WERE TAKING A DRAMATIC TURN FOR THE BETTER. THE FLEDGLING BAND HAD SECURED A SERIES OF GIGS AT THE MARQUEE CLUB IN LONDON'S SOHO, ORGANISED BY AN AMERICAN ENTREPRENEUR, BERNARD STOLLMAN. THEY WERE ESSENTIALLY AN EXTENSION OF A SERIES OF SMALLER SCALE PERFORMANCE EVENTS THAT HAD ALREADY BEEN HELD EITHER SIDE OF CHRISTMAS AT THE GOINGS ON CLUB IN SOHO AND HOSTED BY CREAM LYRICIST AND POET PETE BROWN, WHERE PINK FLOYD HAD ALREADY APPEARED.

The first of these events was held from 4.30pm on Sunday 30 January and was billed as a 'Giant Mystery Happening' and ran every Sunday afternoon thereafter. Pink Floyd's first appearance there was on 13 March and was advertised on handbills simply as 'Trip', although the subsequent shows became more commonly known as 'Spontaneous Underground'.

Apart from the first 'Happening', the shows were never advertised in the press – even the Marquee's weekly advert in *Melody Maker* shows every Sunday as 'Closed For Private Hire'. Instead they relied solely on an audience of the performers' friends and a handful of freaks that had heard the word on the street or found handbills at select outlets. There were never more than fifty or so people at any one event although they did prove to be a turning point in the band's emergence as an original talent. The shows allowed them to get away with almost anything on stage, but more importantly, they brought them to the attention of the people who were beginning to shape 'alternative London'.

Coincidentally, and fortuitously, it was at the last one of these events on 12 June that would-be pop manager Peter Jenner chanced upon the band he had been dreaming of. At the time he was a bored lecturer at the London School of Economics and he and his friend John 'Hoppy' Hopkins were seeking a way of making their

fortune within the booming music industry. The pair had already formed a loose partnership with friends Joe Boyd and Ron Atkins in the shape of DNA Productions and had signed up a group called AMM to a management agreement. Boyd, an expatriate American was working as Elektra Records' UK representative, and signed them to the label, but Jenner soon realised he had obtained a painfully small financial return for his troubles.

It is worth noting that AMM were achieving some notoriety in London. They dressed in white laboratory coats and experimented heavily in infant electronics and unconventional amplification methods, creating a unique sound, which pre-dated 'Krautrock' by several years. They operated out of the Beckenham Arts Lab, not far from Barrett's art school at Camberwell, and they too were regulars on Sundays at the Marquee. Clearly they were an inspiration and in particular for Pink Floyd's more abstract sounds, which were becoming fundamental to their new direction. Nevertheless, their album, *AMMMusic*, now reissued on CD, is an almost continuous drone and one of the most tuneless rackets of all time. Consequently it didn't take DNA long to realise that a more mainstream act would be a wiser investment.

What Jenner heard that day was, for the most part, a very conventional set. 'At that stage they were a blues band who played things like "Louie Louie" and then played wacky bits in the middle. I wandered around trying to work out whether the noise was coming from the keyboards or from the guitar and that was what interested me.'[1] But, as Waters later said, 'We didn't know many songs, so it was a matter of settling on a chord and improvising, if that's the word.'[2] Peter Whitehead, film student and friend of the band from Cambridge, was studying at Slade School of Art in London at the time and joked that he invented the Pink

Floyd sound: 'I was living in this house where the band used to practice in the hall. And their music got louder and louder and my music – lots of Janacek and Bartok – got louder too. Poor old Syd was doing his Chuck Berry and Little Richard and having to compete with my copy of "Das Rheingold".[3]

Jenner may have been rejoicing in his find but his initial offer to manage the band was met with indifference: they were far more concerned with their impending holidays, unsure if they would even bother resuming on their return. But Jenner tried again a few weeks later, in late September, and this time got a more favourable response. As Hopkins was now concentrating on other things, Jenner decided to draft in a new business partner, Andrew King, an old friend. King had time on his hands to book gigs, having recently quit his job at British European Airways, as well as an inheritance with which to buy the band new equipment (reportedly £1,000 worth of new amplifiers!), and a partnership was forged.

Meanwhile, Spontaneous Underground had folded and the party was moving to Notting Hill in west London. It was a fairly run-down multicultural district at the time: its low rents and the easy availability of drugs from the West Indian community attracted its fair share of students and other young people keen to live a bohemian lifestyle.

DNA had also fallen by the wayside and Hopkins' interests, after a recent trip to America, now lay in creating a community identity and spirit by setting up an 'anti-university' in the form of an enlightened night school and citizens advice bureau for the local population. With substantial help from Hopkins' friends Jenner, King, Boyd and many others, the London Free School (LFS) began

life on 8 March 1966.

The LFS was located in a basement flat at 26 Powis Terrace, rented from the notorious British black power activist Michael X. For all its good intentions, it was fraught with funding problems from the outset and by the following year had degenerated into a dope smoking haven and rehearsal space for local bands. If one good thing came from the experiment, it was the fact that it led to the now internationally renowned Notting Hill Carnival, which that July was organised by LFS. Later Boyd recalled above all the 'wild-eyed, slightly condescending idealism, bringing the over-educated elite into healthy contact with the working class'.[4] However, the core group of organisers were reluctant to let their talents go to waste and sought to raise cash in order to publish a more informed, London-wide newspaper than the LFS's community newsletter, *The Grove*. They decided to do this by holding 'social dances' at All Saints Church Hall in nearby Powis Gardens. The vicar was willing to allow the hall to be used for this purpose, because, under the auspices of the LFS, the dances would benefit the whole of the local community.

It wasn't long before Jenner and King's newly signed band were invited to perform, accompanied at the first show by slide projections to enhance their act, and created by Joel and Toni Brown, friends of John Hopkins and visitors to London from Timothy Leary's Millbrook Center in the USA. Word spread on the bush telegraph that something new and exciting was happening in Notting Hill and after only a few appearances by the band the hall was packed to capacity.

Similar lighting effects to the Brown's had been a common feature at concert dances on the West Coast of America for some time, but it is believed that the couple

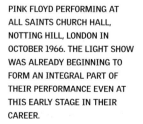

PINK FLOYD PERFORMING AT ALL SAINTS CHURCH HALL, NOTTING HILL, LONDON IN OCTOBER 1966. THE LIGHT SHOW WAS ALREADY BEGINNING TO FORM AN INTEGRAL PART OF THEIR PERFORMANCE EVEN AT THIS EARLY STAGE IN THEIR CAREER.

PETER JENNER << The result was these hugely dramatic shadows behind [the band], which I'm sure everyone thought was brilliant. Of course, it was a complete fuck-up, and mistake, as all the best things are. >>

were responsible for introducing the first psychedelic 'light-show' to the UK. Before long, however, the phenomenon would be viewed as more sinister than mere visual entertainment. The media linked it to the growing availability of psychedelic drugs such as LSD, and suggested that the purpose of light shows was to intensify the multi-sensory effects of hallucinogens.

It was also during the latter part of 1966 that their former landlord, Mike Leonard, had been developing what can only be described as a "sound and light workshop" at Hornsey College of Art. His experiments were based around the control of light by sound. Instead of playing records to his projections, Leonard started to invite the band to perform live. As Mason later recalled, 'The most important starting point for the light show was Mike Leonard and the Hornsey College of Art. That was the idea that the music could be improvised and the lighting could be improvised to go with it. And that definitely was an influence.'[5]

Although far from anything that would later give Pink Floyd its legendary trademark, these rudimentary sessions sowed the seeds for the future and before long many more amateur technicians were busy developing static and moving oil-based slide shows to accompany live music. Pink Floyd's first touring light-show was built by Peter Jenner, his wife Sumi and Andrew King using closed-beam spotlights which they mounted on wooden boards and activated by domestic light switches. 'The result was these hugely dramatic shadows behind [the band], which I'm sure everyone thought was brilliant,' mused Jenner. 'Of course, it was a complete fuck-up, and mistake, as all the best things are.'[6]

Jack Bracelin was the first to take the light-show business seriously and founded Five Acre Lights, which during the next year was to provide the environmental lighting at many 'alternative' venues in London. Over the next few months Pink Floyd used various lighting technicians: Joe Gannon was the first, a former student of the lighting workshop at Hornsey. He was often regarded in the press of the day as the 'fifth Floyd', as he was their first full-time technician on the road. 'I design the slides, basing them on my idea of the music,' explained Gannon, who had also rebuilt Jenner and King's contraption into something more sophisticated. 'The lights work rhythmically, I just wave my hand over the micro-switches and the different colours flash.'[7] Gannon was replaced in the summer of 1967 by Peter Wynne-Wilson and by Christmas 1967, John Marsh. As with most small-scale operations, they also shared the driving between gigs.

Throughout the early autumn Hopkins was busy organising the finance and staff to produce his London-wide newspaper and in October the first edition of *International Times*, or *IT* as it came to be known, was published. Issued fortnightly as an information centre and non-political broadsheet dealing with musical, literary, artistic and social issues, as well as the drug culture, it was produced in the basement of co-editor Barry Miles' influential alternative bookshop Indica Bookshop and Gallery.

A massive launch party was held for *IT* on 15 October, not at All Saints Church Hall, but at the vast Roundhouse in Chalk Farm, north London, a dilapidated Victorian railway turning shed. As Pink Floyd were regarded as the house band, they topped the bill, playing their biggest show to date while securing valuable mainstream media exposure. Indirectly this gig led to a further string of dates at the Roundhouse and by the end of the year they had even appeared at an Oxfam benefit concert at the prestigious Royal Albert Hall.

Pink Floyd were at last making ripples within the

BELOW: PINK FLOYD'S FIRST PUBLICITY PHOTOGRAPH TAKEN BY THEIR MANAGEMENT COMPANY BLACKHILL, IN NOVEMBER 1966. IT WAS SENT TO REGIONAL NEWSPAPERS IN THE HOPE OF PUBLICISING FORTHCOMING GIGS, BUT WAS RARELY PUBLISHED.

alternative music scene and, although they had no record contract yet, they were building a large and faithful London following. In addition, Barrett was becoming a prolific songwriter and over a period of time the band's covers of blues standards were giving way to his songs of childlike wonder and space rituals, with frenzied feedback overlaid at an ever-increasing volume.

It was shortly after the *IT* launch that Jenner was able to relinquish his post at LSE and join King full-time in their management venture, Blackhill Enterprises. The business was run from Jenner's Paddington town house, with June Child (later the wife of Marc Bolan) as its secretary. A six-way partnership was created with the band and, with enthusiasm prevailing over experience, the pair were able to book a series of shows, primarily based on Jenner's contacts, in the period leading up to Christmas.

However, Blackhill were no experts at booking their band into national venues, which is where they needed to spread their wings. Coincidentally, the Bryan Morrison Agency, a small but rapidly expanding firm of booking agents, who also handled The Pretty Things among others, were asked to book Pink Floyd, a band they had never even heard of, for the London based Architectural Association's annual Christmas Ball. The New Year was already looking up for Blackhill and Pink Floyd, and a successful partnership with Bryan Morrison's company began.

Unfortunately, things weren't going so well for Hopkins or Boyd. Boyd was fired from Elektra Records and *IT* was suffering major cash-flow problems, because insufficient advertising revenue was being generated. At the same time, although the All Saints Church Hall events were well attended, the London Free School still couldn't pay its bills. Its financial burdens were ultimately relieved when Boyd and Hopkins realised that a move away from Notting Hill to a more central location would attract a wider audience, increasing their potential income.

In no time at all they had secured the ideal venue: an Irish basement ballroom, located under the Berkeley Cinema, called The Blarney, conveniently located on Tottenham Court Road in the heart of the West End. The landlord, Mr. Gannon, was prepared to hire it out on Friday nights from 10.30pm (when the Irish club closed) until dawn for the grand sum of £15. It was also much larger than All Saints and could therefore cope with the expected increase in attendance.

Initially two dates were booked, one either side of Christmas, and the very last of the combined Hopkins and *IT* money was invested. On 23 and 30 December 1966

THE OPENING NIGHT OF *UFO* ON 23 DECEMBER 1966. PINK FLOYD PERFORMED A TOTAL OF TEN TIMES AT THE UFO CLUB BETWEEN THIS AND ITS CLOSING NIGHT ON 28 JULY 1967.

JOE BOYD   << A vacuum waiting to be filled. Hundreds of freaks looking for a central meeting point. >>

'UFO Presents Night Tripper' was launched at the Blarney.

The club's name was a matter of some debate, 'Unidentified Flying Object' or 'Underground Freak Out', depending on who was asked – either way, the general consensus of opinion was that it was pronounced "You – Foe". Since Boyd elected to manage the venue, it reverted to his preferred title of simply 'UFO'. 'A vacuum waiting to be filled,' he remembered. 'Hundreds of freaks looking for a central meeting point.'[8] As Britain's first, and now legendary, psychedelic club, UFO continued to be held on these premises until the end of July 1967, publicised with large Day-Glo and multicoloured screen-printed posters designed by Michael English and Nigel Waymouth under the moniker of 'Hapshash and The Coloured Coat' and

printed and distributed by Osiris Visions, one of Joe Boyd's other small enterprises. As well as showcasing a huge variety of new underground acts and established bands, including Soft Machine, Arthur Brown and Tomorrow, it also promoted the recently converted-to-psychedelia Move and Procol Harum. The future of *IT* was at last secured and indeed it went on to outlive UFO by many years.

The vast amount of coverage the band was now receiving in the music press and the pressure of engagements were compromising their studies. Now, with a good London following, it seemed only logical that if they were to continue seriously then they should turn their attention to securing a record deal, and this required a demo tape.

Consequently, Jenner and King attempted to record them at a private session on 31 October. Boyd was certain that Elektra would go for the band and played Jac Holzman a tape but he offered them such a paltry deal it wasn't pursued. Indeed Blackhill must have been banking heavily on Elektra, or at least got very close to a deal, as some concert adverts in early November 1966 state Pink Floyd as Elektra recording artists. Undeterred, Boyd even took Island label boss Chris Blackwell to see the band perform, and although he liked what he saw, his label was still mainly concentrating on Jamaican acts (although they had recorded The VIPs – later renamed Art - as their first 'rock' act that same year.)

Finally, Boyd introduced them to Alan Bates of Polydor Records, who was also showing significant interest. Pink Floyd even went so far as to rehearse at their studios in Stratford Place, accompanied at least once by Morrison and two of his staff, Tony Howard and one Steve O'Rourke.

But keeping his cards close to his chest the shrewd Morrison had already been courting EMI producer Norman Smith and was holding out for their decision - after all, that's where The Beatles were and they were the biggest band in the world. Morrison's actions were unbeknown to Boyd, who seeing Polydor as his golden opportunity, had rather impetuously formed Witchseason Productions with the intention of producing Pink Floyd and licensing the recordings to them.

Publicly Morrison suggested they should hold off on the Polydor deal and get themselves into a studio with the aim of selling a finished master tape to a prospective record company rather than going cap in hand with a rough demo tape. Since the ubiquitous Boyd had at his disposal the facilities of Sound Techniques studios in Chelsea, he offered his services as the band's producer

and with Blackhill barely solvent, Morrison financed the sessions starting on 23 January, in return for a percentage of the future publishing. On 29 January they recorded 'Arnold Layne', selected as the standout song of their repertoire, because of its catchy tune and lyric, and 'Candy And A Currant Bun' as its b-side. Within two days the band were signed to EMI and on 1 February 1967 Pink Floyd turned professional.

Curiously, in the middle of all this activity, it was in fact their friend Peter Whitehead who got them into the studio first. He had started to produce his own documentary film, funded by the British Film Institute and needed some soundtrack music. No doubt egged on by Syd Barrett's girlfriend, Jenny Spires, with whom he was having an illicit affair, Whitehead funded a recording session at Sound Techniques studios, again with Boyd in attendance as producer, on the 11 and 12 January. The result was a lengthy take of their live favourite, 'Interstellar Overdrive', which Whitehead used for his snapshot of swinging London, entitled *Tonite Let's All Make Love In London*. Although it didn't receive a cinematic release until 1968 it was premiered at the New York Film Festival on 26 September 1967. Remarkably, when the soundtrack album was being prepared for a re-release in 1990, Whitehead also unearthed a hitherto forgotten instrumental track entitled 'Nick's Boogie' that was also recorded at the same session.

Morrison's master plan had worked, but to Boyd's immense horror EMI weren't so keen on independent producers and insisted on using their own in-house staff and facilities. His days were numbered. 'I was choked when Morrison persuaded them to wait,' he remembers bitterly. 'EMI were very hostile to indie producers at the time.'[9] In reality the band had little choice because the man responsible for signing the cheque, Sidney Arthur Beecher-Stevens (who incidentally, as head of sales at Decca in 1962, was one of the many executives to turn down The Beatles), insisted that as part of the deal staff producer Norman Smith should be responsible for watching over, but not interfering with, Pink Floyd's future recording career. This also allayed certain fears within EMI that some of the more undesirable fringe elements associated with the band would distract them from their professional obligations.

Interestingly, the deal, as bad as it was (a £5,000 advance over five years; a low royalty rate plus studio costs recharged), also included album development, which was very unusual for the time, since the market was very singles-led. EMI knew they had something but, since it was unlike anything else they'd heard before, they

LEFT: SITTING ON THE STAIRS OF LANDLORD MIKE LEONARD'S HOUSE, 22 JANUARY 1967. THE FRONT ROOM DOUBLED AS BOTH ACCOMMODATION AND REHEARSAL SPACE UNTIL NOISE COMPLAINTS FROM NEIGHBOURS FORCED THE BAND TO RELOCATE ELSEWHERE.

OVERLEAF: PINK FLOYD'S FIRST OFFICIAL PHOTO CALL AT EMI RECORDS ON 3 MARCH 1967, AHEAD OF THE RELEASE OF THEIR DEBUT SINGLE 'ARNOLD LAYNE'.

didn't know quite what. They took the decision to just let the band get on with it, and this has been their general policy over the years (Pink Floyd are still with the label having thankfully renegotiated their original deal at an early stage), proving that Beecher-Stevens' gamble more than paid off. 'I classed them as weird, but good,'[10] he confessed.

Having heard the tracks on offer, EMI set about re-recording them at their own studio at 3 Abbey Road in London's St. John's Wood. Although Boyd had been given the nudge, he certainly had the last laugh when his original recordings were used after all. As Norman Smith recalled, 'I told the boys I'd like to have another go at any rate and in fact we set up this recording to do just that along with other titles. It was an all-night session, and I could see that they weren't too keen to attempt a remake, so in fact we never did have a go at that.'[11]

When 'Arnold Layne' came out in March, the band had even made a promo film to back it up. Filmed at Wittering beach on the south coast in the depths of winter it was a comical tribute to the Beatles *Help!* movie. Blackhill even paid to have the single hyped in order to ensure that it reached a favourable chart position. As a result the BBC filmed them for *Top Of The Pops* (although it was not broadcast) and the single was guaranteed plenty of radio airplay. Bizarrely, although the BBC (Radio One didn't start until September 1967) were happy to oblige, the more leftfield pirate station Radio London banned it for being too smutty - in reality a contrived demonstration to display moral standards in their bid for an official government broadcast license. Even Pete Murray reviewed it on BBC TV's *Juke Box Jury*, but his comments infuriated Waters: 'He said we were a con. He thought it was just contrived rubbish to meet

ROGER WATERS << **We are simply a pop group. But because we use light and colour in our act a lot of people seem to imagine that we are trying to put across some message with nasty, evil undertones.** >>

some kind of unhealthy demand.'[12]

Furthermore, a backlash was brewing in certain media circles. It was suggested that Pink Floyd, then spearheading the 'counter-culture', were promoting music sympathetic to certain types of drug abuse. In particular

The News Of The World, then a weekly national broadsheet, set out to alert the general public of the evils of drugs in pop music and set in motion a whole month's worth of investigative reports into this throughout February. The 13 February edition, in particular, started off with a huge heading that read, 'Pop Songs And The Cult Of LSD' above a photo of Pink Floyd with the caption, 'The Pink Floyd group specialise in "psychedelic music" which is designed to illustrate LSD experiences.' The two-page article that followed highlighted the London Free School's apparently subversive activities and Pink Floyd's music in particular. This article alone caused the management of the Southampton Guildhall to cancel one of the band's impending shows.

EMI were then forced to issue a statement to the press to effectively deny all knowledge of the drug connections in Pink Floyd's music, which was also exacerbated by the same article slamming their release of The Smoke's single, 'My Friend Jack'. The newspaper allowed some recourse, and Pink Floyd more-or-less stated that, the term 'psychedelic', to them, meant the use of light and sound in performance rather than an excuse to take LSD. Even as late as July the band were hampered by the sideswipes they received, which caused Waters to air his frustrations in the *NME*: 'We are simply a pop group. But because we use light and colour in our act a lot of people seem to imagine that we are trying to put across some message with nasty, evil undertones.'

Surprisingly, despite all the LSD connotations of their act, the band was a very straight-laced bunch. It was only much later that drugs featured on the agenda: 'None of them did drugs when I met them,' said Jenner, 'except Syd, and we would only smoke dope. Then in the Summer of Love and all that bollocks Syd got very enthusiastic about acid and got into the religious aspect of it. The others were very straight. Rick would take a puff now and again, but Roger and Nick would never go near it.'[13]

If EMI were worried about the drugs issue, they should have been far more concerned about the band's live performance. Both 'Arnold Layne' and its June follow-up, 'See Emily Play', were as far removed from their stage act as they could possibly be. Their quaint pop songs were ignored completely in favour of high-volume, mind-bending workouts lasting in some cases well over ten minutes. While these were acceptable on their home turf of London, provincial audiences were nonplussed, fully expecting to hear their chart hits. Pink Floyd literally hit the audience with a wall of sound verging on 'white noise'.

This reputation had already spread, as *Melody Maker* pointed out: 'Are Pink Floyd being quite honest when they make coy and attractive records like 'See Emily Play' then proceed to make the night hideous with a thunderous, incomprehensible, screaming, sonic torture that five American doctors agree could permanently damage the senses?'

When word got around that they rarely played their chart successes, some promoters insisted on making the band sign a pre-performance clause to ensure that they did so, to avoid audience unrest. Many of the out-of-London bookings would often riot when confronted by this vision from hell. Stories of the reception the band received in some parts of the country are near legendary. Beer glasses (and their contents) were thrown at them, fights broke out and torrents of abuse were hurled, as Nick Mason testified: 'During that period we were

list, forcing this material, rather than 'the hits', on the public was verging on professional suicide. The industry was a very different beast back in the Sixties – records actually climbed the charts and they had to sell significantly more copies than today. Chart positions secured more bookings and higher fees and bands paid their dues by constantly gigging with endless drives day and night along a network of pre-motorway roads. Structured touring such that we know of today wasn't really heard of but there was a thriving live music scene and almost every town the length and breadth of Britain had a venue that hosted weekly beat, soul or jazz dances. The underground psychedelic scene (i.e. not the one created by the mass media or The Beatles) was barely known of in the provinces and publications such as *IT* and *OZ* had almost no distribution outside of London, leaving only a handful of 'freaks' or 'heads' in tune with

NICK MASON   << **During that period we were working at Top Rank circuits and they hated it. Hated it. We could clear halls so fast it wasn't true. I mean they were outraged by what came round on the revolving stage and they lost very little time in trying to make this clear.** >>

working at Top Rank circuits and they hated it. Hated it. We could clear halls so fast it wasn't true. I mean they were outraged by what came round on the revolving stage and they lost very little time in trying to make this clear.'[14] But, he explained, 'we were not demoralised. We rejuvenated every time we came back to London and got that fix of finding that there was an audience for us.'[15]

Such was the band's determination that not once did they cease trying to win over the masses. There was no way they were going to make a single compromise. It was their way or not at all, and this was summed up in a typically ironic comment by Waters at the time: 'We've got the recording side together and not the playing side. So what we've got to do now is get together a stage act that has nothing to do with our records – things like "Interstellar Overdrive" which is beautiful, and instrumentals that are much easier to play,'[16] which of course may also have reflected their ability, or rather lack of it, at that time.

This approach may have paid off in the long run, but at the time, given their then technical prowess and set

an emerging scene to which Pink Floyd was bolted onto. This inevitably took a long time and a lot of hard work to turn around.

With that in mind it wasn't difficult to realise that it was the band's audience in London that held the key and it was that audience that needed to be developed and nurtured first and foremost. Fortunately prominent classical music promoter Christopher Hunt was broad-minded enough to recognise there was great merit in Floyd's performances - assisted no doubt by the fact that Peter Jenner's partner, Sumi, was working for him. Sticking his neck out considerably he first produced a show at the Commonwealth Institute on 17 January and, having been well received, again at the stuffy Queen Elizabeth Hall on 12 May – the latter the reserve of the classical elite. Generally regarded as a critical turning point for Pink Floyd, this show included their first public use of an idea developed in the recording studio: additional speakers were placed at the back of the hall to give an effect of 'sound in the round'. Essentially it was a crude pan pot device made by Bernard Speight, an Abbey

THE PERFORMING RIGHT SOCIETY, LTD
AN ASSOCIATION of COMPOSERS, AUTHORS AND PUBLISHERS of MUSIC
COPYRIGHT HOUSE, 29/33 BERNERS STREET, LONDON, W.I
Telephone: LANgham (six lines)

Name of premises: QUEEN ELIZABETH HALL   Performed from 12th May 1967
Address: S.E.I.
Nature of entertainment during the period: Circuit by THE PINK
Means of performance (e.g. orchestra, pianist, vocalist, etc.)

Note Particulars should be given on this form of ALL MUSIC, WHETHER PUBLISHED OR IN MANUSCRIPT, performed by ANY MEANS, e.g. orchestras, bands, choral singers, pianists, organists, variety artists or vocalists, or by means of gramophone records or tapes. (In the case of performances given in conjunction with cinematograph entertainments, special forms should be used which will be supplied on request.) ALL COLUMNS TO BE COMPLETED WHERE APPLICABLE.

Office use only	TITLE OF WORK PERFORMED	Office use only	COMPOSER	ARRANGER	PUBLISHER	EACH PERFOR A TICK IN
	TAPE DAWN		R. WATERS		MAGDALENE MUSIC	
	MATILDA MOTHER		SYD BARRETT		''	
	FLAMING		''		''	
	SCARECROW		''		''	
	GAMES FOR MAY		''		''	
	BICYCLE		''		''	
	ARNOLD LANE		''		DUNMO MUSIC	
	CANDY & A CURRANT BUN		''		''	
	POW R. TOC H.		THE PINK FLOYD		MAGDALENE MUSIC	
	INTERSTELLAR OVERDRIVE		''	''	''	
	TAPE BUBBLES		R. WRIGHT		''	
	TAPE ENDING		SYD BARRETT		''	
	LUCIFER SAM		''		''	

SPECIAL NOTE. — It is one of the conditions of the Society's licence held in respect of the above-named premises that these programme returns be made, as the royalties collected by the Society are distributed in accordance therewith.

Certified

OT MONEY
His Roll Band

K FLOYD
1 (OR PAY

Road engineer, and in technical jargon consisted of four large rheostats, which were converted from 270-degree rotation to 90-degree. Along with the shift stick, these elements were housed in a large box and enabled the panning of quadraphonic sound. The set-up was, unfortunately, stolen after the show and didn't resurface again until an obscure college dance in Portsmouth in November 1968. It did however make its widespread advertised comeback on the band's 1969 tour and dubbed the 'Azimuth Co-ordinator'. In addition, the Queen Elizabeth Hall show had props that were arranged on stage, bubble machines that let fly and a well-developed light-show which incorporated 35mm film slides and movie sequences. New compositions were also written, including the song 'Games For May', which would form the basis of the band's second single, 'See Emily Play'.

It may not have seemed so at the time, because other matters were beginning to concern the band, but 'See Emily Play' also played a decisive part in the band's history securing them radio play, TV appearances and a healthy chart position. Britain was starting to take note of these rising young stars.

Nevertheless Pink Floyd's meteoric rise to success was having an adverse side effect on Barrett, who was starting to show marked signs of fatigue. The pressure he was under as the band's leader, coupled with the self-inflicted onslaught of constant touring and recording, caused him to withdraw into himself. An increasing use of LSD, both in private and on stage, offered little escape and indeed made matters worse by filling him with chronic stage fright.

The first hint of something going slightly awry came in July, at the BBC TV Studios, where they were recording 'See Emily Play' for Top of The Pops. The single had sold significantly better than their debut, and, as a result of its chart performance, Pink Floyd appeared a remarkable three consecutive weeks on the show. (The BBC managed to erase these historic recordings, along with a substantial amount of other important archive material, in the early Seventies.) As legend has it, Pink Floyd turned out for their first appearance in all their supreme psychedelic King's Road attire. On the second show, Syd's appearance was less immaculate and by the third week he was dishevelled, unshaven and in rags, with a careless attitude, uninterested in performing, and insisting that if John Lennon didn't have to appear on the show, then neither did he.

It was the start of Barrett's increasingly erratic behaviour, which caused a catalogue of professional disasters throughout the rest of the year. The first

occurred literally the day after their final Top Of The Pops appearance at the recording studio for the BBC Light Programme's Saturday Club on 28 July. According to the engineer's report, Syd just 'freaked out'[17] and the session was abandoned. A lengthy correspondence between unimpressed BBC producers and Blackhill ensued which marked their card for future appearances. Hopes were upheld for a return performance at UFO that same night and Boyd in particular was looking forward to seeing the band again but when he made eye contact with Barrett the singer just blanked him. 'It was like somebody had pulled the blinds, you know, nobody home.'[18]

At the Love-In Festival the following day June Bolan observed him on stage: 'Syd just stood there, his arms hanging down. Suddenly he put his hands on the guitar and we thought he's actually going to do it, but he just stood there, tripping out of his mind.'[19] It was a pitiful transformation and one that greatly frustrated the rest of the band since it was becoming an all too familiar occurrence.

For their part, Jenner and King were quick to defuse the situation and ordered the band to have the rest of the month off, cancelling all of their bookings and insisting they take a well-deserved holiday, and so they all decamped to Ibiza. It is ironic that one major music paper greeted the week of their debut album's release date with the headline 'Pink Floyd Flake Out'. Blackhill spent most of the break trying to convince scoop hungry music journalists that the band had not actually split up and that Barrett was merely recuperating from nervous exhaustion on doctor's orders.

Their debut album, The Piper At The Gates Of Dawn, which took its title from a chapter in the Kenneth

OOT
MONEY
d His
g Roll Ban

NK FLOY
£1 (OR PA

FAR LEFT: PINK FLOYD IN PRE-SHOW REHEARSALS FOR THE GAMES FOR MAY CONCERT AT THE QUEEN ELIZABETH HALL, LONDON ON 12 MAY 1967 AND THE PERFORMING RIGHTS SOCIETY ROYALTY RETURN SHEET SHOWING THE SET LIST FROM THE CONCERT.

LEFT: PINK FLOYD'S FINAL APPEARANCE PERFORMING 'SEE EMILY PLAY' FOR BBC TV'S TOP OF THE POPS ON 27 JULY 1967 WAS FRAUGHT WITH BARRETT'S INCREASINGLY ERRATIC BEHAVIOUR AND DRESS SENSE.

Grahame novel *The Wind In The Willows*, was a far more attractive affair than their stage performance, in that it was a perfect mix of psychedelic songs, based largely around Barrett's poetry/storytelling and lengthy instrumentals. These ranged from the poppy 'Flaming' and 'Lucifer Sam' through the hippie I-Ching-style recital of 'Chapter 24' and the whimsical, childlike poetry of 'The Gnome' and 'Scarecrow', to the spacey freak-outs of 'Pow R Toc H' and 'Astronomy Dominé (featuring Peter Jenner reeling off names of planets and stars through a megaphone) – and, of course, the monumentally thunderous 'Interstellar Overdrive'. These last three tracks were possibly the closest representations of their stage act – provided you turned your amplifier up to maximum. It also illustrates a band in development and shows Roger Waters' emergence as a composer. He may not have been the most technically gifted member of the band at that stage, that credit goes to Rick Wright who's talents should never be underestimated, and although this album is largely credited to Barrett, Waters certainly wasn't short of inspiration: 'Pow R Toc H' is an exceptional contribution and a new composition, 'Set The Controls For The Heart Of The Sun', was recorded that August having become a staple of their live shows.

While the album lost many hard-core UFO followers – at least those who preferred the cacophonous, freak-out element – it gained many more followers and was a fine achievement that is regarded to this day as one of the greatest UK psychedelic albums of the Sixties.

Returning to active duty, Pink Floyd plunged straight back into a heavy touring schedule, including their first overseas bookings, in Scandinavia and Ireland. It is noteworthy that, with Barrett effectively no longer fronting the band, Waters acted as spokesman in press and radio interviews of this period and for some time afterwards. It may be that this sudden assumption of responsibility was symptomatic of his already strong sense of leadership.

Blackhill, meanwhile, were keen to break into the lucrative US market. EMI's American sister label, Capitol Records, based in Hollywood, took on the band, assigning them to its subsidiary label, Tower Records, and called for a promotional tour, organised by The General Artists Corporation of Beverly Hills, which would include San Francisco, Los Angeles, New York, Chicago and Boston. The debut album was scheduled for release to coincide with the tour, with Tower heralding them as 'The Light Kings of England'.

With the band chaperoned by King, the tour was due to start in late October at Bill Graham's Fillmore Auditorium in San Francisco. Much to King's distress, and Graham's extreme annoyance, their work permits were delayed and the first set of engagements had to be cancelled. This was exacerbated by a rather complex Musicians Union procedure that dictated a reciprocal tour for a US act had to be arranged by the applicant. When the first set of shows did come together, greatly assisted by Graham reportedly calling the US ambassador in London in the middle of the night to hurry the process, the band were scheduled to support Big Brother and The Holding Company – about as musically incompatible as you could get.

If that wasn't bad enough, their revered light-show was far from exceptional. Lighting the Fillmore (a large ballroom) and Winterland (a converted ice rink with a circular gallery) was a daunting task for Peter Wynne-Wilson more used to lighting small clubs and halls. In all, noted King, 'our lights looked pathetic. The biggest lamp we had was a single kilowatt bulb, but a typical West Coast show had 20. The only things that worked were the more powerful slide projectors.'[20] Although this was a bearable situation, which resulted in Wynne-Wilson merely augmenting the house lights, Syd's condition was

ANDREW KING << **Our lights looked pathetic. The biggest lamp we had was a single kilowatt bulb, but a typical West Coast show had 20. The only things that worked were the more powerful slide projectors.** >>

far from normal. 'Detuning his guitar all the way through one number, striking the strings. He more or less just ceased playing and stood there leaving us to muddle along as best we could,' said Mason.[21]

Three high-profile live TV shows were also scheduled into the tour on three successive days and were equally catastrophic. On the *Pat Boone In Hollywood* show the band attempted to mime their way through 'The Gnome' and 'Chapter 24', before facing the horrors of an interview in which Barrett responded with total silence to the questions asked of him. On Dick Clark's *American Bandstand* (the only surviving footage from this period) Waters struggled to mime lead vocals through 'Apples And Oranges', since Barrett's attention seemed to be focused on a gaping void. On their final TV

FAR LEFT: FOLLOWING THEIR INITIAL CHART SUCCESS PINK FLOYD BECAME UNLIKELY PIN-UPS. THIS PHOTO WAS TAKEN FOR *JACKIE*, A TEENAGER'S MAGAZINE, ON 6 FEBRUARY 1967 AND PUBLISHED IN THE 7 OCTOBER EDITION.

appearance on *Boss City* they once again struggled through 'Apples And Oranges'.

'Syd actually went mad on that first American tour', said Mason. 'He didn't know where he was most of the time. I remember he de-tuned his guitar on stage at Venice, Los Angeles, and just stood there rattling the strings, which was a bit weird, even for us. Another time he emptied a can of Brylcreem on his head because he didn't like his curly hair.'[22]

This chain of events was far more than Capitol could handle since they were relying on these important TV plugs to push the album. In a final, somewhat embarrassing meeting with Capitol's MD, King had to witness the man break down before his eyes. 'He burst

about long enough for three numbers, which nevertheless caused some bewilderment to the majority of fans, who had turned out for Hendrix. 'They got a very mixed reaction,'[24] recalled Noel Redding, Hendrix's bassist.

Syd's behaviour was still a cause for concern; often he would sit alone on the tour bus or wander off into town when he should have been on stage. Mitch Mitchell, drummer with the Experience, recalled that: 'It was actually good fun – lunacy most of the time. However, Syd Barrett didn't talk to anyone during that time.'[25]

Indeed, he was often replaced on stage altogether by the young Davey O'List, guitarist with The Nice. 'I used to stand by the side of the stage to watch the Floyd. They only used to play one number in their set and because it

NICK MASON << Syd actually went mad on that first American tour. He didn't know where he was most of the time. I remember he de-tuned his guitar on stage at Venice, Los Angeles, and just stood there rattling the strings, which was a bit weird, even for us. >>

into tears and asked us what he was going to do'[23] It was the last straw and after fulfilling their shows for Bill Graham in San Francisco Pink Floyd were recalled to the UK, cancelling an important showcase gig in New York.

Remarkably, and despite the obvious stress affecting them all, recuperation was definitely out of the question this time. Ignoring the signs, Blackhill had committed the band to a festival show in the Netherlands almost the moment they landed followed by a month of intense touring, including a slot on what is generally considered to be the last successful UK pop 'package tour' opening for The Jimi Hendrix Experience. Such tours were normally reserved for lightweight entertainment and rock 'n' roll, but this was the first, and probably the last, to showcase 'underground' acts. With Hendrix and The Move headlining, and support from Amen Corner, The Nice, The Outer Limits and Eire Apparent, the bands appeared in descending order of importance, with a stage time to match.

The opening night got off to a flying start when Pink Floyd threatened to walk out of the tour during the afternoon rehearsals at the Royal Albert Hall when they were told they could not use their own lighting gear and projection screen because, being a circular hall, it blocked the view for many in the audience.

The band were allocated a twenty-minute set – just

was a fairly straightforward guitar thing, I was able to pick it up quite quickly. So when Syd didn't turn up one night, Floyd asked me to go on instead.'[26]

Even Barrett's old pal David Gilmour could see little hope: 'It was totally impossible for me to understand the way Syd's mind was working at that time. It was also from having been to two or three of their gigs that it was impossible for me to see how they could carry on like that, because Syd was quite obviously not up to being in that group at that time.'[27]

Waters later spoke of that first US trip and the *American Bandstand* incident, recalling how the rehearsal takes had gone just fine and without incident but, come the final transmission, Barrett just stood there, arms limply hanging by his side. 'He knew of course perfectly well what was going on. He was just being crazy.'[28] Additionally there is also the footage from BBC's *Tomorrow's World*, repeated, for the first time, as part of the BBC *Omnibus* documentary on Pink Floyd in November 1994. Filmed in December 1967 and broadcast in January 1968, it shows Barrett in fine fettle. Regardless of this fact, this may merely serve to highlight the extent of Barrett's apparent schizophrenia.

By now it was also very obvious that Barrett was incapable of continuing to produce the catchy pop songs the band had previously relied on to get them into the

LEFT: PINK FLOYD AS PHOTOGRAPHED BY BARON WOLMAN AT THE CASA MADRONA HOTEL, SAUSALITO, CALIFORNIA ON 11 NOVEMBER 1967 FOR *ROLLING STONE* MAGAZINE. ITS EDITOR, RALPH GLEASON, WAS SO UNIMPRESSED BY THEIR SHOW AT WINTERLAND A PLANNED FEATURE WAS SCRAPPED AND THE SHOTS WERE NEVER USED.

Sources

1. *Days In The Life* by Jonathan Green, Heinemann, 1988
2. *The Daily Mail, You Magazine*, c. 1990
3. *Record Collector*, 1994
4. Authors' interview with Joe Boyd, 1987
5. Danish TV interviews with Pink Floyd, 1992
6. *Dancing In The Streets*, BBC TV, 1996
7. *Pink Floyd – A Visual Documentary* by Miles, Omnibus, 1980
8-9. Authors' interview with Joe Boyd, 1987
10. *Pink Floyd* by Rick Sanders, Futura, 1976
11. *The Pink Floyd Story*, Capital Radio, 17 December 1976
12. *Zig Zag*, Issue 32, July 1973
13. *Mojo*, May 1994
14. *The Pink Floyd Story*, Capital Radio, 17 December 1976
15. *Mojo*, July 1995
16. *Melody Maker*, 5 August 1967
17. *In Session Tonight* by Ken Gardner, BBC, 1994
18. *Pink Floyd – A Visual Documentary* by Miles, Omnibus, 1980
19. *Days In The Life* by Jonathan Green, Heinemann, 1988
20. *Crazy Diamond* by Pete Anderson and Mike Watkinson, Omnibus, 1991
21. *Mojo*, May 1994
22. *Mojo*, May 1994
23. *Crazy Diamond* by Pete Anderson and Mike Watkinson, Omnibus, 1991
24. Letter from Noel Redding to the Author, 1996
25. *The Hendrix Experience* by Mitch Mitchell, Pyramid, 1990
26. *Space Daze* by Dave Thompson, Cleopatra, 1994
27. *The Pink Floyd Story*, Capital Radio, 17 December 1976
28. *Dancing In The Street*, BBC TV, 20 July 1996

47

charts. 'Apples And Oranges', his last single with Pink Floyd, was released in mid-November and failed to gain a good chart placing. But their public had changed too. The band's current live set reflected the emergence of Waters' own brand of science-fiction epics, such as 'Set The Controls For The Heart Of The Sun', which was taking them on a new slant altogether. This inevitably clashed with Barrett's more recent compositions such as 'Scream Thy Last Scream' (featuring Mason's first ever lead vocal), 'Vegetable Man' and 'Jugband Blues', which were doing nothing to advance Floyd's career. The former two are only available to collectors on bootleg recordings as studio out-takes as well as part of the band's 20 December *Top Gear* BBC session. It seemed as if there was a conscious attempt by the rest of the band to radically reinvent themselves, not only in order to survive the collapse of 'Flower Power' but Barrett's own strange new directions.

It is likely that Barrett sensed this redefinition and, aware of the fact that he was not going to be a part of Floyd's new identity, pre-empted the move. Probably in a state of LSD-induced disorientation, whether he meant to

or not, he was making the band's life as awkward as he could. In one particularly well-documented studio session he wilfully teased them with his latest composition, 'Have You Got It Yet?' The song changed with every take, making it impossible to follow. Such tales are legendary and the announcement that he wanted to add a female vocalist, a banjo player and a saxophonist to the line-up left the rest of the band in little doubt as to where this was all leading. He had to go.

Word was put out that an 'additional' guitarist was being sought and although Davey O'List and Jeff Beck were initially considered, it was David Gilmour who attracted the band's attention. He was in attendance at their Royal College of Art show that December, and since he wasn't doing anything better, apart from driving a van around London for clothing designers Quorum, he accepted without hesitation.

Whether it was done this way to limit the hurt to Barrett's feelings is also open to speculation; perhaps it was thought that the addition of a friend would help to stabilize him.

1966

PINK FLOYD / PINK FLOYD SOUND / THE TEA SET

(January 1966 – August 1966)
Roger 'Syd' Barrett: Rhythm Guitar, Vocals
Nick Mason: Drums
Roger Waters: Bass Guitar, Vocals
Richard Wright: Keyboards, Vocals

Sunday 9 January
CONCERT
Goings On Club, Archer Street, London, England
Billed as Pink Floyd.

Friday 11 March & Saturday 12 March
CONCERTS
Rag Ball, Concourse Area, University of Essex, Wivenhoe Park, Colchester, England
Billed as The Tea Set.
Also appearing on 11 March: Marianne Faithfull, Coletrane Union, The Swinging Blue Jeans and Rick & Us (in the Common Room); The Tea Set (9.00pm-9.30pm) with the Cherrie Pickers and Jimmy Pilgrim & The Classics (in the Concourse Area). 12 March with Coletrane Union, Martin Lewis Trad Band and Rick & Us (in the Common Room); The Tea Set (two sets at 2.00am-3.00am and 4.00am-5.00am) with Jimmy Pilgrim & The Classics and The Trends (in the Concourse Area).
The formative Pink Floyd played their first ever gig with a film show on the first night of this two-day university rag weekend. Roger Waters recalled in an interview with *Zig Zag* magazine that, 'Some bright spark down there had done a film with a paraplegic in London, given this paraplegic a film camera and wheeled him round London filming his view. They showed it up on screen behind us as we played.'

Sunday 13 March
CONCERT
Trip, The Marquee, Wardour Street, London, England
Billed as Pink Floyd Sound with AMM. A Spontaneous Underground event.
Although there had already been three Spontaneous Underground events held prior to this one (30 January, 6 and 27 February), this was the first to feature Pink Floyd who thereafter became a regular fixture.

'A Child's Eye View Of Madness' shrieked the headline of *Titbits* in a belated account of these happenings: 'What a rave! A man crawling naked through jelly. Girls stripped to the waist. Off-beat poetry. Weird music. It all adds up to Raving London. For the capital no longer swings. It goes berserk!'

Sunday 27 March
CONCERT
The Marquee, Wardour Street, London, England
Billed as Pink Floyd Sound. A Spontaneous Underground event.

April
AUDITION
Rediffusion TV Studios, Wembley, England
According to Nick Mason, in his book *Inside Out, A Personal History of Pink Floyd*, the band failed a live audition to appear on the music programme *Ready, Steady, Go!* They were invited back the following week with audience tickets and saw the Lovin' Spoonful perform, presumably on their 22 April performance.

Sunday 3 April
CONCERT
The Marquee, Wardour Street, London, England
Billed as Pink Floyd Sound. A Spontaneous Underground event.

Sunday 17 April
CONCERT
The Marquee, Wardour Street, London, England
Billed as Pink Floyd Sound. A Spontaneous Underground event.

Sunday 1 May
CONCERT
The Marquee, Wardour Street, London, England
Billed as Pink Floyd Sound. A Spontaneous Underground event.

Sunday 8 May
CONCERT
The Marquee, Wardour Street, London, England
Billed as Pink Floyd Sound. A Spontaneous Underground event.

Sunday 15 May
CONCERT
The Marquee, Wardour Street, London, England
Billed as Pink Floyd Sound. A Spontaneous Underground event.

Sunday 5 June
CONCERT
The Marquee, Wardour Street, London, England
Billed as Pink Floyd Sound. A Spontaneous Underground event.

Sunday 12 June
CONCERT
The Marquee, Wardour Street, London, England
Billed as Pink Floyd Sound. A Spontaneous Underground event.
This was the last of the regular Marquee appearances but was, by good fortune, the show at which future co-manager Peter Jenner first saw Pink Floyd perform.

PINK FLOYD

(September 1966 – January 1968)
Roger 'Syd' Barrett: Rhythm Guitar, Vocals
Nick Mason: Drums
Roger Waters: Bass Guitar, Vocals
Richard Wright: Keyboards, Vocals

Friday 30 September
CONCERT
London Free School, All Saints Church Hall, Powis Gardens, London, England
With Soft Machine.
Brian Wilcock, DJ at the popular West Hampstead club called Klooks Kleek, recalled that, 'One night a well-dressed guy, probably late twenties, came up to me and said he had a new band playing its first show in Ladbroke Grove the next night; would I take the club record console and some records to play in the interval between two sets, for a fiver. I told him I couldn't take the console, but I had a Dansette type deck that plugged into a PA system and he said, "Fine." So when I get there, it turns out to be Pink Floyd. I told them I only had soul and R&B records but they said that's what they wanted.'

Friday 14 October
CONCERT
London Free School, All Saints Church Hall, Powis Gardens, London, England
Set list: 'Pink' / 'Lets Roll Another' / 'Gimme A Break' / 'Stoned Alone' / 'I Can Tell' / 'The Gnome' / 'Interstellar Overdrive' / 'Lucy Leave' / 'Stethoscope' / 'Flapdoodle Dealing' / 'Snowing' / 'Matilda Mother' / 'Pow R Toc H' / 'Astronomy Dominé'.
As the above set list indicates, by this time Pink Floyd had developed a great deal of original material but were still experimenting within the framework of R&B standards that would feature in their act until the end of the year. John Hopkins later wrote in *International Times* that at this time Pink Floyd were playing, 'Mainly instrumentals and numbers that would sometimes last for half an hour.'

Saturday 15 October
CONCERT
International Times First All Night Rave, The Roundhouse, Chalk Farm, London, England
With Soft Machine.
Set list included: 'Insterstellar Overdrive'.

The launch party for *International Times*, and indeed Pink Floyd, was a festival compressed into one evening. It was billed in the debut issue of *IT* as 'The Greatest Happening Of Them All'. This mad gathering was attended by some 2,500 people and *IT* made sure its coming-out ball was given the fair review it deserved: '...Darkness, only flashing lights, people in masks, girls half naked. Other people standing about wondering what the hell was going on. Pot smoke. Now and then the sound of a bottle breaking. The Pink Floyd, psychedelic pop group did weird things to the feel of the event with their scary feedback sounds, slide projectors playing on their skin - drops of paint run riot on the slides to produce outer space, prehistoric textures - spotlights flashing on them in time with a drum beat... The Soft Machine, another group with new ideas drove a motorbike into the place... a large car in the middle of it all painted bright pop-art stripes... Simon Postuma and Marijke Koger, the Amsterdam couple, designed an interesting cubicle with coloured screens and nets and within the box one of them, in suitable dress, read palms and told fortunes... in another part the London Film Co-op gave an all-night film show featuring films like *Scorpio Rising* and *Towers Open Fire*... famous people turned up: Antonioni and Monica Vitti, Paul McCartney disguised as an Arab, Kenneth Rexroth, Peter Brook, Mickie Most and Tony Secunda. We also saw a well-known junkie, a notorious homosexual... Of course several things went wrong. There was that narrow entrance for an unpleasant start. That communal toilet that ended up in flood (in fact 2,500 people had to share the two toilets in the building!). A giant jelly made in a bath for the party was unfortunately run over by a bicycle. How this happened, or what became of the remains of the jelly or the bicycle, no one knows... Sugar cubes were distributed at the entrance, a favoured way of ingesting LSD, but even though they weren't loaded it did give the recipients the chance to let their hair down. To top it all Pink Floyd were the last group to play: [they] made the most melodramatic of climaxes to the evening by blowing out the power in the middle of "Interstellar Overdrive". It was a resounding finish to their most important appearance so far.' Kenneth Roxreth, the US beat poet, on the other hand wrote in the *San Francisco Chronicle* that the music was ear-splitting and he felt as if he were on the Titanic. He thought that Pink Floyd had not turned up and that the weird sounds coming from the stage were being made by amateurs, who'd assembled from the audience.

Joint manager Andrew King said in an article in the *Sunday Times* that, 'We don't call ourselves psychedelic. But we don't deny it. We don't confirm it either. People who want to make up slogans can do it.' The groups' bass guitarist Roger Waters was a bit less non-committal. 'It's totally anarchistic. But co-operative anarchy if you see what I mean. It's

definitely a complete realisation of the aims of psychedelia. If you take LSD what you experience depends entirely on who you are. Our music may give you the screaming horrors or throw you into screaming ecstasy. Mostly it's the latter. We find our audiences stop dancing now. We tend to get them standing there totally grooved with their mouths open.'

Wednesday 19 October
CONCERT
Top Rank Suite, Brighton, England
Supporting The Graham Bond Organisation and The Artwoods.

Friday 21 October
CONCERT
London Free School, **All Saints Church Hall, Powis Gardens, London, England**

Friday 28 October
CONCERT
London Free School, **All Saints Church Hall, Powis Gardens, London, England**

Monday 31 October
RECORDING SESSION
Thompson Recording Studios, Hemel Hempstead, England
It has been documented, but not substantiated, that on the same day as their management company, Blackhill Enterprises, was set up, Pink Floyd were whisked away to record a demo tape to tout around prospective record companies. The songs 'Let's Roll Another One' and 'I Get Stoned' have been reported as being on this tape but evidently the band would have had little chance of securing a deal presenting these titles. It has often been speculated that this session reaped a take of 'Interstellar Overdrive' that was utilised by film-maker, and Cambridge contemporary, Anthony Stern for his fifteen-minute 'day-in-the-life-of' documentary *San Francisco*.

Friday 4 November
CONCERT
London Free School, **All Saints Church Hall, Powis Gardens, London, England**

Saturday 5 November
CONCERT
Wilton Hall, Bletchley, England
Early show supported by The Torments. The band were billed in advertising as "Elektra Recording Stars The Pink Freud".

Saturday 5 November
CONCERT
The Clubhouse, Five Acres Country Club, Bricket Wood, near Watford, England

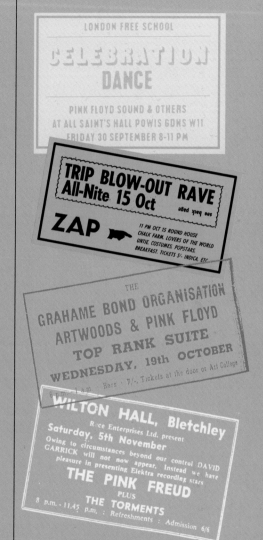

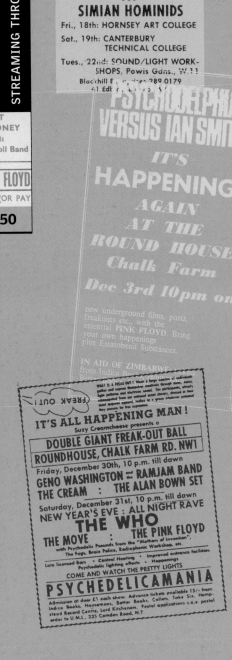

This was one of several caravan parks situated in the area, but the only one that played host to a naturist club. Jack Bracelin, the site manager, and later proprietor of Five Acre Lights, who later supplied lighting for the Free School and UFO Club, invited Pink Floyd to make an informal appearance at the clubhouse. However, there is little chance the audience would have been naked - not in November anyway!

Tuesday 8 November
CONCERT
London Free School, All Saints Church Hall, Powis Gardens, London, England

Friday 11 November
CONCERT
London Free School, All Saints Church Hall, Powis Gardens, London, England

Saturday 12 November
CONCERT
Corn Exchange, Bedford, England
Supported by Something Else.

Tuesday 15 November
CONCERT
London Free School, All Saints Church Hall, Powis Gardens, London, England

Friday 18 November
CONCERT
Rooms A & B, Hornsey College of Art, Hornsey, London, England
With Porrage.
Although Pink Floyd had rehearsed here many times because of their connection with Mike Leonard, who taught at the college, this was their first documented gig there. Students of the Advanced Studies Group let fly with an array of lighting equipment they had built as part of their course work.

Saturday 19 November
CONCERT
Main Hall, Technical College, Canterbury, England
Supported by The Koalas.
The Kentish Times reported that: 'Flashing lights, slide-projection, thunderous atmospheric sounds and incense were the essence of the psychedelic Pink Floyd concert held at Canterbury Technical College on Saturday. A purely physical sensation, psychedelic music either makes your flesh crawl with emotion or leaves you cold. It should be seen and not written about, but it is an experience that should be tried at least once. The Pink Floyd, a London group, comprising two guitars, drums and organ, were super-amplified. Using distortion as a second sound, their music tended to be slow, but not uninteresting, and resembling the sound of a church organ. The opening curtains revealed the group on stage, wearing neutral shirts to reflect the coloured lights, and standing in semi-darkness. Behind was a 15ft high tinfoil Buddha. On either side, sets of filtered spots sprayed varying colours over the stage, whilst modern art slides were projected behind. This weird conglomeration of sights and sound added up to a strange result. Those watching were a little mystified, but after the first rather frightening discordant notes, began dancing, and gradually relaxed. It was an enjoyable if somewhat odd evening.'

Tuesday 22 November
CONCERT
London Free School, All Saints Church Hall, Powis Gardens, London, England

Tuesday 29 November
CONCERT
London Free School, All Saints Church Hall, Powis Gardens, London, England
International Times reported that: 'Since I last saw the Pink Floyd they've got hold of bigger amplifiers, new light gear and a rave from Paul McCartney. This time I saw them at Powis Gardens on Tuesday 29th, the last of their regular shows there. Their work is largely improvisation and lead guitarist Sid Barrett shoulders most of the burden of providing continuity and attack in the improvised parts. He was providing a huge range of sounds with the new equipment, from throttled shrieks to mellow feedback roars. Visually the show was less adventurous. Three projectors bathed the group, the walls and sometimes the audience in vivid colour. But the colour was fairly static and there was no searching for the brain alpha rhythms by chopping up the images. The equipment that the group is using now is infant electronics: let's see what they will do with the grown-up electronics that a colour television industry will make available.'

Saturday 3 December
CONCERT
Psychodelphia Versus Ian Smith, The Roundhouse, Chalk Farm, London, England
With the Ram Holder Messengers and underground film shows, poets and happenings.
The set list included: 'Louie Louie'.
This event was promoted by the Majority Rule for Rhodesia Committee and held in protest at Ian Smith, the Governor of Rhodesia (now Zimbabwe), continuing his policy of white minority rule. The show attracted media interest after advertising posters featured Smith made to resemble Hitler.
NME reported that: 'Last Friday (29 November) the Pink Floyd, a new London group, embarked upon their first happening - a pop dance incorporating psychedelic effects and mixed media - whatever that is! The slides were excellent - colourful, frightening, grotesque, beautiful and the group's trip into outer-space sounds promised very interesting things to come. Unfortunately all fell a bit flat in the cold reality of All Saints Church Hall, but on Saturday night at Chalk Farm's Roundhouse things went better when thousands of people turned up to watch the show. The Floyd need to write more of their own material - psychedelic versions of "Louie Louie" won't come off, but if they can incorporate their electronic prowess with some melodic and lyrical songs - getting away from dated R&B things, they could well score in the near future.'

Monday 12 December
CONCERT
You're Joking - A Benefit Carnival For Oxfam, Royal Albert Hall, Kensington, London, England
This was a marathon four-hour show in aid of Oxfam. Pink Floyd must have felt out of place among a conventional cast that included Peter Cook and Dudley Moore, Paul Jones, Alan Price, Chris Farlowe, Barry Mackenzie, Peter and Gordon and Jackie Trent. Barry Fantoni linked the sets and played clarinet and tenor sax with "The Alberts", a lunacy group, who are said to have contributed some of the best moments of the evening by smashing up a piano on stage. The entire cast joined in a merry chorus finale of 'We All Live On Yellow Margarine'.

Friday 16 December
CONCERT
AA Students Christmas Carnival, The Architects Association, Bedford Square, London, England
The theme for this year's annual Christmas dance was 'Prohibition'.

Thursday 22 December
CONCERT
The Marquee, Wardour Street, London, England
Supported by The Iveys (who later became Apple Records group, Badfinger).

Friday 23 December
CONCERT
UFO Presents Night Tripper, The Blarney Club, Tottenham Court Road, London, England.
Opening night of UFO with Fanta and Ood, The Giant Sun Trolley and Dave Tomlin.

Thursday 29 December
CONCERT
The Marquee, Wardour Street, London, England
With The Syn (featuring future Yes bassist Chris Squire).

Friday 30 December
CONCERT
UFO Presents Night Tripper, The Blarney Club, Tottenham Court Road, London, England.
With Soft Machine.

Saturday 31 December
CONCERT
New Year's Eve Party, Cambridge College of Art & Technology, Cambridge, England
Early show.

Saturday 31 December
CONCERT
New Year's Eve All Night Rave, The Roundhouse, Chalk Farm, London, England
Late show with The Who and The Move.
The set list included: 'Pow R Toc H' / 'Interstellar Overdrive'.
Melody Maker reported that: 'On stage the Pink Floyd, the Who and the Move each attempted to excite the audience into some positive action. The Pink Floyd have a promising sound, and some very groovy picture slides which attract far more attention than the group, as they merge, blossom, burst, grow, divide and die. The Who got on to the stage after an hour wait [and] almost succeeded in winning over the show with an immediate flurry of smoke bombs and sound-barrier smashing. But somebody pulled out the plug and the Who fell quiet as a graveyard. After playing most of their new album tracks rather half-heartedly, Pete Townshend wheeled upon a fine pair of speakers and ground them with his shattered guitar into the stage. It was fair comment. The group had thrice been switched off as well as being constantly being plunged into darkness by a team of lighting men - none of whom seemed to know where, in fact, the stage or the Who were positioned. The Move were more successful. Technically they had no hitches and their act came smoothly to a stage-shaking climax as TV sets with Hitler and Ian Smith pictures were swiped with iron bars, and a car was chopped up. Two girls were incensed enough to strip to the waist and the remaining, shivering crowds surged menacingly towards the stage, the demolished car, and the birds.'

December
CONCERT
Christmas Ball, Royal College of Art, Kensington, London, England
With AMM.
Peter Whitehead, in an interview with *Record Collector*, commented that it was the first time he ever saw Pink Floyd perform live, which led him to invite them to contribute to his documentary film, *Tonite Let's All Make Love In London*. Unfortunately the exact date of this concert could not be found.

1967

Thursday 5 January
CONCERT
The Marquee, Wardour Street, London, England
Supported by Eyes of Blue.
The society magazine *Queen* reported that: 'The Pink Floyd are the most committed psychedelic group I have yet heard in this country. Other groups have been dabbling with light and back projection, but the Floyd have gone into it in some kind of depth and their visuals make a reasonably logical connection with the music. When I caught up with them at the Marquee recently, their apparatus took up more of the club than the audience but the results were quite impressive. There was a giant screen at the back of the stage and the images projected on to it were like something out of *Fantastic Voyage*, great blobs of red and white and purple and blue that diffused and switched and exploded. The effect was like an endless series of action paintings and I found it very enjoyable, although it didn't remotely simulate any drug states that I have ever heard of. Having praised the visuals, I have to say that the actual music wasn't up to much. There was a lot of thumping and crashing and guitar screeching, all of which was presumably meant to signify the intensity and musical explosion. The numbers went on for a long time and they all adopted the same relentless mood. The two guitarists looked moody, the drummer thrashed wildly about and the lights kept flashing. After about twenty minutes it became very boring and after half an hour I left. All in all, I have very mixed feelings about this group. Anyone who can use visuals as well as they do must be talented; anyone who can be so long winded

> january 1967

and tedious must need a lot more time before they are ready to break big. The Pink Floyd at this stage are too cerebral by half. I would like to see them produce a better-balanced, more varied act and I would like to see them project a bit more sex. At the moment they look drab on stage, but if they can only loosen themselves a bit, I could imagine them doing well.'

Dica Productions Present
FREAK OUT ETHEL
at
SEYMOUR HALL, W.1
FRIDAY, JAN. 6th, 7.30
PINK FLOYD
GINGER JOHNSON'S AFRICAN DRUM BAND
WAYGOOD ELLIS & THE ZONE
RICH ST. JOHN
ALEXANDER TROCCHI
KARMA - SIGMA
Dancers • Puppets • Slides • Films
BELLY DANCERS
FULL ELECTRO-COLOUR STIMULI
DOZENS OF PROJECTORS • SLIDES
FULL COLOUR MOVIE FILMS
Tickets 10/- from Collet's, New Oxford Street, Dobell's, Charing Cross Road. Better Books, Charing Cross Road. Karma, Gosfield Street. Indica Books, Southampton Row.
Licensed Bar   Enquiries 455-5360

Friday 6 January
CONCERT
Freak Out Ethel, Seymour Hall, Paddington, London, England
With Ginger Johnson's African Drum Band, Wayward Ellis & The Zone, Rich St John, Alexander Trocchi, Karma-Sigma, belly dancers, light-shows and other happenings.
Having already seen Pink Floyd perform at UFO, Pete Townshend skipped an engagement with The Who in Morecambe in order to take Eric Clapton to see Syd Barrett and Pink Floyd perform.

Sunday 8 January
CONCERT
The Upper Cut, Forest Gate, London, England
Pink Floyd replaced the advertised Mindbenders at short notice.

Monday 9 January
REHEARSAL
London, England

Wednesday 11 & Thursday 12 January
RECORDING SESSIONS
Sound Techniques Studios, Chelsea, London, England
Recording for the soundtrack *Tonite Let's All Make Love In London*.

Friday 13 January
CONCERT
UFO, The Blarney, Tottenham Court Road, London, England
With Marilyn Monroe films and Dave Tomlin's The Giant Sun Trolley.
Pink Floyd's set was filmed by Peter Whitehead and

ABOVE: PERFORMING IN A BLIZZARD OF LIGHT AT *UFO*, LONDON IN JANUARY 1967.

clips appeared in the 1991 video *The Pink Floyd - London 66-67* (UK: See For Miles PFVP1).

Saturday 14 January
CONCERT
Coming-Up Hop, The Great Hall, University of Reading, Whiteknights, Reading, England
The Reading University student newspaper *Shell* received so many complaints about this show, the following letter was published shortly afterwards: 'We would like to express our disgust at the appalling performance given by the Pink Floyd at the "dance" on Saturday. How could people dance to such an offensive din? The Pink Floyd were so cacophonous

that the most cunningly random-noise-making machine could hardly have been more oppressive. The only thing we found to console us was that University dances will never be more debased than this; at least we trust not. We very much regret that certain members of the University degraded themselves by applauding such a performance, and we congratulate the element among the few remaining at the end who gave vent to their indignation by boo-ing.'

Monday 16 January
CONCERT
The Clubroom, Institute of Contemporary Arts, Mayfair, London, England
This was the first time pop music had been allowed at the ICA and *Record Mirror* reported an informal discussion between the band and audience after the show.

Tuesday 17 January
CONCERT
Music In Colour by The Pink Floyd, Commonwealth Institute, Kensington, London, England
The Kensington Post reported that: 'The Pink Floyd had been invited to appear at both the ICA and Commonwealth Institute by a young classical music promoter, Christopher Hunt: "I like what they do", he said to the *Kensington Post*. "I usually just deal with classical chamber music but I believe that the Pink Floyd are something quite different from normal pop groups"'. During the interval between sessions at the Institute there was a performance of NOIT, a mime for paper giants. The creation of artist John Latham this work is, I'm told, a three dimensional representation of Pink Floyd's state of mind.'

Thursday 19 January
CONCERT
The Marquee, Wardour Street, London, England
Supported by Marmalade.

Friday 20 January
CONCERT
UFO, The Blarney Club, Tottenham Court Road, London, England.
With Spectral Audio Olfactory, Karate, Trip Machine and Government Propaganda.

Saturday 21 January
CONCERT
The Birdcage Club, Eastney, Portsmouth, England

Sunday 22 January
REHEARSALS
London, England

Monday 23 - Wednesday 25 January
RECORDING SESSIONS
Sound Techniques Studios, Chelsea, London, England
Recording for the single 'Arnold Layne' / 'Candy And A Currant Bun'.

Thursday 26 January
REHEARSALS
London, England

Friday 27 January
CONCERT
UFO, The Blarney Club, Tottenham Court Road, London, England

With AMM, Five Acre Light, Dave Brown, Plight of the Erogenius and Chapter 1.
Pink Floyd's performance was filmed on this night and clips of 'Interstellar Overdrive' and 'Matilda Mother' were used in the Granada TV documentary arts programme *Scene Special*, subtitled 'It's So Far Out It's Straight Down' and broadcast on the Granada ITV network on 7 February at 10.25pm. It also included coverage of the infamous Albert Hall poetry reading in 1965, performance art at the Roundhouse, a 'happening' in Piccadilly Circus and interviews with various underground figures including Jim Haynes, Barry Miles, John Hopkins and Paul McCartney.

Saturday 28 January
CONCERT
Student Union Common Room, University of Essex, Wivenhoe Park, Colchester, England
Wyvern, the Essex University student newspaper, reported that: 'The psycho-delic dance was a double triumph. The maximum permitted attendance of 500 was achieved and a profit of about £30 was made. Never before has a dance at Essex been fully supported or shown profit. At a social committee meeting on January 30th Mick Gray (Chairman) reported that the dance was by no means trouble free. Several outsiders arrived, and when turned away, lingered on the campus. At about 1am four students from North Essex Technical College, who had been at the dance, were arrested by a police patrol whilst attempting to remove the engine from a motor cycle in the central car park.'

Sunday 29 January
RECORDING SESSION
Sound Techniques Studios, Chelsea, London, England
Recording for the single 'Arnold Layne' / 'Candy And A Currant Bun'.

January
RADIO SHOW
CBC Studios, Great Portland Street, London, England
Roger Waters, Syd Barrett and Nick Mason were interviewed by Nancy Bacal of the Canadian Broadcasting Corporation for part of a magazine item on the underground scene. Pink Floyd also contributed a unique studio recording of 'Interstellar Overdrive' for use in the show – possibly from their recent Sound Techniques session.

Monday 30 January
REHEARSAL
London, England

Tuesday 31 January & Wednesday 1 February
RECORDING SESSIONS
Sound Techniques Studios, Chelsea, London, England
Recording for the single 'Arnold Layne' / 'Candy And A Currant Bun'.

Wednesday 1 February
PRESS RELEASE
London, England
Pink Floyd turned professional having signed a deal with EMI Records on this date.

PINK FLOYD ROAD CREW THROUGH TO SEPTEMBER 1967
Joe Gannon: Lights

Thursday 2 February
CONCERT
Cadenna's Nightclub, Guildford, England.

Friday 3 February
CONCERT
All Nite Rave, Queen's Hall, Leeds, England
Four stages and 10 hours of non-stop entertainment with 12 groups including Cream, Go-Go Dancers, a fairground and a barbecue. This rave went on all night and in the morning breakfast was served. The advertisement announced the release of a live gorilla in the crowd at midnight!

Monday 6 February
PHOTO SESSION
London, England
Pink Floyd were photographed by *Jackie* magazine and a photo from the session eventually appeared as a full page pin-up in the 7 October 1967 edition.

Tuesday 7 February
PHOTO SESSION
London, England
Pink Floyd were photographed by *Fabulous 208* magazine and a photo from the session eventually appeared as a full page pin-up in the 2 September 1967 edition.

Wednesday 8 February
REHEARSAL
London, England

Thursday 9 February
CONCERT
New Addington Hotel, New Addington, Croydon, England

Friday 10 February
CONCERT
Leicester College of Art and Technology, Leicester, England

JANUARY 27 FROM 10.30-6PM & FEBRUARY 3
AMMMUSIC. PINK FLOYD   SOFT MACHINE
FIVE ACRE LIGHT   BROWN'S POETRY
FLIGHT OF THE AEROGENIUS. CHPT 1 CHPT 1
INTERNATIONAL TIMES   BRUCE CONNOR MOVIE
IT GIRL BEAUTY CONTEST. FILM MAKERS CO OP. FOOD
UNDER BERKELY CINEMA. TOT. CT. RD 15/- MEMBERS 10/-

UFO

Saturday 11 February
CONCERT
Old Refectory, Falmer House, University of Sussex, Falmer, Brighton, England
With The Alan Bown Set, The Wishful Thinking and Russell's Clump.

Thursday 16 February
CANCELLED CONCERT
Guildhall, Southampton, England
Supported by Soul Trinity. This concert was cancelled on the day of the show due to the venue management's concerns after an unfavourable article about the band appeared in *The News Of The World*.

Friday 17 February
CONCERT
St. Catherine's College Valentine Ball, Dorothy Ballroom, Cambridge, England
With Bob Kidman, Alexis Korner's Blues Incorporated and Pearl Hawaiians.

Saturday 18 February
CONCERT
California Ballroom, Dunstable, England
Supported by The Equals and Two Of Each.

Monday 20 February
CONCERT
Adelphi Ballroom, West Bromwich, England

Tuesday 21 - Thursday 23 February
RECORDING SESSIONS
Studio 3, EMI Studios, Abbey Road, St. John's Wood, London, England
Pink Floyd's first-ever recording sessions for EMI commenced on 21 February to begin work on their debut album *The Piper At The Gates Of Dawn*. The first track to be recorded was 'Matilda Mother'.

Friday 24 February
CONCERT
Ricky Tick Club, Thames Hotel, Windsor, England
Early show.

Friday 24 February
CONCERT
UFO, The Blarney Club, Tottenham Court Road, London, England
Late show with Brothers Grimm and film shows. Pink Floyd's performance of 'Interstellar Overdrive' and general scenes at UFO were filmed by German TV on this night for inclusion in a one-hour documentary arts programme entitled *Die Jungen Nachtwandler – London Unter 21* that also featured The Who. It was broadcast on the Bayerischer Rundfunk TV network on 3 July 1967 at 11.00pm.

Saturday 25 February
CONCERT
Ricky Tick Club, Hounslow, England

Monday 27 February
RECORDING SESSION
Studio 3, EMI Studios, Abbey Road, St. John's Wood, London, England
Recording for the album *The Piper At The Gates Of Dawn*.

Tuesday 28 February
CONCERT
Blaises Club, Imperial Hotel, Knightsbridge, London, England
Supported by The Majority.

Wednesday 1 March
RECORDING SESSION
EMI Studios, Abbey Road, St. John's Wood, London, England
Mixing for the album *The Piper At The Gates Of Dawn*.

Wednesday 1 March
CONCERT
The Dance Hall, Eel Pie Island Hotel, Twickenham, England

Thursday 2 March
CONCERT
Assembly Hall, Worthing, England
Supporting Geno Washington & The Ram Jam Band.

Friday 3 March
PRESS RECEPTION
EMI Records, Manchester Square, London, England
Pink Floyd attended an afternoon press launch and photo session at EMI Records headquarters at which they also mimed a performance of 'Arnold Layne' and 'Candy And A Currant Bun' complete with light-show.

Friday 3 March
CONCERT
Market Hall, St. Albans, England
Early show supported by Tuppence The TV Dancer.

Friday 3 March
CONCERT
UFO, The Blarney Club, Tottenham Court Road, London, England
Late show with Soft Machine.

Saturday 4 March
CONCERT
Poly Rag Ball, The Large Hall, Regent Street Polytechnic, London, England
Supported by Minor Birds with the Miss Poly Finals and DJ Ed 'Stewpot' Stewart.

West One, the Regent Street Polytechnic student newspaper, reported that: 'As usual the Dance posters and tickets were of the very highest standard. Everyone present at the dance appeared to enjoy themselves but in my opinion the Pink Floyd are not at their best as a "college hop" group. Despite the suggestions of a "freak-out" implied by the dance tickets, the Rag Ball was a glorified "hop". There were more psychedelic effects when the bar flashed the lights on and off to indicate closing time than the rest of the dance put together. The only spontaneous happening I observed was when a young lady who had drunk more than her stomach could bear, had gone out into the cold night air.'

Sunday 5 March
CONCERT
Sunday's At The Saville, Saville Theatre, Shaftesbury Avenue, London, England
With Lee Dorsey, The Ryan Brothers and Jeff Beck.

Monday 6 March
TV SHOW
Granada TV Studios, Manchester, England
Pink Floyd were filmed on this date performing 'Arnold Layne' live for the pilot episode of a new 30-minute Granada TV music programme called *The Rave*. A proposed replacement for Rediffusion's *Ready, Steady, Go!*, and hosted by The Move, the series was not commissioned and this pilot show was never broadcast.

Tuesday 7 March
CONCERT
Malvern Big Beat Sessions, Winter Gardens, Malvern, England
Prior to the show The *Malvern Gazette* reported that: 'The Malvern Winter Gardens has banned the use of the words "It's a freak out, it's a psychedelic happening" in advertising for the appearance of London group, The Pink Floyd. Entertainment's Manager Mr. J.D. Harrison told us that several hundred pamphlets were distributed at Tuesday night's Big Beat session last week advertising the groups' appearance in March. After consulting with the chairman of the Winter Gardens and Publicity Committee, Councillor Ron Holland, decided that the remaining two pamphlets should not be handed out. Also, a poster put up inside the Winter Gardens with similar wording has been taken down. Mr. Harrison said this would be replaced by the London promoters, who do not advertise on billboards in the town. Mr. Harrison said, "It's a word that should not be used. I think it's a trend to the drug world. It's wrong, completely wrong. I rang up Malvern Public Library to find out the meaning of the word and I was told it related to trances induced by the drug LSD."'

Thursday 9 March
CONCERT
The Marquee, Wardour Street, London, England
With The Thoughts.

Friday 10 March
RECORD RELEASE
'Arnold Layne' / 'Candy And A Currant Bun'
UK 7-inch single release. US 7-inch single released on Monday 24 April.
Record Retail And Music Industry News commented: 'This is rather way out and this group with its tremendous visual impact have already built a big following. Number is infectious about Arnold's "strange hobby" with a well-boosted sound behind. Should make the Fifty.' Pink Floyd also made a black and white promotional film for the single which was filmed at Wittering beach on the south coast of England by Derek Nice. Its debut TV broadcast was on the French music programme *Bouton Rouge* broadcast on ORTF2 on 21 May 1967 at 7.43pm. In recent years, following its rediscovery, it has been regularly shown on various global TV shows, and has even been used onscreen by Roger Waters as part of his solo stage shows.

Friday 10 March
CONCERT
UFO, The Blarney Club, Tottenham Court Road, London, England
With Special Guest Robot, films, lights and raids! Pink Floyd's regular slot at UFO was complimented by a screening of the 'Arnold Layne' promotional film.

Saturday 11 March
PRESS REPORT
London, England
Melody Maker reported Pink Floyd as having prepared a thirty-minute television pilot to show to EMI Records in order for the company to decide whether or not to sponsor a series for future broadcast on ITV network television. The project never came to fruition and was described as a 'Monkees-type' TV series. In the same news item it was reported the band would be performing for a whole week in May at the Jeanetta Cochrane Theatre, Long Acre, London, England although evidently this did not come to fruition.

Saturday 11 March
CONCERT
Main Hall, Canterbury Technical College, Canterbury, England
Supported by Specta Quinn Team.

Sunday 12 March
CONCERT
The Agincourt Ballroom, Camberley, England
Supported by Mike Raynor & The Condors.

Tuesday 14 - Thursday 16 March
RECORDING SESSIONS
Studio 3, EMI Studios, Abbey Road, St. John's Wood, London, England
Recording for the album *The Piper At The Gates Of Dawn*. Pink Floyd recorded a short version of 'Interstellar Overdrive' on 16 March that was used exclusively for a French EP released in July.

Friday 17 March
CONCERT
Kingston Technical College, Kingston-upon-Thames, England
Pink Floyd were paid £100 for their performance.

Saturday 18 March
CONCERT
Enfield College of Technology, Enfield, England

Sunday 19 - Wednesday 22 March
RECORDING SESSIONS
Studio 3, EMI Studios, Abbey Road, St. John's Wood, London, England
Recording for the album *The Piper At The Gates Of Dawn*.

Thursday 23 March
CONCERT
Rotherham College of Technology Dance, Clifton Hall, Rotherham, England
Pink Floyd replaced the advertised Shotgun Express at short notice.

Friday 24 March
CONCERT
Ricky Tick Club, Hounslow, England

Saturday 25 March
CONCERT
Ricky Tick Club, Thames Hotel, Windsor, England
Early show.

Saturday 25 March
CONCERT
The New Yorker Discotheque, Swindon, England
Late show. With The Outer Limits.

Saturday 25 March
CONCERT
Shoreline Club, Caribbean Hotel, Bognor Regis, England
With The Shame. Pink Floyd performed in the early hours of 26 March at this Easter weekend all-nighter.

Monday 27 March
RECORDING SESSION
EMI Studios, Abbey Road, St. John's Wood, London, England
Recording for the album *The Piper At The Gates Of Dawn*.

Tuesday 28 March
CONCERT
Chinese R&B Jazz Club, Corn Exchange, Bristol, England

Wednesday 29 March
RECORDING SESSION
EMI Studios, Abbey Road, St. John's Wood, London, England
Mixing for the album *The Piper At The Gates Of Dawn*.

Wednesday 29 March
CONCERT
The Dance Hall, Eel Pie Island Hotel, Twickenham, England

Thursday 30 March
CANCELLED TV SHOW
BBC Lime Grove Studios, Shepherd's Bush, London, England
Pink Floyd were filmed for the UK's most watched pop music show, BBC TV's *Top Of The Pops*, performing 'Arnold Layne' on this date, but its intended broadcast the following week (Thursday 6 April) was cancelled. A statement was issued by the show's producer, Stanley Dorfman, to *Melody Maker*, (published week ending Saturday 8 April), explaining the omission: 'We filmed the Floyd and the Move before last week's show because they were both playing out of town on Thursday night [6 April]. Naturally we wanted the film in the can in case the record entered the chart. In fact, on our combined chart the Floyd dropped three places so it ruled them out of the show.'

Friday 31 March
CONCERT
Top Spot Ballroom, Ross-on-Wye, England
Supported by Group 66.

Saturday 1 April
PRESS RECEPTION
EMI Records, Manchester Square, London, England
Pink Floyd were wheeled out for the press at EMI's headquarters.

Saturday 1 April
CONCERT
The Birdcage Club, Eastney, Portsmouth, England

Monday 3 April
RADIO SHOW
BBC Playhouse Theatre, Charing Cross, London, England
Pink Floyd performed 'Arnold Layne' and 'Candy And A Currant Bun' live for the BBC Radio Light Programme's *Monday, Monday!* broadcast at 1.00pm. Curiously at this time the BBC had a policy of auditioning all bands for live appearance by playing the recordings to a committee for approval for transmission. However, in Pink Floyd's case the BBC archives indicate that their tracks were transmitted and considered a 'live audition' in view of the fact the single was already charting.

Thursday 6 April
CONCERT
City Hall, Salisbury, England
Supported by The Nite Shift.
The set list included: Untitled Instrumental / 'Arnold Layne' / 'Interstellar Overdrive' / 'Matilda Mother'.

Friday 7 April
CONCERT
Floral Hall, Belfast, Northern Ireland
Supported by The Jimmy Johnston Showband.
Rick Wright commented in *Melody Maker* that, 'The best reaction so far to the Floyd's lights and sounds was in Belfast. The kind of place where if they don't like you they let you know in no uncertain manner. We were worried about Belfast, but they really rave over there. We were completely knocked out and stunned at the reaction.' The show featured an unusual lightshow with 35mm slides of the abstract paintings of local artist Cecil McCartney projected over the band as they performed.

Saturday 8 April
CONCERT
Rhodes Centre, Bishops Stortford, England
Early show. Supported by The New Generation.

Saturday 8 April
CONCERT
The Roundhouse, Chalk Farm, London, England
Late show. With The Flies, Earl Fuggle, The Electric Poets [Soft Machine], The Block, Sandy & Narda dancers and Sam Gopal.

Sunday 9 April
CONCERT
Britannia Rowing Club, Nottingham, England

Monday 10 April
CONCERT
The Pavilion, Bath, England
The *Bath & Wilts Evening Chronicle* reported that: 'Three electricians should have taken a bow at the Pavilion last night. Instead four people took the applause - four people who had, apparently haphazardly, thumped out music. The four were the Pink Floyd, one of the most intriguing groups to visit the city. The overall effect created by the noise of those onstage and the lighting from those off-stage was interesting to say the least. Jaundiced blotches ran down mottled multi-coloured backgrounds. Flashing lights transformed the group into ghouls, with giant prancing shadows of distorted beings dwarfing the performers as the lighting changed with the pounding rhythm. The group admits its lighting techniques - which are strictly secret - and sound will and must improve. Roger Waters said, "We are getting better all the time and our techniques are doing the same." But the group denies the "psychedelic" tag it has been branded with. "If psychedelic is producing LSD feelings then we are not," said Nick Mason. "But if psychedelic is light and sound, then we are."'

Tuesday 11 - Thursday 13 April
RECORDING SESSIONS
Studio 3, EMI Studios, Abbey Road, St. John's Wood, London, England
Recording for the album *The Piper At The Gates Of Dawn*. Pink Floyd began recording a song entitled 'Percy The Ratcatcher' which eventually became known as 'Lucifer Sam'.

Thursday 13 April
CONCERT
Tilbury Railway Club, Tilbury, England

Saturday 15 April
CONCERT
Kinetic Arena - K4 Discoteque, Main Ballroom, West Pier, Brighton, England
Set list included: 'Candy And A Currant Bun' / 'Astronomy Dominé' / 'Matilda Mother' / 'Pow R Toc H' / 'Interstellar Overdrive' / 'Lucifer Sam'.
Pink Floyd were invited by Hornsey College of Art's Advanced Studies Group to perform in their 'kinetic audio-visual environments' - collectively entitled 'K4'. They played in front of a sixty-foot-wide white projection screen with a PA system suspended from the ceiling.

ABOVE: PRIOR TO FILMING 'ARNOLD LAYNE' FOR THE *FAN CLUB* TV SHOW IN AMSTERDAM ON 29 APRIL 1967.

Monday 17 & Tuesday 18 April
RECORDING SESSIONS
Studio 3, EMI Studios, Abbey Road, St. John's Wood, London, England
Recording for the album *The Piper At The Gates Of Dawn*. Pink Floyd began recording a new Barrett composition on 18 April entitled 'She Was A Millionaire', which remains unreleased.

Wednesday 19 April
CONCERT
Bromel Club, Court Hotel, Downham, Bromley, England

Thursday 20 April
CONCERT
Queen's Hall, Barnstaple, England
Supported by The Gordon Riots.

Friday 21 April
CONCERT
Starlite Ballroom, Greenford, England
Early show.

Friday 21 April
CONCERT
UFO, The Blarney Club, Tottenham Court Road, London, England
Late show. With The Gas Company.

Saturday 22 April
PRESS REPORT
London, England
Melody Maker reported that Pink Floyd were due to start work on a thirty-minute film called *The Life Story of Percy The Ratcatcher*. Although the project never reached fruition the band had been using this as the working title to the song that eventually became 'Lucifer Sam'.

Saturday 22 April
CANCELLED CONCERT
Sixty Nine Club, Royal York Hotel, Ryde, Isle of Wight, England

Saturday 22 April
CONCERT
Benn Memorial Hall, Rugby, England
The Rugby Advertiser reported that: 'Like mad scientists they wielded their instruments treating each guitar string or drum stick with a fanaticism that rivalled the tantrums of the most despotic dictator. On stage at the Benn Memorial Hall on Saturday was the most weird, frighteningly way-out group fans in Rugby had ever seen - The Pink Floyd. Their experiments went far beyond the realms of pop music and backstage the boys explained why. "We started off as an R&B group, but later decided to adopt our own style", said organist Rick Wright. "Our music is made to represent hallucinatory effects and this is enhanced by the use of lights". The boys appeared only once but the 45-minute stint was about all the average onlooker could take. Flipping through their repertoire, which included 'Interstellar Overdrive', 'Candy And A Currant Bun' and their latest, 'Arnold Layne', they displayed a remarkable dedication to a brand of music which may fade into the past, or could be the next progression in the musical annals of the 20th century.'

Sunday 23 April
CONCERT
Starlight Ballroom, Crawley, England

Monday 24 April
CONCERT
Blue Opera Club, The Feathers public house, Ealing Broadway, London, England
Roger Waters recalled in an interview with *Zig Zag* magazine that, 'The worst thing that ever happened to me was at the Feathers Club, which was a penny, which made a bloody great cut in the middle of my forehead. I bled quite a lot. And I stood at the front of the stage to see if I could see him throw one. I was glowering in a real rage, and I was gonna leap out into the audience and get him. Happily, there was one freak who turned up who liked us, so the audience spent the whole evening beating the shit out of him, and left us alone.'

Tuesday 25 April
CONCERT
The Stage Club, Clarendon Restaurant, Oxford, England
Supported by The Vibratones.

Friday 28 April
CONCERT
The Tabernacle Club, Hillgate, Stockport, England

Saturday 29 April
TV SHOW
Nederland 1 TV Studios, Zaandam, The Netherlands
Pink Floyd travelled to the Netherlands for their first overseas engagement to perform 'Arnold Layne' on the *Fan Club* pop music show. It was broadcast on Nederland 1 TV on 5 May at 7.00pm. The recent discovery of a promotional film circulating on the collectors market showing the band larking about in some woods and in front of a church miming to 'Arnold Layne', has given rise to speculation that this film originates from this date, but it remains unconfirmed.

Saturday 29 April
CONCERT
14-Hour Technicolor Dream, Alexandra Palace, Muswell Hill, London, England
With thirty other groups including The Move, The Pretty Things, Soft Machine, Tomorrow, The Flies, The Creation and The Graham Bond Organisation.
This event was billed as 'The Biggest Party Ever' and every band offered to play for free. In addition there were fairground attractions, igloos dispensing banana-peel joints and the usual giant jellies. It is regarded as an historic event in rock history but, predictably, has grown rosier with age. Mick Farren, quoted in Jonathan Green's book *Days In The Life*, gives an account of The Social Deviants' performance that accurately sums up the evening (clearly it was best appreciated by those who were bombed out of their minds): 'We were the first band on and we were fuckin' terrible. Nobody had ever played a gig this big. It was a rectangle the size of Paddington station with similar acoustics. Because of the helter-skelter we couldn't see the band playing at the other end of the hall, but we could hear it, like a slightly more melodic version of the 3.15 from Exeter pulling in at the platform.'
Pink Floyd turned up at 3.00am after a breakneck journey by van and ferry from The Netherlands. Regardless of the fact that they probably played like bums (certainly Peter Jenner remembers he and Barrett took LSD), it is seen as a magnificent finale to a night of complete madness, the band taking the stage as the dawn sunlight pierced the huge windows of the main hall.
The entire event was documented by three BBC TV film crews for inclusion in a *Man Alive* edition

subtitled 'What Is A Happening?' and broadcast on BBC2 TV on 17 May at 8.05pm although nothing of Pink Floyd's set was captured. Filmmaker Peter Whitehead also took cameras to the show, where he spotted John Lennon, among other celebrities and similarly although he captured the scale of the event as a whole, he failed to pick up Pink Floyd on stage. Segments of Whitehead's work here are also featured on the aforementioned See For Miles 1994 video *The Pink Floyd - London 66-67*.

Sunday 30 April
CONCERT
Plaza Teen Club, Thornton Lodge Hall, Huddersfield, England
Supported by The Match Box and DJ Doc Merwin.

Wednesday 3 May
CONCERT
The Moulin Rouge, Ainsdale, Southport, England
Presented by The Southport Technical College and Old Students' Association.

RIGHT: PINK FLOYD PHOTOGRAPHED IN RUSKIN PARK, DENMARK HILL, LONDON, SUMMER 1967

60

Thursday 4 May
CONCERT
Locarno Ballroom, Coventry, England

Saturday 6 May
CONCERT
Kitson College, Leeds, England

Sunday 7 May
CONCERT
King & Queen Mojo A Go-Go, Mojo Club, Tollbar,
Sheffield, England

Friday 12 May
CONCERT
Games For May, Queen Elizabeth Hall, South Bank,
London, England
Set list: 'Dawn' (tape recording) / 'Matilda Mother' /
'Flaming' / 'Scarecrow' / 'Games For May' / 'Bicycle' /
'Arnold Layne' / 'Candy And A Currant Bun' / 'Pow R
Toc H' / 'Interstellar Overdrive' / 'Bubbles' (tape
recording) / 'Ending' (tape recording) / encore:
'Lucifer Sam'.
Generally regarded as a turning point for the Pink
Floyd, this show included their first public use of an
idea developed in the recording studio: additional

speakers were placed at the back of the hall to give
an effect of 'sound in the round'. A joystick was used
to pan pre-recorded sound effects and instruments
anywhere within the circle formed by the speakers.
The set-up, which was built by technicians at EMI,
was stolen after the show. The idea was resurrected
towards the end of 1968 and used on their 1969 tour
and dubbed the 'Azimuth Co-ordinator'. In addition,
props were arranged on stage and bubble machines
let fly, along with a well developed light show which
incorporated 35mm film slides and movie sequences.
New compositions were also written, including the
song 'Games For May', which would form the basis of
Pink Floyd's second single, 'See Emily Play'. *Financial
Times* reported that: 'Pink Floyd have successfully
grafted vision on to sound in their performance by the
skilful use of projected colours. Last night they
emerged from London's underground life, where they
have been a cult for six months, to explode with the
noisiest and prettiest display ever seen on the South
Bank... The proceedings began with one of the two
acolytes who travel with the four-man group to
superintend the electrical equipment and assist in the
effects, throwing flowers at the audience. Then came
a long period of blackness and hysterical laughter,
which suddenly terminated in the musical sound of

the Floyd. They remained largely invisible in the first
half, their figures dimly deciphered behind the brilliant
colours, which flickered over them. On a backcloth
shapes like amoeba under a microscope ebbed and
flowed with the glimpse of an occasional human form.
The colours were primary and brilliant. Musically the
Floyd are not outstanding. There was good organ and
drumming but the guitars were rarely allowed to
develop a theme. Only on slower numbers was feeling
apparent and here the lyrics, which often invoked
childhood illusions of unicorns and scarecrows,
soothed the mood. In the more strident songs the
words were completely lost, and the sound became
just an accompaniment to the colours rather than a
partnership. A better balance was achieved after the
interval, when the free flow of the psychedelic mind
was given its head. In between some pounding
instrumental excursions, which carried the Floyd close
to the new dimension in experience they aim for, the
group wandered around the stage playing with
friction cars, and water, and blowing bubbles against
a recorded cacophony. With the sound at full blast
and the colours flashing red, blue, green, those who
were at all responsive to the performance succumbed
to the illusion. By the end of the evening music
disappeared and only electronic sounds remained,

filling the hall and the head. Unfortunately with the passing of the music went much of the creativity and instead of using a scalpel on the imagination, the Floyd were using an electric drill... The performance was billed as a salute to spring, but this was far removed from nature. It was instead a triumph of the mechanical and the belligerently avant-garde.'

Saturday 13 May
CONCERT
St. George's Ballroom, Hinckley, England
Show rescheduled from 29 April.

Sunday 14 May
TV SHOW
Studio C, BBC Lime Grove Studios, Shepherd's Bush, London, England
Pink Floyd performed 'Pow R Toc H' and 'Astronomy Dominé' live on the arts programme *The Look Of The Week* broadcast on BBC2 TV at 11.15pm. Barrett and Waters were also interviewed by the classical music critic Professor Hans Keller, who considered their music to be 'terribly loud' and a 'regression to childhood'. This appearance was thankfully archived and various clips have been used in Pink Floyd related retrospectives, most notably in the *Sounds Of The Sixties* BBC 2 series in 1991.

Thursday 18 May
RECORDING SESSION
Sound Techniques Studios, Chelsea, London, England
Recording for the single 'See Emily Play'.

Friday 19 May
CONCERT
Club A' Go Go, Newcastle-upon-Tyne, England
Show rescheduled from 14 April.
Set list included: 'Interstellar Overdrive' / 'Astronomy Dominé' / 'Pow R Toc H' / 'Lucifer Sam' / 'Matilda Mother' / 'Chapter 24' / 'Arnold Layne'.

Saturday 20 May
CONCERT
Floral Hall, Southport, England
Supported by Big Sleep.
Set list included: 'Interstellar Overdrive' / 'Pow R Toc H' / 'Arnold Layne'.

Sunday 21 May
RECORDING SESSION
Studio 3, EMI Studios, Abbey Road, St. John's Wood, London, England
Recording for the album *The Piper At The Gates Of Dawn*. Pink Floyd began recording a song entitled 'The Bike Song' which eventually became known as 'Bike'.

Sunday 21 May
CANCELLED CONCERT
Regent Ballroom, Brighton, England
Show cancelled, presumably due to recording commitments.

Tuesday 23 May
CONCERT
Town Hall, High Wycombe, England
Plus Rod Welling with Top Discs and Prizes.

Wednesday 24 May
CONCERT
Bromel Club, Court Hotel, Downham, Bromley, England
The *Kentish Times* reviewed the show by posing the question, 'Is it music? This is the controversy which has raged about the Pink Floyd, Britain's leading "Psychedelic" group. Certainly their show is unique. They play eerie, electronic music, while a dazzling spectrum of lights is played on to them. The lights could best be described as an illuminated abstract painting on which the patterns move kaleidoscopically, as one watches. They have a hypnotic effect. Their road manager and light operator was unwilling to explain their technique. He said, "I do not tell people how it is done because if groups copy each other, there is no room for originality." The group has two watt amplifiers with beat frequency oscillators. Percussion is provided by a double size drum kit. They are Syd Barrett (lead guitar and vocals), Ric Wright (organ), Roger Waller (bass guitar) and Mick Mason (drums).'

Thursday 25 May
CONCERT
Gwent Constabulary ('A' Division) Spring Holiday Barn Dance, Grosmont Wood Farm, Cross Ash, near Abergavenny, Wales
Supported by Volume IV with MC Eddie Tattersall.

Friday 26 May
CONCERT
General Post Office North West Regional Dance, Empress Ballroom, Winter Gardens, Blackpool, England
Supported by The Koobas, Johnny Breeze & The Atlantics and The Rest. Compered by Jimmy Saville. David Boderke, a member of support band The Rest, recalled that: 'It was through our associations with the Post Office that we got the booking that was to remain the highlight of our brief career. It was at the GPO's (General Post Office) North West Regional Dance at Blackpool's famous Winter Gardens. Topping the bill was the new psychedelic-type band, Pink Floyd. The whole evening was compered by Jimmy Saville in his pre-blonde locks days. Supporting were The Koobas from Liverpool who had toured with The Beatles [in 1965], Johnny Breeze and The Atlantics,

and ourselves (The Rest). After our soundcheck we left our guitars and change of clothing in our dressing room and as were leaving we passed the Pink Floyd's road crew coming in with their equipment. Years later they needed a couple of articulated transporters to carry everything, but even in those days it was still impressive. We stayed behind to watch them setting up and felt more than a little envious as their mountain of equipment dwarfed ours to say the least. Of course everything was bigger and better than our modest collection. Following our set we had a quick chat with Jimmy Saville backstage and then had a couple of drinks before settling down in the balcony to watch the Pink Floyd in action. As they went into their routine, with all the various stage and musical effects, the audience began drifting off the dance floor.'

Saturday 27 May
CONCERT
Bank Holiday Beano, Civic Hall, Nantwich, England
Supported by The SOS.

Monday 29 May
CONCERT
Barbecue 67, Tulip Bulb Auction Hall, Spalding, England
With Jimi Hendrix Experience, Cream, Geno Washington & The Ram Jam Band, Zoot Money & His Big Roll Band and Sounds Force Five. Pink Floyd were the first band on, apparently performing on a smaller side stage at the rear of the hall. About 600 people

attended the show but poor organisation meant that many fans were still queuing to get in as Pink Floyd were performing.

Thursday 1 June
RECORDING SESSION
Studio 3, EMI Studios, Abbey Road, St. John's Wood, London, England
Recording for the album *The Piper At The Gates Of Dawn*.

Friday 2 June
CONCERT
UFO, The Blarney Club, Tottenham Court Road, London, England
With The Soft Machine, Suzy Cream Cheese & Mr. Love, The Hydrogen Jukebox and The Sun Trolley. *International Times* reported that: 'The Pink Floyd played last week to the largest crowd that UFO has ever held. At times queues stretched for yards up Tottenham Court Road, and twice the box office had to close because the floor was completely packed. The audience included Jimi Hendrix, Chas Chandler, Eric Burdon, Pete Townshend and members of the Yardbirds. Appeals by Suzy Creamcheese and Joe Boyd were made to the rather emotional crowd to prevent them taking any action against John Hopkins imprisonment, until after his appeal has been heard. It is a pity that with all this happening the Pink Floyd had to play like bums. The Soft Machine also appeared briefly to perform a poem for John Hopkins. The Tales of Ollin dance group played for about 4 minutes and completely captured the audience imagination, also on the bill was the Hydrogen Jukebox.'

Monday 5 June
RECORDING SESSION
Studio 3, EMI Studios, Abbey Road, St. John's Wood, London, England
Recording for the album *The Piper At The Gates Of Dawn*.

Wednesday 7 June
RECORDING SESSION
Studio 3, EMI Studios, Abbey Road, St. John's Wood, London, England
Recording for the album *The Piper At The Gates Of Dawn*.

Friday 9 June
CONCERT
Students Union, College of Commerce, Queen's Gardens, Hull, England
Supported by The ABC and The Night Starvation.

Saturday 10 June
CONCERT
The Nautilus Club, South Pier, Lowestoft, England

Sunday 11 June
CANCELLED CONCERT
Image Klub, Patronaatsgebouw, Terneuzen, The Netherlands
8.00pm show.

Sunday 11 June
CANCELLED CONCERT
Concertgebouw, Vlissingen, The Netherlands
11.00pm show.

Monday 12 June
RECORDING SESSION
Studio 3, EMI Studios, Abbey Road, St. John's Wood, London, England
Recording for the album *The Piper At The Gates Of Dawn*.

Tuesday 13 June
CONCERT
Blue Opera Club, The Feathers public house, Ealing Broadway, London, England

Friday 16 June
RECORD RELEASE
'See Emily Play' / 'Scarecrow'
UK 7-inch single release. US 7-inch single released on Monday 24 July.
Highest chart position UK No.6
Melody Maker commented, 'The Pink Floyd. I can tell by the horrible organ sound. It's much better than "Arnold Layne". They are the only people doing this kind of scene and they have a very distinctive sound. What the hell is a psychedelic record anyway? Is it something with weird sounds on it? The Beatles use

weird sounds but I wouldn't call them psychedelic.'

Friday 16 June
CONCERT
Tiles, Oxford Street, London, England
Supported by Sugar Simone & The Programme.

Saturday 17 June
CONCERT
The Ballroom, Dreamland Amusement Park, Margate, England
Early show supported by The Tony Merrick Set.

Saturday 17 June
CONCERT
Supreme Ballroom, Ramsgate, England
Late show.

Sunday 18 June
PUBLIC APPEARANCE
Radio London Motor Racing & Pop Festival, Brands Hatch Race Track, Brands Hatch, England
Pink Floyd participated in a pop musicians parade in open top cars around the track with Dave Dee, Dozy, Beaky, Mick & Titch, David Garrick, The Moody Blues, and Tristram – The Seventh Earl of Cricklewood. The event was compered by Radio London DJ's Mark *Roman and Ed Stewart and featured an evening bikini fashion show and pop concert with Chris Farlowe & The Thunderbirds, Episode Six and The Shell Shock at which Pink Floyd did* **not appear.**

Tuesday 20 June
CONCERT
Commemoration Ball, Main Marquee, Magdalen College, Oxford, England
With John Bassett, Georgie Fame, Herbie Goins and comedian Frankie Howerd in the Main Marquee. Also appearing: The De Quincey Discotheque (in the Old Bursary); The Right Track, Steel Band and The Pooh (in the Cloisters Night Club) and the Spike Wells Trio and film shows (in the Junior Common Room). The event began at 10.00pm and ended at 6.00am. Pink Floyd performed two twenty-minute sets, at 11.00pm and again at 3.15am.

Wednesday 21 June
CONCERT
Bolton College of Art Midsummer Ball, Rivington Hall Barn, Horwich, Bolton, England
With The Chasers and Northside Six.

ABOVE: PINK FLOYD, LONDON IN JUNE 1967. PHOTOGRAPHER ANDREW WHITTUCK INVITED THE BAND TO SET UP THEIR GEAR IN HIS BEDROOM AT HIS PARENT'S HOUSE IN HAMPSTEAD ALONG WITH JOE GANNON'S LIGHT-SHOW.

Friday 23 June
CONCERT
Rolls Royce Apprentices Ball, Locarno Ballroom, Derby, England

Early show. Supported by Paperback Edition and Thorndyke Mordikai's Imagination.

Ken Cook, a member of support band Thorndyke Mordikai's Imagination, recalled that: 'My band appeared with Pink Floyd at the annual Rolls Royce Apprentices Ball. The majority of the audience hadn't got a clue what the Pink Floyd were about and the band kept themselves to themselves. Oil slides were projected onto the dance floor and they performed in front of a white sheet on one half of the revolving stage. The other bands on the bill were amazed at the massive PA they used - it was four watt! The backline (with the distinguished Farfisa Organ sound) totally drowned out any vocals that they were trying to get out of the PA, so I think you can probably imagine what the overall sound was like. To conclude, 80% of the audience were totally confused as to the direction of the Floyd whilst the remainder were possible converts to this new sort of music never heard before in the likes of Derby.'

Friday 23 June
CONCERT
The 8-Hour Psycho-Chromatic Fantasy, Great & Small Halls, Bradford University, Bradford, England

Late show. With Soft Machine, Tomorrow, The Children, Cock-A-Hoop, The Roll Movement and film shows.

Saturday 24 June
CANCELLED CONCERT
Civic Centre, Corby, England

It was reported in the *Corby Leader*, a month prior to the proposed date, that Corby Urban Council, owners of the venue, ceased negotiations with Pink Floyd's management claiming that, 'The £260 fee was too high for a group which has no crowd appeal at present.' The article was headlined, 'Visit By Drug Music Group Is Off'.

ABOVE: FILMING 'SEE EMILY PLAY' FOR THE SECOND TIME ON BBC TV'S *TOP OF THE POPS*, 13 JULY 1967.

Saturday 24 June
CANCELLED CONCERT
César's Club, Bedford, England
The Skatalites replaced Pink Floyd at short notice and rescheduled to 14 October 1967.

Sunday 25 June
CANCELLED CONCERTS
Mister Smiths, Manchester, England
With The Measles, Tony Powell and DJ Dave Lee Travis.
Pink Floyd cancelled two sets advertised for the Main Dance Hall and the Drokiweeny Beach Room for unknown reasons.

Monday 26 June
CONCERT
Warwick University, Coventry, England
Melody Maker printed this reader's letter in response to their show in Coventry: 'Having just seen the Pink Floyd [at Warwick University], I am absolutely bewildered. Can someone please explain what this psychedelic crap is about? Their performance bore no connection with music and after three numbers I walked out in disgust.'

Tuesday 27 June
RECORDING SESSION
Studio 3, EMI Studios, Abbey Road, St. John's Wood, London, England
Recording for the album *The Piper At The Gates Of Dawn.*

Wednesday 28 June
CONCERT
The Dance Hall, Eel Pie Island Hotel, Twickenham, England

Thursday 29 & Friday 30 June
RECORDING SESSIONS
Studio 3, EMI Studios, Abbey Road, St. John's Wood, London, England
Recording for the album *The Piper At The Gates Of Dawn.*

Friday 30 June
RADIO SHOW
Studio B15, BBC Broadcasting House, Portland Place, London, England
Nick Mason and Roger Waters were interviewed in the afternoon for the BBC World Service programme *Highlight*. It was broadcast on 2 July at 4.15am.

Saturday 1 July
CONCERT
The Swan public house, Yardley, Birmingham, England
Supported by Blend 5.

Sunday 2 July
CONCERT
Midnight City, Digbeth, Birmingham, England

Monday 3 July
CONCERT
The Pavilion, Bath, England

Wednesday 5 July
RECORDING SESSION
Studio 1, EMI Studios, Abbey Road, St. John's Wood, London, England
Recording for the album *The Piper At The Gates Of Dawn.*

Wednesday 5 July
CONCERT
The Dance Hall, Eel Pie Island Hotel, Twickenham, England

Thursday 6 July
TV SHOW
BBC Lime Grove Studios, Shepherd's Bush, London, England
Pink Floyd performed 'See Emily Play' live for the first of three times on the music programme *Top Of The Pops*. It was broadcast on BBC1 TV at 7.30pm.

Friday 7 July
CONCERT
The Birdcage Club, Eastney, Portsmouth, England

Saturday 8 July
PRESS REPORTS
London, England
Pink Floyd were reported in *Melody Maker* to be making a promotional film of 'Scarecrow' for British Pathe News. Filmed in and around Marbury Country Park in Northwich prior to their show that evening, the clip was then syndicated throughout the ABC cinema circuit in the summer of 1967 and featured the band wandering through wheat fields and having a pretend shoot-out, whilst trying not to collapse into fits of laughter. The same news item reported Pink Floyd's forthcoming album might be called *Astronomy Dominé*. *NME* meanwhile reported that Pink Floyd would be representing Britain in the June 1968 Olympic Games in Mexico City by performing at an official youth culture festival of music, although this never materialised.

Saturday 8 July
CONCERT
Northwich Memorial Hall, Northwich, England
Supported by Phoenix Sound.

Sunday 9 July
CONCERT
Dance, The Roundhouse, Chalk Farm, London, England
Supported by The Moody Blues and The Outer Limits. A BBC 2 TV crew was reported as filming the show for the *Man Alive* series, but it was never broadcast.

Thursday 13 July
TV SHOW
BBC Lime Grove Studios, Shepherd's Bush, London, England
Pink Floyd performed 'See Emily Play' live for the second of three times on the music programme *Top Of The Pops*. It was broadcast on BBC1 TV at 7.30pm.

Saturday 15 July
CONCERT
Stowmarket Carnival, The Cricket Meadow, Stowmarket, England
With Feel For Soul, The Ketas and other bands. DJ John Peel, speaking on *The Pink Floyd Story* broadcast by Capitol Radio on 17 December 1976, recalled that, 'I now live in a little town up in East Anglia, which is near Stowmarket. When I first moved up there I was buying a dustbin at the local Woolworths and this fellow came up to me and said, "It's John Peel, isn't it?" and I said, "Yes". He said, "Having you move into the area is the best thing that's happened since the Pink Floyd played here." And apparently they did a gig in the cricket grounds at Stowmarket back when they were first starting out, and everybody went along expecting a band playing the top 2 and there were about a dozen people who went there who were knocked out with them - the local freaks and loonies. Everyone else hated them, but it's the biggest thing musically that's ever happened in Stowmarket ever, I think.'

Sunday 16 July
CONCERT
Redcar Jazz Club, The Ballroom, Coatham Hotel, Redcar, England
Supported by The Silverstone Set.

Monday 17 July
TV SHOW
Rediffusion TV Studios, Wembley, England
Pink Floyd were reported to be recording for the ITV children's programme *Come Here Often* but the content and broadcast details remain unknown. It was broadcast on the Rediffusion London ITV network on 18 July at 5.25pm

Tuesday 18 July
CONCERT
The Palace Ballroom, Douglas, Isle of Man, England

Wednesday 19 July
CONCERT
Floral Hall, Gorleston, England
Supported by The Alex Wilson Set.
This show was filmed by BBC2 TV for inclusion in a proposed TV show entitled *Impresarios* and subtitled 'Underground Impresarios'. Unfortunately the show was shelved and not broadcast.
Eastern Evening News reported that: 'Determined to

ensure that the Pink Floyd turned up at the Floral Hall - previous bands having let him down - promoter Howard Platt drove to Manchester to escort them back from Manchester Airport. He had a lonely wait. The group changed their plans and flew direct to London, leaving poor Platt in a frustrating psychedelic trance at passenger disembarkation, as they passed overhead at 20,000ft. But in the end they made it to Gorleston on time, one of the first groups to do so of the whole season. The crowd, about 800 strong, were subjected to many mind-expanding (trans-psychedelic) influences before the appearance of the group. A BBC2 camera team were there, preparing to record the freak-out, and at the far side of the hall stood a young girl surrounded by slide projectors - or were they magic lanterns? - preparing instant colour slides with tints and potions from a portable dispensary. The significance of this act was made apparent later. Suddenly it happened. As the curtains of the stage drew back the Pink Floyd launched themselves into a shuddering opening number, sending the decibels flying round the hall. Flashing green lights, the flashes linked to the rumbles of the guitars, burst around the group from all angles so that at times the different shadows thrown gave the impression that there was a whole crowd of people on the stand. Vocally they were disappointing. This wasn't their fault. Their own amplification had broken down and they had to borrow the Set's PA system. In the middle of that gargantuan instrumental sound they sounded very small - I felt the same way. Visually and sound wise the Pink Floyd are interesting, even exciting, but after the initial effect has worn off, it all seemed a bit thin. As one Floral Hall raver told me, "You've seen one freak-out, you've seen them all." To appreciate this further, I think I needed some other influencing factor, not readily available at the bar. The Floral Hall atmosphere didn't help. Stifled by the heat, my eardrums at perforation point, I dropped out of the Floral Scene.'

SCOTLAND & NORTH OF ENGLAND TOUR

Thursday 20 July
CONCERT
Two Red Shoes Ballroom, Elgin, Scotland
Supported by The Copycats.
Set list included: 'See Emily Play'.
Roger Waters commented in *Disc & Music Echo*, who had sent a journalist to accompany the first three shows, that, 'We've never played on a smaller stage. The audience was very cool to us. Some actually danced while we played. What was that guy saying? "Do ye ken I could sing better in ma wee bath!"'

Friday 21 July
CONCERT
Ballerina Ballroom, Nairn, Scotland

Two different adverts show support from either The Rebel Sounds or The T-Set.

Saturday 22 July
PRESS REPORT
London, England
Melody Maker announced Pink Floyd 's follow up single to 'See Emily Play' would be a new Barrett composition entitled 'Old Woman With A Casket' ('Scream Thy Last Scream') or 'Millionaire' released in September.

Saturday 22 July
CONCERT
Beach Ballroom, Beach Leisure Centre, Aberdeen, Scotland
Set list included: 'See Emily Play' / 'Arnold Layne'.

Sunday 23 July
CONCERT
Cosmopolitan Ballroom, Carlisle, England
Supported by The Lemon Line and The Cobwebs. Les Leighton, then manager of the Cosmopolitan Ballroom, recalled that, 'The Pink Floyd arrived late for the show. They were supposed to be on stage at 9.00pm, but didn't arrive until 11.50pm - and my license was up to 1.00am. The Floyd went on stage at 12.50pm and played until 3.00am and all their stuff was cleared by 4.45am. I risked my license! I can remember the oil and water slides - they had a huge amount of gear - it was a tremendous night, the Floyd were a bit special. All that night cost me was £15 - the Floyd and their manager were gentlemen, apologising for their late arrival. They were a bit special, not just another band.'

Monday 24 July
CONCERT
The Maryland Ballroom, Glasgow, Scotland
Set list included: 'Arnold Layne' / 'Interstellar Overdrive'.

Thursday 27 July
TV SHOW
BBC Lime Grove Studios, Shepherd's Bush, London, England
Pink Floyd performed 'See Emily Play' live for the third and final time on the music programme *Top Of The Pops*. It was broadcast on BBC1 TV at 7.30pm. Talking to *Cash Box* magazine some years later, the band's studio producer, Norman Smith, recalled that he accompanied the band to the BBC and that, 'After a hairdresser had spent many hours making Syd look "presentable" and after a make up artist had done the same, Syd looked in the mirror – screamed – and straight away began to mess himself back into his normal self.'

Friday 28 July
CANCELLED RADIO SHOW
BBC Playhouse Theatre, Charing Cross, London, England

The producer abandoned Pink Floyd's recording session for the BBC Radio Light Programme *Saturday Club*, for broadcast on 12 August at 10.00am, when Barrett reportedly 'freaked out' and left the studio during the recording of the first number.

Friday 28 July
CONCERT
UFO, The Blarney Club, Tottenham Court Road, London, England

With Fairport Convention and Shiva's Children. *Melody Maker* reported that: 'In a cacophony of sound played to a background of multi-coloured projected lights the Pink Floyd proved they are Britain's top psychedelic group. In two powerful sets they drew nearly every conceivable note from their instruments but ignored their two hit singles. They included "Pow R Toc H" and a number which received its first hearing called "Reaction In G", which they say was a reaction against their Scottish tour when they had to do "See Emily Play". Bass player Roger Waters gave the group a powerful depth and the lights played on to them to set an impressive scene. Many of the audience found the Floyd's music too much to sit down to and in more subdued parts of the act the sound of jingling bells from their dancing masters joined in. It is clear that the Floyd prefer playing to UFO type audiences rather than provincial ones and are at their best in an atmosphere more acceptable to them.'

Sadly, this was the last time UFO opened at these premises. The following Thursday, the landlord gave Joe Boyd notice to quit having seen a lengthy article in *The News Of The World* published on 30 July under the heading 'Disturbing World Of The Flower Children' that supposedly revealed the sordid nature of the underground gatherings: 'Men danced with men, girls with girls. One girl danced on her own all night,' as well as implying drug use, although by today's standards it seems almost laughable it ever went to print. The article even carried a description of Pink Floyd's live performance: 'A band crashed on to the stage and somebody's Dalmatian dog padded through the crowd looking for its owner. Discordant music belched from multiple stereo speakers set at full volume. Weirdly dressed men and women jerked to its rhythm. The thumping music was so loud the whole floor vibrated and violent coloured lights flashed in odd sequences.'

Although Brian Epstein offered Boyd the Champagne Lounge in his Saville Theatre for later shows, the club moved to the larger and far less intimate Roundhouse, where it remained until financial troubles forced its closure in October.

Saturday 29 July
CONCERT
The Wellington Club, The Dereham Exchange, East Dereham, England

Early show. Supported by The Void.

Roger Waters remembered the show in an interview with *Zig Zag*: 'I'll never forget that night. We did a double header that night. First of all we played to a roomful of about five gypsies, hurling abuse and fighting, and then we did Ally Pally. We actually had broken beer mugs smashing into the drum kit.'

Saturday 29 July
CONCERT
Love in Festival, Alexandra Palace, Muswell Hill, London, England

Late show. With Eric Burdon & The Animals, Brian Auger, Julie Driscoll & The Trinity, Crazy World Of Arthur Brown, The Creation, Blossom Toes, Sam Gopal's Dream and Apostolic Intervention.

An ugly evening to say the least; *Go!* magazine reported the sudden change in atmosphere from previous events: '...what about one fellow who was stabbed and trailed blood in a path outside the Palace early in the morning? Is this a LOVE-IN? No one had planned the tense atmosphere, the robbing, looting and violence. In fact the idea had seemed perfect. Only two groups with top billing got any reaction from the icy crowd. The Pink Floyd got a reaction - a bad one. While the Floyd make ridiculously good records, their music can only be termed boring. When the Animals departed, for thence onwards the music, the people, the atmosphere went abruptly downhill. People floated aimlessly around the hall trying to find where something was at. But "it" just wasn't there.'

Friday 4 August
RECORD RELEASE
The Piper At The Gates Of Dawn
UK album release. US album release on Saturday 21 October.

Cash Box commented that, 'The set is a particularly striking collection of driving, up to date rock ventures. "The Gnome" is an oft-played track. Among the other outstanding efforts included on the LP are "See Emily Play", "Chapter 24" and "Interstellar Overdrive". [Note: the US edition included 'See Emily Play'. Please refer to discography for further information.]

CANCELLED CONCERTS

Pink Floyd were forced to take some time out because of Syd Barrett's deteriorating mental health and the following appearances were cancelled: Town Hall, Torquay, England (31 July); Filming for the *Music For Young People* TV Show, Hamburg, West Germany (1 & 2 August, although it was incorrectly reported in the music press that Jeff Beck replaced Syd Barrett, despite the fact Jeff Beck was indeed in Germany on promotional duties on those dates); Seagull Ballroom, Ryde, Isle of Wight, England (5 August); *Beat Dance*, Skyline Ballroom, Hull, England (10 August); Top Rank, Doncaster, England (11 August); *7th National Jazz Federation Pop Ballads & Blues Festival*, Balloon Meadow, Royal Windsor Racecourse, Windsor, England (12 August) and the Gaiety (Mecca) Ballroom, Grimsby, England (1 September).

Andrew King spoke to *NME* who were speculating, in view of the cancellation of the Torquay and German TV show, on the band having split up: 'It is not true Syd has left the group. He is tired and exhausted, and has been advised to rest for two weeks. We have decided the whole group will holiday for the next fortnight, and any bookings which have to be cancelled will be re-arranged for a later date.' Pink Floyd departed for Ibiza, Spain shortly after 16 August. Additionally, the following two events were also cancelled in this period, that would have included Pink Floyd's participation: *UFO Festival*, Paignton, England (1 September) and *The Rolling Stones Benefit Concert*, Alexandra Palace, Muswell Hill, London, England (8 September) which followed the much publicised arrest of Mick Jagger and Keith Richards, in an unrealised event proposed by manager Andrew 'Loog' Oldham.

Monday 7 & Tuesday 8 August
RECORDING SESSIONS

Studio 3, EMI Studios, Abbey Road, St. John's Wood, London, England
Recording for the album *A Saucerful Of Secrets*. Pink Floyd began recording a new Barrett composition on 7 August entitled 'Scream Thy Last Scream', which remains unreleased, and a new Waters composition on 8 August entitled 'Set The Controls For the Heart Of The Sun'.

Tuesday 15 & Wednesday 16 August
RECORDING SESSIONS

Sound Techniques Studios, Chelsea, London, England
Recording for the album *A Saucerful Of Secrets*. Pink Floyd began recording a new composition entitled 'Reaction In G', which remains unreleased.

PINK FLOYD ROAD CREW THROUGH TO DECEMBER 1967

Peter Watts: Tour Manager / Front of House Sound
Peter Wynne-Wilson: Lights

Friday 1 September
CONCERT

UFO Festival, The Roundhouse, Chalk Farm, London, England
With Arthur Brown, Tomorrow, Fairport Convention and The Nack.

Saturday 2 September
CONCERT

UFO Festival, The Roundhouse, Chalk Farm, London, England
With The Move, Soft Machine, Fairport Convention, The Nack and Denny Laine.

Monday 4 - Wednesday 6 September
RECORDING SESSIONS

Sound Techniques Studios, Chelsea, London, England
Recording for the album *A Saucerful Of Secrets*.

SCANDANAVIAN TOUR

Saturday 9 September
CONCERT

Boom, Åarhus, Denmark
Supported by Wishful Thinking, Step By Step, Shaking Phantoms, Barnet And His Dandy-Bublers. Pink Floyd left some very strong impressions at their first Danish performance in the Boom dancing centre. More than 1,000 people attended the show, and at least the same number were unable to get in. After the microphones failed, the band were forced to play a mainly instrumental set.

Sunday 10 September
CONCERT

Gyllene Cirkeln, Stockholm, Sweden
Supported by The Sleeptones and DJ Errol Devonish. Set list included: 'Reaction In G' / 'Matilda Mother' / 'Pow R Toc H' / 'Arnold Layne'.
Roger Waters was interviewed after the show for a late night magazine programme broadcast live on Tonarskvall 3 Radio, Stockholm, Sweden

Monday 11 September
CONCERT

Starclub, Copenhagen, Denmark
Supported by The Beefeaters, Peter Belli & B. Brothers, Steppeulvene, The Clan, Hitmakers, Ebonies, The Case and The Defenders.
Set list included: 'Set The Controls For The Heart Of The Sun'.

Tuesday 12 September
CONCERT

Starclub, Copenhagen, Denmark
Supported by The Beefeaters, Peter Belli & B. Brothers, Steppeulvene, The Clan, Hitmakers, Ebonies, The Case and Melvis.

Wednesday 13 September
CONCERT

Starclub, Copenhagen, Denmark
Supported by The Beefeaters, Peter Belli & B. Brothers, Steppeulvene, The Clan, Hitmakers, Ebonies, The Case and Melvis.
Set list: 'Reaction In G' / 'Arnold Layne' / 'One In A Million' / 'Matilda Mother' / 'Scream Thy Last Scream' / 'Astronomy Dominé'.

IRISH TOUR

Friday 15 September
CONCERT

The Starlite Ballroom, Belfast, Northern Ireland
Supported by The Fugitives.

Saturday 16 September
CONCERT

Flamingo Ballroom, Ballymena, Northern Ireland
Supported by The Cousins.

Sunday 17 September
CONCERT

The Arcadia Ballroom, Cork, Republic of Ireland
The last night of the tour.

Monday 18 September
TV SHOW

RTB TV Studios, Brussels, Belgium
Pink Floyd were widely reported to have flown straight from Cork to Brussels to participate in a 'TV Spectacular' but the content and broadcast details remain unknown.

Tuesday 19 September
CONCERT

The Speakeasy Club, Margaret Street, London, England

Thursday 21 September
CONCERT
Assembly Hall, Worthing, England
Set list: 'Scream Thy Last Scream' / 'Astronomy Dominé' / 'Set The Controls For The Heart of The Sun' / 'Reaction In G' / 'Interstellar Overdrive'.

Friday 22 September
CONCERT
Tiles, Oxford Street, London, England
Supported by Roger James Explosion.

Saturday 23 September
CONCERT
Saturday Scene, Corn Exchange, Chelmsford, England
Plus supporting group.

Monday 25 September
RADIO SHOW
BBC 201 Piccadilly Studios, Piccadilly, London, England
Pink Floyd recorded a live show on this day for BBC Radio One between 2.30pm and 6.30pm in which they performed, in order, 'The Gnome', 'Scarecrow', 'Set The Controls For The Heart Of The Sun', 'Matilda Mother', 'Reaction In G' (only a few seconds of which was used as a fade-out) and 'Flaming'. It was broadcast on the first ever edition of *Top Gear* on 1 October at 2.00pm, which also marked John Peel's debut appearance on BBC Radio One as a guest presenter with Pete Drummond. 'Set The Controls For The Heart Of The Sun' was repeated on the *David Symmonds Show* on 13 November at 5.33pm and 'Matilda Mother' was repeated on the *David Symmonds Show* on 17 November at 5.33pm. The first complete rebroadcast of the show occurred when a live tape recording of the entire 1 October 1967 show was played on BBC Radio 6 as part of a John Peel retrospective broadcast on 24 October 2005 at 9.00pm.

Tuesday 26 September
FILM PREMIERE
5th New York Film Festival, Philharmonic Hall, Lincoln Center, New York City, New York, USA
The premiere of the film *Tonite Let's All Make Love In London*.

Wednesday 27 September
CONCERT
Fifth Dimension, Leicester, England
The club commissioned a specially designed psychedelic poster by 'Hapshash & The Coloured Coat' for their opening week of shows, which included this date. After the show Pink Floyd were interviewed by *Ripple*, the Leicester University student newspaper.

Thursday 28 September
CONCERT
Top Star Beat Dance, Skyline Ballroom, Hull, England
Supported by The Dimples, The Rats, The Disturbance and DJ Rikki Dobbs.

Friday 30 September
CONCERT
The Imperial Ballroom, Nelson, Lancashire, England
Supported by The Atlantics and The Beatovens.

Sunday 1 October
CONCERTS
Sunday's At The Saville, Saville Theatre, Shaftesbury Avenue, London, England
Two shows at 6.00pm and 8.30pm. Supported by Tomorrow, The Incredible String Band and Tim Rose with compere Joe Boyd.
Set list at second show: 'Astronomy Dominé' / 'Flaming' / 'Lucifer Sam' / 'Matilda Mother' / 'Pow R Toc H' / 'Scarecrow' / 'Candy And A Currant Bun' /

'Interstellar Overdrive'.

NME reported that: 'The beautiful people and hippies turned up in their shawls, embroidered jackets, Indian headbands and beads to see the Pink Floyd at the Saville on Sunday night. Even the compere, Joe Boyd, was from UFO. The Pink Floyd were one of the first groups to experiment with weird effects and they now have it down to a fine art, or rather their lighting man has. The flashing patterns and weaving silhouettes are an integral part of their music, which was very loud and mainly instrumental'

Thursday 5 & Friday 6 October
RECORDING SESSIONS
Sound Techniques Studios, Chelsea, London, England
Recording for the album *A Saucerful Of Secrets*.

Friday 6 October
CONCERT
Miss Teenage Brighton Contest, Top Rank Suite, Brighton, England
Set list included: 'Arnold Layne' / 'See Emily Play' / 'Matilda Mother' / 'Astronomy Dominé'.
Pink Floyd provided the musical interlude at the contest, which was compered by Radio Caroline DJ, Mike Aherne.

Saturday 7 October
PRESS REPORTS
London, England
In a joint report *Record Mirror* and *NME* stated that Pink Floyd were planning to stage a series of 'Spectaculars' in March 1968 with a 100-piece choir and a small chamber orchestra. Provsional dates were even announced: Free Trade Hall, Manchester (2 March), Philharmonic Hall, Liverpool (9 March), Royal Albert Hall, London (15 March) and Town Hall, Birmingham (16 March), but nothing came of these plans. The *NME* also reported that Pink Floyd would be recording for television in Germany and Belgium between 17 and 20 October and giving shows in Paris between 22 and 26 October, but this cannot be confirmed, although there is a gap in known activity between 15 and 18 October. Reported additional dates in the Netherlands between 8 and 12 November were cancelled due to the scheduled US tour.

Saturday 7 October
CONCERT
Victoria Rooms, University of Bristol, Clifton, Bristol, England
Plus support group.

Monday 9 October
RECORDING SESSION
BBC Radiophonic Workshops, Maida Vale, London, England
Pink Floyd made a daytime visit to the Workshops

with a view to co-writing a soundtrack for a new TV series but this never came to fruition.

Monday 9 - Thursday 12 October
RECORDING SESSIONS
De Lane Lea Studios, Holborn, London, England
Recording for the album *A Saucerful Of Secrets*. Pink Floyd began recording a new Barrett composition on 9 October entitled 'Vegetable Man', which remains unreleased.

Friday 13 October
CONCERT
The Pavilion, Weymouth, England
Presented by The Steering Wheel Clubs. Supported by Freddy Mack & The Mack Sound and Denise Scott & The Soundsmen.
Set list: 'Astronomy Dominé' / 'Reaction In G' / 'Set The Controls For The Heart Of The Sun' / 'Matilda Mother' / 'Interstellar Overdrive' / 'Pow R Toc H'.

Saturday 14 October
CONCERT
César's Club, Bedford, England
Supported by The Tecknique.
Journalist Steve Peacock recalled in an article he wrote in the Seventies for *Sounds* that, 'I remember seeing them at Bedford play an aggressive set to a cowed audience. They seemed to take a gloomy kind of pleasure in it: in the dressing-cupboard afterwards, Roger Waters made the grim comment, "At least we frightened a few people tonight."'

Thursday 19 & Friday 20 October
RECORDING SESSIONS
De Lane Lea Studios, Holborn, London, England
Recording for the album *A Saucerful Of Secrets*. Pink Floyd began recording two new Barrett compositions entitled 'John Latham' and 'In The Beechwoods', which remain unreleased.

Saturday 21 October
CONCERT
University of York, Hesslington, York, England

Monday 23 October
RECORDING SESSION
Studio 2, EMI Studios, Abbey Road, St. John's Wood, London, England
Recording for the album *A Saucerful Of Secrets*. Pink Floyd began recording a new composition entitled 'Early Morning Henry', which remain unreleased or was given another title at a later date.

Monday 23 October
CONCERT
The Pavilion, Bath, England

Tuesday 24 October
RECORDING SESSION
Studio 2, EMI Studios, Abbey Road, St. John's Wood, London, England
Recording for the single 'Apples And Oranges'/'Paintbox'.

Thursday 26 & Friday 27 October
RECORDING SESSIONS
Studio 2, EMI Studios, Abbey Road, St. John's Wood, London, England
Recording for the album *A Saucerful Of Secrets* and the single 'Apples And Oranges' / 'Paintbox'.

Saturday 28 October
CONCERT
Dunelm House, University of Durham, Durham, England

NORTH AMERICAN TOUR
Pink Floyd's debut tour was originally set between 23 October and 12 November, but got off to a very shaky start when the late application for work permits by Blackhill forced the cancellation of the following advertised shows: Whisky-A-Go-Go, West Hollywood, Los Angeles, USA (23 and 24 October); Fillmore Auditorium, San Francisco, California, USA (26, 27 and 28 October); Whisky-A-Go-Go, West Hollywood, Los Angeles, California, USA (30, 31 October and 1 November); *KPFA Radio Benefit Halloween Costume Ball*, Fillmore Auditorium, San Francisco, California, USA (late show, 30 October) and *Tower Night Out*, Pacific West High, San Jose, California, USA (late show, 31 October). Dates at The Cheetah, Chicago, Illinois, USA (5 November) and Cage Au Go Go, Manhattan, New York City, New York, USA (7–12 November) were proposed but cancelled before they were advertised.

Pink Floyd finally left the UK on 1 November arriving in Los Angeles where they immediately transferred to San Francisco (checking into the Casa Madrona Hotel in nearby Sausalito). However, their shows on 2 and 3 November at Winterland Auditorium, San Francisco were also cancelled due to the continued delay of their work permits. To appease Bill Graham, the band were added to the bill of an existing run of shows booked for Procol Harum and HP Lovecraft at the Fillmore and Winterland, making the show on 11 November the last night of their tour.

Prior to the arrangement of the US tour an advertised show at the *Caves Club*, Chislehurst Caves, Chislehurst, England on 3 November was cancelled and rescheduled to 8 December. Additionally, an advertised show at The Public Hall, Harpenden, England on 12 November was cancelled due to the extension of the tour, but was not rescheduled.

To add further confusion to this period, and despite reports to the contrary in both *Cash Box* and *Variety* magazines, Pink Floyd also cancelled a show at The

> november 1967

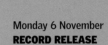

Cheetah Club, Manhattan, New York City, New York, USA on 12 November, which was added to the schedule when the additional San Francisco shows were announced.

It is also understood the band made a number of radio interviews in this period but exact details could not be found.

Saturday 4 November
CONCERT
Winterland Auditorium, San Francisco, California, USA

With Richie Havens and Big Brother & The Holding Company.

Sunday 5 November
CONCERTS
Cheetah Club, Venice, Santa Monica, Los Angeles California, USA

Two shows - afternoon and evening with Smokestack Lightning and The Candymen.

Los Angeles Free Press reported that: 'Pink Floyd, another mind-bending group from England, made its only local appearance last weekend at Santa Monica's Cheetah. Even the seaweed was swinging at the end of their first set. The unbelievable sound of Pink Floyd was first heard through a hurricane of colour, bringing total sensual involvement of audience and performers, each absorbed in the creation of aural/visual experience. The creation belonged to Pink Floyd, but there was ample room for all of us to share their visions, their feelings. At the end, the audience might have been another creation of the facile, collective mind of Pink Floyd. To quote their press release, "There can be no barriers, there can be no predictions."'

Monday 6 November
RECORD RELEASE
'Flaming' / 'The Gnome'
US 7-inch single release.

Monday 6 November
TV SHOW
KHJ TV Studios, Hollywood, Los Angeles, California, USA

Pink Floyd mimed to 'The Gnome' and 'Chapter 24' for the entertainment programme *Pat Boone In*

Hollywood. In a brief interview afterwards, Barrett reportedly returned a mute stare. It was broadcast (in colour) on the independent KHJ TV network Channel 9 on 4 December at 3.30pm.

Tuesday 7 November
TV SHOW
ABC TV Center, Burbank, Los Angeles, California, USA
Pink Floyd mimed to 'Apples And Oranges' for the music programme *American Bandstand*, hosted by Dick Clark, in which the band were also interviewed. It was broadcast (in colour) on the KABC network Channel 7 on 18 November at 11.30am.

Wednesday 8 November
TV SHOW
KHJ TV Studios, Hollywood, Los Angeles, California, USA
Pink Floyd made their third and final US TV

appearance on this tour miming to 'Apples And Oranges' for the teenage magazine programme *Boss City*, hosted by Sam Riddle. It was broadcast (in colour) on the independent KHJ TV network Channel 9 on 11 November at 6.00pm.

Thursday 9 November
CONCERT
Fillmore Auditorium, San Francisco, California, USA
With Procol Harum and HP Lovecraft.

Friday 10 & Saturday 11 November
CONCERTS
Winterland Auditorium, San Francisco, California, USA
With Procol Harum and HP Lovecraft. The show of 11 November was the last night of the tour.

Monday 13 November
CONCERT
Hippy Happy Fair, **De Oude Ahoy Hallen, Ahoy Heliport, Rotterdam, The Netherlands**
With The Jimi Hendrix Experience, The Motions, The Spencer Davis Group, Daddy's Act, The Buffoons, Soft Machine, Golden Earring, Tomorrow, Q65, Armand, The Shoes, Geno Washington & The Ram Jam Band, Rob Hoek's R&B Group and Cuby & The Blizzards and a band talent contest.
Set list: 'Reaction In G' / 'Pow R Toc H' / 'Scream Thy Last Scream' / 'Set The Controls For The Heart Of The Sun' / 'Interstellar Overdrive'.
Pink Floyd appeared on the third evening of this four-day festival starting on 10 November having been rescheduled from the advertised 12 November due to a later return from the US. Coupled with cancellations by some of the other advertised bands Pink Floyd were sandwiched between Group 1850 and the talent contest finals.

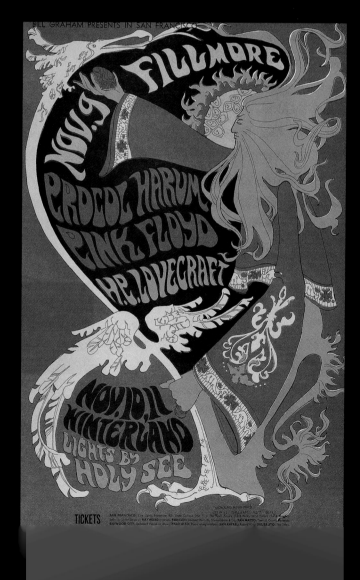

ABOVE: PINK FLOYD, DECEMBER 1967. WERE IT NOT FOR BARRETT'S DEPARTURE SHORTLY AFTER THIS PHOTO WAS TAKEN PINK FLOYD COULD QUITE EASILY HAVE FADED INTO OBSCURITY.

Tuesday 14 November
RECORDING SESSION
EMI Studios, Abbey Road, St. John's Wood, London, England
Mixing for the single 'Apples And Oranges' / 'Paintbox'.

JIMI HENDRIX UK TOUR

Pink Floyd joined a package tour with, in descending order of appearance: The Jimi Hendrix Experience (headliners), The Move, The Nice, Amen Corner, Outer Limits and Eire Apparent. Pink Floyd appeared for 15 to 20 minutes each night slotted between Amen Corner and Outer Limits. The show times given on this and all other dates on the tour are commencement times of the show and not of Pink Floyd's performance.

Tuesday 14 November
CONCERT
The Alchemical Wedding, Royal Albert Hall, Kensington, London, England
One show at 8.00pm.
Disc & Music Echo reported that: 'Possibly the most interesting act was the Pink Floyd's, fresh from playing hippie emporiums on America's West Coast, with what must be the best light-show yet seen in this country and very inventive music... were greeted by silence while most of the audience tried to grasp the "meaning" behind their music - although they played hard rock based material with drummer Nick Mason laying down some beautiful rhythms and guitarist Syd Barrett hitting some incredible flights of fantasy... They won rapturous applause, though from an audience which could have not been in the most part Pink Floyd fans. A very satisfying set.'

Wednesday 15 November
CONCERTS
Winter Gardens, Bournemouth, England

Two shows, at 6.10pm and 8.30pm.
Set list at the late show included: 'Set The Controls For The Heart Of The Sun'.

Friday 17 November
RECORD RELEASE
'Apples And Oranges' / 'Paintbox'
UK 7-inch single release.
NME commented that this was, 'The most psychedelic single the Pink Floyd have yet come up with. It takes several spins before you get to grips with it, and then you realise that a great deal of thought has gone into it. Although much of the track is way-out, there's a catchy and repetitive chorus, which should prove a reliable sales gimmick.

Friday 17 November
CONCERTS
City (Oval) Hall, Sheffield, England
Two shows, at 6.20pm and 8.50pm.

Friday 17 November
CONCERT
All Night Garden Party, Queen's Hall, Leeds, England
Late night show and an off-tour engagement. The event ran from 8.00pm to dawn. Also appearing were John Mayall's Bluesbreakers, The Warren Davis Monday Band, Ivan's Jaguars, The JB's, The Peighton Checks, Roger Bloom's Hammer, The Roll Movement, The Screen, The Syndicate and DJ Dave Cash.

Saturday 18 November
CONCERTS
Empire Theatre, Liverpool, England

Two shows, at 6.00pm and 8.35pm.
Set list at late show included: 'Interstellar Overdrive' / 'Pow R Toc H'.

Sunday 19 November
CONCERTS
Coventry Theatre, Coventry, England
Two shows, at 6.00pm and 8.30pm.
The Coventry Evening Telegraph reported that: 'Jimi Hendrix fans were unmoved - and I guess somewhat bewildered - by the Pink Floyd, a group of whom the new wave is more of a spring tide. The Floyd's extended instrumental/electronic experiments were fascinating, almost hypnotic, but unappreciated by an audience probably expecting their hit tunes.'

Wednesday 22 November
CONCERTS
Guildhall, Portsmouth, England
Two shows, at 6.30pm and 8.50pm.

Thursday 23 November
CONCERTS
Sophia Gardens Pavilion, Cardiff, Wales
Two shows, at 6.15pm and 8.35pm.

Friday 24 November
CONCERTS
Colston Hall, Bristol, England
Two shows, at 6.30pm and 8.45pm.
The Bristol Evening Post reported that: 'There was guitar smashing on-stage at the Colston Hall - and glass smashing off-stage last night. Over-boisterous Welsh teenagers were ejected after incidents in the hall bars in the auditorium. Teenagers from over the Severn Bridge came to yell for Welsh group the Amen Corner. Hall officials repeatedly warned the noisier teenagers as they brandished stools and shouted in the bar. In the hall, youths hurled abuse at performers. There was more weird music by The Pink Floyd and The Nice. Between them they beat up an electric organ, shattered a couple of thousand eardrums and lost themselves in a swirling cloud of coloured lights.'

Saturday 25 November
CONCERTS
Opera House, Blackpool, England
Two shows, at 6.10pm and 8.20pm.
Set list at the early show included: 'See Emily Play' / 'Set The Controls For The Heart Of The Sun'.
Set list at the late show: 'Take Up Thy Stethoscope And Walk' / 'Set The Controls For The Heart Of The Sun' / 'Interstellar Overdrive'.

Sunday 26 November
CONCERTS
Palace Theatre, Manchester, England
Two shows, at 6.10pm and 8.15pm.

Monday 27 November
CONCERTS
Festival '67, Whitla Hall, Queen's College, Belfast, Northern Ireland
Two shows, at 7.00pm and 9.15pm.

Friday 1 December
CONCERTS
Central Hall, Chatham, England
Two shows, at 6.15pm and 8.45pm.
The Chatham Standard reported that: 'Chatham Council's first beat promotion on Friday did not have a

EMPIRE - LIVERPOOL
Manager: Neil Brooks   Tel. Royal 1555
Saturday, 18th November at 6.15 and 8.35

Seat Prices: 15/-   12/6   10/6   7/6

HAROLD DAVISON & TITO BURNS PRESENT

JIMI HENDRIX EXPERIENCE   THE MOVE

THE PINK FLOYD
THE NICE   THE OUTER LIMITS   THE EIRE APPARENT
COMPERE PETE DRUMMOND
THE AMEN CORNER

POSTAL BOOKING SLIP

To Box Office Manager, Empire, Liverpool   Jimi Hendrix/The Move Show
Please forward _____ seats at _____ for the 6.15/8.35 p.m. performance on Saturday, 18th November
I enclose stamped addressed envelope and P.O./Cheque value _____
Name
Address

Printed by Hastings Printing Co., Drury Lane, St. Leonards-on-Sea, Sussex Telephone Hastings 2450

perfect start. While fans sat listening to the Outer Limits - first on the bill - organisers rushed about in quest of the missing groups - they were at the Town Hall, searching for the audience that had already settled itself at the Central Hall a few hundred yards away. With a few changes to the programme order, the groups all managed to arrive in time to prevent any embarrassingly long gaps during the evening, but the confusion at the start seemed somehow to upset the atmosphere. The Pink Floyd was the biggest disappointment, because I was expecting so much more. They performed in near darkness for most of the time, played some very unrecognisable numbers and were completely overshadowed by the entertaining antics of a young man in a bear skin jacket whose task seemed to be to leap about the stage adjusting amplifiers, twisting knobs and retrieving the odd cymbal or microphone.'

Saturday 2 December
CONCERTS
The Dome, Brighton, England
Two shows, at 6.15pm and 8.40pm.
Set list at the late show: 'Astronomy Dominé' / 'Set The Controls For The Heart Of The Sun' / 'Interstellar Overdrive'.
It is said that David Gilmour may have made his first appearance with Pink Floyd at this show to replace an absent Syd Barrett. Whether his involvement went beyond this date is uncertain, but it is worth noting that Mitch Mitchell (drummer with Jimi Hendrix) recalls in his book *The Hendrix Experience* that he joined the tour halfway through, so he may well have been present at several other shows.

Sunday 3 December
CONCERTS
Theatre Royal, Nottingham, England
Two shows, at 5.30pm and 8.00pm.
Set list at late show included: 'Set The Controls For The Heart Of The Sun'.
Tom Croson, a fan in attendance, recalled that, 'I had the misfortune of going to the first one. Syd Barrett didn't make the first show and David O'List, the lead guitarist with The Nice, who were also on the same bill, stepped in and ad-libbed along with the Floyd! He did the best he could under the circumstances. Some friends of mine went to the second house which he arrived in time for.'

Monday 4 December
CONCERTS
City Hall, Newcastle-upon-Tyne, England
Two shows, at 6.15pm and 8.30pm.

Tuesday 5 December
CONCERTS
Green's Playhouse, Glasgow, Scotland
Two shows, at 6.15pm and 8.45pm. The last night of

the tour.
Set list at the late show: 'Interstellar Overdrive' / 'Set The Controls For The Heart Of The Sun'.

PINK FLOYD ROAD CREW THROUGH TO MARCH 1968
Peter Watts: Tour Manager / Front of House Sound
John Marsh: Lights

Wednesday 6 December
CONCERT
Horror Ball, **Royal College of Art, Kensington, London, England**
The Kensington Post reported that: 'When 23 year old Martin Hayden was refused a grant by his local authority to see him through a two-year course at the Royal College of Art, Kensington, he decided he would have no choice but to leave college. Without the £300 a year grant he could not possibly afford to stay on. But help was on the way from his fellow students. They organised a whip round and decided that the profits from last night's Christmas college dance would be given to Martin. Groups playing at the dance were The Pink Floyd, The Bonzo Dog Doo-Dah Band, The Marmalade and Blue Rivers & His Maroons.'

Friday 8 December
CONCERT
Caves Club, **Chiselhurst Caves, Chiselhurst, England**

Saturday 9 December
PRESS REPORT
London, England
Members of Pink Floyd and their managers were reported in *Melody Maker* to be viewing a colour film clip of the newly recorded 'Jugband Blues' at The Central Office of Information for inclusion in a cultural exchange magazine programme. Widely available on the collectors market, this film was networked throughout North America and widely reported to be the band's next single. The recording date and location remains unknown.

Sunday 10 December
CONCERT
Teenagers Sunday Club, **The Birdcage, Harlow, England**

Tuesday 12 December
TV SHOW
Stanhope Gardens, Hampstead, London, England
Pink Floyd were filmed at former landlord Mike Leonard's house for an edition of the *Tomorrow's World* programme that featured his sound and light experiments. To accompany his work the band were seen playing an untitled instrumental piece composed by Waters and Mason. (The soundtrack also included the Floyd jamming a Booker T. & The MG's style

improvisation.) The programme was broadcast on BBC1 TV on 17 January 1968 at 6.40pm and repeated for the very first time as part of the BBC *Omnibus* special on Pink Floyd broadcast on BBC1 TV on 15 November 1994 at 10.00pm.

Wednesday 13 December
CONCERT
Flamingo Ballroom, Redruth, England
Presented by the Cornwall Technical College with support from PP Arnold (although Mike Cotton & Lucas and John L. Watson & The Webb were advertised).
Melody Maker continued to receive complaints about Pink Floyd's show up to the end of the year, including this little gem: 'If any readers are intending to see Pink Floyd, my advice is don't. They played here recently and were so unbelievably bad the supporting group had to be brought back early. It was the opinion of most of the 1000, students at our dance that they were the worst group ever to appear in Cornwall.'

Thursday 14 December
CONCERT
The Pavilion Ballroom, Bournemouth, England
Presented by Poole College Students Union with support from The Clockwork Motion and Caxton.

Friday 15 December
CONCERT
Middle Earth, Covent Garden, London, England
Supported by Fusion Fluff and DJ John Peel.

Saturday 16 December
CONCERT
Ritz Ballroom, King's Heath, Birmingham, England
Early show. Supported by Gospel Garden and The Rare Breed and DJ Dave Terry.

Saturday 16 December
CONCERT
Saturday Spectacular, **The Penthouse, Constitution Hill, Birmingham, England**
Late show. Supported by Gospel Garden and The Rare Breed and DJ's Dave Terry & Haig.

Wednesday 20 December
RADIO SHOW
Studio 4, BBC Maida Vale Studios, Maida Vale, London, England
Pink Floyd recorded a live session in the morning for BBC Radio One, in which they performed, in order, 'Vegetable Man', 'Scream Thy Last Scream', 'Jugband Blues' and 'Pow R Toc H'. It was broadcast on *Top Gear* on 31 December at 2.00pm.

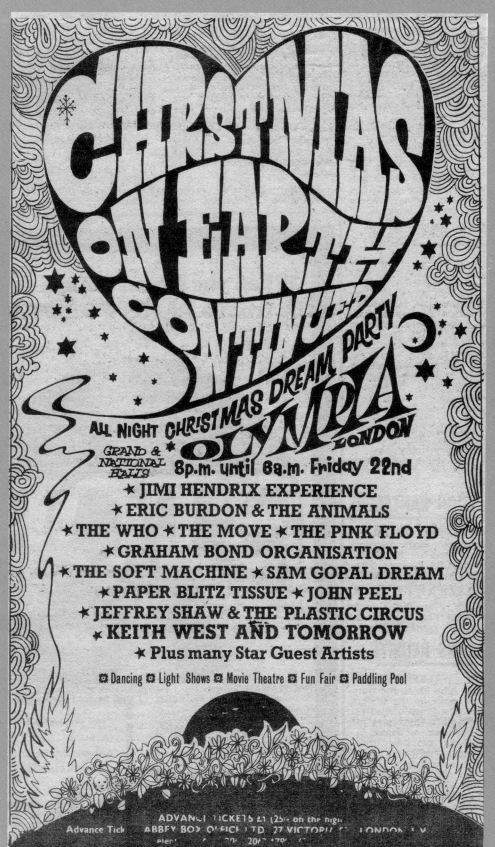

Wednesday 20 December
RECORDING SESSION
Studio 2, EMI Studios, Abbey Road, St. John's
Wood, London, England
Recording for the album *A Saucerful Of Secrets*.

Thursday 21 December
CONCERT
The Speakeasy Club, Margaret Street, London,
England

Friday 22 December
CONCERT
Christmas On Earth Continued, Olympia Exhibition
Halls, Olympia, London, England
With The Jimi Hendrix Experience, Eric Burdon & The
Animals, The Move, Graham Bond Organisation, Soft
Machine, Sam Gopal's Dream, Paper Blitz Tissue,
Keith West & Tomorrow, DJ John Peel and Jeffrey
Shaw & The Plastic Circus and many others. Pink
Floyd took to the stage at 5.00am.
In a preview of the show *The Kensington Post*
reported that: 'It will be one of the most ambitious
pop projects ever undertaken in Britain with an
incredible line up of top groups. By using two large
specially erected stages at either end of the Grand
Hall it is ensured that their music will continue
throughout the night non-stop. A cinema in the
National Hall will show top vintage films on one
screen while a light show is going on two other
screens. In all more than a hundred projectors are
being used throughout the building to make up a
spectacular display of various lighting effects. In the
centre of the hall will be a pool surrounded by sand
where one can laze in a tropical atmosphere to watch
the film shows. Fun-fair attractions will be assembled
around the two halls and there will be an arcade of
boutiques and stalls in the West Hall called
"Portobello Road, Continued". Here the strolling steel
band will provide music. Two three-feet high light
towers with three projection levels incorporating a
dozen radio-controlled follow spots are the centre
feature of the spectacular light show. It is expected
that 15,000 young people will be at Olympia
tomorrow night.'

75

MOTHERS

High St Erdington B'ham..

SATURDAY, OCTOBER 3

ECLECTIO

JOHN PEEL &

SUNDAY. OCT. 6th

SPOOKY TOOTH

Adm. 8/6

set the controls

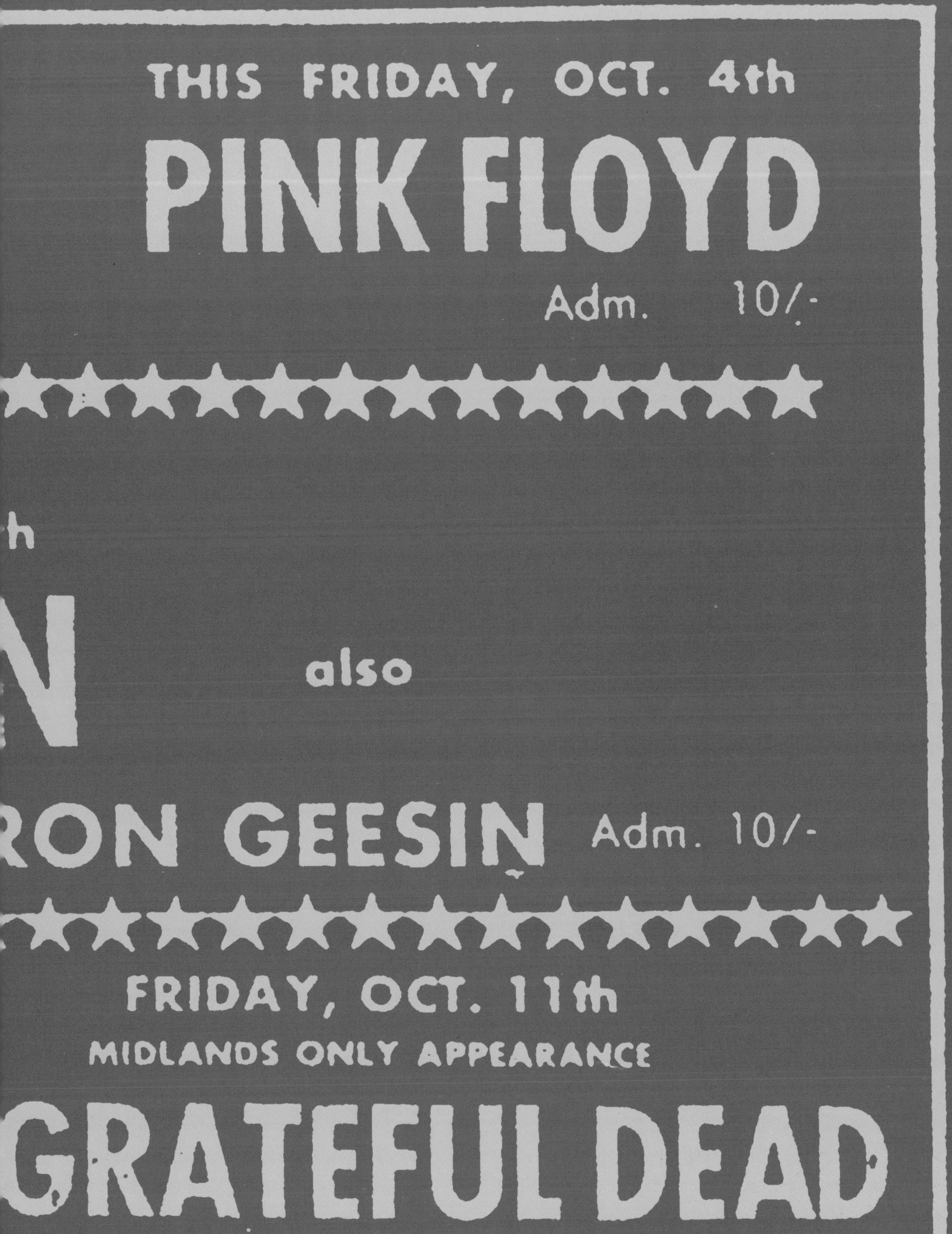

THIS FRIDAY, OCT. 4th

PINK FLOYD

Adm.   10/-

★★★★★★★★★★★★★★★★★★★★

also

N

RON GEESIN   Adm. 10/-

★★★★★★★★★★★★★★★★★★★★

FRIDAY, OCT. 11th

MIDLANDS ONLY APPEARANCE

GRATEFUL DEAD

for the heart of the sun

1968 - 1969

S YD BARRETT WAS CLEARLY NEVER GOING TO COME BACK TO THE REAL WORLD, AND HIS ROLE WITHIN PINK FLOYD WAS ALL BUT OVER. ONE SOLUTION THE BAND THOUGHT OF WAS TO USE HIM AS AN OFF-STAGE SONGWRITER IN THE SAME WAY THAT THE BEACH BOYS RETAINED BRIAN WILSON. BUT ALMOST AT ONCE THEY REALISED THAT THIS WAS AN IMPOSSIBILITY.

Gilmour took some time to settle in as Barrett's replacement, which he evidently found very uncomfortable at first: 'I learnt to sing all Syd's parts and all his guitar parts more or less. My guitar style and Syd's weren't even close, so it was very difficult for me to know what to do and it took me a while to settle in... I'd known Syd since I was fourteen; it was hard dealing with replacing one of my close friends. And having to see one of my close friends no longer functioning as a normal human being.'[1]

To further complicate matters, at that time Barrett was living in the same flat as Rick Wright in Richmond. 'I had to say things like, 'Syd, I'm going out to get some cigarettes', and go off and do a gig and come back the next day. It was awful; a terrible time.'[2]

Even so, the five-piece Floyd did play a handful of shows together throughout January. There are no reliable witness reports or press reviews of these final and fraught performances, but Gilmour does have some recollection of them: 'Sometimes Syd sang a bit and sometimes he didn't. It became very obvious that it wasn't going to continue for very long like that and on the sixth one that we would have done together, which I think was at Southampton University, we just never picked him up. Someone said, "Shall we bother to pick up Syd?" and someone said, "Nah, let's not bother", and that was the end.'[3]

The subsequent guilt, frustration, anger and hopelessness of the situation has haunted the band ever since, deeply affecting Waters, who, Gilmour has said,

'was the one who had the courage to drive Syd out, because he realised that as long as Syd was in the band, they wouldn't keep it together. The chaos factor was too great. Roger looked up to Syd and he always felt very guilty about the fact that he'd blown out his mate.'[4]

Consequently, and despite Barrett's relatively short spell in the group, his spectre has hung over Pink Floyd ever since. There are unmistakable allusions to him in various songs, in particular the haunting 'Shine On You Crazy Diamond' from the 1975 album *Wish You Were Here*. In many respects he has never really left the band.

And, just as the remaining members could no longer see a future with Barrett, their managers, Andrew King and Peter Jenner, could no longer see a future in a Pink Floyd without him. Blackhill Enterprises chose to dissolve their agreement with the band in April 1968 but continued to represent Barrett, who, they felt, would fare better as a solo artist. In the event, Wright very nearly departed at the same time: 'Peter and Andrew thought Syd and I were the musical brains of the group, and that we should form a breakaway band, to try to hold Syd together. And believe me, I would have left with him like a shot if I had thought Syd could do it.'[5]

Given the lack of offers at the time, and the debts the band had accumulated, to Wright this seemed a not unreasonable option. Blackhill were in the same boat financially and had even sought an Arts Council grant for about £5,000 to assist a stage production featuring Pink Floyd. But this was clearly a thinly disguised veil to try to pay off the bills. It was at this point, Mason told *Zig Zag*

FAR RIGHT: THE SHORT-LIVED FIVE PIECE LINE-UP OF PINK FLOYD. WITHIN A FEW DAYS OF THIS PHOTO BEING TAKEN BARRETT MADE HIS FINAL APPEARANCE WITH PINK FLOYD IN HASTINGS ON 20 JANUARY 1968.

PETER JENNER << We didn't have the resources to do anything more for them. They needed someone bigger to look after them. I suspect if they'd stayed with us we'd probably have bogged ourselves down in a trough of doom, which was very much in the air at the time. >>

magazine some years later, that their debts reached a peak, Waters adding that 'cheques were bouncing all the time because there wasn't enough money to pay everybody, so whoever got their cheque first got their money'.

Nevertheless, Wright decided to stay on board, and the Bryan Morrison Agency took over the band's management – specifically under Steve O'Rourke who oversaw the day-to-day management and Tony Howard who took the bookings. O'Rourke in particular had been involved with the band since 1967, and during their tours together had developed a strong bond of trust and friendship. In later years Blackhill would be accused of making their biggest ever business error, but Jenner takes a philosophical view: 'We didn't have the resources to do anything more for them. They needed someone bigger to look after them. I suspect if they'd stayed with us we'd probably have bogged ourselves down in a trough of doom, which was very much in the air at the time'.[6]

Immediate plans were now put into play to revive the band's flagging career. Remarkably, despite this turmoil, the new line-up composed and recorded some new music that April for Peter Sykes' film *The Committee*, which starred Paul Jones and featured Arthur Brown. A limited cinematic release in May further ensured its cult status and the film remained in the archives until the summer of 2005 with the advent of a remastered DVD release. The band's soundtrack, which is a series of improvised instrumental passages, does however include the earliest known version of 'Careful With That Axe, Eugene'. With the film's virtual non-appearance the only option left open to the band, in order to push them up a few rungs and secure more bookings, was to release another single.

However, the release in April of 'It Would Be So Nice', penned by Wright and backed by a new Waters composition, 'Julia Dream', was typically dogged with disaster. For EMI the single was a failure in almost every respect. This was partly thanks to BBC Radio One, who banned it for the mention of the *Evening Standard* newspaper in the lyrics, since product placement was strictly forbidden. Reluctantly, and at a cost of £750 to the band, replacement acetate discs were cut strictly for their benefit and the 'controversial' reference amended to the fictitious *Daily Standard*. But, this change made little difference, for the lapse between its release and airplay promotion had grounded the single. The band weren't entirely convinced this was the only reason – they hated it from the start: 'Nobody ever heard it because it was such a lousy record!' remarked Waters.[7]

The last single the band released in the UK for some eleven years, 'Point Me At The Sky', did no better when released in December, fuelling their conviction that singles were a waste of time, money and effort. Nevertheless, Morrison believed that Pink Floyd's struggles in Britain need not inevitably be repeated in the largely unexplored European market.

Having performed very little outside of the UK in their first professional year, they now had the ideal opportunity to strike out in different territories at the same time as tackling their home ground on their own terms.

1968 saw Pink Floyd undertake an immense amount of promotional work for European TV channels, which slowly built up for them a large and faithful following who were largely unaware of the earlier psychedelic period. Few of them knew who Syd Barrett was, and even at that early stage they had no identifiable front man, so presenting the band to a fresh audience required little explanation of a change of line-up or style. It was the perfect remedy, and before long, by some bizarre quirk of fate, Pink Floyd were being placed high up on the billing at major European pop festivals.

By the summer Blackhill were slowly dragging themselves out of the mire of insolvency by representing, among others, Tyrannosaurus Rex, Roy Harper and the Edgar Broughton Band, and announced that they were to stage the first Hyde Park free concert on 29 June 1968, having been granted a licence by the Royal Parks and Ministry of Works. Naturally they chose Pink Floyd as their headline act and the concert is often regarded as the moment the band successfully re-launched themselves in Britain. Their spellbinding performance was as well received by the press as it was by the assembled crowd and although the band performed some older numbers, these were now greatly reworked to suit their current style. Much of the thanks for Floyd's reassessment in Britain is due to the highly influential broadcaster and journalist John Peel, who, after seeing the show, championed the band for the next few years.

 Coincidentally Pink Floyd's second album, *A Saucerful Of Secrets*, was released in that same week, with a sleeve designed by their old Cambridge chum and graphic designer Storm Thorgerson and his flatmate Aubrey 'Po' Powell. Thorgerson was studying at the Royal College of Art and Powell at the London School of Film Technique, and working under the moniker of Hipgnosis, provided a unique photomontage of some 14 separate superimpositions. This included images of Marvel Comics' *Dr. Strange and the Universal Tribune*; an alchemist and his various bottled potions; various planets; a zodiac chart and a photo of the band sitting in Richmond Park. Hipgnosis would become a renowned Seventies design team and their distinctive work a trademark of Pink

Floyd. Indeed, Thorgerson's relationship with the band, barring a brief hiatus in the Eighties, has endured to the present day.

The album fared well in the charts despite some mixed reactions – *IT*, for example, described the title track as 'too long and boring'. But although it was an album that had no particular formula or real direction, and one that had its fair share of *Piper* leftovers, it nevertheless marked a complete departure from psychedelic pop.

Indeed Barrett's contribution to *A Saucerful Of Secrets* is minimal. He had penned the sadly prophetic 'Jugband Blues' just before his departure. Characteristically, he had invited members of a Salvation Army band who were also recording at Abbey Road into the studio to apparently play whatever they wanted – with no instructions, music or direction and, judging by the resultant track, not entirely the same piece at the

BELOW: PUBLICITY SHOT IN ADVANCE OF PINK FLOYD'S FIRST MAJOR TOUR OF THE NETHERLANDS AND BELGIUM, FEBRUARY 1968.

FAR RIGHT: DAVID GILMOUR'S FIRST PHOTO-CALL WITH PINK FLOYD FOR EMI RECORDS, MARCH 1968.

same time.

The only indication of any other contribution by Barrett came in a surprisingly coherent response to a reader's letter published in *Melody Maker* on 7 June. In his reply he stated that he only played on 'Remember A Day'. He added that there had been complications regarding the album, but hid the fact that his former band mates had made this concession merely to compensate him for the long hours he had spent in the recording studio's reception area waiting to be invited inside. Incidentally it is also on this track that Norman Smith performed drums in place of Mason.

Since the album was already in progress during the autumn of 1967 Gilmour's involvement was also minimal and he reportedly received a £300 flat fee for his performance as well as a quarter share in the publishing rights of the title track. 'I contributed what I could but I was, quite honestly, a little on the outside through it all. I didn't do a single thing. I was pretty paranoid.'[10]

On the subjects of Gilmour and the management split, Jenner says, 'I remember Dave [Gilmour] being auditioned in Abbey Road. Somebody said, "C'mon, Dave, give us your Hendrix." And out came this extraordinary sound, quite breathtaking. That was the thing, though; Dave was a great mimic. He could play like Hendrix, and he could also do Syd. What we underestimated was the power of the band name, the loyalty of the fans. We thought it was all down to creativity.'[11]

In good time, however, Gilmour would introduce his own ideas and unique style. Wright was already regarded as the most talented musician, whereas Waters and Mason were far more concerned with the structure, presentation and overall concept of the band – the 'big picture'. Fortunately this unique relationship worked exceptionally well and over time it became clear that neither element could work adequately without the other.

PETER JENNER << I remember Dave [Gilmour] being auditioned in Abbey Road. Somebody said, "C'mon, Dave, give us your Hendrix." And out came this extraordinary sound, quite breathtaking. That was the thing, though; Dave was a great mimic. He could play like Hendrix, and he could also do Syd. What we underestimated was the power of the band name, the loyalty of the fans. We thought it was all down to creativity. >>

certainly didn't feel like a full member and I wasn't up front contributing all the way on it.'[8]

His suspicions about the band being a pretty weird bunch were confirmed when he saw Waters and Mason 'draw out *A Saucerful Of Secrets* as an architectural diagram, in dynamic form rather than any sort of musical form, with peaks and troughs.'[9]

This was probably very alienating for someone with a raw talent but unlikely there was any clear definition of the extent to which Gilmour was expected to inject his ideas. While there could be no doubting his ability, his playing style and vocal range were quite removed from Barrett's and it took him some time to find his feet – even more so in the recording studio. 'I don't think they – the rest of the band – had fixed ideas of what I should do or how I should do it. I mean I just played rhythm to help it all along. For a good six months – maybe more – I

Surprisingly, their prospects were now looking promising in the USA. The 1967 tour had been a disaster, but Tower kept pushing out singles, despite limited chart success, at a greater frequency than in Britain. As a result the band was gaining a cult following, and a tour of America, mainly on the West Coast, was rather haphazardly arranged for July and August to tie in with *A Saucerful Of Secrets'* release.

It is a very poorly documented period of the band's history as their US booking agent, Premier Talent, struggled to close the gaps between the key bookings even as they were touring. As with the first US tour, their work permits failed to arrive in time and the band had to decamp to Montréal, Canada, in order to square the paperwork. Coupled with so many days off and the rising costs of hotel bills, not to mention mounting boredom, the tour was, not unsurprisingly, cut short.

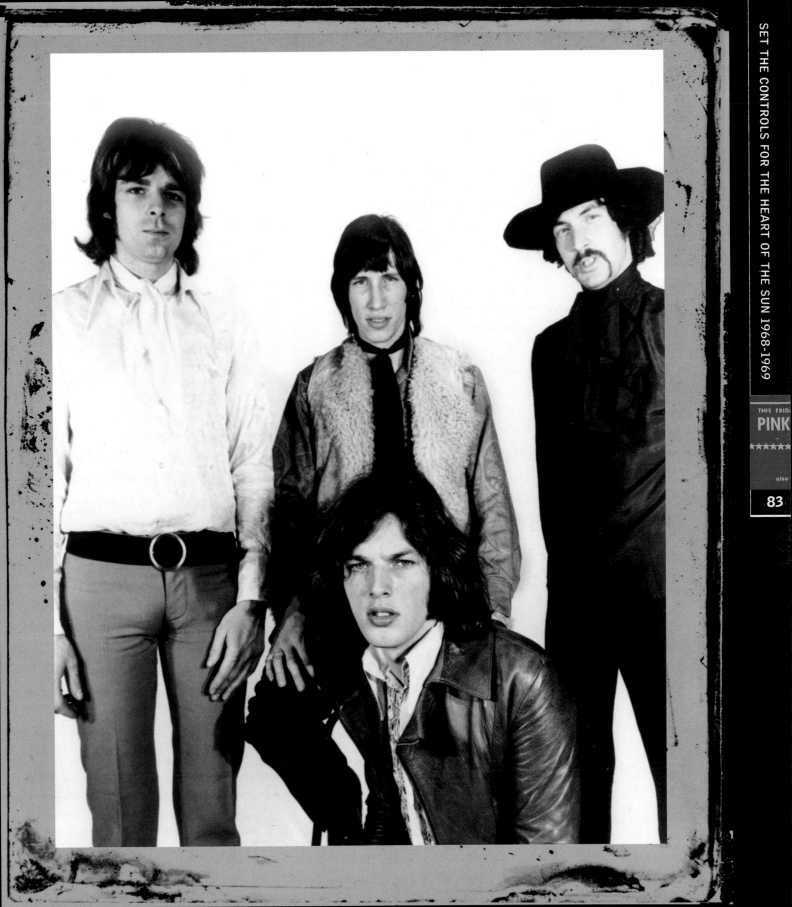

ABOVE: PINK FLOYD MAKING
THEIR DEBUT APPEARANCE IN
NEW YORK AT *STEVE PAUL'S THE
SCENE CLUB*, 15 JULY 1968.

Additionally, and to cut the cost of hefty freight charges, the band didn't take much equipment with them, hiring their drums, amps and speakers for each show, and even borrowed instruments and amplifiers from Jimi Hendrix's Electric Lady studios in New York during their residency at The Scene.

Those shows that did go ahead garnered a flood of rave reviews, from the underground press to the highly influential industry magazines *Cash Box* and *Billboard* and this may have temporarily renewed Tower's faith in the band, despite the fact Pink Floyd did not return to the US for another two years.

Just prior to the tour, and unbeknown to the band at the time, Bryan Morrison was suffering some personal turmoil, and was in the process of selling the business to the NEMS organisation, which should have included both agency and management rights to Pink Floyd. Thankfully the band had never signed a management agreement with Morrison following their transfer from Blackhill and the only document in place was a hastily drawn up agency contract to cover the US tour. When Morrison's sale went ahead they negotiated Steve O'Rourke's release from NEMS to become their personal manager. He later formed his own management company, EMKA (named after his two daughters Emma and Katherine), in a position he retained until his death in October 2003. Tony Howard did however remain at NEMS and continued to book the band and even occasionally tour managed them through the Seventies.

By the end of the year Pink Floyd's presence in Europe, too, was consolidated by further appearances. They were developing a unique style that advanced their career at an impressive pace. Moreover, their finances were stabilising and for the first time in months they were able to pay themselves more than their roadies.

Come the New Year a more mature stage presentation had developed and the Barrett compositions had all but disappeared from the band's repertoire. In addition, most of their earnings from performances now began to be invested in upgrading sound equipment, in an age when bands used to truck their own PA equipment however small the gig. They still carried a small array of projectors but for the most part visual entertainment was provided by the venues. And so the focus shifted towards the perfection of sound over visuals for the next few years. 'Our main thing,' Gilmour said at the time, 'is to improve and we are trying all the time. We are striving to improve our amplification, on stage and in the studios, we want to clean-up the sound equipment.'[12]

At the same time it was becoming clear from the

pattern of bookings that no one was ever going to attempt to dance to the band's music again (a situation that was later wryly satirised in 1981 with the title of the first authorised Floyd compilation *A Collection Of Great Dance Songs*) so it was fortunate that a new audience was prepared to take them on board: the university and college circuit. This 'intellectual' crowd, who revelled in the band's technology and the construction of the songs as pieces of music, would sit down and listen politely and intently. This suited the band just fine, making a welcome change from the initial months of touring to constant heckling and torrents of abuse. Now, during one of their performances you could almost hear a pin drop right up until the last fading note of a song.

Pink Floyd's press had also improved dramatically and at last they were being taken seriously as pioneers of a new and exciting movement capable of pushing back the boundaries. The experimentalism wasn't so much a free-form muddle as it had been in the past, but something more readily defined by the press, which labelled it – ghastly as the term now sounds – 'Progressive Rock' and for the next five years the UK

music press fawned over the band.

The live breakthrough came at a spectacular event held on 14 April 1969 at the 2,500 capacity Royal Festival Hall in London, big sister to the Queen Elizabeth Hall (from which they had been banned two years earlier when their bubble machine had soiled the upholstery and carpets). Billed as 'The Massed Gadgets Of Auximenes – More Furious Madness From Pink Floyd', the event, much to everyone's surprise, sold out well in advance. The show was a high point in Pink Floyd's ability to mix performance, stage and theatrics. The 'Azimuth Co-ordinator', their new 360-degree surround sound-system, made its London debut, as did many new and reworked tracks grouped as two suites, 'The Man' and 'The Journey'.

'The Man' opened with 'Daybreak', an alternative title for 'Grantchester Meadows', performed here as an acoustic instrumental piece that would later appear on the *Ummagumma* album with lyrics. This flowed into 'Work', a Mason-fuelled percussion workout during which the others sawed and nailed pieces of wood to make a table; it closed with a bombardment, from speakers all

ABOVE: APPEARING AT THE *KASTIVAL '68 FESTIVAL*, KASTERLEE, BELGIUM ON 31 AUGUST 1968. BY NOW PINK FLOYD WERE BECOMING A PROMINENT FEATURE ON THE EUROPEAN FESTIVAL CIRCUIT.

around the hall, of tape-recorded clanking machinery, after which the band's roadies served tea on stage. 'Afternoon' followed, enabling Wright to display his ability on trombone; this is a piece that was later known as 'Biding My Time' and later appeared on the *Relics* compilation album. This was followed by 'Doing It' (a crude reference to sex), an instrumental of percussion and taped voices reminiscent of 'The Party Sequence' on the imminent album *More*. Next came 'Sleeping', an electronic instrumental of ethereal keyboards and slide guitars, merging into 'Nightmare', which incorporated tapes of heavy breathing, ticking clocks and alarm bells. (In the clock sequence on the pre-recorded tapes, Waters' voice yells in a mock Scottish accent, 'If you don't eat your meat, you can't have any pudding', which was to appear on *The Wall* album some ten years later.) A reprise of 'Daybreak' ended the cycle and the first half of the show.

After a fifteen-minute intermission tapes of crashing waves and seagulls heralded 'The Journey'. The opening section, 'The Beginning', was later recorded as 'Green Is The Colour', on *More*. 'Beset By Creatures Of The Deep', a reworking of 'Careful With That Axe, Eugene', followed this. 'The Narrow Way' would feature as 'Part 3' of the same track, again on *Ummagumma*. This was followed, as the stage lights dimmed and the band came off stage, by a long taped sequence of footsteps circling the auditorium and doors opening and closing, allowing the audience to appreciate the Azimuth Co-ordinator in all its glory. On their return, 'The Pink Jungle', an instrumental, brought the stage back to explosive life, before giving way to the grand finale of the three-part sequence 'The Labyrinths Of Auximenes', 'Behold The Temple Of Light' and 'The End Of The Beginning' – the latter piece taken from the closing section of 'A Saucerful Of Secrets' – dramatically displayed by Wright as he took controls of the grand Festival Hall pipe organ.

Waters, in a later interview, explained the band's goal at this time: 'We wanted to throw away the old format of the pop show standing on a square stage at one end of a rectangular room and running through a series of numbers. Our idea is to put the sound all around the audience with ourselves in the middle. Then the performance becomes much more theatrical.'[13]

In fact, Pink Floyd had toyed with the idea of offering their audiences a theatrical experience as long ago as 1967, with plans to take an orchestra on the road for a series of one-off spectaculars which would have incorporated a screen fifty feet high and 100 feet wide on which to project films, slides and oil projections. In one of his last band interviews in *Melody Maker*, on 9 December that year, Barrett accurately predicted that 'in the future, groups are going to have to offer much more than just a pop show. They'll have to offer a well-presented theatre show.'

The overall sound quality at the trial run in the Royal Festival Hall disappointed the band. Furthermore, some press reports saw it as no more than a good rehearsal, although the reviewers could at least understand what was being aimed at. On the other hand, the attendance at the concert boosted confidence among venue promoters and remarkably, although there was no new product to promote, the band were booked for their first headline tour of the UK in June, playing not at the usual round of clubs but at large civic halls.

One of the most important shows of this tour was at the Fairfield Halls in Croydon – an auditorium renowned for its excellent acoustics and atmosphere. The venue issued its own press release, which explained very clearly the feelings aroused by the band at that time: 'As groups go, the Pink Floyd are a strange case. You either love them or hate them. Few past their mid-twenties can tolerate them. For the Pink Floyd were one of Britain's first psychedelic pop groups, placing almost as much

RICHARD WRIGHT   << I suppose much of what gives our music a space-like quality is that it is very free-form – especially on stage. We work out basic formats but it's all improvisation on known themes. A lot of people seem to think that on stage we work with tapes – but that's just not true. We spend a lot of time looking for new sounds especially when we're in the recording studios. A lot of it happens when we're on a gig – then we remember the sound and use it afterwards. >>

importance on their light-show as their musical side. Their concert at Croydon's Fairfield Halls on Friday, May 30, promises to be a sell-out, and if their past concerts are a guide, the Croydon show will include, give or take a song, two numbers. The Floyd – if all goes well – will also be introducing their new concept in audience mind blowing, with a new electronic scheme to fill the concert hall with stereo sound from every angle. And to carry off a show based on 360 degree stereo system, the Floyd have decided to include far more than a mere selection of songs. They plan to assault their unsuspecting audience by hurling music, lights, poetry and melodrama in furious succession. He who leaves the concert on steady feet will be constitutionally superhuman.'

Such enthusiasm confirmed that Pink Floyd were becoming very much an 'overground' phenomenon and before long they were in meetings with both the Royal and Boston Philharmonic Orchestras to discuss the possibility of joint recordings and performance. 'Not that we are such a successful group,' explained Waters, 'it's just that our name has got about to people who want to do strange things.'[14]

The tour culminated in a concert at the prestigious Royal Albert Hall in London, with the Royal Philharmonic joining the band to close the show. It was a spectacular moment – such a large and grand environment was the perfect vehicle for encapsulating the full splendour of Pink Floyd's theatrics and their remarkable new sound system, which has made them, through years of constant refinement, the world's leading exponents of concert sound production.

In fact the band had been gaining recognition outside their usual circles for some time: French director Barbet Schroeder commissioned them to score his new film, More, with the soundtrack album of the same name due for release in July 1969. It told a sorry tale of love and drug addiction on the then hippy island retreat of Ibiza.

Recorded at Pye Studios in London, and without the band seeing the finished film, the score was written, recorded and mixed in just eight days during late January and early February. Although what is heard on the album is very different to that on the film – most of the songs are largely incomplete or played in the background – there are at least two tracks, an unidentified instrumental and one other, 'Seabirds', that only ever appeared on the film. The recordings also featured Nick Mason's then wife, Lindy, on penny whistle. Overall it is a delicate, almost entirely acoustic album that is much overlooked and very underrated.

A cinema release in Britain never came, which is just as well, given lines like 'Groovy man, let's get high', although the album did reach a healthy No.9 in the charts. However, the film went down well in America and also did wonders for the band's profile in France, without doubt paving the way for many successful concert appearances there in the coming year.

Although the band failed in their ultimate goal to compose the soundtrack for a film that really inspired them, 2001: A Space Odyssey, their music was unarguably influenced by scenes from outer space, as Wright explained: 'I don't know how conscious that is – I suppose a lot of it is, because Roger is fairly well into science fiction. I suppose much of what gives our music a space-like quality is that it is very free-form – especially on stage. We work out basic formats but it's all improvisation on known themes. A lot of people seem to think that on stage we work with tapes – but that's just not true. We spend a lot of time looking for new sounds especially when we're in the recording studios. A lot of it happens when we're on a gig – then we remember the sound and use it afterwards.'[15]

By now the band's ability to create an extraterrestrial soundscape had caused the BBC and several other major European TV stations to invite them to compose music for their coverage of the Apollo 11 moon landings. The publicity this gained for them was staggering, for countless TV viewers heard their music accompanying the culmination of NASA's historic mission.

In addition, the band were working on the music for an American children's cartoon by Alan Aldridge called Rollo, about a character that travels through outer space collecting animals for his zoo. This project, which would have involved recording the music for twenty-six half-hour instalments, was never concluded except for an unbroadcast pilot film containing some previously recorded material.

Throughout this burst of activity both David Gilmour and Roger Waters assisted in the production of Syd Barrett's debut solo album, The Madcap Laughs, whilst Pink Floyd pressed on with the recording of their next album, the official follow-up to A Saucerful Of Secrets. Called Ummagumma, it was named after a friend of the band's personal slang for copulation and was released at the beginning of November on Harvest, EMI's newly founded subsidiary label specialising in progressive rock.

Ummagumma was a double album, with one disc consisting of live concert recordings and the other of new studio compositions. The receding front cover shot was

ABOVE: ROGER WATERS AND DAVID GILMOUR AT THE *VAN DIKE CLUB*, PLYMOUTH ON 1 AUGUST 1969. FLOYD'S ROADIE, ALAN STYLES, IS SEATED BEHIND GILMOUR. DESPITE ACHIEVING SELL-OUT CONCERTS AT LARGE CIVIC HALLS, PINK FLOYD STILL PERFORMED REGULARLY AT SMALL INDEPENDENT ROCK CLUBS.

taken at the house of Libby January's parents (where Jokers Wild and Pink Floyd performed back in 1965) in Great Shelford, Cambridge – the result of her continuing relationship with Storm Thorgerson. The rear sleeve photo cleverly shows the band's equipment arranged on Biggin Hill aerodrome runway in a parody of a jet fighter with its payload laid out. Floyd roadie, Alan Styles later of 'Alan's Psychedelic Breakfast' fame, stands amid this vast array of equipment in front of what would appear to be a Tardis-like van.

Significantly, it was also the last album Norman Smith would produce for Pink Floyd. Smith and the band had been drifting apart for some time, for he favoured the old pop songs and since they were getting to grips

with recording studio technology they now needed his help much less.

For the purposes of the live set recordings were made during a series of concerts that followed on from the Festival Hall appearance of 14 April and just before the start of the UK tour. These were made at Bromley Technical College, Mothers in Birmingham – a favoured alternative venue of the time – and the College of Commerce in Manchester. The recordings the band eventually selected were taken from the latter two shows and made up entirely of old audience favourites in the belief that they would soon be dropped from the repertoire. Each track on the finished album was of an almost equal length, allowing two per side. The result was respectable versions of 'Astronomy Dominé', 'Careful with That Axe, Eugene', 'Set The Controls For The Heart of The Sun' and 'A Saucerful Of Secrets'.

'The live part of the album we had to record twice,' explained Rick Wright. 'The first time, at Mothers in Birmingham, we felt we'd played really well, but the equipment didn't work so we couldn't use nearly all of that one. The second time, at Manchester College of Commerce, was a really bad gig but as the recording equipment was working really well, we had to use it. Parts of 'Saucer' came from the Birmingham gig which we put together with the Manchester stuff but the stuff on the album isn't half as good as we can play.' [16] In any event a large part of the vocals was overdubbed at a later date at Abbey Road. It is also worth noting that the album sleeve lists incorrect recording dates; correct sleeve notations not being Pink Floyd's strongest point even to the present day.

The studio album was an altogether different affair, comprising, unusually, four equal solo excursions. Best described as experimental, it was developed from existing, or developing, live performance pieces. Wright nearly makes the grade with his four-part concerto 'Sysyphus', while Waters' 'Grantchester Meadows' had lyrics from its earlier incarnation as a live acoustic instrumental – a nostalgic recollection of his youth and lazy summer days spent by the River Cam. He also penned the ridiculously titled 'Several Species of Small Furry Animals Gathered Together In A Cave And Grooving With A Pict', in which he rants away in a mock-Scottish accent, bridging the two tracks with an amusing sequence involving a fly being swatted – in full stereo!

Mason's contribution is no more than an experimental space-filler as well, not dissimilar to the percussion bashing sequence of 'Work' that was incorporated into 'The Man' sequence and, like Wright's piece, it has no lyrics. Gilmour, in enchanting contrast, produced 'The Narrow Way', which was also used as a live piece from early on in the year. Along with 'Grantchester Meadows', it is the strongest material on the studio album.

In fact, the whole idea of this flawed project came from Gilmour, who suggested, 'it was down to a lot of paranoia amongst each other, and thinking we would have a good time doing things on our own for a change, just for a laugh.' [17]

Although the idea may have been suggested with good intentions, it probably alerted Waters to a weakness he could exploit to his own advantage and thus assert himself, in the long term, as the band's chief

DAVID GILMOUR   << It was down to a lot of paranoia amongst each other, and thinking we would have a good time doing things on our own for a change, just for a laugh. >>

lyricist. 'I'd never written anything before,' confessed Gilmour, 'I just went into the studio and started waffling about tacking bits and pieces together. I rang up Roger at one point to ask him to write me some lyrics. He just said "No."' [18] It was the first noticeable friction in a catalogue of disputes between the pair that would continue throughout their career together. Although it was by no means a serious matter it does highlight Gilmour's ability to produce worthwhile material under pressure.

LEFT: FRANK ZAPPA PERFORMING WITH PINK FLOYD ON 'INTERSTELLAR OVERDRIVE' AT THE *ACTUEL FESTIVAL*, AMOUGIES, BELGIUM ON 25 OCTOBER 1969: ONE OF THE VERY RARE OCCASIONS ANOTHER MUSICIAN HAS BEEN ALLOWED TO APPEAR ON STAGE WITH THE BAND.

The overall impression created by the studio album is one of missed opportunity and self-indulgence. Waters admitted himself, with hindsight, that the album could have been improved with group effort. 'It would have been a better album if we'd gone away, done the things, come back together, discussed them and people could have come in and made comments. I don't think it's a good idea to work in total isolation.' [19] Mason's summation reinforces this view: 'I think what this demonstrates, is that our sum is always better than our parts.' [20]

On a more positive note, the album displayed the band's preference to preview new material on stage and develop it to their satisfaction, gauging their own performance as well as the audience reaction, before committing themselves to recording. Although this approach undoubtedly improved many recorded works, it had the unwelcome side effect of attracting the attentions of an ever-expanding army of bootleggers.

Sources
1-3. *Omnibus*, BBC TV, 15 November 1994
4. *The Pink Floyd Story*, Capital Radio, 17 December 1976
5.-6. *Mojo*, May 1994
7. *Pink Floyd* by Rick Sanders, Futura, 1976
8. *The Pink Floyd Story*, Capital Radio, 24 December 1976
9. *Mojo*, May 1994
10. *Sounds*, 6 October 1973
11. *Mojo*, November 2001
12. *Disc & Music Echo*, 22 November 1969
13. *Great Speckled Bird*, 25 May 1970
14. *Melody Maker*, c. 1969
15.-16. Unidentified press articles, c.1970
17. *Beetle*, May 1973
18. *Mojo*, May 1994
19. *Disc & Music Echo*, 8 August 1970
20. *Mojo*, May 1994

1968

PINK FLOYD

(1 January 1968 – 25 January 1968)
Syd Barrett: Guitar, Vocals
David Gilmour: Guitar, Vocals
Nick Mason: Drums
Roger Waters: Bass Guitar, Vocals
Richard Wright: Keyboards, Vocals

Monday 1 January
PRESS REPORT
London, England
Beat Instrumental reported that: 'The Pink Floyd are currently using an 800 watt PA, which has been custom built for them by Watkins Electric Music Limited. The group are very pleased with the sound of the PA and are ordering a range of amplifiers from Watkins which have a 100 watt output.'

Monday 8 & Tuesday 9 January
REHEARSALS
London, England
David Gilmour rehearsed with the band for the first time prior to both studio and touring commitments.

Wednesday 10 & Thursday 11 January
RECORDING SESSIONS
Studio 2, EMI Studios, Abbey Road, St. John's Wood, London, England
Recording for the album *A Saucerful Of Secrets*. The band continued to record versions of the tracks 'Scream Thy Last Scream' and 'Set The Controls For The Heart Of The Sun'.

Friday 12 January
CONCERT
Guild of Students, University of Aston, Birmingham, England
It is widely accepted that this was the first show that Pink Floyd performed as a five-piece with David Gilmour as a permanent member.

Saturday 13 January
CONCERT
Saturday Dance Date, Winter Gardens Pavilion, Weston-super-Mare, England
Supported by The Ken Birch Band and the 3 of Spades Plus.

Monday 15 & Tuesday 16 January
REHEARSALS
London, England

Wednesday 17 & Thursday 18 January
RECORDING SESSIONS
Studio 2, EMI Studios, Abbey Road, St. John's Wood, London, England
Recording for the album *A Saucerful Of Secrets*.

Friday 19 January
CONCERT
Town Hall, Lewes, England
Presented by Lewes Football Club and supported by Granny's Intentions. Two sets were performed.

Saturday 20 January
CONCERT
The Pavilion Ballroom, Hastings Pier, Hastings, England
Supported by Beaufords Image and compered by Pete Drummond.
This was almost certainly Syd Barrett's final live appearance with Pink Floyd.

Monday 22 & Tuesday 23 January
REHEARSALS
London, England

Wednesday 24 & Thursday 25 January
RECORDING SESSIONS
Studio 2, EMI Studios, Abbey Road, St. John's Wood, London, England
Recording for the album *A Saucerful Of Secrets*. The band began recording a new composition entitled 'The Most Boring Song I've Ever Heard Bar 2', which remains unreleased or was given another title at a later date.

PINK FLOYD

(25 January 1968 – November 1979)
David Gilmour: Guitar, Vocals
Nick Mason: Drums
Roger Waters: Bass Guitar, Vocals
Richard Wright: Keyboards, Vocals

Friday 26 January
CONCERT
Old Refectory, Student's Union, Southampton University, Highfield, Southampton, England
With Tyrannosaurus Rex and The Incredible String Band. It was decided by the rest of the band not to pick up Barrett en route to this concert, effectively terminating his tenure with Pink Floyd.

Saturday 27 January
PRESS REPORT
London, England
Melody Maker was the first of the international music

papers to announce that David Gilmour had joined Pink Floyd, increasing its line up to five. A late news report, the article stated that he had rehearsed with the band for several weeks and would join them on their first European tour, beginning in February.

Saturday 27 January
CONCERT
Leicester College of Art and Technology, Leicester, England

Monday 29 January
REHEARSAL
London, England

Tuesday 30 & Wednesday 31 January
RECORDING SESSIONS
EMI Studios, Abbey Road, St. John's Wood, London, England
Recording for the album *A Saucerful Of Secrets*.

Thursday 1 February
RECORDING SESSION
EMI Studios, Abbey Road, St. John's Wood, London, England
Recording for the album *A Saucerful Of Secrets*.

Tuesday 6 February
REHEARSAL
London, England

Wednesday 7 February
RECORDING SESSION
EMI Studios, Abbey Road, St. John's Wood, London, England
Recording for the album *A Saucerful Of Secrets*.

Saturday 10 February
CONCERT
The Imperial Ballroom, Nelson, England
Supported by The Forth Coming and The Atlantics.

Monday 12 & Tuesday 13 February
RECORDING SESSIONS
EMI Studios, Abbey Road, St. John's Wood, London, England
Recording for the album *A Saucerful Of Secrets*.

Thursday 15 February
RECORDING SESSION
EMI Studios, Abbey Road, St. John's Wood, London, England
Recording and mixing for the album *A Saucerful Of Secrets*.

Friday 16 February
CONCERT
ICI Fibres Club, Pontypool, Wales

EUROPEAN TOUR

Essentially a tour of The Netherlands and Belgium, the band made several cancellations to their itinerary in this period including a previously announced date for German TV (13 February), a show in Frankfurt (February) and shows in Stockholm (14 & 15 February). Shows at Jongerencentrum Spola, Amersfoort (25 February) and *Daddle Doofy*, Concertzaal De Jong, Groningen (25 February) were also cancelled and a further rescheduled show in Groningen (31 March) at the same venue was also cancelled.

Saturday 17 February
CONCERT

Immage, Patronaatsgebouw, Terneuzen, The Netherlands

8.00pm show. Supported by Dragonfly, Endatteme Jugband and Living Kick Formation.

Saturday 17 February
CONCERT

Concertgebouw, Vlissingen, The Netherlands

11.00pm show. Supported by Dragonfly, Endatteme Jugband and Living Kick Formation.

Set list included encore: 'Interstellar Overdrive'.

Sunday 18 & Monday 19 February
TV SHOW

RTB TV Studios, Brussels, Belgium

David Gilmour made his film debut with Pink Floyd by recording a series of promotional clips for Belgian TV, which included 'Astronomy Dominé', 'Set The Controls For The Heart Of The Sun', 'Apples And Oranges', 'Corporal Clegg', 'Paintbox', 'Scarecrow' and 'See Emily Play'. All were broadcast in black and white. The first four numbers were shot in the TV studios, with 'Apples And Oranges' in a mock-up of a greengrocer's shop. The latter three were all shot in and around the Parc de Laekan, with the Brussels Atomium clearly visible in the background. All of the tracks were mimed over the original recordings, except for 'Corporal Clegg', which, although mimed, is noticeably different in its earlier incarnation by having a completely different verse ending from that which later appeared on their second album, *A Saucerful Of Secrets*.

'Apples And Oranges' was broadcast on the RTB pop music programme *Vibrato* on 27 February at 8.30pm. 'Astronomy Dominé', 'Scarecrow', 'Corporal Clegg', 'Paintbox', 'Set The Controls For The Heart Of The Sun' and 'See Emily Play' as well as a photo montage accompanying the album recording of 'Bike' was broadcast in a dedicated Pink Floyd TV special as part of the *Tienerklanken* pop music show broadcast on BRT TV on 31 March at 3.40pm.

'See Emily Play' is the only track from these sessions that has ever been semi-officially released, appearing on the 1989 compilation video *Rock & Roll - The Greatest Years - 1967* (UK: Video Collection VC 458).

Tuesday 20 February
TV SHOW

ORTF TV Studios, Buttes Chaumont, Paris, France

Pink Floyd performed 'Astronomy Dominé', 'Flaming', 'Set The Controls For The Heart Of The Sun' and 'Let There Be More Light' live for the music programme *Bouton Rouge*. It was broadcast (in colour) on ORFT2 on 24 February at 6.15pm.

Wednesday 21 February
TV SHOW

ORTF TV Studios, Buttes Chaumont, Paris, France

Pink Floyd mimed to 'Paintbox' for the music programme *Discorama*. It was broadcast (in black and white) on ORTF2 on 17 March at 12.30pm.

Thursday 22 February
CONCERT

Rijschool, Leuven, Belgium

As part of the city carnival, students organised an all-night event featuring Pink Floyd who replaced The Crazy World of Arthur Brown at short notice.

This show was abandoned just as the band was taking to the stage. Nick Mason recalled in a 1970 interview with *Circus*, that it was, 'The worst run-in of our career. Flemish on one side and the French on the other. The Flemish are fond of swigging beer and singing all these old drinking songs. That's fine, except that most of the audience was French. Even the seating was divided. Well, they really got into one of their songs and the French kids started yelling and stamping for Pink Floyd. All of a sudden, as if on cue, all the Flemish side hurled their beer glasses across the room. It was a beautiful sight, actually. Everything was quiet for a moment while the glasses were in the air. I thought it was some sort of Flemish ritual until I heard the screams when the glasses started landing. Even we decided not to stay around to hear Pink Floyd.'

Friday 23 February
CONCERT

Pannenhuis, Antwerp, Belgium

Supported by The Mike Stuart Span.

THIS FRIDAY
PINK F

★★★★★

also

GEESU

92

*pink
floyd*

Het Laatste Nieuws reported that: '400 youngsters experienced "the psychedelic thing" at the Pannenhuis which only holds 200 people! This beat-mecca in Antwerp was literally shaking on the very ground it was built on. A mind-expanding experience that lasted for two hours was given by Pink Floyd and the Mike Stuart Span. Everything was perfectly enhanced by a primitive "sensual laboratory" that provided light and colour explosions all over the stage whilst keeping up with the devilish rhythms of the music, equalling a volcano-like outburst of sight and sound. Pink Floyd merely used the lyrics as excess baggage and most of the times did not bother with vocals at all. They let their incredible electronic organ-improvisations, coupled with wonderful guitar effects and supersonic drum solos, do the talking for them. The whole show was proof of a "total communication through light and sound", a concept that left a beat-loving teenage audience stunned at first but in the end succeeded in drawing everybody into a whirlpool of music, sounds and multi-coloured light effects.'

Saturday 24 February
CONCERT
Cheetah Club, Brussels, Belgium

Sunday 25 February
CONCERT
't Smurf, De Engh, Bussum, The Netherlands
With Set Money and Sun Set. The last night of the tour.

Monday 26 February
CONCERT
Domino Club, Lion Hotel, Cambridge, England
With a scratch band made up of musicians from local bands The Chequers and The Tykes. Pink Floyd were reported in the local press to have replaced the advertised Wages of Sin at the last minute.

Thursday 29 February
REHEARSALS
London, England

PINK FLOYD ROAD CREW THROUGH 1968
Peter Watts: Tour Manager / Front of House Sound

Friday 1 March
PRESS RELEASE
London, England
On or around this date Syd Barrett's departure from Pink Floyd was made official, although he had not been appearing on stage with the band since February. Barrett, however, continued to be managed by Blackhill as a solo artist.

LEFT: PINK FLOYD APPEARING IN THE DUTCH MAGAZINE *MUSIEK EXPRESS*, MARCH 1968.

Monday 4 March
CONCERT
Isleworth Film Studios, Isleworth, London, England
Pink Floyd performed at the invitation of Vanessa Redgrave for the end of filming party for her latest movie, *Isadora*.

Tuesday 5 March
RECORDING SESSION
EMI Studios, Abbey Road, St. John's Wood, London, England
Recording for the single 'It Would Be So Nice'.

Saturday 9 March
CONCERT
Faculty of Technology Union, Manchester Technical College, Manchester, England

Tuesday 12 & Wednesday 13 March
RECORDING SESSIONS
EMI Studios, Abbey Road, St. John's Wood, London, England
Recording for the single 'It Would Be So Nice'.

Thursday 14 March
CONCERTS
Whitla Hall, Queen's College, Belfast, Northern Ireland
Two shows at 7.00pm and 9.30pm with The Spencer Davis Group (headline), The Taste (featuring guitarist Rory Gallagher) and The Freshmen.

Friday 15 March
CONCERT
The Stage Club, Clarendon Restaurant, Oxford, England

Saturday 16 March
CONCERT
Crawdaddy, The Ballroom, Casino Hotel, Taggs Island, Hampton Court, England
Early show.

Saturday 16 March
CONCERT
Middle Earth, Covent Garden, London, England
Late show. With Juniors Eyes, DJ Jeff Dexter and The Explosive Spectrum Light Show.

David Gilmour recalled in an interview with *Zig Zag* magazine that: 'I remember one terrible night when Syd [Barrett] came and stood in front of the stage. He stared at me all night long. Horrible!'

Wednesday 20 March
CONCERT
New Grafton Rooms, Liverpool, England

Thursday 21 March
RECORDING SESSION

EMI Studios, Abbey Road, St. John's Wood, London, England
Recording for the single 'It Would Be So Nice'.

Friday 22 March
CONCERT
Main Hall, Woolwich Polytechnic, Woolwich, London, England
At this poorly publicised all-night event Pink Floyd took to the stage at 2.00am (23 March) in front of an audience of fewer than fifty.

Saturday 23 & Monday 25 March
RECORDING SESSIONS
EMI Studios, Abbey Road, St. John's Wood, London, England
Recording for the single 'It Would Be So Nice'.

Monday 25 March
CANCELLED CONCERT
Zurich, Switzerland
Cancelled due to recording commitments.

Tuesday 26 March
TV SHOW
BBC Lime Grove Studios, Shepherd's Bush, London, England
Pink Floyd performed live for the magazine programme *Late Night Line Up* subtitled 'The Sound Of Change'. It was broadcast on BBC2 TV on 10 September at 8.00pm. The track is marked as 'untitled' in the BBC archives.

> march 1968

Thursday 28 March
TV SHOW
Abbey Mills Pumping Station, East Stratford,
London, England
Pink Floyd performed 'Set The Controls For The Heart
Of The Sun' live at this location for BBC producer
Tony Palmer as part of an *Omnibus* TV special
focusing on the socio-political context of rock music
and subtitled 'All My Loving'. Much of the rest of the
documentary (with the working titles of 'Sound And
Picture City,' 'My Generation' and finally, 'Pop Film')
was filmed in the USA and featured live performances
by The Who, Donovan, Jimi Hendrix and Cream as
well as interviews with Paul McCartney, Eric Burdon,
Derek Taylor, Frank Zappa, Anthony Burgess and even
George Harrison's mother! In addition to their
appearance fee the BBC also had to compensate Pink
Floyd the sum of £90 for damage to their equipment.
Tony Palmer had originally scheduled filming of Pink
Floyd to take place on 26 March at 7.00pm in a
specially erected marquee in the cemetery at Barnes
Common, south west London but this plan was
shelved at short notice.
The film was previewed at a special screening for cast
and crew at the Hanover Grand Film and Arts
Theatre, central London on 1 November at 11.00am
although it is doubtful the band attended having
already attended a screening at BBC TV Centre on 17
September.
The programme was eventually broadcast on BBC1
TV (in black and white) on 3 November at 10.40pm
and first repeated (in colour) on BBC2 TV on 18 May
1969 at 9.30pm and also included a very brief
excerpt from 'A Saucerful Of Secrets' used as
background music which was taken from a session
recorded at the BBC on 11 April.

Friday 29 March
RECORDING SESSION
EMI Studios, Abbey Road, St. John's Wood, London,
England
Recording for the album *A Saucerful Of Secrets.*

Monday 1 & Tuesday 2 April
RECORDING SESSIONS
EMI Studios, Abbey Road, St. John's Wood, London,
England
Recording for the album *A Saucerful Of Secrets.*

Thursday 4 – Sunday 7 April
RECORDING SESSIONS
Belsize Square, Belsize Park, London, England
Pink Floyd spent four days recording the soundtrack
to the avant-garde film *The Committee* in the front
room of the house owned by two of the film's actors,
Michael and Marion Kidner. The music was recorded
live as the band improvised to the film's images
projected onto a screen in the same room. The
soundtrack is comprised entirely of ethereal

instrumental passages but does include the earliest
known version of 'Careful With That Axe, Eugene'.

Thursday 11 April
TV SHOW
Studio 4, BBC TV Centre, White City, London,
England
Pink Floyd recorded 'A Saucerful Of Secrets' as
additional soundtrack music for the programme 'All
My Loving'.

Thursday 11 April
CANCELLED SHOW
Sjok In, Hilversum, The Netherlands

Friday 12, Saturday 13 & Sunday 14 April
TV SHOW
RTB TV Studios, Brussels, Belgium
Pink Floyd were reported to be recording for Belgian
TV but the content and broadcast details remain
unknown.

Friday 19 April
RECORD RELEASE
'It Would Be So Nice' / 'Julia Dream'
UK 7-inch single release. US 7-inch single release on
Monday 3 June.

Thursday 18 & Friday 19 April
CONCERTS
Piper Club, Rome, Italy
This was Pink Floyd's first ever appearance in Italy.

Saturday 20 April
CONCERT
Raven Club, RAF Waddington, Waddington, England
Supported by The Delroy Williams Show (with go-go
girls) and The Individual Set.

Monday 22 - Wednesday 24 April & Friday 26 April
RECORDING SESSIONS
EMI Studios, Abbey Road, St. John's Wood, London,
England
Recording and mixing for the album *A Saucerful Of
Secrets.*

Tuesday 30 April
TV SHOW
Nederland 1 TV Studios, Zaandam, The Netherlands
Pink Floyd performed for the music programme *Moef
Ga Ga* although their contribution is unknown. The
programme was broadcast on Nederland 2 TV on 1
May at 5.03pm.

Tuesday 30 April
CANCELLED CONCERTS
Paradiso, Amsterdam, The Netherlands & Fantasio,
Amsterdam, The Netherlands
Despite having all their equipment set up at the
Paradiso for an early evening show, Pink Floyd were
forced to cancel this and a late evening show at the
Fantasio, also on this date, due to a problem with
work permits. The Paradiso was rescheduled to 23
May and Fantasio to 31 May.

Thursday 2 & Friday 3 May
RECORDING SESSIONS
EMI Studios, Abbey Road, St. John's Wood, London,
England
Recording and mixing for the album *A Saucerful Of
Secrets.*

Friday 3 May
CONCERT
Westfield College, Hampstead, London, England
With Grand Union.

Saturday 4 May
CONCERT
Theatre 140, Brussels, Belgium
Supported by Dragonfly.

Sunday 5 May
CONCERTS
Theatre 140, Brussels, Belgium
Two shows at 3.30pm and 8.30pm.
Supported by Dragonfly.

Monday 6 May
CONCERT
First European International Pop Festival, Palazzo
Dello Sport, EUR, Rome, Italy
With The Move, The Nice and The Association.
Set list: 'Astronomy Dominé' / 'Interstellar Overdrive'
/ 'Set The Controls For The Heart Of The Sun' / 'Pow
R Toc H' / Remember A Day'.
This ambitious festival was first announced for 19-25
February and later for 4-10 May but on both
occasions the event failed to take place, one of the
main problems being the fact that many of the bands
were advertised by the organisers before agreeing to
appear. Only 400 people attended Pink Floyd's show
in the huge Palazzo Dello Sport (many acts were
rescheduled to the much smaller Piper Club).
Italian RAI radio recorded parts of the festival and

broadcast 'Astronomy Dominé', 'Interstellar Overdrive' and 'Set The Controls For The Heart Of The Sun' complete with an interview by Roger Waters shortly after the show. This recording was then made available to Dutch VPRO radio who broadcast the same programme, with Dutch commentary over the Italian, on 7 June at 8.00pm. German ARD network TV filmed parts of the festival and included 'Interstellar Overdrive' in an unidentified programme which was broadcast at a later date.

The most comprehensive coverage of the event was by the BBC who covered the festival for inclusion in the magazine programme *Release* in a feature subtitled 'Rome Goes Pop'. It was broadcast on BBC2 TV (in colour) on 18 May at 9.55pm. The programme featured live performances, filmed at the Palazzo Dello Sport, by Donovan, Brian Auger & The Trinity, Captain Beefheart & His Magic Band, The Nice, The Association, The Giganti and The Samurai. Pink Floyd were also included in this programme and showed the band miming to 'It Would Be So Nice' at the Piper Club, without an audience. It should be noted that although extensive paperwork exists in the BBC archives relating to this programme for all other participants, there is no schedule for the filming of Pink Floyd. It is therefore a possibility that the band may well have been filmed by Italian TV on 18 or 19 April and the footage then licensed to the BBC for use in this programme.

Thursday 9 May
RECORDING SESSION
EMI Studios, Abbey Road, St. John's Wood, London, England
Recording for the album *A Saucerful Of Secrets*.

Saturday 11 May
CONCERT
Brighton Arts Festival - The Gentle Sound of Light, Falmer House Courtyard, University of Sussex, Falmer, Brighton, England
With Soft Machine (who cancelled), volcanos, air raids, monsters and more!
Set list included: Let There Be More Light / Set The Controls For The Heart Of The Sun / Interstellar Overdrive / It Would Be So Nice.
The Wine Press, the Sussex University student newspaper reported that: 'Inclement weather, the non-appearance of one group and numerous technical failures turned the University's main contribution to the Brighton Arts Festival into disappointment both for its organisers and the 1,400 people who flooded into Falmer House Courtyard last Saturday night. Technical troubles started almost immediately after the start of the show when one of the giant 35mm projectors burst into flame. Several fuses burned out and very few if any of the mechanical effects worked. When at about 10.15pm the evening first looked like failing it was arranged that the Pink Floyd who were

originally to have appeared for two half hour spots were to go on at 10.30pm for an hour. This should have solved some problems since this group had stated that they did not wish the University's lights to operate while they were on stage preferring to use just their own. The light crews therefore had an hour in which to organise the rest of the show starting with the air raid sequence as Pink Floyd finished. This, when it came, could not be described as successful as somehow the volume of the sirens had been turned down and the two search lights were lost in the glare of the other lights which were left on. Two young girls were mesmerised by the lights and music and had to be treated by the first aid unit.'

Wednesday 15 & Thursday 16 May
RECORDING SESSIONS
EMI Studios, Abbey Road, St. John's Wood, London, England
Recording for the album *A Saucerful Of Secrets*.

Friday 17 May
CONCERT
Middle Earth, Covent Garden, London, England
With Alexis Korner, Free, DJ Jeff Dexter and Chakra.

NETHERLANDS TOUR

Wednesday 22 May
CONCERT
Hotel Billard Palace, Antwerp, Belgium
With Inez & The Racers.

Thursday 23 May
CONCERT
Whisky A Go Go, RK Verenigingsgebouw, Zaandam, The Netherlands
Early show.

Thursday 23 May
CONCERTS
Paradiso, Amsterdam, The Netherlands
The last night of the tour.
Set list: 'Let There Be More Light' / 'Interstellar Overdrive' / 'Set The Controls For The Heart Of The Sun' / 'A Saucerful Of Secrets'.

Friday 24 May
CONCERT
The Punch Bowl public house, Lapworth, near Birmingham, England

Saturday 25 May
CONCERT
Mayfair Suite, The Belfry Hotel, Wishaw, Sutton Coldfield, near Birmingham, England
Supported by Young Blood and Pineapple Incident. Admission included supper.

Sunday 26 May
CONCERT
OZ Magazine Benefit, Middle Earth, Covent Garden, London, England
One of a series of benefit shows for *OZ* magazine, which was going through its usual round of difficulties with the authorities. Also appearing were The Pretty Things, Social Deviants, Blonde On Blonde, Alexis Korner, Miss Kelly, The Flamingoes, Buzby Lloyd, DJ's John Peel and Jeff Dexter and the Trancendental Aurora Light Show.
Set list included: 'Interstellar Overdrive' / 'Set The Controls For The Heart Of The Sun'.

Monday 27 & Tuesday 28 May
RECORDING SESSIONS
EMI Studios, Abbey Road, St. John's Wood, London, England
Recording for the album *A Saucerful Of Secrets*.

BELGIAN & NETHERLANDS TOUR
An advertised show at Lijn 3, Amsterdam, Netherlands (31 May) was cancelled and reports of an additional show at De Kentering, Rosmalen, The Netherlands on Saturday 1 June cannot be confirmed.

Friday 31 May
CONCERT
Paradiso, Amsterdam, The Netherlands
Evening show. Supported by Circus.
Pink Floyd's performance was filmed and brief excerpts appeared in the arts programme *Open Eye* in a feature about the Paradiso. It was broadcast on NTS Netherlands TV (in black and white) on 5 July 1968.
Set list: 'Keep Smiling People' (an unrecorded instrumental similar to 'Careful With That Axe, Eugege') / 'Let There Be More Light' / 'Set The Controls For The Heart Of The Sun' / 'Flaming' / 'A Saucerful Of Secrets'.

Friday 31 May
CONCERT
Fantasio, Amsterdam, The Netherlands
Evening show. Supported by Circus.

Saturday 1 June
CONCERT
Lijn 3, Amsterdam, The Netherlands
2.00pm show. This show was scheduled at very short notice to replace Captain Beefheart & The Magic Band who cancelled their appearance.

Saturday 1 June
CONCERT
't Smurf, De Engh, Bussum, The Netherlands
8.00pm show. Supported by Living Kick Formation.

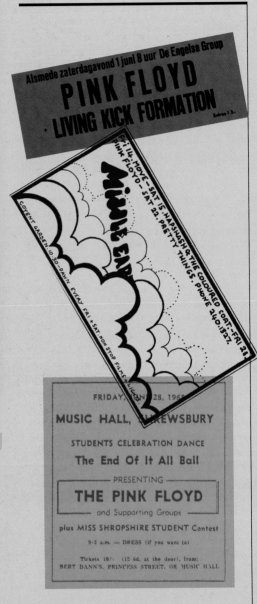

Saturday 1 June
CONCERT
Eurobeurs, Apeldoorn, The Netherlands
Late show. Supported by The Mozarts, Les Copains
and Outlook.
Pink Floyd turned up for this show very late in the
evening, overrunning their allocated slot. When the
promoter turned on the house lights to force the band
to stop playing so that the 'disco' could start, the
resultant argument between the promoter and Roger
Waters was so fierce it had to be broken up by the
local police.

Sunday 2 June
CONCERT
Concertgebouw, Vlissingen, The Netherlands
Supported by Dragonfly.
Set list included: 'Let There Be More Light' / 'Flaming'.

Monday 3 June
CONCERT
De Pas, Heesch, The Netherlands
5.00pm show. Supported by Chockfull, Blaze and The
Bubbles.

Monday 3 June
CONCERT
Parochieel Ontspannings Centrum, Weesp, The
Netherlands
Evening show. Supported by The Motions. The last
night of the tour.

Saturday 8 June
CONCERT
Market Hall, Haverfordwest, Wales
Supported by The Bond.

Wednesday 12 June
CONCERT
Architects Ball, Homerton College, Cambridge,
England
Early show. With Henry Cow.

Wednesday 12 June
CONCERT
May Ball, King's College, Cambridge, England
Late show. With The Fairport Convention, Aynsley
Dunbar, plus dance, jazz, folk, classical guitar and the
King's Choral scholars. At this concert Pink Floyd
reportedly made use of a mind-blowing light show
supplied by Cambridge band White Unicorn.

Friday 14 June
CONCERT
Midsummer Ball, University College London,
Bloomsbury, London, England
Pi, the UCL student newspaper, reported that: 'The
big surprise to everyone when the Pink Floyd
appeared was how little they missed their recently
departed leader Syd Barrett. Now led by bass player
Roger Waters they are far and away the best
psychedelic blues band in the land and frequently play
at Middle Earth (this is a cellar opposite Covent
Garden Market - a den where you can dance, sit,
listen, eat or even attend more pleasing matters. John
Peel is often the compere and makes splendid jokes
about drugs and ever present police in fluent Scouse
which no one can hear, much less understand).'

Saturday 15 June
CONCERTS
Magic Village, Manchester, England
An all-night event at which Pink Floyd performed two
shows at 7.30pm and 11.30pm. Also appearing were
Purple Stone and The Alchemist, The Jack Lancaster -
Bruce Mitchell Quartet and The Inner Light Show.

Friday 21 June
CONCERT
Commemoration Ball, Balliol College, Oxford,
England
Late afternoon show. Pink Floyd were originally
contracted to appear at the *Corpus Summer Ball*,
Corpus Christi College, Oxford (with Uther,
Pendragon, Soft Machine, Wages of Sin and Shell
Steel Band) on this date but by mid-May poor ticket
sales had forced its cancellation. Pink Floyd were then
booked by Balliol College as an additional attraction
to their summer Ball.

Friday 21 June
CONCERT
Middle Earth, Covent Garden, London, England
Evening show. With Hurdy Gurdy, Easy Moses and DJ
Jeff Dexter (billed as Dexasterous).

Friday 21 June
CONCERT
The First Holiness Kitschgarden For The Liberation of Love & Peace in Colours, Houtrusthallen, Den Haag, The Netherlands
Pink Floyd performed on the first day of this two day festival that also featured The Small Faces, The Pretty Things, Dirty Underwear, Group 1850, Chemical Explosions Of Death And War, Living Kick and the Trancendental Aurora Lightshow among others. It was a very poorly attended event (originally scheduled for 14-15 June) at which Pink Floyd didn't appear until 4.00am performing only three songs before returning to the UK.

Saturday 22 June
CONCERT
Lower Common Room, University of East Anglia, Norwich, England
Evening show. With Fairport Convention and The Shell.

Tuesday 25 June
RADIO SHOW
BBC 201 Piccadilly Studios, Piccadilly, London, England
Pink Floyd recorded two live shows on this day for BBC Radio One.
The first show was recorded between 2.30pm and 6.00pm and was broadcast on *Top Gear*, hosted by John Peel, on 11 August at 3.00pm in the following order: 'Careful With That Axe, Eugene' (announced as 'Murderistic Woman'), 'A Saucerful Of Secrets' (announced as 'The Massed Gadgets Of Hercules'), 'Let There Be More Light' and 'Julia Dream'.
The second show was recorded between 6.00pm and 9.30pm and was broadcast on *Top Gear*, hosted by John Peel, on 8 September at 3.00pm in the following order: 'Julia Dream', 'Careful With That Axe, Eugene' (announced as 'Murderistic Woman'), 'Let There Be More Light' and 'A Saucerful Of Secrets' (announced as 'The Massed Gadgets Of Hercules').

Wednesday 26 June
CONCERT
Sheffield Arts Festival, Lower Refectory, Sheffield University, Sheffield, England
Supported by Jethro Tull.

Friday 28 June
RECORD RELEASE
A Saucerful Of Secrets
UK album release. US album released on Saturday 27 July.
Rolling Stone commented that: 'Unfortunately the Pink Floyd's second album, *A Saucerful Of Secrets*, is not as interesting as their first, as a matter of fact, it is rather mediocre. With Barrett gone we are left with the work of bassist Roger Waters and organist Rick Wright. Waters is an uninteresting writer, vocalist and bass player. "Let There Be More Light" and "Set The Controls For The Heart Of The Sun" are boring melodically, harmonically and lyrically. The production work is not as glittery as the first album's, and the instrumental work is shoddy and routine; yet both tracks run for some five minutes, two examples of unnecessary length in rock.'

Friday 28 June
TV SHOW
Studio 7, BBC TV Centre, White City, London, England
Pink Floyd performed 'A Saucerful Of Secrets' live for the magazine programme *Release*. It was broadcast on BBC2 TV on 29 June at 10.10pm and included an interview with Roger Waters by the programme presenter Tony Palmer plus an excerpt of their performance of 'Set The Controls For The Heart Of The Sun' taken from the forthcoming *Omnibus* programme *All My Loving*.
Parts of the *Release* programme, including 'Set The Controls For The Heart Of The Sun', were repeated on BBc2 TV on 5 July at 11.13pm as part of the magazine programme *Late Night Line Up*.

ABOVE: ROY HARPER JOINS PINK FLOYD ON STAGE FOR SOME CYMBAL BASHING DURING 'A SAUCERFUL OF SECRETS' AT THE FIRST HYDE PARK FREE FESTIVAL, 29 JUNE 1968.

Friday 28 June
CONCERT
Students Celebration Dance - The End Of It All Ball, **Music Hall, Shrewsbury, England**
Plus the Miss Shropshire Student Contest and supporting groups.

Saturday 29 June
CONCERT
Midsummer High Weekend, **The Cockpit, Hyde Park, London, England**
Afternoon show, with Tyrannosaurus Rex, Roy Harper and Jethro Tull. Pink Floyd headlined the first ever Hyde Park free concert, organised by Blackhill Enterprises.
Set list: 'Let There Be More Light' / 'Set The Controls For The Heart Of The Sun' / 'A Saucerful Of Secrets' (with Roy Harper on cymbals) / 'Interstellar Overdrive'.

Saturday 29 June
CONCERT
Town Hall, Torquay, England
Evening show. With Phydeaux Lime and The Phaze.

NORTH AMERICAN TOUR
Pink Floyd's second US tour was also beset by problems concerning their work permits, which again had not been issued in time. This meant a delayed start to the tour and their entry to the US in New York on 4 July was on a tourist visa, therefore performing shows through to 17 July illegally. They decamped to Canada to square the paperwork immediately after the shows in New York, returning in time to perform in Boston.
Despite some glowing reviews it was a patchy tour at best and since the band were spending far too much time holed up in hotels between shows it was decided towards the end of August they would cut their losses and return to the UK. This resulted in the cancellation of their appearance at two festival shows (both of which went ahead without Pink Floyd): *Sky River Rock Festival and Lighter Than Air Fair*, Betty Nelson's Organic Raspberry Farm, Sultan, Washington, USA with Kaleidoscope, Muddy Waters, Peanut Butter Conspiracy, Santana, Country Joe & The Fish, John Fahey, HP Lovecraft, Steppenwolf, The Youngbloods and many others (31 August) and the *Oakland Pop Festival*, Baldwin Pavilion, Oakland University, Rochester Hills, Detroit, Michigan, USA with Procol Harum, Howlin' Wolf, Chris Chrysalis, The Rationals, SRC Thyme, MC5, Jagged Edge, Psychedelic Stooges and The Frost Children (1 September).
Additionally, Nick Mason has stated in his book *Inside Out* that the band performed at the Whisky-A-Go-Go,

West Hollywood, Los Angeles, California, USA but venue advertisements in the local press throughout this period do not include Pink Floyd, so this is highly unlikely.
Due to the extension of the existing tour an advertised show in the UK was cancelled at The Royal Lido, Central Beach, Prestatyn, Wales on 24 August.

Monday 8 July
CONCERT
Kinetic Playground, Chicago, Illinois, USA
It was reported that one of Gilmour's guitars was stolen en route to the show.

Tuesday 9 July
PRESS RECEPTION
Michael Mann's, Manhattan, New York City, New York, USA
Tower Records held a press reception for the band at this popular New York restaurant nightclub.

Friday 12 July
CONCERT
Grande Ballroom, Detroit, Michigan, USA
Supported by The Thyme and The Jagged Edge.
Set list: 'Interstellar Overdrive' / 'A Saucerful Of Secrets' / 'Set The Controls For The Heart Of The Sun' / 'Astronomy Dominé' / 'Flaming'.
Detroit City Estate reported that: 'Pink Floyd is a very weird group. I know that they were unbelievably bad at the Grande and I'm not about to try and excuse

them other than say that in every other performance in this country and in England they ably demonstrated that they are the best psychedelic group in the world. They have never claimed to be the world's best musicians, and they are really at best with their own light show, so unless you have a light show of your own - just close your eyes and turn your amplifier fully on, and your parents fully off by putting *A Saucerful Of Secrets* on. Although the album is by no means indicative of what the group is really - oh well, there is absolutely no point in saying this. Either you dig the Floyd or you don't. I do.'

Saturday 13 July
CONCERT
Fifth Dimension, Ann Arbor, Michigan, USA
Supported by The Rationals.

Monday 15, Tuesday 16 & Wednesday 17 July
CONCERTS
Steve Paul's The Scene, Manhattan, New York City, New York, USA
Supported by Fleetwood Mac on 15 July and The John Hammond Trio on 16 & 17 July.
Set list on 15 July: 'Interstellar Overdrive' / 'Let There Be More Light' / 'Set The Controls For The Heart Of The Sun' / 'Astronomy Dominé' / 'Flaming' / 'A Saucerful Of Secrets'.
Billboard reported that: 'Pink Floyd overpowered a packed house at the Scene on Monday in a varied programme with a strong emphasis on space and oriental sounds. In the first night of a three-day engagement the quartet was joined by Fleetwood Mac, which made an excellent impression in its initial set. While both British acts were well received, the inventiveness of Tower Records' Pink Floyd was the most remarkable. From opening "Interstellar Overdrive" to closing "A Saucerful Of Secrets", the group displayed top-flight musicianship and consistent interest. An act that requires top effort from each member, Pink Floyd drew just that. Roger Waters played a mean guitar, but that was only the beginning as he also played gong and cymbals and sang. Drummer Nicky Mason was strong throughout on both sticks and mallets. David Gilmer, the newest member of the unit, not only played guitar and sang well, but showed he knew how to use feedback to advantage, an important part of the Floyd's electronic sound. And Rick Wright clearly is one of the finest organists around. Whether producing high pitch sounds or conventional Bach-like music, Wright's performance was masterful. He also aided in vocals. But, little of what Pink Floyd did was conventional. In "Set The Controls For The Heart Of The Sun", Waters produced vocal sounds from whisper to high-pitched screech after returning to guitar. The number is on the group's latest Tower album *A Saucerful Of Secrets*, whose title song produced the wild ending to the set, which ran for more than an hour. In this

number, Waters assisted Mason by playing one cymbal, then two. He even shattered a glass by flinging it at the gong. But even this number has quiet moments as Mason varied the intensity of his playing and Wright turned to church-like sounds. Gilmer's use of feedback had its greatest use in this number. The selection that made greatest use of church organ effect, however, was "Astronomy Dominé". Gilmer's best vocal was "Flaming". But, it was their inventiveness, musicianship and ability to say something musically, whether playing and vocalising softly or overwhelming with cascades of sound.'

Friday 19 July
RECORD RELEASE
Tonite Let's All Make Love In London
UK album release. The original film soundtrack album, featuring 'Interstellar Overdrive' was recorded on 11 and 12 January 1967. The release date given here is that of the New York cinema opening of the film, as no exact date for a UK record release can be found. It is generally accepted this opening occurred shortly after the release of *A Saucerful Of Secrets* although the film had been previewed at the New York Film Festival on 26 September 1967. Pink Floyd also lent a completely different take of the track 'Interstellar Overdrive' to last the full-length of Anthony Stern's 15-minute rapid-fire day-in-the-life-of documentary entitled *San Francisco*. Funded by the British Film Institute, it was occasionally shown at special screenings at the BFI and also the ICA over the following two years.

Thursday 18, Friday 19 & Saturday 20 July
CONCERTS
The Boston Tea Party, Boston, Massachusetts, USA

Monday 22 July
RECORD RELEASE
'See Emily Play' / 'Scarecrow'
US 7-inch single re-release.

Wednesday 24 July
CONCERT
Philadelphia Music Festival, John F. Kennedy Stadium, Philadelphia, Pennsylvania, USA
With The Who (headline), The Troggs, Pink Floyd (billed as special guests replacing the advertised Procol Harum who cancelled), The Mandala, Friends Of The Family and The Joshua Light Show.
Set list included: 'Set The Controls For The Heart Of The Sun' / 'A Saucerful Of Secrets'.
Friends Of The Family and Pink Floyd were the only two bands to appear at this show. When the third band on the bill, The Mandala, began their set a lightning strike hit the stage and forced the closure of the event.

Friday 26 & Saturday 27 July
CONCERT
Shrine Exposition Hall, Exposition Park, Los Angeles, California, USA
With Blue Cheer (headline) and the Jeff Beck Group (opening).

Set list on 26 July: 'Interstellar Overdrive' / 'Matilda Mother' / 'Set The Controls For The Heart Of The Sun' / 'A Saucerful Of Secrets'.

The LA Free Press reported that: 'The Shrine Hall was so sweltering sticky hot that had you been in some vague bummer frame of mind you might have taken one look at Single Wing Turquoise Bird's light-show, heard Pink Floyd's "Interstellar Overdrive", and imagined you were in some fundamentalist tent-show evangelist's version of hell. What I hadn't counted on was that the Jeff Beck group, sandwiched between the other two, would put both Pink Floyd AND Blue Cheer to shame. Pink Floyd on record is one thing: live, they're something else. Disappointing. It isn't the overdubbing, the reverses, or the sound effects you particularly miss, but studio control and balance. Clarity. At the Shrine, even the maddening celestial cacophony of "Overdrive" came off as listless and muddled, sadly lacking in spark and distinction. Maybe it's Rick Wright's organ which saves the Floyd's concerts from disaster. He wanders into some strange things - hypnotic arabesques in "Matilda Mother", labrynthian flights in "Set The Controls For The Heart Of The Sun", and mystical mazes in "A Saucerful Of Secrets". "Heart Of The Sun" is an object lesson in the disparity between recorded and live Floyd. On disc, it's a belladonna trip through the inner limits of the listeners' body. Nicky Mason's drums beat out steady rays of sunlight, while Wright's organ evokes the dancing of the rays on waves in a sea of blood. Towards the end, the Floyd ingeniously mixes in the sounds of seagulls and breakers. But in concert much of the ethereality is lost. The organ almost obliterates Syd Barrett's guitar, and Roger Waters, the bassist-vocalist tries to imitate the gulls and

breakers vocally. The result is almost embarrassingly inadequate."

Friday 2, Saturday 3 & Sunday 4 August
CONCERTS
Avalon Ballroom, San Francisco, California, USA
Supported by Chrome Syrcus and The Holy Modal Rounders.

Friday 9, Saturday 10 & Sunday 11 August
CONCERTS
Eagles Auditorium, Seattle, Washington, USA
Supported by Blue Cheer with lights by the Retina Circus Light Company.

Friday 16 & Saturday 17 August
CONCERTS
Sound Factory, Sacramento, California, USA
Supported by Initial Shock and AB Skhy Blues Band.

Members of the band went to see The Who perform at The Fillmore West on 15 August.

Monday 19 August
RECORD RELEASE
'Let There Be More Light' / 'Remember A Day'
US 7-inch single release.

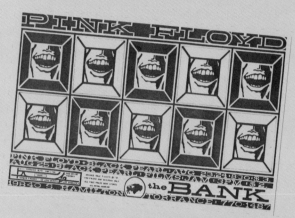

Friday 23 & Saturday 24 August
CONCERTS
The Bank, Torrance, Los Angeles, California, USA
Supported by Black Pearl. The show of 24 August was the last night of the tour.

Open City reported that: 'Top billing this week at the bank, just off the Harbor Freeway at Torrance, went to the Pink Floyd, a psychedelic progressive rock group from England. The PF led by vocalist and lead guitarist David Gilmore, is a four-man outfit, with Rodger Waters on the bass guitar; Rick Wright, organ and piano; and Nicky Mason, drums. Gilmore's vocals were drowned out at times by a wall of electronic gadgetry, but displayed a worthy lyric sound. Gilmore also has a touch at solo feedback work. Waters backs up well on his bass and in vocal sections, and Wright's semi atonal organ solos were simple compared to the tight, involved music of the total group. Mason gave instant stability with a beat steadier than most groups could stand. Lighting design by Bob Stone and Mike Devine is making a tough bid at stealing the show.'

BELGIAN & NETHERLANDS TOUR

Saturday 31 August
CONCERT
Kastival '68 Festival, Kasterlee, Belgium

With The Mike Stuart Span, Patrick, The Pebbles, Rita Reys, The Spencer Davis Group, Status Quo, Elly Nieman, Marie-Thérèse Smets, Roger Whittaker, The Golden Gate Quartet and The Crazy World of Arthur Brown.

Set list included: 'Astronomy Dominé' / A Saucerful Of Secrets.

Pink Floyd performed in the afternoon on the first day of this three-day festival having arrived in Belgium directly from the USA on 30 August. The whole event was filmed by BRT TV and highlights, including an interview with Roger Waters and Pink Floyd's performance of 'Astronomy Dominé', were broadcast in a dedicated 30-minute 'Kastival 1968' TV special as part of the *Tienerklanken* pop music show broadcast on BRT TV on 8 October at 7.00pm.

CANCELLED NETHERLANDS CONCERTS

A series of shows in the Netherlands following the above festival were not fulfilled due to problems with work permits and the band returned to the UK. These included shows at Huis Ter Lucht, Delft (early evening show, 31 August); Globe Theatre, Stadsschouwburg, Eindhoven (late evening show, 31 August at which the supporting bands Living Kick Formation and The New Electric Chamber Music Ensemble had already performed before the venue management made the announcement that Pink Floyd wouldn't be showing, which reportedly caused a riot among the audience) and the Fantasio, Amsterdam (1 September). A further show in this period was also cancelled, possibly for similar reasons, at the *First Fuq Festivity*, Westerkerk, Leeuwarden (14 September).

Wednesday 4 September
CONCERT
Middle Earth, The Club House, Richmond Athletic Club, Richmond, England

FRENCH & BELGIAN TOUR

Friday 6 September
TV SHOW
ORTF TV Studios, Buttes Chaumont, Paris, France
Pink Floyd mimed to 'Let There Be More Light' and 'Remember A Day' for the music programme *Samedi et Compagnie*. It was broadcast (in black and white) on ORTF1 on 5 October at 4.15pm.

Saturday 7 September
TV SHOW
Le Bilboquet, St. Germain des Près, Paris, France
Pink Floyd performed 'Let There Be More Light' live for inclusion in a four-hour TV special entitled *Surprise Partie* that also featured The Who, Joe Cocker, The Troggs, Fleetwood Mac, Small Faces, PP Arnold, The Equals among many other artists. It was broadcast (in colour) on ORTF2 on 31 December at 10.40pm.

Sunday 8 September
CANCELLED APPEARANCE
Châtelet Teenage Festival, Gemeentepark, Châtelet, Belgium
On the last night of this brief tour Pink Floyd were forced to cancel their appearance at this festival because of work permit problems with customs authorities upon entry to Belgium. The event reportedly ended in violence although The Kinks, among other bands, were able to perform.

Friday 13 September
CONCERT
Mothers, Erdington, Birmingham, England

Tuesday 17 September
TV PREVIEW
Theatre 4, BBC Lime Grove Studios, Shepherd's Bush, London, England
Pink Floyd and other guests attended a screening of the finished BBC TV *Omnibus* film 'All My Loving'. (See 28 March for further details).

Friday 20 September
CONCERT
Victoria Rooms, University of Bristol, Clifton, Bristol, England.
Supported by Kevin Ayers.

Thursday 26 September
FILM PREMIERE
Cameo Poly Cinema, Lower Regent Street, London, England
The premiere of the film *The Committee*.

Thursday 26 September
CONCERT
Mayfair Ballroom, Newcastle-upon-Tyne, England
With The Nice, The Sect and Coloured Rain.

Friday 27 September
CONCERT
Queen's Hall, Dunoon, Scotland
Supported by The Poets and DJ Tam Ferrie.
Brian Wilson, now a Labour Party MP, promoted the event and recalled that: 'Pink Floyd had gone to great lengths to get there, because of the terrible weather.

The ferries were off and the band had to hire their own boat from Gourock. It meant they were late and the audience were getting restless. When the audience of 400 heard their futuristic music, the response was less than ecstatic. Although they died on stage, a few people loved it and couldn't believe they were seeing Pink Floyd in Dunoon.'

Saturday 28 September
CANCELLED APPEARANCE
The International Essener Song Tage, Gruga Halle, Essen, West Germany.
After the previous evening's fiasco, and being unable to make travel connections, Pink Floyd cancelled their appearance at the above festival.

Tuesday 1 October
CONCERT
The Maryland Ballroom, Glasgow, Scotland
Staying in Scotland for a few days Pink Floyd reportedly made an impromptu appearance with local band, Mind Excursion.

Thursday 3 October
TV SHOW
Thames TV, London, England
A little known nationally syndicated children's drama, entitled *The Tyrant King*, produced by the London-area independent television channel Thames TV began broadcasting on this date at 5.20pm. It lasted for only six weekly episodes and was designed to encourage teenagers to visit the capital city by featuring various landmark locations within the context of the story. The soundtrack featured many contemporary artists including The Nice, Cream, Moody Blues, Tyrannosaurus Rex and Petula Clark among others. Although taken directly from the album, Pink Floyd's 'Corporal Clegg' was featured in a sequence showing a troop of the Household Division on parade in Hyde Park and the drum sequence of 'A Saucerful Of Secrets' on the closing credits.

Friday 4 October
CONCERT
Mothers, Erdington, Birmingham, England

Sunday 6 October
CONCERT
The Country Club, Belsize Park, London, England

Tuesday 8 & Wednesday 9 October
RECORDING SESSIONS
EMI Studios, Abbey Road, St. John's Wood, London, England
Recording for the 'Point Me At The Sky' single.

Saturday 12 October
TV SHOW
ORTF TV Studios, Buttes Chaumont, Paris, France

101

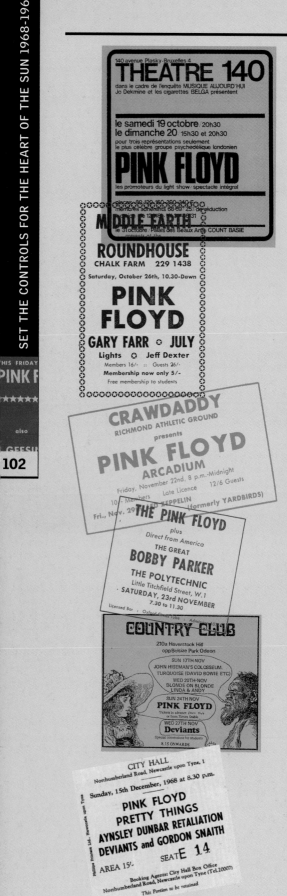

Footage of Pink Floyd larking about on the London underground combined with shots of London landmarks were used as a backdrop to the recording of 'Let There Be More Light' taken from the album *A Saucerful Of Secrets* and shown on the arts programme *A L'Affiche Du Monde* subtitled 'Special Angleterre: La Nouvelle Vogue De La Pop Music', broadcast on ORTF2 on this day at 9.35pm.

Monday 14 & Tuesday 15 October
RECORDING SESSIONS
EMI Studios, Abbey Road, St. John's Wood, London, England
Recording for the 'Point Me At The Sky' single.

Wednesday 16 October
CONCERT
Théâtre du Huitième, Lyon, France
With a psychedelic light show by the London Arts Laboratory.

Friday 18 October
CONCERT
Industrial Club, Norwich, England
This show was booked as a replacement for a cancelled show by a different promoter who had advertised Pink Floyd appearing at the Orford Club, Norwich on 4 October, despite the band's commitment to a show in Birmingham on that date.

Saturday 19 October
CANCELLED CONCERT
Salford University, Salford, Manchester, England
Scaffold replaced the advertised Pink Floyd when they cancelled this concert in order to play in Belgium.

Saturday 19 October
CONCERT
Theatre 140, Brussels, Belgium

Sunday 20 October
CONCERT
Theatre 140, Brussels, Belgium
Two shows at 3.30pm and 8.30pm.

Friday 25 October
CONCERT
The Boat House, Kew, London, England

Saturday 26 October
CONCERT
Union Hall, Imperial College, Kensington, London, England
Early show. With two supporting groups.

Saturday 26 October
CONCERT
Middle Earth, The Roundhouse, Chalk Farm, London, England
Late show 10.30pm till dawn with Gary Farr, July and DJ Jeff Dexter. Rescheduled from 18 October.

Thursday 31 October
TV SHOW
L'Antene du Chapiteau du Kremlin-Bicêtre, Paris, France
Pink Floyd performed 'Let There Be More Light' and 'Flaming' live on the music programme *Tous en Scene*. It was broadcast (in colour) on ORTF2 on 26 November at 8.35pm.

CANCELLED NORTH AMERICAN TOUR
Pink Floyd were reported in the UK music press to be returning to the US to complete a college tour with Tyrannosaurus Rex through November, but this plan never came to fruition. Additionally a series of shows were booked including the following shows that were still being advertised a week prior to the show date that may have ben cancelled due to a problem with work permits: Fillmore East, Manhattan, New York City, New York (two shows at 8.00pm and 11.30pm with Richie Havens and Quicksilver Messenger Service on both 1 & 2 November) and Electric Factory, Philadelphia, Pennylvania (8 & 9 November with The Moody Blues).

Friday 1 November
CONCERT
The Sound of Colours, Highbury Technical College, Portsmouth, England
With The Sonic Invaders and Tangerine Slide.
The Portsmouth News reported that: 'Those going along to the dance could well see pop history made. The Floyd – one of the most progressive groups on the current scene – will not be playing in the usual position on stage. Instead, they will be positioned in the centre of the dance floor, and using an entirely new and revolutionary sound system. Surrounded by speakers the group will be using an eight-track stereo sound system. This gives 360 degrees in stereo – reputed to be 10 times more effective than the normal stereo sound.'

Saturday 2 November
CONCERT
Main Hall, Watford Technical College, Watford, England

Thursday 7 November
CONCERT
Porchester Hall, Queensway, London, England
With Barclay James Harvest, Edgar Broughton Band. Pink Floyd also jammed with Alexis Korner and Arthur Brown after their set.

Friday 8 November
CONCERT
Fishmonger's Arms public house, Wood Green,
London, England
Supported by Closed Cell Sponge and Stranger Than
Yesterday with DJ Jerry Floyd and the Saffron
Rainbow Light Show.
Set list included: 'Careful With That Axe, Eugene' / 'A
Saucerful Of Secrets'.
Record Mirror reported that: 'The turnout - for what
was probably a little-advertised event - was amazing.
The hall was absolutely packed - not with the usual
sort of kid fans but with a seriously attentive and
wildly appreciative crowd. The customers there at a
London suburban pub were the most vivid proof of
the existence of an increasingly large, new-type
audience for intelligent and imaginative pop.'

WEST GERMAN & SWISS TOUR

Friday 15 November
CONCERTS
Blow Up Club, Munich, West Germany
Two evening shows with Morgen Soul Star Band and
Jackie Edwards. This was Pink Floyd's first ever
appearance in Germany.

Saturday 16 November
CONCERT
Restaurant Olten-Hammer, Olten, Switzerland
Early show. Pink Floyd's first ever show in
Switzerland was reportedly attended by over 400
fans.

Saturday 16 November
CONCERT
Grosse Tanzparty, Coca-Cola Halle, Abtwil,
Switzerland
Late show. Supported by The Blues Club, The Axis,
The Wood Chuck and The Ponny's with the Miss
Coca-Cola Competition.

Sunday 17 November
CONCERT
2nd Pop & Rhythm and Blues Festival, Hazyland,
Kongresshaus, Zurich, Switzerland
The last night of the tour.

Friday 22 November
CONCERT
Crawdaddy, The Club House, Richmond Athletic
Club, Richmond, England
Supported by Arcadium.

Saturday 23 November
CONCERT
The Large Hall, Regent Street Polytechnic, London,
England
With Bobby Parker.

Sunday 24 November
CONCERT
The Country Club, Belsize Park, London, England
Supported by Andromeda.

Wednesday 27 November
CONCERT
Keele University, Newcastle-under-Lyme, England
Set list: 'Astronomy Dominé' / 'Flaming' / 'Careful
With That Axe, Eugene' / 'Interstellar Overdrive' /
'Let There Be More Light' / 'Set The Controls For The
Heart Of The Sun' / 'A Saucerful Of Secrets'.

Friday 29 November
CONCERT
Hanover Lodge, Bedford College, Regents Park,
London, England
Supported by Blonde On Blonde.
Correspondence in The Royal Holloway College
Archives noted that: 'In protest of students
establishing for themselves an annual Christmas Ball,
the Social Secretary stated in the minutes of the
General Meeting of the college Union on 6 December
that: 'Three young ladies had done no academic work
for three weeks due to Pink Floyd's dance and the
Christmas Ball on account of all the preparations for
these events.'

Monday 2 December
RADIO SHOW
Studio 4, BBC Maida Vale
Studios, Maida Vale,
London, England
Pink Floyd recorded two
live shows on this day for
BBC Radio One.
The first show was
recorded between 2.30pm
and 6.00pm, in which the
band performed, in order,
'Point Me At The Sky', 'The
Narrow Way Pt.1'
(announced as 'Baby Blue
Shuffle In D Major'), 'The
Embryo' and 'Interstellar
Overdrive'. It was broadcast
on *Top Gear* hosted by John
Peel on 15 December at

RIGHT: PUBLICITY PHOTO FOR
'POINT ME AT THE SKY',
TAKEN AT BIGGIN HILL
AERODROME, NOVEMBER
1968. PINK FLOYD ALSO MADE
A PROMOTIONAL FILM FOR
THE SINGLE SHOWING SOME
OF THE BRAVER MEMBERS OF
THE BAND TAKING TO THE
SKIES IN A GYPSY MOTH BI-
PLANE.

3.00pm.
The second show was recorded between 6.00pm and
9.30pm, in which the band performed, in order, 'Point
Me At The Sky', 'The Embryo' and 'Interstellar
Overdrive'. It was broadcast on *Top Gear* hosted by
John Peel on 19 January 1969 at 3.00pm.

Wednesday 4 December
THEATRE PREMIERE
Jeanetta Cochrane Theatre, Long Acre, London,
England
Pink Floyd provided some specially recorded music for
the production of *Pawn To King 5* by the Ballet
Rambert that premiered on this date.

Thursday 5 December
CONCERT
*Bournemouth College Students Union Christmas
Dance*, Royal Arcade Ballrooms, Boscombe,
Bournemouth, England
With Status Quo and Mouse & The Kats.

Friday 6 December
RECORD RELEASE
'Point Me At The Sky' / 'Careful With That Axe,
Eugene'
UK 7-inch single release.

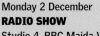

THIS FR
PINK
★★★★★

als

NME commented that: 'Apart from the excessive volume I found it quite intriguing and absorbing – quite the best Floyd single to be issued for some long time.'

Saturday 7 December
CONCERT
Kaleidoscope '68, Liverpool Stadium, Liverpool, England
An all day event commencing mid-day to 1.30am with The Move, Cliff Bennett, The Perfumed Garden, The BJ's, Reason Why, The Klubs, The Mumbles, The New Mojo Band, The Curiosity Shoppe, The Pattern People, The Chapter Six, Mick Burns, The Humphrey Lyttelton Band. The show was compered by BBC Radio 1 DJ's Dave Symonds, Tony Brandon, Rick Dane and Pete Price. Despite the grandeur of its name, the venue was in fact a large ballroom.

Wednesday 11 December
CONCERT
Students Union, St. Andrew's University, St. Andrew's, Scotland

Thursday 12 December
CONCERT
Christmas Revels Ball, College of Art, Dundee, Scotland
With The Sleaz Band.

Friday 13 December
CONCERT
The New Marquee, Leeds, England

Sunday 15 December
CONCERT
City Hall, Newcastle-upon-Tyne, England
Supported by The Pretty Things, Aynsley Dunbar Retaliation, The Deviants and Gordon Snaith. Two shows were scheduled but the earlier one was cancelled because Pink Floyd were delayed on the motorway. They played two numbers in half an hour until, at 10.30pm, the venue management turned off the power, sparking off a near riot in the audience.

Tuesday 17 December
TV SHOW
EMI Studios, Abbey Road, St. John's Wood, London, England
Pink Floyd participated in a live recording session for BBC TV illustrating the recording process for this educational TV programme *Science Session* subtitled 'Let's Make Pop'. It was broadcast on BBC1 TV on 5 March 1969 at 2.05pm and repeated on BBC1 TV on 6 March 1969 at 2.05pm.

Friday 20 December
RADIO SHOW
BBC Paris Cinema, Lower Regent Street, London, England
Pink Floyd recorded a live audience show on this day for BBC Radio One in which the band performed, in order, 'Let There Be More Light', 'Set The Controls For The Heart Of The Sun', 'Point Me At The Sky' and 'Careful With That Axe, Eugene'. It was broadcast on the BBC Radio One programme *Radio One Club*, presented by David Symonds, at midday.

Friday 27 December
CONCERT
Grote Zaal, De Doelen, Rotterdam, Netherlands
With The Outsiders, Barber Green's Fantastic Collection, Misfits, R&B Ltd.4, Eye's Blues Formation, Only's, Joseph Guy, Heads, Panique, WW Dance Girls and featuring the Provadya? Lightshow.

Saturday 28 December
CONCERT
Flight To Lowlands Paradise II, Margriethal-Jaarbeurs, Utrecht, Netherlands
Pink Floyd replaced the advertised Jimi Hendrix Experience at this two-day festival event held over 28 and 29 December. Also appearing were The Jeff Beck Group, Jethro Tull, The Pretty Things, The Bonzo Dog Doo-Dah Band, The Pebbles and around ten other Dutch bands.
Set list: 'Astronomy Dominé' / 'Careful With That Axe, Eugene' / 'Interstellar Overdrive' / 'Set The Controls For The Heart Of The Sun' / 'A Saucerful Of Secrets'.

1969

PINK FLOYD ROAD CREW THROUGH 1969
Alan Styles: Technician / Stage Crew
Peter Watts: Tour Manager / Front of House Sound

January - February
RECORDING SESSIONS
EMI Studios, Abbey Road, St. John's Wood, London, England
Discontinuous recording for the album *Ummagumma*.

Friday 10 January
CONCERT
Fishmonger's Arms public house, Wood Green, London, England
Pink Floyd replaced the advertised Jimi Hendrix Experience at short notice.

Saturday 11 January
CANCELLED APPEARANCE
Kink Pop Festival, Dordrecht, The Netherlands
Pink Floyd cancelled their advertised appearance for unknown reasons.

Sunday 12 January
CONCERT
Mothers, Erdington, Birmingham, England
With DJ John Peel.

Friday 17 January
CANCELLED APPEARANCE
Brunel University (Uxbridge) Rag Week Ball, Royal Albert Hall, Kensington, London, England
With Ten Years After, Family and DJ John Peel. Pink Floyd did not appear at this show, possibly because of the following day's punishing schedule.

Saturday 18 January
CONCERT
Homerton College, Cambridge, England
Afternoon show. With Armageddon, Saffron Knight, discotheque, Southside Jazz Band, Fab-Cab, blues bands and a cabaret.

Saturday 18 January
CONCERT
London College of Printing, Elephant and Castle, London, England
Evening show.

Saturday 18 January
CONCERT
Middle Earth, The Roundhouse, Chalk Farm, London, England
2.15am show (19 January). With Arcadium, Jimmy Scott & His Band, DJ Jeff Dexter and The Explosive Spectrum Lightshow.
Set list included: 'Set The Controls For The Heart Of The Sun'.
Pink Floyd's set was followed by a screening of excerpts from the Tiny Tim film *You Are What You Eat*. The entire band was reported in attendance of the premiere of the film on 29 January at the Windmill Theatre, London.
An unidentified newspaper reported that: 'A large queue began forming outside the Roundhouse from about eleven o'clock at night and by half past one in the morning most of the assembled masses were inside. Under the large central dome there was a large circular floor area. Most of the audience sat on

the floor, but latecomers sat on the colonnaded promenade. To brighten things up a bit the back of the stage, the roof of the dome, and a circular strip all the way round under the dome were draped with white sheets, which were used as projection screens for the lights. An hour of recorded music preceded the band's stage entry. At a quarter past two a tentative probing of the immense gong heralded "Set The Controls For The Heart Of The Sun." A sixty five minute set followed which included the breaking of a milk bottle in a rubbish bin and the frying of eggs, and more gong beating.'

Wednesday 22 January
TV SHOW
ORTF Studios, Buttes Chaumont, Paris, France
Pink Floyd performed 'Set The Controls For The Heart Of The Sun' and 'A Saucerful of Secrets' live for the music programme *Forum Musiques*. David Gilmour was also interviewed in French between the two songs. It was broadcast (in black and white) on ORTF1 on 15 February at 10.35pm.

Saturday 25 January
CONCERT
Sixty Nine Club, **Royal York Hotel, Ryde, Isle of Wight, England**
Supported by The Cherokees.
Set list included: 'Set The Controls For The Heart Of The Sun'.

Late January – Early February
RECORDING SESSIONS
Studio One, Pye Recording Studios, ATV House, Marble Arch, London, England
Discontinuous recording for the album *More*. Studio archives have revealed that other than the released tracks, other titles recorded at the sessions included 'Paris Bar' and 'Stephan's Tit'.

Friday 7 February
CANCELLED CONCERT
University of Hull, Hull, England
This show was cancelled on the night due to heavy snowfalls delaying the arrival of the band and their equipment from London.

Friday 14 February
CONCERT
Valentines Ball, **Edward Herbert Building, University of Loughborough, Loughborough, England**
With Free, DJ Emperor Rosco and The Delroy Williams Show. *International Times* had incorrectly listed Pink Floyd appearing at Warwick University, Coventry on this day.

Monday 17 February
PRESS REPORT
Edinburgh, Scotland

Edinburgh Evening News reported that: 'Pop group Pink Floyd have written the music for a ballet sequence being put on at the Royal Lyceum Theatre [Edinburgh, between 17 and 22 February]. It is part of a programme being presented by The Ballet Rambert and is a piece of improvisation called "Pawn To King Five". The piece will be included in the company's programme, *Number One*, which starts on Monday. The choreography is being handled by John Chesworth.'

Monday 17 February
CONCERT
The Ballroom, Bay Hotel, Whitburn, Sunderland, England

Tuesday 18 February
CONCERT
Manchester & Salford Students' Shrove Rag Ball, **Main Debating Hall, Manchester University, Manchester, England**
With Fairport Convention. Also appearing were John Dummer Blues Band and Bakerloo (in the Open Lounge), Liverpool Scene, Bridget St. John and John Peel (in the Lesser Debating Hall), The Foundations and Simon Dupree (at the Burlington Street site).

Friday 21 February
CONCERT
Alhambra Theatre, Bordeaux, France
Supported by Roland Kirk.

Monday 24 February
CONCERT
The Dome, Brighton, England
Supported by The Pretty Things and Third Ear Band. Also advertised with post-concert 'super-jam' session. Set list included: 'Interstellar Overdrive' / 'Set The Controls For The Heart Of The Sun' / 'A Saucerful Of Secrets' / encore: 'Let There Be More Light'.
The Wine Press, the Sussex University student newspaper reported that: 'On Monday of last week Jimi Hendrix played his second concert at London's Royal Albert Hall. And the Pink Floyd appeared at The Dome. They did not play their "Symphony In Sixteen Parts"[*]. It did not matter. There was no super-jam session. Just who could add anything to the music of the Floyd? They proved themselves once more as the most consistently brilliant group in England. The group are at their best on the two long instrumentals "Interstellar Overdrive" and "A Saucerful Of Secrets". They probably could not count the number of times they have performed the first work; it is an ever-changing tableau of improvisation. At The Dome they played the finest version of it I have ever heard. It is a pity that such live performances are not preserved. "Saucerful" is the title track of their last album. Their version of this was simply incredible - superb drumming from Mason leading onto the centrepiece

of polyphonic chaos, news from the quasars. Waters prowled the stage like a captain on the observation deck of a star ship, penetrating ever deeper into the heart of darkness. At their most brilliant, the group go where no man has gone before. The beautiful organ solo leading to the conclusion of the work, showed Rick Wright to be the best organist in Britain. The group finished with "More Light" - great speed-freak guitar from Gilmore, great bass playing from Waters. This number together with "Set The Controls" show Roger Waters to be an ever better song writer than Sid Barrett, who's departure has not harmed the group, probably helped them. Waters vocal style is curiously hushed; menacing - too quiet to hear the words, loud enough to generate the meaning. What of the future? The next album will not be their symphony, about which they are unenthusiastic at the moment. They will perform it again some time in another form. Set music holds no appeal to them.'
*Note: "Symphony In Sixteen Parts" is a title that has not appeared in any other reference to the band's output and consequently it has not been possible to research this any further.

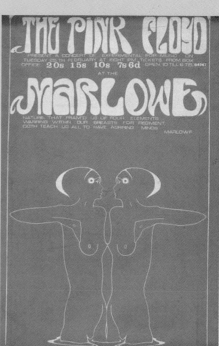

Tuesday 25 February
CONCERT
Marlowe Theatre, Canterbury, England
Set list included: 'Set The Controls For The Heart Of The Sun' / 'Careful With That Axe, Eugene'.
The Kent Herald reported that: 'Pink Floyd began their performance with impromptu coughs into the microphones, building up into the opening number. They used electric organ, grand piano, vibes and two large Chinese gongs as well as guitars and drums, and the music (or rather sounds) definitely attacked the

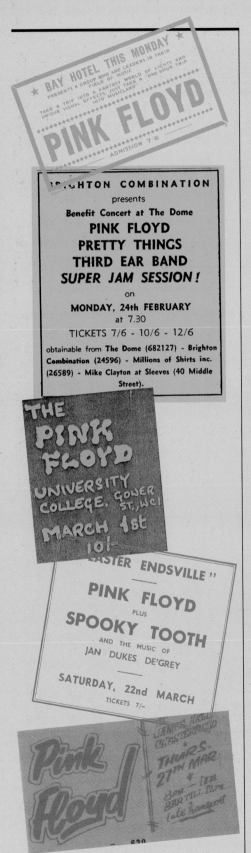

senses as advertised. In the second half the musicians wandered about the stage, playing each other's instruments, and generally seeming to have a good time. Some brilliant piano and organ work came from Rick Wright, and the drums were played magnificently by Nick Mason, who kept the group stable with his good sense of rhythm. On stage, without the flashing lights for which they are renowned, they were informal and obviously musically talented. Perhaps the majority of the audience were flattered, however, to be allowed to see what looked like the group's rehearsal rather than a prepared show.'

Wednesday 26 February
CONCERT
New Cavendish Ballroom, Edinburgh, Scotland
Pink Floyd performed in aid of Shelter, an event organised by the University of Edinburgh's charity campaign, for which £250 was raised.

Thursday 27 February
CONCERT
Glasgow Arts Lab Benefit, The Maryland Ballroom, Glasgow, Scotland
Supported by The Jimmy Mullen Jazz Group.

Friday 28 February
CONCERT
Commemoration Ball, Queen Elizabeth College, Kensington, London, England
With The Moody Blues and The Settlers.

Saturday 1 March
CONCERT
University College London, Bloomsbury, London, England

Monday 3 March
CONCERT
Vic Rooms Dance, Victoria Rooms, University of Bristol, Clifton, Bristol, England
Supported by East of Eden.
Set list included: 'Astronomy Dominé' / 'Interstellar Overdrive' / 'Set The Controls For The Heart Of The Sun' / 'Let There Be More Light' / 'A Saucerful Of Secrets'.
The *Bristol Evening Post* reported that: 'The Pink Floyd played an extraordinary and very different show last night. And they even managed to quieten with their music 1,000 students fresh from the Rag torch light procession through the streets of Bristol.

Electronic sounds one usually only hears on records came through loud and clear at the hall and this remarkable group played a fascinating set. All the numbers were lengthy, eerie meanderings through a pop version of science fiction, with loud guitar and organ interplay's creating the strange effects. Throughout the performance there was a fascinating light-show by Adrian Jones and Keith Wilkins, who managed to produce a blizzard of colours and forms to add even more excitement to a remarkable show.'

Saturday 8 March
CONCERT
Reading University Rag Ball, New Union, University of Reading, Whiteknights, Reading, England
With The Pretty Things, The Gods, Discotheque, folk singing, blues, and the Sound Kitchen light-show.

Tuesday 11 March
CONCERT
Lawns Centre, Cottingham, England
Presented by Huddersfield University.

Friday 14 March
CONCERT
Van Dike Club, Devonport, Plymouth, England
Supported by Afterwards.

Saturday 15 March
CONCERT
Kee Club, Bridgend, Wales

Wednesday 19 March
CONCERT
Going Down Ball, The Refectory, University College, Singleton Park, Swansea, Wales
Set list: 'Astronomy Dominé' / 'Careful With That Axe, Eugene' / 'Set The Controls For The Heart Of The Sun' / 'Interstellar Overdrive' / encore: 'A Saucerful Of Secrets'.

Friday 21 March
CONCERT
Blackpool Technical College & School of Art and St. Anne's College of Further Education Arts Ball, Empress Ballroom, Winter Gardens, Blackpool, England
With The Love Affair, PP Arnold, Carnaby Square, DJ Gary Wild and cabaret.

Saturday 22 March
CONCERT
Easter Endsville, Refectory Hall, University Union, Leeds University, Leeds, England
With Spooky Tooth and Jan Dukes De Grey.

Thursday 27 March
CONCERT
St. James' Church Hall, Chesterfield, England
Supported by King Mob Echo and Gandalf's Garden.
Set list: 'Astronomy Dominé' / 'Careful With That Axe, Eugene' / 'Interstellar Overdrive' / 'Set The Controls For The Heart Of The Sun' / 'A Saucerful Of Secrets'.

April - June
RECORDING SESSIONS
EMI Studios, Abbey Road, St. John's Wood, London, England
Discontinuous recording for the album *Ummagumma*.

Wednesday 9 April
CANCELLED RADIO SHOW
BBC Paris Cinema, Lower Regent Street, London, England
Pink Floyd were due to record a live show for the BBC Radio One programme *Radio One Club* hosted by John Peel at midday but the band failed to turn up due to illness. It was rescheduled to 12 May.

Monday 14 April
CONCERT
Royal Festival Hall, South Bank, London, England

Set list: 'The Man' // 'The Journey' / encore: 'Interstellar Overdrive'.
This show saw the introduction of two new suites of music built around existing and new works: 'The Man' and 'The Journey'.
'The Man' comprised of the following pieces: 'Daybreak' (an alternative title for 'Grantchester Meadows' performed as an acoustic instrumental) / 'Work' (a percussion workout during which the band sawed and nailed pieces of wood to make a table) / 'Afternoon' (an alternate title for 'Biding My Time') / 'Doing It' (an instrumental of percussion and taped voices reminiscent of 'The Party Sequence') / 'Sleeping' (an electronic instrumental) / 'Nightmare' / 'Daybreak (reprise)'.

'The Journey' comprised of the following pieces: 'The Beginning' (an alternate title for 'Green Is The Colour') / 'Beset By Creatures Of The Deep' (a reworking of 'Careful With That Axe, Eugene') / 'The Narrow Way' (as 'Part 3' of the same track) / taped sequences of footsteps and doors opening and closing / 'The Pink Jungle' (an explosive instrumental piece) / 'The Labyrinths Of Auximenes' / 'Behold The Temple Of Light' / 'The End Of The Beginning' (taken from the closing section of 'A Saucerful Of Secrets').
Film director Anthony Stern attended the afternoon rehearsal prior to sound-check and was able to film the band working on parts of their set. A recording emerged, filmed in black and white, on the collectors market in early 2006 and included parts of 'Afternoon' ('Biding My Time'), 'The Beginning' ('Green Is The Colour'), 'Cymbaline', 'Beset By Creatures Of The Deep' ('Careful With That Axe, Eugene'), 'The End of The Beginning' (the closing organ section of 'A Saucerful Of Secrets') and other instrumental passages. Stern had obviously turned up on the off chance with a view to recording the evening show for posterity. Unfortunately the venue management prevented him from filming in the evening and the ensuing discussion with a venue steward is also caught on tape.
The programme for this concert also gave a listing of

Pink Floyd's forthcoming appearances that included the following shows that remain unconfirmed: Sweden (9 June), France (16 June) and The Netherlands (18 June).

Saturday 19 April
TV BROADCAST
SDR TV Villa Berg Studios, Stuttgart, West Germany
Pink Floyd had previously recorded original material for an SDR TV programme entitled *Pink Floyd Mit Einen Neuen Beat Sound* that was broadcast on this day. This show has since been erased from the station's archives and the content and date of the recording cannot be confirmed.

Saturday 26 April
CONCERT
Light & Sound Concert, Main Hall, Bromley Technical College, Bromley Common, Bromley, England
With East of Eden, Third Ear Band and Hippotama (all in the Refectory Hall). Lights by Luminiferous Extravaganza.
Set list: 'Astronomy Dominé' / 'Careful With That Axe, Eugene' / 'Interstellar Overdrive' / 'Green Is The Colour' / 'Pow R Toc H' / 'Set The Controls For The

Heart Of The Sun' / 'A Saucerful Of Secrets'. Pink Floyd's set was recorded for the *Ummagumma* album but not used.

Sunday 27 April
CONCERT
Mothers, Erdington, Birmingham, England
With DJ John Peel.
Set list: 'Astronomy Dominé' / 'Careful With That Axe, Eugene' / 'Interstellar Overdrive' / 'Set The Controls For The Heart Of The Sun' / 'A Saucerful Of Secrets'. Pink Floyd's set was recorded for the *Ummagumma* album.
DJ John Peel wrote in his weekly column for *Disc & Music Echo* that: 'At one moment they are laying surfaces of sound one upon another in symphonic thunder; at another isolated, incredibly melancholy sounds which cross one another sounding like cries of dying galaxies lost in sheer corridors of time and space.' The review earned him a mention in the 'Pseuds Corner' column of the satirical magazine *Private Eye*.

Friday 2 May
CONCERT
Student Union Building, College of Commerce, Manchester, England
With Roy Harper, Pete Brown & His Battered Ornaments, Principal Edwards Magic Theatre, White Trash, Edgar Broughton Band, Smokey Rice and The Groundhogs with the Nova Express Lightshow and a film theatre. Fairground rides were also set up in the grounds of the college.
Set list: 'Astronomy Dominé' / 'Careful With That Axe, Eugene' / 'Interstellar Overdrive' / 'Set The Controls For The Heart Of The Sun' / 'A Saucerful Of Secrets'. Pink Floyd's set was recorded for the *Ummagumma* album.

Saturday 3 May
CONCERT
The Sports Hall, Queen Mary College, Mile End, London, England
Supported by Watch Us Grow.
Set list included: 'Astronomy Dominé' / 'Set The Controls For The Heart Of The Sun' / 'A Saucerful Of Secrets'.

Friday 9 May
CONCERT
Camden Fringe Festival Free Concert, Parliament Hill Fields, Hampstead Heath, London, England
Afternoon show. With Roy Harper, The Pretty Things, Pete Brown's Battered Ornaments and Jody Grind.
Set list: 'Astronomy Dominé' / 'Set The Controls For The Heart Of The Sun' / 'Careful With That Axe, Eugene' / 'A Saucerful Of Secrets'.
International Times reported that: 'The Floyd took to the stage like they were once more taking part in an all too familiar ritual - they looked tired and dispirited, and were obviously pissed off with the Orange equipment which was making the most unbelievably loud grunts and buzzes. After some rather hesitant beginnings they found where they were going and roared into "Astronomy Dominé" - the crowd yelled its approval. "Set The Controls" and "Careful With That Axe, Eugene" were dispensed in hard fashion, though Dave Gilmore had trouble with his amp, and the band announced that it had a gig to do in Southampton and would finish with a "quick" version of "Saucerful". Roger Waters moved into the dark arena of crashing power in a most mysteriously violent way, and Rick Wright's organ, as ever, swept along fluidly with great sweeps and dives across the rest of the band. Nick Mason managed to drum as succinctly as ever, and by the end of "Saucerful" The Floyd had created for the evening its colour - the tone and excitement of their playing was not to be lost. They left the stage to huge applause...'

BELOW: PERFORMING IN THE AFTERNOON AT THE *CAMDEN FRINGE FESTIVAL*, HAMPSTEAD, LONDON ON 9 MAY 1969. PINK FLOYD ARE USING THE FESTIVAL'S ORANGE AMPS INSTEAD OF THEIR OWN WEM SYSTEM WHICH WAS MAKING ITS WAY TO SOUTHAMPTON FOR A SHOW THAT EVENING.

Friday 9 May
CONCERT
Old Refectory, Student's Union, Southampton University, Highfield, Southampton, England
Evening show. Supported by Bridget St. John.
Set list: 'Astronomy Dominé' / 'Careful With That Axe, Eugene' / 'Interstellar Overdrive' / 'The Beginning' / 'Beset By Creatures Of The Deep' / 'A Saucerful Of Secrets'.

Saturday 10 May
CONCERT
Nottingham's Pop & Blues Festival, Notts County Football Ground, Nottingham, England
Pink Floyd closed the day's events, performing in the pouring rain, which was headlined by Fleetwood Mac and featured The Tremeloes, Marmalade, Georgie Fame, Love Sculpture, Keef Hartley, Status Quo, Duster Bennett, Dream Police and Van Der Graaf Generator.

Monday 12 May
RADIO SHOW
BBC Paris Cinema, Lower Regent Street, London, England
Pink Floyd recorded a replacement show for the aborted 9 April session for BBC Radio One on this date. Recorded between 5.30pm and 12.00midnight the band performed, in order, 'Daybreak', 'Cymbaline', 'The Narrow Way, Part 3' and 'Green Is The Colour'. It was broadcast on *Top Gear* on 14 May at 8.15pm and repeated on *Top Gear* on 1 June at 7.00pm in the following order: 'Daybreak', 'Cymbaline', 'Green Is The Colour' and 'The Narrow Way, Part 3'.

Thursday 15 May
CONCERT
It's A Drag - City of Coventry College of Art May Ball, Locarno Ballroom, Coventry, England
With Spooky Tooth and Free (who replaced Wellington Kitch at the last moment).

UK TOUR
Pink Floyd's first nationally advertised tour, complete with generic print and tour programme, was interspersed with many one-off engagements both at home and abroad and comprised of the following shows: Town Hall, Leeds, England (16 May); City Hall, Sheffield, England (24 May); Fairfield Halls, Croydon, England (30 May); Rex Ballroom, Cambridge, England (8 June); Ulster Hall, Belfast, Northern Ireland (10 June); Colston Hall, Bristol, England (14 June); Guildhall, Portsmouth, England (15 June); The Dome, Brighton, England (16 June); Town Hall, Birmingham, England (20 June) Royal Philharmonic, Liverpool, England (21 June); Free Trade Hall, Manchester, England (22 June), Royal Albert Hall, London, England (26 June).
For the tour Pink Floyd performed material previewed

the previous month at the Royal Festival Hall in London. Some fine-tuning was required and as a result 'Nighmare' now incorporated 'Cymbaline,' with an additional middle section of pre-recorded quadraphonic sequence of footsteps and doors opening and closing, which was heard throughout the auditorium. 'The Pink Jungle' was also extended to include a reworking of 'Pow R Toc H'. As at the Royal Festival Hall show, a costumed 'creature' would often lumber around the hall during the set.

Friday 16 May
CONCERT
Town Hall, Leeds, England

CANCELLED NETHERLANDS SHOWS
Pink Floyd cancelled several advertised shows in the Netherlands over the summer period for what is believed to have been difficulties with work permits. These included dates at the Paradiso, Amsterdam (17 May) and Concertzaal de Jong, Groningen (18 May). Rescheduled and additional dates were also cancelled for similar reasons including those at Concertzaal de Jong, Groningen (6 June); Paradiso, Amsterdam, (7 June); Meerpaal, Dronten (8 June); Paradiso, Amsterdam (10 July) and *Popmanifestatie*, Veilinggebouw, Groningen (11 July).

Saturday 24 May
CONCERT
City (Oval) Hall, Sheffield, England
Set list: 'The Man' // 'The Journey' / encore: 'Interstellar Overdrive'.

Sunday 25 May
CONCERT
Benefit For The Fairport Convention, The Roundhouse, Chalk Farm, London, England
With Blossom Toes, The Deviants, Eclection, Family, Mick Fleetwood, Mimi & Mouse, Jack Moore, John Peel and The Pretty Things.
This was a hastily arranged benefit show to help pay for the care of members of Fairport Convention who were injured in a serious accident on the M1 in which drummer Martin Lamble and a female passenger, Gene Franklin, were killed. However, the show was a far from peaceful event marred by crowd violence.

Friday 30 May
CONCERT
Fairfield Halls, Croydon, England
Set list: 'The Man' // 'The Journey'.
The Croydon Advertiser reported that: 'Before a packed and rapturous audience the Pink Floyd were a brilliant success with a two and a half hour programme of their unique brand of happening music. The first half was called simply "The Man". The Floyd took the audience, with music and sound effects, through a day in the life of a man. From "Daybreak" to

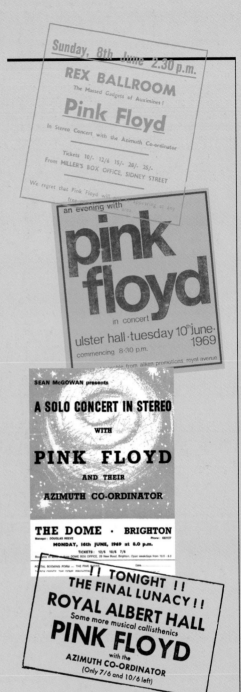

"Daydream" the group went through the whole 24 hours, and in the 24 hours they portrayed and expressed the whole gamut of human experience. "Work", complete with logs being sawed, the dramatic "Doing It!", in which the group gave a musical description of the sex act without once going across the borders into poor taste, and the traumatic "Nightmare" sequence, were all vividly clear. But the real mood-setting half of the programme was Part Two, which described a long and often tortuous journey. And this is where the programme came in useful. With that in front of me, I was able to use it almost as a musical score. Each of the seven sections had a clear a definite division: and it was easy to see the transition from one part to the next. From "The Beginning" the journey was "Beset By Creatures Of The Deep", and progressed through the "Narrow Way" and the "Pink Jungle" - some magnificently atmospheric organ playing here by Richard Wright. "The Labyrinths Of Auximenes" featured a special guest appearance by a monster of gargantuan physical proportions who did the most personal things all over the stage. Pure theatre or gobbledegook: well it certainly did not offend me, though I suppose it could have upset some. But for me it was the least apposite part of the whole programme. After this the four built up a tremendous climax in "Behold The Temple Of Light" and "The End Of The Beginning", with organist Wright moving over to the fine Fairfield organ and creating a breath gasping finale."

Sunday 31 May
CONCERT
Eights Week Ball, Main Marquee, Pembroke College, Oxford, England
• With Juniors Eyes and Dark Blues in the Main Marquee. Also appearing: Sister Ray Disco with light show (in the Cellar), Proteus Projection Workshop with The Acid Show (in the Junior Common Room) Rmas Band and Tropicanas (in the Hall), and Tropicanas with Limbo dancer, fire eater and Alan Rae (in the North Quad).

Sunday 8 June
CONCERT
Rex Ballroom, Cambridge, England
2.30pm show.

Tuesday 10 June
CONCERT
Ulster Hall, Belfast, Northern Ireland

Friday 13 June
RECORD RELEASE
More
UK album release. US album release on Saturday 9 August.
Record Song Book commented that: 'The music is

sometimes purely instrumental, sometimes both instrumental and vocal, *always* extremely interesting and arresting. Quite weird in parts too. Try the 'Main Theme' on side 2 for example. But it's not all like this. There's a super little Spanish bit that sounds almost traditional, and there are other equally contrasting tracks.'

Friday 13 June
CONCERT
Students Dance, Great Hall, Devonshire House, University of Exeter, Exeter, England
Pink Floyd cancelled an advertised appearance at the Van Dike Club, Plymouth (which was rescheduled to 27 June) in order to do this show.

Saturday 14 June
CONCERT
Colston Hall, Bristol, England
The Bristol Evening Post reported that: 'The Pink Floyd unleashed the power of modern electronics, modern pop ideas and modern violence at their concert in Bristol. Electronically the show was brilliant. The Floyd played over recorded tapes, which smashed four channel stereo sounds across, around and under the Colston Hall. The ideas were also exciting. A pop concert by a single group with the guts to drop the package tour format and a concert which followed a musical storyline which wasn't difficult to trace. The concert had its moments. An exciting blues solo by the lead guitarist, which Hendrix would have been proud of, nervous organ solos and some weirdly vicious rock and roll climaxes. But the Floyd pulled the punches and the music played on stage didn't live up to the interesting ideas they have created. The music was only intermittently good. For the Floyd it was a surprise, because they usually play immaculately - and the show had its silly moments. In one weirdo number an unnecessary Caliban staggered on to the stage and went into a music hall lavatory joke routine.'

Sunday 15 June
CONCERT
Guildhall, Portsmouth, England

Monday 16 June
CONCERT
The Dome, Brighton, England
Peter Towner, a fan in attendance, recalled that: 'There was this small guy dressed up in a grey/green warty skinned costume with a cock that would give a donkey a complex and cause serious damage to a mare. I swear the guy was playing this cock, musically, as he moved, cat-like, around the stage after first stealing around the front and sides of the stalls. My eyes were watering at the sight of this enormous chopper being waved around so my vision could have been impaired.'

Tuesday 17 June
RECORDING SESSION
EMI Studios, Abbey Road, St. John's Wood, London, England
Mixing David Gilmour's section of the album *Ummagumma*.

Friday 20 June
CONCERT
Town Hall, Birmingham, England

Saturday 21 June
CONCERT
Royal Philharmonic, Liverpool, England
Set list included: 'Astronomy Dominé' / 'Green Is The Colour' / 'Careful With That Axe, Eugene' / encore: 'A Saucerful Of Secrets'.

ROYAL PHILHARMONIC LIVERPOOL
Saturday, 21st June, at 7.30p.m.

the massed gadgets of auximines
Pink floyd
in stereo concert with the 'azimuth co-ordinator'

The Bryan Morrison Agency

Tickets:- 5/- 7/6 10/6 12/6 15/-
From: Royal Philharmonic, box office [709 3789] and Rushworth & Dreapers [709 8070]

Sunday 22 June
CONCERT
Free Trade Hall, Manchester, England
Set list: 'The Man' // 'The Journey' / encore: 'Set The Controls For The Heart Of The Sun'.

Monday 23 June
RECORDING SESSION
EMI Studios, Abbey Road, St. John's Wood, London, England
Mixing Roger Waters' section of the album *Ummagumma*.

Tuesday 24 June
CONCERT
Commemoration Ball, Main Marquee, Front Quad, Queen's College, Oxford, England
With Ten Years After (who had replaced Procol Harum at the last minute).
Nigel Lewendon, then Steward of Queen's College, recalled that: 'I remember everyone sitting down on the grass, because it's not the sort of music you could dance to. They had an enormous amount of sound equipment and I was standing by one of the speakers when the drummer hit this huge gong - I don't think I heard another thing for three days!'

Thursday 26 June
CONCERT
The Final Lunacy!, Royal Albert Hall, Kensington, London, England
The last night of the UK tour. Set list: 'The Man' // 'The Journey' (with brass and choir) / encore: 'Set The Controls For The Heart Of The Sun'.
The climax to 'The Journey' saw the group joined on stage by a brass section of the Royal Philharmonic and ladies of the Ealing Central Amateur Choir conducted by Norman Smith. One of Pink Floyd's more experimental concerts, it featured Richard Wright playing on the venue's huge pipe organ, a member of their crew dressed up as a gorilla, and even members of the band sawing wood on stage. A pair of Waterloo cannon's were fired from the stage and a huge pink smoke bomb was let off at the finale, which led the hall's management to ban Pink Floyd from the venue for life.

Friday 27 June
CONCERT
Van Dike Club, Devonport, Plymouth, England

Saturday 28 June
CONCERT
Saturday Dance Date, Winter Gardens Pavilion, Weston-super-Mare, England
Supported by The Ken Birch Band and the Mike Slocombe Combo.

Monday 30 June
CONCERT
President's Ball, Top Rank Suite, Cardiff, Wales
Presented by the Llandaff Technical College. Supported by Stop Watch.
Pink Floyd performed a one-hour show and were paid £100.

Friday 4 July
CONCERT
Selby Arts Festival, St. James Street Recreation Ground, Selby, England
Pink Floyd headlined at this open-air concert staged by art students of Bradford University to mark the end of the week-long festival. It was attended by some 2,000 fans.

Sunday 20 July
TV SHOW
Studio 5, BBC TV Centre, White City, London, England
Pink Floyd performed a five-minute live improvisation entitled 'Moonhead' as part of a one-hour BBC1 TV *Omnibus* special entitled 'So What If It's Just Green Cheese?', one of many programmes covering the Apollo 11 moon landing. It was broadcast at 10.00pm and featured appearances by Judi Dench, Ian McKellern, Michael Horden, Roy Dotrice, Marian Montgomery and Dudley Moore & the Dudley Moore Trio.

Tuesday 22 July
TV SHOW
SDR TV Villa Berg Studios, Stuttgart, West Germany
Pink Floyd performed 'Corporal Clegg' and 'A Saucerful Of Secrets' live for the children's programme *P-1*. 'Corporal Clegg' was played over some bizarre footage of the band engaged in a staged restaurant food-fight whilst 'A Saucerful Of Secrets' saw the band performing with their stage equipment set up in the studio. It was broadcast on the SDR TV network on 21 September at 5.15pm.

Wednesday 23 July
TV SHOW
West Germany
Pink Floyd were reported to be appearing on German TV for coverage of the Apollo 11 moon landing but the content and broadcast details remain unknown.

Thursday 24 July
TV SHOW
Nederland 1 TV Studios, Zaandam, The Netherlands
The last of three European TV appearances culminated in a performance for the programme *Apollo 11* subtitled 'Een Man op De Maan' (One Man on The Moon). It was broadcast on Nederland1 TV at 9.20pm. The content details remain unknown but is most likely to have been similar to the music provided for the BBC on 20 July.

Friday 1 August
CONCERT
Van Dike Club, Devonport, Plymouth, England

Monday 4 August
FILM PREMIERE
7th New York Film Festival, Alice Tulley Hall, Lincoln Center, New York City, New York, USA
The premiere of the film *More*.

Friday 8 August
CONCERT
9th National Jazz Pop Ballads & Blues Festival, Plumpton Race Track, Streat, England
With Soft Machine, Keith Tippett, East Of Eden, Bonzo Dog Band, Roy Harper, The Who and many others.
Set list: 'Set The Controls For The Heart Of The Sun' / 'Cymbaline' / 'The Journey' / encore: 'Interstellar Overdrive'.
This three-day festival (8 - 10 August) was originally going to be staged on a derelict site on Horton Road, West Drayton, but the local council refused to grant a license and so the organisers relocated the event to Plumpton. For the bands and the audience in the main arena on the first night, the momentum was lost with power cuts occurring throughout Soft Machine's set. During over an hour of silence the crowd became restless, although most had fallen asleep by the time Pink Floyd came on.

Saturday 9 August
CONCERT
Paradiso, Amsterdam, The Netherlands
Set list: 'Interstellar Overdrive' / 'Set The Controls For The Heart Of The Sun' / 'Careful With That Axe, Eugene' / 'A Saucerful Of Secrets'.
Hilversum 3 Radio was recording this concert for future broadcast but after a microphone failure early in the show the band was forced to perform an instrumental set and as a result the broadcast was aborted.

Saturday 13 September
CONCERT
The Sam Cutler Stage Show - Rugby Rag's Blues Festival, Rainsbrook, Ashlawn Road, Rugby, England
With The Nice, Taste, Free, Edgar Broughton Band, Third Ear Band, Roy Harper, Ralph McTell and many other acts.
This three-day (13 - 15 September), open-air festival offered one day of Blues, one of Pop and one of Folk. It was attended by more than 3,000 people despite heavy downpours of cold rain throughout, and was policed peacefully by the Hell's Angels. Pink Floyd

appeared on the Pop day and, remarkably, given the weather conditions, were accompanied by an impressive light show.

NETHERLANDS & BELGIAN TOUR

Wednesday 17 September
CONCERT
Concertgebouw, Amsterdam, Netherlands
Supported by Dream with the Khaphalous Light Show.
Set list: 'The Man' // 'The Journey'.
Hilversum 3 Radio successfully recorded Pink Floyd's set and an edited version was broadcast later in the year.

Friday 19 September
CONCERT
Grote Zaal, De Doelen, Rotterdam, The Netherlands
Supported by Dream.

Saturday 20 September
CONCERT
Concertzaal de Jong, Groningen, The Netherlands
Two shows at 9.00pm and 11.00pm. Supported by Dream.
Set list at the second show included: 'Astronomy Dominé' / 'Green Is The Colour' / 'Careful With That Axe, Eugene' / 'Interstellar Overdrive' / 'Set The Controls For The Heart Of The Sun' / 'A Saucerful of Secrets'.

Sunday 21 September
CONCERT
Het Kolpinghuis, Nijmegen, The Netherlands
2.00pm show. Show rescheduled from an unknown venue in Tiel.

Supported by Dream with the Khaphalous Lightshow.

Monday 22 & Tuesday 23 September
TV SHOWS
BRT TV Studios, Brussels, Belgium
Pink Floyd were reported to be recording for Belgian TV but the content and broadcast details remain unknown.

Wednesday 24 September
CONCERT
Stadtsgehoorzaal, Leiden, The Netherlands
Show rescheduled from Waarschijnlijk, Nijmegen.

Thursday 25 September
CONCERT
Staargebouw, Maastricht, The Netherlands
Show rescheduled from Stadsschouwberg, Maastricht.

Friday 26, Saturday 27 & Sunday 28 September
CONCERTS
Theatre 140, Brussels, Belgium
The show on 28 September was the last night of the tour.

Friday 3 October
CONCERT
Debating Hall, Birmingham University, Edgbaston, Birmingham, England
Supported by Pegasus and Barnabas.
Set list included: 'Interstellar Overdrive' / 'Set The Controls For The Heart Of The Sun' / 'A Saucerful Of Secrets'.
Redbrick, the Birmingham University student newspaper, reported that: 'Their Floydian majesties did indeed descend on the Union on Friday. They were in a particularly celestial mood, even though the Azimuth was nowhere to be seen. On any occasion the effects of "Interstellar Overdrive" are likely to be rather disconcerting, but when the sequence extends to "Set The Controls For The Heart Of The Sun" and the near legendary "Saucerful Of Secrets" the only wonder is that the floor of the Deb Hall was not littered with the mortal remains of those whose migrant spirits were winging their way to the Heavens. Roger Waters actually attempted to fly, but he was unsuccessful.'

Saturday 4 October
CONCERT
New Union, Reading University, Whiteknights Park, Reading, England
Supported by Quintessence and Zap Gun Smith.

Friday 10 October
CONCERT
Edward Herbert Building, University of Loughborough, Loughborough, England
Supported by Jimmy Powell and Arrival.

Saturday 11 October
CONCERT
Internationales Essener Pop & Blues Festival '69, Grugahalle, Essen, West Germany
With Fleetwood Mac, The Pretty Things, Yes, Muddy Waters, Alexis Korner, The Nice and Deep Purple and many others. Pink Floyd played on the last night of this three-day festival (9-11 October).
Set list: 'Astronomy Dominé' / 'Green Is The Colour' / 'Careful With That Axe, Eugene' / 'Interstellar Overdrive' / 'A Saucerful Of Secrets'.

Saturday 18 October
CONCERT
University College London, Bloomsbury, London, England
With The Edgar Broughton Band and Majority.

Friday 24 October
CONCERT
Fillmore North, Locarno Ballroom, Sunderland, England
Supported by Stone The Crows and DJ John Peel.
Set list: 'Astronomy Dominé' / 'Green Is The Colour' / 'Careful With That Axe, Eugene' / 'Interstellar Overdrive' / 'Set The Controls For The Heart Of The Sun' / 'A Saucerful Of Secrets'.

Saturday 25 October
CONCERT
Actuel Festival, Mont de l'Enclus, Amougies, Belgium
Set list: 'Astronomy Dominé' / 'Green Is The Colour' / 'Careful With That Axe, Eugene' / 'Interstellar Overdrive '(with Frank Zappa) / 'Main Theme' from *More* / 'Set The Controls For The Heart Of The Sun' / 'A Saucerful Of Secrets'.
With Ten Years After, Colosseum, Aynsley Dunbar Retaliation, Alan Jack Civilization, Art Ensemble of Chicago, Sunny Murray, Burton Greene Ensemble, Renaissance, Don Cherry, The Nice, Caravan, Archie Shepp, Yes, The Pretty Things, Keith Tippet, Daevid Allen, Pharoah Sanders, Sonny Sharrock and Captain Beefheart. The event was compered by Frank Zappa who performed with many of the acts including Pink Floyd.
This massive five-day festival was originally intended to be held in St. Cloud, Paris, as the *First Continental Festival* (24-28 October) but the French police refused to grant the event a license, as did the authorities in Pelouses de Reuilly, Vincennes when the organisers, Byg Records, tried to relocate it there. They were left with little option but to move it out of France altogether, to the tiny Belgian village of Amougies. Pink Floyd topped the bill on the main stage, on the second night, which was housed in a massive marquee, playing to an audience of over 2,000.
Melody Maker reported that: 'Pink Floyd - at last something to compare with "2001". They had to battle against a few crackles from the amplifiers, but came over clear and well balanced. Frank Zappa accepted their challenge to join in on "Interstellar Overdrive" and a few new galaxies were discovered.'
Parts of the festival were reportedly broadcast on Europe 1 radio shortly after the event but further details could not be found.
Two documentary films were also made of the festival, directed by Gérome Laperrousaz, entitled *European Music Revolution* and *Music Power*, the latter featuring Pink Floyd, and these were released on the French cinema circuit in June 1970. A clip of 'Careful With That Axe, Eugene' taken from the film

ABOVE: APPEARING AT BRUNEL UNIVERSITY, UXBRIDGE ON 28 NOVEMBER 1969. PINK FLOYD BECAME A POPULAR ATTRACTION ON THE UNIVERSITY CIRCUIT IN THE LATE SIXTIES AND EARLY SEVENTIES.

was shown on the music programme *Samedi et Compagnie* broadcast on ORTF1 on 30 May 1970 at 12.25pm. The film *Music Power* was shown in its entirety on ORTF2 on 24 September 1972 at 9.30pm.

Monday 27 October
CONCERT
Electric Garden, Glasgow, Scotland
Supported by The Stoics.

Friday 31 October
CANCELLED APPEARANCE
Black Magic & Rock & Roll, Olympia Stadium, Detroit, Michigan, USA
With Arthur Brown, The Frost, MC5, Amboy Dukes, The Bonzo Dog Doo-Dah Band, The Stooges, Coven, Kim Fowley, Alice Cooper, Sky, SRC, Bob Seger and many others. Because of contractual difficulties, Pink Floyd, like some of the other acts billed to appear, did not perform.

Saturday 1 November
CONCERT
Main Debating Hall, Manchester University, Manchester, England
Supported by Stone The Crows with Nova Express Lightshow.
Set list: 'Astronomy Dominé' / 'Green Is The Colour' / 'Careful With That Axe, Eugene'/ 'Interstellar Overdrive' / 'Cymbaline' / 'Set The Controls For The Heart Of The Sun' / 'A Saucerful Of Secrets' / 'Pow R Toc H'.
Manchester Independent, the Manchester University student newspaper, reported that: 'It is difficult to imagine the Pink Floyd who played the Free Trade Hall last term fitting their sound into MDH. The Azimuth co-ordinator should compete fairly strongly with the disco in the open lounge. The Floyd are certainly one of the most technically accomplished groups around, even if flying drumsticks are a feature of their act - their drummer's fingers are notoriously slippery. A packed MDH should prove an interesting animal with creaking doors and ominous footsteps all around it. Their performances are not just musical, but an initiation into the theatre of darkness - a goldmine of sound effects. The removal of the light-show from their act accentuates the sophistication of their sound.'

Friday 7 November
RECORD RELEASE
Ummagumma
UK album release. US album release on Saturday 8 November.
International Times commented that: 'These two albums are a really magnificent package. The first disc comprises four pieces from their live repertoire, beautifully played and really well produced by Norman Smith. I think it is probably one of the best live recordings I have ever heard.'

Friday 7 November
CONCERT
Main Hall, Waltham Forest Technical College, Walthamstow, London, England
Supported by Jan Dukes de Grey.
Set list: 'Astronomy Dominé' / 'Interstellar Overdrive' / 'Green Is The Colour' / 'Careful With That Axe, Eugene' / 'Set The Controls For The Heart Of The Sun' / 'A Saucerful Of Secrets' / encore: 'Let There Be More Light'.

Saturday 8 November
CONCERT
Refectory Hall, University Union, Leeds University, Leeds, England
Supported by The Idle Race.

Saturday 15 – Saturday 22 November
RECORDING SESSIONS
Technicolor Sound Services, Rome, Italy
Recording for the album *Zabriskie Point*.

Saturday 22 November
PRESS REPORT
London, England
It was reported in *NME* that Pink Floyd would be joining The Pretty Things and Steamhammer on a tour of West Germany, but Pink Floyd pulled out at the last minute due to recording commitments in Italy and were replaced by Fat Mattress. Fans at some venues were not informed of the change until they were inside the venues and in some cases violence broke out as a result. Known shows that were advertised included Messehalle, Nürnburg, Germany (21 November) and Star Club, Hamburg, Germany (23 November).

Wednesday 26 November
CONCERT
Friars Club, Queensway Hall, Civic Centre, Dunstable, England
Supported by Andy Dunkley with Optic Nerve Superlights.

Thursday 27 November
CONCERT
Mountford Hall, Liverpool University, Liverpool, England
Set list: 'Astronomy Dominé' / 'Green Is The Colour' / 'Careful With That Axe, Eugene' / *'The Man'* / 'Sysyphus' / 'Interstellar Overdrive' / 'Set The Controls For The Heart Of The Sun' / encore: 'A Saucerful Of Secrets'.
Guild Gazette, the Liverpool University student newspaper, reported that: 'The Floyd gave superb renderings of "A Saucerful Of Secrets" and "Set The Controls For The Heart Of The Sun", Richard Wright

giving an excellent piano solo in "Sysyphus", and we all enjoyed the chair-breaking and stage-bashing of Roger Waters which did seem to make some sense in the context of the musical violence. It was amazing, too, seeing him making those weird sounds with his mouth, when it might be thought that the Floyd sound is composed of electronic gimmickry. They are an experience of the Sixties, and will still lead the way for progressive music into the Seventies.'

Friday 28 November
CONCERT
Brunel University Arts Festival Weekend, Refectory Hall, Brunel University, Uxbridge, England
Supported by Gracious with Explosive Spectrum Lightshow.
Set list included: 'Astronomy Dominé' / 'Green Is The Colour' / 'Careful With That Axe, Eugene' / 'A Saucerful Of Secrets' / encore: 'Cymbaline'.

Sunday 30 November
CONCERT
The Lyceum, Strand, London, England
Supported by Audience and Cuby's Blues Band.

Saturday 6 December
CONCERT
Afan Festival of Progressive Music, Afan Lido Indoor Sports Centre, Port Talbot, Wales
Supporting Pentangle, with East of Eden, Sam Apple Pie, Samson, Daddy Long Legs and Solid State.
Set list: 'Interstellar Overdrive' / 'Green Is The Colour' / 'Careful With That Axe, Eugene' / 'Set The Controls For The Heart Of The Sun' / 'Cymbaline' / 'A Saucerful Of Secrets'.

Friday 12, Saturday 13 & Sunday 15 – Tuesday 17 December
RECORDING SESSIONS
EMI Studios, Abbey Road, St. John's Wood, London, England
Completion of recording for the album *Zabriskie Point*. Pink Floyd's first known studio leak resulted in the appearance of a bootleg album that contained outtakes from these sessions that are commonly known to collectors as 'Fingal's Cave', 'One One', 'Corrosion' and 'Rain In The Country'. An expanded soundtrack released by Rhino Records in 1997 included previously unreleased titles including 'Country Song', 'Unknown Song' and 'Love Scene (Versions 6 & 4)'. A further bootleg album released around this time included yet more tracks from the sessions including the previously unreleased 'Red Queen Theme', 'Blues Scene', 'Riot Scene' and 'Love Scene (Versions 1 to 6)'.

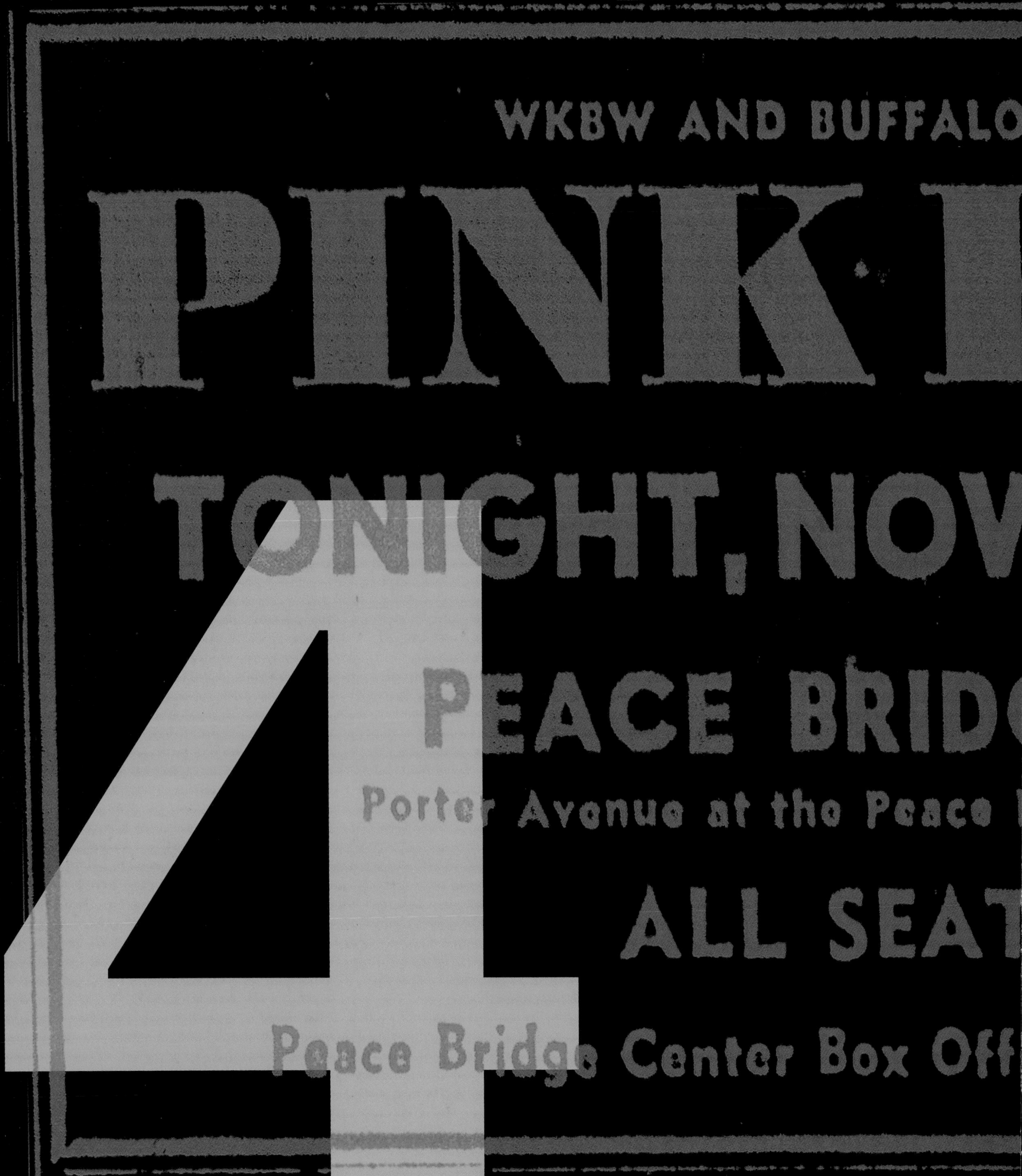

WKBW AND BUFFALO

PINK F

TONIGHT, NOV

4

PEACE BRIDG

Porter Avenue at the Peace

ALL SEAT

Peace Bridge Center Box Off

the sound of

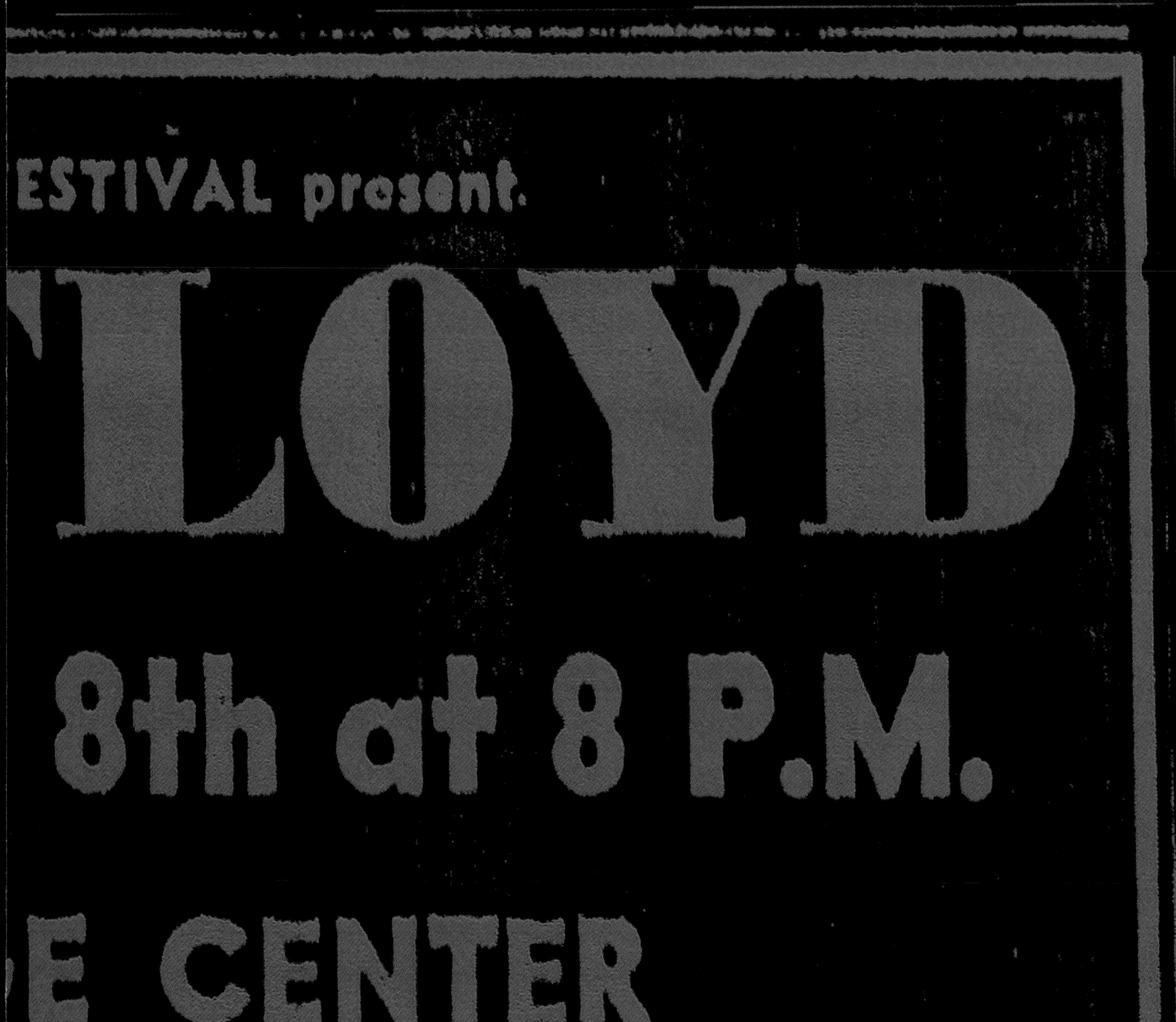

ESTIVAL present.

LOYD

8th at 8 P.M.

E CENTER

dge (Thruway Exit N-9)

$5.00

opens tonight at 6 P.M.

1970-1971

music in my ears

ON 5 FEBRUARY 1970 MICHELANGELO ANTONIONI'S FILM *ZABRISKIE POINT* WAS PREMIERED IN NEW YORK CITY AHEAD OF A GENERAL THEATRICAL RELEASE ON 9 FEBRUARY. IT RECEIVED EXTENSIVE PRESS COVERAGE AND WAS PROPELLED TO GREAT HEIGHTS PARTLY BECAUSE IT WAS ANTONIONI'S EAGERLY AWAITED FOLLOW-UP TO THE 1966 CULT CLASSIC *BLOW UP* AND PARTLY BECAUSE OF ITS FOCUS ON AMERICAN STUDENT REBELLION – A TOPIC OF MUCH CONCERN TO THE MEDIA OF THE DAY.

While it has not aged well in cinematic terms, it has achieved elevated status in rock music circles for one reason alone: Pink Floyd recorded some unique music for its soundtrack.

The band were invited by Antonioni to write, record and mix the entire film score at Technicolor Sound Services in Rome in just one week of sessions in November 1969. The director was present throughout the sessions and, according to Nick Mason, was an impossible man to work for: 'We'd start work at about nine [in the evening]. The studio was a few minutes walk down the road, so we'd stagger down the road. We could have finished the whole thing in about five days because there wasn't too much to do. Antonioni was there and we did some great stuff, but he'd listen and go, and I remember he had this terrible twitch, he'd go, "Eet's very beauteeful but eet's too sad" or "Eet's too strong." It was always wrong consistently. There was always something that stopped it being perfect. You'd still change whatever was wrong and he'd still be unhappy. It was hell. Sheer hell. He'd sit down and fall asleep every so often, and we'd go on working till about seven or eight in the morning.'[1]

'What our theory is,' reckoned Gilmour, 'is that he thought our music was too powerful and would have taken over from the film.'[2]

Eventually Antonioni called a halt to the sessions and settled for a selection of tracks that were then finished off and mixed by the band at EMI Abbey Road. This was then whittled down to just three numbers: 'Heart Beat, Pig Meat', an acoustic number reminiscent in style of the material found on *More*, 'Crumbling Land', an odd country-rock style number; and

'Come In Number 51 Your Time Is Up', a reworking of 'Careful with That Axe, Eugene'. This last track appeared to have been Antonioni's prime motive for choosing the band in the first place and he used the revamped version in the film's climax, when the heroine visualises a TV set and an expensive villa in Death Valley blowing up.

Like the band's previous soundtrack work, the released versions are quite different from those heard on the film, which for the most part appear as convenient edits; for instance, when a radio is switched on Pink Floyd comes blaring out. They also experienced a studio leak for the very first time, when three out-takes appeared on a bootleg album, *Omayyad*, under the assumed titles 'Oneone', 'Fingal's Cave' and 'Rain In The Country'. With the advent of a 1997 deluxe reissue of the film soundtrack on a double CD, four previously unreleased Pink Floyd out-takes were also revealed. And almost simultaneously, a 15-track bootleg CD of the complete sessions appeared that revealed additional works in progress, among them a track that was long referred to by the band as 'The Violent Sequence'. It was penned for a riot scene in the film and although unreleased in any form officially, was incorporated into their live set as an acoustic piano piece in the early part of the year. It was a forerunner to the melody of 'Us And Them', which featured on their 1973 album *Dark Side Of The Moon*.

Ultimately, their efforts were largely wasted, as Antonioni chose to fill the remaining soundtrack with a variety of previously released studio recordings by US artists, including The Grateful Dead, The Youngbloods and Kaleidoscope. Nevertheless, the film sparked off a massive wave of interest in Pink Floyd. Since *More* had

FAR RIGHT: DAVID GILMOUR ON STAGE AT THE THEATRE DES CHAMPS-ELYSÉES, PARIS ON 23 JANUARY 1970. FRANCE WAS ONE OF PINK FLOYD'S MOST POPULAR DESTINATIONS THANKS TO THEIR MANY TV APPEARANCES.

already been a big hit in America, this new exposure led to their first countrywide US tour.

It was also during this time that Gilmour began work on the production of Syd Barrett's second solo album, *Barrett*, and Waters embarked on his first solo project outside of Pink Floyd, collaborating with the avant-garde performer-composer Ron Geesin on a bizarre experimental documentary film called *The Body*. Nick Mason, who had met Geesin through a mutual friend, Sam Cutler, earlier in the year and had enjoyed socialising together, introduced them. When Mason introduced Geesin to Waters, they hit it off instantly – both were ideas men, and in a short space of time they became good friends and golfing partners. It was a natural choice for Geesin to turn to Waters when a lyricist was required for his next project.

'It was intended to be a new style of making a documentary feature,' recalled Geesin, 'a stimulatory film.

RON GEESIN << **I could see the orchestra tuning up and the band playing in all bloody directions, playing different tunes, because I'm not a conductor, simply because I'm self taught. Conductors are now essential in modern music.** >>

The idea in a fundamental way was to get something good with not very much, the ideal was that if you can express everything in a single melody, and variations, that would be very good. But I don't know what they replaced it with because I never actually saw it. The distributors had had an early sight and said it was too radical for their market, to tame it down, so they added some commentary. Roy Battersby, the director was forced to get his mate Vanessa Redgrave, who was in the Workers Revolutionary Party, and they did lots of pansy, posey stuff over it, poems and things, that took the whole heat out of it.'[3]

It was not widely known until recently that the other members of Pink Floyd also appear on the album – on the final track, 'Give Birth To A Smile' – for which they were paid as session musicians and remain uncredited. Waters and Geesin both wanted a four-piece band, and the others willingly obliged, "You want a big sound," Geesin remembers them saying, "well here we are!"' [4]

Back on the touring circuit, during the early months of 1970 Pink Floyd had begun to tour with the

aforementioned out-take from *Zabriskie Point*, 'The Violent Sequence'; some reworked tracks from the studio half of *Ummagumma*, and two new numbers, one of which was called 'The Embryo'. This had first been worked on in the studio during the latter part of 1968 and a version had been recorded for a BBC session in December of that year. The track is surrounded by a certain amount of controversy since it was never officially sanctioned by the band for release, although it is said that a studio recording was unwittingly authorised by then Harvest label manager, Malcolm Jones, for inclusion on the sampler album *Picnic*. Except for its appearance on the 1983 Capitol Records Floyd compilation *Works*, the track has remained unreleased, and *Picnic* is now something of a rarity. Surprisingly, given their reluctance to see it released, the band often played the song live during the early Seventies.

The other number the band had started to work on in the early part of 1970 was an untitled instrumental which in later months became known as 'Atom Heart Mother'. The track was initiated entirely in the studio and would eventually fill one side of their new album of the same title, where it featured a ten-piece choir.

In its earliest live performance it incorporated a lengthy drum solo and featured Gilmour and Wright vocalising on what would develop into the familiar choral section. By March, a basic studio recording had been made at Abbey Road, featuring Waters and Mason on bass and drums.

At this stage Geesin was invited to help out with the track. 'Roger proposed to me that I should help Floyd with their next album. He said he would like me to write the brass and choir pieces... Floyd were off to the States then, and Roger left me with a skeleton tape of rhythm and chords. It was to be a twenty-five minute piece – and that's a hell of a lot of work... Nobody knew what was wanted, they couldn't read music.'[5]

With time running short, having completed a not insignificant tour of the UK, Europe and their longest US tour and a series of French festival dates booked over the summer months plus a second US tour scheduled for the autumn, the piece had to be recorded fast. As Geesin recalled: 'Dave proposed strict ideas for melodies, and then we did the choir section together, both at keyboards collaborating with Rick. We all had sleepless nights, worrying about what was going on... Well, it got done,

but then the thing had to be recorded with the brass band, orchestra and choir.'[6]

It was here that Geesin ran into trouble and came close to a complete breakdown. The pressure of work was piling up and the cantankerous nature of some of the orchestral musicians was driving him to despair. 'I could see the orchestra tuning up and the band playing in all bloody directions, playing different tunes, because I'm not a conductor, simply because I'm self taught. Conductors are now essential in modern music. I was incapable of telling them what to do. Things were looking terrible, nobody knew what was going to happen. But then John Aldiss, who was in charge of the best modern choir in the classical area, came to collect the choir parts, and saw our plight. I became advisor, and he the conductor.'[7]

Even Gilmour couldn't help but notice the problems Geesin was facing with the orchestra. 'In the studio they were pretty annoying sometimes; they always used to rush off to the canteen whenever they had the chance, and split right on the dot when the session was over. Towards the end of recording the album it all seemed to get a bit warped. Some of it seems a bit messy, when I listen to it now little things jump out at

me and I think, "Shouldn't have done that."'[8]

Although Pink Floyd had been performing the piece for some months, the official premiere of 'Atom Heart Mother' took place at the Bath Festival in June, with, for the first time on stage, a full orchestra and choir. This was one of only a handful of occasions over the next year when a brass and choir section would accompany the band live.

The piece was announced as 'The Amazing Pudding' since they still hadn't figured out a suitable title. When the time came to choose one it was all done in the usual comedic fashion: The band were previewing a performance of the piece for a live John Peel BBC Radio One concert session at the BBC Paris Cinema on 16 July, two days before their Hyde Park concert and the title had to be registered for royalties as well as Peel having something by which to introduce the piece. Geesin explained: 'We were sitting in the control room and John Peel had his newspaper [*The Evening Standard*] and we were sitting round with Nick, Roger and the others. I think they were all there saying, "We haven't got a title for this", and I said, "If you look in there you'll find a title", and then Roger picked up the paper and said, "Atom Heart Mother" and the others said, "Yeah, that

ABOVE: PINK FLOYD PHOTOGRAPHED IN LONDON, SUMMER 1971.

sounds good.'"[9] The headline appears on page 9 of the 16 July edition and reads, 'The Atom Heart Mother Is Named' and refers to 56 year-old Mrs. Constance Ladell who received Britain's first plutonium based pacemaker.

Gilmour spoke at the time of the problems in taking the new work on the road: 'Something on the scale of 'Atom Heart Mother' really takes a lot of getting together. The problem is that we've never done it more than twice with the same people. The choir is usually all right because they're used to working together, but some of the brass people have been really hopeless. We had problems with the sound equipment, getting it miked up and balanced and stuff. The trouble was also not having enough rehearsal time everywhere we did it, because we used a different brass and choir group in Europe than the one we used on the East Coast, and another one on the West Coast. So we used three completely different sets of people performing it. We tried to hire musicians from local symphonies, so we'd just get the session musicians.

ROGER WATERS   << **We were all frantically trying to write songs, and initially I thought of just doing something on the rhythm of a dripping tap, then it turned into this whole kitchen thing.** >>

We found our conductor, Peter Philips, by coming over and looking for someone a couple of months before the tour...'[10]

The album *Atom Heart Mother* has contributions from each member of the band except Mason, who is only part-composer of the title track. There are only four other numbers on the album, three of which have a very summery, bluesy feel to them: Waters' 'If' (performed rarely at this time, but more frequently on his later solo tours); Wright's 'Summer '68'; and Gilmour's 'Fat Old Sun', which was performed live throughout the year, and had been written at the same time as Waters' 'Grantchester Meadows'.

The closing track, 'Alan's Psychedelic Breakfast', is a typical but flawed Floyd experimentation. As Waters explained: 'It was the usual thing of an idea coming out of the fact that we'd almost finished an LP but not quite and we needed another so many minutes. We were all frantically trying to write songs, and initially I thought of just doing something on the rhythm of a dripping tap,

RIGHT: PINK FLOYD ON STAGE AT BILL GRAHAM'S FILLMORE EAST, NEW YORK ON 27 SEPTEMBER 1970. EARLIER IN THE YEAR GRAHAM'S LACK OF CONFIDENCE IN THEIR DRAW RESULTED IN THE BAND HAVING TO HIRE THE VENUE FROM HIM.

then it turned into this whole kitchen thing. On the record it's a carefully set up stereo picture of a kitchen with somebody coming in, opening a window, filling a kettle and putting it on the stove. But instead of the gas lighting, there's a chord, so he strikes a match and there's another chord, and so on until it finally goes into a piece of music.'[11]

The kitchen sounds, along with an amusing conversation with Alan Styles, one of the band's roadies, were recorded for the most part in Mason's kitchen. The music was added at Abbey Road. Because of its novelty, the track was rarely performed live – only a handful of UK shows in the run-up to Christmas featured it. Waters was anticipating the problems it would cause when he spoke to *Sounds* about it shortly before the tour: 'The logistics of doing it live are quite difficult – we can't obviously take a set of a kitchen round with us and do it all, but we'll have to have some table arrangement to fry eggs on and boil kettles and everything.' This was a task eventually left to the roadies, who, to the accompaniment of BBC broadcaster and DJ Jimmy Young's trademark 'Oft we jolly well go', fried eggs and bacon and made tea on stage. To round off the festive spirit, Mason often dressed up as Father Christmas.

The album's title track also caught the attention of Stanley Kubrick, who wanted to use the music in his adaptation of Anthony Burgess's novel *A Clockwork Orange*. 'He wanted to use 'Atom Heart Mother', said Waters, 'and chop and change it about. He just phoned up and said that he wanted it and we said, "Well, what do you want to do?" and he didn't know, he just said he wanted to use it, "How I want – when I want". And we said right away, "Right, you can't use it."'[12] It is difficult to imagine the film carrying this music – maybe it is just as well it wasn't used after all.

Atom Heart Mother, with its striking sleeve picture of a cow, was in keeping with Pink Floyd's already established sense of the absurd. Posters for the album depicted herds of cattle on The Mall in London (which was supposedly closed at dawn to create the image). The success of the promotion played a part in gaining the band their very first number one in the UK album chart.

With 1971 barely started there was already mounting pressure on Pink Floyd to release new product hot on the heels of the success of *Atom Heart Mother*. Losing little time, they entered the studio in early January for their usual round of brainstorming sessions. It was the first time they were not contractually obliged to use EMI's facilities at Abbey Road and much of the recording of the new album, *Meddle*, took place at Air,

Command and Morgan Sound studios.

Recognising how long it would take the band to record the album, not least because of their live commitments, which would see extensive touring in the UK, Europe and US but also debut shows in Australia and Japan, EMI decided to sate the appetite of eager fans in the meantime by releasing a budget-priced compilation entitled *Relics – A Collection Of Bizarre Antiques And Curios*. Released in May, this stop-gap album, with a cover illustration by Mason, contained a collection of works from the band's early years, single tracks available for the first time since their deletion and a previously unreleased number, 'Biding My Time'.

The initial *Meddle* sessions at Abbey Road produced some remarkable work. Extending the ideas they had applied on 'Alan's Psychedelic Breakfast', the band proposed making a whole album without using any musical instruments whatsoever. It was a complicated process involving the use of kitchen utensils, bottles, cutlery, glasses, lampshades and even sawing up bits of wood, to replicate conventional sounds.

But the 'household objects' project, as it is often referred to, was never to come to fruition. Despite efforts to revive the idea in 1974, Gilmour felt that it wasn't worth the time and trouble required to complete even the most basic of sequences: 'We actually built a thing with a stretched rubber band this long [about two feet]. There was a g-clamp this end fixing it to a table and this end there was a cigarette lighter for a bridge. And then there

was a set of matchsticks taped down this end. You stretch it and you can get a really good bass sound. Oh, and we used aerosol sprays and pulling rolls of Sellotape out to different lengths – the further away it gets the note changes. We got three or four tracks down. It'd be very hard to make any of them really work as a piece of genuine music.'[13] And contrary to popular belief, it wasn't entirely dispensed with as Gilmour later recalled: 'We did actually use some of the household objects – the wine glasses were in some of the music at the beginning of the *Wish You Were Here* album.'[14]

In addition, the sounds were almost impossible to reproduce live, so it is hardly surprising that the band finally shelved their work on the project.

Over the next few weeks their collective brain developed an epic twenty-minute track with the working title 'Nothing – Parts 1 to 24'. Collecting together twenty-four completely unconnected pieces of music, and using many ideas from the previous sessions, they worked the piece into shape and performed it live for the first time in April as 'Return Of The Son Of Nothing'. The piece had this title for some months until, when released as a full side of *Meddle*, it was retitled 'Echoes'.

Many fans regard this track as Pink Floyd's masterpiece – a calling card for legions of stoned freaks, the ultimate stereophonic blast-off into inner space both in concert and on vinyl. The band's last great outing into the realms of science-fiction fantasy, it was to prove a live favourite for many years to come and was even used in the classic 1973 Australian surfing film *Crystal Voyager* to accompany spectacular underwater shots and wave tunnels – film of which would later accompany their live performances of 'The Great Gig In The Sky' throughout 1974 and 1975.

• Only one other track remains a standout: 'One Of These Days'. Another live stalwart, this pounding, bass-driven instrumental was developed from a studio experiment that originally featured a vocal tape loop of the venerable Jimmy Young and the BBC Radiophonic Workshop's theme for the TV show *Dr. Who*. The track features a rare Mason lead vocal, a garbled one-liner: 'One of these days I'm going to cut you into little pieces', before launching into slide-guitar mayhem. Incidentally, Young was again the butt of Pink Floyd's stoned humour when they chopped up tape recordings of his commentary on his *Family Favourites* BBC2 radio show to make hilarious and nonsensical introductions to their shows throughout the early Seventies.

By comparison, the remaining tracks are subdued and very reminiscent of the material on *Atom Heart Mother*, none of which were ever performed live. 'Fearless' is a successful experiment which segues a football crowd singing the terrace anthem 'You'll Never Walk Alone' into the last few seconds of the song – a reminder of Pink Floyd's collective passion for the sport.

To close side one of the album, another throwaway number, typical of the band's sense of humour when it came to improvisation, featured a howling Irish Wolfhound for lead vocals. 'Dave was looking after Seamus while Steve Marriott [the dog's owner, who was on tour with Humble Pie] was in the States, and he used to bring him into the sessions,' explained Waters, 'and one day he said, "There's something I meant to show you – this dog sings", and he got a harmonica out and blew it at the dog, and as soon as the dog hears a harmonica it starts howling. So we all thought we'd do a short 12-bar and stick him on it.'[15]

Meddle was released in November and featured another Hipgnosis sleeve design featuring a close-up photograph of an ear slightly submerged in rippling water. The gatefold inner sleeve also featured a black and white portrait of the band – the last time Pink Floyd would be visually identified on an album for some sixteen years, an absence which increased their mystique with the public.

With *Meddle* only recently wrapped up and their second US tour of that year just around the corner, the band linked up with Adrian Maben, a French film director backed by German money, who planned to film

them in concert. Keen to avoid the usual 'rockumentary' style presentation, together they hit upon the idea of the band performing without an audience against the spectacular backdrop of the ancient Roman amphitheatre at Pompeii in Italy.

Filming for *Pink Floyd Live At Pompeii* took place between 4 and 7 October 1971 in weather that was still fairly warm. The entire stage set-up was located inside the dusty ruined amphitheatre and complete concert run-throughs, performed live day and night, were successfully filmed.

The most popular numbers from the band's current repertoire were used. These included 'Echoes' (split into two halves to open and close the film), 'Careful With That Axe, Eugene', 'A Saucerful Of Secrets', 'Set The Controls For The Heart Of The Sun', 'One Of These Days (I'm Going To Cut You Into Little Pieces)' and 'Mademoiselle Knobs'. This last track, a retitling of 'Seamus', is an hilarious sequence in which Wright holds the microphone up to the infamous howling dog while Gilmour blasts away on his harmonica.

Some additional live sequences and overdubs, including the above, were shot at Studio Europasinor in Paris between 13 and 20 December and further material from an early 1972 recording at Abbey Road which featured the band at work on what would become *The Dark Side Of The Moon* was added. Finally, and to much surprise, the film opened with that album's prelude, 'Speak To Me', which sets the scene by combining images of the ruined city and the band's road crew assembling their array of equipment. Interspersed throughout the film are brief candid interviews with the band also filmed at Abbey Road. *Pink Floyd Live At Pompeii* was finally previewed at the Edinburgh Film Festival in the summer of 1972, to rave reviews. An official public premiere was then scheduled at the Rainbow Theatre on 24 November but was cancelled on the night due to a contractual glitch and the film, remarkably, didn't see a general theatrical release until the summer of 1974.

As 1971 drew to a close, Pink Floyd's touring schedule was already stretching well into the latter half of 1972. However, they were very aware that their stage material was becoming rather stale – a point that hadn't escaped the music press – and decided to apply themselves to the task of composing an entirely new set of numbers for their imminent UK tour. Free for the moment from pressure to record a new album, they could perfect new material on the road more extensively than they had been able to do so in the past, before going into the studio.

THE SOUND OF MUSIC IN MY EARS 1970-1971

LEFT: PINK FLOYD APPEARING AT THE SPORTPALAST, WEST BERLIN ON 5 JUNE 1971. DESPITE EXTENSIVE TOURING THROUGHOUT WEST GERMANY IN THE SEVENTIES, THE BAND NEVER PERFORMED IN ITS CAPITAL CITY, BONN.

OVERLEAF: PINK FLOYD PHOTOGRAPHED IN LONDON, SUMMER 1971. THE SAME SERIES OF IMAGES WERE USED TO PUBLICISE PINK FLOYD'S UK TOUR OF JANUARY AND FEBRUARY 1972.

Sources
1. *Disc*, 23 August 1975
2. *Beetle*, May 1973
3-7. Authors' interview with Ron Geesin, 16 July 1994
8. Unidentified press article.
9. Authors' interview with Ron Geesin, 16 July 1994
10. *Music Now*, 28 November 1970; *Beetle*, May 1973
11. *Sounds*, 10 October 1970
12. *Great Lake*, April 1973
13. *Sounds*, 1 June 1974
14. *House of Wax*, BBC Radio One, 26 November 1988
15. *NME*, 11 December 1971

1970

PINK FLOYD ROAD CREW THROUGH TO SEPTEMBER 1970

Bobby Richardson: Technician / Stage Crew
Brian Scott: Technician / Stage Crew
Alan Styles: Technician / Stage Crew
Peter Watts: Tour Manager / Front of House Sound

Saturday 10 January
CONCERT
The Ballroom, University of Nottingham, Beeston, Nottingham, England
Set list: 'Astronomy Dominé' / 'Set The Controls For The Heart Of The Sun' / 'Green Is The Colour' / 'Careful With That Axe, Eugene' / 'A Saucerful Of Secrets'.
Both *Time Out* and *NME* incorrectly listed Pink Floyd to be appearing at this venue on 22 October 1969.

Saturday 17 January
CONCERT
Lawns Centre, Cottingham, Hull, England
Presented by Hull University.
Set list included: 'Astronomy Dominé' / 'Green Is The Colour' / 'Careful With That Axe, Eugene' / 'Atom Heart Mother'* / 'Set The Controls For The Heart Of The Sun' / encore: 'A Saucerful Of Secrets'.

*This number has been titled retrospectively for identification purposes; the title was not formally adopted until 16 July 1970 and was often introduced at shows as "a new untitled piece."

Sunday 18 January
CONCERT
Fairfield Halls, Croydon, England
Set list: 'Careful With That Axe, Eugene' / 'The Embryo' / 'Main Theme' from *More* / 'Biding My Time' / 'Astronomy Dominé' / 'The Violent Sequence' / 'Set The Controls For The Heart Of The Sun' / 'Atom Heart Mother' / encore: 'A Saucerful Of Secrets'.
Croydon Advertiser reported that: 'There was a standing ovation, there was an encore... Make no mistake, Pink Floyd are good. More than that, they are originals, and have been so since earlier days when they practically invented psychedelia. They are individually adept as musicians and command a range of instruments, Rick Wright for instance played organ, piano, trombone and vibraphone at Sunday's concert. Anything can be legitimately used in creating the atmosphere: recourse to heavy timpani, violent assault on cymbal, flogging a gargantuan gong and insistent thumping of fingers on microphones. Pink Floyd are obsessed with the mystery of outer space - "Set The Controls For The Heart Of The Sun" and "Interstellar Overdrive" are two titles - and portray it with imagination. Yet the fact remains that their concert on Sunday was marred by repetitive phrasing, by long unmelodic passages, by monotony... Perhaps with the lighting effects they have abandoned the sterile patches would not have been so noticeable... Still it was a long concert- nearly three hours - for Messrs. Waters, Wright, Mason and Gilmore to fill. I liked particularly, the contributions of Wright, including funereal excursions of organ playing in the traumatic "Saucerful Of Secrets" and his unhurried, halcyon piano in "Niagara Dellof"[*], which was like a respite from a storm - and which was deservedly applauded. Drummer Nick Mason has said: "People have the confidence that if we do something extraordinary, it's quite likely not to be a giant con and there's some purpose or meaning behind it." Certainly not a 'con' - but the end product was lamentably, just lacking.'
*Note: 'Niagra Dellof' is a title that has not appeared in any other reference to the bands' output. Although it may have been introduced as such at this concert this could be a reference to 'The Violent Sequence'.

Monday 19 January
CONCERT
The Dome, Brighton, England
Set list included: 'Careful With That Axe, Eugene' / 'The Embryo' / 'Main Theme' from *More* / 'Atom Heart Mother' / 'Astronomy Dominé' / 'Set The Controls For The Heart Of The Sun' / 'A Saucerful Of Secrets'.

Friday 23 January
CONCERT
Theatre des Champs-Elysées, Elysée, Paris, France
Set list: 'Green Is The Colour' / 'Careful With That Axe, Eugene' / 'The Violent Sequence' / 'Biding My Time' / 'Atom Heart Mother' / 'Daybreak' / 'Sleeping' / 'Main Theme' from *More* / 'A Saucerful Of Secrets'.

Saturday 24 January
CONCERT
Theatre des Champs-Elysées, Elysée, Paris, France
Set list included: 'The Man' / 'Set The Controls For The Heart Of The Sun'.

RICHARD WRIGHT AND ROGER WATERS ON STAGE AT THE PALAIS DES SPORTS, LYON, 2 FEBRUARY 1970.

Monday 2 February
CONCERT
Palais des Sports, Lyon, France
Set list included: 'The Man' // 'Astronomy Dominé' / 'The Violent Sequence' / 'Set The Controls For The Heart Of The Sun'.
Europe 1 radio reportedly recorded this show but the content and broadcast details remain unknown.

Thursday 5 February
CONCERT
Cardiff Arts Centre Project Benefit Concert, Sophia Gardens Pavilion, Cardiff, Wales
With Quintessence, Daddy Longlegs, Gary Farr, Heaven, Ron Geesin, Tea & Symphony and Black Sabbath.

Saturday 7 February
CONCERT
Royal Albert Hall, Kensington, London, England
Set list: 'The Embryo' / 'Main Theme' from *More* / 'Careful With That Axe, Eugene' / 'Sysyphus' // 'The Violent Sequence' / 'Atom Heart Mother' / 'Set The Controls For The Heart Of The Sun' / encore: 'A Saucerful Of Secrets'.

Sunday 8 February
CONCERT
Opera House, Manchester, England
Set list: 'The Embryo' / 'Careful With That Axe, Eugene' / 'Main Theme' from *More* / 'Sysyphus' / 'Atom Heart Mother' / 'Set The Controls For The Heart Of The Sun' / 'Astronomy Dominé'.

Wednesday 11 February
CONCERT
Town Hall, Birmingham, England
Set list: 'The Embryo' / 'Main Theme' from *More* / 'Careful With That Axe, Eugene' / 'Sysyphus' / 'improvisations' / 'The Violent Sequence' / 'Set The Controls For The Heart Of The Sun' / 'Atom Heart Mother'.

Saturday 14 February
CONCERT
King's Hall, Town Hall, Stoke-on-Trent, England
Presented by North Staffordshire Polytechnic.

Sunday 15 February
CONCERT
Empire Theatre, Liverpool, England
Set list: 'The Embryo' / 'Careful With That Axe, Eugene' / 'Main Theme' from *More* / 'Atom Heart Mother' / 'Astronomy Dominé' / 'Interstellar Overdrive' / 'Set The Controls For The Heart Of The Sun' / 'A Saucerful Of Secrets'.

Tuesday 17 February
CONCERT
City Hall, Newcastle-upon-Tyne, England

Sunday 22 February
CONCERT
Electric Garden, Glasgow, Scotland
Set list included: 'A Saucerful Of Secrets' / 'Set The Controls For The Heart Of The Sun'.

Monday 23 February
CONCERT
McEwan Hall, University of Edinburgh, Edinburgh, Scotland

Saturday 28 February
CONCERT
Endsville '70, Refectory Hall, University Union, Leeds University, Leeds, England
Supported by Heavy Jelly.
Set list: 'The Embryo' / 'Careful With That Axe, Eugene' / 'Set The Controls For The Heart Of The Sun' / 'Atom Heart Mother' / 'A Saucerful Of Secrets' / encore: 'Interstellar Overdrive'.

Sunday 1 - Thursday 5 March
RECORDING SESSIONS
EMI Studios, Abbey Road, St. John's Wood, London, England
Recording for the album '*Atom Heart Mother*.

Thursday 5 March
TV SHOW
Studio B, BBC TV Centre, White City, London, England
Pink Floyd recorded some original live music (logged as 'Zabriskie Point' in the BBC archives) for the magazine programme *Line Up*. It was broadcast on BBC2 on 13 March at 11.10pm.

Friday 6 March
CONCERT
Great Hall, College Block, Imperial College, Kensington, London, England
Supported by Juicy Lucy with Tom & Jerry cartoons shown between bands.
Set list included: 'Atom Heart Mother' / 'Set The Controls For The Heart Of The Sun' / 'A Saucerful Of Secrets'.

Saturday 7 March
CONCERT
University of Bristol Arts Festival – Timespace, Colston Hall, Bristol, England
Pink Floyd commenced their show at 3.00pm. The Who were originally advertised to perform in the evening at 8.00pm but did not appear.
Set list included: 'Main Theme' from *More*.
'The Floyd's Saturday show was something from an underground siesta. Tea time at the weekend isn't exactly the right moment to suffer the violence and intensity of a Floyd concert (it commenced at 3.00pm). Their music's so involving, sometimes overpowering, that the time of day should have been a positive disadvantage. It didn't matter too much however. They somehow generated the right enthusiasm and turned a lazy afternoon into a full, now and again, frightening experience. This show had its faults. The volume on a couple of their disturbing

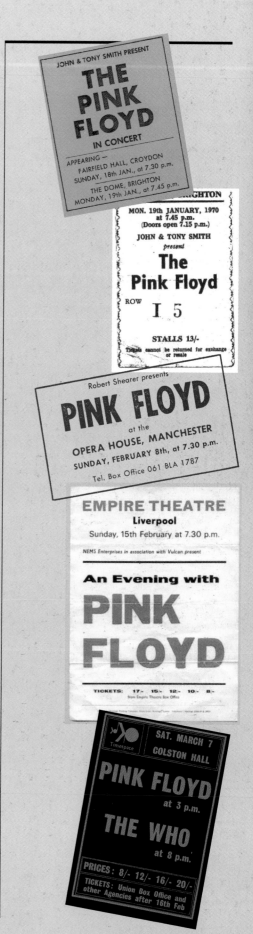

129

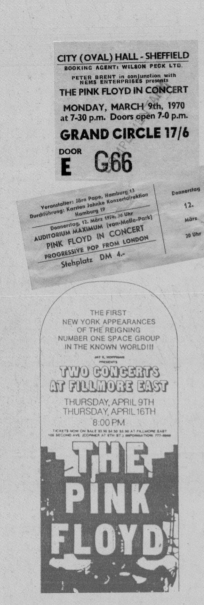

destructive numbers was quite terrifying, enough to make you feel physically ill. Maybe that's what they were after. But in their melancholy numbers - particularly the "Main Theme" from *More* - they created a sumptuous atmosphere of sadness and regret. The music was effective and it was a thoughtful, worthwhile show.' (Review from *Bristol Evening Post*)

Sunday 8 March
CONCERT
Mothers, Erdington, Birmingham, England
Set list: 'The Embryo' / 'A Saucerful Of Secrets' / 'Set The Controls For The Heart Of The Sun' / 'Careful With That Axe, Eugene' / 'Astronomy Dominé' / 'Atom Heart Mother' / encore: 'Blues' *.
*Note: Where 'Blues' appears as a track listing it is merely an improvised 12-bar blues instrumental, a common and often impromptu addition to Pink Floyd's set throughout the next few years.

Monday 9 March
CONCERT
City (Oval) Hall, Sheffield, England

EUROPEAN TOUR

Wednesday 11 March
CONCERT
Stadthalle, Offenbach, West Germany
Set list: 'Astronomy Dominé' / 'Green Is The Colour' / 'Careful With That Axe, Eugene' / 'Cymbaline' / 'A Saucerful Of Secrets' / 'Interstellar Overdrive' / 'Set The Controls For The Heart Of The Sun' / 'Atom Heart Mother'.

Thursday 12 March
CONCERT
Kleiner Saal, Auditorium Maximum, Hamburg Universität, Hamburg, West Germany
Set list: 'Astronomy Dominé' / 'Careful With

That Axe, Eugene' / 'Cymbaline' / 'A Saucerful Of Secrets' / 'The Embryo' / 'Interstellar Overdrive' / 'Set The Controls For The Heart Of The Sun' / 'Atom Heart Mother'.

Friday 13 March
CONCERTS
Konzert Saal, Technische Universität, West Berlin, West Germany
Two shows at 8.00pm and 10.00pm
Set list 10.00pm show: 'Astronomy Dominé' / 'Careful With That Axe, Eugene' / 'Cymbaline' / 'A Saucerful Of Secrets' / 'The Embryo' / 'Interstellar Overdrive' / 'Set The Controls For The Heart Of The Sun' / 'Atom Heart Mother' / encore: 'Blues'.

Saturday 14 March
CONCERT
Meistersinger Halle, Nürnberg, West Germany
Set list: 'Astronomy Dominé' / 'Careful With That Axe, Eugene' / 'Cymbaline' / 'A Saucerful Of Secrets' / 'The Embryo' / 'Interstellar Overdrive' / 'Set The Controls For The Heart Of The Sun' / 'Atom Heart Mother'.

Sunday 15 March
CONCERT
Niedersachsenhalle, Hannover, West Germany
Set list: 'Astronomy Dominé' / 'Careful With That Axe, Eugene' / 'Cymbaline' / 'A Saucerful Of Secrets' / 'The Embryo' / 'Interstellar Overdrive' / 'Set The Controls For The Heart Of The Sun' / 'Atom Heart Mother' (announced by Roger Waters as 'Consequently').

Wednesday 18 March
FILM PREMIERE
Coronet Theater, Manhattan, New York City, New York, USA
The premiere of the film *Zabriskie Point*.

Thursday 19 March
CONCERT
Stora Salen, Konserthuset, Stockholm, Sweden
Show rescheduled from Gothenberg on 18 March.
Set list included: 'Interstellar Overdrive' / 'Main Theme' from *More* / 'A Saucerful Of Secrets' / 'Atom Heart Mother'.

Friday 20 March
CONCERT
Akademiska Föreningens Stora Sal, Lund, Sweden
Set list: 'Astronomy Dominé' / 'Careful With That Axe, Eugene' / 'Cymbaline' / 'A Saucerful Of Secrets' / 'The Embryo' / 'Interstellar Overdrive' / 'Set The Controls For The Heart Of The Sun' / 'Atom Heart Mother'.

Saturday 21 March
CONCERT
Tivolis Koncertsal, Copenhagen, Denmark
The last night of the tour.
Set list included: 'A Saucerful Of Secrets' / 'Interstellar Overdrive' / 'Set The Controls For The Heart Of The Sun'.

Wednesday 25 – Sunday 29 March
RECORDING SESSIONS
EMI Studios, Abbey Road, St. John's Wood, London, England
Recording for the album *Atom Heart Mother*.

Monday 30 March
CONCERT
Le Festival Musique Evolution, Le Bourget (Aéroport de Paris), Siene St. Denis, France
Also appearing were Ginger Baker's Airforce, Procol Harum, Kevin Ayers And The Whole World, Keith Relf's Renaissance, Hawkwind, Edgar Broughton Band, Skin Alley and Le Voyage among others.
Set list: 'Astronomy Dominé' / 'Careful With That Axe, Eugene' / 'Cymbaline' / 'A Saucerful Of Secrets' / 'The Embryo' / 'Interstellar Overdrive' / 'Set The Controls For The Heart Of The Sun'.
This, the first officially sanctioned music festival in France, was staged in an aircraft hangar. It promised to be quite an event, with many top name bands performing with film shows, light shows, cheap food, camping and a 'pop village' with market stalls. As it turned out, two adjoining stages accommodated the live entertainment, but little else materialised. Repeatedly, groups were not ready to play, leaving an audience that was far smaller than anticipated listening to impromptu jams by roadies and stray musicians. In addition, food prices were inflated and no authorisation was given for camping, so that those who did try to pitch tents were evicted by the police. Cold winds blasted through the hangar, which now doubled as accommodation. Pink Floyd performed to a crowd of some 8,000 fans sandwiched between Kevin Ayers and Edgar Broughton, who closed the show to a fast dwindling audience. RTL radio and French TV reportedly recorded parts of this show although the content and broadcast details remain unknown.

Wednesday 1 - Monday 6 April
RECORDING SESSIONS
EMI Studios, Abbey Road, St. John's Wood, London, England
Recording for the album *Atom Heart Mother*. During April and May Ron Geesin worked on the musical score for the orchestrations on the album.

NORTH AMERICAN TOUR
Early drafts of Pink Floyd's tour show the band scheduled to appear at San Diego, California, USA (9 May); Kansas, Missouri, USA (24 May); Aragon Ballroom, Chicago, Illinois, USA (29 & 30 May) and Ludlow Garage, Cincinnati, Ohio, USA (5 & 6 June).

Thursday 9 April
CONCERT
Fillmore East, Manhattan, New York City, New York, USA
Set list: 'Grantchester Meadows' / 'Careful With That Axe, Eugene' / 'Cymbaline' / 'Atom Heart Mother' / 'The Embryo' / 'Set The Controls For The Heart Of The Sun' / encore: 'Interstellar Overdrive'.

Friday 10 April
CONCERT
Aragon Ballroom, Chicago, Illinois, USA
With Rotary Connection, Mason Proffit and Litter.

Saturday 11 April
CONCERT
The Gymnasium, State University of New York, Stony Brook, Long Island, New York, USA
Set list: 'Astronomy Dominé' / 'Careful With That Axe, Eugene' / 'Cymbaline' / 'Atom Heart Mother' / 'Set The Controls For The Heart Of The Sun' / 'A Saucerful Of Secrets'.

Sunday 12 April
CONCERT
Boston Tea Party, Boston, Massachusetts, USA

Thursday 16 April
CONCERT
Fillmore East, Manhattan, New York City, New York, USA
Set list: 'Grantchester Meadows' / 'Astronomy Dominé' / 'Main Theme' from *More* / 'The Violent Sequence' / 'Atom Heart Mother' / 'Set The Controls For The Heart Of The Sun' / encore: 'A Saucerful Of Secrets'.
Billboard reported that: 'Pink Floyd, one of the most distinctive British musical groups, gave a lengthy and imaginative show at Fillmore East. The quartet demonstrated its mastery of sound with speakers at the sides and rear of the theatre and a range from opening acoustic guitars to the most amplified of effects, including tape. Richard Wright on organ, grand piano and 'azimuth co-ordinator' was a key to

the units success. The co-ordinator proved an exceptional electronic device with a variety of effects. A gong, a trademark of this quartet, also was much in evidence as played by bass guitarist Roger Waters, who also played cymbals, aiding drummer Nick Mason, whose playing also was exceptional. Lead guitarist David Gilmour also was in top form. In fact, the entire group gave one of its best performances with such material as "Saucerful Of Secrets" and "Set The Controls For The Heart Of The Sun". An untitled number from the next album was also top-notch as were soundtrack numbers from *More* and *Zabriskie Point*, the latter a number cut out from the film.'

Friday 17 & Saturday 18 April
CONCERTS
Electric Factory, Philadelphia, Pennsylvania, USA
Two shows, at 8.00pm and 11.00pm. Supported by Insect Trust.

Wednesday 22 April
CONCERT
Capitol Theatre, Port Chester, New York, USA
Set List: 'Grantchester Meadows' / 'Astronomy Dominé' / 'Cymbaline' / 'Atom Heart Mother' / 'The Embryo' / 'Green Is The Colour' / 'Careful With That Axe, Eugene' / 'Set The Controls For The Heart Of The Sun' / 'A Saucerful Of Secrets' / encore: 'Interstellar Overdrive'.

Friday 24 & Saturday 25 April
CONCERT
Eastown Theatre, Detroit, Michigan, USA
With The Frost and The Up.

Tuesday 28 April
TV SHOW
KQED TV Studios, San Francisco, California, USA
Set list: 'Atom Heart Mother' / 'Cymbaline' / 'Grantchester Meadows' / 'Green Is The Colour' / 'Careful With That Axe, Eugene' / 'Set The Controls For The Heart Of The Sun'.
Pink Floyd recorded a one-hour live studio recording for the PBS TV network on this day at the KQED TV studios. Although KQED have no copies of this film in their archive, let alone a record of the filming ever taking place, other sources were able to confirm this as the recording date. It was broadcast for the first time in January 1971 on the PBS network KQED channel, and repeated for the first time in August 1981 – the apparent source for copies that have recently emerged on the collectors' market.

Wednesday 29 April
CONCERT
Fillmore West, San Francisco, California, USA
Set List: 'Grantchester Meadows' / 'Astronomy Dominé' / 'Cymbaline' / 'Atom Heart Mother' / 'The Embryo' / 'Green Is The Colour' / 'Careful With That

Axe, Eugene' / 'Set The Controls For The Heart Of The Sun' / encore: 'A Saucerful Of Secrets'.

Friday 1 May
CONCERT
Civic Auditorium, Santa Monica, California, USA
Set list: 'Grantchester Meadows' / 'Astronomy Dominé' / 'Cymbaline' / 'Atom Heart Mother' / 'The Embryo' / 'Set The Controls For The Heart Of The Sun' / encore: 'Interstellar Overdrive'.

Thursday 7 May
CONCERT
Pauley Pavilion, University of California Los Angeles, West Hollywood, Los Angeles, California, USA
This was a completely unscheduled and unadvertised concert in the wake of a call for a general strike by students at campuses throughout the United States beginning 5 May in protest at the killing of four unarmed students by National Guardsmen at Kent State University, Ohio on 4 May. Several hundred campuses closed across the country and UCLA participated in a strike following an attempt by Governor Ronald Reagan to close the University, which he finally succeeded in doing between 8 and 11 May. *Melody Maker* reported that: 'Pink Floyd gave a free concert to 10,000 students which even a detachment of National Guardsmen complete with helmets, riot shields and rifles enjoyed.'

Saturday 9 May
CONCERT
Terrace Ballroom, Salt Lake City, Utah, USA
Supported by Blue Mountain Eagle.

Tuesday 12 May
CONCERT
Municipal Auditorium, Atlanta, Georgia, USA
Supporting The Guess Who.
Set list included: 'Grantchester Meadows' / 'Astronomy Dominé' / 'Cymbaline' / 'A Saucerful Of Secrets'.
Great Speckled Bird reported that: 'The group uses a 360-degree stereo sound system, meaning that speakers are employed throughout the auditorium, as well as on stage. Pink Floyd's sound system is beyond belief - you can physically feel the music (without good old LSD too!). But it isn't just loudness and volume, like so many concerts, where you leave the place with your ears ringing. They are perhaps one of the few groups that knows how to properly use their sound equipment. And they use a shit-load of it too (three tons worth), most of it conventional amplifiers and speakers but also much sophisticated electronic apparatus. Pink Floyd's music could be best described as the natural merging of electronics and psychedelics. Music of the coming age. Most of their music originates from conventional instruments, but then goes through so many incredible electronic alterations that the final sound is hard to associate with the instruments being played. In addition to the live sounds produced on stage, magnetic tapes are used, especially tape loops of such things as bird calls to create rhythmic sounds. The concert also includes a stereo tape solo of giant footsteps which appear to walk around the auditorium, as well as doors opening and closing and a fly which finally gets swatted. Doesn't sound very thrilling on paper, but it was very freaky at the time!'

Thursday 15 & Friday 16 May
CONCERTS
The Warehouse, New Orleans, Louisianna, USA
With The Allman Brothers Band and Country Funk.
Set list on 15 May included: 'Grantchester Meadows' / 'Astronomy Dominé' / 'A Saucerful Of Secrets'.
The band had $40,000 worth of equipment stolen out of their hired truck while they slept in their hotel after the gig on 16 May. The entire contents were taken which comprised of four electric guitars, an electric organ, a 4,000 watt sound system with 12 speaker cabinets, five Italian echo units, microphones, two drum kits and 10 miles of cable. As a result the shows in Houston and Dallas were cancelled and the band returned to the UK shortly after this date.
Nick Mason recalled in an interview with *Melody Maker* that it was, 'Nearly a total disaster. We sat down at our hotel thinking – "Well that's it. It's all over." We were pouring out our troubles to a girl who worked at the hotel and she said her father worked for the FBI. The police hadn't helped us much, but the FBI got to work and four hours later it was found.'

Thursday 22 May
CANCELLED APPEARANCES
Houston Music Theatre, Houston, Texas, USA
Two shows at 7.00pm and 10.00pm supporting Grand Funk Railroad.

Friday 23 May
CANCELLED APPEARANCE
State Fair Music Hall, Dallas, Texas, USA
Supporting Grand Funk Railroad.

Friday 29 May
RECORD RELEASE
Zabriskie Point
UK album release. US album release on Saturday 11 April.
The soundtrack to the Antonioni film featured the previously unreleased Pink Floyd tracks 'Heart Beat Pig Meat', 'Crumbling Land' and 'Come In Number 51 Your Time Is Up'. The remainder of the album features The Grateful Dead, the Youngbloods and The Kaleidoscope among others.

Thursday 11 June – Sunday 5 July
RECORDING SESSIONS
EMI Studios, Abbey Road, St. John's Wood, London, England
Discontinuous recording for the album *Atom Heart Mother*.

made it on stage. They took a very long time to set up but their act was worth it. People were getting tired but the spectacular close to their set woke everyone up. After laying down some good sounds they were joined by a choir, about 12 strong, and a brass section and

went into a 20 minute thing which will be one side of their new album. It was a heavenly sound. The finale saw three flares bursting open the sky with a galaxy of colours - smoke and the light show flooded the stage. It was amazing.'

Sunday 28 June
CONCERT
The Holland Pop Festival '70, Kralingse Bos, Rotterdam, The Netherlands
Featuring Jefferson Airplane, Santana, The Flock, Canned Heat, Hot Tuna, Quintessence, East Of Eden, The Byrds, Family, Dr. John, Country Joe, Tyrannosaurus Rex, Renaissance, Third Ear Band, Al Stewart, Soft Machine, Chicago Art Ensemble, John Surman, Han Bennink, Caravan, Fairport Convention and Fotheringay.
Set list: 'Astronomy Dominé' / 'Green Is The Colour' /

LEFT AND BELOW: PERFORMING AT THE *HOLLAND POP FESTIVAL*, ROTTERDAM, 28 JUNE 1970.

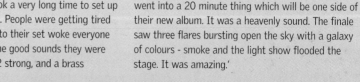

Saturday 27 June
CONCERT
Bath Festival of Blues & Progressive Music '70, Bath & West Showgound, Shepton Mallet, England
This three-day festival (26-28 June) also featured Led Zeppelin, Canned Heat, Steppenwolf, Johnny Winter, It's A Beautiful Day, Fairport Convention, Colosseum, Keef Hartley, Jefferson Airplane, Frank Zappa And The Mothers of Invention, The Moody Blues, The Byrds, The Flock, Santana, Dr. John, Country Joe and Hot Tuna. Compered by DJ's John Peel and Mike Raven.
Set list: 'Green Is The Colour' / 'Careful With That Axe, Eugene' / 'A Saucerful Of Secrets' / 'Set The Controls For The Heart Of The Sun' / 'Atom Heart Mother' (announced as 'The Amazing Pudding' with the Philip Jones Brass Ensemble and the John Aldiss Choir, conducted by John Aldiss).
This huge three-day event, which inspired Michael Eavis to stage the first Glastonbury Festival, featured many of the world's top performing artists and was headlined by Led Zeppelin, attracting twice the anticipated audience. A rough estimate put it at 150,000, which put a terrible strain on maintaining food supplies, not to mention the toilets, of which there were often up to 200 people queuing at any one time! The traffic it generated also caused the biggest jams in Somerset's history. Generally speaking it was a very peaceful weekend. The only reported incident occurred when the Hell's Angels, in their customary role of site security, 'assisted' in the clearance of the VIP/press area in front of the stage to make way for Pink Floyd's light show projectors to be set up, midway through Steppenwolf's set.
Disc & Music Echo reported that: 'We were into the early hours of Sunday morning before Pink Floyd

'Careful With That Axe, Eugene' / 'Atom Heart Mother' / 'Set The Controls For The Heart Of The Sun' / 'A Saucerful Of Secrets' / encore: 'Interstellar Overdrive'.

Sponsored by Coca-Cola, the Holland Pop Festival remains the largest event of its kind in Netherlands with an estimated attendance exceeding 350,000. It ran from the 26 to the 28 June and had a reciprocal agreement with the organisers of the Bath Festival that enabled many of the same artists to perform at both. Pink Floyd finally took to the stage at 4.00am on 29 June but this time minus the special effects, lightshow and orchestra. A film was made of the event that included Pink Floyd's performance of 'Set The Controls For The Heart Of The Sun' and 'A Saucerful Of Secrets' and was released in cinemas as *Stamping Ground*. It has also been released on video under this title and Pink Floyd's performance has also appeared on many Various Artists video compilations including *Psychomania!*

Wednesday 8 – Tuesday 21 July
RECORDING SESSIONS
EMI Studios, Abbey Road, St. John's Wood, London, England
Discontinuous recording for the album *Atom Heart Mother*.

Sunday 12 July
CONCERT
1st Open Air Pop Festival, Reiterstadion Soers, Aachen, West Germany
Pink Floyd headlined on the third and final day of this festival which featured many acts including Taste, Hardin and York, Keef Hartley, If, Fat Mattress, Champion Jack Dupree, Quintessence, Caravan,

Golden Earring, Amon Düül II, Kevin Ayers And The Whole World, Traffic, Edgar Broughton Band, Tyrannosaurus Rex and Deep Purple.
Set list: 'Astronomy Dominé' / 'Green Is The Colour' / 'Careful With That Axe, Eugene' / 'Atom Heart Mother' / 'Set The Controls For The Heart Of The Sun' / 'A Saucerful Of Secrets' / encore: 'Interstellar Overdrive'.

Thursday 16 July
RADIO SHOW
BBC Paris Cinema, Lower Regent Street, London, England
Pink Floyd recorded a live audience show on this day for BBC Radio One in which the band performed in, order, 'The Embryo', 'Fat Old Sun', 'Green Is The Colour', 'Careful With That Axe, Eugene', 'If' and 'Atom Heart Mother' (with the Philip Jones Brass Ensemble and the John Aldiss Choir). It was broadcast on the *Peel Sunday Concert* on 19 July at 4.00pm and repeated on *Sounds of The Seventies* on 22 July at 6.00pm. This show also marked the naming of the track 'Atom Heart Mother' for the first time.

Saturday 18 July
CONCERT
Blackhill's Garden Party - Hyde Park Free Concert, Hyde Park, London, England
With Third Ear Band, Kevin Ayers And The Whole World, Edgar Broughton Band and DJ Jeff Dexter. Set list: 'The Embryo' / 'Green Is The Colour' / 'Careful With That Axe, Eugene' / 'Set The Controls For The Heart Of The Sun' / 'Atom Heart Mother' (announced as 'The Atomic Heart Mother' with the Philip Jones Brass Ensemble and the John Aldiss Choir, conducted by John Aldiss) / encore: 'Atom Heart Mother' (reprise).
Disc & Music Echo reported that: 'Over five hours of varied and contrasting music was topped by a performance from the Pink Floyd, who treated the gathering to a preview of their forthcoming album. But most of all, the weather was kind. The only unusual incident to be witnessed by everybody came just after Edgar Broughton finished his set. A middle-aged father, who had apparently lost his son in the crowd, was handing in a message when he suddenly grabbed the microphone from Jeff Dexter. The bewildered man spluttered into the PA: 'I just want to tell you kids - because that's all you are - that I think this bloody music of yours is a load of rubbish!' The remark was met with uproar, and a shower of empty coke cans rained down on him from the audience... The Pink Floyd gave an hour of beautifully mature music, soothing and inspiring to listen to. They kept the numbers short, apart from the finale, and carefully restrained. With the sun glinting on Nick Mason's drums and the clouds breaking up overhead, it seemed as if the sounds were dropping from the

sky itself. After a quiet and lazy, bluesy, introduction, they went gently into "Green Is The Colour" and "Careful With That Axe, Eugene". Even in the latter the volume was down, and the mood reflective. "Set The Controls For The Heart Of the Sun" was at its most ethereal, the smooth crescendos flying away over the heads of the captivated audience. To end, a brass section and choir were brought on for the 25-minute finale. The piece began with an arrangement for the brass, and then switched into a lengthy choir pattern, followed by a dash of marvellous Floyd rock-jazz. In came the brass again, pursued by incantations from the choir and swirling special effects in twin-channel stereo. A reprise took up the original theme - based on a simple chord progression akin to the finale of "The Man" - and group, choir and orchestra projected it together in fine combination.'

FRENCH FESTIVAL TOUR
Pink Floyd, members of their family and road crew rented a villa in St. Tropez to use as a base for a combined holiday and season of French Riviera festival appearances. Unfortunately many of the festivals, including appearances in Bandol and Le Barcares that never even got beyond the planning stage, were cancelled or disrupted by violence and in the end Pink Floyd appeared at only three events.

Sunday 26 July
CONCERT
XI Festival International de Jazz, Pinède Gould, Antibes Juan-les-Pins, France
As part of this month-long series of events French TV reportedly recorded this show but the content and broadcast details remain unknown.

Saturday 1 August
CANCELLED CONCERT
Festival d'Aix-en-Provence, Parc de Saint Pons, Aix-en-Provence, France
With Derek And The Dominos, Soft Machine, Traffic and Balls. Pink Floyd were due to headline the second day of this three-day festival (30 July – 2 August), organised by local dignitary General Claude Clement but it was abandoned on the first day because of rioting and was closed by the city authorities as a fire hazard and threat to public safety.

Wednesday 5 August
CANCELLED CONCERT
Popanalia Festival, Autoroute De L'Esteral, Biot, France
With Joan Baez, Soft Machine, Eric Clapton, Traffic, Balls, Ex Plastic Ono Band, The Moody Blues, King Crimson, Spencer Davis, Kevin Ayers And The Whole World, Alan Price, Daevid Allen's Gong, Alice, Ame Son, Alan Jack Civilization, Art Ensemble Of Chicago, Archie Shepp, Sonny Scharrock and Don Cherry. Planned to last 36 hours, with Pink Floyd due to

ABOVE: PINK FLOYD ON STAGE AT THE HYDE PARK
FREE CONCERT, LONDON, 18 JULY 1970. ALTHOUGH NOT
PICTURED IT WAS ONE OF THE FEW TIMES THE BAND
PERFORMED 'ATOM HEART MOTHER' WITH A CHOIR
AND ORCHESTRA IN AN OPEN AIR SETTING.

appear on the 6 August, this event was abandoned soon after it started. When Soft Machine were told they wouldn't receive their contracted fee, they refused to perform, and as a result disgruntled fans rioted, many of them members of a hippie cult called 'Les Compagnons de la Route', egged on by a young left-wing political element, who vandalised the stage and equipment. The extensive damage included a Yamaha grand piano that was pushed off the stage and smashed to pieces and two RTL Radio mobile recording trucks that were set on fire. It was consequently dubbed by the French music press as the "Festival maudit de Biot" (The cursed festival of Biot). ORFT TV had planned to dedicate a whole edition of the music programme *Pop 2* to the festival for broadcast on ORTF2 on 20 August at 9.50pm, but in view of events the content of the programme was changed.

Saturday 8 August
CANCELLED CONCERT
Pop Festival Saint Raphael, Stade Municipal, St. Raphaël, France
This two-day event (8 and 9 August) never even got underway, despite extensive publicity, due to local authority objections. Also due to appear were Family, Edgar Broughton Band, Keef Hartley Blues Band, Frank Zappa, Iron Butterfly, Kevin Ayers And The Whole World, Steamhammer, Geno Washington And The Ram Jam Band, Deep Purple, Hardin and York, Little Free Rock and Ginger Johnson's African Drummers.

Saturday 8 August
CONCERT
Festival de St. Tropez, Les Caves du Roy, St. Tropez, France
Set list included: 'Astronomy Dominé' / 'Cymbaline' / 'Atom Heart Mother' / 'The Embryo' / 'Green Is The Colour' / 'Careful With That Axe, Eugene' / 'Set The Controls For The Heart Of The Sun'.
As part of a series of events for the festival, Pink Floyd performed in the grounds of this unusual open-air nightclub. ORTF TV filmed the show and featured parts of the show on the *Pop 2* music programme in two featured instalments subtitled 'Pink Floyd: Premiere Partie'. The first programme was broadcast on ORTF2 on 10 October at 6.15pm and featured 'Atom Heart Mother' and 'The Embryo' and the second programme was broadcast on ORTF2 on 24 October at 6.20pm and featured 'Green Is The Colour', 'Careful With That Axe, Eugene' and 'Set The Controls For The Heart Of The Sun'. Both programmes featured shots of the band and crew during the afternoon soundcheck. Both parts were repeated on *Pop 2* and broadcast on ORTF2 on 4 November 1972 at 5.40pm.

ABOVE: PINK FLOYD PERFORMING IN SAN TROPEZ, 8 AUGUST 1970 - ONE OF THE FEW FESTIVALS IN FRANCE TO GO AHEAD PEACEFULLY THAT SUMMER.

Wednesday 12 August
CONCERT
Fête de St. Raphaël, L'Amphithéâtre Romain, Fréjus, St. Raphaël, France
The last night of Pink Floyd's festival tour was staged at this preserved Roman arena.

Saturday 15 August
CANCELLED APPEARANCE
Yorkshire Folk, Blues & Jazz Festival, Krumlin, Barkisland, Halifax, England

With Atomic Rooster, Juicy Lucy, Elton John, The Pretty Things, Alexis Korner, Pentangle, Fairport Convention, Ralph McTell, The Kinks, Taste, Yes and many other acts.
Pink Floyd's headline show on the second day of this three-day Festival (14-16 August) was cancelled due to fog delaying their departure from Paris airport. In the event the entire festival was abandoned by Sunday morning due to torrential rain on the Saturday. A report was later printed in *The Yorkshire Times* of the disappearance of the promoter, who had suffered financial losses in excess of £12,000.

Saturday 29 August
CANCELLED CONCERT
Open Air Festival Heidelberg, Thingstätte Amphitheatre, Heidelberg, West Germany
Although extensively advertised, this one-day event was cancelled. Also on the bill was Deep Purple, Xhol, Edgar Broughton Band, Embryo, Quintessence, Tangerine Dream, Guru Guru, Groove, Nosferatu and many other acts.
This same weekend saw the staging of the 3rd Isle of Wight Festival for which WEM provided the PA and Peter Watts was the front-of-house sound engineer. David Gilmour was also in attendance and reportedly lent a hand at the desk during what would be Jimi Hendrix's final UK performance.

Monday 31 August
CONCERT
Charlton Park, Bishopsbourne, near Canterbury, England
With Rod Stewart & The Faces, Mott The Hoople, Edgar Broughton Band, Stoneground, Silver Meter, Linda Lewis, Shawn Philips, Daddylonglegs, Al Stewart and comperes Wavy Gravy, General Wastemoreland and DJ Jeff Dexter.
Set list included: 'Set The Controls For The Heart Of The Sun' / 'Cymbaline' / 'Careful With That Axe, Eugene' / 'Atom Heart Mother'.
For many in attendance this was a post Isle of Wight party on the Bank Holiday Monday extending from 11.00am until Pink Floyd's headline set finished well after midnight. The event was filmed for inclusion in a film called the *Medicine Ball Caravan* but none of the footage was used in the finished film.
The Kent Herald reported that: 'The Great Medicine Ball - a hippie caravan that has trekked across America from San Francisco to take part in a film that sets out to explain the hippie philosophy. A film unit from Warner Brothers had followed the extraordinary journey by the 150 hippies, which started on August 4 and ended up on Bank Holiday Monday with a mammoth pop festival in the beautiful grounds of Charlton Park, home of Lt.Col. and Mrs. Michael Underwood. Hundreds of youngsters made their way to the peaceful village to hear non-stop pop from such groups as Pink Floyd, Small Faces, Mott

The Hoople, Edgar Broughton Band and Silver Meter. The hippie hardcore, around whom the film is being made, directed by Frenchman Francois Reichenbach, brought with them multi-coloured tie-dyed tepees which gave the traditionally laid-out English parkland the air of an Indian reservation. As darkness fell on Monday evening Charlton Park was lit by a score or more of small fires started by the audience who by then numbered nearly 1,000.'

Saturday 12 September
CONCERT
Fete de L'Humanite, Grand Scene, Bois de Vincennes, Paris, France
Set list: 'Astronomy Dominé' / 'Green Is The Colour' / 'Careful With That Axe, Eugene' / 'Set The Controls For The Heart Of The Sun' / 'Atom Heart Mother' (with the Philip Jones Brass Ensemble and the John Aldiss Choir, conducted by John Aldiss).
Over 500,000 people reportedly saw Pink Floyd, making it their largest single concert attendance - a record that remains unbeaten, to this day. French TV reportedly recorded the show but the content and broadcast details remain unknown.

NORTH AMERICAN TOUR
Early drafts of Pink Floyd's tour show the band scheduled to appear at The Gymnasium, Gonzaga University, Spokane, Washington (2 October) and Seattle, Washington (4 October).

PINK FLOYD ROAD CREW THROUGH 1970
Seth Goldman: Technician / Stage Crew
Bobby Richardson: Technician / Stage Crew
Brian Scott: Technician / Stage Crew
Alan Styles: Technician / Stage Crew
Peter Watts: Tour Manager / Front of House Sound

Saturday 26 September
CONCERT
Electric Factory, Philadelphia, Pennsylvania, USA
Pink Floyd was a late addition, replacing Chicken Shack as support for Savoy Brown.
Set list: 'Astronomy Dominé' / 'Cymbaline' / 'A Saucerful Of Secrets' / 'Interstellar Overdrive' / 'Fat Old Sun' / 'Green Is The Colour' / 'Careful With That Axe, Eugene' / encore: 'Set The Controls For The Heart Of The Sun'.

Sunday 27 September
CONCERTS
Fillmore East, Manhattan, New York City, New York, USA
Two shows at 6.00pm and 9.00pm.
Set list at both shows: 'Astronomy Dominé' / 'Green Is The Colour' / 'Careful With That Axe, Eugene' / 'Fat

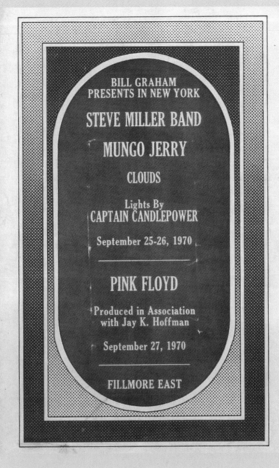

BILL GRAHAM PRESENTS IN NEW YORK

STEVE MILLER BAND
MUNGO JERRY
CLOUDS

Lights By
CAPTAIN CANDLEPOWER

September 25-26, 1970

PINK FLOYD

Produced in Association with Jay K. Hoffman

September 27, 1970

FILLMORE EAST

Old Sun' / 'Set The Controls For The Heart Of The Sun' / 'A Saucerful Of Secrets' / encore: 'Atom Heart Mother' (with brass and choir).
An unidentified newspaper reported that: 'The Pink Floyd trooped out on stage followed by about ten union horn men (dressed 'down' for their gig at the Fillmore!), and a chorus of approximately 20 singers. All of this entourage was fronted by a conductor! They all proceeded to perform a type of rock-classically fused composition that lasted about an hour, and sounded like one of Blood, Sweat and Tears' more ambitious compositions at best. I really feel that if one mixes rock with classical music something more ought to come out of it than merely bad rock or bad classical music. The audience, by the way, enjoyed the show immensely, and were cheering for more at the end of the concert.'

Thursday 1 October
CONCERT
Memorial Coliseum, Portland, Oregon, USA

Friday 2 October
RECORD RELEASE
Atom Heart Mother
UK album release. US album release on Saturday 10 October.

Rolling Stone commented that: *Atom Heart Mother* is a step headlong into the last century and a dissipation of their collective talents, which are considerable. ...If Pink Floyd is looking for some new dimensions, they haven't found them here.' *Circus* magazine received the album in more excited tones by commenting that, 'This is a trip. Most of Floyd is a trip. Trip, trip, trip. Tippy top trip.'

Friday 2 & Saturday 3 October
CONCERTS
Moore Theater, Seattle, Washington, USA
Set list on 2 October included: 'Set The Controls For The Heart Of The Sun' / 'A Saucerful Of Secrets'.
Seattle Sabot reported that: 'If, like me, you'd only heard them on record and went to see them last weekend, the big question was - can they do that live? - Yes they can. They produce a sound that at once gives me fantasies of outer-space (As it obviously is supposed to with such titles as "Set The Controls For The Heart Of The Sun" and "A Saucerful Of Secrets") and puts me at ease, soothes me. Live, there was also the fascination of watching the actions that help produce these wondrous sounds. At times the guitarist was seated with his back almost directly to the audience, doing things to his instrument in a manner reminiscent of the ape with the bone in *2001*.'

Sunday 4 October
CONCERT
The Gymnasium, Gonzaga University, Spokane, Washington, USA

Tuesday 6 October
CONCERT
Central Washington University, Ellensburg, Washington, USA

Wednesday 7 October
CONCERT
Gardens Arena, Vancouver, British Columbia, Canada
Set list: 'Astronomy Dominé' / 'Fat Old Sun' / 'Cymbaline' / 'The Embryo' / 'Atom Heart Mother' / 'Green Is The Colour' / 'Careful With That Axe, Eugene' / 'Set The Controls For The Heart Of The Sun' / 'A Saucerful Of Secrets'.
Roger Waters and David Gilmour were interviewed before the show by Vancouver's *Georgia Straight* magazine.

Thursday 8 October
CONCERT
Jubilee Auditorium, Calgary, Alberta, Canada

Friday 9 October
CONCERT
Sales Pavilion Annex, Edmonton, Alberta, Canada

Saturday 10 October
CONCERT
Centennial Auditorium, Saskatoon, Saskatchewan, Canada

Sunday 11 October
CONCERT
Centre of The Arts, Regina, Saskatchewan, Canada
Set list included: 'Green Is The Colour' / 'Careful With That Axe, Eugene' / 'Cymbaline' / 'A Saucerful Of Secrets' / 'Atom Heart Mother'.

Tuesday 13 October
CONCERT
Centennial Concert Hall, Winnipeg, Manitoba, Canada

Thursday 15 October
CONCERT
Terrace Ballroom, Salt Lake City, Utah, USA
Supported by Blue Mountain Eagle.

Friday 16 & Saturday 17 October
CONCERTS
Pepperland Auditorium, San Rafael, California, USA
Supported by Kimberley and Osceola with lights by Brotherhood of Light.
Set list on 17 October: 'Astronomy Dominé' (with several false starts due to power failures) / 'Fat Old Sun' / 'Green Is The Colour' / 'Careful With That Axe, Eugene' / 'Cymbaline' / 'Atom Heart Mother' / 'The Embryo' / 'Set The Controls For The Heart Of The Sun' / encore: 'A Saucerful Of Secrets' (with power failures towards the end of the song).

Sunday 18 October
CONCERT
University College of San Diego, San Diego, California, USA
An open air event with Hot Tuna (headline) and Leon Russell.

Wednesday 21 October
CONCERT
Fillmore West, San Francisco, California, USA
Set list: 'Astronomy Dominé' / 'Fat Old Sun' / 'Green Is The Colour' / 'Careful With That Axe, Eugene' / 'Cymbaline' / 'Set The Controls For The Heart Of The Sun' / 'A Saucerful Of Secrets' / 'Atom Heart Mother' (with brass and choir conducted by Peter Philips) / encore: 'Ave Maria' (choir only).
Rolling Stone reported that: 'That was Pink Floyd on the Fillmore stage October 21st, along with the Roger Wagner Chorale, three French horns, three trombones, three trumpets, and a tuba. They were performing, for

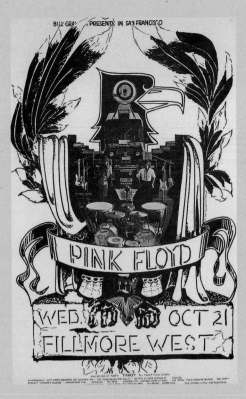

the second time ever on stage, the suite from *Atom Heart Mother*. For an encore the Chorale did an "Ave Maria" written in 1562. "Atom Heart Mother" got a standing ovation, and bassist Roger Waters introduced Wagner. But it was too much for some of the more dazed and die-hard Fillmore freaks: as the Chorale neared the "Amen", scattered give-me-back-my-candy shouts of "we want Pink Floyd" came through from the sides of the auditorium. If they didn't understand what Pink Floyd's music is all about in the first place, it is a bit puzzling why they spent $3 and four hours to come to see them. The music of Pink Floyd evokes images of cold, clear, far interstellar regions, of black moving water, of the exhilarating bleakness of the moon.'

Friday 23 October
CONCERT
Civic Auditorium, Santa Monica, Los Angeles, California, USA
Set list: 'Astronomy Dominé' / 'Green Is The Colour' / 'Careful With That Axe, Eugene' / 'Fat Old Sun' / 'Cymbaline' / 'A Saucerful Of Secrets' / 'Atom Heart Mother' (with brass and choir conducted by Peter Philips) / encore: 'Interstellar Overdrive'.

Sunday 25 October
CONCERT
The Boston Tea Party, Boston, Massachusetts, USA
The last night of the tour.

Saturday 31 October
CANCELLED CONCERT
Black Magic & Rock & Roll, Cincinnati Gardens, Cincinnati, Ohio, USA
Promoters Mike Quattro and Russ Gibb attempted to re-stage their ill-fated *Black Magic & Rock & Roll* concert held in Detroit the previous year, and invited

Pink Floyd as early as April 1970 to perform at this show. It was reported that the American Musicians Union prevented the band from participating at this event in what was described as a 'voodoo and science fiction convention.'

EUROPEAN TOUR

Friday 6 November
CONCERT
Concertgebouw, Amsterdam, The Netherlands
Set list: 'Astronomy Dominé' / 'Fat Old Sun' / 'Cymbaline' / 'Atom Heart Mother' / 'The Embryo' / 'Green Is The Colour' / 'Careful With That Axe, Eugene' / 'Set The Controls For The Heart Of The Sun' / encore: 'A Saucerful Of Secrets'.

Saturday 7 November
CONCERT
Grote Zaal, De Doelen, Rotterdam, The Netherlands
Set list: 'Astronomy Dominé' / 'Fat Old Sun' / 'Cymbaline' / 'Atom Heart Mother' / 'The Embryo' / 'Green Is The Colour' / 'Careful With That Axe, Eugene' / 'Set The Controls For The Heart Of The Sun' / 'A Saucerful Of Secrets' / encore: 'Blues'.

Wednesday 11 November
CONCERT
Konserthuset, Gothenberg, Sweden
Set list: 'Astronomy Dominé' / 'The Embryo' / 'Fat Old Sun' / 'Green Is The Colour' / 'A Saucerful Of Secrets' / 'Atom Heart Mother' / encore: 'Blues'.

Thursday 12 November
CONCERTS
Falkoner Centret, Copenhagen, Denmark
Two shows at 8.00pm and 10.30pm.
Set list at 8.00pm show: 'Astronomy Dominé' / 'Fat
Old Sun' / 'Cymbaline' / 'Atom Heart Mother' / 'Green
Is The Colour' / 'Careful With That Axe, Eugene' /
'Set The Controls For The Heart Of The Sun' / 'A
Saucerful Of Secrets' / encore: 'The Embryo'.

Friday 13 November
CONCERT
Vejlby-Risskov Hallen, Åarhus, Denmark
Set list: 'Astronomy Dominé' / 'Fat Old Sun' /
'Cymbaline' / 'Atom Heart Mother' / 'The Embryo' /
'Green Is The Colour' / 'Careful With That Axe,
Eugene' / 'Set The Controls For The Heart Of The Sun'
/ 'A Saucerful Of Secrets' / encore: 'Blues'.

Saturday 14 November
CONCERT
Ernst-Merck Halle, Hamburg, West Germany
Set list: 'Astronomy Dominé' / 'Fat Old Sun' /
'Cymbaline' / 'improvisations' / 'The Embryo' / 'Atom
Heart Mother' / 'Green Is The Colour' / 'Careful With
That Axe, Eugene' / 'Set The Controls For The Heart
Of The Sun' / encore: 'A Saucerful Of Secrets'.
Pink Floyd gave a five-minute interview at this show
to Keith Altham for the BBC Radio 1 show *Scene And
Heard* that was broadcast at 1.30pm.

Saturday 21 November
CONCERT
Super Pop 70 VII, Casino de Montreux, Montreux,
Switzerland
With Krishna Lights.
Set list: 'Astronomy Dominé' / 'Fat Old Sun' /
'Cymbaline' / 'Atom Heart Mother' / 'The Embryo' /
'Green Is The Colour' / 'Careful With That Axe,
Eugene' / 'Set The Controls For The Heart Of The Sun'
/ 'A Saucerful Of Secrets' / encore: 'Interstellar
Overdrive'.

Sunday 22 November
CONCERT
Super Pop 70 VII, Casino de Montreux, Montreux,
Switzerland
With Krishna Lights. This hastily added show
commenced at 2.30pm.
Set list: 'Astronomy Dominé' / 'Fat Old Sun' /
'Cymbaline' / 'Atom Heart Mother' / 'The Embryo' /
'Green Is The Colour' / 'Careful With That Axe,
Eugene' / 'Set The Controls For The Heart Of The Sun'
/ 'A Saucerful Of Secrets' / encore: 'Just Another 12-
Bar' / 'Blues'.
Both Montreux shows were recorded and EMI
Records pressed white-label acetates entitled *Pink
Floyd Live At Montreux Casino* with the tracks:
Astronomy Dominé / More Blues / The Embryo / Just

Another 12 Bar and included an interview with
Gilmour conducted in French. However, it is likely
these would have been intended as promotional tools,
not for commercial release. 'Just Another 12 Bar' is a
title given on the acetate label and is simply an
improvised blues instrumental.

Monday 23 November
CANCELLED CONCERT
**Grosser Konzerthaussaal, Wiener Konzerthaus,
Vienna, Austria**
This show was cancelled due to snow-drifts blocking
the roads out of Montreux preventing the band's
equipment lorry getting through. A second show was
pencilled in for 29 November, but this too was
cancelled in favour of a booking in Munich on the
same date.

Wednesday 25 November

CONCERT

Friedrich Ebert Halle, Ebertpark, Ludwigshafen, West Germany

Set list: 'Astronomy Dominé' / 'Fat Old Sun' / 'Cymbaline' / 'Atom Heart Mother' / 'The Embryo' / 'Green Is The Colour' / 'Careful With That Axe, Eugene' / 'Set The Controls For The Heart Of The Sun' / encore: 'A Saucerful Of Secrets'.

Thursday 26 November

CONCERT

Killesberg Halle 14, Stuttgart, West Germany

Set list included: 'Fat Old Sun' / 'Cymbaline' / 'Atom Heart Mother' / 'Green Is The Colour' / 'Careful With That Axe, Eugene' / 'The Embryo' / encore: 'A Saucerful Of Secrets'.

Friday 27 November

CONCERT

Niedersachsenhalle, Hannover, West Germany

Shows scheduled for both the Sporthalle and Sartory Saal, Cologne, West Germany on this date were rescheduled to Hannover following local authority concerns over rowdy audiences at previous pop concerts held in the area.

Saturday 28 November

CONCERT

Saarlandhalle, Saarbrücken, West Germany

Sunday 29 November

CONCERT

Circus Krone, Munich, West Germany

The last night of the tour.

Set list: 'Astronomy Dominé' / 'Fat Old Sun' / 'Cymbaline' / 'Atom Heart Mother' / 'The Embryo' / 'Green Is The Colour' / 'Careful With That Axe, Eugene' / 'Set The Controls For The Heart Of The Sun' / encore: 'A Saucerful Of Secrets'.

Friday 4 & Saturday 5 December

TV SHOW

ORTF Studios, Buttes Chaumont, Paris, France

Pink Floyd were reported to be recording for French TV but the content and broadcast details remain unknown.

ATOM HEART MOTHER IS GOING ON THE ROAD - UK TOUR

Friday 11 December

CONCERT

Big Apple, Regent Theatre, Brighton, England

Set list included: 'Atom Heart Mother' / 'Fat Old Sun' / 'Green Is The Colour' / 'Careful With That Axe, Eugene' / 'Cymbaline' / 'Set The Controls For The Heart Of The Sun' / 'A Saucerful Of Secrets' / encore: 'Astronomy Dominé'.

Sounds reported that: 'The Pink Floyd are brilliant musicians, but it is undoubtedly their technical genius that has made them Britain's No.1 truly progressive pop band. This was proved conclusively at Brighton's Big Apple on Friday night when the Floyd made one of their rare club appearances... Thankfully the Floyd are one of the few bands who refuse to be governed by sheer volume. They use more than 30 speakers and they are certainly loud. But they obviously go to a lot of trouble to ensure that every sound is clearly audible. At times they were far out, freaky even. For example they made excellent use of tape recorded sounds ranging from crying babies to galloping horses and explosions.'

Saturday 12 December

CONCERT

Village Blues Club, The Roundhouse public house, Dagenham, England

Set list included: 'The Embryo' / 'A Saucerful Of Secrets' / 'Atom Heart Mother' / 'Blues' / encore: 'Astronomy Dominé'.

Friday 18 December

CONCERT

Town Hall, Birmingham, England

Set list included: 'Alan's Psychedelic Breakfast' / 'Fat Old Sun' / 'A Saucerful Of Secrets' // 'Atom Heart Mother' (with brass and choir conducted by John Aldiss) / encore: 'Atom Heart Mother' (reprise).

Sunday 20 December

CONCERT

Colston Hall, Bristol, England

Set list included: 'Alan's Psychedelic Breakfast' / 'Atom Heart Mother' (with brass and choir conducted by John Aldiss).

Monday 21 December

CONCERT

Free Trade Hall, Manchester, England

Set list: 'Alan's Psychedelic Breakfast' / 'The Embryo' / 'Fat Old Sun' / 'Careful With That Axe, Eugene' / 'Set The Controls For The Heart Of The Sun' / 'A Saucerful Of Secrets' // 'Atom Heart Mother' (with brass and choir conducted by John Aldiss) / encore: 'Atom Heart Mother' (reprise).

Tuesday 22 December

CONCERT

City (Oval) Hall, Sheffield, England

The last night of the tour.

Set list: 'Alan's Psychedelic Breakfast' / 'The Embryo' / 'Fat Old Sun' / 'Careful With That Axe, Eugene' / 'Set The Controls For The Heart Of The Sun' / 'A Saucerful Of Secrets' // 'Atom Heart Mother' (with brass and choir conducted by John Aldiss) / encore: 'Atom Heart Mother' (reprise).

1971

PINK FLOYD ROAD CREW THROUGH 1971

Chris Adamson: Technician / Stage Crew
Seth Goldman: Technician / Stage Crew
Bobby Richardson: Technician / Stage Crew
Brian Scott: Technician / Stage Crew
Alan Styles: Technician / Stage Crew
Peter Watts: Tour Manager / Front of House Sound

Monday 4 – Monday 11 January
RECORDING SESSIONS
EMI Studios, Abbey Road, St. John's Wood, London, England
Recording for the album *Meddle*.

Sunday 17 January
CONCERT
Implosion, The Roundhouse, Chalk Farm, London, England
Supported by Quiver, Nico with John Cale and DJ Jeff Dexter.
Set list: 'The Embryo' / 'Astronomy Dominé' / 'Fat Old Sun' / 'Careful With That Axe, Eugene' / 'Cymbaline' / 'Set The Controls For The Heart Of The Sun' / 'A Saucerful Of Secrets' / encore: 'Atom Heart Mother' (with brass and choir conducted by John Aldiss).

Tuesday 19 - Thursday 21 January
RECORDING SESSIONS
EMI Studios, Abbey Road, St. John's Wood, London, England
Recording for the album *Meddle*.

Saturday 23 January
CONCERT
Refectory Hall, University Union, Leeds University, Leeds, England
Set list included: 'Atom Heart Mother' / 'Careful With That Axe, Eugene' / 'Cymbaline' / 'Set The Controls For The Heart Of The Sun' / 'A Saucerful Of Secrets'.

Sunday 24 - Tuesday 26 January
RECORDING SESSIONS
EMI Studios, Abbey Road, St. John's Wood, London, England
Recording for the album *Meddle*.

Wednesday 3 February
CONCERT
Great Hall, Devonshire House, University of Exeter, Exeter, England
Set list: 'Atom Heart Mother' / 'The Embryo' / 'Astronomy Dominé' / 'Fat Old Sun' / 'Careful With That Axe, Eugene' / 'Cymbaline' / 'Set The Controls For The Heart Of The Sun' / encore: 'A Saucerful Of Secrets'.

Friday 12 February
CONCERT
Lecture Theatre Block 6 & 7, University of Essex, Wivenhoe Park, Colchester, England
Set list: 'Atom Heart Mother' / 'The Embryo' / 'Careful With That Axe, Eugene' / 'Astronomy Dominé' / 'Cymbaline' / 'Set The Controls For The Heart Of The Sun' / encore: 'A Saucerful Of Secrets'.

Saturday 13 February
CONCERT
Student Union Bar, Farnborough Technical College, Farnborough, England
Set List: 'Atom Heart Mother' / 'The Embryo' / 'Careful With That Axe, Eugene' / 'Cymbaline' / 'Astronomy Dominé' / 'Set The Controls For The Heart Of The Sun' / encore: 'A Saucerful Of Secrets'.

Saturday 20 February
CONCERT
Student Union, Queen Mary College, Strawberry Hill, Twickenham, England

EUROPEAN TOUR

Monday 22 February
CANCELLED CONCERT
Théâtre du Huitième, Lyon, France
This show was cancelled because of venue management fears of a repetition of violence at a recent Rolling Stones show in the nearby Palais des Sports.

Wednesday 24 February
CONCERT
Halle Münsterland, Münster, West Germany
Set list: 'The Embryo' / 'Green Is The Colour' / 'Careful With That Axe, Eugene' / 'Fat Old Sun' / 'Set The Controls For The Heart Of The Sun' / 'Cymbaline' / 'A Saucerful Of Secrets' / encore: 'Atom Heart Mother' (with brass and choir conducted by Jeffrey Mitchell). The second half of the show nearly didn't happen since the score for 'Atom Heart Mother' had been left in London and the mistake wasn't discovered until 6.00pm, when the crew were setting up the equipment. A courier flew out to Düsseldorf and a police Porsche waiting on the airfield raced back to the show, arriving at 10.30pm.

Thursday 25 February
CONCERT
Grosser Saal, Musikhalle, Hamburg, West Germany
Set list: 'Astronomy Dominé' / 'Green Is The Colour' / 'Careful With That Axe, Eugene' / 'Cymbaline' / 'The Embryo' / 'Set The Controls For The Heart Of The Sun' / 'A Saucerful Of Secrets' / encore: 'Atom Heart Mother' (with brass and choir conducted by Jeffrey Mitchell).
This show was rescheduled from the Staatsoper, Hamburg, West Germany at a few days notice when the band were told by the venue management they would have less than two hours to set up their equipment. The *Hamburger Abendblatt* commented, 'Never before had that many bootleggers and tape recorder microphones been seen in an auditorium.' German TV crews filmed this show and the following night's show at Offenbach for inclusion in the arts programme *Aspekt* and featured the soundcheck as well as live performance clips of 'Atom Heart Mother', an interview with Jeffrey Mitchell and interviews with the band members on their chartered plane. It was broadcast (in colour) on ZDF network TV on 2 March 1971 at 10.30pm.

Friday 26 February
CONCERT
Stadthalle, Offenbach, West Germany
Set list: 'Astronomy Dominé', 'Green Is The Colour' / 'Careful With That Axe, Eugene' / 'The Embryo' / 'Set The Controls For The Heart Of The Sun' / 'Cymbaline' / 'A Saucerful Of Secrets' // 'Atom Heart Mother' (with brass and choir conducted by Jeffrey Mitchell) / encore: 'Atom Heart Mother' (reprise) / 'Blues'.
This show was rescheduled from Alte Oper, Frankfurt, West Germany for similar reasons as the Hamburg concert.

Saturday 27 February
TV SHOW
ORTF TV Studios, Buttes Chaumont, Paris, France
The end of this European tour culminated in a TV session in which the band performed 'Set The Controls For The Heart Of The Sun' live for the ORTF2 music programme *Pop 2*. It was broadcast (in colour) on 6 March at 6.20pm.

Sunday 7 - Sunday 28 March
RECORDING SESSIONS
EMI Studios, Abbey Road, St. John's Wood, London, England
Discontinuous recording for the album *Meddle*.

Saturday 3 April
CONCERT
Sportpaleis Ahoy, Rotterdam, Netherlands
Set list: 'Astronomy Dominé' / 'Careful With That Axe, Eugene' / 'Fat Old Sun' / 'Set The Controls For The Heart Of The Sun' / 'Cymbaline' / 'The Embryo' / 'A Saucerful Of Secrets' / encore: 'Atom Heart Mother' (with brass and choir conducted by Jeffrey Mitchell).

141

Thursday 8 – Wednesday 14 April
RECORDING SESSIONS
EMI Studios, Abbey Road, St. John's Wood, London, England
Recording for the album *Meddle*.

Friday 16 April
CONCERT
Top Rank Suite, Doncaster, England
Presented by Doncaster College of Technology.
Supported by Forevermore, Quiver, America and DJ Pete.
Set list: 'Atom Heart Mother' / 'A Saucerful Of Secrets' / 'Cymbaline' / 'Fat Old Sun' / 'The Embryo' / 'Green Is The Colour' / 'Careful With That Axe, Eugene' / 'Set The Controls For The Heart Of The Sun' / encore: 'Astronomy Dominé'.
Bill Smythe, a fan in attendance, recalled that, 'At 7.30 we filed into the hall and as there were no seats on the ground floor everyone sat on the floor. The smell of hash was overpowering and the PA pumped out Syd Barrett's "Terrapin". We politely applauded America and the stage revolved exposing the Floyd's instruments - the lovely drum kit with its familiar design and the gong. Then the band came on one by one to great rounds of applause. The sounds of aircraft rose to the crashing chords of "Atom Heart Mother". Straight after that was "Saucerful". After that a lot of heckling broke out from the upstairs gallery - people shouting, "Play some fucking music!" [Another account of the show tells of the quadraphonic 'footsteps' sequence being played during "Cymbaline" for nearly 15 minutes with the band off stage and the hall in total darkness.] The band continued and we on the lower level heckled back to them to shut up, which indeed they did when some of Floyd's roadies who were drinking upstairs sorted them out. But the evening's surprises were not over because during "Fat Old Sun" a jobsworth appeared on stage and walked up to David's mic and said, "would the owner of a grey Morris Minor,

registration number ***** please remove it from the front of house". David and Roger were gobsmacked, but returned to the song.'

Monday 19 - Wednesday 21 April
REHEARSALS
Cecil Sharp House, Camden, London, England

Thursday 22 April
CONCERT
Norwich Lads Club, Norwich, England
Set list included: 'Atom Heart Mother' / 'Fat Old Sun' / 'Set The Controls For The Heart Of The Sun' / 'A Saucerful Of Secrets' / 'Echoes' *.
*This number has been titled retrospectively for identification purposes: It was not formally adopted until the commencement of their Japanese tour on 6 August 1971 and was known both in the studio and on stage as 'The Return Of The Son Of Nothing'.

Monday 26 – Wednesday 28 April
RECORDING SESSIONS
EMI Studios, Abbey Road, St. John's Wood, London, England
Recording for the album *Meddle*.

Saturday 1 & Sunday 2 May
RECORDING SESSIONS
EMI Studios, Abbey Road, St. John's Wood, London, England
Recording for the album *Meddle*.

Wednesday 5 May
REHEARSALS
Granada Cinema, Wandsworth, London, England
Sound On Stage reported that: 'Pink Floyd hired the Wandsworth Granada to evaluate a new two-way passive Bill Kelsey system, which initially incorporated seven-foot, 500-lb. RCA "W" cabinets before switching to Martin's 2 by 15-inch bass bin. Kelsey, who had already built PA's for King Crimson and ELP, recalls: "What happened was indicative of the way the Floyd used to do business in the days when they were more of a cult band. Peter Watts and Steve O'Rourke [Floyd's manager] said they'd like to try a system so I went down with all the gear, and then found there was another PA company there and that it was to be an A/B test. Feeling a bit miffed that I hadn't been told, I set up the gear as did the other company, and they tried it out with the mixing console at the back of the hall. "It seemed to be going all right, but Peter said, 'To be quite frank, I'm disappointed... it's rubbish.' And Steve cut in, 'You realize you've wasted my whole day, not to mention

the cost of the hall.' Peter continued to push up one fader to produce this horrid, muffled sound, while the second fader produced a nice, clear sound. I just wanted the ground to open up. Suddenly they both burst into laughter and admitted they'd crossed the whole thing over." Despite the elaborate wind-up, Kelsey's system was taken on board at the beginning of the following year.'

Thursday 6 May
RECORDING SESSION
Morgan Sound Studios, Willesden, London, England
Recording for the album *Meddle*.

Friday 7 May
CONCERT
Central Hall, University of Lancaster, Bailrigg, Lancaster, England
Supported by Ron Geesin.
Set list included: 'Echoes'.
Although not much is remembered about this concert, Pink Floyd used a psychedelic light show, including slides of an astronaut walking on the moon. After the show Roger Waters was interviewed by the University magazine, *Bullsheet*.

Sunday 9 - Tuesday 11 May
RECORDING SESSIONS
EMI Studios, Abbey Road, St. John's Wood, London, England
Recording for the album *Meddle*.

Friday 14 May
RECORD RELEASE
Relics
UK album release. US album release on Saturday 17 July.

Saturday 15 May
CONCERT
Garden Party, Crystal Palace Bowl, Crystal Palace, London, England
With Quiver, Mountain, The Faces and compere Pete Drummond.
Set list: 'Atom Heart Mother' / 'Careful With That Axe, Eugene' / 'Fat Old Sun' / 'Echoes' / 'Set The Controls For The Heart Of The Sun' / 'The Embryo' / 'A Saucerful Of Secrets' / encore: 'Astronomy Dominé'.
The Croydon Advertiser reported that: 'Cold rain coursing down the neck can dampen anyone's ardour for music. But despite the unwanted delivery from the heavens at Crystal Palace Bowl on Saturday, there was no notable exodus before the end of the pop concert, the first of its kind to be put on there. The throng, about 15,000 at a guess, was soaked by the downpour. But everyone stayed to hear the Pink Floyd top the bill at the so-called "Garden Party". They were certainly worth waiting for. Imaginative, creative musicians, innovators and showmen, the Pink Floyd

ABOVE: PERFORMING AT THE *GARDEN PARTY*, **CRYSTAL PALACE, LONDON, 15 MAY 1971.**

across on first hearing as particularly distinguished. Secondly, the absence of the choir and additional orchestration meant that "Atom Heart" suffered in comparison with the LP and came across rather limply. But the performance as a whole underlined the moving, dramatic epic quality of Floyd music, enhanced by the so called quadraphonic sound, achieved by having speakers at different points on the rim of the arena. Visual aids were effective too: orange smoke bombs misting up the pond and the trees at the end, rockets, and for fun, a giant octopus inflated in the water.'

Tuesday 18 May
CONCERT
University of Stirling, Stirling, Scotland
Supported by Ron Geesin.
Set list: 'Atom Heart Mother' / 'Set The Controls For The Heart Of The Sun' / 'Fat Old Sun' / 'Careful With That Axe, Eugene' / 'Echoes' / encore: 'A Saucerful Of Secrets'.
The surround sound system broke down half way

through the show but continued as a stereo concert. It was fixed in time for the show at Glasgow, but unfortunately broke down again during that show as well. Prior to this show the band were interviewed by the University newspaper, *Pig* and the Lambert High School magazine.

Wednesday 19 May
CONCERT
Caledonian Cinema, Edinburgh, Scotland

Thursday 20 May
CONCERT
The Ballroom, University of Strathclyde, Glasgow, Scotland

Friday 21 May
CONCERT
Students Union, Trent Polytechnic, Nottingham, England
Set list: 'Atom Heart Mother' / 'Fat Old Sun' / 'Careful With That Axe, Eugene' / 'Echoes' / 'The Embryo' / 'Set The Controls For The Heart Of The Sun' / encore: 'A Saucerful Of Secrets'.

can rightly claim to being one of the leading rock groups of the day. But soon after the Floyd struck up with "Atom Heart Mother" the skies opened. The audience huddled under miles of polythene... revellers swam in the muddy pond... and the band played on... There was also a new work, "The Return Of The Son Of Nothing", which didn't come

Monday 24 – Friday 28 May
RECORDING SESSIONS
EMI Studios, Abbey Road, St. John's Wood, London,
England
Recording for the album *Meddle*.

Wednesday 2 June
CONCERT
Student Health Centre Refectory, Edinburgh
University, Edinburgh, Scotland
Set list included: 'Atom Heart Mother' / 'Set The
Controls For The Heart Of The Sun' / 'Echoes'.

EUROPEAN TOUR

Friday 4 June
CONCERT
Philipshalle, Düsseldorf, West Germany
Set list: 'Atom Heart Mother' / 'Careful With That
Axe, Eugene' / 'Fat Old Sun' / 'The Embryo' / 'Echoes'
/ 'Set The Controls For The Heart Of The Sun' /
'Cymbaline' / encore: 'A Saucerful Of Secrets'.

Saturday 5 June
CONCERT
Berliner Sportpalast, West Berlin, West Germany
Show rescheduled from 27 May.
Set list: 'Careful With That Axe, Eugene' / 'Fat Old
Sun' / 'The Embryo' / 'Echoes' // 'Set The Controls For
The Heart Of The Sun' / 'Cymbaline' / 'A Saucerful Of
Secrets' / encore: 'Astronomy Dominé' / 'Blues'.

Saturday 12 June
CONCERT
Palais des Sports, Lyon, France
Set list included: 'Careful With That Axe, Eugene' /
'Set The Controls For The Heart Of The Sun' /
'Cymbaline' / 'A Saucerful Of Secrets' / 'Atom Heart
Mother' (with a 20 piece choir, plus three trombones,
three trumpets and one tuba, conducted by John
Aldiss).
Europe 1 radio reportedly recorded this show but the
content and broadcast details remain unknown.

Tuesday 15 June
CONCERT
Abbaye de Royaumont, Royaumont, France
Set list included: 'Set The Controls For The Heart Of
The Sun' / 'Cymbaline' / 'Atom Heart Mother'.
ORTF TV filmed the show and featured 'Cymbaline'
and 'Set The Controls For The Heart Of The Sun' on
the arts programme *Cinq Grand Sur La Deux*. It was
broadcast (in colour) on ORTF2 on 12 July at 1.00am.

Saturday 19 June
CONCERT
Palazzo Delle Manifestazioni Artistiche, Brescia,
Italy
Set list: 'Atom Heart Mother' / 'Careful With That

ABOVE: PINK FLOYD AT THE PALAZZO DELLO SPORT, ROME, 20 JUNE 1971.

Axe, Eugene' / 'Fat Old Sun' / 'The Embryo' / 'Echoes' / 'Set The Controls For The Heart Of The Sun' / 'Cymbaline' / encore: 'A Saucerful Of Secrets'.
Pink Floyd's first Italian 'tour' was beset by problems from the start: The original plan was to stage the show on the 19 June at the Palazzo Del Ghiaccio in Milano but there had been rioting at a recent Chicago concert and the authorities refused to grant permits for the Pink Floyd show. With the Palazzo in Bologna on hold in the event of a change in schedule, it was thought all would be fine, but literally at the point of signing the contracts to hire the venue the authorities, for reasons best known to themselves, declared the concert 'an unsuitable event'. Eventually, and at short notice, the show was promoted in Brescia. It is also amusing to note that EMI Records informed the Italian music magazine *CIAO 2001*, sponsors of the two dates, that Syd Barrett was reunited with the band for these two engagements!

Sunday 20 June
CONCERT
Palazzo Dello Sport, EUR, Rome, Italy
The last night of the tour. Set list: 'Atom Heart Mother' / 'Careful With That Axe, Eugene' / 'Fat Old Sun' / 'The Embryo' / 'Echoes' / 'Set The Controls For The Heart Of The Sun' / 'Cymbaline' / 'A Saucerful Of Secrets' / encore: 'Astronomy Dominé'.

Tuesday 22 June
CANCELLED APPEARANCE
Glastonbury Fayre, **Worthy Farm, Pilton, England**
Forerunner to the now enormous annual Glastonbury Festival, Pink Floyd were scheduled to appear at 1.00am on the 22 June, on the third day of the event

scheduled to coincide with the summer solstice (20-24 June). Pink Floyd couldn't make it because their equipment was delayed coming back from Italy but other performers included Traffic, David Bowie, Gong, Marc Bolan and Al Stewart. It was attended by approximately 1,500 people; admission was £1 and included free milk from the farm.

Wednesday 23 June
CONCERT
Hatfield Polytechnic, Hatfield, England

Saturday 26 June
CONCERT
Free Concert, **Amsterdamse Bos, Amsterdam, The Netherlands**
With America and Pearls Before Swine.
Set list: 'Careful With That Axe, Eugene' / 'Cymbaline' / 'Set The Controls For The Heart Of The Sun' / 'A Saucerful Of Secrets' / 'The Embryo'.
It was reported in the press that Pink Floyd made a hasty exit from this show in order to catch a flight to America to participate in the festival below, which as it turned out was cancelled. It is uncertain whether Pink Floyd actually boarded their flight.

Monday 28 June
CANCELLED APPEARANCE
Celebration of Life, **Cypress Pointe Plantation, McCrea, near Baton Rouge, Louisianna, USA**
With The Amboy Dukes, BB King, The Allman Brothers Band, Canned Heat, The Chambers Brothers, Chuck Berry, Country Joe McDonald, The Flying Burrito Brothers, Ike & Tina Turner, It's A Beautiful Day, John Lee Hooker, Richie Havens, Roland Kirk and Taj Mahal among many others.
This ambitious project saw the promoters of the Toronto Rock & Roll Revival, Atlanta Pop and New

Orleans Pop Festivals joining forces to stage this huge eight-day festival (21-28 June) on a secluded peninsula off the Atchafalaya River. From the outset it was dogged by problems when the promoters could not obtain a license to open the festival until the 23 June. The first live performance was not until the following day and the festival closed down in the early hours of 28 June following an all-night show at which Pink Floyd are believed not to have played. The event ended a day early after an invasion by two motorcycle gangs, members of which were charged with attempted murder, inciting a riot and assaulting a law officer. Two of the promoters also went missing after IRS officials filed tax liens totalling $700,000 on ticket manifesto's.

Thursday 1 July
CONCERT
Internationale Musikforum Ossiachersee, Congress Center Villach, Stiftshoff, Ossiach, Austria
Set list: 'Echoes' / 'Careful With That Axe, Eugene' / 'Set The Controls For The Heart Of The Sun' / 'Atom Heart Mother' (with brass and choir).
Pink Floyd appeared at this city festival (running 25 June - 5 July), which featured a programme of contemporary orchestras - the only other non-classical group to appear was Tangerine Dream. The event was highlighted on Austrian radio and on the Bayerischer Rundfunk TV channel as *Musikforum Ossiachersee*, although it is not known if Pink Floyd were included. A triple LP of the festival, *Ossiach Live* (BASF 4921119-3), was released later in the year but, for contractual reasons, did not feature Pink Floyd.

Monday 19 – Thursday 22 July
RECORDING SESSIONS
Morgan Sound Studios, Willesden, London, England
Recording for the album *Meddle*.

Saturday 14 August
PRESS REPORT
London England
Sounds reported that Pink Floyd's touring PA and backline comprised of the following equipment: 6 x 100 Watt Hiwatt Amps; 17 x 100 Watt WEM Amps; 1 x 40 Watt WEM Amp; 1 x Leslie 145 Speaker; 4 x WEM 2x15 Speakers; 8 x WEM 4x12 Speakers; 11 x WEM 4x12 Speaker Columns; 8 x WEM 2x15 Speaker Columns; 4 x WEM Horn Units; 2 x WEM Mixers; 5 x Binson Echo Units; 1 x WEM 1x12 Speaker Cabinet; 4 x 3x10 WEM Speaker Columns; 2 x Leslie 147 Speakers; 2 x WEM Horns; 4 x Tannoy Speakers; 1 x HH Electronic 100 Watt Amp; 1 x Leslie Amp; 6 x Sennheiser Mics; 12 x Shure Mics; 12 x Microphone Stands; 2 x Fender Stratocaster Guitars; 2 x Fender Precision Bass Guitars; 1 x Ludwig Drum Kit with 7 x Drums of various sizes; 9 x Cymbals of various sizes; 1 x Hammond M102 Organ; 1 x Farfisa Organ Pack; 3 x Revox Tape recorders; 1 x Gong with stand.

JAPANESE TOUR
Pink Floyd departed for Japan via Hong Kong on 31 July. This, their first visit to the country saw them perform twice at an open-air festival and at one indoor show. Extensive publicity surrounded Pink Floyd's debut performances in Japan with parts of the first show being filmed by Japanese TV although the content and broadcast details remain unknown.

Friday 6 August
CONCERT
Hakone Aphrodite '71, Seikei Gakuen Jofundai [near Lake Ashi], Hakone, Japan
With Buffy Sainte Marie, The 1910 Fruit Gum Company, Mops, Strawberry Path, Happenings Four, Yosuke Yamashita Trio, Masahiko Sato Torio and others.
Set list: 'Green Is The Colour' / 'Careful With That Axe, Eugene' / 'Atom Heart Mother' / 'Echoes' / 'Cymbaline' / encore: 'A Saucerful Of Secrets'.

Saturday 7 August
CONCERT
Hakone Aphrodite '71, Seikei Gakuen Jofundai [near Lake Ashi], Hakone, Japan
With Buffy Sainte Marie, The 1910 Fruit Gum Company, Mops, Strawberry Path, Happenings Four, Yosuke Yamashita Trio, Masahiko Sato Torio and others.
Set list: 'Green Is The Colour' / 'Careful With That Axe, Eugene' / 'Atom Heart Mother' / 'Echoes' / 'Set The Controls For The Heart Of The Sun' / encore: 'A Saucerful Of Secrets'.

Monday 9 August
CONCERT
Festival Hall, Osaka, Japan
The last night of the tour. Supported by Buffy Sainte Marie and The 1910 Fruit Gum Company.
Set list: 'Green Is The Colour' / 'Careful With That

147

BELOW: PINK FLOYD ATTENDING A PRESS CONFERENCE IN TOKYO, JAPAN ON 5 AUGUST 1971.

Axe, Eugene' / 'Fat Old Sun' / 'Atom Heart Mother' / 'Echoes' / 'Set The Controls For The Heart Of The Sun' / 'Cymbaline' / encore: 'A Saucerful Of Secrets'.

AUSTRALIAN TOUR

Pink Floyd's first ever shows in Australia were announced in the Australian music press in June by the promoter, International Booking Corporation, to take place at the Dallas Brooks Hall in Melbourne on 21 and 22 August. Less than a month later a single show was being advertised for the Festival Hall on 13 August.

Friday 13 August
CONCERT
Festival Hall, Melbourne, Australia
Supported by Lindsay Bourke and Pirana.
Set list: 'Atom Heart Mother' / 'Green Is The Colour' / 'Careful With That Axe, Eugene' / 'Set The Controls For The Heart Of The Sun' / 'Echoes' / 'Cymbaline' / encore: 'A Saucerful Of Secrets'.
Go-Set magazine reported that: 'The promoters spent so much time and energy publicising their Rock Concert Club that there was very little mention of the concert actually at hand, the amazing Pink Floyd. The result was a not very full Festival Hall that really didn't do justice to the occasion at all. For a moment, when they first readied themselves on stage before going into "Atom Heart Mother", I wondered whether all those fascinating electric sounds were really going to come from that stage, from those instruments. As soon as they began playing I realised it was indeed so, rock instruments taken into an adventure of Pink Floyd's. The amazing thing was the quality of their sound, exactly like their records, even at Festival Hall. Pink Floyd are very serious and involved as they play. The only showmanship is that of concentration, listening to one another, waiting for their separate parts, weaving those adventurous, inventive space patterns.'

Sunday 15 August
CONCERT
St. Leger Stand, Randwick Racecourse, Randwick, Sydney, Australia
The last night of the tour. 1.00pm afternoon show.
Supported by Lindsay Bourke and Pirana.
Set list included: 'Careful With That Axe, Eugene' / 'Set The Controls For The Heart Of The Sun'.
Pink Floyd were featured three times on the local early evening TV show *Get To Know*, which included two previews of the show. The broadcast on the 15 August at 6.00pm included an interview before this show and included part of their performance of 'Careful With That Axe, Eugene' (with music dubbed from *Ummagumma*) and 'Set The Controls For The Heart Of The Sun' (with, curiously, music dubbed from 'A Saucerful Of Secrets', again from *Ummagumma*). Pink Floyd departed Australia via Hong Kong on the

17 August, arriving back in London on 19 August.

Monday 23 - Friday 27 August
RECORDING SESSIONS
Air Studios, Oxford Street, London, England
Recording for the album *Meddle*.

Saturday 18 September
CONCERT
Festival de Musique Classique, **Pavillon de Montreux, Montreux, Switzerland**
Set list: 'Echoes' / 'Careful With That Axe, Eugene' / 'Set The Controls For The Heart Of The Sun' / 'Cymbaline' / 'Atom Heart Mother' (with members of the London Philharmonic Orchestra and choir) / encore: 'A Saucerful Of Secrets'.

Sunday 19 September
CONCERT
Festival de Musique Classique, **Pavillon de Montreux, Montreux, Switzerland**
Set list included: 'Atom Heart Mother' (with members of the London Philharmonic Orchestra and choir).

Tuesday 21 September
RECORDING SESSION
Command Studios, Piccadilly, London, England
Mixing for the album *Meddle*. Incidentally, Command Studios were situated in the BBC's former 201 Piccadilly Studios, where the band had previously recorded radio sessions in 1967 and 1968.

Wednesday 22 September
CONCERT
Kungliga Tennishallen, Stockholm, Sweden
Set list: 'Careful With That Axe, Eugene' / 'Fat Old Sun' / 'Atom Heart Mother' / 'Set The Controls For The Heart Of The Sun' / 'Cymbaline' / 'Echoes' / 'A Saucerful Of Secrets'.

Thursday 23 September
CONCERT
KB Hallen, Copenhagen, Denmark
The last night of the tour.
Set list: 'Careful With That Axe, Eugene' / 'Fat Old Sun' / 'Set The Controls For The Heart Of The Sun' / 'Atom Heart Mother' / 'Echoes' / 'Cymbaline' / 'A Saucerful Of Secrets' / encore: 'Blues'.

Sunday 26 September
RECORDING SESSION
Command Studios, Piccadilly, London, England
Recording for the album *Meddle*.

Wednesday 29 & Thursday 30 September
REHEARSALS
Granada Cinema, Wandsworth, London, England

Thursday 30 September
RADIO SHOW
BBC Paris Cinema, Lower Regent Street, London, England
Pink Floyd recorded a live audience show between 10.00pm and 11.30pm on this day for BBC Radio One in which the band performed, in order, 'Fat Old Sun', 'One Of These Days', 'The Embryo', 'Echoes' and 'Blues'. It was broadcast on *Sounds Of The Seventies* on 12 October at 10.00pm but omitted 'Blues'. For unexplained reasons this track was only ever broadcast on WNEW radio in New York having been sent the tapes under license by the BBC. Subsequent BBC Transcription Services discs have also omitted 'Blues' as well as 'The Embryo' in order to form a disc suitable for a complete 60 minute broadcast. *Radio Times* commented in a preview of the show that, 'From their inception, The Pink Floyd have been a pleasantly confusing group. Classic Top 20 hits like "See Emily Play" lured many an unsuspecting pop-picker into range of the harsh feedback of the early Floyd stage act; and their recent Ron Geesin aided "Atom Heart Mother" emphasised the relative feebleness of the songs on the other side of the album. Their fine sense of the dramatic lends itself to sound-pictures painted on a big canvas: hopefully, a new work will be unveiled tonight.'

Monday 4 – Thursday 7 October
RECORDING & FILMING SESSIONS
Roman Amphitheatre, Pompeii, Italy
Filming and recording for the film *Pink Floyd Live At Pompeii*.

Sunday 10 October
CONCERT
Great Hall, Bradford University, Bradford, England
Set list: 'Careful With That Axe, Eugene' / 'Fat Old Sun' / 'Set The Controls For The Heart Of The Sun' / 'Atom Heart Mother' // 'Echoes' / 'Cymbaline' / 'One Of These Days' / 'A Saucerful Of Secrets' / encore: 'Blues'.

Monday 11 October
CONCERT
Town Hall, Birmingham, England
Set list: 'Careful With That Axe, Eugene' / 'Fat Old Sun' / 'Atom Heart Mother' / 'Set The Controls For The Heart Of The Sun' / 'Echoes' / 'Cymbaline' / 'One of These Days' / 'A Saucerful Of Secrets' / encore: 'Blues'.

NORTH AMERICAN TOUR

Pink Floyd's most extensive North American tour to date was booked by Allen Frey of the Ashley Famous Agency based in New York. Frey continued to act as Pink Floyd's booking agent in North America right through to *The Wall* shows in 1980. Early drafts of Pink Floyd's tour show the band scheduled to appear at Taft Auditorium, Cincinnati, Ohio (30 October); Music Hall, Boston, Massachusetts (4 November) and Lowes Theatre, Providence, Rhode Island (5 November).

Friday 15 October
CONCERT
Winterland Auditorium, San Francisco, California, USA

Saturday 16 October
CONCERT
Civic Auditorium, Santa Monica, California, USA
Set list: 'Careful With That Axe, Eugene' / 'Fat Old Sun' / 'Set The Controls For The Heart Of The Sun' / 'Atom Heart Mother' / 'The Embryo' / 'Cymbaline' / 'Echoes' / 'A Saucerful Of Secrets' / encore: 'Blues'.

Direct Productions Inc Presents
Pink Floyd
Finnegan
San Diego Community Concourse on Sunday October 17th

Sunday 17 October
CONCERT
Convention Hall, Community Concourse, San Diego, California, USA
Supported by Mike Finnigan and Jerry Woods.
Set list: 'Careful With That Axe, Eugene' / 'Fat Old Sun' / 'Atom Heart Mother' / 'The Embryo' / 'Set The Controls For The Heart Of The Sun' / 'Cymbaline' / 'Echoes' / 'A Saucerful Of Secrets' / encore: 'Blues'.
The San Diego Union reported that: 'The Community Concourse was turned into a space ship for two hours

last night by English group Pink Floyd. Their music, as strange as their name, was an odd mixture of electronic effects, whispers, screams and breathy vocal intonations, which created a 2001 effect. The group showed great sensitivity for balance and continuity. Each set Floyd played created an overpowering feeling of weightlessly drifting in space. The music was uncluttered and flowing. Rarely did Floyd sing while they played their instruments. Unique and welcomed by the enthusiastic audience was the special effects they provided. The sounds of seagulls, crashing waves, footsteps, which seemed to come from all corners of the auditorium, and applause. Pink Floyd is unique and totally electric.'

Tuesday 19 October
CONCERT
National Guard Armory, Eugene, Oregon, USA

Thursday 21 October
CONCERT
Willamette University, Salem, Oregon, USA

Friday 22 October
CONCERT
Paramount Theatre, Seattle, Washington, USA
Set list included: 'Atom Heart Mother' / 'Set The Controls For The Heart Of The Sun' / 'A Saucerful Of Secrets' / 'Careful With That Axe, Eugene' / 'Cymbaline' / 'One Of These Days' / encore: 'Echoes'.

Saturday 23 October
CONCERT
Gardens Arena, Vancouver, British Columbia, Canada
Set list included: 'Set The Controls For The Heart Of The Sun' / 'Atom Heart Mother' / 'Careful With That Axe, Eugene' / 'Cymbaline' / encore: 'Echoes'.

Tuesday 26 October
CONCERT
Eastown Theater, Detroit, Michigan, USA
Set list: 'The Embryo' / 'Fat Old Sun' / 'Set The Controls For The Heart Of The Sun' / 'Atom Heart Mother' / 'One Of These Days' / 'Careful With That Axe, Eugene' / 'Cymbaline' / 'Echoes' / encore: 'A Saucerful Of Secrets'.

Wednesday 27 October
CONCERT
Auditorium Theatre, Chicago, Illinois, USA
Set list: 'The Embryo' / 'Fat Old Sun' / 'Set The Controls For The Heart Of The Sun' / 'Atom Heart Mother' / 'One Of These Days' / 'Careful With That

Axe, Eugene' / 'Cymbaline' / 'Echoes' / encore: 'A Saucerful Of Secrets'.

HOMECOMING 1971
"LET'S WORK TOGETHER!"
THUR OCT 28
PINK FLOYD
GUARDIAN ANGEL
FRI OCT 29
PARLIAMENT FUNKADELIC
BLACK ENSEMBLE
SAT OCT 30
QUICKSILVER
CATFISH+
HILL AUDITORIUM
ANN ARBOR

149

Thursday 28 October
CONCERT
Hill Auditorium, University of Michigan, Ann Arbor, Michigan, USA
Supported by Guardian Angel.
Set list: 'The Embryo' / 'Fat Old Sun' / 'Set The Controls For The Heart Of The Sun' / 'Atom Heart Mother' / 'One Of These Days' / 'Careful With That Axe, Eugene' / 'Cymbaline' / 'Echoes' / encore: 'Blues'.

Sunday 31 October
CONCERT
Fieldhouse, University of Toledo, Toledo, Ohio, USA
Set list: 'The Embryo' / 'Fat Old Sun' / 'Set The Controls For The Heart Of The Sun' / 'Atom Heart Mother' / 'One Of These Days' / 'Careful With That Axe, Eugene' / 'Cymbaline' / 'Echoes' / encore: 'Blues'.

Tuesday 2 November
CONCERT
McCarter Theatre, Princeton University, Princeton, New Jersey, USA
The Daily Princeton reported that: 'The Floyd are something from a different century - rarely smiling, never speaking to their audience except to put down a request with a weary mincingly English, "We'll never play "Astronomy Dominé" again." Unreceptive as they may be, the Floyd are undeniably good musicians with a unique style of composition. Their main strength, and their claim to the kingship of psychedelia, is their

mastery of electronics - they proved perfectly capable of reproducing the synthetic soundstorms and whispery, sibilant, echoing vocals that characterise their albums in concert. In fact, they actually surpassed their studio work by employing a quadraphonic sound system that, piloted by the organist with a modified joystick control, could seemingly place the group's sound effects anywhere in the theatre. The illusion of movement was sufficiently astonishing that anyone attending the concert drugged must have gotten a far bigger dose of psychedelia than he had bargained for. The magnificent six-ton sound system that accomplished this - the stage was piled ten feet high with amplifiers, while more equipment was set up in the balcony - was also quite sufficient to fill a hall the size of, say, the Spectrum. In McCarter, it was literally painfully loud, and I must admit that sheer volume drove me out halfway through a concert that I was otherwise enjoying very much.'

Wednesday 3 November
CONCERT
Central Theatre, Passaic, New Jersey, USA

Thursday 4 November
CONCERT
Lowes Theatre, Providence, Rhode Island, USA

Friday 5 November
RECORD RELEASE
Meddle
UK album release. US album release on Saturday 30 October 1971.
NME commented that, 'Pink Floyd have done it again; something I thought would be difficult after the brilliance they showed with the "Atom Heart Mother Suite", a piece of musical mastery that took great courage to put on record, and even greater courage to perform live – which they did successfully... an exceptionally good album.'

Friday 5 November
CONCERT
Assembly Hall, Hunter College, Columbia University of New York, Brooklyn, New York, USA
Compered by Zach of WPLJ Radio.
Set list: 'The Embryo' / 'Fat Old Sun' / 'Set The Controls For The Heart Of The Sun' / 'Atom Heart Mother' / 'One Of These Days' / 'Careful With That Axe, Eugene' / 'Cymbaline' / 'Echoes' / encore: 'A Saucerful Of Secrets'.

Saturday 6 November
CONCERT
Emerson Gymnasium, Case Western Reserve University, Cleveland, Ohio, USA
Set list: 'The Embryo' / 'Fat Old Sun' / 'Set The

Controls For The Heart Of The Sun' / 'Atom Heart Mother' / 'One Of These Days' / 'Careful With That Axe, Eugene' / 'Cymbaline' / 'Echoes' / encore: 'Blues'.

Monday 8 November
CONCERT
Peace Bridge Exhibition Center, Buffalo, New York, USA
Set list included: 'Set The Controls For The Heart Of The Sun'.

Tuesday 9 November
CONCERT
Centre Sportif, Université de Montréal, Montréal, Québec, Canada

Wednesday 10 November
CONCERT
Pavillon de la Jeunesse, Québec City, Québec, Canada
Set list: 'The Embryo' / 'Fat Old Sun' / 'Set The Controls For The Heart Of The Sun' / 'One Of These Days' / 'Atom Heart Mother' / 'Cymbaline' / 'Careful With That Axe, Eugene' / 'Echoes' / encore: 'A Saucerful Of Secrets'.

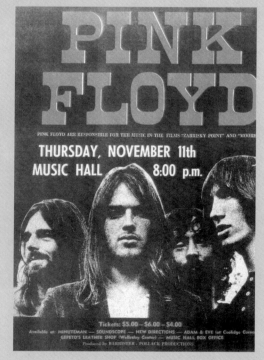

Thursday 11 November
CONCERT
Music Hall, Boston, Massachusetts, USA

Friday 12 November
CONCERT
Irvine Auditorium, University of Pennsylvania, Philadelphia, Pennsylvania, USA
Set list: 'The Embryo' / 'Fat Old Sun' / 'Set The Controls For The Heart Of The Sun' / 'Atom Heart Mother' / 'One Of These Days' / 'Careful With That Axe, Eugene' / 'Cymbaline' / encore: 'Echoes'.

Saturday 13 November
CONCERT
Convention Hall, Asbury Park, New Jersey, USA

Sunday 14 November
CONCERT
The Gymnasium, State University of New York, Stony Brook, Long Island, New York, USA

Monday 15 November
CONCERT
Main Hall, Carnegie Hall, Manhattan, New York City, New York, USA
Set list: 'Set The Controls For The Heart Of The Sun' / 'Atom Heart Mother' / 'One Of These Days' / 'Careful With That Axe, Eugene' / 'Cymbaline' / encore: 'Echoes'.

Tuesday 16 November
CONCERT
Lisner Auditorium, George Washington University, Washington, District of Columbia, USA
Set list: 'The Embryo' / 'Fat Old Sun' / 'Set The Controls For The Heart Of The Sun' / 'Atom Heart Mother' / 'One Of These Days' / 'Careful With That Axe, Eugene' / encore: 'Echoes'.
The Washington Post reported that: 'This was no ordinary rock show - it was the closest thing that

rock music has to show in the way of avant-garde music. Even apart from the strange opening - in which a fellow gifted as magician, juggler and fire-eater, breathed forth flame so white-strobed lady could light her cigarette - there were other novelties in the Pink Floyd show at Lisner Auditorium last night. This English rock group prepared to satisfy a sold-out house, arrived with electronics in the highest. Echo and reverberation units, time delivery devices, synthesisers and taped sound segments were all part of the act. They played into a 32 channel mixing panel that relayed the joy into a public address system completely encircling the audience. Any given instrument, by these means could be 'placed' at any position in the hall and could be mixed with all kinds of taped wonders such as chirping birds and high volume 'white' noise. They did not worry too much with the usual content of music. When they sang, the vocals were not important as words with meanings but rather as aspects of an exciting tension that you could hear in the process of creation. Form and content were replaced by dynamics. The band sounded sometimes like a screaming saw, sometimes like a fleet of intergalactic jets. A guitar, with this group, became a screeching bird. Drums were explosions. "Set The Controls" as they sang (and as the audience did) "For The Heart Of The Sun"'.

Friday 19 November
CONCERT
Syria Mosque Theater, Pittsburgh, Pennsylvania, USA

Saturday 20 November
CONCERT
Taft Auditorium, Cincinnati, Ohio, USA
The last night of the tour.

Set list: 'improvisations' / 'The Embryo' / 'Fat Old Sun' / 'Set The Controls For The Heart Of The Sun' / 'Atom Heart Mother' / 'Careful With That Axe, Eugene' / 'Cymbaline' / 'Echoes' / encore: 'Blues'.

Monday 29 November
RECORD RELEASE
'One Of These Days' / 'Fearless'
US 7-inch single release.

Monday 29 November – Friday 10 December
STUDIO REHEARSALS
Decca Studios, Broadhurst Gardens, West Hampstead, London, England
Pink Floyd spent some time composing, writing and making initial demo recordings for their stage show and album that would eventually become *The Dark Side Of The Moon*. This was the same location the Beatles failed their Decca Records audition in 1962 and where Jonathan King auditioned Jokers Wild in 1965.

Monday 13 – Monday 20 December
RECORDING & FILMING SESSIONS
Studio Europasinor, Paris, France
Additional recording and filming for *Pink Floyd Live At Pompeii*.

Sunday 26 December
TV SHOW
Beat Club, Radio Bremen TV Studios, Bremen, Germany
Pink Floyd were reported to be appearing on the NDR German network TV show *Beat Club* (episode number 74) on this date at 6.00pm but the content details remain unknown.

ROBERT PATERSO...

EARLS C

FRIDAY 18 MAY

Extra Date By P

PINK F

SATURDAY, 19th F

TICKETS: £2.00, £1.75, £1.00 From Box Offic

Postal applications for £2.00 tickets only with S.A.E. to:

We recommend calling at box office p

CHEQUES PAYABLE TO: Advanc

All Profits are being

Please note that ticket applicants are requested not to call the Earls Cou

playing different tunes

announces

OURT

— SOLD OUT

blic Demand

LOYD

AY at 8.00 p.m.

Tel. 01- 371 6638, 10 a.m. to 7 p.m.

K FLOYD BOX OFFICE, EARLS COURT, S.W.5.

nally to avoid disappointment

eservations Agency Ltd.

aid to Shelter

in switchboard number, only the BOX OFFICE: 01-371 6638

1972 - 1973

5

THE INITIAL IDEAS FOR WRITING SOMETHING NEW HAD BEEN DISCUSSED TOWARDS THE END OF 1971 AT A BAND MEETING IN THE USUAL VENUE OF NICK MASON'S KITCHEN, FOLLOWED BY A PERIOD OF STUDIO WRITING AT THE DECCA STUDIOS IN BROADHURST GARDENS, WEST HAMPSTEAD. WATERS, UNDOUBTEDLY THE MAIN SOURCE OF INSPIRATION, BEGAN FURIOUSLY WRITING LYRICS SHORTLY AFTER THE END OF THEIR LAST US TOUR. AN ALBUM'S WORTH OF MATERIAL WOULD ALSO BE OF CONVENIENT LENGTH FOR THE FIRST HALF OF A NEW STAGE SHOW, THE SECOND HALF OF WHICH COULD BE GIVEN OVER TO ESTABLISHED FAVOURITES. AS WATERS EXPLAINED, 'IT HAD TO BE QUICK, BECAUSE WE HAD A TOUR STARTING. IT MIGHT HAVE BEEN ONLY SIX WEEKS BEFORE WE HAD TO HAVE SOMETHING TO PERFORM.'[1]

He came up with the specific idea of dealing with all the things that drive people mad, not to mention a link for some unfinished and unused studio pieces. The album would focus on the enormous pressures the band themselves were experiencing on the road: the strains of travelling and the problems of living, often abroad for great stretches of time, and coping with (and without) money. It would also explore violence, social problems and the comforts of religion – this last theme no doubt prompted by their recent tours through middle America.

It all happened in such a short space of time it is almost unbelievable, as Wright confirmed, 'At the start we only had vague ideas about madness being a theme. We rehearsed a lot just putting down ideas and then in the next rehearsals we used them. It flowed really well. There was a strong thing in it that made it easier to do.'[2]

Lyrically, it was Waters' most profound and focused effort to date, and for the first time he dominated the creative input almost exclusively, conveying a vision all his own. The success of The Dark Side Of The Moon is probably attributed to the fact that it was kept deliberately simple and accessible as possible, with strong dynamics and melodies. It was certainly more down to earth than earlier flights of fancy such as 'Echoes'. Indeed, Waters gave some hint of what to expect on the forthcoming tour when he spoke to Sounds that January under the headline, 'Pink Floyd Have Gone Mental!' 'In concept it's more literal, not as abstract as the things we've done before.'[3]

'I think at that time he [Waters] was finding himself as a lyric writer,' remembers Gilmour. 'He was realising that he could get to grips with more serious issues, some political and others that involved him personally. His style had developed and improved. I remember him saying that he wanted to write this album absolutely straight, clear and direct, for nothing to be hidden in mysteries, to get away from all the psychedelic warblings and say exactly what he wanted for the first time.'[4]

Finally, the new work was given the provisional title Dark Side Of The Moon. But said Gilmour, 'At one time, it was called Eclipse because Medicine Head did an album called Dark Side Of The Moon. But, that didn't sell well, so what the hell. I was against Eclipse and we felt a bit annoyed because we had already thought of the title before Medicine Head came out. Not annoyed at them, but because we wanted to use the title.'[5]

Both on stage and on record the piece would propel the group into the superstar league, severing their underground roots forever. As for Waters, it boosted his confidence as a writer – his skills clearly far outstripped anything any of the others could achieve – and he became the self-appointed lyricist of the band.

With their first country-wide UK tour since 1969 about to commence, they were still working out the last few details and intricacies of the piece and booked a few days' rehearsal at a warehouse owned by the Rolling Stones in Bermondsey, south London. Final dress rehearsals would take place at the Rainbow Theatre, where they would return to perform exactly one month later.

To complete the production, the band purchased a brand-new WEM PA with a twenty-eight channel mixing desk and a four-channel 360-degree quadraphonic sound system. They also had their first complete lighting rig, that to date had still only comprised of a couple of oil projectors, built to specification by their newly acquired lighting designer, Arthur Max who had evidently impressed them as house engineer at Floyd's Fillmore East show in 1970. Max remained with the band through to the end of 1977 and now enjoys a lucrative career as a Hollywood production designer. In addition, specially recorded backing tapes were created to accompany the

RICHARD WRIGHT << Sometimes I look at our huge truck and tons of equipment and think, "Christ, all I'm doing is playing an organ!" >>

music on stage. A total of over nine tons of equipment, which required assembly by a crew of seven each afternoon before the performance, was put together and transported by three trucks. Wright himself remarked on the scale of the operation: 'Sometimes I look at our huge truck and tons of equipment and think, "Christ, all I'm doing is playing an organ!"'[6]

It was also the first time Pink Floyd had taken an entire album on the road, and although they had been used to previewing material before recording it, *Dark Side Of The Moon* was a piece that was vastly improved and refined as a result of the decision to tour with it before its release. It was performed in exactly the same order as on the finished album but the early shows lacked synthesisers: for example, the track 'On The Run' was merely a keyboard and guitar improvisation, sometimes referred to as 'The Travel Sequence' concluding, not in an explosion, but a confused cacophony of sound effects. 'The Great Gig In The Sky', on the other hand, widely known to fans at the time as 'The Mortality Sequence', was an electric piano solo backed by pre-recorded tapes of readings from the Book of Ephesians, the Lord's Prayer and other biblical discourses, along with recordings of the controversial British broadcaster Malcolm Muggeridge in full rant.

Some of the other tracks had been part-written already: The music on 'Brain Damage', for example, was written at the time of *Meddle*, but not used, while 'Us And Them' came out of the previously mentioned 'The Violent Sequence' from the *Zabriskie Point* sessions and was resurrected by Wright.

Despite first-night hitches at the Brighton Dome, caused by an electrical fault that knocked out the tape playback at the start of 'Money', and a total power failure in Manchester, the tour was acclaimed, if not fully comprehended, by the public. And, proving the value of

roadwork, Waters came up with the lyrics for the 'Brain Damage'/'Eclipse' sequence just in time for their show in Leicester - eight dates into the tour. 'The piece felt unfinished to me when we were doing it on the road,' he later recalled. 'I came in one day and said, "Here, I've just written the ending and this is it."'[7]

Undoubtedly the band's pivotal performance came in mid-February at the Rainbow, where the world's press sat in attendance to witness *The Dark Side Of The Moon* in all its seemingly well-rehearsed glory. In a series of presentations, and despite some rather stilted performances, Pink Floyd were heralded as a triumph of the imagination and for the first time greeted by critical acclaim throughout the national press.

For the time being the album's recording was deferred: the French director Barbet Schroeder invited them to write music for *La Vallee*. In two one-week sessions, one before and one after their tour of Japan, the band composed and recorded the entire work at the Strawberry Studios, in the Chateau d'Hérouville near Paris (known as the 'Honky Chateau' thanks to Elton John). The album was released in June as *Obscured By Clouds* and once again the film – about a young woman's spiritual awakening in Papua New Guinea – although not a great success elsewhere, was well received in France.

Obscured By Clouds is as striking as it is subtle, with some remarkable music that would feature on later tours. Perhaps the last true combined effort by the band, the album contains some particularly pensive lyrics by Waters. 'Free Four', for example, deals for the first time with the pressures of touring, well before the subject was taken to a conclusion on *The Dark Side Of The Moon*. His father's death is also discussed, perhaps flippantly, but it was a theme that later recurred on *The Wall* with greater vehemence. Significantly, with 'Childhood's End' Gilmour made his last complete lyrical/musical composition in this line-up of Floyd. The album ends with 'Absolutely Curtains', which includes taped recordings of a religious chant performed by the Mapuga tribe.

The album completed, and their customary August holiday period over with, Pink Floyd continued their extensive tour throughout North America and Europe, playing their largest (and generally sold-out) venues to date on both continents. At one particularly spectacular concert, at the Hollywood Bowl, eight powerful searchlights beamed rays skywards from behind the domed stage of the vast amphitheatre into the night sky,

RIGHT: PINK FLOYD PERFORMING
THE DARK SIDE OF THE MOON
FOR THE FIRST TIME TO A
LONDON AUDIENCE AT THE
RAINBOW THEATRE, FINSBURY
PARK, FEBRUARY 1972.

トリップ・サウンド
ピンク・フロイドが運んできた7トンの光と音

ピンク・フロイドがまたやって来た。今度は7トンの機材で創り出す2時間半の音と光
の演出に　観客はただただ酔いしれ　他には見られないロック・シーンが展開された。

撮影｜小堀篤信

ABOVE: PINK FLOYD ON TOUR IN
JAPAN, MARCH 1972.

and a colourful fireworks display rounded off the evening. Elsewhere on other tours of the time, impressive effects included sheets of flame shooting from cauldrons at the back of the stage during 'Echoes', and a huge Chinese gong that burst into flames at the climax of 'Set The Controls For The Heart Of The Sun'.

It was also the year that Pink Floyd delved into other performing arts to enhance their work. The band had already provided incidental music for the Ballet Rambert in 1969 and plans were now approaching fruition to link up with Europe's foremost contemporary

ABOVE: THE CINEMA POSTER FOR *LA VALLEE / OBSCURED BY CLOUDS*, AUGUST 1972. PINK FLOYD'S SECOND SOUNDTRACK FOR THE FILM DIRECTOR BARBET SCHROEDER FURTHER REINFORCED THEIR POPULARITY IN FRANCE.

ballet school, based in Marseilles and directed by Roland Petit. The band were brought to the attention of Petit by his daughter, a fan, who had suggested marrying a traditional ballet with modern music. The basic idea was discussed by the two parties in the middle of the band's American tours of 1971, when it was suggested that Proust's novel *Remembrance Of Things Past* be adapted for the project. However, this idea floundered almost immediately, having failed to fire anyone's imagination sufficiently, and, after unsuccessful attempts

by the band to read the monumental work, the project was abandoned. Petit even considered adapting either *A Thousand And One Nights* or *Carmen*, but again these ideas were dropped.

Waters recalled, with some disbelief, the farcical planning meeting that took place in London that year: 'First of all it was "Proust", then it was *Aladdin*, then it was something else. We had this great lunch one day - me, Nick [Mason] and Steve [O'Rourke]. We all went to have lunch with Nureyev, Roman Polanski, Roland Petit, some film producer or other. What a laugh. It was to talk about the projected idea for us doing the music, and Roland choreographing it, and Rudy Bryans being the star, and Roman Polanski directing the film, and making this fantastic ballet film. It was all a complete joke because nobody had any idea what they wanted to do.

'We all sat around this table until someone thumped the table and said, "What's the idea then?" and everyone just sat there drinking this wine and getting more and more drunk, with more and more poovery going on around the table, until someone suggested *Frankenstein* and then Nureyev started getting a bit worried. And when Polanski was drunk enough he started to suggest we make the blue movie to end all blue movies, and then it all petered out into cognac and coffee and then we jumped into our cars and split. God knows what happened after we left.'[8]

Although unlikely to have ever reached fruition, there had even been reported plans, combined with a full page advert in *Cash Box*, the US record industry trade magazine, of the staging of the ballet production at the 10,000-seat Great Palais in Paris on 10 June 1971, with a 108-piece orchestra, and have it broadcast on Eurovision.

In what seemed like a sensible conclusion to their encounter it was agreed that the band should compose forty minutes' worth of original material to which Petit

NICK MASON << **The thing to do is to really move people. To turn them on, to subject them to a fantastic experience, to do something to stretch their imagination.** >>

DAVID GILMOUR << **But, the reality of all these people prancing around in tights in front of us didn't feel like what we wanted to do long term.** >>

would provide choreography. But, still pushed for time, Pink Floyd finally agreed on a forty-minute set of existing material from their current repertoire and the performance was finally staged at Marseilles, at a residency mid-way through the band's European tour in November 1972. Waters, for one, approached it with some trepidation: 'Playing live means that we've got to be note-perfect each night, otherwise the dancers are going to get lost, and we won't be using a score, we'll be playing from memory. That might be a bit difficult.'[9]

From here the production moved to Paris for a series of weekend shows in January and February of 1973. Curiously, only four of these featured Pink Floyd performing live: all of the other dates used pre-recorded music. Gilmour even mentioned plans to take the show to Canada, 'but they couldn't because in the Maïakovski ballet that goes before it, there's two pieces both written by the same man, which had something to do with the Russian Revolution and things. In one part of it there's a thing with huge red flags draped on the stage, and the Canadian government wouldn't let them use it.'[10]

The conclusion of this extraordinary project illustrated yet another facet of Pink Floyd's ever-widening talents. Their shows were treated with awe and wonder by fans and critics alike. As Nick Mason said: 'The thing to do is to really move people. To turn them on, to subject them to a fantastic experience, to do something to stretch their imagination.'[11] 'But', concluded Gilmour, 'the reality of all these people prancing around in tights in front of us didn't feel like what we wanted to do long term.'[12]

Nineteen seventy-three was the first year in the band's career that the UK was largely ignored in favour of North America, which received the full-scale sensory assault of a greatly improved 'Dark Side Of The Moon' on two extensive tours.

Additional on-stage personnel were also recruited for the very first time including saxophonist and Cambridge associate Dick Parry, who stayed on board for the next two years. For the two US tours of the year American backing vocalists Nawasa Crowder, Phylliss Lindsey and Mary Ann Lindsey, former members of Black Grass and fresh from a six month US tour with Leon Russell, were recruited to reproduce the deep, soulful harmonies the piece now required. Liza Strike and Vicki Brown took over the duties at the Earl's Court shows in May supplemented by Clare Torry at the Rainbow Theatre shows in November. All were eventually replaced by former Humble Pie backing vocal trio The Blackberries comprising Billie Barnum, Venetta Fields and Clydie King. In June 1974 Fields teamed up with Carlena Williams for Pink Floyd's tour of France and as a vocal duo retaining the name The Blackberries, they remained with the band for the next two years.

Such was the scale of the production, the touring machine was akin to a finely tuned military operation and by now Pink Floyd required a small army of technicians to make it all possible. At its core were Arthur Max and his assistants Graeme Fleming and Rob Murray who were responsible for the lighting, which, beginning with the second US tour of 1973, included a hemispherical mirror ball, which rose above the stage and reflected beams from two batteries of red lasers. Chris Adamson maintained the backline, Mick 'The Pole' Kluczinski operated the effects tapes and looked after the quad system and Alan Parsons was recruited from EMI as the front of house engineer.

At least one week before a show the tour manager and chief technician Peter Watts (who had started with the band back in late 1967), with the assistance of new recruit Robbie Williams, would go to each hall in advance and talk to the promoter and venue staff to ensure that, in particular, the stage and the electrics would be ready on show day.

Additional house staff were also needed to help deal with the equipment and run the show: two fork-lift drivers, six stage hands, two electricians, two soundmen,

PLAYING DIFFERENT TUNES 1972-1973

EARLS
AY 18 MAY
xtra Date By F

IK F
AY, 19th

159

DAVID GILMOUR << It alludes to the human condition and sets the mood for the music which describes the emotions experienced during a lifetime. Amidst the chaos there is beauty and hope for mankind. The effects are purely to help the listener understand what the whole thing is about. >>

eight follow-spot operators and one house electrician.

On a typical day two forty-foot articulated equipment trucks, crewed by two drivers each, would arrive at the venue for ten in the morning, usually after an overnight drive, to be met by the road crew, who would have flown with the band on the show day, to start setting up. This would take until at least four in the afternoon to complete, by which time the band would appear for their customary soundcheck. After the show the equipment would take less than half the time to dismantle and, once it was loaded on the trucks, the process would start all over again.

The Dark Side Of The Moon was finally released in March – a landmark album in every respect. However, all of Pink Floyd except Wright, boycotted the press reception at the London Planetarium because the quadraphonic mix had not been completed in time. Against the band's wishes, EMI presented a stereo playback through an inferior PA system.

Waters had commented to the *NME* shortly after the release of *Meddle* that, 'However long you go on working on an album I don't think you ever come out thinking, "Bugger me, I've done it this time". I don't think it's possible to make an album that you think is definitely all right from beginning to end.' Nevertheless, the album successfully combined every element of Pink Floyd's collective ability that for the first time, was consistent throughout, with strong dynamics and thoughtful lyrics.

It also boasted enough FM radio-friendly tracks, 'Money' in particular, to make a serious dent in the hard-to-crack American market, thus exposing Pink Floyd for the very first time to a mass audience, propelling them out of the weird cult band bracket and into a solidly mainstream rock market that contemporaries such as The Who and Led Zeppelin had been enjoying for some time. But it came at a price as Gilmour ruefully recalled: 'It included an element that wasn't versed in Pink Floyd's

ways. It started from the first show in America [Madison, Wisconsin]. People at the front shouting, "Play Money! Gimme something I can shake my ass to!" We had to get used to it, but previously we'd be playing to 10,000-seaters where, in the quiet passages, you could hear a pin drop.'[13]

'The thing about *Dark Side*,' commented Nick Mason, 'is that I think when it was finished, everyone felt it was the best thing we'd ever done to date, and everyone was very pleased with it, but there's no way that anyone felt it was five times as good as *Meddle*, or eight times as good as *Atom Heart Mother*, or the sort of figures that it has in fact sold. It was something of a phenomena, and was about not only being a good album, but also about being in the right place at the right time.'[14]

No one could quite explain this meteoric success, which took the band by surprise. As Rick Wright commented: 'We approached the album, I would say, in exactly the same way as any other album we've done. Except that this was a concept album. It was about madness, it was about one's fear, it was about the business – whereas none of the other albums had been about that. They may have been musically tied together, but there hadn't been a theme like that running on both sides.'[15]

The album begins and ends, as did the live shows, with a heartbeat – the simple thread that pulls the whole thing together, the essence of what it is all about and, as Gilmour said, 'It alludes to the human condition and sets the mood for the music which describes the emotions experienced during a lifetime. Amidst the chaos there is beauty and hope for mankind. The effects are purely to help the listener understand what the whole thing is about.'[16]

The album's sleeve also follows the idea through. A centre-spread gatefold repeats the central theme, showing a cardiograph blip, while the stunning front cover has an impressive, yet simple, white-light beam and a full spectrum that fans out from a central prism. The mysticism of the prism image continues in the publicity material, which used shots of the Great Pyramids at Giza in Egypt for which Storm Thorgerson and Aubrey 'Po' Powell of Hipgnosis had travelled to Egypt especially to photograph. 'It represented both the diversity and cleanliness of the sound of the music,' said Thorgerson. 'It was Roger's idea to turn the light into a heartbeat inside the sleeve, the sound that starts the music.'[17]

The recorded material itself was significantly altered from the live originals and many tracks featured female backing vocals for the first time, which lent a much softer edge to the overall piece. In addition, 'On The Run' was developed entirely in the studio to replace the comparatively weak guitar and keyboard jams while 'The Mortality Sequence' was changed beyond all recognition with a stunning improvised lead vocal from Clare Torry to form 'The Great Gig In The Sky'. Incidentally Torry, who was paid her standard £30 session fee for her contribution, which was recorded on 23 January 1973, won a half share in the copyright and an undisclosed settlement in royalties in a High Court case she brought against the band and EMI Records in April 2005. Future pressings saw the credits change to Wright/Torry.

The vastly improved production was also largely a result of the different textures used. 'Time', for example, has a creative use of sound effects and the abstract use of total silence as a second instrument to Mason's roto-tom drumming.

It is also interesting to note how Gilmour was influenced at the time and how these influences contributed to the sound of the album. A quick listen to the 1971 Beaver & Krause album *Gandharva* will reveal that the whole approach is undeniably very similar, musically. Gilmour has recently confessed to stealing bit parts such as Eric Clapton's Leslie speaker sound from 'Badge' for 'Any Colour You Like', and, unlikely as it may seem, the echoey and dry sounds on 'Money' from Elton John's earlier work.

Where *Atom Heart Mother* had employed taped voices, now Roger Waters extended this idea much further by devising a system of questions that were written out on a series of cards and presented in such a way as to prevent anticipation and to elicit a definite answer. In all he interviewed about twenty people for this exercise, including Paul and Linda McCartney (although they don't appear on the album) who were

BELOW: EARL'S COURT, LONDON, MAY 1973. EMBRACING THEIR CONTINUED SENSE OF THE THEATRICAL PINK FLOYD NOW EMPLOYED THE JAMES BOND SPECIAL EFFECTS TECHNICIAN DERRICK MEDDINGS TO ADD VISUALS TO THE SHOW WHICH BY NOW INCLUDED CLOUDS OF DRY ICE, A BURNING GONG, FLARES, SMOKE BOMBS, ROCKETS AND EXPLODING AIRCRAFT.

recording *Red Rose Speedway* with Wings in an adjacent studio; crew member Chris Adamson ('I've been mad for fucking years...') and Peter Watts' wife, Pudsey ('That geezer was cruising for a bruising'); the Abbey Road engineers and in particular the studio doorman, Jerry Driscoll, who responded magnificently ('I've always been mad...', 'I'm not frightened of dying...' and 'There is no dark side of the moon really...'). All of the questions were delivered on a one to one basis with very little repetition, to prevent interviewees having prior warning of what to expect from others who may have told them about their

own session. The questions asked about the interviewees' thoughts on life and death, what did the dark side of the moon mean to them, had they ever been violent and, in the case of Henry McCullough (Wings guitarist), 'When did you last thump someone?' According to Alan Parsons his response was 'New Year's Eve'. The next question was, 'Were you in the right?", and he said, 'I don't know, I was drunk at the time.' His wife was also asked, 'When did you last thump someone?' She said 'New Year's Eve too!'[18] Very noticeable on the finished album is a stream of manic laughter from one of the band's roadies known

BELOW: PINK FLOYD RETURNED TO THE RAINBOW THEATRE, LONDON ON 4 NOVEMBER 1973 TO PERFORM TWO BENEFIT SHOWS FOR ROBERT WYATT.

as Roger 'The Hat' Manifold who also delivers the line 'a short, sharp, shock', in describing a particularly memorable moment of road rage.

Despite the length of time the music had been gestating on the road, and the time the band had spent in the studio recording it, people still didn't understand its meaning. 'It's amazing,' said Gilmour. 'At the final mixing stage we thought it was obvious what the album was about, but still a lot of people, including engineers and roadies, when we asked them, didn't know what the LP was about. I really don't know if our things get through, but you have to carry on hoping. Our music is about neuroses. We are able to see it, and discuss it. *The Dark Side Of The Moon* itself is an allusion to the moon and lunacy. The dark side is generally related to what goes on inside people's heads – the subconscious and the unknown.'[19]

The Dark Side Of The Moon is also the highpoint of the band's collaborative powers as Waters recalls with fondness: 'They were very happy times. We discovered what we did, each of us, what our contributions were. We had gelled as a group, we were working very well together and we were working very hard, doing lots of gigs. We were in the springtime of Pink Floyd when it was all good fun and we had a common purpose – we wanted to be popular, we all wanted to be rich and famous and yet we weren't. And I could express myself within that context, and Dave could play his guitar, Rick could play keyboards and write and Nick could do what he did, and we were all content to be together and it was very jolly. A wonderful time.'[20]

The Dark Side Of The Moon was recorded and released in the stereo format, having been mixed by Chris Thomas. A short time later the album was remixed, virtually single-handedly, by Alan Parsons into quadraphonic for the expected rush in trend for the newly available quad hi-fi systems. Obviously due to the limited interest in and cost of the new format it's perhaps only now with the advent of the Hybrid SACD 5.1 version released in 2003 that listeners can fully appreciate the depth of the sonic detail that for some had lain dormant for nigh on 30 years.

By the end of 1973 sales of *The Dark Side Of The Moon* were showing little sign of tailing off on the *Billboard* US Top 100 album chart, and by now over 700,000 copies had been bought in the UK alone. From here the album would just continue to sell and sell and sell. It was calculated, some twenty-five years after its release, the album had sold in excess of thirty-five million copies worldwide, and it is still in the top five best-selling

album titles of all time. Surprisingly, it never made the UK number one spot, being thwarted by Alice Cooper's *Billion Dollar Babies*.

Despite this success, Capitol Records in the USA just weren't shaping up to the band's needs partly because many other artists on the label were being prioritised (though why that should be remains something of a mystery), although it's far more likely the

ROGER WATERS << They were very happy times. We discovered what we did, each of us, what our contributions were. We had gelled as a group, we were working very well together and we were working very hard, doing lots of gigs. >>

band knew the company had insufficient resources to cope with their requirements. Although Pink Floyd was the only modern act with which the label was having any real success – it had spent years slogging away with what was basically a cult band with limited return but was now shifting units – Capitol could do little to prevent Pink Floyd from moving on now that their contract had been fulfilled.

In late 1973 the band's manager, Steve O'Rourke, struck a deal with Clive Davis at the mighty CBS conglomerate, who, like EMI in the UK, were prepared to give Pink Floyd the artistic freedom they wanted and had the financial muscle to successfully market, distribute and promote them on a much larger scale. 'We thought they would be best for us,' explained Rick Wright, 'largely because of their size. They're well organised. When we left Capitol, they were badly organised. Also, we'll be the only act of our type on CBS. When you're competing against similar acts on the same label, someone is bound to be squeezed out. We didn't want that.'[21] Credit must go to O'Rourke for the move since the band had nothing on offer – no new material or plans for a US tour. He pulled off a deal that ensured them essential breathing space and no doubt a hefty advance to go with it.

With such an exhausting period of their career behind them, Pink Floyd went into semi-retirement, not only to catch up with their families, but also reflect on their newfound wealth and the stardom that had been thrust upon the anonymous individuals so suddenly.

Sources
1. *Zig Zag*, Issue 32, July 1973
2. *Disc & Music Echo*, c.1974
3. *Sounds*, 29 January 1972
4. *Mojo*, March 1998
5. *Sounds*, 19 May 1973
6. *Sounds*, 1 June 1974
7. *Mojo*, March 1998
8. *Zig Zag*, Issue 32, July 1973
9. *Sounds*, 29 January 1972
10. *Beetle*, May 1973
11. *Beat Instrumental*, April 1971
12-13. *Mojo*, March 1998
14-15. *The Pink Floyd Story*, Capital Radio, 7 November 1976
16. *Sounds*, 19 May 1973
17-18. *Mojo*, March 1998
19. *Sounds*, 19 May 1973
20. *Mojo*, March 1998
21. *Beetle*, January 1975

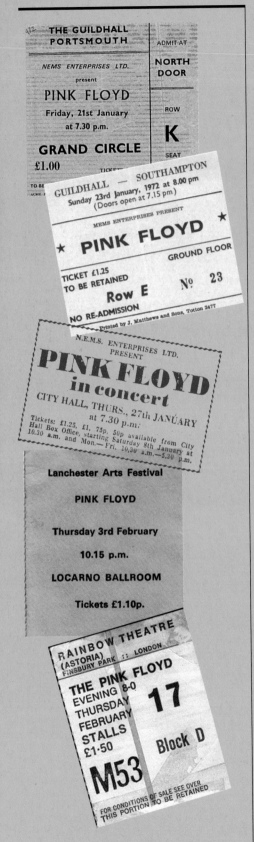

1972

January – February
RECORDING SESSIONS
EMI Studios, Abbey Road, St. John's Wood, London, England
Discontinuous recording for the album *The Dark Side Of The Moon*.

UK TOUR '72

PINK FLOYD ROAD CREW
Chris Adamson: Technician / Stage Crew
Seth Goldman: Technician / Stage Crew
Mick 'The Pole' Kluczynski: PA Technician
Arthur Max: Lighting Technician
Bobby Richardson: Technician / Stage Crew
Brian Scott: Technician / Stage Crew
Peter Watts: Head of PA / Front of House Sound

Pink Floyd premiered a new set piece on this tour that would form the backbone of their 1973 album *The Dark Side Of The Moon*. Show programmes, press reports and adverts generally refer to this piece as being 'The Dark Side Of The Moon' from the start of the UK tour up to the end of March. Thereafter, and commencing with the first US tour of the year on 14 April, the band referred to the piece as 'Eclipse' and did so right up to the end of the second US tour ending 30 September. It finally reverted back to 'The Dark Side Of The Moon' permanently thereafter. To avoid confusion this has been listed as 'The Dark Side Of The Moon' in the set lists throughout the year.

Monday 3 – Saturday 15 January
REHEARSALS
Bermondsey, London, England
Tour preparation and rehearsals took place at this south London warehouse owned by The Rolling Stones. The tour was notable for its brand new lighting and PA system – and the first use of stage monitors by the band!

Monday 17 - Wednesday 19 January
REHEARSALS
Rainbow Theatre, Finsbury Park, London, England
Three days of full production rehearsals were staged at the Rainbow Theatre before embarking on tour.

Thursday 20 January
CONCERT
The Dome, Brighton, England
Set list: *The Dark Side Of The Moon* (abandoned at 'Money' due to technical problems) / 'Atom Heart Mother' // 'Careful With That Axe, Eugene' / 'One Of These Days' / 'Echoes' / encore: 'A Saucerful Of Secrets'.

NME reported that: 'The Floyd opened the first set of the British tour with a new piece, tentatively titled *Dark Side Of The Moon*, and showed that their writing had taken on a new and again innovatory form. A pulsating bass beat, pre-recorded, pounded around the hall's speaker system. A voice declared Chapter Five, verses 15 to 17 from the Book of Ephesians. The organ built up; suddenly it soared like a jumbo jet leaving Heathrow; the lights, just behind the equipment, rose like an elevator. Floyd were on stage playing a medium paced piece. The Floyd inventiveness had returned, and it astounded the capacity house. From the fast-paced tempo, the music gained exuberance, and they went into a racing jazz-based riff. Rick Wright on piano provided some delightful filling, with Gilmour's guitar interweaving well, and the team of Mason and Waters as solid as ever. Not everything in the piece flowed. The church organ part seemed to come all of a sudden, rather than a continuation of the theme. Yet that too added a new dimension to the Floyd music. The instrumentation was truly magnificent, and although the vocals were indistinctive, the harmonisation between Wright and Gilmour was good and emotional. At the beginning we had the quasi-religious element, and this became more apparent in the middle. "Let the Holy Spirit fill you", the voice urged, "Speak to one another. Sing and make music in your hearts with the Lord." Other voices, on the quadraphonic system, professed other feelings. At one time three voices fused into complete confusion, and ended with the Lord's Prayer. Pretty hot stuff. Unfortunately those profound statements were lost as a result of two things. One was that the vocals were none too clear, and secondly, the number broke down 30 minutes through. A drone and a hissing filled the hall as Floyd went through a simple riff. Gilmour turned to Waters and spoke. We didn't catch what it was he said, but it had a staggering effect. Waters removed his guitar, and both he and Gilmour left the stage. When Waters returned to the stage, he explained: "Due to severe mechanical and electric horror we can't do any more of that bit, so we'll do something else." They restarted the show with part of the "Atom Heart Mother" suite. But it was disappointing that such a remarkable new piece should collapse abysmally part way through. Even more disappointing was the fact that they restarted the second half with "Careful With That Axe, Eugene". The nervous pressure on the band resulted in one of the most brilliant sets I have ever heard them perform. "Echoes" was masterful.'

PINK FLOYD TOUR '72

Jan.	20th	The Dome, Brighton
	21st	Guildhall, Portsmouth
	22nd	Winter Gardens, Bournemouth
	23rd	Guildhall, Southampton
	27th	City Hall, Newcastle
	28th	Town Hall, Leeds
Feb.	5th	Colston Hall, Bristol
	10th	De Montfort Hall, Leicester
	11th	Free Trade Hall, Manchester
	12th	City Hall, Sheffield
	13th	Empire, Liverpool

FEBRUARY 17th, 18th & 19th RAINBOW THEATRE, LONDON

Friday 21 January
CONCERT
Guildhall, Portsmouth, England
Set list: *The Dark Side Of The Moon* // 'One Of These Days' / 'Set The Controls For The Heart Of The Sun' / 'Echoes' / encore: 'A Saucerful Of Secrets'.

Saturday 22 January
CONCERT
Winter Gardens, Bournemouth, England
Set list: *The Dark Side Of The Moon* // 'One Of These Days' / 'Set The Controls For The Heart Of The Sun' / 'Echoes' / encore: 'A Saucerful Of Secrets'.

Sunday 23 January
CONCERT
Guildhall, Southampton, England
Set list: *The Dark Side Of The Moon* // 'One Of These Days' / 'Set The Controls For The Heart Of The Sun' / 'Echoes' / encore: 'A Saucerful Of Secrets'.
Frustratingly, this show was filmed in its entirety by the BBC in order to test out some new camera equipment. The film was never intended for broadcast and consequently the tapes were wiped shortly afterwards.

Thursday 27 January
CONCERT
City Hall, Newcastle-upon-Tyne, England
Set list: *The Dark Side Of The Moon* // 'One Of These Days' / 'Set The Controls For The Heart Of The Sun' / 'Echoes' / encore: 'A Saucerful Of Secrets'.

Friday 28 January
CONCERT
City Hall, Leeds, England
Set list: *The Dark Side Of The Moon* // 'One Of These Days'/ 'Careful With That Axe, Eugene' / 'Echoes' / 'Set The Controls For The Heart Of The Sun' / encore: 'Blues'.

Thursday 3 February
CONCERT
Lanchester Polytechnic College Arts Festival, Locarno Ballroom, Coventry, England
With the Mandalla Lightshow. Pink Floyd's show began just after midnight following an earlier evening performance by Chuck Berry.
Set list: *The Dark Side Of The Moon* // 'Careful With That Axe, Eugene' / 'One Of These Days' / 'Echoes' / encore: 'Set The Controls For The Heart Of The Sun'.

Saturday 5 February
CONCERT
Colston Hall, Bristol, England
Set list: *The Dark Side Of The Moon* // 'One Of These Days' / 'Careful With That Axe, Eugene' / 'Set The Controls For The Heart Of The Sun' / encore: 'Echoes'.
The Bristol Evening Post reported that: 'Pink Floyd, armed to the teeth with enough explosive musical gadgetry to cause a minor traffic jam of parked vans behind the Colston Hall, rose above the machinery and gave a memorable concert on Sunday [sic] night. There wasn't a single moment when their battery of tapes, multi-channel stereo systems and robot like banks of rock music technology failed to act as mere servants of the four players' talents. The group began slowly in the first half, playing the slightly less ethereal music they have been composing recently. In the second half things really began to take off as they used more and more beautifully recorded tapes

through a disturbingly effective stereo system placed around the auditorium breaking down the barrier between stage and audience. All the time the band were spotlighted by their own lighting system which ran through rich, harsh contrasts of colour and brightness and reached an extraordinary climax as blinding fireworks burst into clouds of smoke. In the last 45 minutes they ran through their showstoppers, the almost theatrical "Careful With That Axe, Eugene" and the melancholy "Set The Controls". Dave Gilmour's guitar and Rick Wright's keyboard work dominated the performance but the whole group's sympathy with each other has built up to one of today's most original sounds. Bassist Roger Waters and Nicky Mason on drums gave a richly textured rhythm section that was quite as important to the overall effectiveness of Pink Floyd as the guitar - keyboards front line. Tickets for this concert had been the most sought after since the Stones' shows last year. It was easy to see why.'

Sunday 6 February
CANCELLED CONCERT
ABC Theatre, Plymouth, England
Show cancelled for unknown reasons.

Thursday 10 February
CONCERT
De Montfort Hall, Leicester, England
Set list: *The Dark Side Of The Moon* // 'One Of These Days' / 'Careful With That Axe, Eugene' / 'Set The Controls For The Heart Of The Sun' / 'Echoes' / encore: 'Blues'.

Friday 11 February
CONCERT
Free Trade Hall, Manchester, England
Set list: 'One Of These Days' / Careful With That Axe, Eugene'.
About 25 minutes into the show, during 'Careful With That Axe, Eugene', there was a power cut and, despite cries of "Acoustic!" from the audience, the concert was abandoned.

Saturday 12 February
CONCERT
City (Oval) Hall, Sheffield, England
Set list: 'One Of These Days' / 'Careful With That Axe, Eugene' / *The Dark Side Of The Moon* / 'Set The Controls For The Heart Of The Sun' / encore: 'Echoes'.

Sunday 13 February
CONCERT
Empire Theatre, Liverpool, England

Thursday 17 February
CONCERT
Rainbow Theatre, Finsbury Park, London, England
Set list: *The Dark Side Of The Moon* // 'One Of These Days' / 'Careful With That Axe, Eugene' / 'Set The

Controls For The Heart Of The Sun' / encore: 'Echoes'.

Friday 18 February
CONCERT
Rainbow Theatre, Finsbury Park, London, England
Set list: *The Dark Side Of The Moon* // 'One Of These Days' / 'Careful With That Axe, Eugene' / 'Echoes' / encore: 'A Saucerful Of Secrets' / 'Blues' / 'Set The Controls For The Heart Of The Sun'.

Saturday 19 February
CONCERT
Rainbow Theatre, Finsbury Park, London, England
Set list: *The Dark Side Of The Moon* // 'One Of These Days' / 'Careful With That Axe, Eugene' / 'Echoes' / encore: 'A Saucerful Of Secrets' / 'Blues' / 'Set The Controls For The Heart Of The Sun'.

Sunday 20 February
CONCERT
Rainbow Theatre, Finsbury Park, London, England
The last night of the tour.
Set list: *The Dark Side Of The Moon* // 'One Of These Days' / 'Careful With That Axe, Eugene' / 'Echoes', 'A Saucerful Of Secrets' / 'Blues' / encore: 'Set The Controls For The Heart Of The Sun'.

Wednesday 23 – Tuesday 29 February
RECORDING SESSIONS
Strawberry Studios, Chateau d'Hérouville, near Paris, France
Recording for the album *Obscured By Clouds*.
ORTF TV filmed an interview with Roger Waters and David Gilmour at the studios and included background music from the sessions of 'Mudmen' and 'The Gold It's In The...' for the music programme *Pop 2*. It was broadcast on ORTF2 on 4 March at 5.05pm.

JAPANESE TOUR

Monday 6 March
CONCERT
Tokyo-To Taiikukan, Tokyo, Japan
Set list: *The Dark Side Of The Moon* // 'Atom Heart Mother' / 'Careful With That Axe, Eugene' / encore: 'Echoes'.
Tokia FM radio reportedly recorded this show but the content and broadcast details remain unknown.

Tuesday 7 March
CONCERT
Tokyo-To Taiikukan, Tokyo, Japan
Set list: *The Dark Side Of The Moon* // 'One Of These Days' / 'Careful With That Axe, Eugene' / 'Echoes' / encore: 'A Saucerful Of Secrets'.

Wednesday 8 & Thursday 9 March
CONCERTS
Festival Hall, Osaka, Japan
Set list at both shows: *The Dark Side Of The Moon* // 'One Of These Days' / 'Echoes' / 'Atom Heart Mother' / 'Careful With That Axe, Eugene' / encore: 'A Saucerful Of Secrets'.

Friday 10 March
CONCERT
Dai-Sho-Gun Furitsu Taiikukan, Kyoto, Japan
Set list: *The Dark Side Of The Moon* // 'One Of These Days' / 'Careful With That Axe, Eugene' / 'Echoes'.

Saturday 11 March
CANCELLED CONCERT
Kemin Hall, Yokohama, Japan
Show cancelled.

Monday 13 March
CONCERT
Nakajima Sports Center, Sapporo, Japan
The last night of the tour.
Set list: *The Dark Side Of The Moon* // 'One Of These Days' / 'Careful With That Axe, Eugene', 'Echoes'.

Thursday 23 – Monday 27 March
RECORDING SESSIONS
Strawberry Studios, Chateau d'Hérouville, near Paris, France
Pink Floyd complete recording of the album *Obscured By Clouds*.

Wednesday 29 & Thursday 30 March
CONCERTS
Free Trade Hall, Manchester, England
These two shows were arranged to make up for the aborted show at the same venue in February.
Set list on 29 March: *The Dark Side Of The Moon* // 'One Of These Days' / 'Careful With That Axe, Eugene' / 'Echoes' / encore: 'Set The Controls For The Heart Of The Sun'.

Tuesday 4 - Thursday 6 April
RECORDING SESSIONS
Morgan Sound Studios, Willesden, London, England
Final mixing of the album *Obscured By Clouds*.

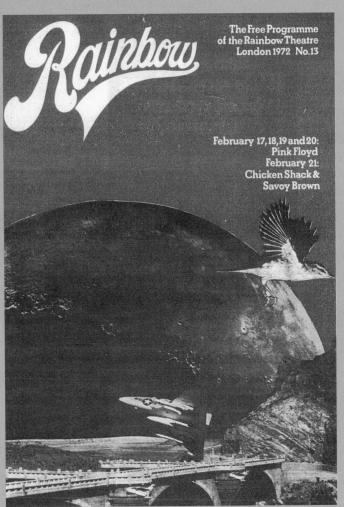

The Free Programme of the Rainbow Theatre London 1972 No.13

February 17, 18, 19 and 20:
Pink Floyd
February 21:
Chicken Shack & Savoy Brown

NORTH AMERICAN TOUR

Early drafts of Pink Floyd's tour show the band scheduled to appear at Pirates Cove, Pirates World Amusement Park, Dania, Hollywood, Florida (15 April); Massey Hall, Toronto, Ontario, Canada (30 April); Franklin-Marshall College, Lancaster, Pennsylvania (6 May) and Spectrum Theater, Philadelphia, Pennsylvania (7 May).

PINK FLOYD ROAD CREW THROUGH 1972

Chris Adamson: Technician / Stage Crew
Seth Goldman: Technician / Stage Crew
Mick 'The Pole' Kluczynski: Tour Manager
Arthur Max: Lighting Technician
Chris Mickie: Front of House Sound Mixer
Bobby Richardson: Technician / Stage Crew
Brian Scott: Technician / Stage Crew
Peter Watts: Head of PA

Friday 14 April
CONCERT
Fort Homer Hesterly Armory Auditorium, Tampa, Florida, USA

Saturday 15 April
CONCERT
Sportatorium, Hollywood, Florida, USA
Set list: *The Dark Side Of The Moon* // 'One Of These Days' / 'Careful With That Axe, Eugene' / 'Echoes' / encore: 'Set The Controls For The Heart Of The Sun'.

Sunday 16 April
CONCERT
Township Auditorium, Columbia, South Carolina, USA
Set list: *The Dark Side Of The Moon* // 'One Of These Days' / 'Careful With That Axe, Eugene' / 'Atom Heart Mother' / encore: 'Echoes'.

Tuesday 18 April
CONCERT
Symphony Hall, Atlanta Memorial Arts Center, Atlanta, Georgia, USA

Thursday 20 April
CONCERT
Syria Mosque Theater, Pittsburgh, Pennsylvania, USA
Set list: *The Dark Side Of The Moon* // 'One Of These Days' / 'Careful With That Axe, Eugene' / 'Echoes'.

Friday 21 April
CONCERT
The Lyric Theatre, Baltimore, Maryland, USA

Saturday 22 April
CONCERT
Civic Theatre, Akron, Ohio, USA
Set list: *The Dark Side Of The Moon* // 'One Of These Days' / 'Careful With That Axe, Eugene' / 'Echoes' / encore: 'A Saucerful Of Secrets'.

Sunday 23 April
CONCERT
Music Hall, Cincinnati, Ohio, USA
Set list: *The Dark Side Of The Moon* // 'One Of These Days' / 'Careful With That Axe, Eugene' / 'Echoes' / encore: 'A Saucerful Of Secrets'.

Monday 24 April
CONCERT
Allen Theatre, Cleveland, Ohio, USA
Show rescheduled from The Sports Arena, Toledo, Ohio, USA.

Wednesday 26 & Thursday 27 April
CONCERTS
Ford Auditorium, Detroit, Michigan, USA
Set list on 27 April: *The Dark Side Of The Moon* // 'One Of These Days' / 'Careful With That Axe, Eugene' / 'Echoes' / encore: 'Blues' / 'Set The Controls For The Heart Of The Sun'.

Friday 28 April
CONCERT
Auditorium Theatre, Chicago, Illinois, USA
Set list: *The Dark Side Of The Moon* // 'One Of These Days' / 'Careful With That Axe, Eugene' / 'Echoes' / encore: 'Set The Controls For The Heart Of The Sun'.

Saturday 29 April
CONCERT
Spectrum Theater, Philadelphia, Pennsylvania, USA

Monday 1 & Tuesday 2 May
CONCERTS
Carnegie Hall, Manhattan, New York City, New York, USA
Set list on 2 May: *The Dark Side Of The Moon* // 'One

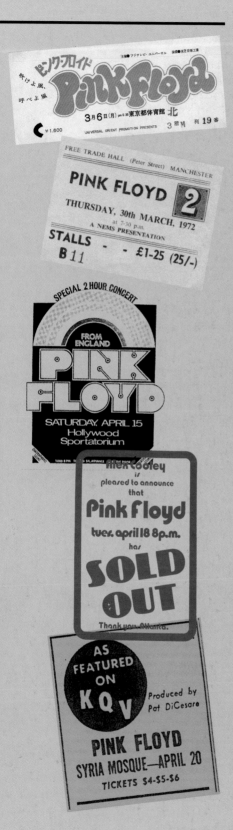

PLAYING DIFFERENT TUNES 1972-1973

Of These Days' / 'Careful With That Axe, Eugene' /
'Echoes' / encore: 'A Saucerful Of Secrets'.

Wednesday 3 May
CONCERT
Concert Hall, John F. Kennedy Center for
Performing Arts, Washington, District of Columbia,
USA

Thursday 4 May
CONCERT
Music Hall, Boston, Massachusetts, USA
The last night of the tour. Rescheduled from the
smaller Orpheum Aquarius Theater, Boston, due to
high ticket demand.
Set list: *The Dark Side Of The Moon* // 'One Of These
Days' / 'Careful With That Axe, Eugene' / 'Echoes' /
encore: 'Blues'.

Thursday 18 May
CONCERT
Deutschlandhalle, West Berlin, West Germany
Set list: *The Dark Side Of The Moon* // 'One Of These
Days' / 'Careful With That Axe, Eugene' / 'Echoes' /
encore: 'Set The Controls For The Heart Of The Sun'.

Sunday 21 May
CONCERT
2nd British Rock Meeting, Insel Grün, Germersheim,
West Germany
This festival was originally scheduled to take place at
Friesenheimer Grün, Mannheim, West Germany but
after local authority objections it was successfully
relocated to Germersheim at short notice. Attended
by over 70,000 people this event

was staged between 20 and 22 May and featured
Humble Pie, The Faces, The Kinks, The Doors, Family,
The Incredible String Band, Atomic Rooster, Osibisa,
Linda Lewis, Buddy Miles Express, Curved Air and
many others. Pink Floyd headlined on the second day
and reportedly received a fee of 60,000 Marks for

their performance.
Set list: 'Atom Heart Mother' / 'Set The Controls For
The Heart Of The Sun' / 'One Of These Days' //
'Careful With That Axe, Eugene' / 'Echoes' / 'A
Saucerful Of Secrets'.

Monday 22 May
CONCERT
The Amsterdam Rock Circus,
Olympisch Stadion, Amsterdam,
The Netherlands
With Donovan, New Riders of The
Purple Sage, Buddy Miles Band
with Carlos Santana, Tom Paxton
and Memphis Slim, Dr. John The
Night Tripper and Spencer Davis
with Sneeky Pete and Gene Clark.
Set list: 'Atom Heart Mother' /
'One Of These Days' / 'Careful
With That Axe, Eugene' / 'Echoes'
/ encore: 'A Saucerful Of Secrets'.

**Wednesday 24 May – Monday
25 June**
RECORDING SESSIONS
Studio 3, EMI Studios, Abbey Road, St. John's
Wood, London, England
Discontinuous recording for the album *The Dark Side
Of The Moon*. Recording notes reveal that by 30 May
the album was still a long way off its final format
with the titles logged as: 'Intro' ['Speak To Me'] /
'Travel' ['Breathe'] / 'Time' / 'Home Again' ['Breathe,

reprise'] / 'Religion' ['The Great Gig In The Sky'] /
'Money' / 'Us And Them' / 'Scat' ['Any Colour You
Like'] / 'Lunatic' ['Brain Damage'] / 'End – All That
You...' ['Eclipse']. The basic tracks for 'Us And Them'
was recorded on 1 June; 'Money' on 7 June; 'Time' on
8 June and 'The Great Gig In The Sky' on 25 June.

Friday 2 June
RECORD RELEASE
Obscured By Clouds
UK album release. US album release on Saturday 17
June.
Crawdaddy commented that: 'The Floyd have
discovered a sense of direction that has been lacking
in their work since *Ummagumma*. If they can follow
this up it may lead them back to their position as the
premier space-rock band.'

Friday 23 June
CANCELLED APPEARANCE
Bièvres Festival, Bièvre, France
Pink Floyd cancelled an advertised appearance at this
three-day festival (23-25 June), which was organised
by the French collective group Crium Delirium. The
event featured Soft Machine, Matching Mole, Amon
Düül II, Kevin Ayers, Hawkwind, Third World War,
Pink Fairies, Gong, Lard Free, Dagon, Catharis,
Komintern, Moving Gelatine Plates, Opus N, Higelin,
Fontaine, Areski and Catherine Ribiero with free jazz,
Magic Circus and Le Cirque Bonjour.

Wednesday 28 & Thursday 29 June
CONCERTS
The Dome, Brighton, England
Set list at both shows: *The Dark Side Of The Moon* // 'One Of These Days' / 'Careful With That Axe, Eugene' / 'Echoes' / 'Set The Controls For The Heart Of The Sun' / encore: 'A Saucerful Of Secrets' (a short version).
As at Manchester, two shows were arranged as a replacement for the concert that had been abandoned in January. The show on the 29 June was professionally filmed and directed by Peter Clifton for inclusion in his epic, 104 minute film *Sound Of The City 1964-1973* (also known as *Music Power*). Clips of this material occasionally appear on television and compilation videos, more recently 'Careful With That Axe, Eugene', which has appeared in the video release, *Superstars In Concert*.

Monday 10 July
RECORD RELEASE
'Free Four' / 'Stay'
US 7-inch single release.

Saturday 26 August
CANCELLED CONCERT
Arena Pop Festival, Arena di Verona, Verona, Italy
Pink Floyd were reported in the music press to be appearing at this event alongside America, Jefferson Airplane and many other groups but the event never got beyond the planning stages due to strong local and press opposition. However, Pink Floyd would perform at this spectacular venue, one of the most preserved Roman arena's in the world, which is mainly devoted to classical music, some 27 years later.

Tuesday 29 August
FILM PREMIERE
Venice International Film Festival, Venice, Italy
The premiere of the film *La Vallee / Obscured By Clouds*.

Saturday 2 September
FILM PREMIERE
26th Edinburgh Film Festival, Cameo Cinema, Tollcross, Edinburgh, Scotland
The premiere of the film *Pink Floyd Live At Pompeii*.

NORTH AMERICAN TOUR

Early drafts of Pink Floyd's tour show the band scheduled to appear at the Community Center Arena, Tucson, Arizona (11 September) and Seattle Arena, Seattle, Washington (29 September).

Friday 8 September
CONCERT
Municipal Auditorium, Austin, Texas, USA

Saturday 9 September
CONCERT
Music Hall, Houston, Texas, USA

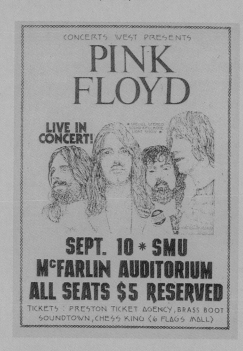

Sunday 10 September
CONCERT
McFarlin Auditorium, Southern Methodist University, University Park, Dallas, Texas, USA
Set list: *The Dark Side Of The Moon* // 'One Of These Days' / 'Careful With That Axe, Eugene' / 'Set The Controls For The Heart Of The Sun' / encore: 'Echoes'.

Monday 11 September
CONCERT
Memorial Hall, Kansas City, Missouri, USA

Tuesday 12 September
CONCERT
Civic Center Music Hall, Oklahoma City, Oklahoma, USA
Set list included: *The Dark Side Of The Moon* // 'One Of These Days' / 'Careful With That Axe, Eugene'.

Wednesday 13 September
CONCERT
Henry Levitt Arena, Wichita, Kansas, USA

Friday 15 September
CONCERT
Community Center Arena, Tucson, Arizona, USA

Saturday 16 September
CONCERT
Golden Hall, Community Concourse, San Diego, California, USA

Sunday 17 September
CONCERT
Big Surf, Tempe, Arizona, USA
Set list: *The Dark Side Of The Moon* // 'One Of These Days' / 'Careful With That Axe, Eugene' / 'Echoes'.
New Times reported that: 'Pink Floyd, chief explorers into the music of Space, appeared oddly in Tempe on Sunday night. A crowd entered Big Surf, looked at the speakers on their four sides, the mountain of equipment onstage surrounded by banks of coloured lights, said "wow" and sat down. Gradually a heartbeat hit them from behind, lights begin to revolve in Mason's clear drums, a dense bank of green fog rolls onto the stage, towers of lights raise themselves high into the air and Pink Floyd begins with words from *Music from the Body*. Using loud effects, Pink Floyd played most of their latest album, *Obscured By Clouds* [reviewer error - this should be *The Dark Side Of The Moon*], ending with the appearance of a yellow disc of light above the band. After intermission, they returned with "One Of These Days", which was so engulfing, the audience could not help but be merged with the flashing lights. At this point we knew something was happening here in music that had needed to happen for a long time - that we couldn't criticise, analyse, evaluate or resist. After the stage exploded with light and flame during a piece from *Ummagumma* and Pink Floyd followed with "Echoes", a long super-mellow thing, it was no wonder that the wind started blowing and the rain falling. Roger Waters stopped, said rain could mean instant death to their sound stage. Pink Floyd was over.'

PLAYING DIFFERENT TUNES 1972-1973

Tuesday 19 September
CONCERT
University of Denver Arena, Denver, Colorado, USA
Set list included: *The Dark Side Of The Moon* / encore: 'Set The Controls For The Heart Of The Sun'.

ON STAGE
Hollywood Bowl / September 22, 1972 / 8 PM
PINK FLOYD

Friday 22 September
CONCERT
Hollywood Bowl, Hollywood, Los Angeles, California, USA
Set list included: *The Dark Side Of The Moon* // 'One Of These Days' / 'Careful With That Axe, Eugene' / 'Set The Controls For The Heart Of The Sun' / 'Echoes' / encore: 'A Saucerful Of Secrets'.

Saturday 23 September
CONCERT
Winterland Auditorium, San Francisco, California, USA
Show rescheduled from Santa Clara Fairground, San Jose, California.
Set list: *The Dark Side Of The Moon* // 'One Of These Days' / 'Careful With That Axe, Eugene' / 'Echoes' / encore: 'A Saucerful Of Secrets'.

Sunday 24 September
CONCERT
Winterland Auditorium, San Francisco, California, USA
Set list: *The Dark Side Of The Moon* // 'One Of These Days' / 'Careful With That Axe, Eugene' / 'Echoes' / encore: 'Set The Controls For The Heart Of The Sun'.

Wednesday 27 September
CONCERT
Gardens Arena, Vancouver, British Columbia, Canada
Set list: *The Dark Side Of The Moon* // 'One Of These Days' / 'Careful With That Axe, Eugene' / 'Echoes' / encore: 'Set The Controls For The Heart Of The Sun'.
Vancouver Free Press reported that: 'Pink Floyd are definitely a band whose multi-sensory stage performance lends them open-air performances; the confines of the Gardens Arena just don't do justice to David Gilmour's brilliant guitar playing - full of floating shadows - or the various lighting and theatric smoke and fire effects that the band have become known for. After a half-hour delay while the stage crew hassled with some of the equipment needed to run the quadraphonic sound system that is being used on this tour, the crowd was silenced by an insistent throbbing beat that passed around the four speakers (two of them situated midway back in the audience) and grew to the guitar introduction of the first number. Smoke had poured from outlets near the back of the stage during the beginning of this number and it hung in the air reflecting various coloured spotlights as the band worked into the second piece which gave the first real glimpses of Gilmour's brilliance on guitar. Madcap shouts and laughter echoed round the sound system and the music started out once more in the cosmic zones. Gently, sawing guitar notes over wailing organ runs and a pulsating bass line. Quietly building creeping up and then exploding into a solid wall of sound as smoke and flame flares up on stage and bright yellow and red spots blow away the darkness. There was a lot of dope doing the rounds and there were a few tripping initiates to Pink Floyd concerts that were heard giving wild shouts at this juncture - the guy next door to me shot bolt upright as if someone had cracked a whole cluster of amyl nitrates under his nostrils. After continuing for a while with the onslaught the musicians cut back and developed a series of floaty guitar runs and breathy scat vocals in amongst the clouds of smoke that are reflecting bands of coloured light. Well received, even my neighbour seemed to wind down sufficiently to get his hands meeting.'

Thursday 28 September
CONCERT
Memorial Coliseum, Portland, Oregon, USA

Friday 29 September
CONCERT
Hec Edmundson Pavilion, University of Washington, Seattle, Washington, USA

Saturday 30 September
CONCERTS
Gardens Arena, Vancouver, British Columbia, Canada
Two shows, at 4.00pm and 8.00pm. The last night of the tour.
Set list at 8.00pm show: *The Dark Side Of The Moon* // 'One Of These Days' / 'Careful With That Axe, Eugene' / 'Echoes' / encore: 'Set The Controls For The Heart Of The Sun'.

Tuesday 10 – Tuesday 17 October
RECORDING SESSIONS
EMI Studios, Abbey Road, St. John's Wood, London, England
Recording for the album *The Dark Side Of The Moon*.

JOHN & TONY SMITH
present
The PINK FLOYD
in concert
Saturday, 21st October
8 p.m. at
EMPIRE POOL - WEMBLEY
ALL PROCEEDS TO: WAR ON WANT, THE ALBANY TRUST DEPTFORD, SAVE THE CHILDREN FUND
Tickets £1 and £1.50 available from Box Office Empire Pool (01-902 1234) and from all branches of Harlequin Record Shops (01-636 1348)

Saturday 21 October
CONCERT
Empire Pool, Wembley, England
A benefit show for War On Want, The Albany Trust Deptford and Save The Children Fund.
Set list: *The Dark Side Of The Moon* // 'One Of These Days' / 'Careful With That Axe, Eugene' / 'Echoes' / encore: 'Set The Controls For The Heart Of The Sun' / 'Blues'.
Sounds reported that: 'From the word go, they gave

the packed stadium a faultless demonstration of what psychedelic music is all about. There wasn't a note, or a sound, out of place during the whole evening. It's a recital more than a concert, and the Floyd don't so much give us numbers as perform pieces of music, lasting up to an hour each. For starters, on Saturday, we had that lengthy work entitled "Dark Side Of The Moon", an eerie title for an equally eerie piece of music that takes the listener through a host of different moods, most of which are accompanied by unusual sounds stretching around his head by way of the group's quadraphonic sound system. The effect is quite stunning. The second half of the recital was composed of three more major pieces, and a couple of encores. The first - the riveting "Set The Controls For The Heart Of The Sun" - was obviously rehearsed, but the second - a bluesy jam - wasn't. It served a useful purpose to show that the group are not confined to playing science fiction soundtrack music all the time. The incendiary gimmicks from the stage frequently obliterated the artists. Flash-bombs erupted here and there at well timed places, and Roger Waters gong actually became a blazing sun during "Set The Controls". All the time the group were effectively illuminated by their imposing lighting tower at the rear of the stage which served a dual purpose - at frequent intervals it belched out smoke which mingled with the coloured lights and the dry ice surface mist to effectively whisk us all away to Planet Floyd.'

Wednesday 25 - Friday 27 October
RECORDING SESSIONS
EMI Studios, Abbey Road, St. John's Wood, London, England
Recording for the album *The Dark Side Of The Moon*.

EUROPEAN TOUR

Friday 10 & Saturday 11 November
CONCERTS
KB Hallen, Copenhagen, Denmark
Set list at both shows: *The Dark Side Of The Moon* // 'One Of These Days' / 'Careful With That Axe, Eugene' / 'Echoes' / encore: 'Set The Controls For The Heart Of The Sun'.

Sunday 12 November
CONCERT
Ernst-Merck-Halle, Hamburg, West Germany
Set list: *The Dark Side Of The Moon* // 'One Of These Days' / 'Careful With That Axe, Eugene' / 'Echoes' / encore: 'Set The Controls For The Heart Of The Sun'.

Tuesday 14 November
CONCERT
Philipshalle, Düsseldorf, West Germany
Set list: *The Dark Side Of The Moon* // 'One Of These Days' / 'Careful With That Axe, Eugene' / 'Echoes' / encore: 'Set The Controls For The Heart Of The Sun'.

Wednesday 15 November
CONCERT
Sporthalle, Böblingen, West Germany
Set list: *The Dark Side Of The Moon* // 'One Of These Days' / 'Careful With That Axe, Eugene' / 'Echoes' (announced by Roger Waters as 'Looking Through The Knotholes In Granny's Wooden Leg') / encore: 'Set The Controls For The Heart Of The Sun'.

Thursday 16 November
CONCERT
Festhalle, Frankfurt, West Germany
Set list: *The Dark Side Of The Moon* // 'One Of These Days' / 'Careful With That Axe, Eugene' / 'Echoes' (announced by Roger Waters as 'The March Of The Dambusters') / encore: 'Set The Controls For The Heart Of The Sun'.

Friday 17 November
CONCERT
Festhalle, Frankfurt, West Germany
Set list: *The Dark Side Of The Moon* // 'One Of These Days' / 'Careful With That Axe, Eugene' / 'Echoes' / encore: 'Set The Controls For The Heart Of The Sun'.

ROLAND PETIT BALLET SHOWS

The following shows, which did not form part of the scheduled European tour, were a series of special collaborations that featured the company of Les Ballets de Marseille, with Roland Petit as Choreographer and Artistic Director, and with the participation of Maïa Plissetskaia, a recent addition from Moscow's Bolshoi Theatre. The programme was divided into three sections:
1. Allumez les Étoiles (Light The Stars). A ballet concerning Maïakovski (1893-1930), a poet of the Russian Revolution, with extracts of the works of Prokofiev, Chostakovitch and Moussorgski.
2. La Rose Malade (The Sick Rose). A ballet in three movements based on the William Blake poem with extracts from Mahler's 2nd and 5th Symphonies.
3. The Pink Floyd Ballet. A ballet in four movements, based on the following set list: 'One Of These Days' / 'Careful With That Axe, Eugene' / 'Obscured By Clouds' / 'When You're In' / 'Echoes'.

Monday 20 & Tuesday 21 November
REHEARSALS
Salle Valliers, Marseille, France
Full production rehearsals for the forthcoming Ballet shows took place on these dates. The rehearsals on 21 November were filmed by ORTF TV for inclusion in the arts programme *JT 20H* and segments, including Pink Floyd's soundcheck and part of their performance of 'One Of These Days', was shown in a feature entitled 'Pink Floyd Et Ballets Roland Petit'. It was broadcast (in black and white) on ORTF1 on 26 November at 7.45pm.

Wednesday 22, Thursday 23, Friday 24, Saturday 25 & Sunday 26 November
CONCERTS
Salle Valliers, Marseille, France
The Pink Floyd Ballet based on the following set list at all five shows: 'One Of These Days' / 'Careful With That Axe, Eugene' / 'Obscured By Clouds' / 'When You're In' / 'Echoes'.

Saturday 25 November
FILM PREMIERE
Rainbow Theatre, Finsbury Park, London, England
The scheduled cinematic premiere of *Pink Floyd Live At Pompeii* was cancelled because the owners of the theatre, the Rank Organisation, gave the promoter just one day's notice of a previously ignored clause in the lease forbidding the promotion of any event that may be deemed to be competitive with its own operations. Rank further claimed that the film had not yet been given a certificate by the British Board of Film Censors, and all 3,000 ticket-holders who were not made aware of the problems had to be turned away.

EUROPEAN TOUR (Continued)

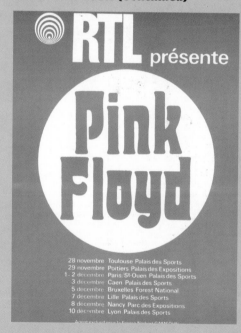

Tuesday 28 November
CONCERT
Palais des Sports, Toulouse, France

Wednesday 29 November
CONCERT
Les Arènas, Parc des Expositions, Poitiers, France
Set list: *The Dark Side Of The Moon* // 'One Of These Days' / 'Careful With That Axe, Eugene' / 'Echoes'.

Friday 1 December
CONCERT
Centre Sportif, Ile Des Vannes, St. Ouen, Paris, France
Set list: *The Dark Side Of The Moon* // 'One Of These Days' / 'Careful With That Axe, Eugene' / 'Blues' / 'Echoes' / 'Childhood's End' / encore: 'Set The Controls For The Heart Of The Sun'.
RTL radio, sponsors of the French tour, broadcast the entire show live in a two-hour presentation from 8.30pm.

Saturday 2 December
CONCERT
Centre Sportif, Ile Des Vannes, St. Ouen, Paris, France
Set list: *The Dark Side Of The Moon* // 'One Of These Days' / 'Careful With That Axe, Eugene' / 'Echoes' / encore: 'Set The Controls For The Heart Of The Sun'.

Sunday 3 December
CONCERT
Parc des Expositions, Caen, France

Tuesday 5 December
CONCERT
Sport Palais Vorst Nationaal, Brussels, Belgium
Set list included: *The Dark Side Of The Moon* // 'Careful With That Axe, Eugene'.
VRT Radio 1 Belgium broadcast an audience recording of the show including excerpts of 'Time', 'Breathe (reprise)' and 'Careful With That Axe, Eugene' as part of a Pink Floyd documentary broadcast on 1 November 2005.

Thursday 7 December
CONCERT
Palais des Sports, Lille, France
Set list: *The Dark Side Of The Moon* // 'One Of These Days' / 'Careful With That Axe, Eugene' / encore: 'Echoes'.
This show was very nearly cancelled due to inadequate power supplies to meet Pink Floyd's demands. The show went ahead with a reduced lighting rig.

Friday 8 December
CONCERT
Parc des Expositions, Nancy, France

Saturday 9 December
CONCERT
Hallenstadion, Zurich, Switzerland
Set list: *The Dark Side Of The Moon* // 'One Of These Days' / 'Careful With That Axe, Eugene' / encore: 'Echoes' / 'Childhood's End'.

Sunday 10 December
CONCERT
Palais des Sports, Lyon, France
The last night of the tour. Set list: *The Dark Side Of The Moon* // 'One Of These Days' / 'Careful With That Axe, Eugene' / encore: 'Echoes.'
The band was held up by customs authorities at the Swiss border and took the stage two hours later than scheduled, at 8.00pm.

Tuesday 9 January – Thursday 1 February
RECORDING SESSIONS
Studios 2 & 3, EMI Studios, Abbey Road, St. John's Wood, London, England
Discontinuous recording and mixing for the album *The Dark Side Of The Moon* took place at almost every opportunity outside of live performance commitments. Clare Torry recorded her vocal for 'The Great Gig In The Sky' on 21 January.

PINK FLOYD ROAD CREW THROUGH TO JUNE 1973
Chris Adamson: PA / Stage Technician
Graeme Fleming: Lighting Technician
Mick 'The Pole' Kluczynski: Tour Manager
Arthur Max: Production Manager / Lighting
Robin Murray: Lighting Technician
Alan Parsons: Front of House Sound Engineer
Robbie Williams: PA / Stage Technician
Peter Watts: Head of PA

ROLAND PETIT BALLET SHOWS
An additional season of Ballet shows was staged in Paris, following the success of the shows in Marseille. However, due to recording commitments Pink Floyd only appeared at eight of the 16 shows, the remainder featured an audio playback only.
These shows also featured the company of Les Ballets de Marseille with Roland Petit as Choreographer and Artistic Director, and with the participation of Maïa Plissetskaia:
1. Allumez les Étoiles (Light The Stars)
A ballet concerning Maïakovski (1893-1930), a poet of the Russian Revolution, with extracts of the works of Prokofiev, Chostakovitch and Moussorgski.
2. La Rose Malade (The Sick Rose)
A ballet in three movements based on the William Blake poem with extracts from Mahler's 2nd and 5th Symphonies.
3. The Pink Floyd Ballet
A ballet in four movements, based on the following set list: 'One Of These Days' / 'Careful With That Axe, Eugene' / 'Obscured By Clouds' / 'When You're In' / 'Echoes'.

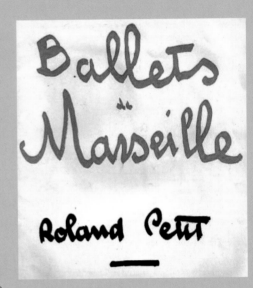

Thursday 11 and Friday 12 January
REHEARSALS
Palais des Sports de la Porte de Versailles, Paris, France
The rehearsals on 12 January were filmed by ORTF TV for inclusion the arts programme *JT 20H* and segments of 'Echoes' and 'Careful With That Axe, Eugene' were shown in a feature entitled 'Pink Floyd Ballet'. It was broadcast (in colour) on ORTF1 on 12 January 1973 at 7.45pm.
A complete 38-minute show filmed in rehearsals was broadcast for the first time, over four years later (in colour), in a programme entitled *Pink Floyd Ballet* on ORTF2 on 19 December 1977 at 10.30pm.

Saturday 13 January
CONCERT
Palais des Sports de la Porte de Versailles, Paris, France
Two shows, at 5.00pm and 8.45pm. The Pink Floyd Ballet based on the following set list at both shows: 'One Of These Days' / 'Careful With That Axe, Eugene' / 'Obscured By Clouds' / 'When You're In' / 'Echoes'.

Sunday 14 January
CONCERT
Palais des Sports de la Porte de Versailles, Paris, France
Two shows, at 2.30pm and 6.00pm. The Pink Floyd Ballet based on the following set list: 'One Of These Days' / 'Careful With That Axe, Eugene'

/ 'Obscured By Clouds' / 'When You're In' / 'Echoes'.

Saturday 20 January
PLAYBACK CONCERT
Palais des Sports de la Porte de Versailles, Paris, France
Two shows, at 5.00pm and 8.45pm, with audio playback only.

Sunday 21 January
PLAYBACK CONCERT
Palais des Sports de la Porte de Versailles, Paris, France
Two shows, at 2.30pm and 6.00pm, with audio playback only.

Saturday 27 January
PLAYBACK CONCERT
Palais des Sports de la Porte de Versailles, Paris, France
Two shows, at 5.00pm and 8.45pm, with audio playback only.

Sunday 28 January
PLAYBACK CONCERT
Palais des Sports de la Porte de Versailles, Paris, France
Two shows, at 2.30pm and 6.00pm, with audio playback only.

Saturday 3 February
CONCERT
Palais des Sports de la Porte de Versailles, Paris, France
Two shows, at 5.00pm and 8.45pm. The Pink Floyd Ballet based on the following set list at both shows: 'One Of These Days' / 'Careful With That Axe, Eugene' / 'Obscured By Clouds' / 'When You're In' / 'Echoes'.

Sunday 4 February
CONCERT
Palais des Sports de la Porte de Versailles, Paris, France
Two shows, at 2.30pm and 6.00pm. The Pink Floyd Ballet based on the following set list at both shows: 'One Of These Days' / 'Careful With That Axe, Eugene' / 'Obscured By Clouds' / 'When You're In' / 'Echoes'.
Sounds reported that: 'Dry ice was fuming quietly all over an apron stage and the Pink Floyd, standing above it all amongst their sound equipment and lighting towers, seemed suspended about ten feet up in the blackness. An unsteady, bright shaft of light opened up beneath them and slowly a stiff, bowed figure moved out and, gradually unbending, took command of the stage. Rudy Bryans, star soloist with the Ballets de Marseille, danced to the Pink Floyd's "Echoes". The audience is strange, hardly a typical crush of Floyd devotees, but a mixture of people who obviously came because it was the band, people who

obviously came because it was the ballet, and people who didn't look quite sure why they'd come. The opening movement, "One Of These Days" was fairly short, a kind of introduction with the whole troupe dancing, and it struck me at the time that that was what organised dance to rock music should look like, it was essentially rhythmic and fast. "Obscured By Clouds" was a solo for Rudy Bryans and Daniele Jossi, beautifully lit, which had a hesitant, slightly menacing air. "Careful With That Axe" was the troupe again, moving through various tableaux and sequences, featuring the exploding flares. "Echoes" was the finale, a constantly changing sequence of short pieces, the most spectacular of which were Rudy's entrance from the tunnel, and a dance where he pulled Daniele right across the width of the stage with her in the splits position.'

Monday 19 - Wednesday 21 February
REHEARSALS
Rainbow Theatre, Finsbury Park, London, England
Full production rehearsals for their upcoming US tour were staged at the Rainbow prior to their equipment being shipped.

Tuesday 27 February
PRESS RECEPTION
London Planetarium, Marylebone, London, England
EMI records held a press reception at the Planetarium in London to preview the band's new album *The Dark Side Of The Moon*. Richard Wright was the only band member in attendance, the rest having boycotted the event due to an inferior sound system having been brought in by EMI.

NORTH AMERICAN TOUR
Early drafts of Pink Floyd's tour show the band scheduled to appear at Charlotte Park Center, Charlotte, North Carolina (21 March) and Littlejohn Coliseum, Clemson Agricultural College, Clemson, South Carolina (23 March).

ADDITIONAL TOUR PERSONEL
Nawasa Crowder: Backing vocals
Mary Ann Lindsey: Backing vocals
Phyllis Lindsey: Backing vocals
Dick Parry: Saxophone

Sunday 4 March
CONCERT
Dane County Memorial Coliseum, Madison, Wisconsin, USA
Set list included: 'Obscured By Clouds' / 'When You're In' / 'Careful With That Axe, Eugene' // *The Dark Side Of The Moon*.
The Wisconsin State Journal reported that: 'They began with a song called "Obscured By Clouds" and before it was over the Coliseum had been obscured in a pinkish-coloured cloud emanating from the

footlights and taking the audience of 9,000 completely by surprise. Pink Floyd, an English experimental rock group, kicked off their current American tour at Dane County Coliseum Sunday night showing a definite grasp of the visual and electronic potential of their music. Once referred to as psychedelic music, Pink Floyd has updated and come around into something loosely labelled space-rock, a mixture of some hard-driving sets, electronic gimmickry and quadraphonic sound. The gimmickry was Floyd's focal point Sunday and they exploited it to its fullest to add an unusual dimension to their performance. The smoke turned from green to purple as Floyd broke into one of their more recognisable hits, "Careful With That Axe Eugene", a song interrupted by blinding, flashing lights. The group used several special video effects ranging from the sound of cash registers in a piece called "Money", to a soundtrack of what was apparently an Apollo flight in a song called "Breathe". The accompanying light show; which received a second billing and can only be described as overwhelming, tended to dwarf some of the more sensitive lyrics.'

Monday 5 March
CONCERT
Cobo Arena, Detroit, Michigan, USA
Set list: 'Echoes' / 'Obscured By Clouds' / 'When You're In' / 'Careful With That Axe, Eugene' // *The Dark Side Of The Moon* / encore: 'One Of These Days'.
During 'Careful With That Axe, Eugene' the stage pyrotechnics damaged the PA system, showering the crowd with debris. After a short break to assess the damage the second half continued without incident.

Tuesday 6 March
CONCERT
Kiel Opera House, St. Louis, Missouri, USA
Set list: 'Echoes' / 'Obscured By Clouds' / 'When You're In' / 'Childhood's End' / 'Careful With That Axe, Eugene' // *The Dark Side Of The Moon* / encore: 'One Of These Days'.

Wednesday 7 March
CONCERT
International Amphitheatre, Chicago, Illinois, USA
Set list: 'Echoes' / 'Obscured By Clouds' / 'When You're In' / 'Childhood's End' / 'Careful With That Axe, Eugene' // *The Dark Side Of The Moon* / encore: 'One Of These Days'.

Thursday 8 March
CONCERT
University of Cincinnati Fieldhouse, Cincinnati, Ohio, USA
Set list: 'Echoes' / 'Obscured By Clouds' / 'When You're In' / 'Childhood's End' / 'Careful With That Axe, Eugene' // *The Dark Side Of The Moon* / encore: 'One Of These Days'.

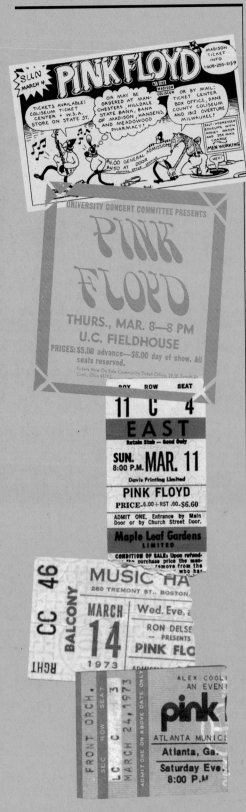

Saturday 10 March
CONCERT
Memorial Gymnasium, Kent State University, Kent, Ohio, USA
Set list: 'Echoes' / 'Obscured By Clouds' / 'When You're In' / 'Childhood's End' / 'Careful With That Axe, Eugene' // *The Dark Side Of The Moon* / encore: 'One Of These Days'.

Sunday 11 March
CONCERT
Maple Leaf Gardens, Toronto, Ontario, Canada
Set list: 'Echoes' / 'Obscured By Clouds' / 'When You're In' / 'Set The Controls For The Heart Of The Sun' / 'Careful With That Axe, Eugene' // *The Dark Side Of The Moon* / encore: 'One Of These Days'.
Nick Mason recalled in his book *Inside Out* that, 'We discovered one of our backing singers had disappeared, the reason being that she had been arrested with her boyfriend for holding up a grocery store.' Unfortunately it cannot be confirmed which singer it was or whether the tour was completed with or without her, but reviews from New York on 17 March indicate three backing vocalists on stage.

Monday 12 March
CONCERT
The Forum, Montréal, Québec, Canada
Set list included: 'Echoes' / 'Set The Controls For The Heart Of The Sun' // *The Dark Side Of The Moon*.

Wednesday 14 March
CONCERT
Music Hall, Boston, Massachusetts, USA

ABOVE: SOUNDCHECK AT RADIO CITY MUSIC HALL, 17 MARCH 1973.

Set list: 'Careful With That Axe, Eugene' / 'Obscured By Clouds' / 'When You're In' / 'Set The Controls For The Heart Of The Sun' / 'Echoes' // *The Dark Side Of The Moon* / encore: 'One Of These Days'.

Thursday 15 March
CONCERT
Spectrum Theater, Philadelphia, Pennsylvania, USA
Set list included: 'Obscured By Clouds' / 'When You're In' // *The Dark Side Of The Moon*.

Saturday 17 March
CONCERT
Radio City Music Hall, Manhattan, New York City, New York, USA
Set list: 'Obscured By Clouds' / 'When You're In' / 'Set The Controls For The Heart Of The Sun' / 'Careful With That Axe, Eugene' / 'Echoes' // *The Dark Side Of The Moon* / encore: 'One Of These Days'.
Sounds reported that: 'Pink Floyd turned out an exciting set last week with a stage half a block long, and a 6,200 seat theatre on four levels as their basic props. At one-thirty in the morning the lights dimmed, the audience stood, clouds of steam shot upwards from the vents in the stage, and the Floyd rose into view on one of the elevators; three light towers with

Friday 23 March
CONCERT
Charlotte Park Center, Charlotte, North Carolina, USA

Saturday 24 March
CONCERT
Municipal Auditorium, Atlanta, Georgia, USA
The last night of the tour.
Set list: 'Obscured By Clouds' / 'When You're In' / 'Set The Controls For The Heart Of The Sun' / 'Careful With That Axe, Eugene' / 'Echoes' // *The Dark Side Of The Moon* / encore: 'One Of These Days'.

Sunday 25 March
CANCELLED CONCERT
Bayfront Center, St. Petersburg, Florida, USA
This hastily arranged show was proposed for the end of the tour but was cancelled because Santana were scheduled to appear at the nearby Tampa Stadium on the same night and the promoter considered that this would reduce the audience for Pink Floyd.

Monday 7 May
RECORD RELEASE
'Money' / 'Us And Them'
US 7-inch single release.

Friday 18 & Saturday 19 May
CONCERTS
Earl's Court Exhibition Hall, Earl's Court, London, England
Set list at both shows: 'Obscured By Clouds' / 'When You're In' / 'Set The Controls For The Heart Of The Sun' / 'Careful With That Axe, Eugene' / 'Echoes' // *The Dark Side Of The Moon* / encore: 'One Of These Days'.
Pink Floyd were supplemented by Vicki Brown (backing vocals), Dick Parry (saxophone) and Liza Strike (backing vocals).
John Baxter and Martin Whicker-Kempton, fans in attendance, recalled that: 'After the reportedly dismal failure of David Bowie's Earls Court fiasco, when he could be seen by a few and heard by fewer, we approached last night with mixed emotions, anticipation and slight apprehension of what was to come. However, from the moment Rick Wright's synthesiser played the droning beginning of "Obscured By Clouds" amidst appropriate clouds of smoke, we knew we need fear no more. The Floyd's sound system incorporated their famous quadraphonic effects. They have perfected it to such an extent that it resembles a giant hi-fi system. One feels that the Floyd have used their vast technical knowledge and financial resources in a good way, and built a PA of such crystal clarity that it may be equalled but never bettered. Of the rest of their brilliant set, "Eugene"

OVERLEAF: ON STAGE AT EARL'S COURT, LONDON, MAY 1973.

a reflecting dish mounted on the centre one, created a glowing, hypnotic effect as you looked at the stage. The elevated stage section reached its full height then began to inch forward, and the crowd roared approval. Special mention ought to be made of the Floyd's lighting and sound crews who seemed never to miss a cue, and the 20 speaker quad system with speakers on all levels of the hall gave a close almost headphone sound. The music started with some of their well known older pieces with "Echoes" ending the first half. The second half was the new album *The Dark Side Of The Moon* (on which they used three black singers) with an encore of "One Of These Days". The fifteen-foot dish hanging from the centre tower glowed and steamed in the lights, and at one point as the red spots caught it the effect was of red laser beams flashing through the dark hall. Other times when the lights caught it, it looked like one of those mirrored globes they had at 30's balls. The Floyd were at their best and the stage presentation was one of the best I've seen in a hell of a long time.'

Sunday 18 March
CONCERT
Palace Theatre, Waterbury, Connecticut, USA
Set list: 'Obscured By Clouds' / 'When You're In' / 'Set The Controls For The Heart Of The Sun' / 'Careful With That Axe, Eugene' / 'Echoes' // *The Dark Side Of*

The Moon / encore: 'One Of These Days'.

Monday 19 March
CONCERT
Providence Civic Center, Providence, Rhode Island, USA

Thursday 22 March
CONCERT
Hampton Coliseum, Hampton, Virginia, USA

Friday 23 March
RECORD RELEASE
The Dark Side Of The Moon
UK album release. US album release on Saturday 10 March.
Lloyd Grossman, future TV personality, wrote in his review for *Rolling Stone* that: 'Throughout the album the band lays down a solid framework which they embellish with synthesisers, sound effects and spoken voice tapes. The sound is lush and multi-layered while remaining clear and well structured. *The Dark Side Of The Moon* is a fine album with a textural and conceptual richness that not only invites, but demands involvement. There is a certain grandeur here that exceeds mere musical melodramatics and is rarely attempted in rock.'

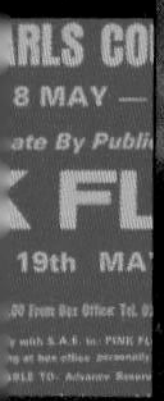
ARLS CO
8 MAY —
ate By Publi
FL
19th MA

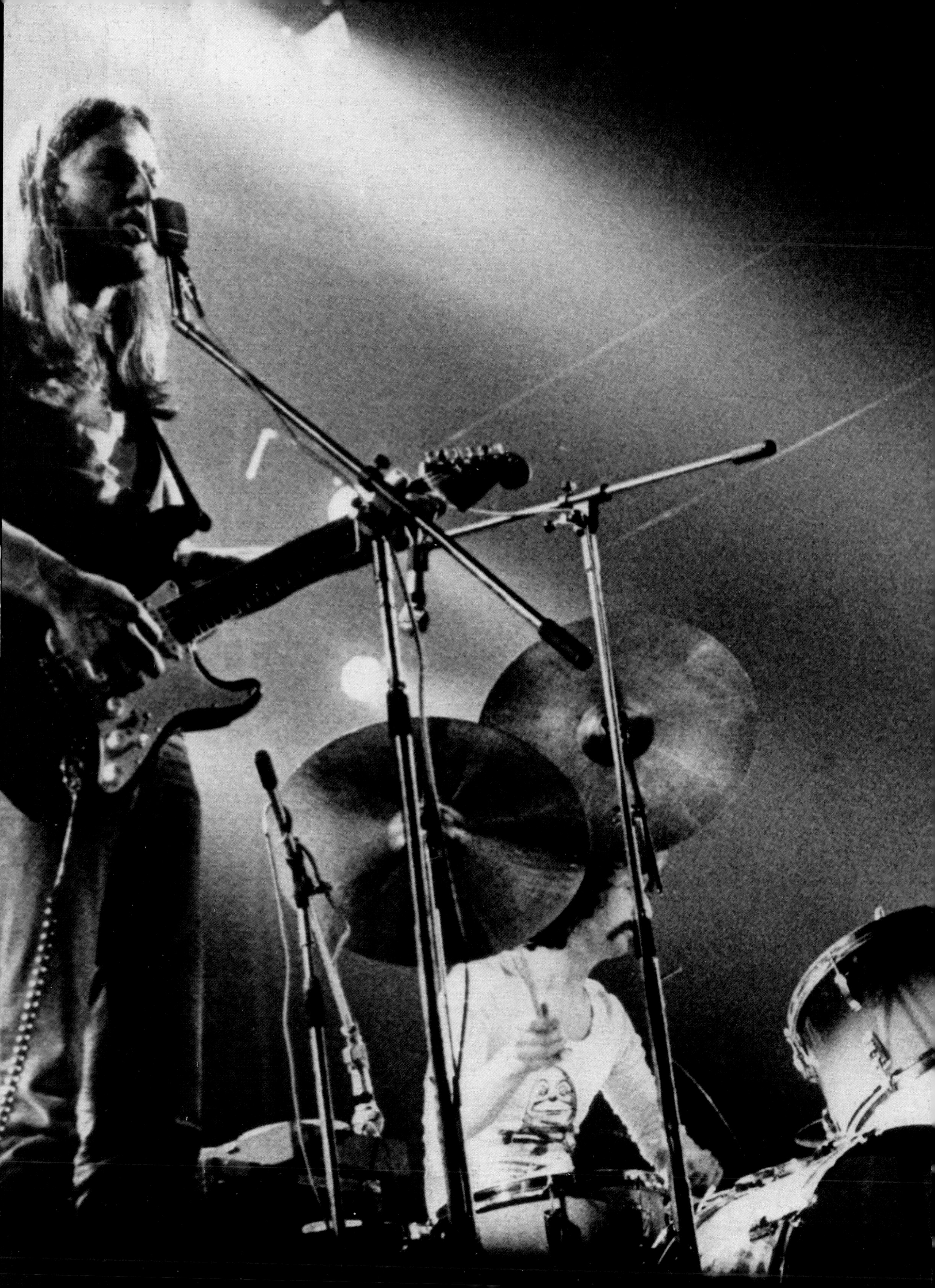

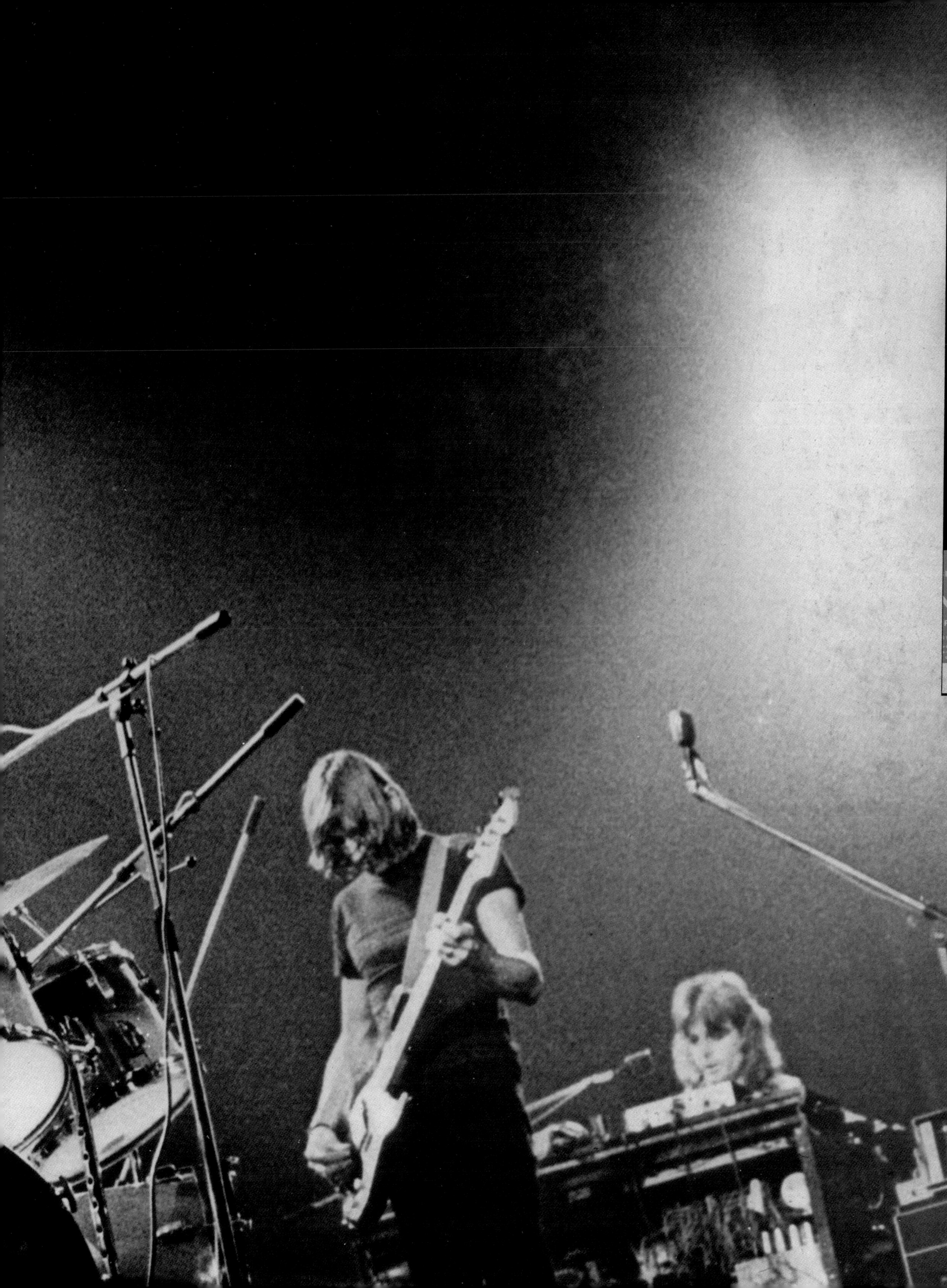

and "Set The Controls" are still there, but given a new freshness with the aid of burning gongs and a spaceman whose eyes lit up, and the inevitable smoke bombs after the by now legendary "Careful With That Axe, Eugene". Then came "Echoes" when, during the wind and crows sequence, tons of dry ice poured on to the stage and swirled around the feet of the group and into the 18,000 strong audience giving a very effective *Macbeth*-ian "blasted heath" scene. The second half featured *The Dark Side Of The Moon*, complete with girl singers, a saxophonist and insane laughter which made full use of the quadraphonic sound system. It has been said that the Floyd have relied too heavily on taped effects to liven up their performances. Now they have integrated them into their performance so well that the tape deck becomes another instrument contributing to a homogenous group sound rather than a group entity. The only disappointment for me was "Great Gig In The Sky" which failed to get off the ground. The end of *The Dark Side Of The Moon* came along with rockets being fired into the roof of the hall and the tolling of the iron bell, and the knowledge that we had been fortunate, nay privileged, to witness this evening. All however was not over. To greet us at the door was the Army, complete with wartime-type searchlights which panned across the faces of the people leaving, then raked into the sky to form the all too familiar criss-cross patterns which have not been with us over London since 1945.'

NORTH AMERICAN TOUR

PINK FLOYD ROAD CREW THROUGH 1973

Chris Adamson: Backline Technician
Graeme Fleming: Lighting Technician
Mick 'The Pole' Kluczynski: Tape Operator, Drum Kit, Quad Sound
Arthur Max: Lighting and Effects
Paul Padun: Lighting Technician
Alan Parsons: Front of House Sound Engineer
Bobby Richardson: PA / Stage Technician

Peter Watts: Road Manager
Robbie Williams: PA / Stage Technician
On Tour: Trucking Crew - Four drivers and two forty-foot trailer tractors
At Gig: 2 fork lift drivers, 6 stage hands, 2 electricians, 2 soundmen, 8 follow spot operators, 1 house electrician

ADDITIONAL TOUR PERSONEL

Nawasa Crowder: Backing vocals
Mary Ann Lindsey: Backing vocals
Phyllis Lindsey: Backing vocals
Dick Parry: Saxophone

Saturday 16 June
CANCELLED CONCERT
Roosevelt Stadium, Union City, New Jersey, USA
The opening night of the tour was rescheduled to a previously held 'rain date' on 18 June due to severe inclement weather.

Sunday 17 June
CONCERT
Saratoga Performing Arts Center, Saratoga Springs, New York, USA
Set list: 'Obscured By Clouds' / 'When You're In' / 'Set The Controls For The Heart Of The Sun' / 'Careful With That Axe, Eugene' / 'Echoes' // *The Dark Side Of The Moon* / encore: 'One Of These Days'.

Monday 18 June
CONCERT
Roosevelt Stadium, Union City, New Jersey, USA
Set list: 'Obscured By Clouds' / 'When You're In' / 'Set The Controls For The Heart Of The Sun' / 'Careful With That Axe, Eugene' / 'Echoes' // *The Dark Side Of The Moon* / encore: 'One Of These Days'.
Amusement Business reported that: 'Pink Floyd overcame a rain-out and further downpours on the rain date to set a record gross at the Roosevelt Stadium where 22,113 fans contributed to the $110,565 gross box office with tickets at $5 each.

LEFT: THE GONG EXPLODES INTO FLAMES DURING 'SET THE CONTROLS FOR THE HEART OF THE SUN' AT EARL'S COURT, LONDON, MAY 1973..

The Floyd date was initially set for June 16, but was called off at 4pm, with several thousand fans in the stands. On the rain date, the rains came down until about 2pm with a full stop about 4pm. At 8pm the group went on stage and played two one-hour and 15-minute sets until 10.45pm. All but 500 of the sold tickets sold in advance. Date had a potential of 25,000 audience. During the performance, a 7ft airplane crashed on stage from its harbor in the stands, as one of several stage effects employed by Pink Floyd.'

Tuesday 19 June
CONCERT
Civic Center Arena, Pittsburgh, Pennsylvania, USA
Set list: 'Obscured By Clouds' / 'When You're In' / 'Set The Controls For The Heart Of The Sun' / 'Careful With That Axe, Eugene' / 'Echoes' // *The Dark Side Of The Moon* / encore: 'One Of These Days'.

Wednesday 20 & Thursday 21 June
CONCERT
Merriweather Post Pavilion, Columbia, Maryland, USA
Set list at both shows: 'Obscured By Clouds' / 'When You're In'/ 'Set The Controls For The Heart Of The Sun'/ 'Careful With That Axe, Eugene' / 'Echoes' // *The Dark Side Of The Moon* / encore: 'One Of These Days'.
The Washington Post reported that: 'The British foursome opened a two-night stand before 9,000 people at the Pavilion last night, ranging their way through an amalgam of synthesisers, echo chambers, tape units, fog machines, incendiary bombs, flaming gongs and a giant rotating mirrored ball. The effect of all this was certainly dazzling, a real show in a rock world frequently low on entertainment and performance value. The problem is to decide whether Pink Floyd creates music or merely extols advances in audio engineering.'

Friday 22 June
CONCERT
Buffalo Memorial Auditorium, Buffalo, New York, USA
Show rescheduled from 15 June.
Set list: 'Obscured By Clouds' / 'When You're In' / 'Set The Controls For The Heart Of The Sun' / 'Careful With That Axe, Eugene' / 'Echoes' // *The Dark Side Of The Moon* / encore: 'One Of These Days'.

Saturday 23 June
CONCERT
Olympia Stadium, Detroit, Michigan, USA
Set list: 'Obscured By Clouds' / 'When You're In' / 'Set The Controls For The Heart Of The Sun' / 'Careful

With That Axe, Eugene' / 'Echoes' // *The Dark Side Of The Moon* / encore: 'One Of These Days'.

Sunday 24 June
CONCERT
Blossom Music Center, Cuyahoga Falls, Ohio, USA
Set list: 'Obscured By Clouds' / 'When You're In' / 'Set The Controls For The Heart Of The Sun' / 'Careful With That Axe, Eugene' / 'Echoes' // *The Dark Side Of The Moon* / encore: 'One Of These Days'.

Monday 25 June
CONCERT
Convention Center, Louisville, Kentucky, USA

Tuesday 26 June
CONCERT
Lake Spivey Park, Jonesboro, Georgia, USA

Wednesday 27 June
CONCERT
Jacksonville Coliseum, Jacksonville, Florida, USA

Thursday 28 June
CONCERT
The Sportatorium, Hollywood, Florida, USA
This show was originally scheduled for Pirates Cove, Pirates World Amusement Park, Dania, Hollywood, Florida and then switched to Miami Baseball Stadium, Miami, Florida before finally going ahead at The Sportatorium.
Set list: 'Obscured By Clouds' / 'When You're In' / 'Set The Controls For The Heart Of The Sun' / 'Careful With That Axe, Eugene' / 'Echoes' // *The Dark Side Of The Moon* / encore: 'One Of These Days'.

Friday 29 June
CONCERT
Tampa Stadium, Tampa, Florida, USA
The last night of the tour.
Set list: 'Obscured By Clouds' / 'When You're In' / 'Set The Controls For The Heart Of The Sun' / 'Careful With That Axe, Eugene' / 'Echoes' // *The Dark Side Of The Moon* / encore: 'One Of These Days'.

Sunday 23 September
CANCELLED CONCERT
3rd British Rock Meeting, Sandrennbahn Altrip, Frankfurt, West Germany
Pink Floyd were heavily advertised to headline on the closing day of this huge two-day festival (22-23 September) that was cancelled. Among the scheduled acts were Frank Zappa and The Mothers of Invention, Beck, Bogert and Appice, Chuck Berry, Wishbone Ash, Fumble, Suzy Quatro, Lou Reed, Greenslade, Jerry Lee Lewis, Rare Earth and Albert Hammond.

Monday 1 – Thursday 4 October
RECORDING SESSIONS
EMI Studios, Abbey Road, St. John's Wood, London, England
Discontinuous recording for the abandoned *Household Objects* project.

Monday 8 – Wednesday 10 October
RECORDING SESSIONS
EMI Studios, Abbey Road, St. John's Wood, London, England
Discontinuous recording for the abandoned *Household Objects* project.

Friday 12 October
CONCERT
Münchener Olympiahalle, Olympia Park, Munich, West Germany
Supported by Fumble.
Set list: 'Obscured By Clouds' / 'When You're In' / 'Set The Controls For The Heart Of The Sun' / 'Careful With That Axe, Eugene' / 'Echoes' // *The Dark Side Of The Moon* / encore: One Of These Days'.
Pink Floyd were supplemented at this and the following show in Vienna by Billie Barnum (backing vocals), Venetta Fields (backing vocals), Clydie King (backing vocals) and Dick Parry (saxophone).

Saturday 13 October
CONCERT
Stadthalle, Vienna, Austria
The last night of the tour. Set list: 'Obscured By Clouds' / 'When You're In' / 'Set The Controls For The Heart Of The Sun' / 'Careful With That Axe, Eugene' / 'Echoes' // *The Dark Side Of The Moon* / encore: One Of These Days'.

Monday 22 – Wednesday 31 October
RECORDING SESSIONS
EMI Studios, Abbey Road, St. John's Wood, London, England
Discontinuous recording for the abandoned *Household Objects* project.

Saturday 3 November
REHEARSAL
St. Augustine's Road, Camden, London, England
A pre-concert rehearsal from 12 noon to 2.00pm was arranged for backing vocalists Vicki Brown, Liza Strike and Clare Torry at Nick Mason's house.

Sunday 4 November
CONCERT
A Benefit For Robert Wyatt, Rainbow Theatre, Finsbury, London, England
Two shows at 5.00pm and 9.00pm. With Soft Machine.
Set list at both shows: *The Dark Side Of The Moon* // 'Obscured By Clouds' / 'When You're In'.
Pink Floyd were supplemented by Vicki Brown (backing vocals), Liza Strike (backing vocals), Clare Torry (backing vocals) and Dick Parry (saxophone).
Melody Maker reported that: 'It was a splendid evening of rock co-operation, in which both groups gave their services in aid of disabled drummer Robert Wyatt, and compere John Peel was pleased to announce that some 10,000 pounds was raised. Heartbeats in fact commenced proceedings, pulsating through the auditorium and stilling the more excitable elements in the crowd. Clocks ticked mysteriously and with perfect precision the Floydmen slotted their live instruments into the recorded sound, combining quadraphonic pre-recorded tapes, lights, smoke and theatrical effects into a kind of rock *Son et Lumiere*. Overhead was suspended a huge white balloon to represent the moon, on which spotlights played, and not long after performance began, searchlights began to pierce the gloom, and yellow warning lights began revolving in banks on the speaker cabinets. A choir of ladies cooed like angels of mercy and as a silver ball reflecting myriad beams of light began to revolve and belch more smoke, the audience rose to give them an ovation. They deserved a Nobel prize or at least an Oscar.'

Monday 12 November – Wednesday 5 December
RECORDING SESSIONS
EMI Studios, Abbey Road, St. John's Wood, London, England
Discontinuous recording for the abandoned *Household Objects* project.

Wednesday 5 December
FILM PREMIERE
Sydney Opera House, Sydney, Australia
The premiere of the film *Crystal Voyager*.

Friday 21 December
RADIO SHOW
Room 605, BBC World Service, Chandos Street, London
Roger Waters gave an interview to Michael Wale for the BBC Radio One show *Rockspeak* that was broadcast at 10.00pm.

running over the same old ground

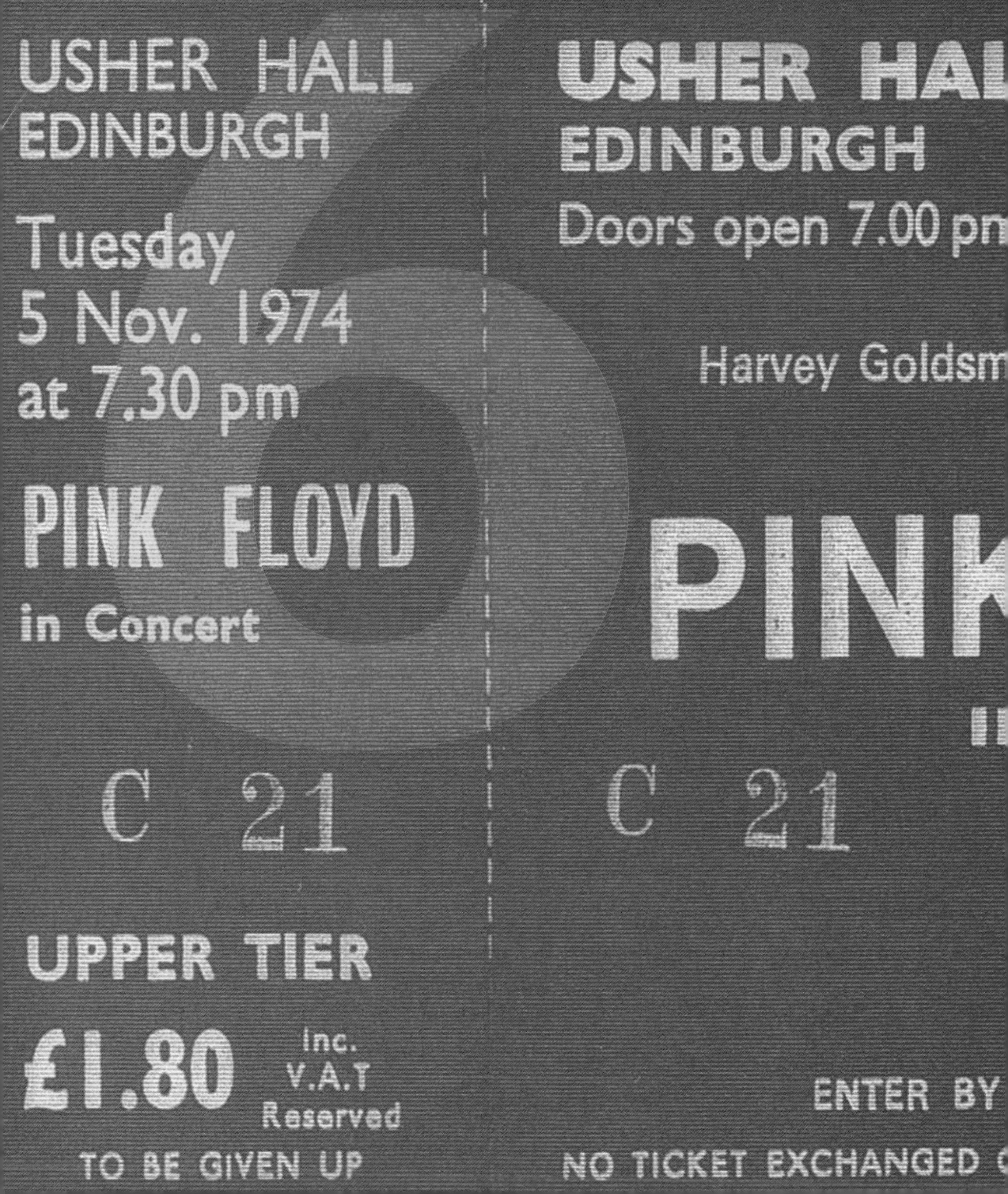

USHER HALL
EDINBURGH

Tuesday
5 Nov. 1974
at 7.30 pm

PINK FLOYD
in Concert

C 21

UPPER TIER

£1.80 Inc.
V.A.T
Reserved
TO BE GIVEN UP

USHER HAL
EDINBURGH
Doors open 7.00 pm

Harvey Goldsm

PINK

C 21

ENTER BY
NO TICKET EXCHANGED

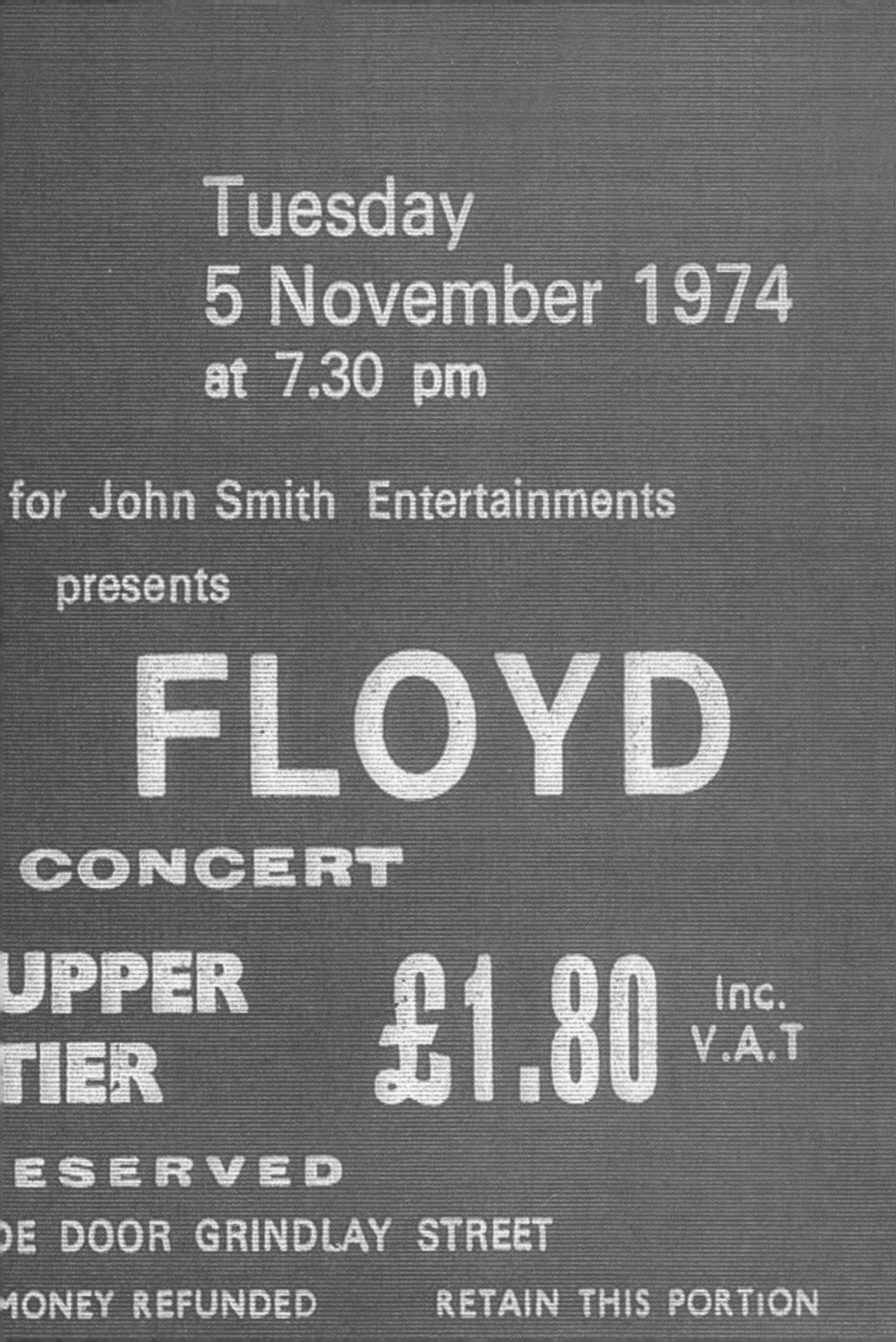

Tuesday
5 November 1974
at 7.30 pm

for John Smith Entertainments

presents

FLOYD

CONCERT

UPPER
TIER

£1.80 inc. V.A.T

ESERVED

DE DOOR GRINDLAY STREET

MONEY REFUNDED   RETAIN THIS PORTION

1974 – 1975

PINK FLOYD'S BREAK FROM BOTH LIVE PERFORMANCE AND RECORDING FROM LATE 1973 INTO EARLY 1974 SAW GILMOUR AND MASON, FOR THE FIRST TIME, INVOLVED IN PROJECTS OUTSIDE THE BAND. GILMOUR HAD BEEN INTRODUCED TO A TALENTED YOUNG SINGER-SONGWRITER CALLED KATE BUSH, AND HE EVENTUALLY INFLUENCED EMI'S DECISION TO SIGN HER. SINCE THEN GILMOUR HAS FREQUENTLY GUESTED ON BUSH'S WORK.

He had also spotted a band called Unicorn at a friend's wedding reception. After inviting them to test out his new home studio on a farm in the Essex countryside, he financed some recording sessions at Olympic studios in London, and produced their debut album, *Blue Pine Trees*. Steve O'Rourke became Unicorn's manager and the band was signed to the Chrysalis label, for whom they went on to make three albums.

Mason, meanwhile, lent his hand to producing Principal Edward's Magic Theatre as well as Robert Wyatt. With Wyatt he performed at London's Theatre Royal, as well appearing on BBC TV's *Top of The Pops* miming Wyatt's cover of the Monkees' 'I'm A Believer' in a pick up band that also featured Andy Summers, later of The Police.

It wasn't long before Pink Floyd themselves were back in the studio. Despite having promised themselves more leisure time, they found it hard to let go of the routine of constant activity, and by spring they were already working hard on new material. They booked rehearsal time at a studio in King's Cross, London, where many of the songs for the next two albums would emerge, not least a stunning new title, 'Shine On' (later changed to 'Shine On You Crazy Diamond'), an ode to Syd Barrett.

'We started playing together and writing in the way we'd written a lot of things before. In the same way that "Echoes" was written,' Waters remembered. '"Shine On You Crazy Diamond" was written in exactly the same way, with odd little musical ideas coming out of various people. The first one, the main phrase, came from Dave, the first loud guitar phrase you can hear on the album was the starting point and we worked from there until we had the various parts of "Shine On You Crazy Diamond".[1]

A second number, entitled 'Raving And Drooling', was also worked out, and both tracks were premiered in June during a tour of France – the only country outside the UK where Pink Floyd would perform this year.

The entourage was also expanded by the hiring of many extra road hands, including Phil Taylor, who remained with the band through their last tour of 1994 and continues to be Gilmour's chief technician at both his studio and on solo performances to this day.

The band had also gone to considerable effort and expense to redesign their stage presentation to create a far greater visual impact than ever before. The show now featured, at the centre rear of the stage, a forty-foot circular screen, which was used to back-project specially prepared film and animation sequences. The screen also served as a backdrop at the close of 'Shine On', when a huge rotating mirror-ball was raised in front of it and hit with a spotlight to produce blinding shards of white light, under cover of which the band exited. Fireworks and rockets also provided some spectacular visual effects.

The French tour, however, was dogged by an enormous amount of problems. A succession of cancelled and rescheduled dates occurred when promoters realised just how much electrical power the band's new equipment required and the ceiling height that was needed to accommodate the huge circular screen. However, the shows that did go ahead in the five cities in which Pink Floyd performed were complete sell-outs, setting new records for audience attendance in France.

Whereas problematic dates were eventually straightened out, a sponsorship campaign into which the band entered with the French soft drinks company Gini two years previously reared its head at this time and turned decidedly sour. The agreement required a photo-shoot in Morocco for press adverts and the recording of a song for the TV ads, which Waters penned, called 'Bitter Love'. The band was offered the princely sum of £50,000 and although it seemed a good idea at the time and would go some way to lining their pockets, the band became increasingly wary of the implications it would have for their image – not to mention the fact that Waters was told he wouldn't be allowed to sing on it. Their position was clearly compromised and although nothing could stop the press advertisements coming out, it is not clear whether the TV ad was ever aired. It is an incident that the band has chosen to put down to experience, and all the monies were subsequently donated to charity.

Even so, the episode left a bad taste in Waters' mouth and, after taking a short break following the tour, he started writing a new song, 'How Do You Feel', which remains unreleased, expressing his feelings about the experience. But the band were still inviting sponsorship of sorts, and all of the band members were seen sporting Guinness T-shirts on stage throughout the year, although no hint of a deal has ever been made public. An advertising campaign launched in 1973 by Avis rental vehicles also attracted the band's name, with the slogan 'Make tracks like Pink Floyd – Rent An Avis truck'.

The 1974 British Winter Tour, as it was called, was booked to start in November, and was planned to coincide with important football games in the cities on the itinerary, in order that the band could enjoy watching a good afternoon match before each show.

By now 'Shine On' had become 'Shine On You Crazy Diamond' and, like 'Raving And Drooling', had been knocked into better shape. The band also added a third new song to the set, 'Gotta Be Crazy', that Waters had penned at home to which Gilmour added the chord sequence at a later date. All three songs were very harsh in comparison to the softer melodies of *The Dark Side Of The Moon* and the

lyrics were an unforgiving tirade against society's current values. It certainly laid to rest the last traces of Floyd's psychedelic past.

The choice of films the band had projected onto the circular screen for *The Dark Side Of The Moon* half of the show in France was now extensively refined, with whole new sequences being produced throughout the rest of the summer. In addition, a three-week rehearsal period was booked at the Elstree film studios, north of London, before the tour to allow the band to work out the intricate timings that were required to keep the music in sync with the visual material.

Audiences in Britain were treated to a version of *The Dark Side Of The Moon* with greater dimension and visual impact than ever before, including specially commissioned animation by Ian Eames. The piece now began with quadraphonic sound blasting out the taped maniacal laughter that appears on the album and the spoken line of 'I've been mad for fucking years' repeated over and over again at deafening volume. A picture of the moon grew bigger and bigger until it occupied the whole screen and then, with the underlying heart beat now very

BELOW: PERFORMING AT THE EMPIRE POOL, WEMBLEY, NOVEMBER 1974. USING THE CIRCULAR FILM SCREEN FOR THE FIRST TIME THAT YEAR, IT WAS TO BECOME A TRADEMARK OF PINK FLOYD'S LIVE SHOWS.

audible, this gave way to a darting cardiograph blip, allowing the band to launch into 'Breathe'.

Perhaps the most outstanding feature of all was the sequence for 'On The Run' and 'Time'. A series of flashing street, car, airport and aircraft lights, in bewildering and dazzling succession, led the viewer into a tunnel with a planet at the far end. As this image seemed to rush towards the viewer, the film switched to animation, skimming across the planet's surface and then sweeping through urban landscapes to reveal scenes of utter destruction.

The 'Time' sequence, again animated, was equally remarkable: flights of clock faces were seen passing across a cloudy sky, then piling up against one another and peeling away, squadrons of them flying through the air as their hands raced around. The final scene focussed on a pendulum sweeping the sky to introduce the opening line of the song.

'The Great Gig In The Sky' featured underwater shots taken from the film *Crystal Voyager* and 'Money' had a series of rapid-fire shots of banknotes, women parading in fur coats, a lyrically appropriate Lear jet and even copies of *The Dark Side Of The Moon* coming off the production line.

'Us And Them', the dreamy blues number from the album, featured slow-motion footage of the rush hour in the City of London in contrast with the diamond miners of South Africa. As *The Dark Side Of The Moon* came to its grand finale with 'Brain Damage', film images of politicians were used to compliment the accompanying insane laughter. The eclipse of the sun by the moon concluded the epic piece.

The UK tour was a complete success, with every venue sold out. BBC Radio One even recorded a show at Wembley for a complete broadcast of *The Dark Side Of the Moon* (having first edited out the introductory voiceover!) wowing many more fans. However, it was also the first time that a noticeable backlash against the band had occurred within the national music press. Throughout the early Seventies Pink Floyd had reigned supreme, but the concerts at Wembley's Empire Pool brought disdain from a younger generation of critics, principally Nick Kent of the *NME*, who described their show as 'a pallid excuse for creative music' and not only suggested they lived a bourgeois existence, but also attacked Gilmour's personal appearance.

On Monday 13 January 1975 Pink Floyd entered EMI's newly refitted Studio 3 at Abbey Road to start work on their seventh studio album, *Wish You Were Here*. Because of their touring commitments, the sessions took

place either side of and between two tours of the USA. As a result, the recording process became very protracted, and ultimately pushed the album's release back to September. One by-product of this delay was that the band was again able to refine new works on stage.

The first US tour was announced in March and, in a new departure, carried no national advertising. Instead, CBS Records used FM radio to alert fans to a specially prepared Pink Floyd show which was simulcast early that month to the seven major cities where they were booked to play. Within hours, all of the dates had completely sold out, breaking all the venues' box office records, including those of the Los Angeles Sports Arena, which in a single day sold all of its 67,000 tickets for the band's scheduled four-night run. Even an extra fifth show sold out within hours, and indeed the demand for tickets was so great that the band's residency could easily have been extended still further.

Overall, the American fans' response to the tour was simply overwhelming. It bewildered many city newspapers that a band, whom many had never even heard of, could have such a rabid following and do better business than The Rolling Stones, who were also on tour, yet be completely anonymous personalities. It also didn't go unnoticed by the band's former label, Capitol, that the band had no new product which prompted them to issue a promotional compilation album, *Tour '75*, to radio stations in order to boost back catalogue sales.

On stage Pink Floyd chose to play a different set from that of the UK tour of the previous year. *The Dark Side Of The Moon* still formed the mainstay of the second half of the show, with 'Echoes' as an encore, but the first half, although still opening with 'Raving And Drooling' and 'Gotta Be Crazy' now divided the lengthy 'Shine On You Crazy Diamond' into two halves which straddled another new composition, 'Have A Cigar', a dig at the corporate music industry.

For the first time American fans witnessed the full visual impact of the new stage show, complete with circular film screen, giant mirror ball, crashing model aircraft and obligatory pyrotechnics – in addition to the trademark quadraphonic sound system. It was a large-scale operation in every sense: over thirty tons of equipment, much of it shipped over from England, was transported around the country, and it took a full-time road crew of seventeen to make the event possible. The band also chartered a private jet to travel between shows, while the road crew moved the gear in a convoy of articulated trucks.

Although this vast array of visual effects was

spectacular in indoor venues, the band ran into serious trouble when they began their East Coast leg of the tour in June. Their still primitive staging – small-scale compared with the vast scaffolding structures of today's outdoor concerts (although not quite as rudimentary as the Beatles' set-up at New York's Shea Stadium in the mid Sixties) – looked decidedly lost in the vast expanses of the huge sports stadiums in which they were now performing.

In an attempt to boost the visual impact and lend the outdoor stadium shows a more impressive scale, Pink Floyd turned to Mark Fisher and Jonathan Park, two accomplished London-based architectural designers with experience of advanced inflatable and pneumatic structures. Their brief was to construct a huge pyramid that would sail above the stage and radiate light beams in a way that was reminiscent of the cover of *The Dark Side Of The Moon*.

BELOW AND OVERLEAF: PERFORMING AT THE NASSAU VETERANS MEMORIAL COLISEUM, LONG ISLAND, NEW YORK, JUNE 1975 ON PINK FLOYD' FIRST STADIUM AND ARENA TOUR OF NORTH AMERICA.

CHIEF DAVIS (LAPD) << **I'm the meanest chief of police in the history of the United States. >>**

Assembled in record time, the structure made its maiden flight at the Atlanta Stadium on 7 June, but having failed to work properly didn't resurface again until the band's show at the Three Rivers Stadium in Pittsburg, on 20 June. The huge pyramid, its base sixty-foot square, was held by guides and launched from the back of the stage at the climax of the show and rose some distance before a heavy wind blew it over, dislodging the helium balloon inside. The balloon was never seen again; nor was the pyramid, which, after crashing into a number of vehicles in the stadium car park, was shredded in minutes by souvenir-hungry fans.

Despite the overall success of the tour, it is also remembered for the heavy-handed actions of the Los Angeles Police Department, which arrested over 500 fans during the five-night run at the Sports Arena. Police

Chief Ed Davis, in a speech to businessmen a week before the concerts, described the forthcoming shows as an 'illegal pot festival' and gave the assurance that his force was committed to bringing the full weight of the law to bear on even the most minor of offences committed at or in the grounds of the venue. Inevitably, many innocent fans were also stopped and questioned.

This confrontation had been brewing for some time; the LAPD had been waiting eagerly to deal with a big music event in the city. *Rolling Stone*, in its June 1975 edition, ran an extensive report that gave evidence that many other venues in the greater Los Angeles area had been subjected to the heavy-handed actions of Chief Davis, who was quoted as saying, 'I'm the meanest chief of police in the history of the United States.' The article also contained an allegation that the 'bust' had been planned well in advance: 'One young man arrested at the Shrine Auditorium's Robin Trower concert of 16 March claimed an officer told him, "If you think this is something, you ought to see what we're going to do at

BELOW: FORMER BRITISH PRIME MINISTER (CONSERVATIVE, OCTOBER 1963 – OCTOBER 1964) ALEC DOUGLAS HOME ON SCREEN DURING A SEQUENCE FROM 'BRAIN DAMAGE' DURING A SHOW AT THE NASSAU VETERANS MEMORIAL COLISEUM, LONG ISLAND, NEW YORK, JUNE 1975.

the Sports Arena.'"

Officially only seventy-five police officers were deployed at the shows on each of the five nights Pink Floyd played, but venue management estimated the figure at nearer 200. Of the 511 arrests made, the majority were for possession of marijuana. The police justified their actions by claiming that there were a couple of more serious offences, including cocaine dealing and possession of a loaded gun. This fact made more headline news in the *LA Times* than the concerts themselves. Despite the tense atmosphere, the fans behaved well in the view of the Arena's management, who later praised them.

Back in Britain, with the US tour just a few days behind them, in July Pink Floyd were due to give their long-awaited 'homecoming' open-air concert at Knebworth Park in rural Hertfordshire in July. The concert was dogged by problems from the start, among which was the arrival of the road crew, jet-lagged from the US tour only a day or so beforehand. Because of the scale of the event, Pink Floyd's own PA system had to be used by all the other bands, which due to the late delivery of some new components was still being rigged up on the morning of the show. Not surprisingly, by the time the band came to use it themselves it had taken a serious pounding.

In addition, their stage entrance had been precisely scheduled to coincide with the fly-past of two Second World War Spitfires, but in the event the fighters buzzed the audience at low level while the roadies were still frantically trying to prepare the stage. As a result the band came on stage unprepared and their set was tired, uninspired and marred throughout by technical breakdowns mainly due to insufficient generator power. The most noticeable result of this occurred during 'Raving And Drooling', when the stage-right PA stack failed altogether. This problem was later rectified, but the mains power was not coming through at the correct frequency and this put Rick Wright's Hammond organ out of tune. The instrument couldn't be retuned and Wright was forced to use his Farfisa instead, which gave the rest of the show a very hard, mechanical feel.

It may have been a wonderful day out for the estimated 100,000 crowd: the concert was only licensed

for 40,000, but so great was the turn-out that the perimeter fencing was eventually removed. And yet, all in all, it was not quite the return the fans had been expecting from Pink Floyd, especially as it was their first British show for seven months.

Predictably, the band again fell foul of the UK music press. Some reviewers accused them of turning in a poor performance and others for playing *The Dark Side Of The Moon* yet again; others took them to task for playing in their own country all too infrequently. Whereas Pink Floyd had once been seen as stalwarts of the British rock-underground, regular performers at festivals and small UK venues, the view now was that the industry machine had taken over and the band had overreached themselves. What the journalists failed to realise was that their own overwhelming support over the years had contributed to this massive expansion. The audiences had swelled considerably, which prevented the band from playing small-scale concerts ever again. Besides, as much as the band disliked it, they and their management recognised that a US tour was far more lucrative than its UK counterpart could ever be. Underlining this difference, the American tour had ensured enough album sales to propel *The Dark Side Of The Moon* back into the

ROGER WATERS << I cast myself back into how fucking dreadful I felt on the last American tour with all those thousands and thousands and thousands of drunken kids smashing each other to pieces. I felt dreadful because it had nothing to do with us – I didn't think there was any contact between us and them. >>

Billboard Top 100 album chart on 12 April 1975, where it resided until 6 March 1977.

Money issues aside, the US tour had left the band cold. There was a distinct feeling of isolation, with the back row getting further and further away. The fans' intense enthusiasm and ability to make plenty of noise meant that attending a Pink Floyd concert in the States was akin to an FA Cup Final back home. Their shows had ceased to become an intimate performance for the fans and more like a large-scale party for the masses, regardless of the entertainment.

Such was this sense of alienation, at least in Roger

190

Waters' mind, that it led him to believe there may as well have been a brick wall between band and audience. 'I cast myself back into how fucking dreadful I felt on the last American tour with all those thousands and thousands and thousands of drunken kids smashing each other to pieces. I felt dreadful because it had nothing to do with us – I didn't think there was any contact between us and them.'[2]

It was an idea that he would nurture over the next few years, but for the moment there was a deadline looming for the release of *Wish You Were Here*. Both record company and management were now exerting greater pressure than ever before on the band to deliver an album that would equal the massive success of its predecessor. But the truth was, their hearts just weren't in it. In fact, they were very close to splitting up. Indeed Waters has, on many occasions, stated in print that *The Dark Side Of The Moon* had more or less finished the group as a creative force, since they had fulfilled at a stroke the shared ambition of fame and fortune.

He spoke quite frankly of these fraught times shortly after the later album's release: 'I definitely think that at the *Wish You Were Here* recording sessions most of us didn't wish we were there at all, we wished we were somewhere else. I wasn't happy being there because I got the feeling we weren't together. The album is about none of us really being there, or being there only marginally. About our non-presence in the situation we had clung to through habit, and are still clinging to through habit – being Pink Floyd.

'We pressed on regardless of the general ennui for a few weeks and then things came to a bit of a head. I felt that the only way I could retain interest in the project was to try to make the album relate to what was going on there and then – i.e. the fact that no one was really looking each other in the eye, and that it was all very

"Have A Cigar" came in.'[3]

'Welcome To The Machine' offers very little respite from the storm – another pounding epic, its throbbing beat building slowly through the use of the favoured VCS3 synthesiser, which sets the tone. Perhaps the only light relief comes in the shape of the anthem 'Wish You Were Here' – a latter-day sing-along but none the worse for its intelligent, reflective lyric. Musically, its masterstroke is the use of a tinny transistor radio being tuned in that gives way to Gilmour's delicate guitar work.

Speaking of the recording sessions Waters later commented: 'We all sat round and unburdened ourselves a lot, and I took notes on what everybody was saying. It was a meeting about what wasn't happening and why. Dave was always clear that he wanted to do the other two songs – he never quite copped what I was talking about. But Rick did and Nicky did and he was outvoted, so we went on.'[4]

In the studio, Waters' vocal sessions on 'Shine On You Crazy Diamond' in the early part of the year had already been a nightmare: 'It was right on the edge of my range. I always felt very insecure about singing anyway because I'm not naturally able to sing well. I know what I wanna do but I don't have the ability to do it well. It was fantastically boring to record, 'cos I had to do it line by line, doing it over and over again just to get it sounding reasonable.'[5]

The final sessions, occurring after Knebworth, saw much of the same difficulty. By the time they had reached 'Have A Cigar', Waters' singing was beyond a joke and as a last resort their friend Roy Harper was drafted in. 'Roy was recording in the studio anyway,' recalled Waters, 'and was in and out all the time. I can't remember who suggested it, maybe I did, probably hoping everybody would go "Oh no Rog, you do it", but they didn't! They all went, "Oh yeah that's a good idea". And he did it (as well as takes with Gilmour duetting with Harper) and everybody went, "Oh, terrific!" So that was that.' [6] It seems to be a decision that Waters has regretted to this day.

Also present on the album's title track was Stephane Grapelli, who was recording with Yehudi Menuhin at Abbey Road. It is often claimed that the tapes were lost or recorded over but, according to Waters, Grapelli definitely appears at the very end of the song, although his contribution is barely audible. He wasn't credited on the sleeve, but he reportedly received a small fee.

ROGER WATERS << I'm very sad about Syd. I wasn't for years. For years I suppose he was a threat because of all that bollocks written about him and us. >>

mechanical. So I suggested we change it – that we didn't do the other two songs ['Raving And Drooling' and 'Gotta Be Crazy'] but tried somehow to make a bridge between the first and second halves of "Shine On", which is how "Welcome To The Machine", "Wish You Were Here" and

One final incident at those sessions has passed into Pink Floyd lore: the sudden and uncanny appearance of Syd Barrett in the studio at precisely the moment the band was going through the final playbacks of 'Shine On You Crazy Diamond', their extended tribute to him. The date was 5 June 1975, just before the Floyd's departure for their second American tour. It was all the more bizarre because none of them recognised Barrett at first, assuming he was a caretaker. His appearance had changed dramatically: he had a shaven head, was extremely overweight and was wearing tatty clothes. He hardly spoke a word and after a short time merely wandered off. It was the last time the band ever saw him.

'I'm very sad about Syd,' Waters declared. 'I wasn't for years. For years I suppose he was a threat because of all that bollocks written about him and us. Of course he was very important and the band would never have fucking started without him but on the other hand it couldn't have gone on with him. He may or may not be important in rock 'n' roll anthology terms but he's certainly not nearly as important say in terms of Pink Floyd. "Shine On" is not really about Syd, he's just a symbol for the extremes of absence some people have to indulge in because it's the only way they can cope with how fucking sad it is – modern life, to withdraw completely.'[7]

As on all Pink Floyd's albums, the artwork was quite unique again designed by Storm Thorgerson and friends at Hipgnosis. It acted as a very specific visual representation of the subject matter and continues the theme of alienation and absence throughout. Even the sleeve was concealed by a black shrink-wrap outer covering, which made the whole album look appropriately anonymous.

Wish You Were Here was finally released on 15 September and went straight to the top of the album charts on both sides of the Atlantic. No doubt CBS in the USA gave a huge sigh of relief on learning that their investment had paid off.

ABOVE: DICK PARRY AND ROGER WATERS ON STAGE AT KNEBWORTH PARK, STEVENAGE ON 5 JULY 1975.

Sources
1–5. *Pink Floyd Lyric Book*, Blandford, 1982 (contains a 1975 interview with Nick Sedgwick)
6. *The Pink Floyd Story*, Capital Radio, 14 January 1977
7. *Pink Floyd Lyric Book*, Blandford, 1982 (contains a 1975 interview with Nick Sedgwick)

1974

R HALL
RGH
en 7.00 pm
vey Goldsmith

INK
IN
1

Sunday 13 January
RECORDING SESSIONS
Studio 3, EMI Studios, Abbey Road, St. John's Wood, London, England
Discontinuous recording commences on the album *Wish You Were Here* on this date and continues throughout the year in the newly refitted Studio 3 at EMI Studios, Abbey Road.

Friday 18 January
RECORD RELEASE
A Nice Pair
UK album release. US album released on Saturday 8 December 1973.
NME commented that, 'This tastefully wrapped double album is a repackaging of the first two Floyd albums *The Piper At The Gates Of Dawn* and *A Saucerful Of Secrets*. Somewhere in between these two albums Syd Barrett left the band, ridding them temporarily of their raison d'etre and thus while *Piper* is crammed full of Syd's devastatingly original, witty humorous and incisive songs, *Saucerful* is very much a transitional album, revealing elements of both what was and what was to be.'

Monday 4 February
RECORD RELAESE
'Time' / 'Us And Them'
US 7-inch single release.

1974 FRENCH TOUR
Many conflicting dates for shows were advertised in the French music press. This situation was caused by the additional difficulty in locating suitable venues to accommodate Pink Floyd's new stage show that used, for the first time, their trademark circular projection screen. As a result the following shows were either rescheduled or cancelled: Palais des Sports, Cambrai (14 June); Palais des Sports, Lyon (14 June); Strasbourg (16 June); Nancy (16 June); Palais des Sports, Lyon (16 June); Palais des Sports, Cambrai (18 June); Les Arènas, Parc des Expositions, Poitiers (20 June); Palais des Sports, Lyon (21 June); Parc des Expositions, Toulouse (22 June).

PINK FLOYD ROAD CREW
Rufus Cartwright: Front of House Sound Engineer
Bernie Caulder: PA / Stage Technician
Alan Conway: Quad Technician

Graeme Fleming: Lighting Technician
Seth Goldman: Monitor Sound Engineer
Mick 'The Pole' Kluczynski: PA / Stage Technician
Mick Marshall: Lighting Technician
Arthur Max: Production Manager / Lighting
Paul Murray: Film Projection
Robin Murray: Lighting Technician
Peter Revell: Film Projection
Nick Rockford: PA / Stage Technician
Phil Taylor: Backline Technician
Robbie Williams: PA / Stage Technician

ADDITIONAL TOUR PERSONNEL THROUGH 1974
Venetta Fields: Backing vocals
Dick Parry: Saxophone
Carlena Williams: Backing vocals

Tuesday 18 June
CONCERT
Hall 1, Parc des Expositions, Toulouse, France
Set list: 'Shine On You Crazy Diamond' * / 'Raving And Drooling' / 'Echoes' // *The Dark Side Of The Moon* // encore: 'Careful With That Axe, Eugene.'

GINI... PINK FLOYD...GINI
Un goût... une musique étranges venus d'ailleurs.

Bitter lemon ton
à boire glace

* 'Shine On You Crazy Diamond' is an early version of the later recorded piece 'Shine On You Crazy Diamond, Parts 1-9'.
Europe 1 Radio reportedly recorded parts of this show together with band interviews but the content and broadcast details remain unknown.

Wednesday 19 June
CONCERT
Les Arènas, Parc des Expositions, Poitiers, France
Set list: 'Shine On You Crazy Diamond' / 'Raving And Drooling' / 'Echoes' // *The Dark Side Of The Moon* / encore: 'Careful With That Axe, Eugene'.

Friday 21 June
CONCERT
Hall 1, Palais des Expositions, Dijon, France
Set list: 'Shine On You Crazy Diamond' / 'Raving And Drooling' / 'Echoes' // *The Dark Side Of The Moon* / encore: 'Careful With That Axe, Eugene'.

Saturday 22 June
CONCERT

Théâtre de Plein Air, Parc des Expositions, Colmar, France
Set list: 'Shine On You Crazy Diamond' / 'Raving And Drooling' / 'Echoes' // *The Dark Side Of The Moon* / encore: 'Careful With That Axe, Eugene'.

Monday 24, Tuesday 25 & Wednesday 26 June
CONCERTS
Palais des Sports de la Porte de Versailles, Paris, France
Set list at all three shows: 'Shine On You Crazy Diamond' / 'Raving And Drooling' / 'Echoes' // *The Dark Side Of The Moon* / encore: 'One Of These Days'.
French TV reportedly filmed the show on 24 June but the content and broadcast details remain unknown.
During the afternoon of 25 June French journalists challenged Pink Floyd and their crew to a football match that was held at the University Campus, Paris. The journalists scored a 4-3 victory over Pink Floyd.

BRITISH WINTER TOUR '74'

PINK FLOYD ROAD CREW
Rufus Cartwright: Front of House Sound Engineer (4 – 14 November)
Bernie Caulder: PA / Stage Technician
Alan Conway: Quad Technician
Paul Devine: PA / Stage Technician
Graeme Fleming: Lighting Technician
Seth Goldman: Monitor Sound Engineer
Brian Humphries: Front of House Sound Engineer (15 November – 14 December)
Mick 'The Pole' Kluczynski: PA / Stage Technician
Mick Marshall: Lighting Technician
Arthur Max: Production Manager / Lighting
Paul Murray: Film Projection
Robin Murray: Lighting Technician
Peter Revell: Film Projection
Nick Rockford: PA / Stage Technician
Phil Taylor: Backline Technician
Coon Thompson: PA / Stage Technician
Robbie Williams: PA / Stage Technician

October
REHEARSALS
Elstree Film Studios, Borehamwood, England & Unit Studios, Kings Cross, London, England
Pink Floyd set up full production rehearsals during the last three weeks of October in a sound stage at Elstree film studios – in part to work out the synching of their new backing films. The musicians had further rehearsals at Unit Studios in north London for a further week.

Friday 25 October
RADIO SHOW
Room 605, BBC World Service, Chandos Street, London
Richard Wright gave an interview to Michael Wale for the BBC Radio One show *Rockspeak* that was broadcast at 10.00pm.

Monday 4 & Tuesday 5 November
CONCERTS
Usher Hall, Edinburgh, Scotland
Set list at both shows: 'Shine On You Crazy Diamond' / 'Raving And Drooling' / 'Gotta Be Crazy' // *The Dark Side Of The Moon* / encore: 'Echoes'.

Friday 8 & Saturday 9 November
CONCERTS
Odeon, Newcastle-upon-Tyne, England
Set list at both shows: 'Shine On You Crazy Diamond' / 'Raving And Drooling' / 'Gotta Be Crazy' // *The Dark Side Of The Moon* / encore: 'Echoes'.

Thursday 14 November
CONCERT
Empire Pool, Wembley, England

Set list: 'Shine On You Crazy Diamond' / 'Raving And Drooling' / 'Gotta Be Crazy' // *The Dark Side Of The Moon* / encore: 'Echoes'.

NME reported that: 'After approximately five minutes of slightly laboured tuning up, the band start their first number of the set - a new composition entitled "Shine On You Crazy Diamond". It is very slow, rather low on melodic inventiveness, each note hanging in that archetypal ominous stunted fashion that tends to typify the Floyd at their most uninspired. This thoroughly unimpressive beginning is duly followed by the second of the three new numbers to be showcased in this section. "Raving And Drooling" is motivated by a rhythm somewhat akin to that of the human heartbeat with further references gathered from numerous Floyd stylised devices. So then there was "Gotta Be Crazy", the magnum opus of this dubious triumvirate, which features a fairly decent melody; a fetching minor chord strummed out by Gilmour who also sings over it. Unfortunately, the Floyd as always, let the song sprawl out to last twice as long as it should. The second half is, of course, taken up by the whole *Dark Side Of The Moon* presentation, to be graced by the projection of a special film made as a visual complement to the music. Finally the set is completed and the band walk off to ecstatic applause. They eventually return for an encore - no 'thank-you's' or anything, and the band do

"Echoes". Visuals are now relegated to luminous green orbs of circular light projected on the big screen.'

Friday 15 November
CONCERT
Empire Pool, Wembley, England
Set list: 'Shine On You Crazy Diamond' / 'Raving And Drooling' / 'Gotta Be Crazy' // *The Dark Side Of The Moon* / encore: 'Echoes'.

Saturday 16 November
CONCERT
Empire Pool, Wembley, England
Set list: 'Shine On You Crazy Diamond' / 'Raving And Drooling' / 'Gotta Be Crazy' // *The Dark Side Of The Moon* / encore: 'Echoes'.
BBC Radio One recorded the show and the entire second half of *The Dark Side Of The Moon* (with the, 'I've been mad for fucking years' in 'Speak To Me' removed from the mix) was broadcast, on the *Alan Freeman Show* on 11 January 1975 at 2.00pm.

Sunday 17 November
CONCERT
Empire Pool, Wembley, England
Set list: 'Raving And Drooling' / 'Gotta Be Crazy' / 'Shine On You Crazy Diamond' // *The Dark Side Of The Moon* / encore: 'Echoes'.
This show was originally scheduled to commence at 3.00pm but in the event didn't start until 6.00pm, still two hours earlier than all of the other Wembley shows.

Tuesday 19 November
CONCERT
Trentham Gardens, Stoke-on-Trent, England
Set list: 'Shine On You Crazy Diamond' / 'Raving And Drooling' / 'Gotta Be Crazy' // *The Dark Side Of The Moon* / encore: 'Echoes'.
An unauthorised recording of this concert found its way onto a vinyl bootleg album entitled *British Winter Tour '74*. Reports in the *NME* suggested it had been pressed in Germany or the Netherlands in upwards of 100,000 copies. In reality, very small quantities were being distributed from a small record shop on London's Carnaby Street known very well to music journalists of the time.

Friday 22 November
CONCERT
Sophia Gardens Pavilion, Cardiff, Wales
Set list: 'Shine On You Crazy Diamond' / 'Raving And Drooling' / 'Gotta Be Crazy' // *The Dark Side Of The Moon* / encore: 'Echoes'.

Thursday 28, Friday 29 & Saturday 30 November
CONCERTS
Empire Theatre, Liverpool, England
Set list at all three shows: 'Shine On You Crazy

Diamond' / 'Raving And Drooling' / 'Gotta Be Crazy' // *The Dark Side Of The Moon* / encore: 'Echoes'.

Tuesday 3, Wednesday 4 & Thursday 5 December
CONCERTS
The Hippodrome, Birmingham, England
Set list at all three shows: 'Shine On You Crazy Diamond' / 'Raving And Drooling' / 'Gotta Be Crazy' // *The Dark Side Of The Moon* / encore: 'Echoes'.

Monday 9 & Tuesday 10 December
CONCERTS
Palace Theatre, Manchester, England
Set list at both shows: 'Shine On You Crazy Diamond' / 'Raving And Drooling' / 'Gotta Be Crazy' // *The Dark Side Of The Moon* / encore: 'Echoes'.

Friday 13 & Saturday 14 December
CONCERTS
The Hippodrome, Bristol, England
Set list at both shows: 'Shine On You Crazy Diamond' / 'Raving And Drooling' / 'Gotta Be Crazy' // *The Dark Side Of The Moon* / encore: 'Echoes'.
The show on 14 December was the last night of the tour.
The Bristol Evening Post reported that: 'Floyd flopped in Bristol last night. The hardware and the talent had been trucked to Bristol by lorry and limousine, and the show had sold out within hours of the box-office opening. That eager audience was presented with a tepid mixture of well-worn material slightly spiced by a first half of new numbers. Floyd appeared uninterested, uninvolved and uninspired, and the band - who've given me more pleasure in concert than practically anyone over the years - left me cold last night. You could have stayed at home, played the albums and you would have lost nothing, because it was a note by note recreation and that's something one doesn't go to concerts for. *Dark Side Of The Moon* was accompanied by some banal movies contrasting piles of cash - of which the Floyd have plenty - with faces of elderly, clearly less affluent citizens. Big deal. It was an irritating, disappointing show, which never even looked like taking off. Rory Gallagher was playing down the road at the Colston Hall, and I wished I had been there instead.'

1975

Monday 6 January - Monday 3 March
RECORDING SESSIONS
EMI Studios, Abbey Road, St. John's Wood, London, England
Discontinuous recording for the album *Wish You Were Here*.

NORTH AMERICAN TOUR

PINK FLOYD US ROAD CREW THROUGH 1975
Bernie Caulder: PA / Stage Technician
Paul Devine: Lighting Technician
Graeme Fleming: Lighting Technician
Jed Frost: Lighting Technician
Seth Goldman: Monitor Sound Engineer
Brian Humphries: Front of House Sound Engineer
Mick 'The Pole' Kluczynski: Tour Manager
Mick Marshall: Film Projection
Arthur Max: Production Manager
Paul Murray: Film Projection
Robin Murray: Lighting Technician
Nick Rockford: PA / Stage Technician
Shamus: Front Man
Peter Sherriden: Lighting Technician
Phil Taylor: Stage Technician
Jim Thompson: Intercom
Carlos Trenidry: PA / Stage Technician
Robbie Williams: PA / Stage Technician

ADDITIONAL TOUR PERSONNEL THROUGH 1975
Venetta Fields: Backing Vocals
Dick Parry: Saxophone
Carlena Williams: Backing Vocals

Tuesday 8 April
CONCERT
Pacific National Exhibition Coliseum, Vancouver, British Columbia, Canada
Set list: 'Raving And Drooling' / 'Gotta Be Crazy' / 'Shine On You Crazy Diamond, Parts 1-5' / 'Have A Cigar' / 'Shine On You Crazy Diamond, Parts 6-9' // *The Dark Side Of The Moon* / encore: 'Echoes'.
The Vancouver Sun reported that: '[Pink Floyd] did a live show that depends on gadgets and an excellent 360 degree sound system. This system, co-ordinated with four light towers and spotlights, transformed the sold-out Coliseum on Tuesday night into psychedelic concrete earphones. When guitarist Dave Gilmour stood in a green light and strummed a simple chord, the chord circled the Coliseum like an electronic bat. The sound effects are maximised by keeping the

music simple in structure as pop art - naive, with all nuance banished. Clear melodic phrases are slow, pseudo-stately tempo's are piled up like building blocks. Ideas are repeated, not developed. The four musicians stood in a row on a cluttered stage, as casual and businesslike as the technicians at the centre-ice master control board. Both Gilmour and bassist Roger Waters have undistinguished voices, much inferior to the two black women of their backing chorus. On the other hand, nothing they play or sing is actively unpleasant. The gimmicks, some of them, were slightly more impressive. The audience cheered a huge disc, shaped to suggest a cruel circular saw, as it revolved far above the stage in a spotlight. Movies were projected on to a circular screen to illustrate the *Dark Side Of The Moon* suite: a flying squad of clock faces disappeared into the heavens on a song called "Time", and there were stacks of silver coins for "Money". Trusty light show clichés - rumpus room sea and sky posters, for example - tended to dominate the few good ideas, and if you have seen one close-up of the human eye, you have seen them all. A fitfully pleasing, consistently dull show, in other words. A better than average pop band lost in a lifeless farrago of tape loops and quad demo record effects. There was a silver model airplane in one corner of the Coliseum that looked poised to swoop down on a cable to the stage, but it never moved. A saxophone player occasionally came on stage for the best solos of the night, but he might well have been a robot and a tape.'

Thursday 10 April
CONCERT
Seattle Center Coliseum, Seattle, Washington, USA
Set list: 'Raving And Drooling' / 'Gotta Be Crazy' / 'Shine On You Crazy Diamond, Parts 1-5' / 'Have A Cigar' / 'Shine On You Crazy Diamond, Parts 6-9' // *The Dark Side Of The Moon* / encore: 'Echoes'.

Saturday 12 & Sunday 13 April
CONCERTS
Cow Palace, Daly City, San Francisco, California, USA
Set list at both shows: 'Raving And Drooling' / 'Gotta Be Crazy' / 'Shine On You Crazy Diamond, Parts 1-5' / 'Have A Cigar' / 'Shine On You Crazy Diamond, Parts 6-9' // *The Dark Side Of The Moon* / encore: 'Echoes'.

Thursday 17 April
CONCERT
Denver Coliseum, Denver, Colorado, USA
Set list: 'Raving And Drooling' / 'Gotta Be Crazy' / 'Shine On You Crazy Diamond, Parts 1-5' / 'Have A Cigar' / 'Shine On You Crazy Diamond, Parts 6-9' // *The Dark Side Of The Moon* / encore: 'Echoes'.

Saturday 19 April
CONCERT
Tucson Community Center Arena, Tucson, Arizona, USA
Set list: 'Raving And Drooling' / 'Gotta Be Crazy' / 'Shine On You Crazy Diamond, Parts 1-5' / 'Have A Cigar' / 'Shine On You Crazy Diamond, Parts 6-9' // *The Dark Side Of The Moon* / encore: 'Echoes'.

Sunday 20 April
CONCERT
University Activity Center, Arizona State University, Tempe, Arizona, USA
Set list: 'Raving And Drooling' / 'Gotta Be Crazy' / 'Shine On You Crazy Diamond, Parts 1-5' / 'Have A Cigar' / 'Shine On You Crazy Diamond, Parts 6-9' // *The Dark Side Of The Moon* / encore: 'Echoes'.
This show was rescheduled from 15 April because when the band's crew first arrived at the venue they deemed the stage unsafe and the power supply inadequate. After the concert there were allegations of ticket fraud when head counts by both the promoter and Pink Floyd's management put the attendance at 1,000 over the 9,000 capacity. Nevertheless it was regarded as a successful concert. *State Press*, the ASU student newspaper, reported that: 'The audience went wild when the light show began. Concertgoers were particularly impressed by a parabolic mirror, which reflected spots of light on the ceiling and walls of the Activity Center. Smoke rose from the stage. Imitation snow fell from above. A huge screen hung from the ceiling showed scenes of an operating room to accompany cuts from *Dark Side*. Hundreds of yellow clock dials were projected moving in time to the music. The crowd liked it, and that should be reason enough. But I think the crowd is wrong. A light show is a good addition to most rock shows, but when special effects are carried to the extreme they can only detract from the music and create a carnival atmosphere. The music was good enough to outweigh the gimmicks, however. And let it be said that their 32 tons of equipment was enough. My ears were ringing for hours after the show.'

Monday 21 April
CONCERT
Sports Arena, San Diego, California, USA
Set list: 'Raving And Drooling' / 'Gotta Be Crazy' / 'Shine On You Crazy Diamond, Parts 1-5' / 'Have A Cigar' / 'Shine On You Crazy Diamond, Parts 6-9' // *The Dark Side Of The Moon* / encore: 'Echoes'.

Tuesday 22, Wednesday 23, Thursday 24, Friday 25, Saturday 26 & Sunday 27 April
CONCERTS
Los Angeles Memorial Sports Arena, Exposition Park, Los Angeles, California, USA
Set list at all six shows: 'Raving And Drooling' / 'Gotta Be Crazy' / 'Shine On You Crazy Diamond, Parts 1-5' /

'Have A Cigar' / 'Shine On You Crazy Diamond, Parts 6-9' // *The Dark Side Of The Moon* / encore: 'Echoes'. The show of 27 April was the last night of the tour.

Monday 5 May – Thursday 5 June
RECORDING SESSIONS
EMI Studios, Abbey Road, St. John's Wood, London, England
Discontinuous recording for the album *Wish You Were Here*. It was at the final session on 5 June that Syd Barrett turned up out of the blue just as the final playbacks of 'Shine On You Crazy Diamond' were being heard by the band. The occasion marks the last time any member of the band saw their former bandmate.

NORTH AMERICAN TOUR

Saturday 7 June
CONCERT
Atlanta Stadium, Atlanta, Georgia, USA
Set list: 'Raving And Drooling' / 'Gotta Be Crazy' / 'Shine On You Crazy Diamond, Parts 1-5' / 'Have A Cigar' / 'Shine On You Crazy Diamond, Parts 6-9' // *The Dark Side Of The Moon* / encore: 'Echoes'.
Pink Floyd had arranged for the construction of a huge inflatable pyramid to be launched at the climax of *The Dark Side Of The Moon* but it failed to operate on the night. Using the next set of indoor dates to rectify the problem, the giant structure was launched on its maiden flight at Pittsburg on 20 June.

Monday 9 & Tuesday 10 June
CONCERTS
Capital Centre, Landover, Maryland, USA
Set list at both shows: 'Raving And Drooling' / 'Gotta Be Crazy' / 'Shine On You Crazy Diamond, Parts 1-5' / 'Have A Cigar' / 'Shine On You Crazy Diamond, Parts 6-9' // *The Dark Side Of The Moon* / encore: 'Echoes'.

Thursday 12 & Friday 13 June
CONCERTS
Spectrum Theater, Philadelphia, Pennsylvania, USA
Set list at both shows: 'Raving And Drooling' / 'Gotta Be Crazy' / 'Shine On You Crazy Diamond, Parts 1-5' / 'Have A Cigar' / 'Shine On You Crazy Diamond, Parts 6-9' // *The Dark Side Of The Moon* / encore: 'Echoes'.

Sunday 15 June
CONCERT
Roosevelt Stadium, Union City, New Jersey, USA
Set list: 'Raving And Drooling' / 'Gotta Be Crazy' / 'Shine On You Crazy Diamond, Parts 1-5' / 'Have A Cigar' / 'Shine On You Crazy Diamond, Parts 6-9' // *The Dark Side Of The Moon* / encore: 'Echoes'.

Monday 16 & Tuesday 17 June
CONCERTS
Nassau Veterans Memorial Coliseum, Uniondale, Long Island, New York, USA
Set list at both shows: 'Raving And Drooling' / 'Gotta Be Crazy' / 'Shine On You Crazy Diamond, Parts 1-5' / 'Have A Cigar' / 'Shine On You Crazy Diamond, Parts 6-9' // *The Dark Side Of The Moon* / encore: 'Echoes'.

Wednesday 18 June
CONCERT
Boston Gardens, Boston, Massachusetts, USA
Set list: 'Raving And Drooling' / 'Gotta Be Crazy' / 'Shine On You Crazy Diamond, Parts 1-5' / 'Have A Cigar' / 'Shine On You Crazy Diamond, Parts 6-9' // *The Dark Side Of The Moon* / encore: 'Echoes'.

Friday 20 June
CONCERT
Three Rivers Stadium, Pittsburgh, Pennsylvania, USA
Set list: 'Raving And Drooling' / 'Gotta Be Crazy' / 'Shine On You Crazy Diamond, Parts 1-5' / 'Have A Cigar' / 'Shine On You Crazy Diamond, Parts 6-9' // *The Dark Side Of The Moon* / encore: 'Echoes'.
Pittsburgh Press reported that: 'From virtually every angle, incredible was the word for Pink Floyd's Three Rivers Stadium concert last night. It was incredible how a first-place baseball team with the third best record in the majors drew only 8,200 there Thursday evening, yet a band with no hit singles to its credit attracted nearly 50,000, a stadium rock show record. Police reported no more than the usual number of underage drinkers, fist-fights and injuries from "jumping from ramp to ramp", although one would-be gatecrasher fell a goodly distance when the rope he was using to scale a wall broke and another youth was badly cut after being slugged in the face with a bottle by an attacker who melted into the mob in the home plate area. It was still light when they started, detracting from the mood so vital to appreciating Pink Floyd's music. Call it what you will - space-rock, cerebral-rock, thinking man's rock - it needs darkness so the lights and props can raise the sound into a real sensory experience. Using the bulk of *Dark Side* as the second part of their show was the same format they employed two years ago - but what a difference this time. A huge "tambourine" behind the band proved to be a screen on which were shown clips "describing" each song. And to top it all off, a monstrous white pyramid that had hovered behind them all night rose slowly from its moorings as spotlights beamed off it and rose high above the crowd (on wires), riding completely out of the stadium.'

Sunday 22 June
CONCERT
County Stadium, Milwaukee, Wisconsin, USA
Set list: *The Dark Side Of The Moon* / encore: 'Echoes'.

This concert was cut short due to heavy rainfall and was blighted by stoppages throughout.

Monday 23 & Tuesday 24 June
CONCERTS
Olympia Stadium, Detroit, Michigan, USA

Set list at both shows: 'Raving And Drooling' / 'Gotta Be Crazy' / 'Shine On You Crazy Diamond, Parts 1-5' / 'Have A Cigar' / 'Shine On You Crazy Diamond, Parts 6-9' // *The Dark Side Of The Moon* / encore: 'Echoes'.
Detroit Free Press reported that: 'Just about everything was working against Pink Floyd at its Monday night concert at Olympia Stadium. Fortunately, the one thing that was perfectly right was the music. Pink Floyd is not nearly as well known to the general public as some groups that attract legions of hard-core rock fans, but nevertheless it has been hugely successful since 1964. Monday, the four members of Floyd were put to the test. Could their music, without many of their infamous special effects, make 17,000 people forget the misery of being crammed into a building that felt like a steam bath gone mad? As part of the contract with Pink Floyd, Olympia used festival-style seating for the Floyd's Monday and Tuesday concerts, and the result was sweaty thigh jammed against sweaty thigh on the main floor where fans sat cross-legged like sweltering Indians. As if the heat weren't enough, Monday's audience was denied a special film by Peter Medak, director of *Ruling Class*. The film, an interpretation of Floyd's *Dark Side Of The Moon*, was on the premises, but the projector was soaked during a downpour at an outdoor date in Milwaukee on Sunday, and was out of commission. The group turned the old ballroom mirrored globe to its own use, bathing the crowd in a swirl of stars. Pink Floyd's futuristic but never garish music shows the polish over 10 years together, with only one personnel change, and the group proved Monday that its music, nothing more, is the foundation of its long success.'

Thursday 26 June
CONCERT
Autostade, Montréal, Québec, Canada

Set list: 'Raving And Drooling' / 'Gotta Be Crazy' / 'Shine On You Crazy Diamond, Parts 1-5' / 'Have A Cigar' / 'Shine On You Crazy Diamond, Parts 6-9' // *The Dark Side Of The Moon* / encore: 'Echoes'.

Saturday 28 June
CONCERT
Ivor Wynne Stadium, Hamilton, Ontario, Canada

The last night of the tour.
Set list: 'Raving And Drooling' / 'Gotta Be Crazy' / 'Shine On You Crazy Diamond, Parts 1-5' / 'Have A Cigar' / 'Shine On You Crazy Diamond, Parts 6-9' // *The Dark Side Of The Moon* / encore: 'Echoes'.
In a dramatic finale to the tour, Pink Floyd's crew decided to go out with a bang and used up all of their

remaining pyrotechnic charges around the stadium scoreboard. The resultant explosion at the climax of the show blew it to pieces and the blast even shattered the glass in a number of neighbouring houses. Additionally all the remaining unsold copies of the tour programme were handed out free of charge, apparently in the hundreds, most of them ending up unwanted and trodden into the grass pitch.

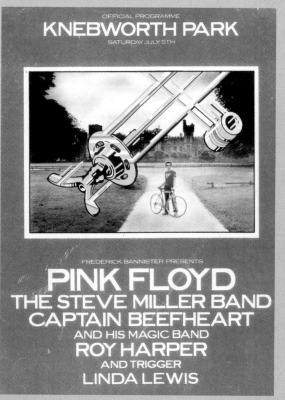

Saturday 5 July
CONCERT
Knebworth Park, Stevenage, England

With The Steve Miller Band, Captain Beefheart And His Magic Band, Roy Harper, Linda Lewis, and Monty Python. Compered by John Peel and Pete Drummond.
Set list: 'Raving And Drooling' / 'Gotta Be Crazy' / 'Shine On You Crazy Diamond, Parts 1-5' / 'Have A Cigar' (with Roy Harper on guest vocals) / 'Shine On You Crazy Diamond, Parts 6-9' // *The Dark Side Of The Moon* / encore: 'Echoes'.
Pink Floyd was supplemented by Venetta Fields (backing vocals), Carlena Williams (backing vocals) and Dick Parry (saxophone).
Sounds reported that: 'There was a long delay before the Floyd arrived while the mechanics of their production were mobilised: the giant circular screen, the lofty lighting towers, the three articulated trucks that carried their sound system and finally the brace of Spitfires that passed overhead. Their set was divided, as usual, into two halves, the first offering the newer, unrecorded material that one assumes will form the basis of their next album, and the second

devoted to *Dark Side Of The Moon* in its entirety, followed again as usual, by "Echoes" as an encore. In short, the first part was poor. *Dark Side* hit occasional highs and "Echoes" was pretty superb. Tuning problems hampered the early songs and Roger Waters hit many a bum note in his vocals as the group laboured along with what appeared to be little enthusiasm for the event. With the darkness falling, they appeared to gain new life and "Crazy Diamond", the last of the three early songs, picked up as their lighting columns bathed the band in a sea of colours. At last it seemed as if an Event would happen. A model plane on a wire heralded the onset of *Dark Side* which picked up as it went along, a majestic piece of music that the group must be over-familiar with by now. Nevertheless, "Any Colour You Like" developed into a tremendous jam, Dave Gilmour especially shining on his Stratocaster, trading lines with Waters and Wright that moved through a spectrum of ideas not contained on the record. The closing two songs, unfortunately, suffered again through Waters' vocals and it limped, rather than romped, to its usually stunning climax. At a rough estimate that's the sixth time I've seen the Floyd play this piece over the last three years. Truth of the matter is that I honestly enjoyed it the most when I heard it at the Rainbow in 1972 - when the piece was still in the formative stages. "Echoes" as stated, ended the day and predictably this was played flawlessly.'

Monday 7 – Saturday 19 July
RECORDING SESSIONS
EMI Studios, Abbey Road, St. John's Wood, London, England

Discontinuous recording and mixing for the album *Wish You Were Here*.

Friday 12 September
RECORD RELEASE
Wish You Were Here

UK album release. US album release on Saturday 13 September.
Melody Maker commented that: 'I am not enthralled. I did try though to acclimatise myself to its bleak, emotionally barren landscape. I keep missing the connection somehow. From whichever direction one approaches *Wish You Were Here* it still sounds unconvincing in its ponderous sincerity and displays a critical lack of imagination in all departments. The Floyd amble somnambulantly along their star struck avenues arm in arm with some pallid ghost of creativity. *Wish You Were Here* sucks. It's as simple as that.'

HARVEY GOLDSMITH ENTER

presents

PINK FLO

IN CONCERT

SATURDAY, 19 MAR

at 8 p.m.

7

SOUTH GRA

£4.25

TO BE RETAINED See condition

a certain unease in the air

AINMENTS

YD

H, 1977

ID TIER

on back

ENTER AT
SOUTH DOOR
ENTRANCE
74
ROW
D
SEAT
98★

1976-1977

ENTERTAIN
nts
'LOY
ICERT
MARCH,
.m.
GRAND

1976 WAS THE FIRST FULL YEAR THE BAND DIDN'T PERFORM ANY LIVE DATES SINCE THEIR INCEPTION. FACED WITH THE PROSPECT OF A HUGE AMOUNT OF PA AND LIGHTING EQUIPMENT LYING IDLE AND HAVING THEIR SENIOR CREW STILL ON THE PAYROLL, THE BAND DECIDED TO EMPLOY THEM TO RENT THEIR GEAR OUT TO OTHER TOURING BANDS.

Based at their newly acquired warehouse premises at Britannia Row in Islington, north London two companies were formed: Britannia Row Audio run by Robbie Williams and Mick Kluczynsky and Britannia Row Lighting run by Graeme Fleming. The band eventually sold the whole business to Robbie Williams and Bryan Grant in 1984, which continues to this day as a leading PA rental company.

Britannia Row itself also had sufficient space for the band to build their own twenty-four-track recording studio within the same complex, and their 1977 album *Animals* was produced entirely in the seclusion of their own facility, marking their first break from EMI Studios at Abbey Road. Recording commenced in the spring of 1976 and was completed in November – a relatively short space of time for the band. The recording was marked by Waters' exercise of an ever-increasing power over the three other members. This led to a noticeable rift in the working unit, which in any case was by now merely serving as a vehicle for his lyrical output.

Wright, being less assertive than the others, was more susceptible to such divisive pressure. It is only in recent years that he has spoken of this fraught period at all: 'I didn't really like a lot of the music on the album. I have to say I didn't fight very hard to put my stuff on,

and I didn't have anything to put on. I played on it. I think I played well, but I didn't contribute to the writing of it but I think that also Roger was kind of not letting me do that. This was the start of the whole ego thing in the band.'[1]

Waters' dominance would, according to other members of the band, reduce it to a mere shadow of its former self. His ability to write cutting lyrics expressing sheer hatred and blind fury was faultless. But excluding others from the process to pursue his own vision – a trend that would continue over the next two studio albums – ultimately worked to the detriment of both Waters and the band itself.

It was also during the recording of *Animals* that Waters slowly developed a collection of unconnected songs into a conceptual piece that described the apparent social and moral decay of society, likening the human condition to that of mere animals. Surprisingly, the two previously ditched songs that had formed the mainstay of the band's 1974-75 tour were revived and extensively reworked for the album. 'Raving And Drooling' and 'Gotta Be Crazy' mutated into the tracks 'Sheep' and 'Dogs' respectively. As Waters explained: 'Sometime during the middle of recording it, it seemed like the right thing to tie it all together. It gave me the lead to re-write the lyrics to "Raving And Drooling" into "Sheep", 'cos "Raving And Drooling" was just another shout, but it was a rather incoherent shout of abuse in a way that "Pigs" is a kind of fairly compassionate scream of abuse. I've had the idea of *Animals* in the back of my mind for years... many years. It's a kind of old chestnut, really.'[2]

Despite the tensions within the band, *Animals* contains one of their best-recorded performances. It is a dark and powerful album, even violent at times. 'Sheep', for example, bastardises Psalm 23 and 'Pigs' makes a scathing attack on, in particular, Mary Whitehouse, the self-appointed protector of the nation's morals (another verse was later revised by Waters as a sideswipe at the rising MP Margaret Thatcher). The more strident songs caught the air of depression and gloom of the times. Despite a strong economy and high employment, there was a growing social unrest in Britain, particularly in the inner cities. Football and street violence was increasing, partially fuelled by rampaging gangs of punks and skinheads, as was racial violence initiated by right-wing organisations such as the National Front; both expressions of discontent contributed to a feeling of unease, even oppression. By complete contrast, 'Pigs On The Wing', with which the album opens and closes, is a very personal message of love from Waters to his then wife Carolyne and remains a live favourite on his solo tours.

It's surprising how well *Animals* fared with the music press, considering its attempts to push rock supergroups like Pink Floyd out of favour once and for all now that it had the likes of the Sex Pistols to fawn over. Perhaps the sheer vehemence of the attack on society won over the more radical critics, although some reviewers thought it was simply just too much to stomach.

Waters visualised the sleeve design as depicting a

(including one in a helicopter) who had been assembled at the location would capture it for posterity on launch day, 2 December. A marksman had also been hired: to shoot the pig down should it break free from its moorings and escape. However, for one reason or other the creature couldn't be inflated. The following day, a bright, sunny morning, a successful launch was made, only for a gust of wind to snap the pig's mooring cables. Unfortunately, nobody had told the marksman to return that day.

It's difficult to say whether this was an intentional

ABOVE: ROGER WATERS AND DAVID GILMOUR PERFORMING AT THE SPORTPALEIS, ANTWERP ON 20 FEBRUARY 1977.

RICHARD WRIGHT ‹‹ I didn't really like a lot of the music on the album. I have to say I didn't fight very hard to put my stuff on, and I didn't have anything to put on. I played on it. I think I played well, but I didn't contribute to the writing of it but I think that also Roger was kind of not letting me do that. ››

large inflatable pink pig hovering between two of the four towering chimneys of south London's Battersea power station. Hipgnosis were commissioned to realise Waters' vision but suggested that an inflatable pig could be photographed in any location and the shot then superimposed into a separate photograph of the power station. However, Waters insisted that the shoot be done for real and a forty-foot inflatable pig was shipped over from designers, Eventstructure Research Group in Amsterdam. (The pig was actually made in Germany by Ballon Fabrik, which had constructed the original Zeppelin airships.) Once it had been inflated with helium and raised on cables, it would be tethered in position and eleven stills photographers and an eight-man film crew

publicity stunt or not but later that morning the pig, having been spotted by an astonished commercial pilot coming into Heathrow, was tailed by a police helicopter as far as Crystal Palace, south-east London. By mid-afternoon it was seen at 18,000 feet over Chatham, in Kent, by which time everybody concerned assumed it was heading for home. Eventually it deflated and crashed, rather appropriately, into a barn at East Stour Farm at Godmersham in Kent. By next morning the story was in all the national newspapers.

In a final, ironic twist the pictures of the power station on the first day were thought to be more interesting because of the contrasting skies – it had been rather overcast that morning – and the pig ended up

TERENCE 'SNOWY' WHITE << **Can we have a bit of a play or a jam or something?" and he [Gilmour] said, "Well you wouldn't be here if you couldn't play would you?" and I replied, "Well, no not really." So he said, "Well that's alright then. You start in November for rehearsals" – and that was it. >>**

said, "Well that's alright then. You start in November for rehearsals" – and that was it.'[3]

But, just before White departed, Waters said, 'Well as you're here you might as well play something,'[4] so Snowy turned in the delicate guitar solo that was used to bridge the two parts of 'Pigs On The Wing'. Although this was only ever used on the eight-track cartridge release, it completed the tape loop that brought the album back to its starting point.

The album was released on the day of the opening show of the tour, in Dortmund, West Germany on 23 January 1977. Each show consisted of the whole of *Animals* and, for the first time, the complete *Wish You Were Here*, as first and second half performances. On stage, a transistor radio was placed on a stand and miked up ready for Mason to scan the airwaves randomly, often with hilarious results, for the introduction of the title track of the latter album. The encores, which depended to a great extent on the collective mood of the band, varied between 'Money' and 'Us And Them', although on occasion both were performed and always featured the familiar back-projected films of the previous tours.

'With the "Animals" tour it was interesting because I played bass a lot of the time in the first half. I used to walk on stage on my own and start the show with this bass thing and then the others used to walk on. Then in the second half of the show they did "Wish You Were Here" and various other tracks where sometimes I'd play the odd bit of harmony with Dave, sometimes I'd play rhythm, sometimes lead. Then towards the end it got a bit more freer and Dave and I would swap licks and things... "Shine On You Crazy Diamond", I used to be able to let fly a little bit on that. There was a certain amount of freedom and I think I managed to keep my own sound through most of it. There were times when there were echoes and fuzzes and those sorts of things: it was nice to do all that.'[5]

A large part of the rehearsals had taken place at

RIGHT: TERENCE 'SNOWY' WHITE ON STAGE AT THE EMPIRE POOL, WEMBLEY, MARCH 1977.

being 'dropped in' after all. Many of the photos taken during the shoot were used for the subsequent tour publicity, programme, and songbook and, much later, for the remastered CD booklet. However, the film footage has, except for the occasional TV clip, only ever been seen as a backdrop film for Waters' much later solo tours, which incorporated material from the album.

An extensive tour of much of Europe and North America followed, in support of the album, and as a result the band's concert entourage needed to be expanded. Sax player Dick Parry was re-employed and a new support guitarist, Terence 'Snowy' White, was brought in. 'I hadn't heard of *Dark Side Of The Moon* even,' White recalled. 'I must have been the only person in England that hadn't heard it – so I went down to the studio to see the boys and that was right at the end of the *Animals* album. It was funny, when I walked in the atmosphere was terrible... I thought, "Fucking hell!" but I discovered that they'd accidentally rubbed out one of Dave Gilmour's favourite solos they were really pleased with and they'd just lost it – and that's when I walked in! Dave took me in the office and told me what the gig was all about and asked me if I fancied doing it and I said, "Can we have a bit of a play or a jam or something?" and he said, "Well you wouldn't be here if you couldn't play would you?" and I replied, "Well, no not really." So he

RIGHT: ROGER WATERS ON STAGE AT THE EMPIRE POOL, WEMBLEY, MARCH 1977.

H ENTERTA
sents

FLO

NCERT
9 MARCH
p.m.

H GRAN

LEFT: PINK FLOYD ON STAGE
DURING THE CLOSING SECTION
OF 'SHINE ON YOU CRAZY
DIAMOND' AS A GIANT
FLOWERING MIRRORBALL IS
RAISED BEHIND THEM AT THE
EMPIRE POOL, WEMBLEY,
MARCH 1977.

RIGHT: LOOKING OUT TO THE CROWD AT ANAHEIM STADIUM, CALIFORNIA, MAY 1977: AN INFLATABLE PIG JUST BEFORE BEING BLOWN TO BITS AT THE CULMINATION OF THE TRACK 'PIGS'.

Britannia Row in early November and the final dress rehearsals at the Olympia Exhibition Hall in London, from where the production was shipped out to Germany. For the first time, Pink Floyd now truly tackled the problem of the stadium environment. Conscious of the fact that many of the larger venues would tend to isolate the audience, they attempted to make the back row feel as involved as the front – to increase the element of spectacle for everyone present.

In order to realise this ideal, again largely conceived by Waters, the Fisher-Park design team were once more mobilised and set to work on the design and construction of various large-scale inflatables to symbolise the typical 'nuclear-age' family. This comprised of a businessman and his wife, reclining on a sofa and, as statistics would have it, 2.5 children. These characters were inflated by industrial fans and hoisted into position by hydraulic rigging halfway through 'Dogs', to be quickly deflated at the end of the song. They were first used at the shows in London, but by the time the tour had reached America a

during 'Pigs'. In indoor shows it would travel the length of the auditorium suspended by steel cables. At outdoor shows it was floated on a cable to a position high above the stage, where the propane charge it carried was detonated to dramatic effect.

Another new element was a compressed-air 'sheep-cannon' that fired small sheep made from tea bag material deep into the audience. But the most striking addition was the awe-inspiring animation film designed by the English satirical cartoonist Gerald Scarfe, which accompanied 'Welcome To The Machine'. The band had spotted Scarfe's work as early as 1972, when he was sent to Los Angeles by BBC TV to try out a new cartoon animation method. This resulted in the *Long-Drawn-Out-Trip*, a parody that let rip at every cliché of American life and is best remembered for its depiction of Mickey Mouse whacked out on drugs. His first work for Pink Floyd, however, had been his caricature of the band for the centrespread of their 1974-75 tour programmes.

Scarfe's film for Pink Floyd was every bit as heart-warming as the song itself and featured a constantly changing series of environments which included a huge, lizard-like metallic creature roaming a geometric landscape; a head that is brutally severed and slowly decays; and a city enveloped by a sea of blood whose lapping waves transform into a mass of bloody, outstretched hands worshipping a huge monolithic structure.

It was reported in *Melody Maker* that the band had allocated a budget of around £100,000 to produce the animation sequence for the concerts alone and that Scarfe had taken some six months to produce it. The result was certainly amazing when seen on the big screen.

Another piece of Scarfe animation was used for the closing section of 'Shine On You Crazy Diamond', which ended the show. This depicted a naked, faceless and sexless body somersaulting through the air as it transformed into a falling leaf and back again until the screen was slowly blanked out by a huge mirror ball, revived from the previous tour. American shows also featured a waterfall of fireworks that stretched the full width of the stage and provided a spectacular conclusion to the extravaganza.

When the UK tour went ahead some minor technical problems were reported at Wembley, assisted by some local authority wrangling over the special

ROGER WATERS << In the end I called him over and, when he got close enough, spat in his face. I shocked myself with that incident enough to think: "Hold on a minute. This is all wrong. I'm hating this". >>

Cadillac, a fridge and a TV set, all in relative scale, had also been added.

Appropriately, the tour motif and newly acquired mascot, the giant inflatable pig, was also used. Not as benign as the Battersea model, the helium-filled balloon sported an ugly snarl as it poked its head from out behind the stage through a massive burst of smoke effects. This was coupled with a date switch but otherwise the tour proceeded well. Incidentally, the band were said to be disappointed at having to play this venue again rather than Earl's Court, where they had had better success on previous occasions. The tour then progressed to the New Bingley Hall, Stafford – an unusual choice of venue and, unusually for the time, an all-standing show. But it was not altogether inappropriate, since it was formerly a livestock market. (Similarly, the shows in Paris were held in a converted abattoir.)

The following month, as the show now dubbed 'Pink Floyd – In The Flesh?' laboured across America, things started to go wrong. Overexcited fans were yelling and screaming throughout the performances, a habit which destroyed the relatively rapt atmosphere that had existed at the shows in Europe. This, along with the fact that firecrackers were being hurled about in abundance - especially in New York where the band were performing throughout Independence Day celebrations - contributed to a growing frustration in Waters that no one was actually listening to his songs, and eventually he came to nurse a hatred for the impersonal nature of stadium touring.

The crunch came at the final show, in Montreal, where the crowd were unusually rowdy. 'I was on stage and there was one guy in the front row shouting and screaming all the way through everything,' Waters recalled. 'In the end I called him over and, when he got close enough, spat in his face. I shocked myself with that incident enough to think: "Hold on a minute. This is all wrong. I'm hating this."'[6]

The whole incident struck a devastating chord in Waters' psyche. Although Gilmour recalled that neither he nor the others had been aware at the time of the effect on their band mate, 'I just thought it was a great shame to end up a six-month tour with a rotten show', he said. 'In fact, I remember going back to the sound mixing board in the middle of the audience to watch the encore while Snowy played guitar.'[7] 'It was quite a long jam,' White recalls. 'I was enjoying myself, and then the crew started dismantling the equipment as we were playing. In the end Nick was just left with a bass drum!'"[8]

Close to a nervous collapse after the tour, Waters felt that the best therapy would be to write about his own experiences. He would attempt to trace his feelings of alienation back to his childhood; his sense of solitude as a consequence of his father's death during the war; the tyranny of his schooling; and the break up of his marriage.

Leaving Waters to his own devices, the rest of the band began recording solo albums. Gilmour's eponymous album featured his former Cambridge band mates Willie Wilson and Rick Wills whereas Wright's *Wet Dream* featured Snowy White among others. Meanwhile, Mason put his name to an album entitled *Fictitious Sports*, essentially a Carla Bley solo record, but given Mason's name as a stronger marketing tool. Gilmour and Wright's were released in 1978 whilst Mason's didn't see the light of day until 1981. It was only when these projects were finished did they turn their attention to Waters' proposal for a new Pink Floyd album.

TERENCE 'SNOWY' WHITE   << It was quite a long jam. I was enjoying myself, and then the crew started dismantling the equipment as we were playing. In the end Nick was just left with a bass drum! >>

Sources
1. *Omnibus*, BBC TV, 15 November 1994
2. *The Pink Floyd Story*, Capital Radio, 21 January 1977
3-4. Author's interview with Terence 'Snowy' White, September 1996.
5. *Snowy White Goldtop*, CD booklet, 1995
6. Unidentified press article, c.1982
7. *Musician*, c.1982
8. Author's interview with Terence 'Snowy' White, September 1996.

BELOW: WNEW RADIO PUBLICISING PINK FLOYD'S FORTHCOMING MADISON SQUARE GARDEN SHOWS AT AN EVENT IN SHEEP MEADOW, CENTRAL PARK, NEW YORK, MAY 1977.

1976

April - December
RECORDING SESSIONS
Britannia Row Studios, Islington, London, England
Discontinuous recording for the album *Animals* began at the band's own purpose build studios in north London. Work here continued throughout the rest of the year and into early 1977.

Thursday 2 & Friday 3 December
FILMING
Battersea Power Station, Battersea, London, England
Sleeve designers Hipgnosis assembled a crew of photographers and cameramen to record the launch of a 40-foot helium-filled inflatable pig for the cover of the bands' forthcoming album *Animals*. On 3 December the inflatable broke its moorings and floated across the south east of England before crashing into a barn at East Stour Farm in Godmersham in Kent.

Friday 17 December
RADIO SHOW
Capital Radio, Euston Tower, London, England
Capital Radio commenced broadcasting its authoritative documentary, *The Pink Floyd Story* over the next six consecutive weeks as follows: Part 1 – 'The Early Years' broadcast 17 December; Part 2 – '*Piper At The Gates Of Dawn* to *Atom Heart Mother*' broadcast 24 December; Part 3 – '*More* to *Dark Side Of The Moon*' broadcast 31 December; Part 4 – 'The *Dark Side Of The Moon*' broadcast 7 January 1977; Part 5 – '*Wish You Were Here*' broadcast 14 January 1977; Part 6: '*Animals*' broadcast 21 January 1977. Each programme was at least 45 minutes long and was the most detailed study of the band to date featuring exclusive interviews with all its current members and notable associates as well their music, including some studio out-takes and live segments.

1977

January
REHEARSALS
Olympia Exhibition Halls, Olympia, London, England
The final production rehearsals for the tour were staged at the halls prior to the production shipping to Germany for the start of the tour.

Wednesday 19 January
PRESS CONFERENCE
Sports & Social Club, Battersea Power Station, Battersea, London, England
The album *Animals* was played at an evening press reception held on the site of the power station.

Thursday 20 January
RADIO SHOW
BBC Broadcasting House, London, England
John Peel played the new Pink Floyd album *Animals* in its entirety on his BBC Radio One show beating, much to his dismay, Capital Radio's Nicky Horne, who had promised an exclusive airing at the conclusion of his epic six-part series, *The Pink Floyd Story*.

Friday 21 January
RECORD RELEASE
Animals
UK album release. US album release on Saturday 12 February.
In France, EMI Records came up with a special promotional campaign for the album by manufacturing 600 life-size plastic display pigs, each with a capacity of 100 albums, which were supplied to the major record retailers.
Sounds commented that: 'Those in search of a new musical trend will probably criticise *Animals* for failing to provide a great leap forward. They've slammed the previous two albums for exactly the same reason but the argument is pointless. The Floyd have got a formula that appeals to millions of people around the world and I can't see any of them being disappointed with this album.'

ANIMALS - EUROPEAN TOUR

PINK FLOYD ROAD CREW THROUGH 1977
Bernie Caulder: PA / Stage Technician
Alan Conway: Quad Technician
Graeme Fleming: Lighting Director
Seth Goldman: Monitor Sound Engineer
Brian Humphries: Front of House Sound
Mick 'The Pole' Kluczynski: Tour Manager
Mick Marshall: Lighting Technician
Arthur Max: Production Manager
Paul Murray: Film Projection
Robin Murray: Lighting Technician
Peter Revell: Film Projection
Nick Rockford: PA / Stage Technician
Nigel Taylor: PA / Stage Technician
Phil Taylor: Stage Technician
Robbie Williams: Head of PA

ADDITIONAL TOUR PERSONNEL THROUGH 1977
Snowy White: Rhythm Guitar, Bass Guitar
Dick Parry: Saxophone

GUITAR CONTRIBUTIONS THROUGH 1977
The guitar contributions for each show on the whole tour ran as follows:
'Sheep': Gilmour on lead guitar; Waters on rhythm guitar; White on bass guitar.
'Pigs On The Wing, Part 1': Waters on acoustic guitar.
'Dogs': Gilmour on lead guitar; Waters on rhythm guitar; White on bass guitar.
'Pigs On The Wing, Part 2': Waters on acoustic guitar.
'Pigs (3 Different Ones)': Gilmour on lead guitar; Waters on rhythm guitar; White on bass guitar.
'Shine On You Crazy Diamond, Parts 1-5': Gilmour on lead guitar; Waters on bass guitar; White on rhythm guitar.
'Welcome To The Machine': Gilmour on lead guitar; Waters on bass guitar; White on acoustic guitar.
'Have A Cigar': Gilmour on rhythm guitar; Waters on bass guitar; White on lead guitar.
'Wish You Were Here': Gilmour on lead guitar; White on acoustic guitar.
'Shine On You Crazy Diamond, Parts 6-9': Gilmour on lap steel guitar; Waters on bass guitar; White on rhythm guitar.
'Money': Gilmour on lead guitar; Waters on bass guitar; White on rhythm guitar.
'Us And Them': Gilmour on lead guitar; Waters on bass guitar; White on rhythm guitar.
'Careful With That Axe, Eugene': Gilmour on lead guitar; Waters on bass guitar; White on rhythm guitar.

Sunday 23 January
CONCERT
Westfalenhalle, Dortmund, West Germany
Set list: 'Sheep' / 'Pigs On The Wing, Part 1' / 'Dogs' / 'Pigs On The Wing, Part 2' / 'Pigs (Three Different Ones)' // 'Shine On You Crazy Diamond, Parts 1-5' / 'Welcome To The Machine' / 'Have A Cigar' / 'Wish You Were Here' / 'Shine On You Crazy Diamond, Parts 6-9' / encore: 'Money' / 'Us And Them'.

Monday 24 January
CONCERT
Westfalenhalle, Dortmund, West Germany
Set list: 'Sheep' / 'Pigs On The Wing, Part 1' / 'Dogs' / 'Pigs On The Wing, Part 2' / 'Pigs (Three Different Ones)' // 'Shine On You Crazy Diamond, Parts 1-5' / 'Welcome To The Machine' / 'Have A Cigar' / 'Wish You Were Here' / 'Shine On You Crazy Diamond, Parts 6-9' / encore: 'Money'.

Wednesday 26 January
CONCERT
Festhalle, Frankfurt, West Germany
Set list: 'Sheep' / 'Pigs On The Wing, Part 1' / 'Dogs' / 'Pigs On The Wing, Part 2' / 'Pigs (Three Different Ones)' // 'Shine On You Crazy Diamond, Parts 1-5' / 'Welcome To The Machine' / 'Have A Cigar' / 'Wish You Were Here' / 'Shine On You Crazy Diamond, Parts 6-9' / encore: 'Money' / 'Us And Them'.

Thursday 27 January
CONCERT
Festhalle, Frankfurt, West Germany
Set list: 'Sheep' / 'Pigs On The Wing, Part 1' / 'Dogs' / 'Pigs On The Wing, Part 2' / 'Pigs (Three Different Ones)' // 'Shine On You Crazy Diamond, Parts 1-5' / 'Welcome To The Machine' / 'Have A Cigar' / 'Wish You Were Here' / 'Shine On You Crazy Diamond, Parts 6-9' / encore: 'Money'.
Melody Maker reported that: 'It had been an evening totally without mishaps. The 12,000 natives packed into Frankfurt's Festhalle for the second successive night on Thursday were in a generally friendly mood, for the Floyd hardly attract the standard aggro crowd of people like Zep or Purple. But in an audience that size, it is a statistical certainty there are bound to be some nutters, like those who were throwing cans and bottles during the first set. An announcement in the first interval asked them to desist, bitte, because delicate equipment was getting damaged. I saw another bottle smash on Nick Mason's Hokusai painted drum kit - evidently a full one, for it sprayed his face with foam. In the shadow of the PA columns, a group of "plain clothes" polizei, about as inconspicuous as a panzer armoured division in their uniform anoraks and regulation length haircuts, took photographs of the crowd to see if anyone was smoking dope. Their American counterparts in the Military Police also ranged through the crowd, checking the ID's of hapless GI's out of camp for a little night music, searching if they were AWOL or carrying exotic substances. The band's special effects department still hadn't got the highpoint of their contribution to the show quite right yet. In the middle of the "Pigs" section, which closed the first half, a gigantic inflated porker is meant to fly over the PA, emerging out of a cloud of smoke, clearing the stacks by a few inches, and making a circuit of the hall over the heads of the audience. Well, Mr. Pig made it over the stack all right without toppling the driver horns on the top, but the trouble was the smoke. The first three nights of the tour they couldn't get enough product out of the rented fog-machine, so they tried a smoke bomb instead. That worked rather too well for comfort, filling the hall with billowing clouds of acrid, throat strangling murk, through which it was barely possible to see that something was happening on stage.'

Saturday 29 & Sunday 30 January
CONCERTS
Deutschlandhalle, West Berlin, West Germany
Set list at both shows: 'Sheep' / 'Pigs On The Wing, Part 1' / 'Dogs' / 'Pigs On The Wing, Part 2' / 'Pigs (Three Different Ones)' // 'Shine On You Crazy Diamond, Parts 1-5' / 'Welcome To The Machine' / 'Have A Cigar' / 'Wish You Were Here' / 'Shine On You Crazy Diamond, Parts 6-9' / encore: 'Money'.

Tuesday 1 February
CONCERT
Stadthalle, Vienna, Austria
Set list: 'Sheep' / 'Pigs On The Wing, Part 1' / 'Dogs' / 'Pigs On The Wing, Part 2' / 'Pigs (Three Different Ones)' // 'Shine On You Crazy Diamond, Parts 1-5' / 'Welcome To The Machine' / 'Have A Cigar' / 'Wish You Were Here' / 'Shine On You Crazy Diamond, Parts 6-9' / encore: 'Money' / 'Us And Them'.

Thursday 3 & Friday 4 February
CONCERTS
Hallenstadion, Zurich, Switzerland
Set list at both shows: 'Sheep' / 'Pigs On The Wing, Part 1' / 'Dogs' / 'Pigs On The Wing, Part 2' / 'Pigs (Three Different Ones)' // 'Shine On You Crazy Diamond, Parts 1-5' / 'Welcome To The Machine' / 'Have A Cigar' / 'Wish You Were Here' / 'Shine On You Crazy Diamond, Parts 6-9' / encore: 'Money'.

Thursday 17, Friday 18 & Saturday 19 February
CONCERTS
Sportpaleis Ahoy, Rotterdam, The Netherlands
Set list at all three shows: 'Sheep' / 'Pigs On The Wing, Part 1' / 'Dogs' / 'Pigs On The Wing, Part 2' / 'Pigs (Three Different Ones)' // 'Shine On You Crazy Diamond, Parts 1-5' / 'Welcome To The Machine' / 'Have A Cigar' / 'Wish You Were Here' / 'Shine On You Crazy Diamond, Parts 6-9' / encore: 'Money'.

Sunday 20 February
CONCERT
Sportpaleis, Antwerp, Belguim
Set list: 'Sheep' / 'Pigs On The Wing, Part 1' / 'Dogs' / 'Pigs On The Wing, Part 2' / 'Pigs (Three Different Ones)' // 'Shine On You Crazy Diamond, Parts 1-5' / 'Welcome To The Machine' / 'Have A Cigar' / 'Wish You Were Here' / 'Shine On You Crazy Diamond, Parts 6-9' / encore: 'Money'.

Tuesday 22, Wednesday 23, Thursday 24 & Friday 25 February
CONCERTS
Pavillon de Paris, Porte de Pantin, Paris, France
Set list at all four shows: 'Sheep' / 'Pigs On The Wing, Part 1' / 'Dogs' / 'Pigs On The Wing, Part 2' / 'Pigs (Three Different Ones)' // 'Shine On You Crazy Diamond, Parts 1-5' / 'Welcome To The Machine' / 'Have A Cigar' / 'Wish You Were Here' / 'Shine On You Crazy Diamond, Parts 6-9' / encore: 'Money'.
ORTF TV broadcast a pre-recorded interview with David Gilmour and Roger Waters for the arts programme *JA2 20H*. It was broadcast on ORTF2 on 21 February at 8.00pm.

Sunday 27 & Monday 28 February
CONCERTS
Olympiahalle, Munich, West Germany
Set list at both shows: 'Sheep' / 'Pigs On The Wing, Part 1' / 'Dogs' / 'Pigs On The Wing, Part 2' / 'Pigs (Three Different Ones)' // 'Shine On You Crazy Diamond, Parts 1-5' / 'Welcome To The Machine' / 'Have A Cigar' / 'Wish You Were Here' / 'Shine On You Crazy Diamond, Parts 6-9' / encore: 'Money'.

Tuesday 1 March
CONCERT
Olympiahalle, Munich, West Germany
The last night of the tour.

ANIMALS - UK TOUR

Tuesday 15 March
CONCERT
Empire Pool, Wembley, England
Set list: 'Sheep' / 'Pigs On The Wing, Part 1' / 'Dogs' / 'Pigs On The Wing, Part 2' / 'Pigs (Three Different Ones)' // 'Shine On You Crazy Diamond, Parts 1-5' / 'Welcome To The Machine' / 'Have A Cigar' / 'Wish You Were Here' / 'Shine On You Crazy Diamond, Parts 6-9' / encore: 'Money'.

Wednesday 16 March
CONCERT
Empire Pool, Wembley, England
This show was rescheduled from 20 March due to a badminton tournament commencing on 21 March leaving insufficient time for the courts to be prepared. The show of 15 March was the last show to be announced.
Set list: 'Sheep' / 'Pigs On The Wing, Part 1' / 'Dogs' / 'Pigs On The Wing, Part 2' / 'Pigs (Three Different Ones)' // 'Shine On You Crazy Diamond, Parts 1-5' / 'Welcome To The Machine' / 'Have A Cigar' / 'Wish You Were Here' / 'Shine On You Crazy Diamond, Parts 6-9' / encore: 'Money'.

Thursday 17 March
CONCERT
Empire Pool, Wembley, England
Set list: 'Sheep' / 'Pigs On The Wing, Part 1' / 'Dogs' / 'Pigs On The Wing, Part 2' / 'Pigs (Three Different Ones)' // 'Shine On You Crazy Diamond, Parts 1-5' / 'Welcome To The Machine' / 'Have A Cigar' / 'Wish You Were Here' / 'Shine On You Crazy Diamond, Parts 6-9' / encore: 'Us And Them'.

Friday 18 March
CONCERT
Empire Pool, Wembley, England
Set list: 'Sheep' / 'Pigs On The Wing, Part 1' / 'Dogs' / 'Pigs On The Wing, Part 2' / 'Pigs (Three Different Ones)' // 'Shine On You Crazy Diamond, Parts 1-5' / 'Welcome To The Machine' / 'Have A Cigar' / 'Wish You Were Here' / 'Shine On You Crazy Diamond, Parts 6-9' / encore: 'Us And Them'.

Saturday 19 March
CONCERT
Empire Pool, Wembley, England
Set list: 'Sheep' / 'Pigs On The Wing, Part 1' / 'Dogs' / 'Pigs On The Wing, Part 2' / 'Pigs (Three Different Ones)' // 'Shine On You Crazy Diamond, Parts 1-5' / 'Welcome To The Machine' / 'Have A Cigar' / 'Wish You Were Here' / 'Shine On You Crazy Diamond, Parts 6-9' / encore: 'Money'.

The Financial Times reported that: 'It gets easier and easier to review a Pink Floyd concert without mentioning the music. The group has always exploited theatrical effects and now, as it stands passively playing in the background, the lights swoop around the stadium; the smoke oozes along the sides; inflatable pigs and persons slide down wires suspended above the audience; images splash on to a giant screen. And all the time the expensively amplified Floyd sound of soaring guitar notes and free-flowing keyboards fills any senses not satiated with the sight. Whether the music is any good or not is a more difficult question - the Floyd is the Cecil B. DeMille of the pop world, which is probably enough. But it is not just the props that create a barrier between the Pink Floyd's music and the reviewer, nor even the elusive, but basically inhuman, nature of the music itself. It is the fascination of the Floyd success, for the Pink Floyd must be among the half dozen top acts to come out of the contemporary music phenomenon. Not only did the Floyd pack the 10,000 seat Empire Pool five times last week, but the crowds of loitering hopefuls, nestling close outside the auditorium to catch the remnants of the sound, would have been considered a healthy audience in themselves by most artists. As for the new music, the lyrics seem unnaturally aggressive for a band which is now extremely rich and mature, but then lyrics have

RIGHT: ROGER WATERS IN FULL SNARL AT THE EMPIRE POOL, WEMBLEY, MARCH 1977.

H ENTERT
sents
FLO
NCERT
9 MARC
p.m.
H GRAM
211

never been important to its success. The actual sounds have changed little, still managing to stimulate one minute and bore the next. The Pink Floyd has made a serious contribution to popular music, but whether it deserves to command such devotion without developing much musically is doubtful. The fact that the Pink Floyd's appeal is to a specific audience may be commercially fortunate but musically very limiting.'

Monday 28, Tuesday 29, Wednesday 30 & Thursday 31 March
CONCERTS
New Bingley Hall, Staffordshire County Showground, Stafford, England
Set list at all four shows: 'Sheep' / 'Pigs On The Wing, Part 1' / 'Dogs' / 'Pigs On The Wing, Part 2' / 'Pigs (Three Different Ones)' // 'Shine On You Crazy Diamond, Parts 1-5' / 'Welcome To The Machine' / 'Have A Cigar' / 'Wish You Were Here' / 'Shine On You Crazy Diamond, Parts 6-9' / encore: 'Money'.

NEW BINGLEY HALL, STAFFORD, 30 MARCH 1977. CLOCKWISE FROM TOP: ROGER WATERS, NICK MASON, RICHARD WRIGHT, SNOWY WHITE, DAVID GILMOUR.

IN THE FLESH - NORTH AMERICAN TOUR – PART 1

Friday 22 April
CONCERT
Miami Baseball Stadium, Miami, Florida, USA
Set list: 'Sheep' / 'Pigs On The Wing, Part 1' / 'Dogs' / 'Pigs On The Wing, Part 2' / 'Pigs (Three Different Ones)' // 'Shine On You Crazy Diamond, Parts 1-5' / 'Welcome To The Machine' / 'Have A Cigar' / 'Wish You Were Here' / 'Shine On You Crazy Diamond, Parts 6-9' / encore: 'Money' / 'Us And Them'.
Because of technical problems, the circular film screen couldn't be lowered into place and the pig, which was tethered to a flagpole throughout the show, merely caught fire instead of dramatically exploding when detonated.

Sunday 24 April
CONCERT
Tampa Stadium, Tampa, Florida, USA
Set list: 'Sheep' / 'Pigs On The Wing, Part 1' / 'Dogs' / 'Pigs On The Wing, Part 2' / 'Pigs (Three Different Ones)' // 'Shine On You Crazy Diamond, Parts 1-5' / 'Welcome To The Machine' / 'Have A Cigar' / 'Wish You Were Here' / 'Shine On You Crazy Diamond, Parts 6-9' / encore: 'Money'.

Tuesday 26 April
CONCERT
The Omni Coliseum, Atlanta, Georgia, USA
Set list: 'Sheep' / 'Pigs On The Wing, Part 1' / 'Dogs' / 'Pigs On The Wing, Part 2' / 'Pigs (Three Different Ones)' // 'Shine On You Crazy Diamond, Parts 1-5' / 'Welcome To The Machine' / 'Have A Cigar' / 'Wish You Were Here' / 'Shine On You Crazy Diamond, Parts 6-9' / encore: 'Money'.

Thursday 28 April
CONCERT
Assembly Center, Louisiana State University, Baton Rouge, Louisiana, USA
Set list: 'Sheep' / 'Pigs On The Wing, Part 1' / 'Dogs' / 'Pigs On The Wing, Part 2' / 'Pigs (Three Different Ones)' // 'Shine On You Crazy Diamond, Parts 1-5' / 'Welcome To The Machine' / 'Have A Cigar' / 'Wish

You Were Here' / 'Shine On You Crazy Diamond, Parts 6-9' / encore: 'Money'.

Saturday 30 April
CONCERT
Jeppesen Stadium, University of Houston, Houston, Texas, USA
Set list: 'Sheep' / 'Pigs On The Wing, Part 1' / 'Dogs' / 'Pigs On The Wing, Part 2' / 'Pigs (Three Different Ones)' // 'Shine On You Crazy Diamond, Parts 1-5' / 'Welcome To The Machine' / 'Have A Cigar' / 'Wish You Were Here' / 'Shine On You Crazy Diamond, Parts 6-9' / encore: 'Money' / 'Us And Them'.

Sunday 1 May
CONCERT
Tarrant County Convention Center Arena, Fort Worth, Texas, USA
Set list: 'Sheep' / 'Pigs On The Wing, Part 1' / 'Dogs' / 'Pigs On The Wing, Part 2' / 'Pigs (Three Different Ones)' // 'Shine On You Crazy Diamond, Parts 1-5' / 'Welcome To The Machine' / 'Have A Cigar' / 'Wish You Were Here' / 'Shine On You Crazy Diamond, Parts 6-9' / encore: 'Money' / 'Us And Them'.

Wednesday 4 May
CONCERT
Veterans Memorial Coliseum, Phoenix, Arizona, USA

Friday 6 May
CONCERT
Anaheim Stadium, Anaheim, Los Angeles, California, USA
Set list: 'Sheep' / 'Pigs On The Wing, Part 1' / 'Dogs' / 'Pigs On The Wing, Part 2' / 'Pigs (Three Different Ones)' // 'Shine On You Crazy Diamond, Parts 1-5' / 'Welcome To The Machine' / 'Have A Cigar' / 'Wish You Were Here' / 'Shine On You Crazy Diamond, Parts 6-9' / encore: 'Money'.

Saturday 7 May
CONCERT
Anaheim Stadium, Anaheim, Los Angeles, California, USA
Set list: 'Sheep' / 'Pigs On The Wing, Part 1' / 'Dogs' / 'Pigs On The Wing, Part 2' / 'Pigs (Three Different Ones)' // 'Shine On You Crazy Diamond, Parts 1-5' / 'Welcome To The Machine' / 'Have A Cigar' / 'Wish

You Were Here' / 'Shine On You Crazy Diamond, Parts 6-9' / encore: 'Money'.

Rolling Stone reported that: 'On their last tour, Pink Floyd lugged along a shell of an airplane as a prop. At Anaheim Stadium they had a real plane buzz overhead with the salutation WELCOME PINK FLOYD ablaze in computerized lights on the underside. Underneath such a display and the towering hoists and cranes that flanked the outfield stage, the Floyd were mere specks, incidental dwarfs in the making of their own music. The music was typically full of splendour, seeming to come from the sky rather than from their arsenal of sound equipment. David Gilmour modified his double-line style of lead guitar with flangers and tape delays, imparting a gripping, appropriate tone of dissonance to the opening *Animals* segment. Underneath, Rick Wright's lazy synthesiser fills and tense organ textures mixed deftly with Roger Waters' repetitive bass lines and Nick Mason's tuneful rhythmic flurries. But ultimately a Pink Floyd concert is as much an optical show as a musical one, and it is in this respect that their stance can seem coldest and most frightening. When a ghostly pig is floated over the cheering crowd and then sacrificed in a gratuitous burst of flame, the commentary couldn't be more obvious or repulsive. During a rabid Escher-like animation sequence they present a decapitation scene (the head then rots away to a grimy skull), a sea of blood spurting tentacles that turn into clawing hands, and a raw muscle twitching on a hook. One can't help but wonder why they impose such nightmares on an audience. Interestingly, while their music has become more humanistically cynical and melodious, their concerts grow more and more perfunctory and aloof, amounting to little more than a bombastic insult.'

Monday 9 May
CONCERT
Oakland Coliseum Arena, Oakland, California, USA
Set list: 'Sheep' / 'Pigs On The Wing, Part 1' / 'Dogs' / 'Pigs On The Wing, Part 2' / 'Pigs (Three Different Ones)' // 'Shine On You Crazy Diamond, Parts 1-5' / 'Welcome To The Machine' / 'Have A Cigar' / 'Wish You Were Here' / 'Shine On You Crazy Diamond, Parts 6-9' / encore: 'Money' / 'Us And Them' / 'Careful With That Axe, Eugene'.

Tuesday 10 May
CONCERT
Oakland Coliseum Arena, Oakland, California, USA
Set list: 'Sheep' / 'Pigs On The Wing, Part 1' / 'Dogs' / 'Pigs On The Wing, Part 2' / 'Pigs (Three Different Ones)' // 'Shine On You Crazy Diamond, Parts 1-5' / 'Welcome To The Machine' / 'Have A Cigar' / 'Wish You Were Here' / 'Shine On You Crazy Diamond, Parts 6-9' / encore: 'Money'.

Thursday 12 May
CONCERT
Memorial Coliseum, Portland, Oregon, USA
The last night of the tour.

IN THE FLESH - NORTH AMERICAN TOUR – PART 2

Wednesday 15 June
CONCERT
County Stadium, Milwaukee, Wisconsin, USA
Set list: 'Sheep' / 'Pigs On The Wing, Part 1' / 'Dogs' / 'Pigs On The Wing, Part 2' / 'Pigs (Three Different Ones)' // 'Shine On You Crazy Diamond, Parts 1-5' / 'Welcome To The Machine' / 'Have A Cigar' / 'Wish You Were Here' / 'Shine On You Crazy Diamond, Parts 6-9' / encore: 'Money'.

Friday 17 June
CONCERT
Freedom Hall, Louisville, Kentucky, USA
Set list included: 'Sheep' / 'Pigs On The Wing, Part 1' / 'Dogs' / 'Pigs On The Wing, Part 2' / 'Pigs (Three Different Ones)' // 'Shine On You Crazy Diamond, Parts 1-5' / 'Welcome To The Machine' / 'Have A Cigar' / 'Wish You Were Here' / 'Shine On You Crazy Diamond, Parts 6-9'.

The Louisville Courier Journal reported that: 'A 30 by 15 foot helium-filled pig with glowing amber eyes. Two human counterparts in a helium husband and wife. Billowing green smoke and fireworks. A spellbinding animation film in which a raw nerve is strung up on a meat hook only to be ripped off by a wild animal, who is then devoured himself. That and more made up the spectacular fusion of music and theatre that was the Pink Floyd concert at Freedom Hall last night. It was an evening that not many of the 19,000 who attended the sell-out show are likely to forget, and they spared no show of appreciation for the eyes and ears that was the Pink Floyd performance. From almost every aspect, it was an unusual concert. Never once wavering in professionalism, the band began the show promptly at 8pm, launching into all of its newest album, *Animals*, and trotting out the helium props at precisely the right moment to compliment the lyrics. After the break they returned to play all of their "Wish You Were Here" album from 1975. With the helium balloons packed away, the band then began the mesmerising animation sequence that was anything but your basic, average background light show. Everyone enjoyed it last night, and part of that had to be because of the superb quad sound system (including 80, 400-watt amplifiers) around the cavernous Freedom Hall (The music drowned out the vocals for much of the first half, but that problem

RIGHT: PINK FLOYD PERFORMING AT OAKLAND COLISEUM ARENA ON 10 MAY 1977.

H ENTERTA
sents

FLO

NCERT
9 MARCH
p.m.

H GRAN

215

was cleared up by the second). But there's another irony in the Floyd performance, too. For all their anguish over mechanisation and technology, Pink Floyd delivers a show that is very much like what they sing about in "Welcome To The Machine"... Music was not really the point of the show last night, though, and if anyone went to hear the precision musicianship Pink Floyd is known for, they found it. But they were probably too distracted by the band's trappings, which guided the audience away from the musicians themselves and into the metaphysical. And that's probably what Pink Floyd wanted.'

PINK FLOYD
IN CONCERT
JUNE 19
SOLDIER FIELD
8:30 PM
On Sale Now
Tickets at all 5 Flip-Side Stores, Hegewich Records & Tapes;Hear,Hear, Sears,Montgomery Wards,and all Ticketron Locations.
ADVANCE PRICE $10.60
IN THE FLESH
DANNY KRESKY ENTERPRISES, INC
CELEBRATION FLIP SIDE

Sunday 19 June
CONCERT
Super Bowl of Rock 'n' Roll, Soldier Field, Chicago, Illinois, USA
Set list: 'Sheep' / 'Pigs On The Wing, Part 1' / 'Dogs' / 'Pigs On The Wing, Part 2' / 'Pigs (Three Different Ones)' // 'Shine On You Crazy Diamond, Parts 1-5' / 'Welcome To The Machine' / 'Have A Cigar' / 'Wish You Were Here' / 'Shine On You Crazy Diamond, Parts 6-9' / encore: 'Money'.
Despite the success of the concert, a Federal Grand Jury investigated allegations of mail fraud, wire fraud, kickbacks and other financial irregularities connected with this concert. On the day itself, the official box-office figure showed attendance of about 67,000, but Pink Floyd, doubting its accuracy, hired a helicopter,

with a photographer on board, to carry out a head count. The aerial estimate was around 95,000, which meant a shortfall in the takings of several hundred thousand dollars.

Tuesday 21 June
CONCERT
Kemper Arena, Kansas City, Missouri, USA
Set list: 'Sheep' / 'Pigs On The Wing, Part 1' / 'Dogs' / 'Pigs On The Wing, Part 2' / 'Pigs (Three Different Ones)' // 'Shine On You Crazy Diamond, Parts 1-5' / 'Welcome To The Machine' / 'Have A Cigar' / 'Wish You Were Here' / 'Shine On You Crazy Diamond, Parts 6-9' / encore: 'Money'.

Thursday 23 June
CONCERT
Riverfront Coliseum, Cincinnati, Ohio, USA
Set list: 'Sheep' / 'Pigs On The Wing, Part 1' / 'Dogs' / 'Pigs On The Wing, Part 2' / 'Pigs (Three Different Ones)' // 'Shine On You Crazy Diamond, Parts 1-5' / 'Welcome To The Machine' / 'Have A Cigar' / 'Wish You Were Here' / 'Shine On You Crazy Diamond, Parts 6-9'.

Saturday 25 June
CONCERT
World Series of Rock, **Municipal Stadium, Cleveland, Ohio, USA**
Supported by Mother's Finest.
Set list: 'Sheep' / 'Pigs On The Wing, Part 1' / 'Dogs' / 'Pigs On The Wing, Part 2' / 'Pigs (Three Different Ones)' // 'Shine On You Crazy Diamond, Parts 1-5' / 'Welcome To The Machine' / 'Have A Cigar' / 'Wish You Were Here' / 'Shine On You Crazy Diamond, Parts 6-9' / encore: 'Money.' / 'Us And Them'.

Monday 27 June
CONCERT
Boston Garden, Boston, Massachusetts, USA
Set list: 'Sheep' / 'Pigs On The Wing, Part 1' / 'Dogs' / 'Pigs On The Wing, Part 2' / 'Pigs (Three Different Ones)' // 'Shine On You Crazy Diamond, Parts 1-5' / 'Welcome To The Machine' / 'Have A Cigar' / 'Wish You Were Here' / 'Shine On You Crazy Diamond, Parts 6-9' / encore: 'Money.' / 'Us And Them'.

Tuesday 28 June
CONCERT
Spectrum Theater, Philadelphia, Pennsylvania, USA

Set list: 'Sheep' / 'Pigs On The Wing, Part 1' / 'Dogs' / 'Pigs On The Wing, Part 2' / 'Pigs (Three Different Ones)' // 'Shine On You Crazy Diamond, Parts 1-5' / 'Welcome To The Machine' / 'Have A Cigar' / 'Wish You Were Here' / 'Shine On You Crazy Diamond, Parts 6-9' / encore: 'Money'.

Wednesday 29 June
CONCERT
Spectrum Theater, Philadelphia, Pennsylvania, USA
Set list: 'Sheep' / 'Pigs On The Wing, Part 1' / 'Dogs' / 'Pigs On The Wing, Part 2' / 'Pigs (Three Different Ones)' // 'Shine On You Crazy Diamond, Parts 1-5' / 'Welcome To The Machine' / 'Have A Cigar' / 'Wish You Were Here' / 'Shine On You Crazy Diamond, Parts 6-9' / encore: 'Money' / 'Us And Them' (this song performed without Roger Waters).

Friday 1 July
CONCERT
Madison Square Garden, Manhattan, New York City, New York, USA
Set list: 'Sheep' / 'Pigs On The Wing, Part 1' / 'Dogs' / 'Pigs On The Wing, Part 2' / 'Pigs (Three Different Ones)' // 'Shine On You Crazy Diamond, Parts 1-5' / 'Welcome To The Machine' / 'Have A Cigar' / 'Wish You Were Here' / 'Shine On You Crazy Diamond, Parts 6-9' / encore: 'Money' / 'Us And Them'.
The New York shows were sponsored by WNEW Radio who announced the shows in April at an event held on Sheep Meadow, Central Park featuring the inflatable pig which had been recovered and repaired from its earlier escapade over Battersea Power Station in London the previous year.

Saturday 2 July
CONCERT
Madison Square Garden, Manhattan, New York City, New York, USA
Set list: 'Sheep' / 'Pigs On The Wing, Part 1' / 'Dogs' / 'Pigs On The Wing, Part 2' / 'Pigs (Three Different Ones)' // 'Shine On You Crazy Diamond, Parts 1-5' / 'Welcome To The Machine' / 'Have A Cigar' / 'Wish You Were Here' / 'Shine On You Crazy Diamond, Parts 6-9' / encore: 'Money'.

Sunday 3 July
CONCERT
Madison Square Garden, Manhattan, New York City, New York, USA
Set list: 'Sheep' / 'Pigs On The Wing, Part 1' / 'Dogs' / 'Pigs On The Wing, Part 2' / 'Pigs (Three Different Ones)' // 'Shine On You Crazy Diamond, Parts 1-5' / 'Welcome To The Machine' / 'Have A Cigar' / 'Wish You Were Here' / 'Shine On You Crazy Diamond, Parts 6-9' / encore: 'Money.' / 'Us And Them'.
NME reported that: 'Not only was it the eve of July 4th, but also it was the week that marijuana had been

decriminalised in New York State. The surprisingly young audience was thus inevitably out of it. Blitzed young men from the Bronx would periodically rise to their feet, extend their clenched fist and bellow "Floiiiiid!" before sinking exhausted back to their seats. July 4th is, of course, the US equivalent to November 5th - it's when all the fireworks go off. Quite a few had brought them to the Garden, and even before the concert began firecrackers were spluttering in the upper tiers. They didn't stay up there long though, because they soon realised what fun it was to throw them down to the part I was sitting in. One rolled under my seat but didn't ignite - another set fire to the T-shirt of a guy five seats away while on stage Roger Waters was playing "Pigs On The Wing". The fireworks were making the audience a bit edgy - those of them that could still feel anything - and it was a while before the Floyd were able to pull together the 20,000 sell-out crowd and get them involved. Gilmour seemed able to use the tension to put an edge on his guitar licks, but Waters was obviously not happy. Roger's lyrics came through clearer and louder than any others of the evening: "You stupid motherfucker!" he bellowed. "And anyone else in here with fireworks - just fuck off and let us get on with it." Then the Floyd filled the place with smoke and brought out a huge inflatable pig which cruised about the vast space of the auditorium, the pencil beams of light from its eyes casting a malevolent gaze over the stalls. On "Have A Cigar" a lulling repetitive riff was suddenly terminated by a quadraphonic sound sweep of the hall like being nosedived by Concorde, which must have stopped the hearts of dozens of space cadets who were cruising their own contemplative mind space. Little girls screamed in shock and micro-thugs roared their approval.'

Monday 4 July
CONCERT
Madison Square Garden, Manhattan, New York City, New York, USA
Set list: 'Sheep' / 'Pigs On The Wing, Part 1' / 'Dogs' / 'Pigs On The Wing, Part 2' / 'Pigs (Three Different Ones)' // 'Shine On You Crazy Diamond, Parts 1-5' / 'Welcome To The Machine' / 'Have A Cigar' / 'Wish You Were Here' / 'Shine On You Crazy Diamond, Parts 6-9' / encore: 'Money.' / 'Us And Them'.

Wednesday 6 July
CONCERT
Stade Du Parc Olympique, Montréal, Québec, Canada
The last night of the tour.
Set list: 'Sheep' / 'Pigs On The Wing, Part 1' / 'Dogs' / 'Pigs On The Wing, Part 2' / 'Pigs (Three Different Ones)' // 'Shine On You Crazy Diamond, Parts 1-5' / 'Welcome To The Machine' / 'Have A Cigar' / 'Wish You Were Here' / 'Shine On You Crazy Diamond, Parts 6-9' / encore: 'Money' / 'Us And Them' / 'Blues' (this

number performed without David Gilmour).
Vibrations reported that: 'Anytime you get 80,000 people at a function, you've got a major happening of sorts, the terrific excitement crackling around the stadium, almost as tangible as the sweet smell of marijuana and cheap wine; secondly, the thousands of animated bodies and faces - like ants in a jar, and thirdly, that somewhere, miles off, a group was playing, not very loudly. Things did improve of course, but in the first half hour, with the sun not fully set and the audience not fully settled, Pink Floyd seemed more like incidental entertainment at a be-in. With darkness came a softening sense of the senses and a heightened receptivity on the audience's part. Floyd naturally obliged, floating sheep down and other characters including the famous pig up, as they broke into material from their album *Animals*.
Unfortunately, the gas menagerie, instead of looming melodramatically over the crowd as it would in a smaller stadium, floated irreverently against the mammoth backdrop of the stadium like children's toys gone astray. As for the music itself, when you could hear it clearly it wasn't bad... tumbling chromatic Moog licks of Rick Wright on keyboards and the strong Clapton-esque solos of guitarist Dave Gilmour. The high points of the concert were when one or both of these two were amplified through the 360 degree sound system, producing great whooshing and screaming effects that would start up at one end of the stadium, then whip around behind you, gaining speed and volume until they faded out back where they started, only to come roaring back again from the other direction. The pity was the size of the stadium made compatibility between the two sound systems (the circular speakers and those on stage) difficult. From the opposite end of the stadium two beats could be discerned. Toe tapping became complicated. Still, most people seemed to enjoy the concert. Even the burly arm-banded security guards keeping law and order seemed content, in spite of (or maybe because of) the cotton wool in their ears. There were memorable vignettes: two skinny St. John's Ambulance men struggling off the field with the heaviest stretcher case they'd probably ever seen between them; an entertaining young man who somehow conceived that the back bleachers needed an MC and filled the role very well, and another fellow on the field who understood that all the applause after each number was for him and acknowledged the ovation most graciously. So why complain? Well the sight lines were not so good at the concert, the sound tower was in the way, the sound was uneven and Pink Floyd themselves didn't care too much for the gig, admonishing some fans at one point to stop screaming. Imagine ranking out 80,000 people. You can't have your cake and eat it too.'

the show must go on

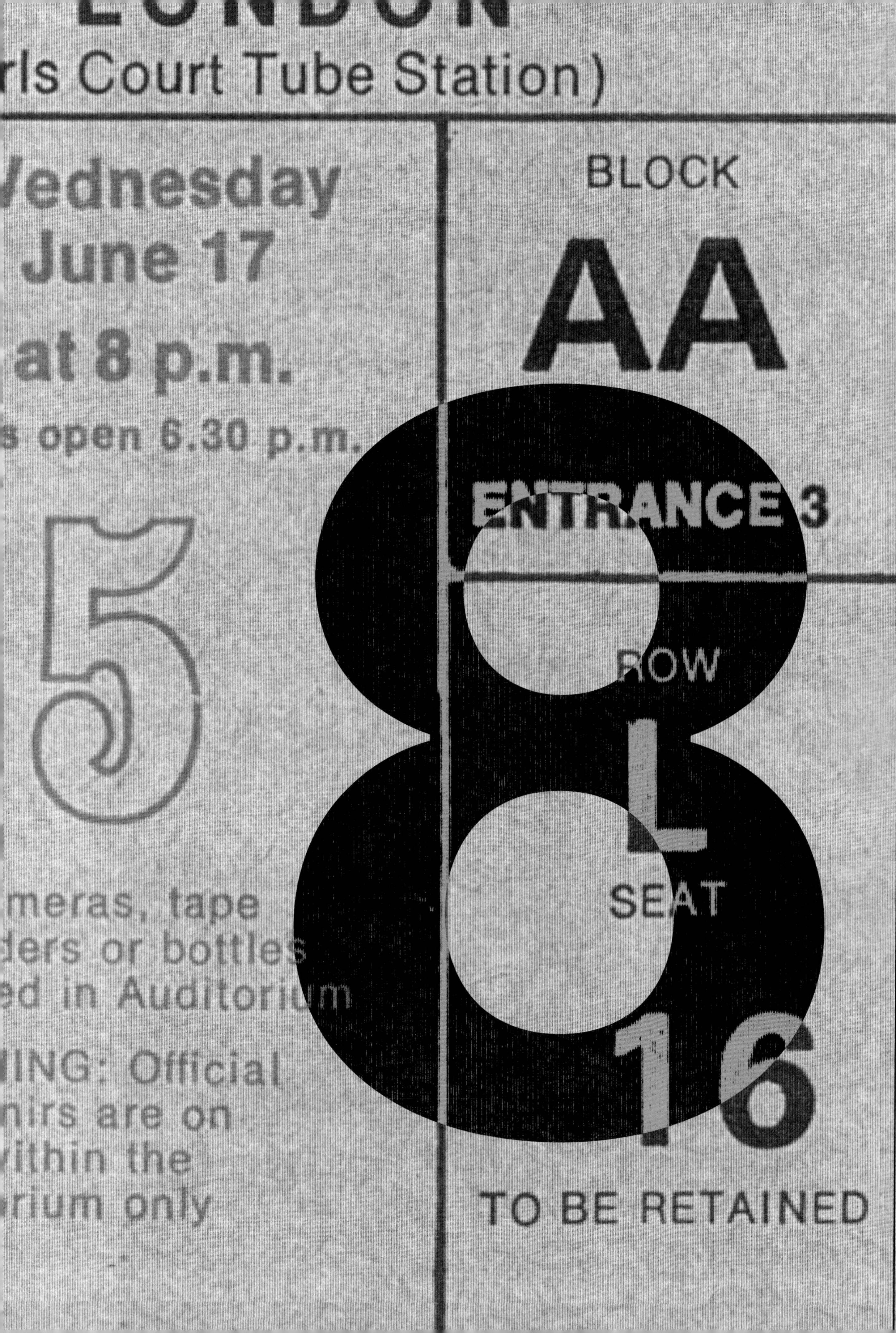

LONDON
(Earls Court Tube Station)

Wednesday June 17
at 8 p.m.
Doors open 6.30 p.m.

Cameras, tape recorders or bottles not allowed in Auditorium

WARNING: Official souvenirs are on sale within the auditorium only

5

BLOCK
AA

ENTRANCE 3

8

ROW

L

SEAT

16

TO BE RETAINED

dESPITE MASSIVE BOX-OFFICE AND ALBUM SALES IN RECENT YEARS, PINK FLOYD WAS VERY MUCH IN THE RED IN THE LATE SEVENTIES. DESPITE HAVING REPORTEDLY SIGNED A DEAL WORTH SEVERAL MILLIONS OF POUNDS WITH PUBLISHING GIANT CHAPPELL IN JANUARY 1980 THEY HAD PREVIOUSLY TEAMED UP WITH CITY BROKERS NORTON-WARBURG WHO BETWEEN 1972 AND 1978 HAD HANDLED THE BAND'S FINANCIAL AFFAIRS AND INVESTED HUGE SUMS INTO VARIOUS HIGH-RISK CAPITAL VENTURE SCHEMES.

The company crashed after nearly all of their investments had failed, coupled with vast sums paid out in director's dividends and loans. The net result was that investments for some 400 clients totalling £15 million were completely wiped out. It also meant that the exact opposite of the scheme had succeeded in working, leaving the band at the hands of a myriad of accountants trying frantically to reduce their now enormous tax exposure.

It wasn't until March 1981 that the full extent of their losses became apparent. At a creditors' meeting it was claimed that Norton-Warburg had managed to lose the band some £2.5 million and as a company had only £800,000 in remaining assets to pay off its creditors, of which Pink Floyd was only one. In short, almost everything Pink Floyd had earned from their record sales and tours over the past few years was wiped out in an instant and they were effectively flat broke – if not bankrupt – and on top of that were facing a huge income tax bill.

Using this misfortune as a convenient lever, the ever-resourceful Waters proposed bailing the band out with one of two possible album projects that he had envisaged and part written in demo form since the *Animals* tour: *Bricks In The Wall* (later known simply as *The Wall*) and *The Pros And Cons Of Hitch-Hiking*, one of which he expected to complete as a solo album at a later date. Barely resembling what would later evolve into one of their most successful albums Gilmour, at odds with Waters' later view, remembered them well: 'The demos for both *The Wall* and *Pros And Cons* were unlistenable; a shitty mess. [They] sounded exactly alike, you couldn't tell them apart. We thought of recording *Pros And Cons* at a later date, but as it turned out Roger preferred to go off and do it as a solo project.'[1]

In the end it was decided that *The Wall* was the better prospect. The finished album told a desperate story of isolation and fear, far more complex than anything previously tackled by Waters. Inevitably the work is seen as partly autobiographical: Pink, the central character, played by Waters, is a successful rock star facing the break-up of his marriage while on tour. This leads him to review his whole life and to begin to build a protective wall around himself, each brick representing the things that have caused him to suffer: a suffocating, over-protective mother, vicious schoolteachers, a faithless wife and stupid groupies. Pink imagines himself elevated to the position of a fascist dictator, with the audience his obedient followers. Hitler-like, he wields his power to persecute the 'unclean'. At the story's climax he faces up to his tormentors and the wall finally crumbles. However, as soon as this wall has fallen, so another slowly begins to rise, suggesting, in a bleak conclusion, a perpetual cycle of imprisonment.

Many of the scenes in the album also represented actual events in Waters' or the band's personal history. There were obvious references to Syd Barrett and Pink Floyd's hippie heyday; the loss of Waters' father in the war; and the rioting at the LA Sports Arena in 1975. The trashing of a motel room recalled an all too common aspect of the Seventies rock star's lifestyle. There were even a few backward messages concealed in the mix – the start of a Pink Floyd tradition.

It was an ambitious project by any stretch of the imagination. From its inception Waters envisaged a three-pronged attack: album, tour and film. Initially it was hoped that all three would be in simultaneous production, but almost at once it became evident that the sheer magnitude of effort in the recording process alone would make this plan unfeasible.

It was obvious the album had to come first and an initial process of selecting and reviewing the best parts of Waters demos took place at his home studio. 'Just sitting around and bickering, frankly, says Gilmour. 'Someone would say, "I don't like that one very much," someone else might agree, and then Roger would look all sulky and the next day he'd come back with something brilliant. He was pretty good about that during *The Wall*. I remember "Nobody Home" came along when we were well into the thing and he'd gone off in a sulk the night before and came back in the next day with something fantastic.'[2]

'From the off Waters asserted full control over the entire project. It was also true that he felt the other band members could not appreciate or contribute in any great way to his vision. Aside from the sheer complexity of the project that lay ahead, Waters needed an outside producer to collaborate on ideas, to help co-ordinate efforts and in many cases act as arbiter between himself and Gilmour once they had started the recording process. That job fell to Canadian-born producer Bob Ezrin.

Ezrin's task was a formidable one, but he succeeded in moulding the then sorry story into a workable shape. Much later he said, 'In an all night session I re-wrote the record. I used all of Roger's elements, but I rearranged their order and put them in a different form. I wrote *The Wall* out in 40 pages, like a book, telling how the songs segued. It wasn't so much re-writing as re-directing.'[3] That script, which incidentally, is now on display at the Rock And Roll Hall Of Fame in Cleveland, undoubtedly focused the task ahead. However, even by the late stages of the recording process, significant changes were made – mainly imposed by the time constraints of the vinyl format. This explains why the album sleeve lists a different running order from that of the two discs and also why there are lyrics to tracks including the 'Empty Spaces'/'What Shall We Do Now' sequence that are not included on the records. Indeed it is often said that the recorded material would have filled three discs before it was carefully edited down.

'I could see that it was going to be a long and complex process and I needed a collaborator who I could talk to about it,' said Waters. 'Because there's nobody in the band that you can talk to about any of this stuff – Dave's just not interested, Rick was pretty closed down at that point, and Nick would be happy to listen because we were pretty close at that time but he's more interested in his racing cars. I needed somebody like Ezrin who was musically and intellectually in a more similar place to where I was.'[4]

'There was an awful lot of confusion as to who was actually making this record when I first started,' recalled Ezrin, complicated by the fact that a young producer, James Guthrie, was also drafted in to act as co-producer/engineer. 'So he brought me in, I think, as an ally to help him to mange this process through. As it turns out, my perception of my job was to be the advocate of the work itself and that very often meant disagreeing with Roger and other people and being a catalyst for them to get past whatever arguments might exist.'[5]

The whole recording process lasted from September 1978 until just before the release of the double album in November 1979 with initial pre-recording demos beginning in earnest at Britannia Row in London. This quickly shifted to France as the band were forced to retreat into tax exile following the Norton-Warburg crash with their families in tow and all relocated to various rented accommodations in and around the city of Nice. Sessions began at Superbear in Berre-des-Alpes and for Waters vocal parts in particular, not suiting the mountain air, Studio Miravel in Le Val. Curiously, the band chose to

DAVID GILMOUR << Just sitting around and bickering, frankly. Someone would say, "I don't like that one very much," someone else might agree, and then Roger would look all sulky and the next day he'd come back with something brilliant. >>

work within civilised office hours, commencing at ten in the morning and finishing by six in the evening. Tensions however started to run high even at this early stage as Ezrin recalls: 'There was tension between band members, even tension between the wives of the band members. Roger and I were having a particularly difficult time. During that period I went a little bit mad and really dreaded going in to face the tension. I preferred not to be there while Roger was there.'[6]

'Most of the arguments came from artistic disagreements.' remembers Gilmour. 'It wasn't total war, though there were bad vibes – certainly towards Rick, because he didn't seem to be pulling his weight.'[7] Despite

BOB EZRIN   << There was tension between band members, even tension between the wives of the band members. Roger and I were having a particularly difficult time. During that period I went a little bit mad and really dreaded going in to face the tension. >>

this fact the band soldiered on and after the customary August vacations production shifted to The Producers Workshop in Los Angeles where some final recording and the entire mixing continued apace. It was here that additional session musicians were recruited by Waters to compliment Mason, whose drum parts had already been completed in France, but in particular Wright's less than able performances and included the talents of Freddie Mandell, Jeff Porcaro, Peter Woods and Lee Ritenour. At one stage it was even hoped to include all of The Beach Boys on vocal harmonies but this was cancelled at the last moment. Additionally Michael Kamen was also drafted in to arrange the orchestrations, which he recorded at CBS in New York.

Whereas Mason and Wright's contributions were minimal to say the least, Gilmour did at least contribute some outstanding music for the album's three more tuneful compositions, 'Young Lust', 'Run Like Hell' and 'Comfortably Numb', (the latter derived from an unused demo from his solo album) for which he received the only other and apparently hard-fought for shared writing credit on the album: the other went to Ezrin for his contribution to 'The Trial'.

The summer break undoubtedly saved the Ezrin - Waters partnership but the same could not be said of Wright who was, by his increasing lack of commitment becoming the brunt of Waters' hostility. Already frustrated by his belief that he should continue to be paid a quarter share of the production credits when it was clear he was in no way contributing to this element at all, the crunch finally came when Waters realised that the volume of work still required to complete the record in time for delivery in October could not be met. Via manager Steve O'Rourke, Waters requested that Wright join Ezrin a week ahead of the rest of the band in Los Angeles in order to catch up on the backlog of work. Ezrin reluctantly agreed but Wright refused outright commenting that he had seen very little of his children when they were in France and was also going through a

tough divorce and that he was not prepared to go.

Waters found this unacceptable. He contacted the other members and decided to communicate to Wright that he would take him to court unless he agreed to finish the album in the timeframe suggested. The get-out clause for Wright, if he did not agree, was that he would be guaranteed his full share of the sales royalties but would have to leave the band quietly at the conclusion of the project.

'I did not go along with it,' said Gilmour. 'I went out to dinner with Rick after Roger had said this to him and said if he wanted to stay in the band I would support him in that. I did point out to Rick that he hadn't contributed anything of any value whatsoever to the album and that I was not over-happy with him myself – he did very, very little, an awful lot of the keyboard parts were done by me, Roger, Bob Ezrin, Michael Kamen, Freddie Mandell.'[8]

Wright wrestled with this ultimatum for some time, wondering if he should call Waters' bluff. In the end he resolved to leave the band but in a final, yet illogical, act of commitment agreed to stay and perform on the live shows. 'It's quite simple,' Wright explained. 'It started because Roger and I didn't get on. There was a lot of antagonism during The Wall and he said either you leave or I'll scrap everything we've done and there won't be an album. Normally I would have told him to get lost, but at that point we had to earn the money to pay off the enormous back-taxes we owed. Anyway, Roger said that if I didn't leave he would re-record the material. I couldn't afford to say no, so I left.'[9]

It would appear that the two men's differences went back right to the start of Pink Floyd. Wright went on to say that the situation began during their student days at the Regent Street Polytechnic: 'The two of us didn't really get on. Being the kind of person he is, Roger would try to... rile you, if you like, try to make you crack. Definitely mental things going on between us and big political disagreements. Him being an armchair socialist... the only time I'd ever get angry with Roger on stage was when he'd be playing out of tune; we'd be in D and he was still banging away in E because he couldn't hear it. I had to tune his bass onstage, you know. In those days there were no strobe tuners, so after every number he'd stick the head of the bass guitar over my keyboards and I'd tune it up for him.' [10]

With the album barely concluded much of the final planning of the live shows was carried out in an intensive effort during the Christmas '79 period, when Pink Floyd were enjoying a number one chart placing with the album across the globe and a surprise top position in the UK with the preceding single, 'Another Brick In The Wall Pt.2'.

But 'Another Brick' was controversial in every respect, having been banned by the less than tolerant

BELOW: PRODUCTION REHEARSALS FOR *THE WALL* SHOWS AT THE LOS ANGELES SPORTS ARENA, JANUARY 1980. IT WAS THE MOST COMPLEX STAGE SHOW OF ITS KIND REQUIRING PERFECTLY TIMED SONGS TO SYNC WITH THE SOUND EFFECTS, FILM SEQUENCES, PUPPETS AND CONSTRUCTION OF THE WALL.

governments of South Africa and Korea, among others, for its anti-establishment message, as well as attracting accusations in the UK media of exploiting children from a nearby school who were brought to Britannia Row for the chorus. (The issue even raised its head again in early 2005 as former pupils contacted each other on the Friends Reunited website with a view to suing for royalties.)

On stage, *The Wall* was Pink Floyd's most overwhelming spectacle to date; presented exclusively at indoor arenas and opening in Los Angeles and New York in February 1980, it skilfully combined every aspect of the rock theatre genre. A wall was literally constructed from hundreds of cardboard bricks before the audience's eyes, and by the close of the first half it spanned the entire width of the auditorium to a height of some forty feet.

playing his monumental guitar solo in 'Comfortably Numb'.

As for the sound, the system was by far the band's best yet, producing a desk reading of 106 decibels in perfect quadraphonic arrangement. An unexpected feature was additional speaker cabinets under the tiered seating to accentuate the rumbling collapse of the wall – the show's grand finale – and give the impression that the very arena itself was crumbling.

But what pleased Waters most about the whole production was that it was pleasantly removed from the stadium environment he so hated. 'I went and walked all the way around the top row of seats at the back of the arena. And my heart was beating furiously and I was getting shivers right up and down my spine. And I thought it was so fantastic that people could actually see and hear something from everywhere they were seated. Because after the 1977 tour I became seriously deranged – or maybe arranged – about stadium gigs. Because I do think they are awful.'[11]

ROGER WATERS << **I went and walked all the way around the top row of seats at the back of the arena. And my heart was beating furiously and I was getting shivers right up and down my spine. And I thought it was so fantastic that people could actually see and hear something from everywhere they were seated.** >>

The whole production called for massive effort to punishing deadlines and it's a miracle it ever happened at all: 'We were all working furiously up until the first night,' Waters recalled. 'And the first time we had the wall right up across the arena with some film on it was four days before the first show!'[12]

The band again went to the Fisher-Park team with the problem of the wall's design, construction and eventual onstage collapse. The show also incorporated a crashing Stuka dive-bomber for the culmination of 'In The Flesh?'; a circular screen on which hideous and newly designed animations by Gerald Scarfe were projected; and three 35mm projectors, used in horizontal configuration, to throw a triptych of animated images on to the wall itself.

In addition, three giant puppets, further products of Scarfe's twisted imagination, made appearances at key points, representing the villains of the piece. These were a twenty-five foot high model of the Schoolteacher, a smaller one of the wife and an inflatable Mother. Even the familiar helium filled pig made a mad dash around the hall during 'Run Like Hell', which Waters regularly introduced as their 'disco' number.

There was even a set built into the face of the wall itself, depicting the motel room where Pink sits comatose before a TV showing an old war film. But one of the most visually striking elements was Gilmour atop the wall

And that task was a nightmare because the editors employed to cut the animation film had the additional job of transforming the projections from a single screen to three in order to project the film across the full width of the auditorium. Peter Hearn, who was working on this recalled: 'Just before the show he [Waters] decided it should be on three screens. Quite a task. A screaming hurry to do that... we also had something went wrong with the time code and they went into rehearsal in Los Angeles and the picture and sound went out, and I tell you what happened was we were having this conversation over the phone from London with this guy in Los Angeles who was sitting in a hotel bedroom spilling film all over the floor telling him what to cut and what to look for.'[13]

There were further problems. Because of some dissatisfaction with their existing lighting designer, Marc Brickman was hired to replace long-time crew member

ABOVE: ROGER WATERS AND
DAVID GILMOUR ON STAGE AT
THE NASSAU VETERANS
MEMORIAL COLISEUM, NEW
YORK, FEBRUARY 1980.

OVERLEAF: PERFORMING *THE
WALL* AT THE
WESTFALENHALLE, DORTMUND,
FEBRUARY 1981. BY THE END OF
THE FIRST HALF OF THE SHOW
THE AUDIENCE WERE FACED
WITH A HUGE WHITE EDIFICE
STRETCHING THE FULL WIDTH
OF THE AUDITORIUM.

PINK
FLOYD
THE
WALL

226

Graeme Fleming at twenty-four hours notice before the opening night in Los Angeles. Believing the call by Steve O'Rourke to be an invitation to watch the show he was horrified to be plunged into the deep end and recalls this as, 'one of the most shocking experiences of my life.'[14] Before that day he hadn't even heard the album.

With immediate sell-outs in both locations and an oversubscribed attendance it was hardly surprising that the promoter offered to extend the band's residency in New York, but this was turned down. In addition, an offer to take the show elsewhere prompted yet another bust-up within the band, as Waters explained: 'Larry Magid the promoter, a Philadelphia promoter, offered us a guaranteed million dollars a show plus expenses to go and do two dates at JFK stadium with *The Wall*. To truck straight from New York to Philadelphia. And I wouldn't do it. I had to go through the whole story with the other members. I said, "You've all read my explanation of what

ALAN PARKER << **In that period I was allowed to develop my vision, and I really made that film with a completely free hand. I had to have that. I couldn't be second-guessed by Roger, and he appreciated that.** >>

The Wall is about. It's three years since we did that last stadium and I saw then that I'd never do one again. And *The Wall* is entirely sparked off by how awful that was and how I didn't feel that the public or the band or anyone got anything out of it that was worthwhile. And that's why we've produced this show strictly for arenas where everybody does get something out of it that is worthwhile. Blah-blah-blah. And, I ain't fuckin' going!" So there was a lot of talk about whether Andy Bown could sing my part. Oh, you may laugh, and in the end, they bottled out. They didn't have the balls to go through with it.'[15]

With the US tour over without further incident, a string of London *Wall* shows were scheduled for June at the Empire Pool, Wembley. In the event, the tour reached its conclusion at London's Earl's Court in August 1980 because the band had learned in the meantime that, for tax reasons, they would have to delay returning to the UK. In addition, a one-off production of the work at the Milton Keynes National Bowl on 26 May was announced in the music press, as well as a 'greatest hits' show at the same venue in August, but neither reached fruition.

Shortly after the end of the tour, EMI began work on a compilation of material to be culled from the band's archive. However, the efforts of the Harvest label's A&R head, Colin Miles, to provide fans with an interesting and varied package of rarities were thwarted when both band and EMI opted for an inferior greatest hits compilation in the shape of 1981's *A Collection Of Great Dance Songs*. The only unusual item this contained was a re-recording of 'Money', carried out for the express purpose of the album and prompted, it would appear, by some dispute with Capitol Records in the USA.

Pressure was now mounting on the band to start work on the full-length movie adaptation – the third and final instalment – of *The Wall* and Waters began planning out the script with Gerald Scarfe and Michael Seresin as directors and film-maker Alan Parker as producer. However, Seresin was soon ousted in favour of Parker as sole director and Waters retained the role of producer. As with the live shows, financing the film (£6 million of it) fell to the band who persuaded MGM via Alan Parker to provide funds although it is said that this was achieved with a little help from other sources and a secured loan from Barclay's bank.

The announcement of a further string of *Wall* shows, in Dortmund in February and London in June 1981, came as a big surprise to fans. But the band had an ulterior motive: they intended to use the events to film themselves in concert, as called for by the original script.

Production began at Pinewood Film Studios in Buckinghamshire during September that same year. However, Parker was not satisfied with the results of the filming at the UK shows, although he captured a competent (as yet unreleased) concert movie. Having decided on a change of plan, he persuaded a reluctant Waters to both drop the live scenes and relinquish his role as Pink. Parker's change of plan also upset Scarfe in that his stage-show puppets would be sacrificed to the creation of an entirely new piece of work separate from the stage presentation, although about twenty minutes of his animation would be retained.

It is well documented that the three men were given to lengthy rows and walk-outs during the filming. Parker resolved the matter by forcing Waters to take a six-week holiday so that he could work unhindered. 'In that period I was allowed to develop my vision,' he said, 'and I really made that film with a completely free hand.

I had to have that. I couldn't be second-guessed by Roger, and he appreciated that. The difficulty came when I'd finished. I'd been shooting for sixty days, fourteen hours a day – that film had become mine. And then Roger came back to it, and I had to go through the very difficult reality of having it put over to me that actually it was a collaborative effort.'[16]

Waters was exceptionally pragmatic about the situation, describing it as 'the most unnerving, neurotic period in my life – with the possible exception of my divorce in 1975. Parker is used to sitting at the top of his pyramid, and I'm used to sitting at the top of mine. We're both pretty much used to getting our own way. If I'd have directed it – which I'd never have done – it would have been much quieter than it is. He paints in fairly bold strokes; he is very worried about boring his audience. It suits us very well, because we did want a lot of this to be a punch in the face.'[17]

The film, which had had its world premier at the Cannes Film Festival on 23 May 1982, opened in London on 14 July. It surprised many by featuring Bob Geldof, the leader of the pop-punk band The Boomtown Rats, as Pink, ranting the parts of 'In The Flesh?' to great effect.

The band also re-recorded some of their works for the soundtrack, using new Michael Kamen orchestrations on 'Mother', 'Bring The Boys Back Home' (with a Welsh male choir) and an expanded 'Empty Spaces', which this time, like the stage shows, included the segue of 'What Shall We Do Now?'. In addition, a completely new track was introduced to act as an overture to the film: 'When The Tigers Broke Free'. It was inspired by the death of Waters' father on the ill-fated Anzio bridgehead in southern Italy during the Second World War.

When it opened in London, the film was generally seen as a powerful piece of celluloid rock music, but it did receive a few unfavourable reviews. Some of the more sensitive writers felt they had been subjected to a battering from start to finish, while a few, misreading it completely, accused it of being neo-Nazi propaganda – a view no doubt inspired by the scenes in which menacing gangs of specially recruited Tilbury skinheads paraded as Pink's 'Hammer Guard'. Scarfe was particularly shocked to find that some of the extras now had his hammer logo tattooed on their skin.

Soon after the film's release, the band announced the release of additional material used on the soundtrack, as well as some that had been cut from both the album and film. As Waters explained: 'We were contracted to make a soundtrack album but there really wasn't enough new material in the movie to make a record that I

ABOVE: PINK FLOYD PERFORMING *THE WALL* AT THE WESTFALENHALLE, DORTMUND, FEBRUARY 1981. DURING THE SECOND HALF OF THE SHOW THE WALL ITSELF BECAME THE BACKDROP TO A SERIES OF ANIMATED FILMS.

THE SHOW MUST GO ON 1978-1985

PINK
FLOYD
THE
WALL

230

thought was interesting. The project then became *Spare Bricks*, and was meant to include some of the film music, like "When The Tigers Break Through" [the working title of 'When The Tigers Broke Free'] and the much less ironic version of "Outside The Wall" which finishes the movie, the sequence with the kids playing with the milk bottles, plus some music written for the movie but left on the cutting room floor. I decided not to include the new version of "Mother" from the movie because it really is film music and it doesn't stand up. It's a very long song, and besides, I'm bored with all that now. I've become more interested in the remembrance and requiem aspects of the thing, if that doesn't sound too pretentious. Anyway, it all seemed a bit bitty then I came up with a new title for the album: *The Final Cut*.' [18]

When the album of this name was eventually released, in the spring of 1983, it was very different from what had been predicted. Waters, inspired by the British Government's military retaliation against Argentina's invasion of the Falkland Islands in the South Atlantic, had composed and recorded new pieces of music that related to the Falkland's conflict, almost without consulting the rest of the band. It was a decisive departure from normal policy and, in the light of Wright's recent exit, it seemed that Waters had assumed unilateral responsibility for the direction of the band.

As a result, this was Pink Floyd's most turbulent period, with arguments apparently raging constantly over band policy, and album quality and content. 'It got to the point on *The Final Cut*,' said Gilmour, 'that Roger didn't want to know about anyone else submitting material.' [19] It seemed that much of what the rest of the band had cherished as a democracy was fast disappearing, as Gilmour went on to explain: 'There was at one time a great spirit of compromise within the group. If someone couldn't get enough of his vision on the table to convince the rest of us, it would be dropped. *The Wall* album, which started off as unlistenable and turned into a great piece, was the last album with this spirit of compromise. With *The Final Cut*, Waters became impossible to deal with.' [20]

Waters himself admitted that it was a highly unpleasant time, but his overriding feeling was frustration at the others' unwillingness – and this applied to Gilmour in particular – to submit to his complete control. 'We were all fighting like cats and dogs. We were finally realising – or accepting, if you like – that there was no band and had not been a band in accord for a long time. Not since 1975, when we made *Wish You Were Here*. Even then there were big disagreements

about content and how to put the record together. I had to do it more or less single-handed, with Michael Kamen, my co-producer. That's one of the few things that the "boys" and I agreed about.' [21]

Gilmour submitted in the sense that he refused to have anything more to do with the album's production, and was less than happy with the personal and political content for it to be anything other than a Waters solo piece, agreeing merely to perform, as required, opting for an easy life in preference to endless rows. 'I came off the production credits because my ideas weren't the way Roger saw it. It is not personally how I would see a Pink Floyd record going.' [22] The power this granted Waters gratified his now tremendous ego, leaving him free to act as if his band mates were no more than mere hired hands. Gilmour later recalled how Waters, at the end of recording, told him, 'the only way he'd ever consider doing another Pink Floyd album was on that basis.' [23]

Even the sleeve, under Waters' artistic control, carried the subtitle 'A Requiem For The Post War Dream by Roger Waters – *performed* by Pink Floyd'. The obvious lack of Wright's name gave fans their first indication of his departure, confirmation of which did not emerge until three years after the album's release and the full details of which were not revealed until press interviews surrounding the release of *The Wall Live* CD set in 2000.

The Final Cut was dedicated to Waters' late father Eric Fletcher Waters, and at last laid his ghost to rest. It was Pink Floyd's worst-selling record in recent years, scraping the top five, a point which Gilmour has gleefully raised time and again to underline the fact that the material was exceptionally weak in comparison with previous albums and obviously lacked cohesive effort. Strong or not, Waters has also been at great pains to point out that Gilmour had nothing to contribute to it and certainly didn't object to this being a Pink Floyd album in favour of a Waters solo piece.

In recent years Waters has been, quite rightly, very defensive towards critics of his control in this period: 'The fact is, we all had the opportunity to write as much as we wanted. There was never any question of me saying, "Don't write. I don't want your stuff." I was desperately keen for everybody in the band to produce as much as possible. But Nick doesn't write at all, and Dave and Rick are not prolific writers. They've written very, very little over the years. They've written some great stuff, but very little of it. So it fell to me as a more prolific writer to fill in the gaps, to actually produce the material.' [24]

If Pink Floyd's history was to come to an end with this album – and there was every indication that it would

– it was hardly the best offering to go out on. It did contain some memorable pieces with some superb lyrics, 'The Fletcher Memorial Home' and 'Two Suns In The Sunset' (with Andy Newmark on drums) in particular, while also spawning the low-charting single, 'Not Now John'. However, it was merely a soundtrack to Waters' often-vicious dialogue, some of its subject matter seems little more than a political rant and an unnecessary extension of some of the themes explored in *The Wall*.

It's therefore hardly surprising that the album's title is seen as prophetic in marking Waters' departure and his wish to dissolve Pink Floyd.

With absolutely no intention of touring the album, the band were now on permanent holiday, and this state of affairs, along with solo albums and extensive tours from both Waters and Gilmour during the early part of 1984, furthered the growing public belief that Pink Floyd had all but split up.

Sources
1. Author's interview with David Gilmour, 25 September 1987
2. *Mojo*, December 1999
3. *Circus*, 15 April 1980
4-8. *Mojo*, Dec 1999
9. *South China Sunday Morning Post*, 17 January 1988
10. *Mojo*, Dec 1999
11-12. *Q Magazine*, August 1987
13. Author's interview with Peter Hearn, 2 July 1986
14. *Q Magazine*, August 1987
15-16. *Rolling Stone*, 16 Sept 1982
17-18. Unidentified press report c.1982
19. *Washington Post*, 19 October 1987
20-21. *Q Magazine*, August 1987
22. *The Sun*, 27 April 1983
23. *Washington Post*, 19 October 1987
24. *Uncut*, June 2004

1978

September – December
RECORDING SESSIONS
Britannia Row Studios, Islington, London, England
Throughout August Roger Waters retreated to his home studio to demo two new pieces of work, one of which would eventually become *The Wall*, the other his first solo album *The Pros And Cons Of Hitch-Hiking*. The initial rough sessions and compilation of the album were pieced together in sessions at Britannia Row in London from September through to the end of the year.

18 November
PRESS REPORT
London, England
In an article headlined 'Pink Floyd Go Camping', the *NME* reported that Pink Floyd were planning to build their own 5,000 capacity inflatable concert hall, which they had nicknamed 'The Slug' because of its shape. This would supposedly avoid the problems the band had previously experienced of playing at existing indoor venues. Despite the design plans being well advanced the project never reached fruition.

1979

January – July
RECORDING SESSIONS
Super Bear Studios, Berre des Alpes, France & Miravel Studios, Le Val, France
Discontinuous recording for *The Wall* took place at Super Bear with Waters vocal sessions taking place at Miravel Studios.

Friday 6 July
RECORD RELEASE
Pink Floyd: First XI
UK album release.

September
RECORDING SESSIONS
CBS Studios, Manhattan, New York City, New York, USA
Pink Floyd made brief use of the CBS Studios for further recording sessions with the New York City Opera and the New York Philharmonic Orchestra conducted by Michael Kamen.

Saturday 1 September – Wednesday 31 October
RECORDING SESSIONS
Cherokee Recording Studios, Los Angeles, California, USA & The Village Recorder, Los Angeles, California, USA
Discontinuous recording and mixing for the album *The Wall*.

Tuesday 2 October
CANCELLED RECORDING SESSION
Sundance Productions, Los Angeles, California, USA
A recording session was booked to record The Beach Boys for backing vocals but was cancelled on the day.

Thursday 1 – Tuesday 6 November
RECORDING SESSIONS
Producers Workshop, Los Angeles, California, USA
Discontinuous recording and mixing for the album *The Wall* plus TV and radio spots and mixing backing tracks for the live show.

Friday 23 November
RECORD RELEASE
'Another Brick In The Wall, Part 2' / 'One Of My Turns'
UK 7-inch single release. US 7-inch single release on Monday 7 January 1980.
NME commented that: 'It's fairly cunningly conceived, complete with easily memorable moron-chorus parts, simple enough for the thickest of terrace terrorists. Expect to hear it accompanying the sound of bladders (human or swine) being kicked around on Saturday afternoons.'

Friday 30 November
RECORD RELEASE
The Wall
UK album release. US album release on Saturday 8 December 1979.
Melody Maker commented that: 'Quite obviously *The Wall* is an extraordinary record. I'm not sure whether it's brilliant or terrible, but I find it utterly compelling. Despite the inevitable expensive production it can't be dismissed as comfortable easy listening, and anyone who takes ideas as challenging and uncomfortable (and pessimistic?) as Roger Waters' deep into the AOR market is worth listening to. Pink Floyd are still relevant, still important and above all, still thinking.'

Friday 30 November
RADIO SHOW
BBC Radio One, Broadcasting House, London, England
DJ Tommy Vance interviewed Roger Waters in a track-by-track commentary from the Beverly Hills Hotel in Los Angeles for his *Friday Rock Show* broadcast on this day at 10.00pm. Much to the horror of Pink Floyd's UK concert promoter, Harvey Goldsmith, Roger Waters announced on air that the band would be performing in the UK at Wembley Arena between 9 and 13 June 1980. Needless to say switchboards were jammed both at the radio station and venue until a statement was issued denying this fact. Rumours were also rife in the music press in the forthcoming year for Pink Floyd shows including a single concert production of *The Wall* to be held at the open-air setting of Milton Keynes National Bowl, Milton Keynes, England on 26 May 1980 and again at the same venue in August 1980 when it was suggested that plans were afoot to stage a single 'greatest hits' concert.

PINK FLOYD
(November 1979 – October 1985)
David Gilmour: Guitar, Vocals
Nick Mason: Drums
Roger Waters: Bass Guitar, Vocals

1980

THE WALL PERFORMED LIVE

PINK FLOYD ROAD CREW THROUGH 1980
Marc Brickman: Lighting Designer
Mark Fisher: Set Design & Effects
Seth Goldman: Monitor Sound Engineer
Pat Griffiths: Wardrobe
James Guthrie: Front of House Sound Engineer
Rick Hart: PA Technician
Don Joce: Special Effects
Jonathan Park: Set Design & Effects
Rocky Paulson: Special Effects
Andy Shields: Projectionist
Nigel Taylor: PA Technician
Phil Taylor: Backline Technician
Mick Treadwell: Special Effects

Greg Walsh: PA Technician
Robbie Williams: Head of PA

ADDITIONAL TOUR PERSONNEL
Musician:
Richard Wright: Keyboards, Vocals
The Surrogate Band:
Andy Bown: Bass Guitar
Snowy White: Guitars
Willie Wilson: Drums
Peter Woods: Keyboards
Backing Vocals:
Joe Chemay
Stan Farber
Jim Haas
John Joyce
Master of Ceremonies:
Cynthia Fox: 7, 9, 12, 13 February
Ace Young: 8 February
Jim Ladd: 10, 11 February

January
REHEARSALS
Leeds Rehearsal Studios, Hollywood, Los Angeles, USA
At least two weeks of music rehearsals took place prior to the production rehearsals.

January
REHEARSALS
MGM Studios, Culver City, Los Angeles, USA
Running parallel to the musician's rehearsals construction rigging and wall building rehearsals took place inside a sound stage prior to the production rehearsals moving to the venue.

Monday 21 January - Wednesday 6 February
REHEARSALS
Los Angeles Memorial Sports Arena, Exposition Park, Los Angeles, California, USA
Three weeks of full production rehearsals were staged at the Sports Arena right up to the opening night.

Monday 4 February & Monday 11 February
RADIO SHOWS
KMET Studios, Los Angeles, California, USA
Jim Ladd interviewed Roger Waters for his two-part *Inner-View* show in a track-by-track commentary on *The Wall* that was recorded in Los Angeles prior to this date. Both shows were broadcast on KMET 94.7 at 10.00pm.

Thursday 7, Friday 8, Saturday 9, Sunday 10, Monday 11, Tuesday 12 & Wednesday 13 February
CONCERT
Los Angeles Memorial Sports Arena, Exposition Park, Los Angeles, California, USA
Set list at all seven shows: 'In The Flesh' / 'The Thin Ice' / 'Another Brick In The Wall, Part 1' / 'The Happiest Days Of Our Lives' / 'Another Brick In The Wall, Part 2' / 'Mother' / 'Goodbye Blue Sky' / 'What Shall We Do Now?' / 'Empty Spaces' / 'Young Lust' / 'One Of My Turns' / 'Don't Leave Me Now' / 'Another Brick In The Wall, Part 3' / 'The Last Few Bricks' * / 'Goodbye Cruel World' // 'Hey You' / 'Is There Anybody Out There?' / 'Nobody Home' / 'Vera' / 'Bring The Boys Back Home' / 'Comfortably Numb' / 'The Show Must Go On' / 'In The Flesh?' / 'Run Like Hell' / 'Waiting For The Worms' / 'Stop' / 'The Trial' / 'Outside The Wall'.
* 'The Last Few Bricks' is a title used to describe an instrumental filler, usually lasting about five minutes in order for the wall construction crews to catch up. At the first few shows this was primarily a blues instrumental with the melody of 'Another Brick' coming through. In later shows it developed into an atmospheric synthesiser-based instrumental with elements of 'Another Brick', 'Young Lust' and 'Empty Spaces'.
The show on 7 February was temporarily halted during 'What Shall We Do Now?' in order to extinguish flames caused by pyrotechnics setting fire to the stage drapes.

THE WALL PERFORMED LIVE

ADDITIONAL TOUR PERSONNEL
Musician:
Richard Wright: Keyboards, Vocals
The Surrogate Band:
Andy Bown: Bass Guitar
Snowy White: Guitars
Willie Wilson: Drums
Peter Woods: Keyboards
Backing Vocals:
Joe Chemay
Stan Farber
Jim Haas
John Joyce
Master of Ceremonies:
Gary Yudman: All shows

LEFT: PERFORMING 'ANOTHER BRICK IN THE WALL, PART 2'
AT EARL'S COURT, LONDON, 7 AUGUST 1980.

Monday 16 – Monday 23 February
REHEARSALS
Nassau Veterans Memorial Coliseum, Uniondale,
Long Island, New York, USA
A full week of production rehearsals and set up.

**Sunday 24, Monday 25, Tuesday 26, Wednesday 27
& Thursday 28 February**
CONCERTS
Nassau Veterans Memorial Coliseum, Uniondale,
Long Island, New York, USA
Set list at all five shows: 'In The Flesh' / 'The Thin Ice'
/ 'Another Brick In The Wall, Part 1' / 'The Happiest
Days Of Our Lives' / 'Another Brick In The Wall, Part
2' / 'Mother' / 'Goodbye Blue Sky' / 'What Shall We
Do Now?' / 'Empty Spaces' / 'Young Lust' / 'One Of
My Turns' / 'Don't Leave Me Now' / 'Another Brick In
The Wall, Part 3' / 'The Last Few Bricks' / 'Goodbye
Cruel World' // 'Hey You' / 'Is There Anybody Out
There?' / 'Nobody Home' / 'Vera' / 'Bring The Boys
Back Home' / 'Comfortably Numb' / 'The Show Must
Go On' / 'In The Flesh?' / 'Run Like Hell' / 'Waiting For
The Worms' / 'Stop' / 'The Trial' / 'Outside The Wall'.

Monday 9 June
RECORD RELEASE
'Run Like Hell' / 'Don't Leave Me Now'
US 7-inch single release.

Monday 23 June 1980
RECORD RELEASE
'Comfortably Numb' / 'Hey You'
US 7-inch single release.

Monday 30 June 1980
RECORD RELEASE
'Run Like Hell' / 'Comfortably Numb'
US 7-inch single release.

THE WALL PERFORMED LIVE

ADDITIONAL TOUR PERSONNEL
Musician:
Richard Wright: Keyboards, Vocals
The Surrogate Band:
Andy Bown: Bass guitar
Snowy White: Guitars
Willie Wilson: Drums
Peter Woods: Keyboards
Backing Vocals:
Joe Chemay
Stan Farber
Jim Haas
John Joyce
Master of Ceremonies:
Gary Yudman: All shows

**Monday 4, Tuesday 5, Wednesday 6, Thursday 7,
Friday 8 & Saturday 9 August**
CONCERTS
Earl's Court Exhibition Hall, Earl's Court, London,
England
Set list at all six shows: 'In The Flesh' / 'The Thin Ice'
/ 'Another Brick In The Wall, Part 1' / 'The Happiest
Days Of Our Lives' / 'Another Brick In The Wall, Part
2' / 'Mother' / 'Goodbye Blue Sky' / 'What Shall We
Do Now?' / 'Empty Spaces' / 'Young Lust' / 'One Of
My Turns' / 'Don't Leave Me Now' / 'Another Brick In
The Wall, Part 3' / 'The Last Few Bricks' / 'Goodbye
Cruel World' // 'Hey You' / 'Is There Anybody Out
There?' / 'Nobody Home' / 'Vera' / 'Bring The Boys
Back Home' / 'Comfortably Numb' / 'The Show Must
Go On' / 'In The Flesh?' / 'Run Like Hell' / 'Waiting For
The Worms' / 'Stop' / 'The Trial' / 'Outside The Wall'.
Sounds reported that: 'If *The Wall* turns out to be the
Pink Floyd's epitaph they've bowed out with a
grandiose, impressive, overblown and provocative
spectacle that typified every prejudice, good or bad,
that anyone could hold about them. No other band
could have conceived, let alone executed, the
extravaganza that packed out Earl's Court for six
consecutive nights last week. While other rock
dinosaurs have tried to get hip to evolution and
trimmed their garish sails to fit the winds of change,
the Floyd have defiantly made their last stand in the
gigantic stadiums that they were partly responsible
for turning into rock venues in the first place. And
true to form they dwarfed the biggest indoor rock
venue in the country with a dazzling array of effects
and a 360° sound system that was the finest I have
ever heard anywhere, let alone the cavernous wastes
of Earl's Court. We knew what we'd come to hear - a
presentation of their latest and massive selling album.
We knew we'd get a wall too but even the
expectation of it didn't prepare you for the sheer scale
of the 40ft high white edifice that eventually
stretched the width of the hall. The start was
unexpected and deliberately confusing. An announcer
came on to wind us up for the show (as if we needed
it). He built up the atmosphere to fever pitch before
giving the band their cue. The Floyd kicked off to the
accompaniment of thunder flashes and a Spitfire that
sailed from one end of the hall to the other, crashing
spectacularly into the half-built wall to roars from the
audience... except that the band wasn't the Floyd but
four clones giving an Americanised version of what
the Floyd ought to look like on stage. The Floyd
emerged behind them and took over after a couple of
minutes. And as the wall built up so did Roger
Waters' bleak tale of indoctrination and alienation,
aided by huge grotesque figures of schoolteachers
and judicial mothers and a series of cartoons, all the
work of Gerald Scarfe who clearly shares Waters'
own sense of the paranoid. The symbolism of the wall
veered between the subtle and the sledgehammer but
you couldn't miss the point as it closed in on the band,

eventually leaving them visible through a couple of
holes while the light show raged on regardless.
Waters made one last attempt at communication
through the gap before the final brick was slotted
into place and the audience was allowed 20 minutes
to get their necks back into position. The second half
began with the Floyd firmly entrenched behind the
wall and for a while it looked as if it might stay that
way until the end but eventually a chink was opened
up to let Waters through. The supreme moment came
when Dave Gilmour appeared on the top of the wall
to sing "Comfortably Numb" while in another corner
Roger Waters sat in a living room which materialised
out of the wall drinking beer and watching television.
The MC reappeared to repeat his introduction in a
slowed down mechanical fashion while the road crew
set up a back line in front of the wall and a whole
new lighting rig descended from the ceiling. But this
time it was the real Floyd in front of the wall and
they got down to some serious playing while the pig,
an old friend from the last tour, glided above gazing
down with cross-eyed searchlights. It took this touch
of pork to induce some unaccustomed warmth into
Waters demeanour and he asked if "you still like our
pig?" The Scarfe/Floydian school of acid eroticism had
itself one more fling before the wall finally crumbled
and Waters marched the entire ensemble across the
debris Pied Piper style. Without necessarily being a
breakthrough, it's the most ambitious spectacle so far
attempted under the auspices of rock and roll.'
It was reported that cartoonist/designer Gerald
Scarfe had 10 of his original pieces of artwork for
The Wall stolen from their glass frames in the foyer
of the Earl's Court arena in the early hours of Sunday
10 August. Insurers put a price tag of more than
£30,000 on the drawings and paintings one of which
was the original artwork for the cover of *The Wall*
album.

1981

THE WALL PERFORMED LIVE

PINK FLOYD ROAD CREW THROUGH 1981
Marc Brickman: Lighting Designer
Mark Fisher: Set Design & Effects
Seth Goldman: Monitor Sound Engineer
Pat Griffiths: Wardrobe

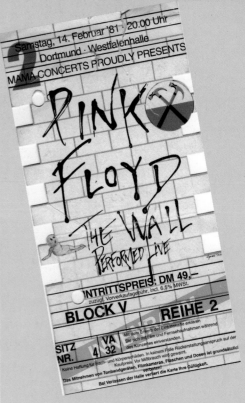

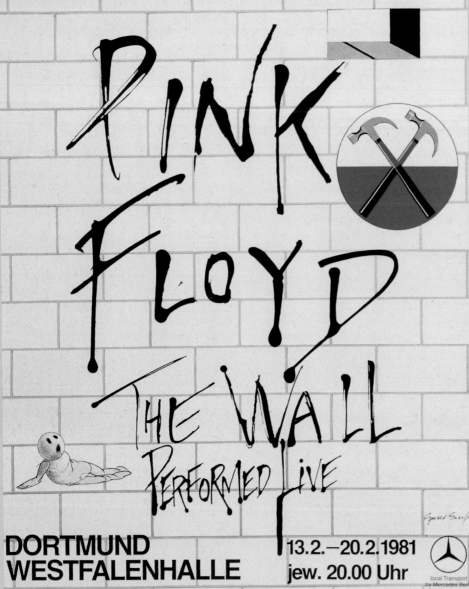

236

Friday 13, Saturday 14, Sunday 15, Monday 16, Tuesday 17, Wednesday 18, Thursday 19 & Friday 20 February

CONCERTS

Westfalenhalle, Dortmund, West Germany

Set list at all eight shows: 'In The Flesh' / 'The Thin Ice' / 'Another Brick In The Wall, Part 1' / 'The Happiest Days Of Our Lives' / 'Another Brick In The Wall, Part 2' / 'Mother' / 'Goodbye Blue Sky' / 'What Shall We Do Now?' / 'Empty Spaces' / 'Young Lust' / 'One Of My Turns' / 'Don't Leave Me Now' / 'Another Brick In The Wall, Part 3' / 'The Last Few Bricks' / 'Goodbye Cruel World' // 'Hey You' / 'Is There Anybody Out There?' / 'Nobody Home' / 'Vera' / 'Bring The Boys Back Home' / 'Comfortably Numb' / 'The Show Must Go On' / 'In The Flesh?' / 'Run Like Hell' / 'Waiting For The Worms' / 'Stop' / 'The Trial' / 'Outside The Wall'.

German ARD network TV filmed this show and a segment of 'The Happiest Days Of Our Lives' was featured in a news item broadcast at a later date.

THE WALL PERFORMED LIVE

ADDITIONAL TOUR PERSONNEL

Musician:

Richard Wright: Keyboards, Vocals

The Surrogate Band:

Andy Bown: Bass Guitar

Andy Roberts: Guitars

Willie Wilson: Drums

Peter Woods: Keyboards

Backing Vocals:

Joe Chemay

Stan Farber

Jim Haas

John Joyce

Master of Ceremonies:

Gary Yudman: All shows

James Guthrie: Front of House Sound Engineer

Rick Hart: PA Technician

Don Jole: Special Effects

Jonathan Park: Set Design & Effects

Rocky Paulson: Special Effects

Andy Shields: Projectionist

Nigel Taylor: PA Technician

Phil Taylor: Backline Technician

Mick Treadwell: Special Effects

Greg Walsh: PA Technician

Robbie Williams: Head of PA

ADDITIONAL TOUR PERSONNEL

Musician:

Richard Wright: Keyboards, Vocals

The Surrogate Band:

Andy Bown: Bass Guitar

Andy Roberts: Guitars

Willie Wilson: Drums

Peter Woods: Keyboards

Backing Vocals:

Joe Chemay

Stan Farber

Jim Haas

John Joyce

Master of Ceremonies:

Wili Tomsik: All shows

Saturday 13, Sunday 14, Monday 15, Tuesday 16, Wednesday 17 & Thursday 18 June 1981
CONCERTS
Earl's Court Exhibition Hall, Earl's Court, London, England
Set list at all six shows: 'In The Flesh' / 'The Thin Ice' / 'Another Brick In The Wall, Part 1' / 'The Happiest Days Of Our Lives' / 'Another Brick In The Wall, Part 2' / 'Mother' / 'Goodbye Blue Sky' / 'What Shall We Do Now?' / 'Empty Spaces' / 'Young Lust' / 'One Of My Turns' / 'Don't Leave Me Now' / 'Another Brick In The Wall, Part 3' / 'The Last Few Bricks' / 'Goodbye Cruel World' // 'Hey You' / 'Is There Anybody Out There?' / 'Nobody Home' / 'Vera' / 'Bring The Boys Back Home' / 'Comfortably Numb' / 'The Show Must Go On' / 'In The Flesh?' / 'Run Like Hell' / 'Waiting For The Worms' / 'Stop' / 'The Trial' / 'Outside The Wall'. The show of the 17 June marked the last night of the tour, and significantly, the last time Waters would

play with Pink Floyd for some 24 years.
It was reported in the music press that second drummer Willie Wilson was taken ill just before the opening show. Clive Brooks, a Floyd roadie who happened to also be a former drummer of The Groundhogs, was given a crash-course in the set's requirements by Nick Mason who replaced Wilson for that one concert.

September
FILMING
Pinewood Film Studios, Iver Heath, England
Production filming began here with Alan Parker on the film *Pink Floyd The Wall* and continued throughout the year and at various locations in London including the Royal Horticultural Society Hall, Victoria, London (for the rally), The Keighley & Worth Valley Railway, Yorkshire (for the steam railway scenes) and Saunton Sands, Devon (for the Anzio beach-head battlefield scenes).

Monday 23 November
RECORD RELEASE
A Collection Of Great Dance Songs
UK album release. US album release on Saturday 21 November.
NME commented that: 'Exactly what form of body movement goes with Pink Floyd is anyone's guess – that slow, steady, rocking motion that you see in people falling asleep on buses I should think.'

1982–1985

1982

Monday 26 July
RECORD RELEASE
'When The Tigers Broke Free' / 'Bring The Boys Back Home'
UK and US 7-inch single releases.

Sunday 23 May
FILM PREMIERE
35th Festival International Du Film, Palais des Festivals, Cannes, France
The world premiere of the film *Pink Floyd The Wall* was held at this prestigious annual film festival although it was not entered into the competition.

July – December
RECORDING SESSIONS
Mayfair Studios, London, England; Olympic Studios, London, England; EMI Abbey Road Studios, London, England; Eel Pie Studios, London, England; Audio International, London, England; RAK Studios, London, England; Hookend Studios, London, England & The Billiard Room Studios, London, England
Discontinuous recording and mixing for the album *The Final Cut*.

1983

Monday 21 March
RECORD RELEASE
The Final Cut
UK album release. US album release on Saturday 2

April 1983.
NME commented that: 'No matter how much Waters may burn and struggle over the sad, sick world he finds himself in along with the rest of us, his diagnoses sit in a stasis of unresolved, unmoving bitterness. Underneath the whimpering meditation and exasperated cries of rage it is the old, familiar rock beast: a man who is unhappy in his work.'

Wednesday 23 March
PRESS RECEPTION
Madison Square Garden, Manhattan, New York City, New York, USA
Columbia Records held a reception in one of the function suites at this venue to launch *The Final Cut* to the US media.

Tuesday 3 May
RECORD RELEASE
'Not Now John' / 'The Hero's Return (Parts 1 & 2)'
UK 7-inch single release.
'Not Now John' (single version) / 'The Hero's Return (Parts 1 & 2)' / 'Not Now John' (album version)
UK 12-inch single release.
Sounds commented that: 'The dinosaur roars, part 365. More crushing misery from Roger Waters and the boys executed with all the consummate skill of Hadean craftsmen.'

Monday 18 June
RECORD RELEASE
Works
US album release.

1984

Pink Floyd were inactive during 1984.

1985

October
PRESS RELEASE
London, England
Roger Waters issued a High Court application to prevent the Pink Floyd name ever being used again considering it to be a spent force. Thus began a bitter legal dispute as Gilmour prepared to defend this action. Shortly afterwards Roger Waters terminated his contract with both EMI and CBS Records invoking his 'leaving member' clause. A year later the case was finally heard.

PINK FLOYD
(October 1985 – January 1994)
David Gilmour: Guitar, Vocals
Nick Mason: Drums

IN PRODUCTION PRES

PINK FLOYD
***
UPPER PRESS BOX

PONTIAC SILVERDOME
NOV. 10, 1987 9:0

9

SS BOX   COMP

GEN   ADMCA
ROW   SEAT

CN 31361.

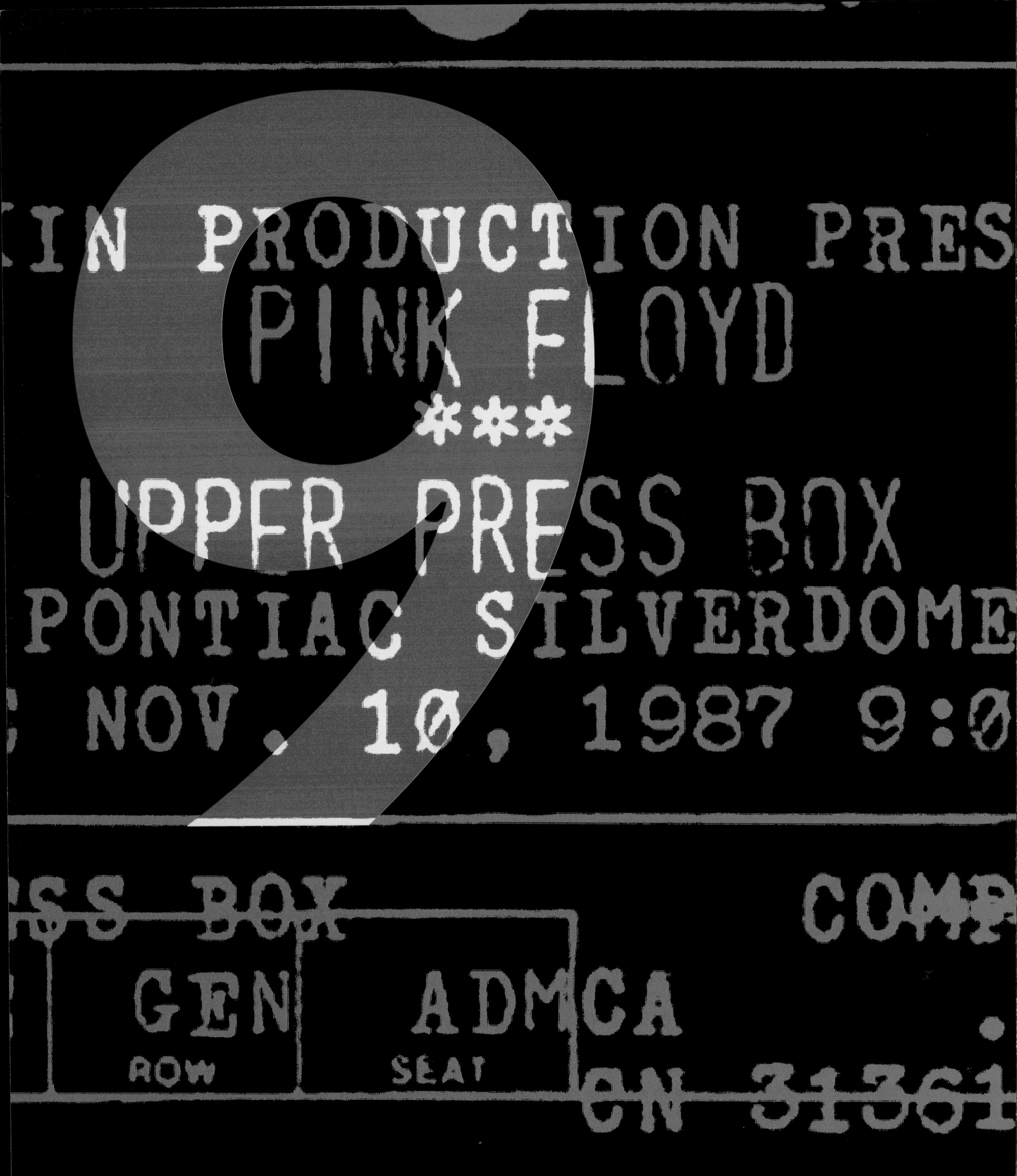

a new machine

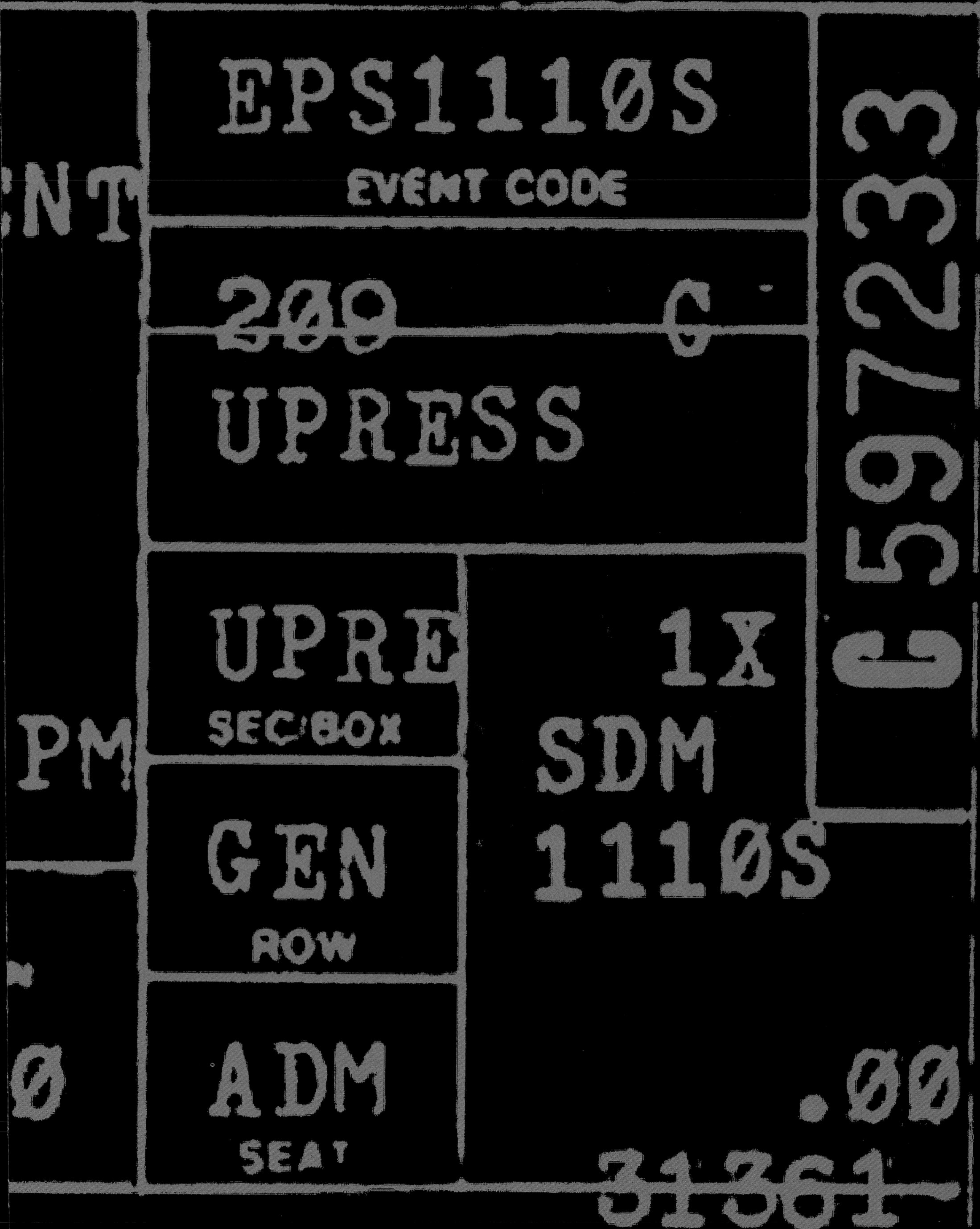

EPS1110S

EVENT CODE

CNT

200   G

UPRESS

UPRE

SEC·BOX

PM

GEN

ROW

1X

SDM

1110S

ADM

SEAT

0

.00

31361

C 5972233

1986 – 1993

UNBEKNOWN TO THE GENERAL PUBLIC, TECHNICALLY, WATERS HAD DISMISSED HIMSELF FROM PINK FLOYD IN LATE 1985, AFTER HIS *FINAL PROS AND CONS OF HITCH-HIKING* TOUR. HE HAD ISSUED A STATEMENT TO EMI AND CBS RECORDS INVOKING HIS 'LEAVING MEMBER' CLAUSE ON THEIR CONTRACT SAYING THAT HE CONSIDERED THE BAND A 'SPENT FORCE' AND THAT HE WOULDN'T RECORD WITH GILMOUR AND MASON EVER AGAIN, OR WITH ANYONE ELSE AS PINK FLOYD. WHEN HE DECLARED THIS HE HAD APPARENTLY NOT BELIEVED THAT THE OTHERS HAD THE NECESSARY QUALITIES TO CARRY ON UNDER THE NAME.

He was wrong. Gilmour did not accept it could be Waters sole decision to dissolve a band he had been a member of for some 17 years, and called his bluff. Waters had to concede: 'They threatened me with the fact that we had a contract with CBS Records and that part of the contract could be construed to mean that we had a product commitment with CBS and if we didn't go on producing product, they could a) sue us and b) withhold royalties if we didn't make any more records. So they said, "that's what the record company are going to do and the rest of the band are going to sue you for all their legal expenses and any loss of earnings because you're the one that's preventing the band from making any more records." They forced me to resign from the band because, if I hadn't, the financial repercussions would have wiped me out completely.'[1]

Even then Waters could not have expected the others to carry on without him. However, about a year later, at a routine board meeting of Pink Floyd Music Limited, he learnt that Gilmour and Mason were about to open a new bank account to pay out and receive money on what was being termed 'the new Pink Floyd project'. He was outraged, and in a much-publicised chain of events, including plenty of mud slinging, he claimed that the group was defunct and that Gilmour and Mason's pursuit, with or without his involvement, of any further projects was simply not acceptable.

As a result, Waters instigated High Court proceedings to legally determine the nature of the Pink Floyd partnership. Therefore, on 31 October 1986, exactly twenty years after the band had first entered a recording studio, there began a court case which, Waters hoped, would uphold his belief that, since he had written the bulk of its songs, he was entitled to prevent others' commercial exploitation of the name 'Pink Floyd'.

Within days, every British national newspaper was carrying headlines saying that Pink Floyd had split up, but Gilmour and Mason countered with a statement issued by their record company, saying 'Pink Floyd are alive, and well, and recording in England', which gave some hope to fans at the same time as increasing their puzzlement and that of the media.

For his part, Gilmour reluctantly countered Waters' legal action. Speaking to Nicky Horne on London's Capital Radio in early 1987, he said: 'I think it's rather unnecessary. There's been many, many years together when we have achieved a lot together, and it's a shame when anyone wants to leave of course. But, everyone has to do what they want to do, and of course that's their decision. What is sad and unnecessary about it is trying to prevent anyone else from carrying on with their legitimate artistic and business endeavours.'

Waters eventually dropped his legal action, conceding that Gilmour could continue to use the name 'Pink Floyd'. As Gilmour explained: 'The situation is that Virgin wanted to release his soundtrack [Waters' *When The Wind Blows*] and in order to do so, EMI made him sign a piece of paper on the case saying, essentially, if you want to put this soundtrack out on another label, not to interfere with Pink Floyd being Pink Floyd, or pursue any activities in the name of Pink Floyd – which Roger signed and agreed to.'[2] The mutual sniping continued throughout the next few years but the two parties agreed terms on their business affairs at a meeting on Gilmour's houseboat studio, Astoria, on 23 December 1987.

Meanwhile, Gilmour and Mason, who had been recording together since the autumn of 1986, had long been convinced that a new album was a better idea than just taking a greatest hits show out on the road. It was a shrewd gamble and, although over the next few months the going was tough, the result was an album that became a worldwide success. *A Momentary Lapse Of Reason*, the recording of which was completed in March 1987, followed by three months post-production in Los Angeles, was released in September of that year. The album was mainly recorded at Gilmour's River Thames studio houseboat Astoria, with Bob Ezrin producing (much to Waters' consternation, since he had hoped Ezrin would work on his own *Radio KAOS* album for him). Significantly, it was the first Pink Floyd album in some fourteen years that didn't follow a conceptual path.

Not that a concept album wasn't attempted. Eric Stewart, formerly of 10cc, had been drawn in via Nick Mason's second solo album, and recalled: 'Dave Gilmour and I got together around August or September 1986 to work on a concept that was definitely intended for the next Pink Floyd album. We sat around writing for a period of time, but we couldn't get the different elements to gel. The songwriting itself was acceptable in certain parts, but not as a whole, so the concept was eventually scrapped.'[3]

Also drafted in were the English poet Roger McGough and Canadian songwriter Carole Pope. 'The idea to contact me came from Bob Ezrin,' explained Pope. 'It was January 1987, and they were looking for somebody to rewrite a batch of Dave Gilmour's material, so I went over to England for a few weeks to lend assistance. Bob and David asked me if I had suggestions for concept albums in the Pink Floyd style. By the time I left England in February, they still couldn't decide what to do.'[4]

Eventually, however, the idea of a concept album was abandoned in favour of a conventional approach, with songs not linked thematically. Gilmour, who selected musicians whom he had met in recent years to help complete *A Momentary Lapse Of Reason,* had become a respected session player and had performed at many charity events including *Live Aid* (where he was the only Floyd member in attendance), and *The Secret Policeman's Ball.*

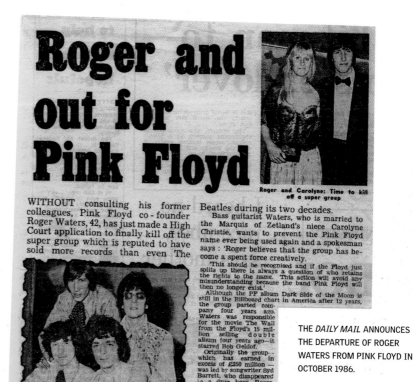

Roger and out for Pink Floyd

WITHOUT consulting his former colleagues, Pink Floyd co-founder Roger Waters, 42, has just made a High Court application to finally kill off the super group which is reputed to have sold more records than even The Beatles during its two decades.

Bass guitarist Waters, who is married to the Marquis of Zetland's niece Carolyne Christie, wants to prevent the Pink Floyd name ever being used again and a spokesman says: 'Roger believes that the group has become a spent force creatively.

'This should be recognised and if the Floyd just splits up there is always a question of who retains the rights to the name. This action will avoid any misunderstanding because the band Pink Floyd will then no longer exist.'

Although the PF album Dark Side of the Moon is still in the Billboard chart in America after 12 years, the group parted company four years ago. Waters was responsible for the movie The Wall from the Floyd's 15 million selling double album four years ago—it starred Bob Geldof.

Originally the group—which has earned in excess of £250 million—was led by songwriter Syd Barrett, who disappeared in a drug haze. Roger, guitarist David Gilmour, keyboard Rick Wright and drummer Nick Mason. It is not clear if any of the others will defend the court action.

Roger and Carolyne: Time to kill off a super group

Pink Floyd in the pink. Back: Roger Waters and Syd Barrett. Front: Nick Mason and Rick Wright

THE *DAILY MAIL* ANNOUNCES THE DEPARTURE OF ROGER WATERS FROM PINK FLOYD IN OCTOBER 1986.

As for Rick Wright, the chance to return to the fold was very welcome, particularly since he had all but given up playing, his confidence, like Mason's, having been shattered during Waters' rule. For legal reasons, however, Wright couldn't officially rejoin the band and, in any case, the album was almost complete by the time he rejoined Gilmour and Mason.

When *A Momentary Lapse Of Reason* appeared, much of Waters' expected criticism focused on the amount of supporting musicians used, which infuriated Gilmour: 'Roger never used to credit anyone. Yet he was always fussy about the credit for himself. I never had the

DAVID GILMOUR << Roger never used to credit anyone. Yet he was always fussy about the credit for himself. I never had the time to worry about it, that sort of thing. >>

time to worry about it, that sort of thing. On *Animals* for instance Roger took the credits for everything. Let's say that I wrote 70% of "Sheep". At least half of that album I played bass on and Roger was hardly in the studio during its recording. I played bass on almost all of the Pink Floyd albums, which is where Roger forgets that

other people had huge, vast amounts of input, but at the time I never worried, so long as the product was completed. On *The Wall* there was a song that Bob Ezrin never got credited for, "Is There Anybody Out There?", Roger never credited him for that."[5]

The album came over as a strange cross between the cold and sterile aspects of *Wish You Were Here* and the bleakness of *Animals*. Although it's basically a dolled-up Gilmour solo album, as a first effort with a new line-up, it is an accomplished piece. At the least it offered a chance for the post-Waters band to gain self-confidence and start touring again, in addition to recording. The artwork saw Storm Thorgerson returning to the fold once more. He turned Gilmour's 'visions of empty beds' lyric into an arrangement of some 800 old hospital beds lined up on Saunton Sands beach in Devon as the basis for the cover shot. Additional artwork was also provided for the ensuing singles, tour programme, promo videos and tour backdrop films, completing the overall theme.

In order to make the comeback complete in this respect, Gilmour wanted to recreate the spectacle of the world-renowned Pink Floyd shows with a breathtaking production. With Mason (who used his valuable 1962 GTO Ferrari as security), they invested several millions of their personal wealth into the project.

Finding a promoter willing to take on an almost equal risk without knowing Pink Floyd's pulling power was likely to be a harder task than they first imagined since they had been redundant for so long. It had been over six years since the band had given a nationwide tour in either Europe or America and in addition, Waters' absence and legal threat was always going to be at the forefront of their minds. But for Michael Cohl, of the CPI Agency in Canada, who was about to have a similar success with The Rolling Stones, there was little doubt about their potential, and undaunted he took the band on.

Cohl's complete confidence was proven when on 27 April 1987, tickets went on sale for a single show at the CNE Stadium in Toronto on 21 September. The result was that all 60,000 tickets went as fast as they could be printed, resulting in the fastest sell-out in the history of the venue. Hardly believing it, he put a second show on sale, with exactly the same result, then a third show, which was also a sell-out, thus securing a gross income of over US$3 million.

In no time at all local promoters across North America were queuing up to take on the show, well before the album was released to radio or the public, and a massive tour was set in motion to run until the end of the year. In almost every location box-office records fell,

making it the most successful US tour, by any band, that year.

To further complicate matters, Waters, who was still attempting to obstruct his former band mates at every turn, issued a threat of legal action to any promoter if they dared put a Pink Floyd show on sale. Heavyweight US promoters aren't easily discouraged, but Gilmour and Mason played it safe by having a team of expert lawyers on hand at every city they played in.

The bankability of the name Pink Floyd had become increasingly apparent, and the tour simply snowballed. Tours of Australia, Japan, Europe and the UK followed, with two more tours of the US thrown in for good measure, and the band sold out at almost every venue.

For Waters, by contrast, the going was tough. He had released *Radio KAOS* slightly ahead of *A Momentary Lapse Of Reason* and decided to tour the US simultaneously. Whereas his former band mates succeeded in selling out huge auditoria, he was struggling to pull a crowd even a third of the size. Overall, however, fans benefited from seeing and hearing twice as much Floyd music as they had anticipated, and a strong debate raged between hardcore fans over who was the rightful heir to the name. Waters fuelled much of this by having T-shirts printed for his tour with the defiant motif 'Which One's Pink?' emblazoned on the front. Even the media were confused. The only certainty was that Pink Floyd's success was enduring, if baffling – a twenty-year-old rock band outstripping any other artist for sales and concert attendances the world over.

Putting Pink Floyd on the road was another matter entirely. A great deal had happened in the world of stadium touring, from stage designs through to PA and lighting technology, since they had last hit the road and a massive investment had to be made to bring the show up to and beyond the fans' expectations. The Fisher-Park design team declined to design the stage-show, favouring the confines of Waters' *Radio KAOS*, and the task was given to theatre set designer Paul Staples and *The Wall* lighting man Marc Brickman. Whereas in Waters' day the band had employed a handful of technicians, a crew of about 200 was now required to maintain three separate stages which leap-frogged across continents to keep the show moving.

The concerts themselves incorporated many of the old trademarks: the giant circular film-screen displayed much of the vintage footage, a flowering mirror ball, green and red lasers and over a hundred other lights. All of this was housed within a vast steel framework, which measured some eighty feet high, a hundred and sixty-

FAR LEFT: PINK FLOYD'S SPECTACULAR STAGE SHOW REACHES MADISON SQUARE GARDEN, NEW YORK, OCTOBER 1987.

eight feet wide and ninety-eight feet deep. Suspended from this were 'pods' of lights and smoke machines attached to four moving units that were suspended from tracks above the stage, as well as smaller 'Floyd Droids', as they became known, reminiscent of R2-D2 in *Star*

DAVID GILMOUR **<< We wanted to leave no one in any doubt that we were still in business and meant business – and no one was going to stop us. >>**

Wars, that rose from the stage to throw out light into the audience. Quadraphonic sound was also used with some 240 speaker units making up the system, a crashing aeroplane during 'On The Run' (later replaced by a crashing bed to make further use of the tour motif), an inflatable pig and a strange winged creature that launched skywards in 'Learning To Fly'.

It all made for a visually striking comeback, so much so that many reports suggested that the spectacle distracted from the music, which combined old and new. It came as a huge surprise that 'Echoes' opened the show, albeit only in the early concerts, followed by selections of the new album in the first half and a 'greatest hits' package in the second. The only frustrating aspect was that the set list remained unchanged throughout the tour, despite a rich heritage of numbers to choose from.

On 22 November 1988, after the US tour, Pink

Floyd released an album derived from recordings made at their New York concerts. *Delicate Sound Of Thunder* also appeared as a video, in June the following year, and acted as a promotional tool for the current round of European dates.

A few days after the album's release, Gilmour and Mason accompanied President François Mitterrand of France to the Baykonur Cosmodrome, in Kazakstan, USSR, to attend the launch of the Soyuz-7 space rocket, which was piloted by a Franco-Soviet crew. The cosmonauts had requested a cassette of the album to listen to when they rendezvoused with the orbiting MIR station. Pink Floyd thus made history as the first rock band to be played in space.

The comeback tour finally came to its official conclusion with a one-off show at Knebworth Park, north of London, in September 1990. There had been some 200 shows, attracting over 4.25 million fans and taking more than £60 million at the box office alone (merchandising revenues were separate). It certainly rammed the point home to a retreating Waters. Gilmour later summed up their return quite simply: 'We wanted to leave no one in any doubt that we were still in business and meant business – and no one was going to stop us.'[6]

Completing the reunion, Wright was now playing full time with the band. In this role he contributed substantially to the soundtrack for Gilmour, Mason and O'Rourke's self-produced film of their vintage motor-car racing exploits across Mexico, *La Carrera Panamericana*, which was released on video in April 1992.

RIGHT AND FAR RIGHT: NICK MASON AND DAVID GILMOUR PERFORMING AT THE NEWLY OPENED LONDON ARENA ON 8 JULY 1989. DESPITE A SELL-OUT RUN OF SIX NIGHTS, PINK FLOYD'S CHOICE OF VENUE WAS POORLY RECEIVED BY FANS AND CRITICS ALIKE.

Sources
1. *Uncut*, June 2004
2. Author's interview with David Gilmour 25 September 1987
3-4. *Rock Lives*, Timothy White, Henry Holt 1990
5. Author's interview with David Gilmour 25 September 1987
6. *Q Magazine*, September 1990

1986

Friday 31 October
PRESS RELEASE
London, England
Proceedings began in the High Court, London on this day that were brought about by Roger Waters in order to legally determine the nature of the Pink Floyd partnership in order to seek its dissolution. Waters eventually dropped the action and both David Gilmour with Nick Mason began work on a new Pink Floyd album.

November – December
RECORDING SESSIONS
The Astoria, Hampton, England & Britannia Row Studios, Islington, London, England
Discontinuous recording for the album *A Momentary Lapse Of Reason*.

1987

January – February
RECORDING SESSIONS
The Astoria, Hampton, England & Britannia Row Studios, Islington, London, England
Discontinuous recording for the album *A Momentary Lapse Of Reason*.

February
RECORDING SESSIONS
Mayfair Studios, Primrose Hill, London, England & Audio International Studios, London, England
Discontinuous recording and mixing for the album *A Momentary Lapse Of Reason*.

February - March
RECORDING SESSIONS
A&M Studios, Los Angeles, USA; Village Recorder, Los Angeles, USA & Can Am Studios, Los Angeles, USA
Discontinuous recording and mixing for the album *A Momentary Lapse Of Reason*.

A MOMENTARY LAPSE OF REASON – NORTH AMERICAN TOUR

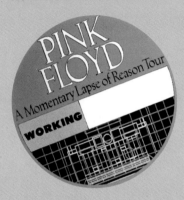

PINK FLOYD CORE ROAD CREW THROUGH TO 1988
Marc Brickman: Lighting Designer
Seth Goldman: Monitor Sound Engineer
Howard Hopkins: Stage Manager
Buford Jones: Front of House Sound Engineer
Morris Lyda: Production Manager
Phil Taylor: Backline Chief
Robbie Williams: Production Director

Since Pink Floyd's last stadium tour of 1977, where the band would have employed a core crew of around 20 persons, the touring machine had taken on a whole new dimension in sound, lighting and set design. To keep up with this demand stadium tours now carried crews in excess of 200 personnel including personal security, instrument technicians, sound and lighting technicians, laser technicians, pyrotechnicians, projectionists, caterers and even wardrobe assistants. All this and not including the truck and bus drivers, site co-ordinators, scaffolders, electricians, riggers and even carpenters and a whole host of peripheral crew members involved with the various contractors and companies providing all manner of technical equipment as well as the backroom staff developing and modifying equipment for specific use, managers and accountants. If you really must know all of their names for this and all subsequent Pink Floyd tours, please consult the tour programmes!

ADDITIONAL TOUR PERSONNEL TO 3 NOVEMBER 1987
Jon Carin: Keyboards and vocals
Rachel Fury: Backing vocals

Scott Page: Saxophones and guitars
Guy Pratt: Bass guitar and vocals
Tim Renwick: Guitars
Margaret Taylor: Backing vocals
Gary Wallis: Percussion
Richard Wright: Keyboards and vocals

August
REHEARSALS
Lester B. Pearson International Airport, Toronto, Ontario, Canada
Pink Floyd made four weeks' use of a bonded warehouse, at a reported cost of $70,000, to rehearse their stage show. A huge flying saucer, hovering over the audience's heads, was intended to have been a feature of the special effects for the outdoor shows, but insurance difficulties prevented its use.

Monday 7 September
CANCELLED CONCERT
Buffalo Memorial Auditorium, Buffalo, New York, USA
Show cancelled from initial tour schedule for unknown reasons - no tickets ever went on sale.

Monday 7 September
RECORD RELEASE
A Momentary Lapse Of Reason
UK album release. US album release on Tuesday 8 September.
Q Magazine commented that: '*A Momentary Lapse Of Reason* is Gilmour's album to much the same degree that the previous four under Floyd's name were dominated by Waters (Mason's probably glad just to be along for the ride). Clearly it wasn't only business sense and repressed ego but repressed talent which drove the guitarist to insist on continuing under the band brand name.'

Wednesday 9 September
CONCERT
Lansdowne Park Stadium, Lansdowne Park, Ottawa, Ontario, Canada
Set list: 'Echoes' / 'Signs Of Life' / 'Learning To Fly' / 'Yet Another Movie' / 'Round And Around' / 'A New Machine, Part 1' / 'Terminal Frost' / 'A New Machine, Part 2' / 'Sorrow' / 'The Dogs Of War' / 'On The Turning Away' // 'One Of These Days' / 'Time' / 'On The Run' / 'Wish You Were Here' / 'Welcome To The Machine' / 'Us And Them' / 'Money' / 'Another Brick In The Wall, Part 2' / 'Comfortably Numb' / encore: 'One Slip' / 'Run Like Hell'.
The Canadian Press reported that: 'Pink Floyd opened its world tour before about 25,000 fans Wednesday night with a multi-media extravaganza that soared during older songs, but bogged down on new material that made the absence of Roger Waters glaringly obvious. From the beginning, guitarist David Gilmour,

drummer Nick Mason and keyboardist Richard Wright did not set out at Lansdowne Park to prove the new Pink Floyd was better than the old one. In fact, except for the sheer timelessness of songs like "Money", it teetered perilously close to being an anachronism. For all its new hi-tech toys, the 21 year-old British band is rooted firmly in the days of space-rock and psychedelic light shows. It even opened with "Echoes" - a 17-minute epic instrumental that featured enough fog to blanket a small airport. The trio - augmented by a seven-member band - made no mention of Waters, who is on a solo tour and performing many Floyd songs. As an entertainment, it was a vintage spectacular; a comfortably numb experience enhanced by visual treats and pleasant 19 degree temperatures. For its first public performance in about five years, and first without Waters, the band trotted out many of the favourite tricks from its 1970's shows like the giant inflated pig. And the plane. A replica flew across the football stadium on a guide wire and crashed beside the mammoth stage. Lighting modules descended from the ceiling like flying saucers. Voices and sound effects made heads turn sharply at the back of the stadium where additional speakers were set up as part of the band's quadraphonic sound system. But the band needs help. Except for Gilmour none of the musicians displayed much flash and everyone stands almost still. Many new songs are best described as droning dirges where the excitement is waiting for the monumental chord change. During the hour-long opening set, the aisles were busy with bored fans. Clearly everyone was waiting for the old stuff. It mesmerised those fans who consider a Pink Floyd concert the ultimate concert experience - especially on various recreational and industrial-strength drugs. In the end, the band delivered just what the fans wanted. Pink Floyd is no longer a leading creative entity, but as entertainment, a Floyd concert is still an aural and visual treat that any rock fan shouldn't miss.'

Saturday 12, Sunday 13, Monday 14 September
CONCERTS
Forum de Montréal, Montréal, Quebec, Canada
Set list at all three shows: 'Echoes' / 'Signs Of Life' / 'Learning To Fly' / 'Yet Another Movie' / 'Round And Around' / 'A New Machine, Part 1' / 'Terminal Frost' / 'A New Machine, Part 2' / 'Sorrow' / 'The Dogs Of War' / 'On The Turning Away' // 'One Of These Days' / 'Time' / 'On The Run' / 'Wish You Were Here' / 'Welcome To The Machine' / 'Us And Them' / 'Money' / 'Another Brick In The Wall, Part 2' / 'Comfortably Numb' / encore: 'One Slip' / 'Run Like Hell' / second encore: 'Shine On You Crazy Diamond, Parts 1-5'.

Monday 14 September
RECORD RELEASE
'Learning To Fly' (edit) / 'Terminal Frost'
US 7-inch single release.

Wednesday 16 September
CONCERT
Municipal Stadium, Cleveland, Ohio, USA
Set list: 'Echoes' / 'Signs Of Life' / 'Learning To Fly' / 'Yet Another Movie' / 'Round And Around' / 'A New Machine, Part 1' / 'Terminal Frost' / 'A New Machine, Part 2' / 'Sorrow' / 'The Dogs Of War' / 'On The Turning Away' // 'One Of These Days' / 'Time' / 'On The Run' / 'Wish You Were Here' / 'Welcome To The Machine' / 'Us And Them' / 'Money' / 'Another Brick In The Wall, Part 2' / 'Comfortably Numb' / encore: 'One Slip' / 'Run Like Hell' / second encore: 'Shine On You Crazy Diamond, Parts 1-5'.

Thursday 17 September
CONCERT
Municipal Stadium, Cleveland, Ohio, USA
Set list: 'Echoes' / 'Signs Of Life' / 'Learning To Fly' / 'Yet Another Movie' / 'Round And Around' / 'A New Machine, Part 1' / 'Terminal Frost' / 'A New Machine, Part 2' / 'Sorrow' / 'The Dogs Of War' / 'On The Turning Away' // 'One Of These Days' / 'Time' / 'On The Run' / 'Wish You Were Here' / 'Welcome To The Machine' / 'Us And Them' / 'Money' / 'Another Brick In The Wall, Part 2' / 'Comfortably Numb' / encore: 'One Slip' / 'Run Like Hell'.

Saturday 19 September
CONCERT
John F. Kennedy Stadium, Philadelphia, Pennsylvania, USA
Set list: 'Echoes' / 'Signs Of Life' / 'Learning To Fly' / 'Yet Another Movie' / 'Round And Around' / 'A New Machine, Part 1' / 'Terminal Frost' / 'A New Machine, Part 2' / 'Sorrow' / 'The Dogs Of War' / 'On The Turning Away' // 'One Of These Days' / 'Time' / 'On The Run' / 'Wish You Were Here' / 'Welcome To The Machine' / 'Us And Them' / 'Money' / 'Another Brick In The Wall, Part 2' / 'Comfortably Numb' / encore: 'Run Like Hell' / second encore: 'Shine On You Crazy Diamond, Parts 1-5'.

Monday 21, Tuesday 22, Wednesday 23 September
CONCERTS
Canadian National Exhibition Stadium, Toronto, Ontario, Canada
Set list at all three shows: 'Echoes' / 'Signs Of Life' / 'Learning To Fly' / 'Yet Another Movie' / 'Round And Around' / 'A New Machine, Part 1' / 'Terminal Frost' / 'A New Machine, Part 2' / 'Sorrow' / 'The Dogs Of War' / 'On The Turning Away' // 'One Of These Days' / 'Time' / 'On The Run' / 'Wish You Were Here' / 'Welcome To The Machine' / 'Us And Them' / 'Money' / 'Another Brick In The Wall, Part 2' / 'Comfortably Numb' / encore: 'One Slip' / 'Run Like Hell' / second encore: 'Shine On You Crazy Diamond, Parts 1-5'.

Friday 25 September
CONCERT
Rosemont Horizon, Rosemont, Chicago, Illinois, USA
Set list: 'Echoes' / 'Signs Of Life' / 'Learning To Fly' / 'Yet Another Movie' / 'Round And Around' / 'A New Machine, Part 1' / 'Terminal Frost' / 'A New Machine, Part 2' / 'Sorrow' / 'The Dogs Of War' / 'On The Turning Away' // 'One Of These Days' / 'Time' / 'On The Run' / 'Wish You Were Here' / 'Welcome To The Machine' / 'Us And Them' / 'Money' / 'Another Brick In The Wall, Part 2' / 'Comfortably Numb' / encore: 'One Slip' / 'Run Like Hell'.

Saturday 26, Sunday 27 & Monday 28 September
CONCERTS
Rosemont Horizon, Rosemont, Chicago, Illinois, USA
Set list at all three shows and all remaining shows on this tour: 'Shine On You Crazy Diamond, Parts 1-5' / 'Signs Of Life' / 'Learning To Fly' / 'Yet Another Movie' / 'Round And Around' / 'A New Machine, Part 1' / 'Terminal Frost' / 'A New Machine, Part 2' / 'Sorrow' / 'The Dogs Of War' / 'On The Turning Away' // 'One Of These Days' / 'Time' / 'On The Run' / 'Wish You Were Here' / 'Welcome To The Machine' / 'Us And Them' / 'Money' / 'Another Brick In The Wall, Part 2' / 'Comfortably Numb' / encore: 'One Slip' / 'Run Like Hell'.

Wednesday 30 September
CONCERT
County Stadium, Milwaukee, Wisconsin, USA
The show featured, for the last time, a crashing replica World War II German Stuka dive-bomber hurtling on a wire across the sky for the culmination of the 'On The Run' sequence. Hereafter, the tour motif, a large bed, replaced it. In addition, the huge scaffolding stage carried revolving radar dishes, flashing beacons and radio masts were not present at any of the later shows.

Saturday 3 October
CONCERT
Carrier Dome, Syracuse University, Syracuse, New York, USA

Monday 5, Tuesday 6 & Wednesday 7 October
CONCERTS
Madison Square Garden, Manhattan, New York City, New York, USA

Saturday 10, Sunday 11 & Monday 12 October
CONCERTS
Brendan Byrne Meadowlands Arena, East Rutherford, New Jersey, USA
After the show of 11 October Gilmour, Mason, Scott Page, Rachel Fury, Margaret Taylor, Guy Pratt and Tim Renwick made an impromptu appearance at The World Club in New York, where they performed a 40 minute set of R&B standards.

248

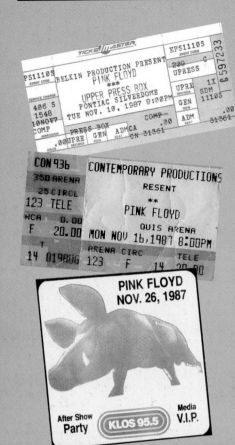

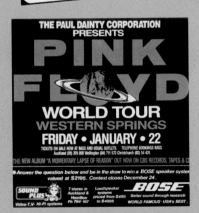

Wednesday 14 & Thursday 15 October
CONCERTS
Hartford Civic Center, Hartford, Connecticut, USA

Friday 16 & Saturday 17 October
CONCERTS
Providence Civic Center, Providence, Rhode Island, USA

Monday 19, Tuesday 20, Wednesday 21 & Thursday 22 October
CONCERTS
Capital Centre, Landover, Maryland, USA

Sunday 25 & Monday 26 October
CONCERTS
Dean E. Smith Student Activities Center, University of North Carolina, Chapel Hill, North Carolina, USA

Friday 30 October
CONCERT
Tampa Stadium, Tampa, Florida, USA

Sunday 1 November
CONCERT
Orange Bowl, Miami, Florida, USA
Heavy rainfall at the concert prevented the inflatable pig from making an appearance at this show.

ADDITIONAL TOUR PERSONNEL THROUGH 1987 - 1988
Jon Carin: Keyboards and vocals
Rachel Fury: Backing vocals
Durga McBroom: Backing vocals
Scott Page: Saxophones and guitars
Guy Pratt: Bass guitar and vocals
Tim Renwick: Guitars
Margaret Taylor: Backing vocals
Gary Wallis: Percussion
Richard Wright: Keyboards and vocals

Tuesday 3, Wednesday 4 & Thursday 5 November
CONCERTS
The Omni Coliseum, Atlanta, Georgia, USA
All three shows were filmed using twenty-three Panavision video cameras for promotional use including videos comprising 'The Dogs Of War', 'On The Turning Away' and 'One Slip' for international use. In addition, tracks from this concert, including 'Run Like Hell', 'The Dogs Of War' and 'On The Turning Away', were used as B-sides of a number of singles. The entire concert film was due to be screened on various European networks, but was withdrawn at the last minute for unknown reasons.

Saturday 7 & Sunday 8 November
CONCERTS
Rupp Arena, Civic Center, Lexington, Kentucky, USA

Tuesday 10 November
CONCERT
Pontiac Silverdome, Pontiac, Detroit, Michigan, USA

Thursday 12 November
CONCERT
Hoosier Dome, Indianapolis, Indiana, USA

Sunday 15 & Monday 16 November
CONCERTS
St. Louis Arena, St. Louis, Missouri, USA

Wednesday 18 November
CONCERT
Astrodome, Houston, Texas, USA

Thursday 19 & Friday 20 November
CONCERTS
Frank Erwin Center, University of Texas, Austin, Texas, USA

Saturday 21, Sunday 22 & Monday 23 November
CONCERTS
Reunion Arena, Reunion Park, Dallas, Texas, USA

Thursday 26, Friday 27, Saturday 28, Sunday 29, Monday 30 November and Tuesday 1 December
CONCERTS
Los Angeles Memorial Sports Arena, Exposition Park, Los Angeles, California, USA

Thursday 3, Friday 4, Saturday 5 & Sunday 6 December
CONCERTS
Oakland Coliseum Arena, Oakland, California, USA

Tuesday 8 December
CONCERT
Kingdome, Seattle, Washington, USA

Thursday 10 & Friday 11 December
CONCERTS
Pacific National Exhibition Coliseum, Vancouver, British Columbia, Canada
The show of the 11 December was the last night of the tour.

Monday 14 December
RECORD RELEASE
'On The Turning Away' / 'Run Like Hell' (live)
UK 7-inch single release. US 7-inch single release on Monday 24 November.
'On The Turning Away' / 'Run Like Hell' (live) / 'On The Turning Away' (live)
UK 12-inch single release.
The live tracks were all recorded at The Omni Coliseum, Atlanta between 3 and 5 November.

1988

A MOMENTARY LAPSE OF REASON - NEW ZEALAND & AUSTRALIAN TOUR

Set list at all shows on this tour: 'Shine On You Crazy Diamond, Parts 1-5' / 'Signs Of Life' / 'Learning To Fly' / 'Yet Another Movie' / 'Round And Around' / 'A New Machine, Part 1' / 'Terminal Frost' / 'A New Machine, Part 2' / 'Sorrow' / 'The Dogs Of War' / 'On The Turning Away' // 'One Of These Days' / 'Time' / 'On The Run' / 'Wish You Were Here' / 'Welcome To The Machine' / 'Us And Them' / 'Money' / 'Another Brick In The Wall, Part 2' / 'Comfortably Numb' / encore: 'One Slip' / 'Run Like Hell'.

Friday 22 January
CONCERT
Western Springs Stadium, Auckland, New Zealand

Wednesday 27, Thursday 28, Friday 29, Saturday 30, Sunday 31 January and Monday 1, Tuesday 2, Wednesday 3, Thursday 4 & Friday 5 February
CONCERTS
Sydney Entertainment Centre, Darling Harbour, Sydney, New South Wales, Australia

Sunday 7 & Monday 8 February
CONCERTS
Entertainment Centre, Boondall, Brisbane, Queensland, Australia

Thursday 11 February
CONCERT
Thebarton Oval, Adelaide, South Australia, Australia

Saturday 13, Sunday 14, Monday 15, Tuesday 16, Wednesday 17, Thursday 18, Friday 19 & Saturday 20 February
CONCERTS
National Tennis Centre, Melbourne, Victoria, Australia
Members of the touring party including David Gilmour, Guy Pratt, Gary Wallis, Tim Renwick, Scott Page, Margaret Taylor, Rachel Fury, Durga McBroom and Jon Carin performed under the name The Fishermen's on 17 February and again on 19 February in after-show gigs at the

Corner Hotel in Richmond, Melbourne to crowds of about 200. The first show also featured the late Roy Buchanan and Seventies Floyd backing vocalist Venetta Fields, who reportedly sang an amazing version of 'Little Red Rooster'. The second show saw The Fishermen's perform a set that included 'Respect', 'I Shot The Sheriff', 'Unchain My Heart', 'Superstition', 'Reeling In The Years', 'Good Lovin' Gone Bad' and 'Pick Up The Pieces'.

Wednesday 24 February
CONCERT
Fremantle Oval, Perth, Western Australia, Australia
The last night of the tour.

A MOMENTARY LAPSE OF REASON - JAPANESE TOUR

Set list at all shows on this tour: 'Shine On You Crazy Diamond, Parts 1-5' / 'Signs Of Life' / 'Learning To Fly' / 'Yet Another Movie' / 'Round And Around' / 'A New Machine, Part 1' / 'Terminal Frost' / 'A New Machine, Part 2' / 'Sorrow' / 'The Dogs Of War' / 'On The Turning Away' // 'One Of These Days' / 'Time' / 'The Great Gig In The Sky' / 'Wish You Were Here' / 'Welcome To The Machine' / 'Us And Them' / 'Money' (extended version) / 'Another Brick In The Wall, Part 2' / 'Comfortably Numb' / encore: 'One Slip' / 'Run Like Hell'.

Wednesday 2 & Thursday 3 March
CONCERTS
Budokan Grand Hall, Tokyo, Japan

Friday 4, Saturday 5 & Sunday 6 March
CONCERTS
Yoyogi Olympic Pool, Tokyo, Japan

Tuesday 8 & Wednesday 9 March
CONCERTS
Joh Hall, Osaka, Japan

Friday 11 March
CONCERT
Rainbow Hall, Nagoya, Japan
The last night of the tour.

A MOMENTARY LAPSE OF REASON - NORTH AMERICAN TOUR

Set list at all shows on this tour: 'Shine On You Crazy Diamond, Parts 1-5' / 'Signs Of Life' / 'Learning To Fly' / 'Yet Another Movie' / 'Round And Around' / 'A New Machine, Part 1' / 'Terminal Frost' / 'A New Machine, Part 2' / 'Sorrow' / 'The Dogs Of War' / 'On The Turning Away' // 'One Of These Days' / 'Time' / 'On The Run' / 'The Great Gig In The Sky' / 'Wish You Were Here' / 'Welcome To The Machine' / 'Us And Them' / 'Money' (extended version) / 'Another Brick In The Wall, Part 2' / 'Comfortably Numb' / encore: 'One Slip' / 'Run Like Hell'.

Friday 15 April
CONCERT
Memorial Coliseum, Los Angeles, California, USA

Monday 18 April
CONCERT
Mile High Stadium, Denver, Colorado, USA

Wednesday 20 April
CONCERT
Hughes Stadium, California State University at Sacramento, California, USA

Friday 22 & Saturday 23 April
CONCERTS
Oakland Coliseum Stadium, Oakland, California, USA

Monday 25 & Tuesday 26 April
CONCERTS
Municipal Stadium, Phoenix, Arizona, USA

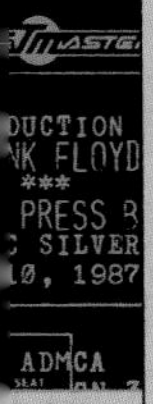
DUCTION
NK FLOYD
PRESS B
C SILVER
10, 1987
ADMCA

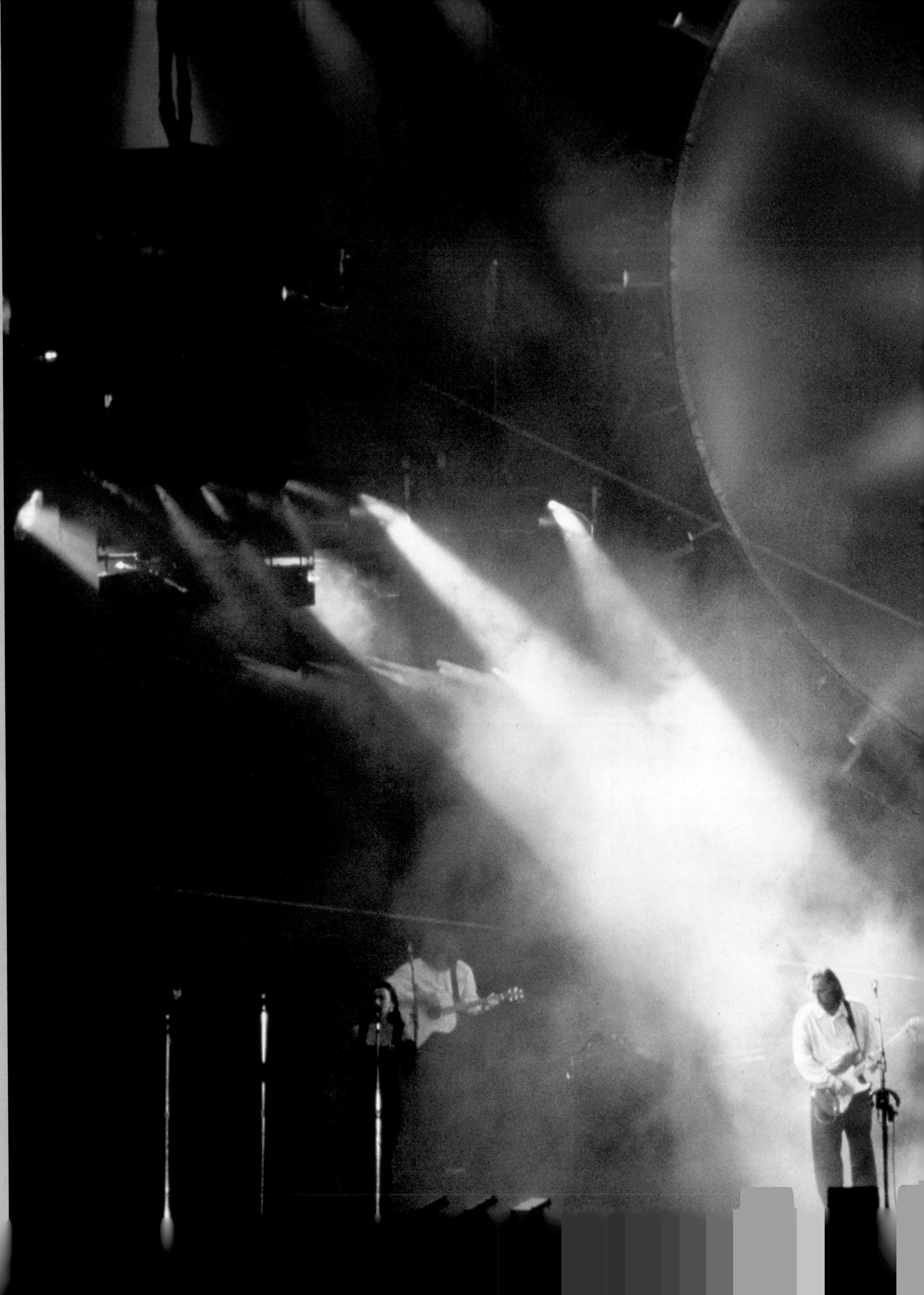

Thursday 28 April
CONCERT
Texas Stadium, Dallas, Texas, USA

Saturday 30 April
CONCERT
Citrus Bowl, Orlando, Florida, USA
A shortened set was performed due to inclement weather: 'Signs Of Life' / 'Learning To Fly' / 'Yet Another Movie' / 'Round And Around' / 'A New Machine, Part 1' / 'Terminal Frost' / 'A New Machine, Part 2' / 'Sorrow' / 'The Dogs Of War' / 'On The Turning Away' // 'One Of These Days' / 'Time' / 'On The Run' / 'The Great Gig In The Sky' / 'Wish You Were Here' / 'Us And Them' / 'Money' (extended version) / 'Another Brick In The Wall, Part 2' / 'Comfortably Numb' / encore: 'One Slip' / 'Run Like Hell'.

Wednesday 4 May
CONCERT
Carter-Finley Stadium, North Carolina State University, Raleigh, North Carolina, USA

Friday 6 & Saturday 7 May
CONCERTS
Foxboro Stadium, Foxboro, Boston, Massachusetts, USA

Wednesday 11 May
CONCERT
Stade du Parc Olympique, Montréal, Canada

Friday 13 May
CONCERT
Canadian National Exhibition Stadium, Toronto, Canada

Sunday 15 & Monday 16 May
CONCERTS
Veterans Stadium, Philadelphia, Pennsylvania, USA

Wednesday 18 May
CONCERT
University of Northern Iowa Dome, Cedar Falls, Iowa, USA

Friday 20 May
CONCERT
Camp Randall Stadium, University of Madison-Wisconsin, Madison, Wisconsin, USA

Saturday 21 & Sunday 22 May
CONCERTS
Rosemont Horizon, Rosemont, Chicago, Illinois, USA

Tuesday 24 May
CONCERT
Metrodome, Minneapolis, Minnesota, USA

Thursday 26 May
CONCERT
Arrowhead Stadium, Kansas City, Kansas, USA

Saturday 28 May
CONCERT
Ohio State University Stadium, Colombus, Ohio, USA

Monday 30 May
CONCERT
Three Rivers Stadium, Pittsburgh, Pennsylvania, USA

Wednesday 1 June
CONCERT
Robert F. Kennedy Stadium, Washington, District of Columbia, USA

Friday 3, Saturday 4 & Sunday 5 June
CONCERTS
Giants Stadium, East Rutherford, New Jersey, USA
The show of the 5 June was the last night of the tour.

A MOMENTARY LAPSE OF REASON - EUROPEAN TOUR
Set list at all shows on this tour: 'Shine On You Crazy Diamond, Parts 1-5' / 'Signs Of Life' / 'Learning To Fly' / 'Yet Another Movie' / 'Round And Around' / 'A New Machine, Part 1' / 'Terminal Frost' / 'A New Machine, Part 2' / 'Sorrow' / 'The Dogs Of War' / 'On The Turning Away' // 'One Of These Days' / 'Time' / 'The Great Gig In The Sky' / 'Wish You Were Here' / 'Welcome To The Machine' / 'Us And Them' / 'Money' (extended version) / 'Another Brick In The Wall, Part 2' / 'Comfortably Numb' / encore: 'One Slip' / 'Run Like Hell'.

Friday 10 June
CONCERT
Stade de la Beaujoire, Nantes, France

Monday 13 June
RECORD RELEASE
'One Slip' / 'Terminal Frost'
UK 7-inch single release.
'One Slip' // 'Terminal Frost' / 'The Dogs Of War' (live)
UK 12-inch single release.

Monday 13 & Tuesday 14 June
CONCERTS
Stadion Feyenoord, Rotterdam, The Netherlands
'A New Machine, Part 1', 'Terminal Frost' and 'A New Machine, Part 2' were not performed at these shows.

Thursday 16 June
CONCERT
Reichstagsgelände, Platz der Republik, West Berlin, West Germany

Saturday 18 June
CONCERT
Maimarktgelände, Mannheim, West Germany

Tuesday 21 & Wednesday 22 June
CONCERTS
Place d'Armee, Chateau de Versailles, France
Both shows were filmed for use on the *Delicate Sound of Thunder* concert video, but only a small segment of 'The Great Gig In The Sky' and audience shots were used in the finished film.

Saturday 25 June
CONCERT
Niedersachsenstadion, Hannover, West Germany

Monday 27, Tuesday 28 & Wednesday 29 June
CONCERTS
Westfalenhalle, Dortmund, West Germany

Friday 1 July
CONCERT
Praterstadion, Vienna, Austria
'A New Machine, Part 1', 'Terminal Frost' and 'A New Machine, Part 2' were not performed at this show.

Sunday 3 July
CONCERT
Olympiastadion, Munich, West Germany
'A New Machine, Part 1', 'Terminal Frost' and 'A New Machine, Part 2' were not performed at this show.

Wednesday 6 July
CONCERT
Stadio Comunale, Turin, Italy

Friday 8 & Saturday 9 July
CONCERTS
Stadio Comunale Braglia, Modena, Italy

Monday 11 & Tuesday 12 July
CONCERTS
Stadio Flaminio, Rome, Italy

Friday 15 July
CONCERT
Stade du Municipal Charles Berty, Grenoble, France
Show rescheduled from Stade Gerland, Lyon.

Sunday 17 July
CONCERT
Stade de l'Ouest, Nice, France

Wednesday 20 July
CONCERT
Estadio Sarria Espanol FC, Barcelona, Spain

Friday 22 July
CONCERT
Estadio Vincente Calderon, Madrid, Spain

Sunday 24 July
CONCERT
Espace Richter, Montpellier, France

Tuesday 26 July
CONCERT
Fussballstadion St. Jakob, Basel, Switzerland

Thursday 28 July
CONCERT
Stadium du Nord, Villeneuve d'Ascq, Lille, France

Sunday 31 July
CONCERT
Gentofte Stadion, Copenhagen, Denmark
Members of the touring party including David
Gilmour, Richard Wright, Guy Pratt, Gary Wallis,
Scott Page and Durga McBroom performed under the
name The Fishermen's in an after-show gig at
Annabel's Night Club, Copenhagen, Denmark.

Tuesday 2 August
CONCERT
Valle Hovin Stadion, Oslo, Norway
Show rescheduled from 19 August. 'A New Machine,
Part 1', 'Terminal Frost' and 'A New Machine, Part 2'
were not performed at this show.

Friday 5 & Saturday 6 August
CONCERTS
Wembley Stadium, Wembley, England
'A New Machine, Part 1', 'Terminal Frost' and 'A New
Machine, Part 2' were not performed at these shows.

Monday 8 August
CONCERT
Maine Road Football Club, Moss Side, Manchester,
England
The last night of the tour. Show rescheduled from 1
and 2 August. 'A New Machine, Part 1', 'Terminal
Frost' and 'A New Machine, Part 2' were not
performed at this show.

Wednesday 10 August
CANCELLED CONCERT
Jumping Arena, Royal Dublin Showgrounds, Dublin,
Republic of Ireland
Show cancelled, allegedly due to poor ticket sales.

A MOMENTARY LAPSE OF REASON - NORTH AMERICAN TOUR

Set list at all shows on this tour: 'Shine On You Crazy
Diamond, Parts 1-5' / 'Signs Of Life' / 'Learning To Fly'
/ 'Yet Another Movie' / 'Round And Around' / 'A New
Machine, Part 1' / 'Terminal Frost' / 'A New Machine,
Part 2' / 'Sorrow' / 'The Dogs Of War' / 'On The
Turning Away' // 'One Of These Days' / 'Time' / 'The
Great Gig In The Sky' / 'Wish You Were Here' /
'Welcome To The Machine' / 'Us And Them' / 'Money'
(extended version) / 'Another Brick In The Wall, Part
2' / 'Comfortably Numb' / encore: 'One Slip' / 'Run
Like Hell'.

Friday 12, Saturday 13 & Sunday 14 August
CONCERTS
The Coliseum, Richfield, Cleveland, Ohio, USA

Tuesday 16 & Wednesday 17 August
CONCERTS
Palace of Auburn Hills, Auburn Hills, Detroit,
Michigan, USA

Friday 19, Saturday 20, Sunday 21, Monday 22 &
Tuesday 23 August
CONCERTS
Nassau Veterans Memorial Coliseum, Uniondale,
Long Island, New York, USA
The show of the 23 August was the last night of the
tour. All five shows were recorded and filmed for the
Delicate Sound Of Thunder concert video and live
album.

Monday 21 November
RECORD RELEASE
Delicate Sound Of Thunder
UK and US album release.
Q Magazine commented that: 'The album will work
best for people who were there. With no more than
the mantelpiece to stir the imagination, the pomposity
of the standard Floyd intro starts to grate: huge
single drumbeats or bass chords left to hang in the air
while you prepare your mind for blowing. "Get on
with it!" cries the voice from the armchair.'

Saturday 26 November
SPACE LAUNCH
Baikonur Cosmodrome, Kasakhstan, USSR
Gilmour and Mason attended the launch of a Soyuz
TM-7 rocket bound for the Russian space station MIR.
The three-man crew took with them a cassette of the
album *Delicate Sound Of Thunder* (minus the cassette
box, for weight reasons) and played it in orbit; this
was thought to have been the first rock music
recording played in space.

1989

ANOTHER LAPSE - EUROPEAN TOUR

Set list at all shows on this tour: 'Shine On You Crazy Diamond, Parts 1-5' / 'Signs Of Life' / 'Learning To Fly' / 'Yet Another Movie' / 'Round And Around' / 'A New Machine, Part 1' / 'Terminal Frost' / 'A New Machine, Part 2' / 'Sorrow' / 'The Dogs Of War' / 'On The Turning Away' // 'One Of These Days' / 'Time' / 'The Great Gig In The Sky' / 'Wish You Were Here' / 'Welcome To The Machine' / 'Us And Them' / 'Money' (extended version) / 'Another Brick In The Wall, Part 2' / 'Comfortably Numb' / encore: 'One Slip' / 'Run Like Hell'.

PINK FLOYD CORE ROAD CREW THROUGH 1989

Marc Brickman: Lighting Designer
Malcolm Craggs: Tour Manager
Seth Goldman: Monitor Sound Engineer
Tony Howard: Road Manager
Buford Jones: Front of House Sound Engineer
Morris Lyda: Production Manager
Phil Taylor: Backline Chief
John Thomson: Stage Manager
Robbie Williams: Production Director

ADDITIONAL TOUR PERSONNEL

Jon Carin: Keyboards and Vocals
Rachel Fury: Backing Vocals
Durga McBroom: Backing Vocals
Lorelei McBroom: Backing Vocals
Scott Page: Saxophones and Guitars
Guy Pratt: Bass Guitar and Vocals
Tim Renwick: Guitars
Gary Wallis: Percussion
Richard Wright: Keyboards and Vocals

Monday 8 & Tuesday 9 May
REHEARSALS
London Arena, Isle of Dogs, London, England
Full production rehearsals for the upcoming European tour were staged at the same London venue they were to return to in July. On 9 May a press reception was held at the venue and the band's handprints were taken in cement for display in the venue's 'Hall of Fame'.

Friday 12 May
REHEARSAL
Festivalweise, Werchter, Belgium
Many fans were already waiting patiently outside the festival grounds for the following day's show and were treated to a full production rehearsal despite not being allowed in. At the conclusion of a complete run through of the show David Gilmour said to the crowds, 'thanks for listening, we'll let you in tomorrow!'

Saturday 13 May
CONCERT
Festivalweise, Werchter, Belgium

Tuesday 16, Wednesday 17 & Thursday 18 May
CONCERTS
Arena di Verona, Verona, Italy

Saturday 20 May
CONCERT
Arena Concerti, Autodromo Di Monza, Monza, Italy

Monday 22 & Tuesday 23 May
CONCERTS
Stadio Comunale Ardenza, Livorno, Italy

Tuesday 23 May
PRESS RECEPTION
CFS Conference Centre, Marylebone, London, England
EMI Records video division, PMI, held a press reception followed by a screening of the *Delicate Sound Of Thunder* video. To celebrate the fact that the band was about to play in Moscow for the first time, organisers laid on complimentary Russian beer!

Thursday 25 & Friday 26 May
CONCERTS
Stadio Simonetta Lamberti, Cava De' Tirreni, Italy

Wednesday 31 May
CONCERT
Olympic Stadium Spiridon Spiros Louis, Athens, Greece

Saturday 3, Sunday 4, Monday 5, Tuesday 6 & Wednesday 7 June
CONCERTS
Bol' Šaja Sportivnaja Arena, Lushniki, Moscow, USSR

Saturday 10 June
CONCERT
Lahden Surhali, Lahti, Finland

Monday 12 June
VIDEO RELEASE
Delicate Sound Of Thunder
UK and US video release.

Monday 12, Tuesday 13 & Wednesday 14 June
CONCERTS
Globe Arena, Stockholm, Sweden

Friday 16 June
CONCERT
Festweisse Im Stadtpark, Hamburg, West Germany

Sunday 18 June
CONCERT
Mungersdorfer Stadion, Cologne, West Germany

Tuesday 20, Wednesday 21 & Thursday 22 June
CONCERTS
Festhalle, Frankfurt, West Germany

Friday 23 June
CONCERT
Linzer Stadion, Linz, Austria

Sunday 25 June
CONCERT
Neckarstadion, Stuttgart, West Germany

Tuesday 27, Wednesday 28, Thursday 29, Friday 30 June & Saturday 1 July
CONCERTS
Palais Omnisports de Paris-Bercy, Paris, France

Tuesday 4, Wednesday 5, Thursday 6, Friday 7, Saturday 8 & Sunday 9 July
CONCERTS
London Arena, Isle of Dogs, London, England
The Guardian summed up the sentiments of many fans at this series of poorly received shows at the newly built London Arena: 'The ticket said the concert would start at 7.30pm sharp. By 8.10pm the embryonic Dockland's infrastructure, and a bizarre decision to make everyone enter the building in single file, had just about half filled the new Arena, and appropriately enough for a building whose

RIGHT: DAVID GILMOUR AT THE LONDON ARENA, 8 JULY 1989.

25

architectural heritage is Heathrow out-buildings, the first sound we heard was an aircraft buzzing across the public address. This excited an audience made up, you may be surprised to hear, not of hairy hangovers, but of gangs of tattooed youths dressed in garish Bermuda shorts with lager overhang. But the enthusiastic cheering was the second indication of the level of critical agility that brings someone to a Floyd concert. The first was the run on the Arena's shrewdly marketed refreshment package: "5oz hamburger, relishes and lager: £3". For those who were still scurrying into their seats halfway through the first section, the part of the lot you missed is a familiar one. Some middle-aged men, drained by legal confrontations with one of their number, return to the stage when the school fees become too much for compact disc sales of their back catalogue to sustain, and hide their shortcomings behind an extravaganza pyrotechnics and excess hardware. If only the likeable Dave Gilmour and his team had a tenth of the energy of their acidic descendants, we might have had some fun. Instead there was smoke billowing from the ceiling, lasers cutting across the auditorium, a galaxy of spotlights picking out men hunched over keyboards playing uninspired dirges that would not have been out of place backing wildlife films. At the side of the stage three refugees from a Robert Palmer video swayed in tight dresses, occasionally moaning into the microphone in unison, unable to find a rhythm to latch their syncopated shuffle on to. This despite the fact there were two drummers on display: that two were deemed necessary for a band whose rhythmic complexities would not tax a clockwork monkey summed up the whole bloated enterprise. For the first half, Gilmour said he would like to play "some new stuff" then "lots of oldies after the break". "You play whatever you like mate," said the chap behind me, who was clearly a veteran Floyd watcher, because that is what Gilmour appeared to be doing throughout: random guitar doodling that bore no relation to received ideas of melody. Some critics have complained that the dire evening service provided by the Dockland's Light Railway is killing the Arena at birth. I, however, owe the railway a debt of thanks. When, during the interval, it was announced that the last train left at 9.30pm, I had a genuine excuse to miss most of the second half.'

Monday 10 July
CONCERT
Goffertpark, Nijmegen, The Netherlands

Wednesday 12 July
CONCERT
Stade Olympique de la Pontaise, Lausanne, Switzerland

Saturday 15 July
CONCERT
Canale di San Marco, Piazza San Marco, Venice, Italy
Set list: 'Shine On You Crazy Diamond, Parts 1-5.' / 'Learning To Fly' / 'Yet Another Movie' / 'Sorrow' / 'The Dogs Of War' / 'On The Turning Away' / 'Time' / 'The Great Gig In The Sky' / 'Wish You Were Here' / 'Money' / 'Another Brick In The Wall, Part 2' / 'Comfortably Numb' / 'Run Like Hell.'
An abbreviated 90 minute show was staged on a huge barge moored off Piazza San Marco and broadcast live on TV to over 20 countries, and seen by an estimated 100 million people. In the UK the show was broadcast live on BBC2 TV at 10.45pm. In 1992 two council officers were faced with charges for allowing the concert to go ahead. A far greater number than anticipated attended the concert, and facilities were vastly inadequate. It was estimated the clean up bill alone reached a cost in excess of £25,000 to the local authorities.

Tuesday 18 July
CONCERT
Stade Vélodrome, Marseille, France
The last night of the tour.

1990—1993

1990

Saturday 30 June
CONCERT
The Silver Clef Award Winners Show, Knebworth Park, Stevenage, England
With Tears For Fears, Status Quo, Cliff Richard, Robert Plant with Jimmy Page, Phil Collins, Genesis, Eric Clapton, Dire Straits, Elton John and Paul McCartney.
Set list: 'Shine On You Crazy Diamond, Parts 1-5' / 'The Great Gig In The Sky' / 'Wish You Were Here' / 'Sorrow' / 'Money' / 'Comfortably Numb' / 'Run Like Hell'.
This charity event in aid of the Nordoff-Robbins Music

Therapy Centre featured 11 hours of continuous entertainment. Although a year on, Pink Floyd officially declared this as the final date of the 'Momentary Lapse Of Reason' world tour and closed the day with a brief set in torrential rain without their circular screen. During a heavy storm earlier in the day, it had collected water and ripped while suspended above the stage.

Pink Floyd were supplemented by Sam Brown (backing vocals), Vicki Brown (backing vocals), Candy Dulfer (saxophone on 'Shine On You Crazy Diamond' and 'Money'), Michael Kamen (keyboards on 'Comfortably Numb'), Guy Pratt (bass guitar), Durga McBroom (backing vocals) and Claire Torry (backing vocals on 'Great Gig In The Sky').

BBC Radio One broadcast the entire event live from 1.00pm and Castle Music Pictures released a three-video set of highlights, entitled *Knebworth - The Event*, and featuring 'Comfortably Numb' and 'Run Like Hell', on 6 August 1990. Polydor released an album of highlights, including these two tracks, at the same time (see discography for further details).

1991

Tuesday 24 December
TV SHOW
BBC TV Centre, White City, London, England
BBC2 TV broadcast at 9.30pm a film entitled *La Carrera Panamericana* which documented David Gilmour and Nick Mason's participation that October in the 3,000-mile South American classic car race of the same name. Both were driving replica Proteus 1952 C-type Jaguars – Mason was co-driving with Lindsay Valentine and Gilmour with manager Steve O'Rourke who, incidentally, broke both his legs when their car veered off the road near San Luis Potosi in Mexico. The soundtrack featured existing and newly reworked Pink Floyd tracks and was officially released on video in 1992. Some of the interview footage was actually filmed after the race in a suitably looking Hispanic bar in Notting Hill, London.

1992

Monday 13 April
VIDEO RELEASE
La Carrera Panamericana
UK video release. US video release on Monday 1 June 1992.

Monday 2 November
RECORD RELEASE
Shine On
UK and US album release.
Universally panned by fans, *Q Magazine* commented that: 'A box of eight Pink Floyd albums lovingly inlaid in their black casket, with a "bonus" CD of early singles along with an envelope of postcards no serious collector would ever actually send to anyone, and a cut-out cardboard shape which one is evidently meant to fold, but your reviewer has so far failed to work out how - still less what it is supposed to be when finished. There are no instructions, and that's not the only thing conspicuously absent from this recession-flouting (£100 plus) package... Storm [Thorgerson] comes unstuck with the design of *Shine On*'s book: the text is treated as just so much grey matter, unclearly laid out and in dire need of a good edit, or even a quick proofreading. Not only is it littered with typographical errors but the odd factual howler too. Most annoyingly, the final piece of text, an unsigned music industry piece on the enduring appeal of *Dark Side Of The Moon*, actually stops mid-sentence.'

1993

January - September
RECORDING SESSIONS
Britannia Row Studios, Islington, London England & The Astoria, Hampton, England
Discontinuous recording for the album *The Division Bell*.

September - December
RECORDING SESSIONS
Metropolis Studios, Chiswick, London England & The Creek Recording Studios, London, England
Discontinuous recording and mixing for the album *The Division Bell*.

Saturday 18 September
CONCERT
Cowdray Ruins Concert 1993, Cowdray Castle, Midhurst, England
Set list: 'Run Like Hell' / 'Wish You Were Here' / 'Comfortably Numb'.
This was a celebrity charity event sponsored by Virgin Radio to raise £200,000 for the King Edward VII hospital in Midhurst. With a ticket price of £140 for the main arena and £80 the outer picnic zones, it was an exclusive gathering, out of the reach of the band's usual fans. The concert opened with a set from Queen, comprising on this occasion, Roger Taylor (lead vocals), John Deacon (bass), Tim Renwick (guitar) and Gary Wallis (drums). Also appearing were Genesis, made up of Phil Collins (lead vocals), Mike Rutherford (bass), Tony Banks (keyboards), Tim Renwick (guitar) and Gary Wallis and Roger Taylor (drums). Pink Floyd headlined with a fairly standard set with the unusual addition of Mike Rutherford (bass), Paul Young of Mike & The Mechanics (vocals on 'Run Like Hell'), Tim Renwick (guitar) and Gary Wallis (drums). Nick Mason sat behind Roger Taylor's drum kit, complete with the famous Queen emblem. The last act to appear was Eric Clapton playing lead guitar on a two-song encore with Gilmour, Taylor, Young, Collins and Renwick.

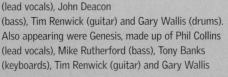

COWDRAY RUINS CONCERT 1993

the nights of wonder

VO
P R

PINK

M

IN C

Produced by HARVEY G

EARLS COURT

FRIDAY 21st OCTOBER

DOORS OPEN 6.15 pm   SHOW STA

NO SUPPORT

BLOCK   ENT   ROW   SEAT

KSWAGEN
SENTS

FLOYD

NCERT

DSMITH ENTERTAINMENTS

1994 – 2006

994

S 7.45 pm

£25

GROUND
LEVEL ARENA

Fig. 1
M

W

THE PREVIOUS YEAR'S SOUNDTRACK MATERIAL PROVIDED A SOLID BASE FOR GILMOUR WHEN, BEGINNING IN JANUARY 1993, HE BEGAN RECORDING A NEW PINK FLOYD ALBUM AT HIS STUDIO ABOARD THE ASTORIA. IT WAS NOT NEARLY AS PAINSTAKING A TASK AS MAKING THE LAST ALBUM, ESPECIALLY NOW THAT MASON AND WRIGHT WERE, IN THEORY, BACK ON FORM.

The Division Bell, released in March 1994, took its title from the bell located in the UK's House of Commons that summons Members of Parliament to debate. (The idea was suggested to Gilmour by his friend, the science-fiction writer Douglas Adams, in exchange for a £5,000 charity donation to the Environmental Investigation Agency.) Many took the title to be a final message to the doubters: it's time to make your mind up. The phenomenal success of the album suggested that the vote had gone decisively in Gilmour, Mason and Wright's favour: it was one of the most successful in Pink Floyd's near-thirty-year history.

The Division Bell, with its distinctive artwork by Storm Thorgerson, saw a classic return to form, and the result was a much warmer and inviting work than the previous album. Moreover, it had stronger lyrics which took the listeners back to the classic Seventies album feel – almost in the tradition of *The Dark Side Of The Moon*.

The reason for the regained sense of shared purpose that characterises the album, Gilmour suggested, was, 'because we're all playing and functioning much better than we were after the trials and tribulations of the late Roger years. Recording *A Momentary Lapse Of Reason* was a very, very difficult process. We were all sort of catatonic. Unfortunately, we didn't really work together an awful lot. But the success of that album and the success of the supporting tour and the enjoyment that we got out of working together meant that this one could be made in a different way.[1] On this album both Nick and Rick are playing all the stuff they should be playing which is why it sounds much more like a genuine Pink Floyd record to me than anything since *Wish You Were Here*. It has a sort of theme about non-communication, but we're not trying to bash anybody over the head with it. We went out last time with the intention of showing the world, 'Look we're still here,' which is why we were so loud and crash-bangy. This is a much more reflective album.' [2]

Indeed, using communication as a general theme enabled Gilmour to lay many ghosts to rest. Chief among these were the recent breakdown of his marriage and his personal recovery, in 'Coming Back To Life'; the collapse of his relationship with Waters, in 'Lost For Words' – in which he buries the hatchet and offers a (refused) olive branch; and the hopelessness of Barrett's condition in 'Poles Apart'. But the album also had a deep focus on the problem of communication, on a global as well as personal level, and this theme is explored in 'A Great Day For Freedom' and the upbeat 'Take It Back'. But, without doubt, the highlights are the anthemic and highly emotive 'High Hopes', a nostalgic return by Gilmour to his Cambridge roots and the passing of the years and 'Keep Talking', which features the voice of mathematician Professor Stephen Hawking, who due to Lou Gehrig's Disease speaks through a speech synthesiser. The instrumental track 'Marooned' went on to be awarded a Grammy for 'Best Rock Instrumental Performance' of that year.

Although Anthony Moore and Nick Laird-Clowes made some contribution to the writing of the album, and Rick Wright received his first writing credit in 19 years for co-writing 'Wearing The Inside Out', it is particularly apt that Gilmour's present wife, ex-journalist Polly Samson, should have co-written much of the material. She performed wonders in hauling Gilmour out of the mire of depression after his battles with Waters. Gilmour, given his admitted diffidence as a wordsmith, greatly valued her close reading of his work. 'After I would write some lyrics, it just seemed natural to have her look though them. In the beginning she tried not to interfere at all, and tried to encourage me to do it on my own. But, of course, that isn't the way things stay. And as time went by, she got more and more involved with the process that was beginning to absorb me 24 hours a day. Her involvement with the lyric writing process – and, in fact, with the music – grew. Her assistance was invaluable.'[3]

Since the band now had a sizeable repertoire to

choose from for the inevitable tour, a new strategy was employed. Now, they presented a pot-pourri of songs, some new and some dating right back to their first album, discarding the usual format of playing the whole of the current album during one half of the show. In addition, a system was adopted whereby the band changed their set list constantly, making it less rigid and thus reducing the risk of boredom for themselves and their fans alike – many of whom, they realised, were seeing them at more than one location throughout the tour.

In staging the show Pink Floyd welcomed back on board designer Mark Fisher, who, along with Marc Brickman, came up with what was inevitably seen as the band's most impressive stage show to date. (An unwritten Floyd tradition seems to demand that each tour should be more spectacular than the previous one). A large semicircular shell now housed the production, replacing a monolithic steel frame, and this was equipped with a much larger circular projection screen. Overall the design was strongly reminiscent of the Hollywood Bowl, while the lighting effects and the fantastical newly generated film sequences – both live action and computer generated – were nothing short of awe inspiring.

It was therefore not surprising that band manager Steve O'Rourke announced to the press that 'David, Rick and Nick have put no limit on the budget. It is a matter of however much it takes to create the best show we can possibly do.'[4] And it certainly showed: a much improved Turbosound PA system provided the best quadraphonic sound available, using some 300 speakers, a raised forty-foot circular projection screen with a 35mm back-projector, a 70mm IMAX front projector, a vast mirror ball that raised from the centre of the now giant slug-like construction that housed the front-of-house soundboard and projectors, and an array of lighting that included 400 Vari-Lites and two copper-vapour pulse lasers that, for the first time, included a variety of colours, including emerald green, lime green, gold, yellow and blood red – this last innovation originally developed for NASA by the Hughes Corporation. The band even recalled one of their original lighting men Peter Wynne-Wilson to re-create liquid-oil patterns to illuminate the revival of the classic Barrett-era anthem 'Astronomy Dominé'.

The new projection films, which alone cost a small fortune, were spectacular. The most impressive were those used for 'Shine On You Crazy Diamond', based largely on the Barrett legend; 'Money', with an untypical hilarious alien monster theme and 'Time', a computer-generated masterpiece that seemed to suck viewers into the vast workings of a hugely intricate mechanical timing device. Reworked scenes also accompanied the classic footage used during 'Us And Them', and the renditions of *The Dark Side Of The Moon* were updated with appropriate inserts of modern-day politicians for the 'Brain Damage'/'Eclipse' finale. Also, much greater attention to detail was given to lighting effects, with the Vari-Lite production being the largest ever taken on the road. Then there was the usual battery of fireworks and props, including a crashing plane for 'On The Run' and two massive comic hogs that launched out of the tops of the twin speaker columns during 'One Of These Days'. It was a show to please every type of Pink Floyd fan, with its visuals that were a mixture of both mainstream rock lighting, full-on psychedelia and not without its fair share of humour. With these complemented by a more creative use of the quad system and mind-mashing sound effects, it was a total sensory bombardment calculated to blow the fans right out of their seats.

The statistics of such a large-scale touring machine are mind-boggling, and the amount of materials and

STEVE O'ROURKE   << David, Rick and Nick have put no limit on the budget. It is a matter of however much it takes to create the best show we can possibly do. >>

manpower required to take the band on the road simply are too fantastic to be ignored: 200 crew members, three separate touring stages (although only one set of lights was carried on tour, since it was the most expensive single element to hire), forty-nine container trucks, 700 tons of steel to build the set – a task which took four days – and a daily running cost of some US$500,000. Two Boeing 747 cargo planes and a chartered Russian Antonov military freight plane were used to transfer the equipment from the USA for the European tour.

Robbie Williams, once the band's roadie and now Production Manager, looked on this complexity with a

ROBBIE WILLIAMS   << We used to get away with a main lighting effect that consisted of four Genie towers, which came up with flashing police beacons on top and 24 par cans – and that was seen as absolutely astonishing. >>

RIGHT: PINK FLOYD'S VISUALLY STUNNING SHOW ENTERS EUROPE AT THE ESTÁDIO DE ALVALADE IN LISBON ON 22 JULY 1994.

mixture of awe and disbelief. 'We used to get away with a main lighting effect that consisted of four Genie towers, which came up with flashing police beacons on top and 24 par cans – and that was seen as absolutely astonishing. Now, to get the same effect on an audience you have to have 20 million dollars' worth of stuff out there. It sometimes amazes me, going back into stadiums we played in the Seventies, when it was a lot more basic. Fax machines? We didn't even have telephones on some

DAVID GILMOUR << Meeting and greeting Volkswagen people. I was not a popular chappy with Volkswagen. I don't want them to be able to say they have a connection with Pink Floyd, that they are part of our success. >>

of those gigs yet we did stadium tours. Sometimes I look around and think, we're ordering 21 phone lines at every venue, and as for computers – we didn't even have calculators.'[5]

At a press conference held in London on 30 November 1993 to announce the European tour, Pink Floyd said they would be performing in Greece, Turkey and Israel in addition to the shows already announced, but none of these locations was confirmed. A show in front of the Great Pyramids at Giza in Egypt was frequently touted by the press as well as additional concerts in Australia in 1995 but these plans never reached fruition.

BELOW: AS SPONSORS OF PINK FLOYD'S 1994 EUROPEAN TOUR, VOLKSWAGEN EVEN PRODUCED A LIMITED EDITION PINK FLOYD VOLKSWAGEN GOLF WITH NEW INTERIORS CO-DESIGNED BY NICK MASON. THIS ONE IS PICTURED AT A DEALERSHIP IN WEIMAR.

To assist with the spiralling costs of the tour the band, perhaps rather hastily, struck a deal with the German car manufacturer Volkswagen. (The company even went so far as to produce a special limited edition 'Pink Floyd' VW Golf with interiors part-designed by Nick Mason.) Although it seemed like a good idea at the time, Gilmour regretted this, 'not having thought it through entirely. Meeting and greeting Volkswagen people. I was not a popular chappy with Volkswagen. I don't want them to be able to say they have a connection with Pink Floyd, that they are part of our success. We will not do it again. I didn't like it, and any money I made from it went to charity. We should remain proudly independent, that's my view, and we will in the future.'[6] Little, it seems, had been learnt from the Gini episode some twenty years earlier.

If one thing set *The Division Bell* and the related stage show apart from all others, it was the sheer power of the delivery – and with such an audio and visual feast, it's difficult to imagine Pink Floyd ever topping this achievement. Most striking was the fact that the band had captured the imagination of a new generation with whole families attending the concerts. A huge number of teenagers who might well have been steeping themselves in rave or grunge were committing themselves to Pink Floyd. As one industry observer put it, 'It's hard to tell how they attract a younger demographic. Unlike Neil Young or Aerosmith, they have no connection to Nineties music. I can't even think of an act that has caught younger consumers' favour that would even lead them to Pink Floyd. This is a unique situation.'[7]

At the close of the tour it was calculated that over 5.3 million tickets had been sold, grossing some US$100 million. To commemorate their efforts, a live album and video, both entitled *Pulse*, were released. These not only gave a balanced and well-recorded picture of Pink Floyd's then current repertoire but, for the first time, contained a complete official rendition of the whole of *The Dark Side Of The Moon*, which they had revived towards the close of the US tour and performed as a complete second half in shows throughout Europe.

'We were bitterly disappointed that we didn't make a proper record of *Dark Side Of The Moon* at Earls Court in '73,'[8] said Mason. Inevitably, some critics would have much preferred that they had done this in the first place rather than present a rehashed latter-day version. After all, while Pink Floyd's last two tours were now fully documented, there still remained an unforgivable void between 1969's *Ummagumma* and 1988's *Delicate Sound Of Thunder*.

Not even the BBC sessions from the late Sixties or early Seventies have been officially released to date. Even the prospect of an anthology set, similar to the trawl of archives undertaken by The Beatles, The Who or Led Zeppelin, among many high-profile acts, seems to this day decidedly remote.

¶ The only concession to this has been the March 2000 release of *Is There Anybody Out There: The Wall Live*, a thoughtfully presented and packaged set derived from those legendary 1980-81 concerts. Speaking of this release Mason commented that, 'It's very difficult to find things from the vaults. A while back the BBC wanted to release some *Top Gear* tapes, and they really weren't good enough. These tapes were almost a surprise, because I didn't realise they even existed.'[9] Needless to say the CD age has created a glut of re-masters and reissues in order to extend their shelf life, including a mono edition of *The Piper At The Gates Of Dawn* and a superb 5.1 remix of *The Dark Side Of The Moon*.

As for original material, remarkably it was Wright that made the first post-*Division Bell* move by releasing a solo album, *Broken China*, in 1996. However, his initial desire to tour the record was thwarted by relatively moderate sales.

Waters is now engaged in what could be described as his most successful and prolific solo period to date, having embarked on world tours that have secured a solid fanbase and he is now enjoying a new found sense of personal and professional freedom: 'I had a lot of negative feelings later on when the boys went off

marching round the world with my songs,' Waters said in a recent interview in *Uncut* Magazine. 'That was problematic for me for a number of years. I'm completely over it now. I couldn't care less, and also I feel much less bullish about the notion that I was right and they were wrong. I absolutely did the right thing, difficult as it was for the first few years when I was making records on my own. It was very hard for me to carve out a niche for myself outside the context of the band.'

Mason renewed his friendship with Waters in 2001 and even appeared as a guest at his solo shows in London the following year. Overall Mason appears to have done very little apart from tinker with his beloved cars but in 2004 he published his memoirs in a hugely entertaining, but not especially revealing, tome entitled *Inside Out – A Personal History Of Pink Floyd*.

Gilmour seems perfectly content to involve himself in family affairs and occasionally pops up as a guest player – his most significant efforts having been with The Pretty Things and Paul McCartney toward the end of the Nineties. Remarkably, he was persuaded by his old friend Robert Wyatt to perform a solo show at London's Royal Festival Hall in June 2001 to great reviews. This was followed by four more shows the next year: two each in Paris and London with Wright as guest performer, offering a faint glimmer of hope that a full-scale tour might follow.

With that in mind the prospect of Pink Floyd being resurrected was decidedly remote for the fans as it was for Gilmour. 'It's a lumbering great behemoth to rouse from its torpor,' he said to *Classic Rock* back in 2000. '*The Division Bell* was better than *A Momentary Lapse...* and it had Rick and Nick working properly together again. Maybe that's proved all I needed to prove. I don't have any hard and fast ideas about it. I haven't got myself in the mood for doing another one yet. I don't know if I want to do all that again. Certainly I'll make another record, but what it is, whether it's Pink Floyd or me, I don't know.'

On a sad note, Pink Floyd's long-serving manager, Steve O'Rourke unexpectedly passed away in October 2003. Although Waters chose not to attend the service at Winchester Cathedral, Gilmour, Mason and Wright all attended and joined together in a rendition of 'Fat Old Sun' as a tribute to their professional and personal relationship. A month later Gilmour was awarded the CBE for his not insubstantial charitable donations and services to music.

I had originally drafted the final few paragraphs of this book by saying that for Pink Floyd, whatever their

DAVE GILMOUR << **Like most people I want to do everything I can to persuade the G8 leaders to make huge commitments to the relief of poverty and increased aid to the third world.** >>

view might be, surely to retire gracefully at this stage is a far more fitting tribute to the band's overwhelming legacy and achievement than to be overshadowed by the internal conflict that raged some ten years ago.

However, in a most surprising turn of events that began in May 2005, Bob Geldof miraculously brought together the two sparring parties to reform the classic Pink Floyd line-up for a one-off performance at his *Live 8* concert in London's Hyde Park on 2 July. Pink Floyd's participation was officially announced on 12 June and it quickly became apparent to the fans and media alike this was almost eclipsing the importance of the event itself. Despite being a free ticket, applications, which had to be submitted via a mobile phone lottery, were closing within the day, and many fans overseas had very little chance to act on this news. Meanwhile a fierce debate raged as the Internet auction site eBay took almost a week to act on Geldof's requests to remove unscrupulous sellers on what was effectively a transferable ticket.

† Their reunion had doubtless been brewing for some time and was almost inevitable at some stage. When Waters played the 2002 Glastonbury Festival he told the official programme that a reunion was on the cards. 'Nick Mason and I have rekindled our friendship to some extent,' he explained, 'so it's possible. It might be a laugh.'

Gilmour, meanwhile, was the first of the band members to issue an official statement: 'Like most people I want to do everything I can to persuade the G8 leaders to make huge commitments to the relief of poverty and increased aid to the third world. It's crazy that America gives such a paltry percentage of its GNP to the starving nations. Any squabbles Roger and the band have had in the past are so petty in this context, and if re-forming for this concert will help focus attention then it's got to be worthwhile.'

Waters in a later communiqué was similarly focused on the event but significantly appeared to be more excited at the prospect of the band reforming than anyone else: 'It's great to be asked to help Bob raise public awareness on the issues of third world debt and poverty. The cynics will scoff, screw 'em! Also, to be given the opportunity to put the band back together, even if it's only for a few numbers, is a big bonus.'

As Nick Mason concluded, 'You can't carry on World War Three forever. If we hadn't reformed for *Live 8* we'd have done it for another charity event, I suspect. It's a good reason to do it; a way of building bridges for the right reasons rather than burning them down.'[10]

Pink Floyd took to the stage, after a two-hour over-run at 11.00pm, following the familiar sight of a cardiograph blip racing across the three screens that covered the stage's rear and sides. David Gilmour, Roger Waters, Nick Mason and Richard Wright took to the stage for the first time together in 24 years and arguably turned in one of their finest ever performances to date as they wowed a 250,000 plus audience and several millions watching on TV across the globe. It was in every aspect a truly historical event.

Waters was perhaps the most vocal of the band after the event as he was actively promoting his *Ça Ira* opera immediately afterwards, giving many candid interviews. 'I enjoyed playing bass [at *Live 8*],' reflected Waters. 'It was more fun than I can remember having with Pink Floyd twenty-five years ago. I was there to enjoy myself. I was very happy, I definitely felt warm and cuddly toward everyone in the band. I decided that if anything came up in rehearsals - any difference of opinion - I would just roll over. And I did.' Elaborating on the split with his former band mates, Waters has certainly

ROGER WATERS << It was more fun than I can remember having with Pink Floyd twenty-five years ago. I was there to enjoy myself. I was very happy, I definitely felt warm and cuddly toward everyone in the band. >>

mellowed in the wake of the event by saying that, 'I would have preferred it if Dave and Nick had not gone around the world using my songs, but it wasn't to be. And in a way it wasn't that bad a thing that they did, as regards keeping Pink Floyd's music alive'. [11]

Of the prospect of future appearances and tours, despite the reported $150 million pay day on offer from several US concert promoters, Waters was hardly tempted: 'I don't really need it. It would be a very hot ticket. That said, I didn't mind rolling over for one day, but I couldn't roll over for a whole fucking tour.' Asked what he thought David Gilmour felt: 'He did send me an e-mail afterward, saying, "Hi, Rog, I'm glad you made that phone call. It was fun, wasn't it?" So he obviously had

fun.'[12]

The two have rarely spoken since and whilst it is almost unthinkable for fans to contemplate a full-scale reunion not expanding beyond this, their *Live 8* performance has, in general terms, been characteristically downplayed by all concerned as strictly a one-off event.

Gilmour, perhaps more forcefully than the others, and in view of the success of his recent solo album and contentment with his family lifestyle, has categorically stated that Pink Floyd is over and that *Live 8* was, in many ways, a convenient vehicle to achieve closure.

For the future then, fans will have to content themselves with continuing solo projects from both of the main protagonists.

ABOVE AND OVERLEAF: PINK FLOYD AND ROGER WATERS ON STAGE ONCE MORE AT *LIVE 8*, LONDON, 2 JULY 2005.

Sources
1. *Guitar World,* September 1994
2. *Mojo,* May 1994
3. *Guitar World,* September 1994
4. *The Evening Standard,* 30 November 1993
5. *Live,* September 1994
6. *Mojo,* July 1995
7. *USA Today,* c.July 1994
8. *Mojo,* July 1995
9. *Classic Rock,* January 2000
10. *Radio Times,* 2-8 July 2005
11. *Word,* October 2005
12. *Rolling Stone,* August 2005

PIN

EARLS
FRIDAY 21st OC
OPEN 6.15 pm

ROW

26

1994

THE NIGHTS OF WONDER 1994-2006

PINK FLOYD

(January 1994 – To Date)
David Gilmour: Guitar, Vocals
Nick Mason: Drums
Richard Wright: Keyboards, Vocals

Thursday 10 January
PRESS RECEPTION
US Naval Air Station, Weeksville, North Carolina, USA

A press reception was held to announce Pink Floyd's new album and world tour at this location with the launch of a specially built Skyship 600 airship. Flown from its manufacturers in the UK to the US, it was specially painted by Burt Dodge in Elizabeth City, North Carolina. It then took off on a round US tour and was acclaimed in the aviation industry for its performance against the jet stream in some of the worst weather for the time of year. It was sighted over many key cities over the next few weeks and even made appearances at some shows. The airship returned to Weeksville, where it was destroyed by a sudden thunderstorm on 27 June 1994, the remnants of which were sold off as souvenirs to fans.

Tuesday 8 – Thursday 24 March
REHEARSALS
Norton Air Force Base, San Barnardino, California, USA

Pink Floyd made use of an aircraft hangar at this US military airbase for their tour rehearsals.

Monday 21 March
PRESS RECEPTION
White Waltham Airfield, Maidenhead, England

A press reception was held to announce Pink Floyd's new album and world tour aboard a specially painted A60 Airship that took off on a circular trip over central London with journalists aboard. In the run up to the European tour the airship later made a promotional tour of the UK and northern Europe. Painted to resemble a large fish, it was fabricated from a translucent material and illuminated from the inside by two large 1000w bulbs giving an eerie effect as it travelled the night sky.

Monday 28 March
RECORD RELEASE
The Division Bell

UK album release. US album release on Monday 4 April.

Teen Ink commented that: 'If you are looking for another *Dark Side* or *Wish* or any of their string of hit records, you will not find it here. A band has to move on to new sounds, to a new stage in their music, or else they become redundant. However the elements are there. You can even find a bit of the old Floyd psychedelia buried in the middle of "Poles Apart". Overall, the album is a bittersweet memoir of friends past, and future hopes.'

THE DIVISION BELL - NORTH & SOUTH AMERICAN TOUR

PINK FLOYD CORE ROAD CREW THROUGH 1994

Marc Brickman: Lighting Designer
Seth Goldman: Monitor Sound Engineer
Tony Howard: Tour Manager
Andy Jackson: Front of House Sound Engineer
Paul Mauradian: Stage Manager
Dave Russell: Production Manager
Phil Taylor: Backline Chief
Robbie Williams: Production Director

ADDITIONAL TOUR PERSONNEL

Sam Brown: Backing Vocals
Jon Carin: Keyboards and Vocals
Claudia Fontaine: Backing Vocals
Durga McBroom: Backing Vocals
Dick Parry: Saxophones
Guy Pratt: Bass Guitar and Vocals
Tim Renwick: Guitars
Gary Wallis: Percussion

Tuesday 29 March
REHEARSAL
Joe Robbie Stadium, Miami, Florida, USA

A full production rehearsal for the upcoming tour was staged prior to the opening night of the tour.

Wednesday 30 March
CONCERT
Joe Robbie Stadium, Miami, Florida, USA

Set list: 'Astronomy Dominé' / 'Learning To Fly' / 'What Do You Want From Me' / 'Take It Back' / 'Lost For Words' / 'Sorrow' / 'A Great Day For Freedom' / 'Keep Talking' / 'One Of These Days' // 'Shine On You Crazy Diamond, Parts 1-5' / 'Breathe' / 'Time' / 'Breathe (reprise)' / 'High Hopes' / 'Wish You Were Here' / 'Another Brick In The Wall, Part 2' / 'The Great Gig In The Sky' / 'Us And Them' / 'Money' (extended version) / 'Comfortably Numb' / encore: 'Hey You' / 'Run Like Hell'.

Sunday 3 April
CONCERT
Alamo Dome, San Antonio, Texas, USA

Set list: 'Astronomy Dominé' / 'Learning To Fly' / 'What Do You Want From Me' / 'Poles Apart' / 'Sorrow' / 'Take It Back' / 'Lost For Words' / 'Keep Talking' / 'On The Turning Away' // 'Shine On You Crazy Diamond, Parts 1-5' / 'Breathe' / 'Time' / 'Breathe (reprise)' / 'High Hopes' / 'Wish You Were Here' / 'One Of These Days' / 'The Great Gig In The Sky' / 'Us And Them' / 'Money' (extended version) / 'Comfortably Numb' / encore: 'Hey You' / 'Run Like Hell'.

Tuesday 5 April
CONCERT
Rice University Stadium, Houston, Texas, USA

Set list: Astronomy Dominé / 'Learning To Fly' / 'What Do You Want From Me' / 'Take It Back' / 'Lost For Words' / 'Sorrow' / 'A Great Day For Freedom' / 'Keep Talking' / 'One Of These Days' / 'Another Brick In The Wall, Part 2' // 'Shine On You Crazy Diamond, Parts 1-5' / 'Breathe' / 'Time' / 'Breathe (reprise)' / 'High Hopes' / 'Wish You Were Here' / 'The Great Gig In The Sky' (partially) / 'Money' (extended version) / encore: 'Run Like Hell' (partially).
Heavy rain seriously damaged the electrics, curtailing the second set.

Saturday 9 April
CONCERT
Autodromo Hnos. Rodriguez, Mexico City, Mexico

Set list: 'Astronomy Dominé' / 'Learning To Fly' / 'What Do You Want From Me' / 'A Great Day For Freedom' / 'Sorrow' / 'Take It Back' / 'Keep Talking' / 'One Of These Days' // 'Shine On You Crazy Diamond, Parts 1-5' / 'Breathe' / 'Time' / 'Breathe (reprise)' / 'High Hopes' / 'Another Brick In The Wall, Part 2' / 'The Great Gig In The Sky' / 'Us And Them' / 'Money' (extended version) / 'Comfortably Numb' / encore: 'Hey You' / 'Run Like Hell'.

Sunday 10 April
CONCERT
Autodromo Hnos. Rodriguez, Mexico City, Mexico

Set list: 'Astronomy Dominé' / 'Learning To Fly' / 'What Do You Want From Me' / 'A Great Day For Freedom' / 'Sorrow' / 'Take It Back' / 'Another Brick In The Wall, Part 2' / 'Keep Talking' / 'On The Turning Away' // 'Shine On You Crazy Diamond, Parts 1-5' / 'Breathe' / 'Time' / 'Breathe (reprise)' / 'High Hopes' / 'Wish You Were Here' / 'One Of These Days' / 'The Great Gig In The Sky' / 'Us And Them' / 'Money' (extended version) / 'Comfortably Numb' / encore: 'Hey You' / 'Run Like Hell'.

Thursday 14 April
CONCERT
Jack Murphy Stadium, San Diego, California, USA

Set list: 'Astronomy Dominé' / 'Learning To Fly' / 'What Do You Want From Me' / 'A Great Day For Freedom' / 'Sorrow' / 'Take It Back' / 'On The Turning Away' / 'Keep Talking' / 'One Of These Days' // 'Shine On You Crazy Diamond, Parts 1-5' / 'Breathe' / 'Time'

/ 'Breathe (reprise)' / 'High Hopes' / 'Wish You Were Here' / 'Another Brick In The Wall, Part 2' / 'Us And Them' / 'Money' (extended version) / 'Comfortably Numb' / encore: 'Hey You' / 'Run Like Hell'.

Saturday 16 April
CONCERT
The Rose Bowl, Pasadena, Los Angeles, California, USA
Set list: 'Astronomy Dominé' / 'Learning To Fly' / 'What Do You Want From Me' / 'Poles Apart' / 'Sorrow' / 'On The Turning Away' / 'Keep Talking' / 'Take It Back' / 'One Of These Days' // 'Shine On You Crazy Diamond, Parts 1-5' / 'Breathe' / 'Time' / 'Breathe (reprise)' / 'High Hopes' / 'Wish You Were Here' / 'Another Brick In The Wall, Part 2' / 'The Great Gig In The Sky' / 'Us And Them' / 'Money' (extended version) / 'Comfortably Numb' / encore: 'Hey You' / 'Run Like Hell'.

Sunday 17 April
CONCERT
The Rose Bowl, Pasadena, Los Angeles, California, USA
Set list: 'Astronomy Dominé' / 'Learning To Fly' / 'What Do You Want From Me' / 'A Great Day For Freedom' / 'Sorrow' / 'Take It Back' / 'On The Turning Away' / 'Keep Talking' / 'One Of These Days' // 'Shine On You Crazy Diamond, Parts 1-5' / 'Breathe' / 'Time' / 'Breathe (reprise)' / 'High Hopes' / 'Wish You Were Here' / 'Another Brick In The Wall, Part 2' / 'The Great Gig In The Sky' / 'Us And Them' / 'Money' (extended version) / 'Comfortably Numb' / encore: 'Hey You' / 'Run Like Hell'.

Monday 18 April
CANCELLED CONCERT
Silver Bowl, Las Vegas, Nevada, USA
Show cancelled for unknown reasons before tickets went on sale.

Wednesday 20 April
CONCERT
Oakland Coliseum Stadium, Oakland, California, USA
Set list: 'Astronomy Dominé' / 'Learning To Fly' / 'What Do You Want From Me' / 'On The Turning Away' / 'Poles Apart' / 'Sorrow' / 'Take It Back' / 'Keep Talking' / 'One Of These Days' // 'Shine On You Crazy Diamond, Parts 1-5' / 'Breathe' / 'Time' / 'Breathe (reprise)' / 'High Hopes' / 'Wish You Were Here' / 'Another Brick In The Wall, Part 2' / 'The Great Gig In The Sky' / 'Us And Them' / 'Money' (extended version) / 'Comfortably Numb' / encore: 'Hey You' / 'Run Like Hell'.

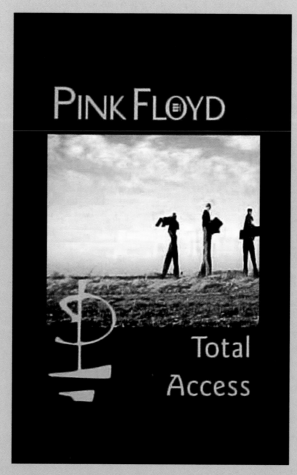

Thursday 21 April
CONCERT
Oakland Coliseum Stadium, Oakland, California, USA
Set list: 'Astronomy Dominé' / 'Learning To Fly' / 'What Do You Want From Me' / 'On The Turning Away' / 'A Great Day For Freedom' / 'Sorrow' / 'Take It Back' / 'Keep Talking' / 'One Of These Days' // 'Shine On You Crazy Diamond, Parts 1-5' / 'Breathe' / 'Time' / 'Breathe (reprise)' / 'High Hopes' / 'Wish You Were Here' / 'Another Brick In The Wall, Part 2' / 'The Great Gig In The Sky' / 'Us And Them' / 'Money' (extended version) / 'Comfortably Numb' / encore: 'Hey You' / 'Run Like Hell'.

Friday 22 April
CONCERT
Oakland Coliseum Stadium, Oakland, California, USA
Set list: 'Astronomy Dominé' / 'Learning To Fly' / 'What Do You Want From Me' / 'On The Turning Away' / 'Poles Apart' / 'Sorrow' / 'Take It Back' / 'Keep Talking' / 'One Of These Days' // 'Shine On You Crazy Diamond, Parts 1-5' / 'Breathe' / 'Time' / 'Breathe (reprise)' / 'High Hopes' / 'The Great Gig In The Sky' / One Slip / 'Us And Them' / 'Wish You Were Here' / 'Money' (extended version) / 'Another Brick In The Wall, Part 2' / 'Comfortably Numb' / encore: 'Hey You' / 'Run Like Hell'.

Sunday 24 April
CONCERT
Sun Devil Stadium, Arizona State University, Tempe, Phoenix, Arizona, USA
Set list: 'Astronomy Dominé' / 'Learning To Fly' / 'What Do You Want From Me' / 'On The Turning Away' / 'Lost For Words' / 'Sorrow' / 'Take It Back' / 'Keep Talking' / 'One Of These Days' // 'Shine On You Crazy Diamond, Parts 1-5' / 'Breathe' / 'Time' / 'Breathe (reprise)' / 'High Hopes' / 'The Great Gig In The Sky' / 'Wish You Were Here' / 'Us And Them' / 'Money' (extended version) / 'Another Brick In The Wall, Part 2' / 'Comfortably Numb' / encore: 'Hey You' / 'Run Like Hell'.

Tuesday 26 April
CONCERT
Sun Bowl Stadium, University of Texas at El Paso, El Paso, Texas, USA
Set list: 'Astronomy Dominé' / 'Learning To Fly' / 'What Do You Want From Me' / 'On The Turning Away' / 'Lost For Words' / 'Sorrow' / 'Take It Back' / 'Keep Talking' / 'One Of These Days' // 'Shine On You Crazy Diamond, Parts 1-5' / 'Breathe' / 'Time' / 'Breathe (reprise)' / 'High Hopes' / 'The Great Gig In The Sky' / 'Wish You Were Here' / 'Us And Them' / 'Money' (extended version) / 'Another Brick In The Wall, Part 2' / 'Comfortably Numb' / encore: 'Hey You' / 'Run Like Hell'.

Thursday 28 April
CONCERT
Texas Stadium, Irving, Dallas, Texas, USA
Set list: 'Astronomy Dominé' / 'Learning To Fly' / 'What Do You Want From Me' / 'On The Turning Away' / 'Poles Apart' / 'Sorrow' / 'Take It Back' / 'Keep Talking' / 'One Of These Days' // 'Shine On You Crazy Diamond, Parts 1-5' / 'Breathe' / 'Time' / 'Breathe (reprise)' / 'High Hopes' / 'The Great Gig In The Sky' / 'Wish You Were Here' / 'Us And Them' / 'Money' (extended version) / 'Another Brick In The Wall, Part 2' / 'Comfortably Numb' / encore: 'Hey You' / 'Run Like Hell'.

Friday 29 April
CONCERT
Texas Stadium, Irving, Dallas, Texas, USA
Set list: 'Astronomy Dominé' / 'Learning To Fly' / 'What Do You Want From Me' / 'On The Turning Away' / 'Coming Back To Life' / 'Sorrow' / 'Take It Back' / 'Keep Talking' / 'One Of These Days' // 'Shine On You Crazy Diamond, Parts 1-5' / 'Breathe' / 'Time' / 'Breathe (reprise)' / 'High Hopes' / 'The Great Gig In The Sky' / 'Wish You Were Here' / 'Us And Them' / 'Money' (extended version) / 'Another Brick In The Wall, Part 2' / 'Comfortably Numb' / encore: 'Hey You' / 'Run Like Hell'.

Sunday 1 May
CONCERT
Legion Field, University of Alabama, Birmingham, Alabama, USA
Set list: 'Astronomy Dominé' / 'Learning To Fly' / 'What Do You Want From Me' / 'On The Turning Away' / 'Take It Back' / 'Lost For Words' / 'Sorrow' / 'Coming Back To Life' / 'Keep Talking' / 'One Of These Days' // 'Shine On You Crazy Diamond, Parts 1-5' / 'Breathe' / 'Time' / 'Breathe (reprise)' / 'High Hopes' / 'The Great Gig In The Sky' / 'Wish You Were Here' / 'Us And Them' / 'Money' (extended version) / 'Another Brick In The Wall, Part 2' / 'Comfortably Numb' / encore: 'Hey You' / 'Run Like Hell'.

Tuesday 3 May
CONCERT
Bobbie Dodd Stadium, Georgia Institute of Technology, Atlanta, Georgia, USA
Set list: 'Astronomy Dominé' / 'Learning To Fly' / 'What Do You Want From Me' / 'On The Turning Away' / 'Take It Back' / 'Lost For Words' / 'Sorrow' / 'Coming Back To Life' / 'Keep Talking' / 'One Of These Days' // 'Shine On You Crazy Diamond, Parts 1-5' / 'Breathe' / 'Time' / 'Breathe (reprise)' / 'High Hopes' / 'The Great Gig In The Sky' / 'Wish You Were Here' / 'Us And Them' / 'Money' (extended version) / 'Another Brick In The Wall, Part 2' / 'Comfortably Numb' / encore: 'Hey You' / 'Run Like Hell'.

Wednesday 4 May
CONCERT
Bobbie Dodd Stadium, Georgia Institute of Technology, Atlanta, Georgia, USA
Set list: 'Astronomy Dominé' / 'Learning To Fly' / 'What Do You Want From Me' / 'On The Turning Away' / 'Coming Back To Life' / 'Sorrow' / 'Take It Back' / 'Keep Talking' / 'One Of These Days' // 'Shine On You Crazy Diamond, Parts 1-5' / 'Breathe' / 'Time' / 'Breathe (reprise)' / 'High Hopes' / 'The Great Gig In The Sky' / 'Wish You Were Here' / 'Us And Them' / 'Money' (extended version) / 'Another Brick In The Wall, Part 2' / 'Comfortably Numb' / encore: 'Hey You' / 'Run Like Hell'.

Friday 6 May
CONCERT
Tampa Stadium, Tampa, Florida, USA
Set list: 'Astronomy Dominé' / 'Learning To Fly' / 'What Do You Want From Me' / 'On The Turning Away' / 'Take It Back' / 'A Great Day For Freedom' / 'Sorrow' / 'Keep Talking' / 'One Of These Days' // 'Shine On You Crazy Diamond, Parts 1-5' / 'Breathe' / 'Time' / 'Breathe (reprise)' / 'High Hopes' / 'The Great Gig In The Sky' / 'Wish You Were Here' / 'Us And Them' / 'Money' (extended version) / 'Another Brick In The Wall, Part 2' / 'Comfortably Numb' / encore: 'Hey You' / 'Run Like Hell'.

Sunday 8 May
CONCERT
Vanderbilt University Stadium, Nashville, Tennessee, USA
Set list: 'Astronomy Dominé' / 'Learning To Fly' / 'What Do You Want From Me' / 'On The Turning Away' / 'Take It Back' / 'A Great Day For Freedom' / 'Sorrow' / 'Keep Talking' / 'One Of These Days' // 'Shine On You Crazy Diamond, Parts 1-5' / 'Breathe' / 'Time' / 'Breathe (reprise)' / 'High Hopes' / 'The Great Gig In The Sky' / 'Wish You Were Here' / 'Us And Them' / 'Money' (extended version) / 'Another Brick In The Wall, Part 2' / 'Comfortably Numb' / encore: 'Hey You' / 'Run Like Hell'.

Tuesday 10 May
CONCERT
Carter-Finley Stadium, North Carolina State University, Rayleigh, North Carolina, USA
Set list: 'Astronomy Dominé' / 'Learning To Fly' / 'What Do You Want From Me' / 'A Great Day For Freedom' / 'Sorrow' / 'Take It Back' / 'On The Turning Away' / 'Keep Talking' / 'One Of These Days' // 'Shine On You Crazy Diamond, Parts 1-5' / 'Breathe' / 'Time' / 'Breathe (reprise)' / 'High Hopes' / 'Wish You Were Here' / 'Another Brick In The Wall, Part 2' / 'The Great Gig In The Sky' / 'Us And Them' / 'Money' (extended version) / 'Comfortably Numb' / encore: 'Hey You' / 'Run Like Hell'.

Thursday 12 May
CONCERT
Death Valley Stadium, Clemson University, Clemson, South Carolina, USA
Set list: 'Astronomy Dominé' / 'Learning To Fly' / 'What Do You Want From Me' / 'On The Turning Away' / 'Take It Back' / 'Poles Apart' / 'Keep Talking' / 'One Of These Days' // 'Shine On You Crazy Diamond, Parts 1-5' / 'Breathe' / 'Time' / 'Breathe (reprise)' / 'High Hopes' / 'The Great Gig In The Sky' / 'Wish You Were Here' / 'Us And Them' / 'Money' (extended version) / 'Another Brick In The Wall, Part 2' / 'Comfortably Numb' / encore: 'Hey You' / 'Run Like Hell'.

Saturday 14 May
CONCERT
Louisiana Superdrome, New Orleans, Louisiana, USA
Set list: 'Astronomy Dominé' / 'Learning To Fly' / 'What Do You Want From Me' / 'On The Turning

Away' / 'Take It Back' / 'Coming Back To Life' / 'Sorrow' / 'Keep Talking' / 'One Of These Days' // 'Shine On You Crazy Diamond, Parts 1-5' / 'Breathe' / 'Time' / 'Breathe (reprise)' / 'High Hopes' / 'The Great Gig In The Sky' / 'Wish You Were Here' / 'Us And Them' / 'Money' (extended version) / 'Another Brick In The Wall, Part 2' / 'Comfortably Numb' / encore: 'Hey You' / 'Run Like Hell'.

Monday 16 May
RECORD RELEASE
'Take It Back' (edit) / 'Astronomy Dominé' (live)
UK 7-inch single release. US 7-inch single release on Tuesday 31 May.

Wednesday 18 May
CONCERT
Foxboro Stadium, Foxboro, Boston, Massachusetts, USA
Set list: 'Astronomy Dominé' / 'Learning To Fly' / 'What Do You Want From Me' / 'On The Turning Away' / "Coming Back To Life" / 'Sorrow' / 'Take It Back' / 'Keep Talking' / 'One Of These Days' // 'Shine On You Crazy Diamond, Parts 1-5' / 'Breathe' / 'Time' / 'Breathe (reprise)' / 'High Hopes' / 'The Great Gig In The Sky' / 'Wish You Were Here' / 'Us And Them' / 'Money' (extended version) / 'Another Brick In The Wall, Part 2' / 'Comfortably Numb' / encore: 'Hey You' / 'Run Like Hell'.

Thursday 19 May
CONCERT
Foxboro Stadium, Foxboro, Boston, Massachusetts, USA
Set list: 'Astronomy Dominé' / 'Learning To Fly' / 'What Do You Want From Me' / 'On

The Turning Away' / 'Take It Back' / 'Poles Apart' / 'Sorrow' / 'Keep Talking' / 'One Of These Days' // 'Shine On You Crazy Diamond, Parts 1-5' / 'Breathe' / 'Time' / 'Breathe (reprise)' / 'High Hopes' / 'The Great Gig In The Sky' / 'Wish You Were Here' / 'Us And Them' / 'Money' (extended version) / 'Another Brick In The Wall, Part 2' / 'Comfortably Numb' / encore: 'Hey You' / 'Run Like Hell'.
MTV filmed the entire concert and clips of 'High Hopes' and 'Keep Talking' were broadcast during a Pink Floyd special broadcast on 28 July.

Friday 20 May
CONCERT
Foxboro Stadium, Foxboro, Boston, Massachusetts, USA
Set list: 'Astronomy Dominé' / 'Learning To Fly' / 'What Do You Want From Me' / 'On The Turning Away' / 'Take It Back' / 'A Great Day For Freedom' / 'Sorrow' / 'Keep Talking' / 'One Of These Days' // 'Shine On You Crazy Diamond, Parts 1-5' / 'Breathe' / 'Time' / 'Breathe (reprise)' / 'High Hopes' / 'The Great Gig In The Sky' / 'Wish You Were Here' / 'Us And Them' / 'Money' (extended version) / 'Another Brick In The Wall, Part 2' / 'Comfortably Numb' / encore: 'Hey You' / 'Run Like Hell'.

Sunday 22 May
CONCERT
Stade du Parc Olympique, Montréal, Quebéc, Canada
Set list: 'Astronomy Dominé' / 'Learning To Fly' / 'What Do You Want From Me' / 'Poles Apart' / 'Sorrow' / 'On The Turning Away' / 'Take It Back' / 'Keep Talking' / 'One Of These Days' // 'Shine On You Crazy Diamond, Parts 1-5' / 'Breathe' / 'Time' / 'Breathe (reprise)' / 'High Hopes' / 'The Great Gig In The Sky' / 'Wish You Were Here' / 'Us And Them' / 'Money' (extended version) / 'Another Brick In The Wall, Part 2' / 'Comfortably Numb' / encore: 'Hey You' / 'Run Like Hell'.

Monday 23 May
CONCERT
Stade du Parc Olympique, Montréal, Quebéc, Canada
Set list: 'Astronomy Dominé' / 'Learning To Fly' / 'What Do You Want From Me' / 'On The Turning Away' / 'A Great Day For Freedom' / 'Take It Back' / 'Sorrow' / 'Keep Talking' / 'One Of These Days' // 'Shine On You Crazy Diamond, Parts 1-5' / 'Breathe' / 'Time' / 'Breathe (reprise)' / 'High Hopes' / 'The Great Gig In The Sky' / 'Wish You Were Here' / 'Us And Them' / 'Money' (extended version) / 'Another Brick In The Wall, Part 2' / 'Comfortably Numb' / encore: 'Hey You' / 'Run Like Hell'

Tuesday 24 May
CONCERT
Stade du Parc Olympique, Montréal, Quebéc, Canada
Set list: 'Astronomy Dominé' / 'Learning To Fly' / 'What Do You Want From Me' / 'On The Turning Away' / 'Coming Back To Life' / 'Sorrow' / 'Take It Back' / 'A Great Day For Freedom' / 'Keep Talking' / 'One Of These Days' // 'Shine On You Crazy Diamond, Parts 1-5' / 'Breathe' / 'Time' / 'Breathe (reprise)' / 'High Hopes' / 'The Great Gig In The Sky' / 'Wish You Were Here' / 'Us And Them' / 'Money' (extended version) / 'Another Brick In The Wall, Part 2' / 'Comfortably Numb' / encore: 'Hey You' / 'Run Like Hell'.

Thursday 26 May
CONCERT
Municipal Stadium, Cleveland, Ohio, USA
Set list: 'Astronomy Dominé' / 'Learning To Fly' / 'What Do You Want From Me' / 'On The Turning Away' / 'Take It Back' / 'Poles Apart' / 'Sorrow' / 'Keep Talking' / 'One Of These Days' // 'Shine On You Crazy Diamond, Parts 1-5' / 'Breathe' / 'Time' / 'Breathe (reprise)' / 'High Hopes' / 'The Great Gig In The Sky' / 'Wish You Were Here' / 'Us And Them' / 'Money' (extended version) / 'Another Brick In The Wall, Part 2' / 'Comfortably Numb' / encore: 'Hey You' / 'Run Like Hell'.

Friday 27 May
CONCERT
Municipal Stadium, Cleveland, Ohio, USA
Set list: 'Astronomy Dominé' / 'Learning To Fly' / 'What Do You Want From Me' / 'On The Turning Away' / 'Sorrow' / 'Take It Back' / 'Keep Talking' / 'One Of These Days' / 'Shine On You Crazy Diamond, Parts 1-5' / 'Breathe' / 'Time' / 'Breathe (reprise)' / 'High Hopes' / 'The Great Gig In The Sky' / 'Wish You Were Here' / 'Us And Them' / 'Money' (extended version) / 'Another Brick In The Wall, Part 2' / 'Comfortably Numb' / encore: 'Hey You' / 'Run Like Hell'.

Sunday 29 May
CONCERT
Ohio State University Stadium, Columbus, Ohio, USA
Set list: 'Astronomy Dominé' / 'Learning To Fly' / 'What Do You Want From Me' / 'On The Turning Away' / 'Coming Back To Life' / 'Sorrow' / 'Take It Back' / 'Keep Talking' / 'One Of These Days' // 'Shine On You Crazy Diamond, Parts 1-5' / 'Breathe' / 'Time' / 'Breathe (reprise)' / 'High Hopes' / 'The Great Gig In The Sky' / 'Wish You Were Here' / 'Us And Them' / 'Money' (extended version) / 'Another Brick In The Wall, Part 2' / 'Comfortably Numb' / encore: 'Hey You' / 'Run Like Hell'.

Tuesday 31 May
CONCERT
Three Rivers Stadium, Pittsburgh, Pennsylvania, USA
Set list: 'Astronomy Dominé' / 'Learning To Fly' / 'What Do You Want From Me' / 'On The Turning Away' / 'Coming Back To Life' / 'Sorrow' / 'Take It Back' / 'Keep Talking' / 'One Of These Days' // 'Shine On You Crazy Diamond, Parts 1-5' / 'Breathe' / 'Time' / 'Breathe (reprise)' / 'High Hopes' / 'The Great Gig In The Sky' / 'Wish You Were Here' / 'Us And Them' / 'Money' (extended version) / 'Another Brick In The Wall, Part 2' / 'Comfortably Numb' / encore: 'Hey You' / 'Run Like Hell'.

Thursday 2 June
CONCERT
Veterans Stadium, Philadelphia, Pennsylvania, USA
Set list: 'Astronomy Dominé' / 'Learning To Fly' / 'What Do You Want From Me' / 'On The Turning Away' / 'Take It Back' / 'Poles Apart' / 'Sorrow' / 'Keep Talking' / 'One Of These Days' // 'Shine On You Crazy Diamond, Parts 1-5' / 'Breathe' / 'Time' / 'Breathe (reprise)' / 'High Hopes' / 'The Great Gig In The Sky' / 'Wish You Were Here' / 'Us And Them' / 'Money' (extended version) / 'Another Brick In The Wall, Part 2' / 'Comfortably Numb' / encore: 'Hey You' / 'Run Like Hell'.

Friday 3 June
CONCERT
Veterans Stadium, Philadelphia, Pennsylvania, USA
Set list: 'Astronomy Dominé' / 'Learning To Fly' / 'What Do You Want From Me' / 'On The Turning Away' / 'Take It Back' / 'A Great Day For Freedom' / 'Sorrow' / 'Keep Talking' / 'One Of These Days' // 'Shine On You Crazy Diamond, Parts 1-5' / 'Breathe' / 'Time' / 'Breathe (reprise)' / 'High Hopes' / 'The Great Gig In The Sky' / 'Wish You Were Here' / 'Us And Them' / 'Money' (extended version) / 'Another Brick In The Wall, Part 2' / 'Comfortably Numb' / encore: 'Hey You' / 'Run Like Hell'.

Saturday 4 June
CONCERT
Veterans Stadium, Philadelphia, Pennsylvania, USA
Set list: 'Astronomy Dominé' / 'Learning To Fly' / 'What Do You Want From Me' / 'On The Turning Away' / 'Coming Back To Life' / 'Sorrow' / 'Take It Back' / 'Keep Talking' / 'One Of These Days' / 'Shine On You Crazy Diamond, Parts 1-5' / 'Breathe' / 'Time' / 'Breathe (reprise)' / 'High Hopes' / 'The Great Gig In The Sky' / 'Wish You Were Here' / 'Us And Them' / 'Money' (extended version) / 'Another Brick In The Wall, Part 2' / 'Comfortably Numb' / encore: 'Hey You' / 'Run Like Hell'.

Monday 6 June
CONCERT
Carrier Dome, Syracuse, New York, USA
Set list: 'Astronomy Dominé' / 'Learning To Fly' / 'What Do You Want From Me' / 'Take It Back' / 'On The Turning Away' / 'Coming Back To Life' / 'Sorrow' / 'Keep Talking' / 'One Of These Days' // 'Shine On You Crazy Diamond, Parts 1-5' / 'Breathe' / 'Time' / 'Breathe (reprise)' / 'Wish You Were Here' / 'Us And Them' / 'High Hopes' / 'Money' (extended version) / 'The Great Gig In The Sky' / 'Another Brick In The Wall, Part 2' / 'Comfortably Numb' / encore: 'Hey You' / 'Run Like Hell'.

Friday 10 June
CONCERT
Yankee Stadium, Bronx, New York City, New York, USA
Set list: 'Astronomy Dominé' / 'Learning To Fly' / 'What Do You Want From Me' / 'On The Turning Away' / 'Poles Apart' / 'Take It Back' / 'Sorrow' / 'Keep Talking' / 'One Of These Days' // 'Shine On You Crazy Diamond, Parts 1-5' / 'Breathe' / 'Time' / 'Breathe (reprise)' / 'High Hopes' / 'The Great Gig In The Sky' / 'Wish You Were Here' / 'Us And Them' / 'Money' (extended version) / 'Another Brick In The Wall, Part 2' / 'Comfortably Numb' / encore: 'Hey You' / 'Run Like Hell'.

Saturday 11 June
CONCERT
Yankee Stadium, Bronx, New York City, New York, USA
Set list: 'Astronomy Dominé' / 'Learning To Fly' / 'What Do You Want From Me' / 'On The Turning Away' / 'Take It Back' / 'Coming Back To Life' / 'Sorrow' / 'Keep Talking' / 'One Of These Days' // 'Shine On You Crazy Diamond, Parts 1-5' / 'Breathe' / 'Time' 'Breathe (reprise)' / 'High Hopes' / 'The Great Gig In The Sky' / 'Wish You Were Here' / 'Us And Them' / 'Money' (extended version) / 'Another Brick

In The Wall, Part 2' / 'Comfortably Numb' / encore: 'Hey You' / 'Run Like Hell'.

Tuesday 14 June
CONCERT
Hoosier Dome, Indianapolis, Indiana, USA
Set list: 'Astronomy Dominé' / 'Learning To Fly' / 'What Do You Want From Me' / 'On The Turning Away' / 'Take It Back' / 'A Great Day For Freedom' / 'Sorrow' / 'Keep Talking' / 'One Of These Days' // 'Shine On You Crazy Diamond, Parts 1-5' / 'Breathe' / 'Time' / 'Breathe (reprise)' / 'High Hopes' / 'The Great Gig In The Sky' / 'Wish You Were Here' / 'Us And Them' / 'Money' (extended version) / 'Another Brick In The Wall, Part 2' / 'Comfortably Numb' / encore: 'Hey You' / 'Run Like Hell'.

Thursday 16 June
CONCERT
Cyclone Stadium, Iowa State University, Ames, Iowa, USA
Set list: 'Astronomy Dominé' / 'Learning To Fly' / 'What Do You Want From Me' / 'On The Turning Away' / 'Take It Back' / 'A Great Day For Freedom' / 'Sorrow' / 'Keep Talking' / 'One Of These Days' // 'Shine On You Crazy Diamond, Parts 1-5' / 'Breathe' / 'Time' / 'Breathe (reprise)' / 'High Hopes' / 'The Great

Gig In The Sky' / 'Wish You Were Here' / 'Us And Them' / 'Money' (extended version) / 'Another Brick In The Wall, Part 2' / 'Comfortably Numb' / encore: 'Hey You' / 'Run Like Hell'.

Saturday 18 June
CONCERT
Mile High Stadium, Denver, Colorado, USA
Set list: 'Astronomy Dominé' / 'Learning To Fly' / 'What Do You Want From Me' / 'On The Turning Away' / 'Take It Back' / 'Coming Back To Life' / 'Sorrow' / 'Keep Talking' / 'One Of These Days' // 'Shine On You Crazy Diamond, Parts 1-5' / 'Breathe' / 'Time' / 'Breathe (reprise)' / 'High Hopes' / 'The Great Gig In The Sky' / 'Wish You Were Here' / 'Us And Them' / 'Money' (extended version) / 'Another Brick In The Wall, Part 2' / 'Comfortably Numb' / encore: 'Hey You' / 'Run Like Hell'.

Monday 20 June
CONCERT
Arrowhead Stadium, Kansas City, Missouri, USA
Set list: 'Astronomy Dominé' / 'Learning To Fly' / 'What Do You Want From Me' / 'On The Turning Away' / 'Poles Apart' / 'Take It Back' /'Sorrow' / 'Keep Talking' / 'One Of These Days' // 'Shine On You Crazy Diamond, Parts 1-5' / 'Breathe' / 'Time' /

'Breathe (reprise)' / 'High Hopes' / 'The Great Gig In The Sky' / 'Wish You Were Here' / 'Us And Them' / 'Money' (extended version) / 'Another Brick In The Wall, Part 2' / 'Comfortably Numb' / encore: 'Hey You' / 'Run Like Hell'.

Wednesday 22 June
CONCERT
Hubert H. Humphrey Metrodome, Minneapolis, Minnesota, USA
Set list: 'Astronomy Dominé' / 'Learning To Fly' / 'What Do You Want From Me' / 'On The Turning Away' / 'Take It Back' / 'Coming Back To Life' / 'Sorrow' / 'Keep Talking' / 'One Of These Days' // 'Shine On You Crazy Diamond, Parts 1-5' / 'Breathe' / 'Time' / 'Breathe (reprise)' / 'High Hopes' / 'The Great Gig In The Sky' / 'Wish You Were Here' / 'Us And Them' / 'Money' (extended version) / 'Another Brick In The Wall, Part 2' / 'Comfortably Numb' / encore: 'Hey You' / 'Run Like Hell'.

Saturday 25 June
CONCERT
British Columbia Place Stadium, Vancouver, British Columbia, Canada
Set list: 'Astronomy Dominé' / 'Learning To Fly' / 'What Do You Want From Me' / 'Coming Back To Life' / 'Sorrow' / 'On The Turning Away' / 'Take It Back' / 'Keep Talking' / 'One Of These Days' // 'Shine On You Crazy Diamond, Parts 1-5' / 'Breathe' / 'Time' / 'Breathe (reprise)' / 'High Hopes' / 'Wish You Were Here' / 'Another Brick In The Wall, Part 2' / 'The Great Gig In The Sky' / 'Us And Them' / 'Money' (extended version) / 'Comfortably Numb' / encore: 'Hey You' / 'Run Like Hell'.

Sunday 26 June
CONCERT
British Columbia Place Stadium, Vancouver, British Columbia, Canada
Set list: 'Astronomy Dominé' / 'Learning To Fly' / 'What Do You Want From Me' / 'A Great Day For Freedom' / 'Sorrow' / 'On The Turning Away' / 'Take It Back' / 'Keep Talking' / 'One Of These Days' // 'Shine On You Crazy Diamond, Parts 1-5' / 'Breathe' / 'Time' / 'Breathe (reprise)' / 'High Hopes' / 'Wish You Were Here' / 'Another Brick In The Wall, Part 2' / 'The Great Gig In The Sky' / 'Us And Them' / 'Money' (extended version) / 'Comfortably Numb' / encore: 'Hey You' / 'Run Like Hell'.

Tuesday 28 June
CONCERT
Commonwealth Stadium, Edmonton, Alberta, Canada
Set list: 'Astronomy Dominé' / 'Learning To Fly' / 'What Do You Want From Me' / 'Sorrow' / 'On The Turning Away' / 'Take It Back' / 'Keep Talking' / 'One Of These Days' // 'Shine On You Crazy Diamond, Parts

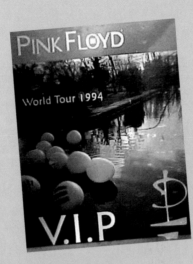

1-5' / 'Breathe' / 'Time' / 'Breathe (reprise)' / 'High Hopes' / 'The Great Gig In The Sky' / 'Wish You Were Here' / 'Money' (extended version) / 'Us And Them' / 'Another Brick In The Wall, Part 2' / 'Comfortably Numb' / encore: 'Hey You' / 'Run Like Hell'.

Friday 1 July
CONCERT
Winnipeg Stadium, Winnipeg, Manitoba, Canada
Set list: 'Astronomy Dominé' / 'Learning To Fly' / 'What Do You Want From Me' / 'On The Turning Away' / 'Poles Apart' / 'Take It Back' / 'Sorrow' / 'Keep Talking' / 'One Of These Days' // 'Shine On You Crazy Diamond, Parts 1-5' / 'Breathe' / 'Time' / 'Breathe (reprise)' / 'High Hopes' / 'Wish You Were Here' / 'The Great Gig In The Sky' / 'Us And Them' / 'Money' (extended version) / 'Another Brick In The Wall, Part 2' / 'Comfortably Numb' / encore: 'Hey You' / 'Run Like Hell'.

Sunday 3 July
CONCERT
Camp Randall Stadium, University of Madison-Wisconsin, Madison, Wisconsin, USA
Set list: 'Astronomy Dominé' / 'Learning To Fly' / 'What Do You Want From Me' / 'On The Turning Away' / 'Take It Back' / 'A Great Day For Freedom' / 'Sorrow' / 'Keep Talking' / 'One Of These Days' // 'Shine On You Crazy Diamond, Parts 1-5' / 'Breathe' / 'Time' / 'Breathe (reprise)' / 'High Hopes' / 'The Great Gig In The Sky' / 'Wish You Were Here' / 'Us And Them' / 'Money' (extended version) / 'Another Brick In The Wall, Part 2' / 'Comfortably Numb' / encore: 'Hey You' / 'Run Like Hell'.

Tuesday 5 July
CONCERT
Canadian National Exhibition Stadium, Toronto, Ontario, Canada
Set list: 'Astronomy Dominé' / 'Learning To Fly' / 'What Do You Want From Me' / 'On The Turning

Away' / 'Take It Back' / 'Coming Back To Life' / 'Sorrow' / 'Keep Talking' / 'One Of These Days' // 'Shine On You Crazy Diamond, Parts 1-5' / 'Breathe' / 'Time' / 'Breathe (reprise)' / 'High Hopes' / 'The Great Gig In The Sky' / 'Wish You Were Here' / 'Us And Them' / 'Money' (extended version) / 'Another Brick In The Wall, Part 2' / 'Comfortably Numb' / encore: 'Hey You' / 'Run Like Hell'.

Wednesday 6 July
CONCERT
Canadian National Exhibition Stadium, Toronto, Ontario, Canada
Set list: 'Astronomy Dominé' / 'Learning To Fly' / 'What Do You Want From Me' / 'On The Turning Away' / 'Take It Back' / 'Sorrow' / 'Keep Talking' / 'One Of These Days' // 'Shine On You Crazy Diamond, Parts 1-5' / 'Breathe' / 'Time' / 'Breathe (reprise)' / 'High Hopes' / 'The Great Gig In The Sky' / 'Wish You Were Here' / 'Us And Them' / 'Money' (extended version) / 'Another Brick In The Wall, Part 2' / 'Comfortably Numb' / encore: 'Hey You' / 'Run Like Hell'.

Thursday 7 July
CONCERT
Canadian National Exhibition Stadium, Toronto, Ontario, Canada
Set list: 'Astronomy Dominé' / 'Learning To Fly' / 'What Do You Want From Me' / 'On The Turning Away' / 'Take It Back' / 'A Great Day For Freedom' / 'Sorrow' / 'Keep Talking' / 'One Of These Days' // 'Shine On You Crazy Diamond, Parts 1-5' / 'Breathe' / 'Time' / 'Breathe (reprise)' / 'High Hopes' / 'The Great Gig In The Sky' / 'Wish You Were Here' / 'Us And Them' / 'Money' (extended version) / 'Another Brick In The Wall, Part 2' / 'Comfortably Numb' / encore: 'Hey You' / 'Run Like Hell'.

Saturday 9 July
CONCERT
Robert F. Kennedy Stadium, Washington, District of Columbia, USA
Set list: 'Astronomy Dominé' / 'Learning To Fly' / 'What Do You Want From Me' / 'On The Turning Away' / 'Poles Apart' / 'Take It Back' / 'Sorrow' / 'Keep Talking' / 'One Of These Days' // 'Shine On You Crazy Diamond, Parts 1-5' / 'Breathe' / 'Time' / 'Breathe (reprise)' / 'High Hopes' / 'The Great Gig In The Sky' / 'Wish You Were Here' / 'Us And Them' / 'Money' (extended version) / 'Another Brick In The Wall, Part 2' / 'Comfortably Numb' / encore: 'Hey You' / 'Run Like Hell'.

Sunday 10 July
CONCERT
Robert F. Kennedy Stadium, Washington, District of Columbia, USA
Set list: 'Astronomy Dominé' / 'Learning To Fly' /

'What Do You Want From Me' / 'On The Turning Away' / 'Take It Back' / 'Coming Back To Life' / 'Sorrow' / 'Keep Talking' / 'One Of These Days' // 'Shine On You Crazy Diamond, Parts 1-5' / 'Breathe' / 'Time' / 'Breathe (reprise)' / 'High Hopes' / 'The Great Gig In The Sky' / 'Wish You Were Here' / 'Us And Them' / 'Money' (extended version) / 'Another Brick In The Wall, Part 2' / 'Comfortably Numb' / encore: 'Hey You' / 'Run Like Hell'.

Tuesday 12 July
CONCERT
Soldier Field, Chicago, Illinois, USA
Set list: 'Astronomy Dominé' / 'Learning To Fly' / 'What Do You Want From Me' / 'On The Turning Away' / 'Lost For Words' / 'Sorrow' / 'Take It Back' / 'Keep Talking' / 'One Of These Days' // 'Shine On You Crazy Diamond, Parts 1-5' / 'Breathe' / 'Time' / 'Breathe (reprise)' / 'High Hopes' / 'The Great Gig In The Sky' / 'Wish You Were Here' / 'Us And Them' / 'Money' (extended version) / 'Another Brick In The Wall, Part 2' / 'Comfortably Numb' / encore: 'Hey You' / 'Run Like Hell'.

Thursday 14 July
CONCERT
Pontiac Silverdome, Pontiac, Detroit, Michigan, USA
Set list: 'Astronomy Dominé' / 'Learning To Fly' / 'What Do You Want From Me' / 'On The Turning Away' / 'Poles Apart' / 'Take It Back' / 'Sorrow' / 'Keep Talking' / 'One Of These Days' // 'Shine On You Crazy Diamond, Parts 1-5' / 'Breathe' / 'Time' / 'Breathe (reprise)' / 'High Hopes' / 'The Great Gig In The Sky' / 'Wish You Were Here' / 'Us And Them' / 'Money' (extended version) / 'Another Brick In The Wall, Part 2' / 'Comfortably Numb' / encore: 'Hey You' / 'Run Like Hell'.

Friday 15 July
CONCERT
Pontiac Silverdome, Pontiac, Detroit, Michigan, USA
Set list: 'Shine On You Crazy Diamond, Parts 1-5' / 'Learning To Fly' / 'High Hopes' / 'Coming Back To Life' / 'Take It Back' / 'Sorrow' / 'Keep Talking' / 'Another Brick In The Wall, Part 2' / 'One Of These Days' // *The Dark Side Of The Moon* / encore: 'Wish You Were Here' / 'Comfortably Numb' / 'Run Like Hell'.

Sunday 17 July
CONCERT
Giants Stadium, East Rutherford, New Jersey, USA
Set list: 'Shine On You Crazy Diamond, Parts 1-5' / 'Learning To Fly' / 'High Hopes' / 'Take It Back' / 'Coming Back To Life' / 'Sorrow' / 'Keep Talking' / 'Another Brick In The Wall, Part 2' / 'One Of These Days' // *The Dark Side Of The Moon* / encore: 'Wish You Were Here' / 'Comfortably Numb' / 'Run Like Hell'.

Monday 18 July
CONCERT
Giants Stadium, East Rutherford, New Jersey, USA
The last night of the tour.
Set list: 'Shine On You Crazy Diamond, Parts 1-5' / 'Learning To Fly' / 'High Hopes' / 'Take It Back' / 'Coming Back To Life' / 'Sorrow' / 'Keep Talking' / 'Another Brick In The Wall, Part 2' / 'One Of These Days' // *The Dark Side Of The Moon* / encore: 'Wish You Were Here' / 'Comfortably Numb' / 'Run Like Hell'.

THE DIVISION BELL - EUROPEAN TOUR

ADDITIONAL TOUR PERSONNEL:
Sam Brown: Backing Vocals
Jon Carin: Keyboards and Vocals
Claudia Fontaine: Backing Vocals
Durga McBroom: Backing Vocals
Dick Parry: Saxophones
Guy Pratt: Bass Guitar and Vocals
Tim Renwick: Guitars
Gary Wallis: Percussion

Friday 22 July
CONCERT
Estádio de Alvalade, Lisbon, Portugal
Set list: 'Astronomy Dominé' / 'Learning To Fly' / 'What Do You Want From Me' / 'On The Turning Away' / 'Take It Back' / 'Coming Back To Life' / 'Lost For Words' / 'Sorrow' / 'Keep Talking' / 'One Of These Days' // 'Shine On You Crazy Diamond, Parts 1-5' / 'Breathe' / 'Time' / 'Breathe (reprise)' / 'High Hopes' / 'The Great Gig In The Sky' / 'Wish You Were Here' / 'Us And Them' / 'Money' (extended version) / 'Another Brick In The Wall, Part 2' / 'Comfortably Numb' / encore: 'Hey You' / 'Run Like Hell'.

Saturday 23 July
CONCERT
Estádio de Alvalade, Lisbon, Portugal
Set list: 'Shine On You Crazy Diamond, Parts 1-5' / 'Learning To Fly' / 'What Do You Want From Me' / 'On The Turning Away' / 'Poles Apart' / 'Take It Back' / 'Sorrow' / 'Keep Talking' / 'One Of These Days' // Astronomy Dominé / 'Breathe' / 'Time' / 'Breathe (reprise)' / 'High Hopes' / 'The Great Gig In The Sky' / 'Wish You Were Here' / 'Us And Them' / 'Money' (extended version) / 'Another Brick In The Wall, Part 2' / 'Comfortably Numb' / encore: 'Hey You' / 'Run Like Hell'.
Melody Maker reported that: 'You cannot begin to imagine. I'm taking about scene and spectacle. About time and place. About the most exorbitantly expensive and expansive stadium show since whatever the last one was. Somebody has just handed me a fact-sheet detailing the logistics of the tour - improbable statistics about rigs and trucks, roadies and cooks, coolies and navvies, the thousands of Nubian slaves who perished in the making of the stage, the scores of elephants it took to drag the fucker over the Alps. I'm talking about You Had To Be There. 70,000 people were there, and another 70,000 the previous night. What is it about Pink Floyd that ensures, wherever they go, multitudes will assemble to worshipfully watch them? Do they fill Antarctic arenas with dizzy, cheering penguins? But I understand. Pink Floyd today may be trademark, a cipher, a hologram of a band who never captured the spirit of the times in the first place, but I understand. I understand because they open with "Shine On You Crazy Diamond", which I still hold to be one of the most perfect and beautiful pieces of music ever written, and they perform it on the scale of the fall of Rome. You don't even have to watch the band. Floyd's old circular screen rises above the filament (yes, the Planetarium slides are back too), but now it's huge, 40 feet across, circled with spotlights - engorged basically, with enormous injections of cash - and an allegorical film by Storm Thorgerson plays upon it. Following "Shine On", the band play a sonic porridge from the last two Floyd albums, the ones which didn't even have the grace to be screamingly, unforgettably awful, like the two before that. I utilised this lengthy aural penumbra - almost half the show - to write the review. I don't know what to suggest you do with yourself during this bit. Bring some knitting, perhaps. David Gilmour has reassembled a Pink Floyd which is more of a showband than a rock 'n' roll group. To even consider it in terms of rock 'n' roll is to miss the point. Pink Floyd belong in the same league as "Holiday on Ice" - massive, mythic, meticulous showbiz, an orgy of stupendous and silly SFX. I have become uncomfortably numb when, at the climax, the very metaphor presents itself in the form of the world's largest revolving mirrored disco ball. It then transforms into the world largest electric palm tree. This show is no less than the exultant culmination of three decades of hi-tech kitsch.'

Monday 25 July
CONCERT
Estadio Anoeta, San Sebastián, Spain
Set list: 'Shine On You Crazy Diamond, Parts 1-5' / 'Learning To Fly' / 'What Do You Want From Me' / 'On The Turning Away' / 'Take It Back' / 'A Great Day For Freedom' / 'Sorrow' / 'Keep Talking' / 'One Of These Days' // Astronomy Dominé / 'Breathe' / 'Time' / 'Breathe (reprise)' / 'High Hopes' / 'The Great Gig In The Sky' / 'Wish You Were Here' / 'Us And Them' / 'Money' (extended version) / 'Another Brick In The Wall, Part 2' / 'Comfortably Numb' / encore: 'Hey You' / 'Run Like Hell'.

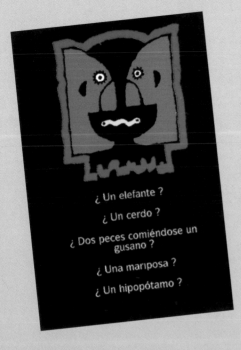

¿ Un elefante ?

¿ Un cerdo ?

¿ Dos peces comiéndose un gusano ?

¿ Una mariposa ?

¿ Un hipopótamo ?

Wednesday 27 July
CONCERT
Estadi Olímpic, Barcelona, Spain
Set list: 'Shine On You Crazy Diamond, Parts 1-5' / 'Learning To Fly' / 'What Do You Want From Me' / 'On The Turning Away' / 'Take It Back' / 'Coming Back To Life' / 'Sorrow' / 'Keep Talking' / 'One Of These Days' // Astronomy Dominé / 'Breathe' / 'Time' / 'Breathe (reprise)' / 'High Hopes' / 'The Great Gig In The Sky' / 'Wish You Were Here' / 'Us And Them' / 'Money' (extended version) / 'Another Brick In The Wall, Part 2' / 'Comfortably Numb' / encore: 'Hey You' / 'Run Like Hell'.

Saturday 30 July
CONCERT
Chateau de Chantilly, Chantilly, France
Set list: 'Shine On You Crazy Diamond, Parts 1-5' / 'Learning To Fly' / 'What Do You Want From Me' / 'On The Turning Away' / 'Take It Back' / 'Lost For Words' / 'Sorrow' / 'Keep Talking' / 'One Of These Days' // Astronomy Dominé / 'Breathe' / 'Time' / 'Breathe (reprise)' / 'High Hopes' / 'The Great Gig In The Sky' / 'Wish You Were Here' / 'Us And Them' / 'Money' (extended version) / 'Another Brick In The Wall, Part 2' / 'Comfortably Numb' / encore: 'Hey You' / 'Run Like Hell'.

Sunday 31 July
CONCERT
Chateau de Chantilly, Chantilly, France
Set list: 'Shine On You Crazy Diamond, Parts 1-5' / 'Learning To Fly' / 'What Do You Want From Me' / 'On The Turning Away' / 'Poles Apart' / 'Take It Back' / 'Sorrow' / 'Keep Talking' / 'One Of These Days' // Astronomy Dominé / 'Breathe' / 'Time' / 'Breathe (reprise)' / 'High Hopes' / 'The Great Gig In The Sky' / 'Wish You Were Here' / 'Us And Them' / 'Money' (extended version) / 'Another Brick In The Wall, Part 2' / 'Comfortably Numb' / encore: 'Hey You' / 'Run Like Hell'.

Tuesday 2 August
CONCERT
Müngersdorfer Stadion, Cologne, Germany
Set list: 'Astronomy Dominé' / 'Learning To Fly' / 'What Do You Want From Me' / 'On The Turning Away' / 'Take It Back' / 'A Great Day For Freedom' / 'Sorrow' / 'Keep Talking' / 'One Of These Days' // 'Shine On You Crazy Diamond, Parts 1-5' / 'Breathe' / 'Time' / 'Breathe (reprise)' / 'High Hopes' / 'The Great Gig In The Sky' / 'Wish You Were Here' / 'Us And Them' / 'Money' (extended version) / 'Another Brick In The Wall, Part 2' / 'Comfortably Numb' / encore: 'Hey You' / 'Run Like Hell'.

Thursday 4 August
CONCERT
Olympiastadion, Munich, Germany
Set list: 'Astronomy Dominé' / 'Learning To Fly' / 'What Do You Want From Me' / 'On The Turning Away' / 'Take It Back' / 'A Great Day For Freedom' / 'Keep Talking' / 'Sorrow' / 'One Of These Days' // 'Shine On You Crazy Diamond, Parts 1-5' / 'Breathe' / 'Time' / 'Breathe (reprise)' / 'High Hopes' / 'The Great Gig In The Sky' / 'Wish You Were Here' / 'Us And Them' / 'Money' (extended version) / 'Another Brick In The Wall, Part 2' / 'Comfortably Numb' / encore: 'Hey You' / 'Run Like Hell'.

Saturday 6 August
CONCERT
Fussballstadion St. Jakob, Basel, Switzerland
Set list: 'Shine On You Crazy Diamond, Parts 1-5' / 'Learning To Fly' / 'High Hopes' / 'Take It Back' / 'Coming Back To Life' / 'Sorrow' / 'Keep Talking' / 'Another Brick In The Wall, Part 2' / 'One Of These Days' // *The Dark Side Of The Moon* / encore: 'Wish You Were Here' / 'Comfortably Numb' / 'Run Like Hell'.

Sunday 7 August
CONCERT
Fussballstadion St. Jakob, Basel, Switzerland
Set list: 'Astronomy Dominé' / 'Learning To Fly' / 'What Do You Want From Me' / 'On The Turning Away' / 'Poles Apart' / 'Take It Back' / 'Sorrow' / 'Keep Talking' / 'One Of These Days' // 'Shine On You Crazy Diamond, Parts 1-5' / 'Breathe' / 'Time' / 'Breathe (reprise)' / 'High Hopes' / 'The Great Gig In The Sky' / 'Wish You Were Here' / 'Us And Them' / 'Money' (extended version) / 'Another Brick In The Wall, Part 2' / 'Comfortably Numb' / encore: 'Hey You' / 'Run Like Hell'.

Tuesday 9 August
CONCERT
Amphitheatre du Chateau de Grammont, Montpellier, France
Set list: 'Astronomy Dominé' / 'Learning To Fly' / 'What Do You Want From Me' / 'On The Turning Away' / 'Take It Back' / 'Coming Back To Life' / 'Sorrow' / 'Keep Talking' / 'One Of These Days' // 'Shine On You Crazy Diamond, Parts 1-5' / 'Breathe' / 'Time' / 'Breathe (reprise)' / 'High Hopes' / 'The Great Gig In The Sky' / 'Wish You Were Here' / 'Us And Them' / 'Money' (extended version) / 'Another Brick In The Wall, Part 2' / 'Comfortably Numb' / encore: 'Hey You' / 'Run Like Hell'.

Thursday 11 August
CONCERT
Esplanade des Quinconces, Bordeaux, France
Set list: 'Astronomy Dominé' / 'Learning To Fly' / 'What Do You Want From Me' / 'On The Turning Away' / 'Take It Back' / 'Coming Back To Life' / 'Sorrow' / 'Keep Talking' / 'One Of These Days' // 'Shine On You Crazy Diamond, Parts 1-5' / 'Breathe' / 'Time' / 'Breathe (reprise)' / 'High Hopes' / 'The Great Gig In The Sky' / 'Wish You Were Here' / 'Us And Them' / 'Money' (extended version) / 'Another Brick In The Wall, Part 2' / 'Comfortably Numb' / encore: 'Hey You' / 'Run Like Hell'.

Saturday 13 August
CONCERT
Hockenheimring, Hockenheim, Germany
Set list: 'Astronomy Dominé' / 'Learning To Fly' / 'What Do You Want From Me' / 'On The Turning Away' / 'Take It Back' / 'Sorrow' / 'A Great Day For Freedom' / 'Keep Talking' / 'One Of These Days' // 'Shine On You Crazy Diamond, Parts 1-5' / 'Breathe' / 'Time' / 'Breathe (reprise)' / 'High Hopes' / 'The Great Gig In The Sky' / 'Wish You Were Here' / 'Us And Them' / 'Money' (extended version) / 'Another Brick In The Wall, Part 2' / 'Comfortably Numb' / encore: 'Hey You' / 'Run Like Hell'.

Tuesday 16 August
CONCERT
Neidersachsenstadion, Hannover, Germany
Set list: 'Shine On You Crazy Diamond, Parts 1-5' / 'Learning To Fly' / 'Take It Back' / 'Sorrow' / 'High Hopes' / 'Keep Talking' / 'Another Brick In The Wall, Part 2' / 'One Of These Days' // *The Dark Side Of The Moon* / encore: 'Wish You Were Here' / 'Comfortably Numb' / 'Run Like Hell'.

Wednesday 17 August
CONCERT
Neidersachsenstadion, Hannover, Germany
Set list: 'Astronomy Dominé' / 'Learning To Fly' / 'What Do You Want From Me' / 'On The Turning Away' / 'Take It Back' / 'A Great Day For Freedom' / 'Sorrow' / 'Keep Talking' / 'One Of These Days' // 'Shine On You Crazy Diamond, Parts 1-5' / 'Breathe' / 'Time' / 'Breathe (reprise)' / 'High Hopes' / 'The Great Gig In The Sky' / 'Wish You Were Here' / 'Money' (extended version) / 'Another Brick In The Wall, Part 2' / 'Comfortably Numb' / encore: 'Hey You' / 'Run Like Hell'.

Friday 19 August
CONCERT
Flugfeld Wiener Neustadt, Vienna, Austria
Set list: 'Shine On You Crazy Diamond, Parts 1-5' /
'Learning To Fly' / 'What Do You Want From Me' / 'On
The Turning Away' / 'Take It Back' / 'Coming Back To
Life' / 'Sorrow' / 'Keep Talking' / 'One Of These Days'
// Astronomy Dominé / 'Breathe' / 'Time' / 'Breathe
(reprise)' / 'High Hopes' / 'The Great Gig In The Sky' /
'Wish You Were Here' / 'Us And Them' / 'Money'
(extended version) / 'Another Brick In The Wall, Part
2' / 'Comfortably Numb' / encore: 'Hey You' / 'Run
Like Hell'.

Sunday 21 August
CONCERT
Maifeld am Olympiastadion, Berlin, Germany
Set list: 'Astronomy Dominé' / 'Learning To Fly' /
'What Do You Want From Me' / 'On The Turning
Away' / 'Take It Back' / 'A Great Day For Freedom' /
'Sorrow' / 'Keep Talking' / 'One Of These Days' //
'Shine On You Crazy Diamond, Parts 1-5' / 'Breathe' /
'Time' / 'Breathe (reprise)' / 'High Hopes' / 'The Great
Gig In The Sky' / 'Wish You Were Here' / 'Money'
(extended version) / 'Another Brick In The Wall, Part
2' / 'Comfortably Numb' / encore: 'Hey You' / 'Run
Like Hell'.

Tuesday 23 August
CONCERT
Parkstadion, Gelsenkirchen, Germany
Set list: 'Astronomy Dominé' / 'Learning To Fly' /
'What Do You Want From Me' / 'On The Turning
Away' / 'Poles Apart' / 'Take It Back' / 'Sorrow' /
'Keep Talking' / 'One Of These Days' //
'Shine On You Crazy Diamond, Parts 1-
5' / 'Breathe' / 'Time' / 'Breathe
(reprise)' / 'High Hopes' / 'The Great
Gig In The Sky' / 'Wish You Were
Here' / 'Us And Them' / 'Money'
(extended version) / 'Another Brick In
The Wall, Part 2' / 'Comfortably
Numb' / encore: 'Hey You' / 'Run Like
Hell'.
The number 19 appeared prominently
on the circular backdrop screen at the
end of this show. All subsequent
shows showed one number less
counting down to the final date of the
tour.

Thursday 25 August
CONCERT
Parken, Copenhagen, Denmark
Set list: 'Shine On You Crazy Diamond,
Parts 1-5' / 'Learning To Fly' / 'What
Do You Want From Me' / 'On The
Turning Away' / 'Take It Back' /
'Coming Back To Life' / 'Sorrow' /

'Keep Talking' / 'One Of These Days' // Astronomy
Dominé / 'Breathe' / 'Time' / 'Breathe (reprise)' / 'High
Hopes' / 'The Great Gig In The Sky' / 'Wish You Were
Here' / 'Us And Them' / 'Money' (extended version) /
'Another Brick In The Wall, Part 2' / 'Comfortably
Numb' / encore: 'Hey You' / 'Run Like Hell'.

Saturday 27 August
CONCERT
Ullevi Stadion, Gothenberg, Sweden
Set list: 'Astronomy Dominé' / 'Learning To Fly' /
'What Do You Want From Me' / 'On The Turning
Away' / 'Take It Back' / 'Sorrow' / 'Keep Talking' /
'One Of These Days' // 'Shine On You Crazy Diamond,
Parts 1-5' / 'Breathe' / 'Time' / 'Breathe (reprise)' /
'High Hopes' / 'The Great Gig In The Sky' / 'Wish You
Were Here' / 'Us And Them' / 'Money' (extended
version) / 'Another Brick In The Wall, Part 2' /
'Comfortably Numb' / encore: 'Hey You' / 'Run Like
Hell'.

Monday 29 August
CONCERT
Valle Hovin Stadion, Oslo, Norway
Set list: 'Astronomy Dominé' / 'Learning To Fly' /
'What Do You Want From Me' / 'On The Turning
Away' / 'Take It Back' / 'Coming Back To Life' /
'Sorrow' / 'Keep Talking' / 'One Of These Days' //
'Shine On You Crazy Diamond, Parts 1-5' / 'Breathe' /
'Time' / 'Breathe (reprise)' / 'High Hopes' / 'The Great
Gig In The Sky' / 'Wish You Were Here' / 'Us And
Them' / 'Money' (extended version) / 'Another Brick
In The Wall, Part 2' / 'Comfortably Numb' / encore:
'Marooned' / 'Run Like Hell'.

Tuesday 30 August
CONCERT
Valle Hovin Stadion, Oslo, Norway
Set list: 'Astronomy Dominé' / 'Learning To Fly' /
'What Do You Want From Me' / 'On The Turning
Away' / 'Take It Back' / 'Poles Apart' / 'Sorrow' /
'Keep Talking' / 'One Of These Days' // 'Shine On You
Crazy Diamond, Parts 1-5' / 'Breathe' / 'Time' /
'Breathe (reprise)' / 'High Hopes' / 'The Great Gig In
The Sky' / 'Wish You Were Here' / 'Us And Them' /
'Money' (extended version) / 'Another Brick In The
Wall, Part 2' / 'Comfortably Numb' / encore:
'Marooned' / 'Run Like Hell'.
The two Oslo shows were the only occasions on which
'Marooned' was performed on the whole tour. A new
projection film accompanied the track that featured
whales - clearly a dig at Norway's whaling policy.
Incidentally, Gilmour's habit of inserting riffs from the
Beatles song, 'Norweigian Wood', into the intro
sequence to 'Run Like Hell' dates from this time.

Wednesday 1 September
CANCELLED CONCERT
Olympiastadion, Helsinki, Finland
Show cancelled, before tickets went on sale,
apparently due to the difficulty in transporting the
show to Finland.

BELOW: PINK FLOYD'S LASER LIGHT SHOW COMPETING
WITH THE EVENING LIGHT AT OSLO'S VALLE HOVIN
STADION, 29 AUGUST 1994.

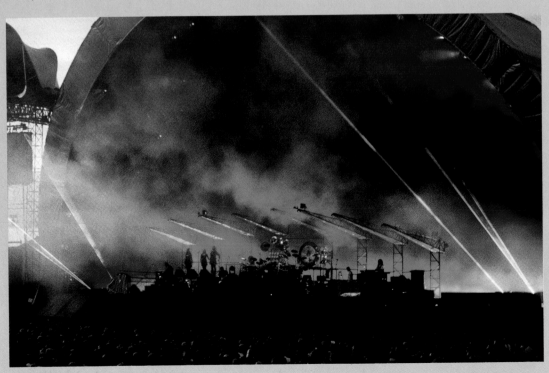

Thursday 2 September
CONCERT
Festivalweise, Werchter, Belgium
Set list: 'Shine On You Crazy Diamond, Parts 1-5' / 'Learning To Fly' / 'What Do You Want From Me' / 'On The Turning Away' / 'Take It Back' / 'A Great Day For Freedom' / 'Sorrow' / 'Keep Talking' / 'One Of These Days' // Astronomy Dominé / 'Breathe' / 'Time' / 'Breathe (reprise)' / 'High Hopes' / 'The Great Gig In The Sky' / 'Wish You Were Here' / 'Money' (extended version) / 'Another Brick In The Wall, Part 2' / 'Comfortably Numb' / encore: 'Hey You' / 'Run Like Hell'.

Friday 3 September
CONCERT
Stadion Feyenoord, Rotterdam, The Netherlands
Set list: 'Astronomy Dominé' / 'Learning To Fly' / 'What Do You Want From Me' / 'On The Turning Away' / 'Poles Apart' / 'Take It Back' / 'Sorrow' / 'Keep Talking' / 'One Of These Days' // 'Shine On You Crazy Diamond, Parts 1-5' / 'Breathe' / 'Time' / 'Breathe (reprise)' / 'High Hopes' / 'The Great Gig In The Sky' / 'Wish You Were Here' / 'Us And Them' / 'Money' (extended version) / 'Another Brick In The Wall, Part 2' / 'Comfortably Numb' / encore: 'Hey You' / 'Run Like Hell'

Saturday 4 September
CONCERT
Stadion Feyenoord, Rotterdam, The Netherlands
Set list: 'Shine On You Crazy Diamond, Parts 1-5' / 'Learning To Fly' / 'Take It Back' / 'Sorrow' / 'Keep Talking' / 'Wish You Were Here' / 'Another Brick In The Wall, Part 2' / 'One Of These Days' // *The Dark Side Of The Moon* / encore: 'High Hopes' / 'Comfortably Numb' / 'Run Like Hell'.

Sunday 5 September
CONCERT
Stadion Feyenoord, Rotterdam, The Netherlands
Set list: 'Shine On You Crazy Diamond, Parts 1-5' / 'Learning To Fly' / 'Take It Back' / 'Sorrow' / 'High Hopes' / 'Keep Talking' / 'Another Brick In The Wall, Part 2' / 'One Of These Days' // *The Dark Side Of The Moon* / encore: 'Comfortably Numb' / 'Wish You Were Here' / 'Run Like Hell'.

Tuesday 7 September
CONCERT
Strahov Stadion, Prague, Czech Republic
Set list: 'Shine On You Crazy Diamond, Parts 1-5' / 'Learning To Fly' / 'What Do You Want From Me' / 'On The Turning Away' / 'Take It Back' / 'A Great Day For Freedom' / 'Sorrow' / 'Coming Back To Life' / 'One Of These Days' // 'Astronomy Dominé' / 'Breathe' / 'Time' / 'Breathe (reprise)' / 'High Hopes' / 'The Great Gig In The Sky' / 'Wish You Were Here' / 'Us And Them' / 'Money' (extended version) / 'Another Brick In The

Wall, Part 2' / 'Comfortably Numb' / encore: 'Hey You' / 'Run Like Hell'.

Thursday 9 September
CONCERT
Stade de la Meinau, Strasbourg, France
Set list: 'Astronomy Dominé' / 'Learning To Fly' / 'What Do You Want From Me' / 'On The Turning Away' / 'Take It Back' / 'Coming Back To Life' / 'Sorrow' / 'Keep Talking' / 'One Of These Days' // 'Shine On You Crazy Diamond, Parts 1-5' / 'Breathe' / 'Time' / 'Breathe (reprise)' / 'High Hopes' / 'The Great Gig In The Sky' / 'Wish You Were Here' / 'Us And Them' / 'Money' (extended version) / 'Another Brick In The Wall, Part 2' / 'Comfortably Numb' / encore: 'Hey You' / 'Run Like Hell'.

Saturday 11 September
CONCERT
Stade du Gerland, Lyon, France
Set list: 'Shine On You Crazy Diamond, Parts 1-5' / 'Learning To Fly' / 'What Do You Want From Me' / 'On The Turning Away' / 'Poles Apart' / 'Take It Back' / 'Sorrow' / 'Keep Talking' / 'One Of These Days' // 'Astronomy Dominé' / 'Breathe' / 'Time' / 'Breathe (reprise)' / 'High Hopes' / 'The Great Gig In The Sky' / 'Wish You Were Here' / 'Us And Them' / 'Money' (extended version) / 'Another Brick In The Wall, Part 2' / 'Comfortably Numb' / encore: 'Hey You' / 'Run Like Hell'.

Monday 13 September
CONCERT
Stadio Delle Alpi, Turin, Italy
Set list: 'Astronomy Dominé' / 'Learning To Fly' / 'What Do You Want From Me' / 'On The Turning Away' / 'Take It Back' / 'A Great Day For Freedom' / 'Sorrow' / 'Keep Talking' / 'One Of These Days' // 'Shine On You Crazy Diamond, Parts 1-5 & 7' / 'Breathe' / 'Time' / 'Breathe (reprise)' / 'High Hopes' / 'The Great Gig In The Sky' / 'Wish You Were Here' / 'Us And Them' / 'Money' (extended version) / 'Another Brick In The Wall, Part 2' / 'Comfortably Numb' / encore: 'Hey You' / 'Run Like Hell'.

Wednesday 15 September
CONCERT
Stadio Friuli, Udine, Italy
Set list: 'Shine On You Crazy Diamond, Parts 1-5 & 7' / 'Learning To Fly' / 'What Do You Want From Me' / 'On The Turning Away' / 'Coming Back To Life' / 'Take It Back' / 'Sorrow' / 'Keep Talking' / 'One Of These Days' // 'Astronomy Dominé' / 'Breathe' / 'Time' / 'Breathe (reprise)' / 'High Hopes' / 'The Great Gig In The Sky' / 'Wish You Were Here' / 'Us And Them' / 'Money' (extended version) / 'Another Brick In The Wall, Part 2' / 'Comfortably Numb' / encore: 'Hey You' / 'Run Like Hell'.

Friday 17 September
CONCERT
Festa Nazionale Dell' Unità, Modena, Italy
Set list: 'Shine On You Crazy Diamond, Parts 1-5 & 7' / 'Learning To Fly' / 'High Hopes' / 'Take It Back' / 'Coming Back To Life' / 'Sorrow' / 'Keep Talking' / 'Another Brick In The Wall, Part 2' / 'One Of These Days' // *The Dark Side Of The Moon* / encore: 'Wish You Were Here' / 'Comfortably Numb' / 'Run Like Hell'.

Sunday 19 September
CONCERT
Studi Di Cinecittá, Rome, Italy
Set list: 'Shine On You Crazy Diamond, Parts 1-5 & 7' / 'Learning To Fly' / 'High Hopes' / 'Take It Back' / 'Coming Back To Life' / 'Sorrow' / 'Keep Talking' / 'Another Brick In The Wall, Part 2' / 'One Of These Days' // *The Dark Side Of The Moon* / encore: 'Wish You Were Here' / 'Comfortably Numb' / 'Run Like Hell'.

Monday 20 September
CONCERT
Studi Di Cinecittá, Rome, Italy
Set list: 'Shine On You Crazy Diamond, Parts 1-5 & 7' / 'Learning To Fly' / 'High Hopes' / 'Take It Back' / 'Coming Back To Life' / 'Sorrow' / 'Keep Talking' / 'Another Brick In The Wall, Part 2' / 'One Of These Days' // *The Dark Side Of The Moon* / encore: 'Wish You Were Here' / 'Comfortably Numb' / 'Run Like Hell'.

Tuesday 21 September
CONCERT
Studi Di Cinecittá, Rome, Italy
Set list: 'Astronomy Dominé' / 'Learning To Fly' / 'What Do You Want From Me' / 'On The Turning Away' / 'Take It Back' / 'A Great Day For Freedom' / 'Sorrow' / 'Keep Talking' / 'One Of These Days' // 'Shine On You Crazy Diamond, Parts 1-5 & 7' / 'Another Brick In The Wall, Part 2' / 'High Hopes' / 'Wish You Were Here' / *The Dark Side Of The Moon* / encore: 'Comfortably Numb' / 'Run Like Hell'.

Thursday 23 September
CONCERT
Stade de Gerland, Lyon, France
Set list: 'Shine On You Crazy Diamond, Parts 1-5 & 7' / 'Learning To Fly' / 'High Hopes' / 'Take It Back' / 'Coming Back To Life' / 'Sorrow' / 'Keep Talking' / 'Another Brick In The Wall, Part 2' / 'One Of These Days' // *The Dark Side Of The Moon* / encore: 'Wish You Were Here' / 'Comfortably Numb' / 'Run Like Hell'.

Saturday 25 September
CONCERT
Stade de la Pontaise, Lausanne, Switzerland
The last night of the tour.
Set list: 'Shine On You Crazy Diamond, Parts 1-5 & 7'
/ 'Learning To Fly' / 'What Do You Want From Me' /
'On The Turning Away' / 'Take It Back' / 'Coming Back
To Life' / 'Sorrow' / 'Keep Talking' / 'One Of These
Days' // 'Astronomy Dominé' / 'Breathe' / 'Time' /
'Breathe (reprise)' / 'High Hopes' / 'The Great Gig In
The Sky' / 'Wish You Were Here' / 'Us And Them' /
'Money' (extended version) / 'Another Brick In The
Wall, Part 2' / 'Comfortably Numb' / encore: 'Hey You'
/ 'Run Like Hell'.

THE DIVISION BELL – UK SHOWS

ADDITIONAL TOUR PERSONNEL:
Sam Brown: Backing Vocals
Jon Carin: Keyboards and Vocals
Claudia Fontaine: Backing Vocals
Durga McBroom: Backing Vocals
Dick Parry: Saxophones
Guy Pratt: Bass Guitar and Vocals
Tim Renwick: Guitars
Gary Wallis: Percussion

Wednesday 12 October
CONCERT
**Earl's Court Exhibition Hall, Earl's Court, London,
England**
The opening night of Pink Floyd's record-breaking run
at Earl's Court was marred by the unfortunate
collapse of a 1,200-capacity seating stand at the rear
of the hall immediately after the lights went down as
Pink Floyd took the stage. No one was seriously hurt,
although eight people were rushed to hospital with
spinal injuries, cuts, bruises and shock, some having
fallen almost twenty feet to the ground. BBC TV were
filming the show for a news item and consequently
covered the accident in time for the 9.00pm news on
BBC1. The show was rescheduled to 17 October on
what was supposed to be a day off for the band. A
free T-shirt and a note of apology from Pink Floyd
was given to everyone who had been sitting in the
collapsed stands.

Thursday 13 October
CONCERT
**Earl's Court Exhibition Hall, Earl's Court, London,
England**
Set list: 'Astronomy Dominé' / 'Learning To Fly' /
'What Do You Want From Me' / 'On The Turning
Away' / 'Take It Back' / 'Coming Back To Life' /
'Sorrow' / 'Keep Talking' / 'One Of These Days' //
'Shine On You Crazy Diamond, Parts 1-5 & 7' /
'Breathe' / 'Time' / 'Breathe (reprise)' / 'High Hopes' /
'The Great Gig In The Sky' / 'Wish You Were Here' /
'Us And Them' / 'Money' (extended version) / 'Another

Brick In The Wall, Part 2' / 'Comfortably Numb' /
encore: 'Hey You' / 'Run Like Hell'.
The Guardian reported that: 'A huge circular screen
sinisterly whirred up to the ceiling and Gilmour spent
10 minutes tweaking out what turned out to be the
introduction to "Shine On You Crazy Diamond". Pink
Floyd will never play one note where 50 will do. They
also never miss a chance to lob in a special effect,
such as lighting the stage a brilliant white when
Gilmour sang the word "shine". Let me admit here
that the "show" part of the show was spectacular. As
well as the expected laser display, there were films,
multi-coloured strobe lights, pyrotechnics and a row
of monitors that lit up into mysterious runes. Oh, and
the giant inflatable pigs, which popped out of boxes
at either side of the stage and shook their trotters
balefully. Good thing the light show was so exciting,
because the music wasn't. Floyd's brand of rockerdelia
is newly back in fashion due to young bands like The
Orb. But it still boils down to the same thing:
portentous synth-pop dressed up with keening female
vocals, saxophones and long, languid guitar passages.
Apart from new songs and technical advances, this is
pretty much the show they've been doing since the
early Seventies. The pigs could have been intended
ironically, but, knowing this band, there was probably
some grumpy symbolism involved. *The Division Bell*
album consumed much of the two-hour set's first half.
The songs are better on record, where Gilmour's
singing and the layers of sound are subtly wrought.
Live, the nuances were squashed under the roar of
two keyboardists, two percussionists, guitarists and
three backing vocalists. To add insult to injury, each
number went on for what seemed like days at a time.
Half a dozen selections from *Dark Side Of The Moon*
were much better. Was it that Gilmour, Mason and
Wright wrote better tunes in 1973, or just that they
were familiar? The loftiness of things like "Breathe"
and "Time" and their co-ordinated laser
accompaniment was truly impressive. But six
numbers don't make a gig. By the end, you were
wishing you had rented a seat cushion, and
bemusedly wondering what the Floyd's electricity bill
was going to be.'

Friday 14 October
CONCERT
**Earl's Court Exhibition Hall, Earl's Court, London,
England**
Set list: 'Shine On You Crazy Diamond, Parts 1-5 & 7'
/ 'Learning To Fly' / 'High Hopes' / 'Take It Back' / 'A
Great Day For Freedom' / 'Sorrow' / 'Keep Talking' /
'Another Brick In The Wall, Part 2' / 'One Of These
Days' // *The Dark Side Of The Moon* / encore: 'Wish
You Were Here' / 'Comfortably Numb' / 'Run Like
Hell'.

Saturday 15 October
CONCERT
Earl's Court Exhibition Hall, Earl's Court, London, England
Set list: 'Astronomy Dominé' / 'Learning To Fly' / 'What Do You Want From Me' / 'On The Turning Away' / 'Take It Back' / 'Coming Back To Life' / 'Sorrow' / 'Keep Talking' / 'One Of These Days' // 'Shine On You Crazy Diamond, Parts 1-5 & 7' / 'Breathe' / 'Time' / 'Breathe (reprise)' / 'High Hopes' / 'The Great Gig In The Sky' / 'Wish You Were Here' / 'Us And Them' / 'Money' (extended version) / 'Another Brick In The Wall, Part 2' / 'Comfortably Numb' / encore: 'Hey You' / 'Run Like Hell'.

Sunday 16 October
CONCERT
Earl's Court Exhibition Hall, Earl's Court, London, England
Set list: 'Shine On You Crazy Diamond, Parts 1-5 & 7' / 'Learning To Fly' / 'High Hopes' / 'Take It Back' / 'Coming Back To Life' / 'Sorrow' / 'Keep Talking' / 'Another Brick In The Wall, Part 2' / 'One Of These Days' // The Dark Side Of The Moon / encore: 'Wish You Were Here' / 'Comfortably Numb' / 'Run Like Hell'.

Monday 17 October
RECORD RELEASE
'High Hopes' (radio edit) / 'Keep Talking' (radio edit)
UK 7-inch single release.
'High Hopes' (album version) / 'Keep Talking' (album version) / 'One Of These Days' (live)
UK CD single release and 12-inch single release.

Monday 17 October
CONCERT
Earl's Court Exhibition Hall, Earl's Court, London, England
Show rescheduled from 12 October.
Set list: 'Astronomy Dominé' / 'Learning To Fly' / 'What Do You Want From Me' / 'On The Turning Away' / 'Poles Apart' / 'Take It Back' / 'Sorrow' / 'Keep Talking' / 'One Of These Days' // 'Shine On You Crazy Diamond, Parts 1-5 & 7' / 'Breathe' / 'Time' / 'Breathe (reprise)' / 'High Hopes' / 'The Great Gig In The Sky' / 'Wish You Were Here' / 'Us And Them' / 'Money' (extended version) / 'Another Brick In The Wall, Part 2' / 'Comfortably Numb' / encore: 'Hey You' / 'Run Like Hell'.

Wednesday 19 October
CONCERT
Earl's Court Exhibition Hall, Earl's Court, London, England
Set list: 'Shine On You Crazy Diamond, Parts 1-5 & 7' / 'Learning To Fly' / 'High Hopes' / 'Lost For Words' / 'A Great Day For Freedom' / 'Keep Talking' / 'Coming Back To Life' / 'Sorrow' / 'Another Brick In The Wall,

Part 2' / 'One Of These Days' // The Dark Side Of The Moon / encore: 'Wish You Were Here' / 'Comfortably Numb' / 'Run Like Hell'.

Thursday 20 October
CONCERT
Earl's Court Exhibition Hall, Earl's Court, London, England
Set list: 'Shine On You Crazy Diamond, Parts 1-5 & 7' / 'Learning To Fly' / 'High Hopes' / 'Take It Back' / 'Coming Back To Life' / 'Sorrow' / 'Keep Talking' / 'Another Brick In The Wall, Part 2' / 'One Of These Days' // The Dark Side Of The Moon / encore: 'Wish You Were Here' / 'Comfortably Numb' / 'Run Like Hell'.
The entire concert was recorded and filmed for the official release of the tour video, Pulse. An edited version of this was broadcast in the USA on Pay-Per-View on 1 November and in the UK on BBC1 TV on 15 November at 10.55pm.

Friday 21 October
CONCERT
Earl's Court Exhibition Hall, Earl's Court, London, England
Astronomy Dominé / 'Learning To Fly' / 'What Do You Want From Me' / 'On The Turning Away' / 'Poles Apart' / 'Take It Back' / 'Sorrow' / 'Keep Talking' / 'One Of These Days' // 'Shine On You Crazy Diamond, Parts 1-5 & 7' / 'Breathe' / 'Time' / 'Breathe (reprise)' / 'High Hopes' / 'The Great Gig In The Sky' / 'Wish You Were Here' / 'Us And Them' / 'Money' (extended version) / 'Another Brick In The Wall, Part 2' / 'Comfortably Numb' / encore: 'Hey You' / 'Run Like Hell'.

Saturday 22 October
CONCERT
Earl's Court Exhibition Hall, Earl's Court, London, England
Set list: 'Astronomy Dominé' / 'Learning To Fly' / 'What Do You Want From Me' / 'On The Turning Away' / 'Take It Back' / 'A Great Day For Freedom' / 'Sorrow' / 'Keep Talking' / 'One Of These Days' // 'Shine On You Crazy Diamond, Parts 1-5 & 7' / 'Breathe' / 'Time' / 'Breathe (reprise)' / 'High Hopes' / 'The Great Gig In The Sky' / 'Wish You Were Here' / 'Us And Them' / 'Money' (extended version) / 'Another Brick In The Wall, Part 2' / 'Comfortably Numb' / encore: 'Hey You' / 'Run Like Hell'.

Sunday 23 October
CONCERT
Earl's Court Exhibition Hall, Earl's Court, London, England
Set list: 'Shine On You Crazy Diamond, Parts 1-5 & 7' / 'Learning To Fly' / 'High Hopes' / 'Take It Back' / 'Coming Back To Life' / 'Sorrow' / 'Keep Talking' / 'Another Brick In The Wall, Part 2' / 'One Of These

Days' // The Dark Side Of The Moon / encore: 'Wish You Were Here' / 'Comfortably Numb' / 'Run Like Hell'.

Wednesday 26 October
CONCERT
Earl's Court Exhibition Hall, Earl's Court, London, England
Set list: 'Astronomy Dominé' / 'Learning To Fly' / 'What Do You Want From Me' / 'On The Turning Away' / 'Take It Back' / 'Coming Back To Life' / 'Sorrow' / 'Keep Talking' / 'One Of These Days' // 'Shine On You Crazy Diamond, Parts 1-5 & 7' / 'Breathe' / 'Time' / 'Breathe (reprise)' / 'High Hopes' / 'The Great Gig In The Sky' / 'Wish You Were Here' / 'Us And Them' / 'Money' (extended version) / 'Another Brick In The Wall, Part 2' / 'Comfortably Numb' / encore: 'Hey You' / 'Run Like Hell'.

Thursday 27 October
CONCERT
Earl's Court Exhibition Hall, Earl's Court, London, England
Set list: 'Shine On You Crazy Diamond, Parts 1-5 & 7' / 'Learning To Fly' / 'What Do You Want From Me' / 'On The Turning Away' / 'Take It Back' / 'A Great Day For Freedom' / 'Sorrow' / 'Keep Talking' / 'One Of These Days' // 'Astronomy Dominé' / 'Breathe' / 'Time' / 'Breathe (reprise)' / 'High Hopes' / 'The Great Gig In The Sky' / 'Wish You Were Here' / 'Us And Them' / 'Money' (extended version) / 'Another Brick In The Wall, Part 2' / 'Comfortably Numb' / encore: 'Hey You' / 'Run Like Hell'.

Friday 28 October
CONCERT
Earl's Court Exhibition Hall, Earl's Court, London, England
Set list: 'Shine On You Crazy Diamond, Parts 1-5 & 7' / 'Learning To Fly' / 'High Hopes' / 'Take It Back' / 'Poles Apart' / 'Sorrow' / 'Keep Talking' / 'Another Brick In The Wall, Part 2' / 'One Of These Days' // The Dark Side Of The Moon / encore: 'Wish You Were Here' / 'Comfortably Numb' / 'Run Like Hell'.
David Gilmour's friend, the science-fiction author, Douglas Adams joined Pink Floyd on stage during 'Brain Damage' to play acoustic guitar. It was a birthday present to Adams, although his participation was unannounced and he remained in the background.

Saturday 29 October
CONCERT
Earl's Court Exhibition Hall, Earl's Court, London, England
The last night of the tour.
Set list: 'Shine On You Crazy Diamond, Parts 1-5 & 7' / 'Learning To Fly' / 'High Hopes' / 'Take It Back' / 'Coming Back To Life' / 'Sorrow' / 'Keep Talking' / 'Another Brick In The Wall, Part 2' / 'One Of These

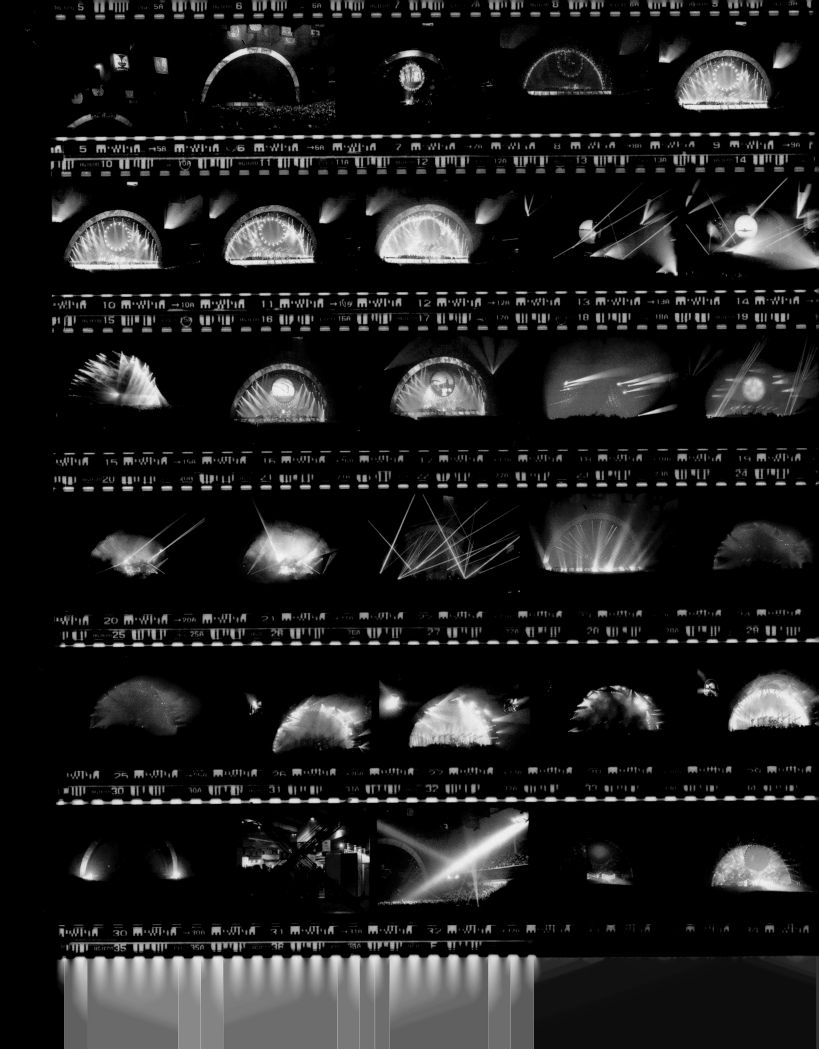

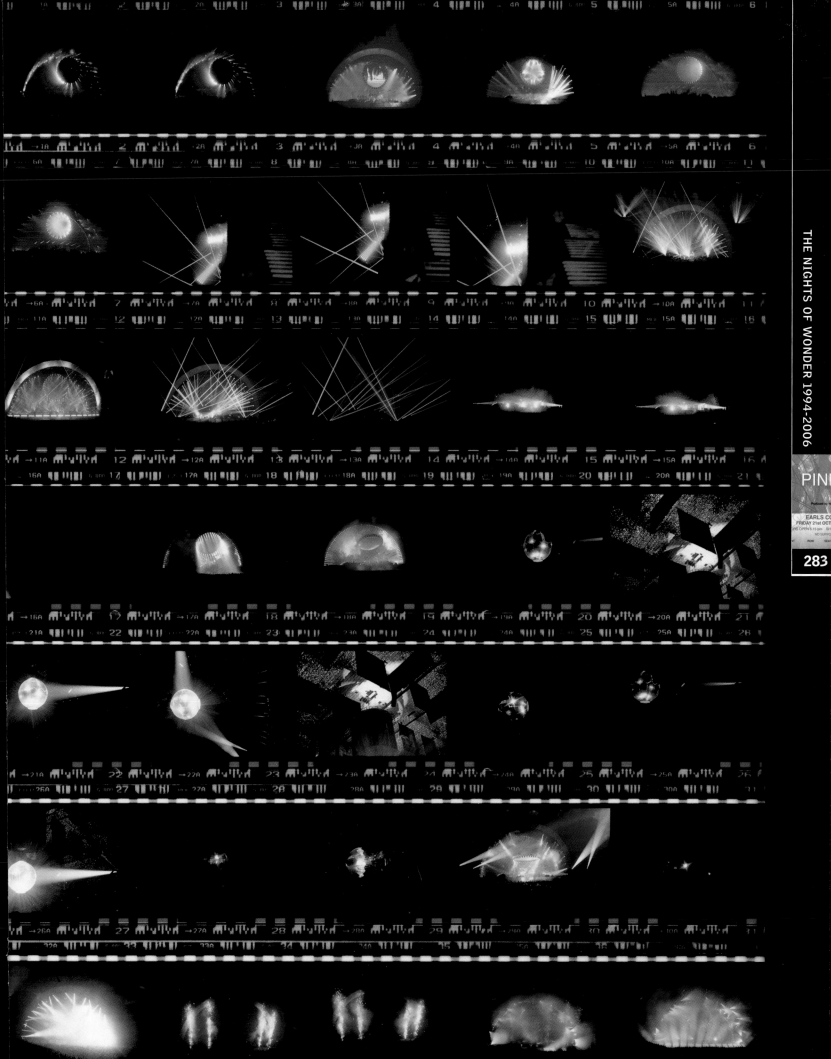

> november 1994

PREVIOUS PAGE AND LEFT: PINK FLOYD ON STAGE DURING THEIR RECORD-BREAKING 15 NIGHT RUN AT EARLS COURT ON 14 OCTOBER 1994.

Days' // *The Dark Side Of The Moon* / encore: 'Wish You Were Here' / 'Comfortably Numb' / 'Run Like Hell'.

Tuesday 15 November
TV SHOW
BBC Television Centre, White City, London, England
BBC1 TV broadcast a 40-minute official history of Pink Floyd entitled 'Pink Floyd – The Story' for its *Omnibus* documentary programme featuring previously unseen archive footage and interviews with members of the band. It was broadcast on BBC1 at 10.15pm. The programme was followed by a complete broadcast of the previously mentioned Earl's Court concert, filmed on 20 October and broadcast at 10.55pm.

1995

Monday 5 June
RECORD RELEASE
Pulse
UK and US album release.
Mojo commented that: 'Far from peddling limp live renderings of the Floyd classics *Pulse*, propels familiar old favourites into new dimensions. *Dark Side Of The Moon* sounds more accomplished and vital now than on any bootleg from the '70's; *The Wall*'s "Comfortably Numb" is more wildly emotive in its masturbatory guitar splendour. Forget the stoopid flashing light on the box or the predictable ageist snipes, feed the corporate rock leviathan and nourish your ears with two transcendent hours of Big Rock history.'

Monday 12 June
VIDEO RELEASE
Pulse
UK and US VHS video release.
The Daily Mail commented that: 'They've got the technology, but as performers Pink Floyd come over as passionate as Thunderbirds puppets. Despite all

the slick projected images and lasers a go-go filmed at Earl's Court last October, the exercise is curiously one-dimensional. It includes the entire *Dark Side Of The Moon* set but at two and half hours, keep your knitting close by.'

1996

Wednesday 17 January
AWARDS CEREMONY
11th Annual Rock And Roll Hall of Fame, The Main Ballroom, Waldorf-Astoria Hotel, Manhattan, New York City, New York, USA
Pink Floyd were inducted into the prestigious Hall of Fame at a ceremony also celebrating the induction of David Bowie, Jefferson Airplane, Little Willie John, Gladys Knight and The Pips, The Shirelles, The Velvet Underground, Pete Seeger and Tom Donahue. The band were presented with the award by Billy Corgan of the Smashing Pumpkins, after which Gilmour and Wright (Mason stood down) were joined on stage by Corgan for a rendition of 'Wish You Were Here', in 'Unplugged' fashion. Gilmour remained on stage for the presentation finale, joining Arlo Guthrie, members of Jefferson Airplane, Stevie Wonder and David Byrne for a rendition of Pete Seeger's 'Goodnight Irene'. A 29-track promotional CD (EMI DPRO 10467) to mark the event that included Pink Floyd's 'Wish You Were Here', 'Money' and 'See Emily Play', was presented to attending guests.

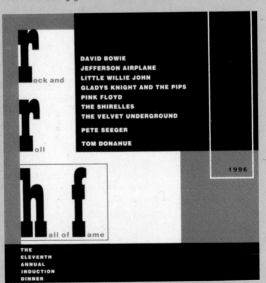

1997-2002

1997

Monday 18 August
RECORD RELEASE
1997 Vinyl Collection
UK album release.

1998 – 1999
Pink Floyd were inactive in 1998 and 1999.

2000

Monday 27 March
RECORD RELEASE
Is There Anybody Out There? The Wall Live: Pink Floyd 1980-81
UK album release. US release on Monday 17 April 2000.
Rolling Stone commented that: 'Pink Floyd's 1980-81 stadium presentations of *The Wall* barely qualified as live rock: They were a theatrical pageant, with a wall built and demolished on stage. The sparkling clarity of this set, assembled from several London performances, only makes it obvious how slavishly the sound of the stage show followed the studio album. This is the most pointless album of its kind since Depeche Mode's *Songs Of Faith And Devotion Live*.' EMI Records held a press launch at The Imperial War Museum, Elephant & Castle, London, England on 9 March 2000.

2001
Pink Floyd were inactive in 2001.

2002

Monday 4 November
RECORD RELEASE
Echoes – The Best Of Pink Floyd
UK & US album release.
Pop Matters commented that: 'Is there a middle ground when it comes to liking the music of Pink Floyd? Can one be a "casual" Pink Floyd fan? Personal experience would seem to dictate not, but perhaps times have changed. After all, we are talking about a "Best Of" collection here, something that usually doesn't settle well with Floyd fans, or that does the

original albums any justice whatsoever. It would seem that the undoable task of creating a successful Pink Floyd "Best Of" has finally been taken care of. Somehow, the Floyd have managed to keep their music going in that rare fashion that suggests they'll never go out of style, without releasing "new" material on a regular basis. *Echoes* is ultimately a testament to that fact.'

2003-2006

2003

Monday 24 March
RECORD RELEASE
The Dark Side Of The Moon
UK & US 30th anniversary 5.1 SACD album release.
High Fidelity Review commented that: 'It is a sparkling success, defying the gravity of expectations that inevitably tug at such a staple of popular music. James Guthrie, the sound engineer responsible for the new 5.1 mix of the album, found a way to succeed where there were ten thousand ways to fail. It is the most important multi-channel disc ever made.'

Friday 10 October – Sunday 25 January 2004
EXHIBITION
Pink Floyd Interstellar, Cité de la Musique, Porte de Pantin, Paris, France
Organised by the Paris Museum of Music, this was an officially sanctioned exhibition tracing Pink Floyd's career with many display items of memorabilia, instruments and stage props loaned by band members and associates. It was officially opened by the French Minister of Culture, Jean-Jacques Aillagon, at an invitation-only preview on 9 October. Over the first three days of the exhibition there was also a programme of film screenings in the museum's theatre including on 10 October the BBC's 1994 Pink Floyd *Omnibus* documentary, Peter Whitehead's *London 1966-67* film and Barbet Schroeder's film *More*; on 11 October *Pink Floyd The Wall*, Anthony Stern's *San Francisco*, *Pink Floyd Live At Pompeii*, the BBC's 2001 *Omnibus* documentary 'Syd Barrett,

Crazy Diamond' and the documentary film *Behind The Wall*; on 12 October the 1977 French TV broadcast of the Pink Floyd-Roland Petit ballet from 1973, a collection of TV clips including 'Astronomy Dominé' from BBC TV's *Look Of The Week*, the 'Arnold Layne' promotional film, 'See Emily Play' from Belgian TV Febraury 1968, 'Flaming' from ORTF's *Bouton Rouge*, 'Set The Controls For The Heart Of The Sun' from BBC TV's *All My Loving*, 'Let There Be More Light' from ORTF's *Surprise Partie*, 'A Saucerful Of Secrets' from ORTF's *Forum Musiques*, 'One Of These Days' from BBC TV's *Old Grey Whistle Test* and an edited screening of the concert film *Pulse*.

2004

Pink Floyd were inactive in 2004.

2005

THE LIVE 8 REUNION CONCERT

Roger Waters reunited with Pink Floyd to perform at this spectacular global awareness event that saw similar concerts staged in Berlin, Paris, Philadelphia, Rome, Barrie (Toronto) and Tokyo. More than 1,000 musicians performed at the concerts, which was broadcast on 182 television networks and 2,000 radio networks worldwide. The show in London was attended by over 200,000 people and ran for almost 12 hours and featured performances by Paul McCartney, U2, Coldplay, Richard Ashcroft, Elton John, Pete Doherty, Dido, Youssou N'Dour, Stereophonics, REM, Ms Dynamite, Keane, Travis, Bob Geldof, Annie Lennox, UB40, Snoop Dogg, Razorlight, Madonna, Snow Patrol, The Killers, Joss Stone, The Scissor Sisters, Velvet Revolver, Sting, Mariah Carey, Robbie Williams and The Who alongside a whole host of other incidental guests and speakers. Pink Floyd were the penultimate act followed by Paul McCartney who then led an all-star finale to the show.

Tuesday 28, Wednesday 29 & Thursday 30 June
REHEARSALS
Black Island Studios, Acton, London, England
Pink Floyd and Roger Waters rehearsed for just three days prior to their performance at Live 8, the first time the four members of this line-up had performed since the final show of *The Wall* concerts held at London's Earl's Court on 17 June 1981. As with most of the other performers a final 'dress' rehearsal was held at Hyde Park on the evening prior to show day.

Saturday 2 July
CONCERT
Live 8, Hyde Park, London, England
Set List: 'Breathe' / 'Money' / 'Wish You Were Here' / 'Comfortably Numb'.
Pink Floyd and Roger Waters were supplemented on stage by Jon Carin (keyboards), Dick Parry (saxophones), Tim Renwick (guitars) and Carol

Kenyon (backing vocals).
Gilmour, Mason and Wright also joined in the all-star finale of 'Hey Jude', led by Paul McCartney.
The entire show was transmitted live on BBC TV (BBC 2 from 1.00pm and then BBC 1 from 4.00pm) and BBC Radio One in a 12-hour presentation from 1.00pm, as well as various other TV and radio networks worldwide. The entire concert featuring all of Pink Floyd's set, plus a studio rehearsal of 'Wish You Were Here' was released as a four DVD set entitled *Live 8* on 7 November 2005.
Brain Damage reported that: 'With the concert overrunning two and a half hours over its extended finish, the band didn't manage to hit the stage until around 11pm, but it was worth the wait. Many reports in the media attested to the fact that the Floyd, reunited for this one, special occasion with Roger Waters, were one of the bands that stole the show at *Live 8*. Despite the late running of the show (which was to eventually finish at midnight), the band performed their complete rehearsed set of "Breathe"/"Breathe (reprise)", "Money", "Wish You Were Here", and "Comfortably Numb". And what a performance! The band were stripped back down to a basic line-up, with only the addition of Tim Renwick on guitar, lurking in the shadows; Dick Parry on sax and Carol Kenyon on backing vocals during "Money' and "Comfortably Numb" and Jon Carin, heavily to the rear of the stage, unlit, shrouded in smoke, playing keyboards during their set! To see and hear the band back chiefly to their core unit was a sheer joy, and got even the non-Floyd fans in the audience applauding for more. In one touching moment, during the introductory guitar work of "Wish You Were Here", Roger said: "It's actually quite emotional, standing up here with these three guys after all these years. Standing to be counted with the rest of you. Anyway, we're doing this for everyone who's not here, particularly, of course for Syd."'

Wednesday 16 November
AWARDS CEREMONY
UK Music Hall Of Fame Induction Ceremony,
Alexandra Palace, Muswell Hill, London, England
The induction ceremony of the second annual UK

ABOVE: THE END OF AN ERA: PINK FLOYD BOW OUT AT *LIVE 8*, HYDE PARK, LONDON, 2 JULY 2005.

Music Hall of Fame saw Pink Floyd members David Gilmour and Nick Mason in attendance (with Roger Waters on screen via video-link from Rome) to accept their place in recognition of their contribution to popular music with an introductory speech given by Pete Townshend. Other inductees included Aretha Franklin, Bob Dylan, The Eurythmics, Joy Division/New Order, Jimi Hendrix, The Kinks, The Who, Black Sabbath and John Peel. The event was filmed and broadcast on Channel 4 TV on 17 November 2005 at 9.00pm.

2006

Sunday 6 January 1946 - Friday 7 July
ROGER KEITH 'SYD' BARRETT
Pink Floyd's founding member, Roger Keith 'Syd' Barrett, passed away on this day due to complications arising from a prolonged battle with diabetes. He was 60 years old. The current members of Pink Floyd together with Roger Waters issued a brief statement following the news saying that, 'The band are naturally very upset and sad to learn of Syd Barrett's death. Syd was the guiding light of the early band line up and leaves a legacy which continues to inspire.' A private family service was held in Cambridge on 17 July.

Monday 10 July
VIDEO RELEASE
Pulse
UK DVD video release. US DVD video release on 11 July.
Brain Damage commented that: 'From various comments made over the years, the band was keen for this to be seen as one of the best music DVD's ever released. I think they've succeeded admirably. Again, Pink Floyd have raised the bar, and produced a DVD that sets new standards in the realm of music.'
EMI records held a press launch attended by David Gilmour, Nick Mason and Richard Wright in which they participated in a Q&A session hosted by BBC Radio 2 DJ Stuart Maconie at the Vue Cinema, Leicester Square, London, England on 3 July.

solo careers and discography

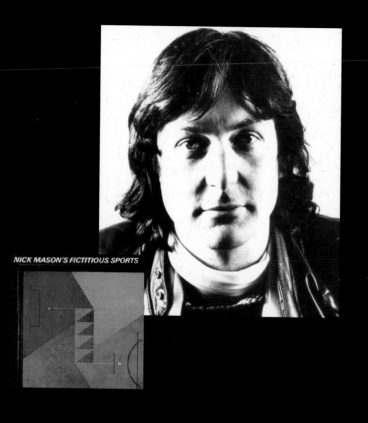

NICK MASON'S FICTITIOUS SPORTS

Richard Wright
Wet Dream

syd barrett

Roger Keith 'Syd' Barrett was born in Cambridge on 6 January 1946. He was the fourth of five children to Dr. Arthur Max Barrett, a Pathologist at Addenbrooke's Hospital in Cambridge, and Winifred Barrett. He attended the Morley Memorial Junior School where he was taught by Roger Waters' mother and continued his education at the Cambridge County High School.
In December 1961 his father unexpectedly passed away and this profoundly affected him in later life. However, in 1962 he won a scholarship to attend a two-year art and design foundation course at the Cambridge College of Arts And Technology where, in his second year, he met David Gilmour. After leaving college he moved to London to take up a degree course at Camberwell School of Art in the summer of 1964. Shortly thereafter he reacquainted himself with Roger Waters and joined the fledgling bands that ultimately became Pink Floyd.
His brief solo career after leaving Pink Floyd in early 1968 was hampered by his continuing emotional problems. Throughout the 1970s he remained in London, where he was the subject of many press reports, or 'Syd sightings' as they became known. None of these suggested any improvement in his mental health and in the late Seventies Barrett retired to his native Cambridge, where he continued to lead a reclusive life. He succumbed to complications arising from a long battle with diabetes on Friday 7 July, 2006.

DISCOGRAPHY

THE MADCAP LAUGHS
Barrett's solo career began on 13 May 1968, when Peter Jenner booked EMI Studios at Abbey Road, London, to start work on a new album. The initial results were disappointing and recording was suspended, but when sessions resumed on 10 April 1969 the work proved good enough to compile as Syd's first solo album. Interviewed in *Melody Maker* in early 1970, Barrett announced he would be doing a solo tour in May of that year, but this never materialised.

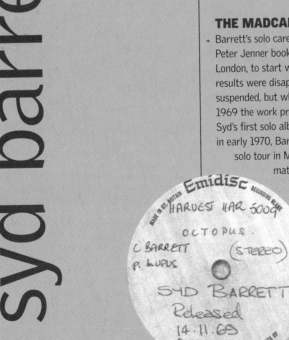

Friday 14 November 1969
'Octopus' / 'Golden Hair'
UK: EMI Harvest HAR 5009 (7-inch single).

Friday 2 January 1970
THE MADCAP LAUGHS
UK: EMI Harvest EMI SHVL 765 (vinyl album).

Track list: 'Terrapin' / 'No Good Trying' / 'Love You' / 'No Man's Land' / 'Dark Globe' / 'Here I Go' / 'Octopus' / 'Golden Hair' / 'Long Gone' / 'She Took A Long Cold Look' / 'Feel' / 'If It's In You' / 'Late Night'.
Additional musicians on 'No Good Trying' and 'Love You' Elton Dean (alto, saxello, electric piano), Mike Ratledge (organ, electric piano), Hugh Hopper (bass guitar) and Robert Wyatt (drums).
Recorded and mixed at EMI Studios, Abbey Road, London, England. Engineered by Peter Bown. Produced by Syd Barrett, Malcolm Jones, Peter Jenner, David Gilmour and Roger Waters.

Engineered by Jeff Jarratt, Pete Mew, Mike Sheady, Phil McDonald and Tony Clark.
Artwork by Hipgnosis.
Highest chart position UK No.40.
Reissued:
UK: Harvest CDP 7466072 (CD album, 1985).
UK: EMI CD GO2053 (CD album with revised packaging and bonus tracks as per *Crazy Diamond* box set edition released, 1993).
UK: EMI 724385566318 (Limited edition vinyl album in original packaging as part of the EMI 100 series celebrating EMI Records' centenary. Pressed on 180-gram virgin vinyl released, 1997).
UK: EMI Simply Vinyl SVLP 289 (Limited edition vinyl album pressed on 180 gram virgin vinyl with original packaging, 2000).
US: Capitol CDP 7466072 (CD album, 1990).
US: Capitol D 102644 (CD album, 1991).

BARRETT
Barrett's second solo album was less bleak than its predecessor, and even incorporated the whimsical 'Effervescing Elephant', written in his youth. The

.... TOGETHER IN A SPECIAL DOUBLE ALBUM PACKAGE

Syd Barrett

Produced by David Gilmour, Roger Waters, Richard Wright and Malcolm Jones.

Featuring –
Syd Barrett – Vocals and Guitars
David Gilmour – Bass
Richard Wright – Keyboards
Jerry Shirley – Drums (courtesy of A&M Records Inc.)

'Syd Barrett' is the complete collection of recorded solo works by the founder member of Pink Floyd, often described, with some justification, as one of the greatest song-writers of our time.

Available on HARVEST SHDW 404 at the special price of £3.25

album was recorded at EMI's Abbey Road Studios and produced entirely by David Gilmour and Richard Wright, who also played bass and keyboards respectively. Sadly, this was to be Barrett's last original release. Despite Peter Jenner's efforts in the summer of 1974 to get him back in the studio the sessions were aborted after four days when it became obvious that nothing of any value would come from them.

Friday 13 November 1970
BARRETT
UK: EMI Harvest SHSP 4007 (vinyl album).
Track list: 'Baby Lemonade' / 'Love Song' / 'Dominoes' / 'It Is Obvious' / 'Rats' / 'Masie' / 'Gigolo Aunt' / 'Waving My Arms In The Air' / 'I Never Lied To You' / 'Wined And Dined' / 'Wolfpack' / 'Effervescing Elephant'.
Additional musicians: Jerry Shirley (Drums and Percussion on 'Gigolo Aunt'); David Gilmour (Bass and 12-string guitar on 'Baby Lemonade', drums on 'Dominoes', second organ on 'It Is Obvious' and 'Gigolo Aunt' and all instruments except lead guitar on 'Wined And Dined'); Richard Wright (organ, piano and harmonium); Vic Saywell (Tuba on 'Effervescing Elephant'); Willey (Percussion on 'Gigolo Aunt').
Recorded and mixed at EMI Studios, Abbey Road, London, England.
Produced by David Gilmour.
Artwork by Hipgnosis.
Reissued:
UK: EMI CDP7466062 (CD album, 1985).
UK: EMI CD GO2054 (CD album with revised packaging and bonus tracks as per *Crazy Diamond* box set edition, 1993).
UK: EMI 724382145011 (Limited edition vinyl album in original packaging as part of the EMI 100 series celebrating EMI Records' centenary. Pressed on 180-gram virgin vinyl, 1997).
UK: EMI Simply Vinyl SVLP 281 (vinyl album limited edition pressed on 180 gram virgin vinyl with original packaging, 2000).
US: CDP 7466062 (CD album, 1990).

COLLECTIONS

Interest in Syd Barrett continues to the present day and many recording artists cite him as a major inspiration. One aspect of this adulation was a huge public demand for EMI to release additional archive material and in response, the company eventually issued a collection of rarities on a single album, *Opel*, which comprised alternate takes and previously unavailable tracks. A further archive discovery resulted in the *Best Of* collection in 2002, which has effectively exhausted all useable material from the vaults.

Monday 8 November 1974
SYD BARRETT
UK: EMI Harvest SHDW 404 (double vinyl album).
US: Harvest SABB-11314 (double vinyl album, released on Saturday 20 July 1974).
Reissue package of *The Madcap Laughs* and *Barrett* albums with new artwork.

Monday 15 February 1988
THE PEEL SESSIONS
UK: Strange Fruit SFPSCD 043 (CD EP).
UK: Strange Fruit SFPS 043 (12-inch EP).
US: Dutch East India DEI8307-2 (CD EP).
Track list: 'Terrapin' / 'Gigolo Aunt' / 'Baby Lemonade' / 'Effervescing Elephant' / 'Two Of A Kind'.

An EP release of the BBC session from 24 February 1970. The 12-inch EP was also released in a limited edition gold tinted sleeve.
Reissued:
UK: Strange Fruit SFPSCD 043 (CD EP with revised sleeve notes, 1995).

Monday 17 October 1988
OPEL

UK: EMI Harvest CZ 144 (CD album).
UK: Harvest EMI SHSP 4126 (vinyl album).
US: Capitol C1-91206 (vinyl album, released on Monday 17 April 1989).
US: Capitol CDP 7912062 (CD album).
Track list: 'Opel' / 'Clowns And Jugglers' ('Octopus') / 'Rats' / 'Golden Hair' / 'Dolly Rocker' / 'Word Song' / 'Wined And Dined' // 'Swan Lee' ('Silas Lang') / 'Birdie Hop' / 'Let's Split' / 'Lanky, Part 1' / 'Wouldn't You Miss Me' ('Dark Globe') / 'Milky Way' / 'Golden Hair' (instrumental).
Reissued:
UK: EMI CD GO2055 (CD album with revised packaging and bonus tracks as per Crazy Diamond box set edition, 1993).
UK: EMI Simply Vinyl SVLP 153 (Limited edition vinyl album pressed on 180 gram virgin vinyl with original packaging, 2000).

April 1989
'Wouldn't You Miss Me' ('Dark Globe') / 'Wouldn't You Miss Me' ('Dark Globe')

US: Capitol SPRO 79606 (promotional 12-inch single for Opel).

Monday 26 April 1993
CRAZY DIAMOND - THE COMPLETE SYD BARRETT

UK: EMI Harvest SYDBOX 1 (CD box set).
US: Harvest CDS 7814122 (CD box set).
Disc 1: The Madcap Laughs. Track list: 'Terrapin' / 'No Good Trying' / 'Love You' / 'No Man's Land' / 'Dark Globe' / 'Here I Go' / 'Octopus' / 'Golden Hair' / 'Long

Gone' / 'She Took A Long Cold Look' / 'Feel' / 'If It's In You' / 'Late Night' / 'Octopus' (takes 1 & 2) / 'It's No Good Trying' (take 5) / 'Love You' (take 1) / 'Love You' (take 3) / 'She Took A Long Cold Look At Me' (take 4) / 'Golden Hair' (take 5).
Disc 2: Barrett. Track list: 'Baby Lemonade' / 'Love Song' / 'Dominoes' / 'It Is Obvious' / 'Rats' / 'Maisie' / 'Gigolo Aunt' / 'Waving My Arms In The Air' / 'I Never Lied To You' / 'Wined And Dined' / 'Wolfpack' / 'Effervescing Elephant' / 'Baby Lemonade' (take 1) / 'Waving My Arms In The Air' (take 1) / 'I Never Lied To You' (take 1) / 'Love Song' (take 1) / 'Dominoes' (take 1) / 'Dominoes' (take 2) / 'It Is Obvious' (take 2).
Disc 3: Opel. Track list: 'Opel' / 'Clowns & Jugglers' ('Octopus') / 'Rats' / 'Golden Hair' / 'Dolly Rocker' / 'Word Song' / 'Wind And Dined' / 'Swan Lee' ('Silas Lang') / 'Birdie Hop' / 'Let's Split' / 'Lanky, Part 1' / 'Wouldn't You Miss Me' ('Dark Globe') / 'Milky Way' / 'Golden Hair' (instrumental) / 'Gigolo Aunt' (take 9) / 'It Is Obvious' (take 3) / 'It Is Obvious' (take 5) / 'Clowns And Jugglers' (take 1) / 'Late Night' (take 2) / 'Effervescing Elephant' (take 2).
A box set of The Madcap Laughs, Barrett and Opel, with yet more out-takes. The sleeves and 24 page booklet feature new artwork based on Barrett's lyrics. The three above CD's were later released separately.

April 1993
SYD BARRETT - CRAZY DIAMOND

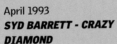

US: Capitol NR 724385818677 (promotional 7-inch EP single on pink vinyl).
Track list: 'Terrapin' / 'Octopus' // 'Baby Lemonade' // 'Effervescing Elephant'.

Monday 16 March 1992
THE BEST OF SYD BARRETT

US: Cleopatra CLEO 57712 (CD album limited edition of 1500 pressings packaged in a printed cloth pouch with a button badge).
Track list: 'Octopus' / 'Swan Lee' ('Silas Lang') / 'Baby Lemonade' / 'Late Night' / 'Wined And Dined' / 'Golden Hair' / 'Gigolo Aunt' / 'Wolf Pack' / 'It Is Obvious' / 'Lanky, Part 1' / 'No Good Trying' / 'Clowns And Jugglers' / 'Waiving My Arms In The Air' / 'Opel'.
Reissued:
US: Cleopatra CLEO 57712 (CD album without special packaging but with a new revised booklet, 1993).

Monday 15 April 2002
WOULDN'T YOU MISS ME - THE BEST OF SYD BARRETT

UK: EMI 5323202 (CD album).
US: Capitol 724353232023 (CD album).
Track list: 'Octopus' / 'Late Nite' / 'Terrapin' / 'Swan Lee' / 'Wolfpack' / 'Golden Hair' / 'Here I Go' / 'Long Gone' / 'No Good Trying' / 'Opel' / 'Baby Lemonade' / 'Gigolo Aunt' / 'Dominoes' / 'Wouldn't You Miss Me' / 'Wined And Dined' / 'Effervescing Elephant' / 'Waving My Arms In The Air' / 'I Never Lied To You' / 'Love Song' / 'Two Of A Kind' (from the BBC sessions) / 'Bob Dylan Blues' (a newly discovered track from the archives) / 'Golden Hair' (instrumental from Opel).
A CD collection with just one newly discovered track, 'Bob Dylan Blues' retrieved from David Gilmour's personal archive. With this release all the useable solo work is ostensibly now available.

Monday 29 March 2004
THE RADIO ONE SESSIONS

UK: Strange Fruit SFRSCD127 (CD album).
Track list: 'Terrapin' / 'Gigolo Aunt' / 'Baby Lemonade' / 'Effervescing Elephant' / 'Two Of A Kind' / 'Baby Lemonade' / 'Dominoes' / 'Love Song'.
A CD album release of the BBC sessions of 24 February 1970 and 16 February 1971.

FILMS

July 1993
SYD'S FIRST TRIP

UK: UFO / Vex Films (VHS PAL video).
US: Music Video Distribution DR 2780 (DVD NTSC video, released 2001).
A limited edition release of poor quality 8-mm silent home movies. The first, shot by Nigel Lesmoir Gordon which lasts only a few minutes, shows a teenage Barrett in the Gog Magog hills in the Cambridgeshire

countryside with friends; some clips of the Pink Floyd, co-manager Andrew King and the group's multicoloured van outside EMI Studios, Abbey Road, London, during the *Piper* sessions in spring 1967; and material from around the same time shot on the balcony of the infamous London flat at Cromwell Road that Barrett and Gordon shared. It is said that David Gilmour purchased the rights from the producers in order to remove this somewhat exploitative film from public circulation.

Monday 24 March 2003
THE PINK FLOYD & SYD BARRETT STORY
UK: Direct Video Distribution DVDUK009D (DVD PAL video).
UK: Direct Video Distribution DVDUK010V (VHS PAL video).
Directed by John Edginton.
An officially sanctioned documentary focussing on Pink Floyd's formative years. Includes newly recorded Roger Waters and David Gilmour interviews; Robyn Hitchcock performing 'Dominoes' and 'It Is Obvious'; Graham Coxon performing 'Love You' and a biography of Syd Barrett. The documentary was first broadcast on BBC2 TV on 24 November 2001.
Reissued:
UK: Direct Video Distribution DVDSD002D (double DVD PAL video, 2006).
An expanded and repackaged version of the above documentary: Disc 1 includes *The Pink Floyd & Syd Barrett Story* and a newly recorded Roger Waters interview. Disc 2 includes newly recorded interviews with David Gilmour, Richard Wright, Nick Mason and Robyn Hitchcock. Bonus material includes Syd Barrett's 'Love You' performed by Graham Coxon, Quiz, Tour of Abbey Road, Biographies, Discographies and a Pink Floyd time-line.

February 2006
SYD BARRETT - UNDER REVIEW
UK: Chrome Dreams CVIS398 (DVD PAL video).
US: Music Video Distribution (DVD NTSC video).
An unauthorised documentary featuring archive clips of the early Pink Floyd in action: Granada TV from the UFO club; BBC *Look Of The Week* footage; *American Bandstand* appearance and a rare clip of the 'Jugband Blues' performance for the Central Office Of Information and includes commentary from various music journalists.

COMPILATIONS

1970
PICNIC - A BREATH OF FRESH AIR
UK: EMI Harvest EMI SHSS 1/2 (double vinyl album).
Compilation includes 'Terrapin'.

1977
HARVEST HERITAGE - 20 GREATS
UK: EMI Harvest SHSM 2020 (vinyl album).
Compilation includes 'Octopus'.

1984
HARVEST STORY VOL.1
UK: EMI Harvest EG 2600971 (vinyl album).
Compilation includes 'Love You'.

1988
THE JOHN PEEL SESSIONS
US: Dutch East India Trading DEI8601-2 (CD album).
Promotional compilation includes 'Two Of A Kind'.

1994
SPACE DAZE
US: Cleopatra Records CLEO 079162 (double CD album).
Compilation includes 'Lanky'.

1994
BEFORE THE FALL 67-77
UK: Strange Fruit SFRLP 203 (vinyl album).
Compilation of BBC sessions includes 'Baby Lemonade' taken from the *Peel Sessions* release.

1995
PROG ROCK - THE AGE OF ENLIGHTENMENT
UK: Chrysalis 724383226313 (CD album).
Compilation includes 'Baby Lemonade'.

1999
HARVEST FESTIVAL
UK: EMI Harvest 724352119820 (five CD album box set).
Compilation includes 'Octopus' and 'Golden Hair'.

2002
ART SCHOOL DANCING
UK: Harvest 5387762 (CD album).
Compilation includes 'Love You'.

GUEST APPEARANCES

2003
KEVIN AYERS - JOY OF A TOY
UK: EMI Harvest 07243-582776-2-3 (CD album).
Barrett plays guitar on the previously unreleased bonus track 'Religious Experience (Singing A Song In The Morning)' on this remastered and repackaged CD.

LIVE PERFORMANCE
If Barrett's solo material is any indication of his mental condition in the years after he left Pink Floyd, it is hardly surprising that he made few public appearances. His most notable achievement was as a member of the extremely short-lived band Stars who performed in Cambridge in the early part of 1972.

Tuesday 24 February 1970
RADIO SHOW
BBC Maida Vale Studios, Maida Vale, London, England
Two live studio recording sessions were performed on this day for BBC Radio 1. The first was recorded between 2.30pm and 6.00pm, in which Barrett, assisted by David Gilmour (organ, bass guitar and guitar) and Jerry Shirley (drums), performed, in order, 'Baby Lemonade', 'Effervescing Elephant', 'Gigolo Aunt', 'Terrapin' and 'Two Of A Kind'. It was first broadcast on *Top Gear* on 14 March 1970 at 3.00pm, except 'Two Of A Kind', which was first broadcast on *Top Gear* on 30 May 1970 at 3.00pm. The complete session was officially released on vinyl and CD in 1988 (see Discography above).
The second session, recorded between 6.00pm and 9.00pm, remains unbroadcast.

Saturday 6 June 1970
CONCERT
Extravaganza 70 - Music and Fashion Festival, The Grand Hall, Olympia Exhibition Hall, Olympia, London, England
With Colosseum, Mungo Jerry, The Move, Mike Raven, The Pretty Things, Rare Bird, Steamhammer, Jackson Heights with Lee Jackson and Fairfield Parlour.
Barrett's first major performance was as a late addition on the last evening of this four-day festival (3-6 June 1970). He was joined on stage by David Gilmour (bass guitar) and Jerry Shirley (drums) and played a rushed set that included 'Terrapin', 'Gigolo Aunt', 'Effervescing Elephant' and 'Octopus'. His vocals were barely audible throughout and even before the last track was finished he left the stage to scattered applause.

Thursday 30 July 1970
CANCELLED APPEARANCE
VPRO Pik Nik Festival, Gemeendecentrum, Drijbergen, Netherlands
With Kevin Ayers And The Whole World.
Barrett was advertised to appear at this VPRO Radio sponsored event but he never appeared.

Tuesday 16 February 1971
RADIO SHOW
BBC Transcription Service Studios, Kensington House, Shepherd's Bush, London, England
Barrett's second and final radio session for BBC Radio 1, recorded between 6.00pm and 9.30pm, in which he performed, in order, 'Baby Lemonade', 'Dominoes' and 'Love Song'. It was first broadcast on *Bob Harris Sounds Of The Seventies* on 1 March 1971 at 6.00pm.

Thursday 20 January 1972
CONCERT
Union Society Cellars, Cambridge, England
Promoted by the Cambridge University Blues Society. Barrett played guitar on an impromptu jam session with Twink (drums) and Jack Monck (bass) at this concert headlined by the Eddie Byrns Combo.

Thursday 27 January 1972
CONCERT
Corn Exchange, Cambridge, England
Billed as The Last Minute Put Together Boogie Band with Twink (drums), Jack Monck (bass), Bruce Paine (guitar) and Fred Frith (guitar). Supporting Hawkwind and Pink Fairies. None of the songs performed by the band were Barrett compositions and were all blues based numbers. Barrett was reported not to have been on the best of form at this show repeatedly playing the riff to Howlin' Wolf's 'Smokestack Lightning' regardless of what his band mates were

trying to play. From surviving tapes the set list included the titles 'Number Nine', 'Gotta Be A Reason', 'Let's Roll' and 'Sweet Little Angel'.

Saturday 5 February 1972
CONCERT
The Dandelion café, Cambridge, England
1.00pm show. Billed as Stars with Twink (drums) and Jack Monck (bass).
Stars debut show was at this small café in the centre of Cambridge. None of the songs performed by the band were Barrett compositions but were instead all blues based numbers.

Saturday 12 February 1972
CONCERT
The Dandelion café, Cambridge, England
1.00pm show. Billed as Stars with Twink (drums) and Jack Monck (bass).

February 1972
CONCERT
Market Square, Cambridge, England
Billed as Stars with Twink (drums) and Jack Monck (bass).
The band performed in what was essentially an impromptu busking session with their equipment powered from a friend's shop called What's In A Name? located in Petty Cury, a side street off the Market Square.

Thursday 24 February 1972
CONCERT
Corn Exchange, Cambridge, England
Billed as Stars with Twink (drums) and Jack Monck (bass). Supporting MC5 and Skin Alley.
Set list: 'Octopus' / 'Dark Globe' / 'Baby Lemonade' / 'Waving My Arms In The Air' / 'Lucifer Sam' / improvised blues jams.
Stars' appearance, which closed the show, was a complete disaster and the situation was not improved when the house lights were accidentally switched on to reveal an audience of fewer than 30 people.

Saturday 26 February 1972
CONCERT
Corn Exchange, Cambridge, England
Billed as Stars with Twink (drums) and Jack Monck (bass). Supporting Nektar.
This was Barrett's last advertised public appearance. Roy Hollingsworth had written a fair account of the 24 February show for the following week's edition of *Sounds* but Barrett was said to have been so upset by it that he refused to perform live ever again.

October 1973
CONCERT
Union Society Cellars, Cambridge, England
Barrett reportedly joined Pete Brown, with guest Jack Bruce, at a jazz/poetry event organised by the Cambridge University Union in what was to become his last ever public appearance.

RIGHT: SYD BARRETT PERFORMING AT OLYMPIA, LONDON ON 6 JUNE 1970.

david gilmour

David Jon Gilmour was born in Cambridge on 6 March 1943 to Douglas Gilmour, a senior lecturer in Zoology at Cambridge University and Sylvia, a teacher and has two brothers and one sister. He was educated at the Perse Preparatory School for Boys and in 1963 attended Cambridge College of Art and Technology for a year to re-sit Modern Languages, where he met Roger 'Syd' Barrett. After leaving school in 1964, Gilmour played in several local bands, including one of the most successful on the Cambridge scene, Jokers Wild. Moving to London in the summer of 1967 he was, among other things, a delivery driver for the clothing designers Quorum before accepting an invitation to join Pink Floyd starting in January 1968.

Of all the Pink Floyd members, past and present, David Gilmour was throughout the Eighties and Nineties the most active as a solo artist. As well as playing on the albums of many other musicians, he has also acted as producer. In addition, he has performed widely, in many cases for charity, and has written and recorded soundtrack material for television. His solo tours have been few and far between, with only one solo tour in 1984 to promote his *About Face* album and six shows over 2001/02. In 2003 David donated the £3.6 million proceeds of the sale of his London house to Crisis; the charity for the homeless of which he is a vice president and in November 2005 was awarded the CBE for philanthropy and services to music.

In 2006 he released a third solo album, *On An Island* and embarked on a small-tour of the UK, Europe and North America. Although he continues to guest on stage and in the studio, this has been to a much lesser extent; having turned the focus of his attention largely to his family.

DISCOGRAPHY

JOKERS WILD

The first recordings made by Jokers Wild were completed at Regent Sound Studios in Denmark Street, Soho, London in the autumn of 1965 and were then pressed in runs of approximately 50 copies each and distributed mainly to friends and family. The line-up of the band at this time would have been David Gilmour (guitar, vocals, harmonica), David Altham (guitar, saxophone, keyboards, vocals), John Gordon (rhythm guitar, vocals), Tony Sainty (bass guitar, vocals) and Clive Welham (drums, vocals). Original pressings occasionally come up for sale in the collectors market although they have been frequently bootlegged.

1965
'Don't Ask Me What I Say' / 'Why Do Fools Fall In Love?'
UK: Regent Sound Recordings RSR 0031 (7-inch acetate single).

1965
JOKERS WILD
UK: Regent Sound Recordings RSLP 007 (one-sided 12-inch mini-album).
Track list: 'Why Do Falls Fall In Love?' / 'Walk Like A Man' / 'Don't Ask Me What I Say' / 'Big Girls Don't Cry' / 'Beautiful Delilah'.

1965
'You Don't Know Like I Know' / 'That's How Strong My Love Is'
These unreleased recording session tapes were produced by Jonathan King at Decca Studios, Broadhurst Gardens, West Hampstead, London in either late 1965/early '66 for a proposed single release on Decca Records. The single was aborted and the tapes are reportedly now in David Gilmour's possession.

DAVID GILMOUR

This well-received guitar-based album was the product of a regrouping of his former band mates Rick Wills (bass, vocals) and Willie Wilson (drums, percussion). Recorded at the Super Bear Studios in France, it was self-produced and featured Carlena Williams, Debbie Doss and Shirley Roden (backing vocals) and Mick Weaver (piano on 'So Far Away'). All of the songs were written by Gilmour, except for 'Cry From The Street' by Gilmour and Eric Stewart and 'Short And Sweet' by Gilmour and Roy Harper. 'There's No Way Out Of Here', was written by Ken Baker of Unicorn, which first appeared on that band's album *Too Many Crooks*.

On 25 May 1978 a press reception was held at the Hotel Prince de Galles, Paris to launch the album. It is said that the manager of the hotel recognised Gilmour and quizzed him over an unpaid bill from 1967 when he was touring with Jokers Wild.

Friday 26 May 1978
DAVID GILMOUR
UK: EMI Harvest SHVL 817 (vinyl album).
US: Columbia JC 35388 (vinyl album, released Saturday 16 June 1984).
Track list: 'Mihalis' / 'There's No Way Out Of Here' / 'Cry From The Street' / 'So Far Away' // 'Short And Sweet' / 'Raise My Rent' / 'Deafinitely' / 'I Can't Breathe Anymore'.
Recorded at Super Bear Studios, Berre des Alpes, France.
Produced by David Gilmour. Engineered by John Etchells and Nick Griffiths.
Artwork by Hipgnosis.
Highest chart position UK No.17, US No. 29.

Certified Gold in the US on 17 November 2000.
Reissued:
US: Columbia CK 35388 (CD album, 2003).
US: Sony 82876815162 (remastered CD album, 2006).
UK: EMI 37084328 (remastered CD album, 2006).

May 1978
DAVID GILMOUR – PROMOTIONAL FILMS
Six tracks from the album *David Gilmour* were filmed at Super Bear Studios, France for TV promotion including 'So Far Away', 'There's No Way Out Of Here', 'Mihalis', 'I Can't Breathe Anymore' and 'No Way'. Gilmour was joined by his brother Mark (rhythm guitar) for the session, which also featured Rick Wills and Willie Wilson. The track 'No Way' was broadcast on BBC2 TV's contemporary rock music programme *The Old Grey Whistle Test* on 5 December 1978 at 11.30pm.

Friday 26 May 1978
'There's No Way Out Of Here' (edit) / 'Deafinately'
UK: EMI Harvest HAR 5226 (7-inch single).
US: Columbia 310803 (7-inch single, released on Monday 21 August 1978).
'There's No Way Out Of Here' (edit) / 'There's No Way Out Of Here' (edit - stereo)
US: Columbia 310803 (promotional only 7-inch single).

ABOUT FACE
Many of the songs on this album leaned towards middle-of-the-road adult pop-rock as opposed to the guitar rock of *David Gilmour*. It was co-produced by

Bob Ezrin and featured an array of guest musicians including Ray Cooper (percussion), Anne Dudley (synthesisers), Bob Ezrin (keyboards), Louis Jardine (percussion), Ian Kewley (Hammond organ and piano), Jon Lord (synthesisers), Pino Palladino (bass guitar), Jeff Porcaro (drums and percussion), Steve Rance (Fairlight programming), Steve Winwood (piano and organ), The Kick Horns: Roddy Lorimer, Barbara Snow, Tim Sanders and Simon Clark (brass), Vicki Brown, Sam Brown, Micky Feat and Roy Harper (backing vocals) and The National Philharmonic arranged by Michael Kamen and Bob Ezrin. Both Pete Townshend and Nick Laird-Clowes co-wrote many of the tracks.

Monday 13 February 1984
'Blue Light' (edit) / 'Cruise'
UK: EMI Harvest HAR 5226 (7-inch single).
'Blue Light' (album version) / 'Cruise'
UK: EMI Harvest 12 HAR 5226 (12-inch single).
'Blue Light' (extended US remix) / 'Blue Light' (instrumental)
UK: EMI Harvest DG1 A/B (promotional 12-inch single).
'Blue Light' (edit) / 'Cruise'
US: Columbia 38-04378 (7-inch single, released on Monday 26 March 1984).
'Blue Light' (edit) / 'Blue Light' (edit)
US: Columbia 38-04378 (promotional 7-inch single).
'Blue Light' (vocal) / 'Blue Light' (instrumental)
US: Columbia 44-04983 (promotional 12-inch single).
'Blue Light' / 'All Lovers Are Deranged'
US: Columbia XSS 169591 (promotional 12-inch single).

Highest chart position US No.62.

Monday 5 March 1984
ABOUT FACE
UK: EMI Harvest SHSP 24 0079 1 (vinyl album).
US: Columbia FC 39296 (vinyl album, released on Monday 5 March 1984).
Track list: 'Until We Sleep' / 'Murder' / 'Love On The Air' / 'Blue Light' / 'Out Of The Blue' // 'All Lovers Are Deranged' / 'You Know I'm Right' / 'Cruise' / 'Let's Get Metaphysical' / 'Near The End'.
Recorded at Pathe Marconi Studios, Paris, France and EMI Abbey Road Studios, London, England.
Produced by David Gilmour and Bob Ezrin. Recorded by Andrew Jackson and Kit

Woolven. Mixed by James Guthrie at Mayfair Studios, London. Orchestra recorded by Eric Tomlinson at EMI Abbey Road Studios. Mastered by Doug Sax and Mike Reese at The Mastering Lab, Los Angeles, USA.
Artwork by Storm Thorgerson.
Highest chart position UK No.21.
Certified Gold in the US on 19 April 1995.
Reissued:
US: Sony 82876815172 (remastered CD album, 2006).
UK: EMI 37084229 (remastered CD album, 2006).

Tuesday 24 April 1984
'Love On The Air' / 'Let's Get Metaphysical'
UK: EMI Harvest HAR 5229 (7-inch single).
'Love On The Air' / 'Let's Get Metaphysical'
UK: EMI Harvest HARP 5229 (radio-shaped picture disc single).
'Love On The Air' / 'Near The End'
US: Columbia 38-04490 (7-inch single, released on Monday 23 April).
'Love On The Air' / 'Love On The Air'
US: Columbia 38-04490 (promotional 7-inch single).
'Love On The Air' / 'Love On The Air'
US: Columbia AS 1875 (promotional 12-inch single).

DAVID GILMOUR
An official document of Gilmour's Hammersmith Odeon show of 30 April 1984 and only released in the US.

Saturday 26 May 1984
DAVID GILMOUR
US: CBS Fox Video Music 7078 (VHS NTSC video).
Track list: 'Until We Sleep' / 'All Lovers Are Deranged' / 'There's No Way Out Of Here' / 'Short And Sweet' / 'Run Like Hell' / 'Out Of The Blue' / 'Blue Light' / 'Murder' / 'Comfortably Numb'.
Produced by Martin Wyn Griffith.
It was broadcast on MTV's *Saturday Night Special* on 26 May 1984 and simulcast nationally on the *Westwood One* radio network.

DAVID GILMOUR – IN CONCERT
A live concert DVD release that was culled from his critically acclaimed concerts at the Royal Festival Hall, London in June 2001 and January 2002.

Monday 21 October 2002
DAVID GILMOUR - IN CONCERT
UK: Capitol EMI 4929589 (DVD PAL video).
US: Capitol C9724349296091 (DVD NTSC video, released on Monday 4 November 2002).
Track list: 'Shine On You Crazy Diamond, Parts 1-5' / 'Terrapin' / 'Fat Old Sun' / 'Coming Back To Life' / 'High Hopes' / 'Je Crois Entendre Encore' / "Smile" / 'Wish You Were Here' / 'Comfortably Numb' (with Robert Wyatt) / 'The Dimming Of The Day' / 'Shine On You Crazy Diamond, Parts 6-9' / 'A Great Day For Freedom' / 'Hushabye Mountain' / 'Dominoes' /

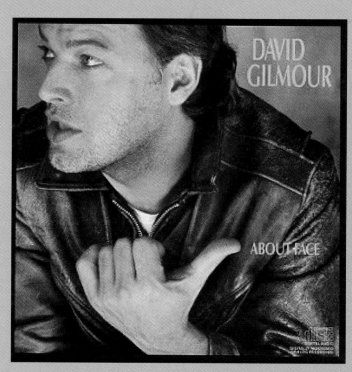

'Breakthrough' / 'Comfortably Numb' (with Bob Geldof).

Also includes extra features: Spare Digits: 'Coming Back To Life' / 'High Hopes', 'Breakthrough' / 'Comfortably Numb' / 'Shine On You Crazy Diamond, Parts 1-5' / 'A Great Day For Freedom' (alternate live versions from the concerts) / Home Movie: 'Je Crois Entendre Encore' in rehearsals / Miscellaneous: 'I Put A Spell On You' (with Mica Paris and Jools Holland from the Channel 4 TV show *Mister Roadrunner* 6 June 1992) / 'Don't' (from the Leiber & Stoller tribute show at The Hammersmith Apollo, 29 June 2001) / 'Sonnet 18' (with Michael Kamen) / 'High Hopes' (choral from the concerts) / Lyrics for all the songs performed at the concert and a 5.1 surround sound tester.

Produced by David Gilmour.

The DVD concert was also screened on Channel 4 TV (UK) on 15 April 2006 at 1.30am and RTP1 (Portugal) on 22 April 2006.

ON AN ISLAND

A complete departure from his previous works both as a solo artist and with Pink Floyd, Gilmour's third solo album is an introspective and very personal piece of work, with many songs co-written with his wife Polly. It was recorded mostly at Gilmour's Astoria studio and was co-produced with Phil Manzanera and Chris Thomas. The album features orchestral arrangements by Zbigniew Preisner conducted by Robert Ziegler and features an accomplished list of guest musicians including: B.J. Cole (Weissenborn guitar), David Crosby and Graham Nash (vocal harmonies), Caroline Dale (cello), Ilan Eshkeri

(programming), Georgie Fame (vocals), Jools Holland (piano), Rado 'Bob' Klose (guitar – from Pink Floyd's earliest incarnation), Chris Laurence (double bass), Ged Lynch (drums), Phil Manzanera (piano), Leszek Modzer (piano), Alasdair Molloy (glass harmonica), Andy Newmark (drums), Guy Pratt (bass), Polly Samson (piano), Chris Stainton (Hammond organ), Chris Thomas (keyboards), Lucy Wakeford (harp), Willie Wilson (drums), Richard Wright (Hammond organ) and Robert Wyatt (cornet).

Monday 6 March 2006
ON AN ISLAND

UK: EMI 3556952 (CD album).
UK: EMI 3556951 (limited edition virgin vinyl album, with poster insert and new artwork, released 5 June 2006).
US: Sony 1CK680280 (CD album, released on Tuesday 7 March 2006).
Track list: 'Castellorizon' / 'On An Island' / 'The Blue' / 'Take A Breath' / 'Red Sky At Night' / 'This Heaven' / 'Then I Close My Eyes' / 'Smile' / 'A Pocketful Of Stones' / 'Where We Start'.
Recorded at The Astoria, Hampton, England; EMI Abbey Road Studios, London, England; British Grove, London, England; Gallery Studio, London, England and David Gilmour's home.
Produced by David Gilmour, Phil Manzanera and Chris Thomas.
Artwork by Blade.
Highest chart position UK No.1.

Monday 30 January 2006
'On An Island' (radio edit) / 'On An Island' (album version)

UK: EMI CDEM 688 (CD single).
US: Sony 82876809762 (CD single, released Tuesday 31 January 2006).

Tuesday 7 March 2006
'Island Jam'

US: Sony (An exclusive bonus CD given away with sales of the regular CD album at Best Buy record stores).
Produced by David Gilmour.
Musicians include Ged Lynch (drums), Guy Pratt (bass) and Paul 'Wix' Wickens (keyboards).

Monday 5 June 2006
'Smile' / 'Island Jam'

UK: EMI CDEM 696 (CD single).
UK: EMI EM 696 (limited edition clear vinyl 7-inch single).

SOUNDTRACKS

1984
GIVE MY REGARDS TO BROAD STREET

Gilmour played guitars on the track 'No More Lonely Nights (Ballad)' featured on the soundtrack to this ill-received film by Paul McCartney. The movie premiered in the US in October 1984 (a month later in the UK) and was also broadcast on the ITV network on 2 January 1994 at 3.50pm.

1991
THE CEMENT GARDEN

Gilmour composed and performed the song 'Me And J.C'. for the soundtrack of this acclaimed cinematic film. It was released on DVD in 2004 (UK: Cinema Club CCD 9011).

1991
RUBY TAKES A TRIP

Gilmour composed and performed the soundtrack music featured on this TV programme, featuring comedienne Ruby Wax heading for California and taking a semi-serious look at the search for the meaning of life in the land of the New Age. It was broadcast on BBC2 TV on 31 December 1991 at 8.55pm.

1992
THE LAST SHOW ON EARTH

Gilmour composed and performed the soundtrack music featured on this TV programme - a two-hour environmental spectacular produced to coincide with the Earth Summit, which also included music by Kate Bush, Soul II Soul, Peter Gabriel, Elton John and Seal. It was broadcast on the ITV network in the UK on 27 May 1992 at 8.00pm.

1993
WITHOUT WALLS: THE ART OF TRIPPING

Gilmour composed and performed the soundtrack music featured on a two-part edition of this TV documentary. The programme was devised by Storm Thorgerson and dealt with the relationship between drug taking and the arts. It was broadcast on Channel 4 in the UK on 23 February and 2 March 1993 at 9.00pm.

1994
COLOURS OF INFINITY

Gilmour composed and performed the soundtrack music featured on this made-for-video educational film (UK: Prism Leisure Video PLATV 956) based on fractal geometry and hosted by Arthur C. Clarke. It was shown a year later on Channel 4 TV in the UK but the broadcast details remain unknown. A book and an accompanying DVD was released in 2004 (UK: Clear Press ISBN 1904555055), featuring the original documentary plus an additional 30-minute fractal animation set to the music of Quintessence.

RADIO SHOWS

1984

IN CONCERT – DAVID GILMOUR

US: *In Concert* (double vinyl album). Show No.84-18, broadcast 31 August 1984.

Track list: 'Until We Sleep' / 'All Lovers Are Deranged' / 'Money' / 'Love On The Air' / 'Short And Sweet' / 'You Know I'm Right' / 'Run Like Hell' / 'Blue Light' / 'Comfortably Numb'.

A double album radio show of David Gilmour's performance recorded at Lehigh University, Allentown on 12 July 1984.

1984

INNER-VIEW – DAVID GILMOUR – ABOUT FACE

US: *Inner-View* (vinyl album). Show No.28-2, broadcast 1984.

Documentary includes music and interviews with David Gilmour.

1984

PFM – GUEST DJ – DAVID GILMOUR

US: PFM (vinyl album). Show No.122, broadcast 23 July 1984.

Radio show where a guest musician acts as DJ. Gilmour selects: 'Blue Light' (by himself) / 'Heartbreak Hotel' (Elvis Presley) / 'Jump' (Van Halen) / 'Out Of The Blue' (by himself) / 'All Along The Watchtower' (Jimi Hendrix) / 'Like A Rolling Stone' (Bob Dylan) / 'Comfortably Numb' (Pink Floyd) / 'Disco Apocalypse' (Jackson Browne) / 'Until We Sleep' (by himself) / 'Across The Universe' (The Beatles) / 'You Know I'm Right' (by himself).

1984

THE SOURCE – DAVID GILMOUR PROFILE

US: NBC Radio Young Adult Network (triple vinyl album). Show No.84-12, broadcast 6 - 8 April 1984.

Documentary includes music and interviews with David Gilmour.

1994

SUPERSTAR CONCERT SERIES – PINK FLOYD

US: Westwood One (double CD album). Show No.94-19, broadcast 2 May 1994.

Compilation of Pink Floyd and solo live recordings including Pink Floyd at BBC Paris Theatre, London on 30 September 1971: 'One Of These Days' / 'Echoes' / David Gilmour at Hammersmith Odeon, London on 30 April 1984: 'Money' / 'Run Like Hell' / 'Comfortably Numb' / Roger Waters at Colisee de Québec, Québec City on 7 November 1987: 'Wish You Were Here' / 'Another Brick in the Wall, Part 1' / 'The Happiest Days Of Our Lives' / 'Another Brick In The Wall, Part 2'.

2003

SUPERSTAR CONCERT SERIES – ROGER WATERS / DAVID GILMOUR

US: Westwood One (double CD album). Show No.03-15, broadcast 12 April 2003.

Compilation of David Gilmour and Roger Waters live recordings including David Gilmour at Lehigh University, Allentown on 12 July 1984: 'Money' / 'Run Like Hell' / 'Short And Sweet' / 'Comfortably Numb' and Roger Waters at Colisee de Québec, Québec City on 7 November 1987: 'Welcome To The Machine' / 'In The Flesh?' / 'Have A Cigar' / 'Pigs (Three Different Ones)' / 'Another Brick In The Wall, Part 1' / 'The Happiest Days Of Our Lives' / 'Another Brick In The Wall, Part 2'.

FREE DOWNLOADS

December 2005

ON AN ISLAND

DavidGilmour.Com made available video clips of every track on the album *On An Island* filmed mostly as works in progress at his Astoria studio and EMI Studios, Abbey Road.

March 2006

ON AN ISLAND

DavidGilmour.Com made available audio clips of every track on the album and a video clip of the track 'On An Island' (extended version).

May 2006

ON AN ISLAND - PODCAST

DavidGilmour.Com made available an interview of Gilmour discussing the making of the album *On An Island*.

June 2006

'Smile'

DavidGilmour.Com made available the video of 'Smile' and iTunes made available the audio of the single 'Smile' and the track 'Island Jam' (demo); the latter featuring Gilmour on guitar with Paul 'Wix' Wickens on keyboards, Guy Pratt on bass and Ged Lynch on drums.

December 2006

'Arnold Layne' / 'Dark Globe'

DavidGilmour.Com made available two versions of 'Arnold Layne' (with David Bowie lead vocals recorded at the Royal Albert Hall on 29 May 2005 and Richard Wright lead vocals recorded on 30 May 2005) and 'Dark Globe' (recorded at Burg Clam, Austria on 27 July 2006).

GUEST APPEARANCES, PRODUCTION & CO-WRITING

(UK Catalogue numbers and original format only)

1969

SYD BARRETT - 'Octopus' / 'No Good Trying'

UK: EMI Harvest HAR 5009 (7-inch single).
Produced by Gilmour, Waters and others.

1970

SYD BARRETT - *THE MADCAP LAUGHS*

UK: EMI Harvest SHVL 765 (vinyl album).
Produced by Gilmour, Waters and others.

1970

SYD BARRETT - *BARRETT*

UK: EMI Harvest SHSP 4007 (vinyl album).
Produced by Gilmour who also played bass on the album.

1974

UNICORN - *BLUE PINE TREES*

UK: Charisma CAS 1092 (vinyl album).
Produced by Gilmour, who played guitar on 'Electric Night'; pedal steel guitar on 'Sleep Song', 'Autumn Wine', 'Just Wanna Hold You' and 'The Farmer' and backing vocals on 'Nightingale Crescent'. In 1993 the track 'Oooh Mother' was included on the four-CD Charisma retrospective, *The Famous Charisma Box* (UK: Charisma CASBOX1).

1974

SYD BARRETT - *SYD BARRETT*

UK: EMI Harvest SHDW 404 (double vinyl album).
Reissue of *The Madcap Laughs* and *Barrett* with new artwork. Details as above. See Syd Barrett section for further reissues and additional out-take compilations.

1975

DAVID COURTNEY - *FIRST DAY*

UK: United Artists UA LASS3-G (vinyl album).
Gilmour played guitars on 'When Your Life Is Your Own'.

1975

ROY HARPER - *HQ*

UK: EMI Harvest SHSP 4046 (vinyl album).
Gilmour played guitars on 'The Game, Parts 1-5'.
Produced by Peter Jenner.

1975

SUTHERLAND BROTHERS & QUIVER - *REACH FOR THE SKY*

UK: CBS 69191 (vinyl album).
Gilmour played pedal steel guitar on 'Ain't Too Proud'.

1976

UNICORN - *TOO MANY CROOKS*

UK: EMI Harvest SHSP 4054 (vinyl album).
Gilmour produced the album and played pedal steel guitar on the title track. He covered 'No Way Out Of Here' on his debut solo album as 'There's No Way Out Of Here'.

1977

RACHID BAHRI - *RACHID BAHRI*

FRANCE: EMI France 2C068-14398 (vinyl album released only in France).

Gilmour played guitars on 'Olivier de Cromwell Road' and 'Il Survivra'.

1977
UNICORN - *ONE MORE TOMORROW*
UK: EMI Harvest SHSP 4067 (vinyl album).
Gilmour produced all but the first four tracks on this album and played uncredited guitar on the tracks 'The Way It Goes' and 'So Hard To Get Through' and pedal steel guitar on 'I'm Alright (When I'm With You)'.

1977
UNICORN - 'Slow Dancing' / 'Give And Take'
UK: EMI Harvest HAR 5126 (7-inch single).
Gilmour produced and engineered the non-album B-side.

1978
KATE BUSH - 'The Man With The Child In His Eyes' / 'Moving'
UK: EMI 2806 (7-inch single).
Gilmour is credited as executive producer.

1979
WINGS - *BACK TO THE EGG*
UK: MPL PCTC 257 (vinyl album).
Gilmour played guitars on 'Rockestra Theme' and 'So Glad To See You Here' as part of the supergroup Rockestra.

1980
KATE BUSH - 'Army Dreamers' / 'Passing Through Air'
UK: EMI 5106 (7-inch single).
Gilmour played guitars, produced and engineered the B-side, which was recorded in 1973. Also available exclusively on CD as part of the Kate Bush box set *This Woman's Work* (UK: EMI CDKBBX 1).

1980
ROY HARPER - *UNKNOWN SOLDIER*
UK: EMI Harvest SHVL 820 (vinyl album)
Gilmour co-wrote and played guitars on 'Playing Games', 'True Story', 'Old Faces', 'Short And Sweet', and 'You (The Game, Part 2)'. Peter Jenner was executive producer.

1982
KATE BUSH - *THE DREAMING*
UK: EMI EMC 3419 (vinyl album)
Gilmour provided backing vocals on 'Pull Out The Pin'.

1982
DOLL BY DOLL - *GRAND PASSION*
UK: MAGL 5047 (vinyl album).
Gilmour played guitars on 'Boxers Hit Harder When Women Are Around'.

1983
ATOMIC ROOSTER - *HEADLINE NEWS*
UK: Towerbell TOW LP4 (vinyl album).
Gilmour played guitars on 'Hold Your Fire', 'Metal Minds', 'Land Of Freedom' and 'Time'.

1984
PAUL MCCARTNEY - *GIVE MY REGARDS TO BROAD STREET*
UK: EMI Parlophone UK-PCTC-2 (vinyl album).
Gilmour played guitars on 'No More Lonely Nights (Ballad)'. Also on the A-side of the 7-inch single 'No More Lonely Nights (Ballad)' / 'No More Lonely Nights (Playout Version)' (UK: EMI Parlophone R6080) and the A-side of the 12-inch single 'No More Lonely Nights (Ballad)' / 'Silly Love Songs' / 'No More Lonely Nights (Playout Version)' (UK: EMI Parlophone 12 R-6080).

1984
KATE BUSH - *THE SINGLES FILE 1978 - 1983*
UK: EMI KBS1 (box set).
A limited edition numbered box set of Kate Bush's first 11 singles. It was later reissued in un-numbered box sets. The set includes the singles containing 'Man With The Child In His Eyes' and 'Passing Through Air,' both of which feature contributions from Gilmour.

1985
ROY HARPER – *WHATEVER HAPPENED TO JUGULAR?*
UK: BBL 60 (vinyl album).
Gilmour co-wrote the track 'Hope' with Harper.

1985
ARCADIA - *SO RED THE ROSE*
UK: EMI Parlophone PCSD 101 (album).
Gilmour played guitars on 'The Promise' and 'Missing'. Also on the A-side of the 12-inch single 'Promise' / 'Rose Arcana' (UK: EMI Parlophone 12 NSR 2).

1985
JOHN 'RABBIT' BUNDRICK - *THE RABBIT ARCHIVE VOL. 5*
UK: Private release on cassette.
Gilmour produced the track 'Rabbit Gets Loose'. The cassette was only available through the Free Appreciation Society.

1985
THE DREAM ACADEMY - 'Life In A Northern Town' / 'Test Tape No.3'
UK: Blanco Y Negro NEG 10T (12-inch single).
Co-produced by Gilmour.

1985
THE DREAM ACADEMY – 'Please, Please Let Me Get What I Want' / 'In Places On The Run'
UK: Blanco Y Negro NEG 20T (7-inch single).
Non-album track co-produced by Gilmour.

1985
THE DREAM ACADEMY - *DREAM ACADEMY*
UK: Blanco Y Negro BYN6 (album).
Gilmour played guitars on 'Bound To Be' and 'The Party'. All tracks except one were co-produced by Gilmour.

1985
BRYAN FERRY - *BOYS AND GIRLS*
UK: EG EGLP 62 (album).
Gilmour played guitars on the title track, 'The Chosen One', 'Sensation' and possibly others.

1985
GRACE JONES - *SLAVE TO THE RHYTHM*
UK: Island GRACE 1 (album).
Gilmour played guitars on the title track and 'The Fashion Show' but was not credited. Also on the A-side of the 12-inch single 'Slave To The Rhythm' / 'G.I. Blues' (UK: Island 1215 206).

1985
MASON & FENN - *PROFILES*
UK: EMI Harvest MAF 1 (vinyl album).
Gilmour provided vocals on 'Lie For A Lie'. Also on the A-side of the 7-inch single 'Lie For A Lie' / 'And The Address' (UK: EMI Harvest HAR 5238) and the A-side of the 12-inch single 'Lie For A Lie' / 'And The Address' / 'Mumbo Jumbo' (UK: EMI Harvest 12HAR 5238).

1985
SUPERTRAMP - *BROTHER WHERE YOU BOUND*
UK: A&M AMA 5014 (vinyl album).
Gilmour played guitar solo on the title track.

1985
PETE TOWNSHEND - *WHITE CITY*
UK: ATCO 252 392-1 (vinyl album).
Gilmour played guitars on and co-wrote 'White City Fighting' and played guitars on 'Give Blood'. Also on the double A-side promotional 7-inch single 'Give Blood' / 'Give Blood' (US: ATCO 7-95577) and the 7-inch and 12-inch singles 'Give Blood' / 'Face The Face' (UK: WEA U8744 / WEA U8744T).

1986
PETE TOWNSHEND – *DEEP END LIVE!*
UK: ATCO 7-905531 (CD album).
Gilmour played throughout the live album of the Deep End concerts recorded at the Brixton Academy on 1 November. Also the 12-inch single 'Give Blood' (from *White City*) / 'Won't Get Fooled Again' (live) / 'Magic Bus' (live) (UK: ATCO U8744T), the 7-inch single 'Give Blood' (from *White City*) / 'Magic Bus' (live) (UK: ATCO U8744) and a promotional 12-inch single 'After The Fire' (live) / 'Barefootin'' (live) / 'I Put A Spell On You' (live) / 'Save It For Later' (live) (US: ATCO PR940).

The full concert was re-released on the Pete Townshend 'Signature Series' as a CD album in November 2004.
.

1986

ROY HARPER – *IN BETWEEN EVERY LINE*

UK: EN 5004 (vinyl album).

Gilmour co-wrote the tracks 'Short And Sweet', 'True Story' and 'The Game' with Harper.

1986

BERLIN - *COUNT 3 AND PRAY*

UK: Mercury LP 830 586-1 (vinyl album).

Gilmour played guitars on 'Pink And Velvet'. Also on the double A-side of the 12-inch promotional single of the same track (UK: Mercury PRO-A-2632).

1986

LIONA BOYD – *PERSONA*

UK: CBS FM 42120 (vinyl album).

Gilmour played guitars on 'L'Enfant', 'Sorceress' and 'Persona'.

1987

WETTON / MANZANERA – *ONE WORLD*

UK: Geffen 924 147-1 (vinyl album).

Gilmour co-wrote 'Talk To Me' with John Wetton, Phil Manzenera and Billy Nicolls.

1987

BRYAN FERRY - 'Is Your Love Strong Enough?' / 'Windswept'

UK: EG FERRY 4 (7-inch single).

Gilmour played guitars on the A-side. Also on the 12-inch single 'Is Your Love Strong Enough?' (full version) / 'Is Your Love Strong Enough?' (7-inch single version) / 'Windswept' (UK: EG FERRX 4). The track was also used for the soundtrack of the film *Legend* and Gilmour also appeared in the promotional video for the single. The film is also included on the VHS video release *Bryan Ferry and Roxy Music - Video Collection* (UK: Virgin VID 2791).

1987

DALBELLO - *SHE*

UK: EMI CDP 564-7482862 (CD album).

Gilmour played guitars on 'Immaculate Eyes'.

1987

BRYAN FERRY - *BÊTE NOIRE*

UK: Virgin V2474 (vinyl album).

Gilmour played guitars on 'Seven Deadly Sins', 'Day For Night', 'New Town', 'Kiss And Tell', 'Limbo' and possibly 'The Right Stuff'. Also on the A-side of the 7-inch single 'Kiss And Tell' / 'Zamba' (UK: Virgin VS 1034), the A-side of the 12-inch single 'Kiss And Tell' / 'Zamba' (UK: Virgin VST 1034), the A-side of the 7-inch single 'Limbo' (Latin Mix) / 'Limbo' (Brooklyn Mix) (UK: Virgin VS 1066), and the A-side of the 12-inch

single 'Limbo' (Latin Mix) / 'Bête Noire' (instrumental) (UK: Virgin VST 1066).

1987

VARIOUS ARTISTS - *THE SECRET POLICEMAN'S THIRD BALL - THE MUSIC*

UK: Virgin 2458 (vinyl album) / UK: Virgin VVD 270 (VHS PAL video).

Gilmour played on 'Running Up That Hill' with Kate Bush's band on this album of highlights from the charity event of the same name.

1988

SAM BROWN - *STOP!*

UK: A&M AMA 5195 (vinyl album) / UK: A&M CDA 5195 (vinyl album).

Gilmour played guitars on 'This Feeling' and 'I'll Be In Love'. Also the A-side of the 7-inch single 'This Feeling' / 'Soldiers' (UK: A&M AM 455) and the A-Side of the 12-inch and CD single 'This Feeling' / 'Window People' / Soldiers' / 'Pitiful World' (UK 12-inch single: A&M AMY 455 / UK CD single: A&M AMCD 455).

1988

JOHN 'RABBIT' BUNDRICK - *DREAM JUNGLE*

UK: Lumina Music LUM CD2 (CD album).

Gilmour played guitars on 'Through The Clouds' and 'Conquest' and is credited as 'Studio Visitor'.

1988

PETER CETERA - *ONE MORE STORY*

UK: Warner Brothers WB 925 704-1 (vinyl album).

Gilmour played guitars on 'You Never Listen To Me' and 'Body Language (There In The Dark)'. Also on the double A-side of the 12-inch promotional single 'You Never Listen To Me' (UK: WB PRO-A-3216).

1989

VICKI BROWN - *LADY OF TIME*

UK: RCA PL 74522 (vinyl album).

Gilmour played guitars on 'Can't Let Go' credited as Mr. E. Guest.

1989

KATE BUSH - *THE SENSUAL WORLD*

UK: EMI EMD 1010 (vinyl album) / UK: EMI CDEMD 1010 (vinyl album).

Gilmour played guitars on 'Love And Anger' and 'Rocket's Tail (For Rocket)'.

Also on the A-side of the 7-inch single 'Love And Anger' / 'Ken' (UK: EMI EM134) and the A-side of the 12-inch single 'Love And Anger' / 'Ken' / 'The Confrontation' / 'One Last Look Around The House Before We Go' (UK: EMI 12 EM134). This track also appears on the VHS video *Sensual World* (UK: Music Club MC 2114) and the video CD *The Whole Story* (UK: PMI PMCD 4912882).

1989

KIRSTY MACCOLL - *KITE*

UK: Virgin KMLP1 (vinyl album) / UK: Virgin CDKM1 (CD album).

Gilmour played guitars on 'You And Me Baby' and 'No Victims'. Also on the second track of the 12-inch single 'Innocence' / 'No Victims (Guitar Heroes Mix)' / 'Don't Run Away From Me Now' / 'Clubland'/ (UK: Virgin KMAT 3).

1989

PAUL MCCARTNEY - *FLOWERS IN THE DIRT*

UK: EMI Parlophone PCSD 106 (vinyl album).

Gilmour played guitars on 'We Got Married'.

1989

VARIOUS ARTISTS - *SPIRIT OF THE FOREST*

UK: Virgin VS 1191 (7-inch single).

Gilmour provided vocals for this multi-artist production. This track was also included on the *Earthrise* album (UK: Polygram TV 515 419-1) and VHS video (UK: Weinnerworld WNR 2027). Gilmour was interviewed and filmed recording his contribution for BBC2 TV's *Nature* programme, which was broadcast in the UK on 2 May 1989 at 8.30pm.

1989

WARREN ZEVON - *TRANSVERSE CITY*

UK: Virgin America VUS LP 9 (vinyl album).

Gilmour played guitars on 'Run Straight Down'.

1990

BLUE PEARL - *NAKED*

UK: Big Life BLR LP4 (vinyl album).

Gilmour played guitars on 'Running Up That Hill' and 'Alive'. Also on the 12-inch single 'Alive' (Goa Mix) / 'Down To You' (Massey Mix) / 'Alive' (Organapella Mix) (UK: Big Life BLR T44) and the CD single 'Alive' (Edit) / 'Alive' (Goa Mix) / 'Down To You' (Massey Mix) (UK: Big Life BLR D44).

1990

SAM BROWN - *APRIL MOON*

UK: A&M AMA 9014 (vinyl album).

Gilmour provided backing vocals on 'Troubled Soul'.

1990

VICKI BROWN - *ABOUT LOVE AND LIFE*

UK: Polydor 847 266-2 (vinyl album).

Gilmour played guitars on 'I'll Always Be Waiting'.

1990

THE DREAM ACADEMY - *A DIFFERENT KIND OF WEATHER*

UK: Blanco Y Negro BYN 23 (vinyl album).

All tracks co-produced by Gilmour (except 'Love'). He also co-wrote the music for 'Twelve-Eight Angel' with Nick Laird-Clowes on which he also played guitar, bass-synth and vocals; played guitar on 'Mercy Killing';

played guitar solo, bass and vocals on 'It'll Never Happen Again' and guitar on 'Forest Fire'. The same contributions feature on the 7-inch single 'Angel Of Mercy' [a retitled version of 'Twelve-Eight Angel'] / 'Immaculate Heartache' (UK: Blanco Y Negro NEG 50) and the 12-inch single 'Angel Of Mercy (12/8 Mix)' / 'Immaculate Heartache' / 'In Suspendium' (UK: Blanco Y Negro NEG 50T).

1990
ROY HARPER - *ONCE*
UK: Awareness AWL 1018 (vinyl album)
Gilmour played guitars on 'Once', 'Once In The Middle Of Nowhere' and 'Berliners (A Better World)'.

1990
MICHAEL KAMEN - *CONCERTO FOR SAXOPHONE*
UK: Warner Brothers WB 7599-26157-2 (vinyl album)
Gilmour played guitars on 'Sasha'.

1990
PROPAGANDA - *1234*
UK: Virgin V2625 (vinyl album).
Gilmour played guitars on 'Only One Word' and on the A-side of the 12-inch single 'Only One Word (Mirror Mix)' / 'La Carne La Morte E Il Diavolo' / 'Open Spaces' (UK: Virgin VST 1271) and the A-side of the 10-inch limited edition box set single 'Only One Word' / 'Only One Word (demo)' / 'Open Spaces' (UK: Virgin VSAX 1271).

1990
ANDRES ROÉ - *ROÉ*
France: Barclay 841 628-2 (CD album – released in France only).
Gilmour played guitars on 'Como El Agua'.

1990
VARIOUS ARTISTS - *ONE WORLD, ONE VOICE*
UK: Virgin V2632 (vinyl album).
Gilmour contributed one short, untitled piece to this musical 'chain letter' recorded for *One World Week*. This piece also appears in the Howard Jones segment of the VHS video of the same title (UK: BMG 74321-1054-3). The segment was broadcast on BBC TV in the UK before the video's release.

1990
VARIOUS ARTISTS - *ROCK AID ARMENIA - THE EARTHQUAKE ALBUM*
UK: Carrere 30004 (vinyl album).
Gilmour played guitars on 'Smoke On The Water'. Also on the A-side of the 7-inch single 'Smoke On The Water' / 'Paranoid' (UK: Carrere ARMEN 001 / Carrere ARMEN T001), the A-side of the 12-inch single 'Smoke On The Water (Mega Rock Remix)' / 'Paranoid' (UK: ARMEN T001), the same track on the CD single 'Smoke On The Water (Radio Mix)' / 'Smoke

On The Water (Extended Mix)' / 'Paranoid' (UK: Carerre ARMEN CD001) and the 12-inch single 'Smoke On The Water '90' / 'Smoke On The Water (Mayhem Mix)' (UK: ARMEN T002). A VHS video compilation derived from the album also featured Gilmour (UK: Virgin Music Video VVD 636).

1990
PAUL YOUNG - *OTHER VOICES*
UK: CBS 466917-1 (vinyl album) / UK: CBS 466917-2 (CD album).
Gilmour played guitars on 'Heaven Can Wait' and 'A Little Bit Of Love'. Also on the A-side of the 12-inch single 'Heaven Can Wait' / 'Heaven Can Wait (7-inch remix)' (UK: CBS Young T6) and the same track on the CD single 'Heaven Can Wait' / 'Come Back And Stay' / 'Wonderland' / 'Everything Must Change' (UK: CBS Young D6).

1991
ALL ABOUT EVE - *TOUCHED BY JESUS*
UK: Vertigo 510 146-19 (vinyl album).
Gilmour played guitars on 'Wishing The Hours Away' and 'Are You Lonely?' Both tracks appear on the retrospective album *Keepsakes – A Collection* (UK: Mercury 9837781 CD album 2006).

1991
THE LAW - *THE LAW*
UK: Atlantic 7567-82195-1 (vinyl album).
Gilmour played guitars on 'Stone'.

1991
VARIOUS ARTISTS - COMIC RELIEF – The Stonk' (Hale And Pace and The Stonkers) / 'The Smile Song' (Victoria Wood)
UK: London LON 296 (7-inch single)
Gilmour played guitars on the title track of this charity record by comedians Hale And Pace as a member of the backing band The Stonkers and also appeared in the promotional video film of the same title. Also on the same track on the CD single and 12-inch single 'The Stonk' (7-inch version) / 'The Smile Song' / 'The Stonk' (extended version) (UK: London LONCD 296 - CD single / UK: LONX 296 - 12-inch single).

1992
ELTON JOHN - *THE ONE*
UK: Phonogram Rocket 512 360-1 (vinyl album).
Gilmour played guitars on 'Understanding Women' - a track originally recorded for the box set *To Be Continued...* (UK: Phonogram Rocket 848 236-2).

1992
JOHN MARTYN - *COULDN'T LOVE YOU MORE*
UK: Permanent CD9 (CD album).
Gilmour played guitars on 'One World', 'Could've Been Me' and 'Ways To Cry'.

1992
JIMMY NAIL - *GROWING UP IN PUBLIC*
UK: East-West 4509-90144-1 (CD album).
Gilmour played guitars on 'Waiting For The Sunshine' and 'Only Love (Can Bring Us Home)'. The album was co-produced by Guy Pratt.

1993
JOHN MARTYN - *NO LITTLE BOY*
UK: Permanent PERM 14 (CD album).
Gilmour played guitars on 'Could've Been Me', 'One World' and 'Ways To Cry'.

1993
PAUL RODGERS - *MUDDY WATERS BLUES*
UK: Victory 383 480 013-2 (CD album).
Gilmour played guitars on 'Standing Around Crying'.

1994
CHRIS JAGGER - *ATCHA*
UK: Sequel NEX CD 258 (CD album).
Gilmour played guitars on 'Steal The Time'.

1994
SNOWY WHITE - *HIGHWAY TO THE SUN*
UK: Bellaphon 290-07-205 (CD album).
Gilmour played guitars on 'Love, Pain And Sorrow'.

1995
JOHN MARTYN – *LIVE*
UK: Permanent PERM CD33 (CD album).
Gilmour played guitar on 'Easy Blues', 'Dealer', 'Sapphire', 'Fisherman's Dream', 'Big Muff', 'John Wayne' and 'Johnny Too Bad' at this John Martyn concert recorded at The Shaw Theatre, London, England on 31 March 1990.

1995
SNOWY WHITE - *GOLDTOP*
UK: RPM 154 (CD album).
Gilmour played guitars on 'Love, Pain And Sorrow'. This retrospective collection also includes the only official release of Pink Floyd's 'Pigs On The Wing, Parts 1 & 2', on which Snowy played guitars.

1997
BB KING – *DEUCES WILD*
UK: MCD 11722 (CD album).
Gilmour played guitar on 'Cryin' Won't Help You Babe'.

1997
PAUL MCCARTNEY – 'Young Boy' / 'I Love This House'
UK: Capitol 724388395/20 (CD single).
Gilmour played guitar on 'I Love This House'. It was probably recorded in 1984 and his contribution is not credited on the sleeve. Also on the US CD single 'The World Tonight' (UK: Capitol 724685865022).

1998
PEGGY SEEGER – *PERIOD PIECES*
UK: TCD 1078 (CD album).
Gilmour played guitar on 'Winnie And Sam'.

1998
THE PRETTY THINGS - *RESURRECTION (DIED 1968 BORN 1998 AT ABBEY ROAD)*
UK: Snapper Music 160042 (CD album).
Gilmour played guitars on 'She Says Good Morning', 'I See You', 'Well Of Destiny', 'Trust', 'Old Man Going'. This was Gilmour's contribution to the live Internet broadcast (and this subsequent limited edition of 10,000 numbered copies CD release) of a 30th anniversary performance of The Pretty Things' album *SF Sorrow*.

1999
THE PRETTY THINGS - *RAGE BEFORE BEAUTY*
UK: Snapper Music SMACD 814 (CD album).
Gilmour played guitars on 'Love Keeps Hanging On'. Since the album was begun in 1981, it is uncertain when his part was recorded.

1999
TOM NEWMAN (& FRIENDS) – *SNOW BLIND*
UK: RFCD 006 (CD album).
Gilmour played guitar on 'Nowhere To Go', recorded in 1983.

1999
PAUL MCCARTNEY - *RUN DEVIL RUN*
UK: EMI Parlophone 523 3042 (Boxed CD album) / EMI Parlophone 522 3512 (CD album) / EMI Parlophone 523 2291 (7-inch singles box set). Gilmour played guitar on this album of rock 'n' roll originals and covers. Also on the 7-inch single 'No Other Baby' / 'Brown Eyed Handsome Man' (UK: EMI Parlophone R6527) and the CD single 'No Other Baby' / 'Brown Eyed Handsome Man' / 'Fabulous' (UK: EMI Parlophone CDR 6527) and the mono CD single 'No Other Baby' / 'Brown Eyed Handsome Man' / 'Fabulous' (UK: EMI Parlophone CDR 6527).

2000
JOHN MARTYN – *CLASSICS*
UK: Artful CD31 (CD album).
Gilmour played guitar on 'Could've Been Me', 'One World', 'Ways To Cry', 'Johnny Too Bad', 'Sapphire', 'Fisherman's Dream', 'Big Muff', 'Easy Blues', 'Dealer' and 'John Wayne'.

2000
UNICORN – *THE BEST OF UNICORN*
UK: See For Miles SEECD 715 (CD album).
Gilmour played pedal steel guitar on 'Oak Mother', 'Just Wanna Hold You', 'Electric Night', 'Blue Pine Trees', 'Sleep Song' and 'Too Many Crooks', a compilation from the band's two albums *Blue Pine*

Trees and *Too Many Crooks*.

2001
JOOLS HOLLAND – *SMALL WORLD BIG BAND*
UK: Warner 0927426562 (CD album).
Gilmour played guitar on 'I Put A Spell On You' with Mica Paris.

2002
UNICORN – *SHED NO TEAR (THE SHED STUDIO SESSIONS)*
UK: Mad Dog MDR 1001 (CD album).
Gilmour produced this album at his Astoria recording studio. Includes a session out-take of 'So Far Away' from Gilmour's first solo album.

1991
DONOVAN – *CELTIA*
UK: Durga 2002 (CD album).
Gilmour played guitar on 'Lover, O Lover', 'Everlasting Sea' and 'Rock Me'. Gilmour's contributions were recorded in 1990.

2001
JASON OSBORN – *IL TRIONFO DELL' AMORE*
UK: CAM 502447-2 (CD album).
Gilmour played guitar on the soundtrack to this film, translated as *Triumph Of Love*, on 'Follow That Young... Person', 'Agis And The Phocion: The Archery', 'I Am Aspasie', 'The Grotto, 'Phocion!' and 'Phocion! (reprise)'.

2002
CAROLINE DALE – *SUCH SWEET THUNDER*
UK: KARMACD 7 (CD album).
Gilmour co-wrote and played guitar on 'Babbie's Daughter'.

2003
ROBERT WYATT – *CUCKOOLAND*
UK: Hannibal Records HNCD 1468 (CD album).
Gilmour played guitar on 'Forest'.

2003
RINGO STARR – *RINGO RAMA*
UK: Koch Records 2384292 (CD album and limited edition enhanced CD with a DVD making-of documentary).
Gilmour played guitar on 'Missouri Loves Company' and 'I Think, Therefore I Rock 'n' Roll'.

2004
PHIL MANZANERA – *6PM*
UK: HNCD 1471 (CD album).
Gilmour played guitar on 'Always You' and 'Sacred Days'.

2004
ALAN PARSONS – *A VALID PATH*
UK: Eagle Rock EAGCD 221 (CD album).
Gilmour played guitar on 'Return To Tunguska'.

2005
VARIOUS ARTISTS – 'Ever Fallen In Love (With Someone You Shouldn't've)' / THE BUZZCOCKS – 'Ever Fallen In Love (With Someone You Shouldn't've)'
UK: EMI Peel CD1 (CD single).
Gilmour played guitar on this tribute single to the late DJ John Peel, which also featured Roger Daltrey, Peter Hook, Robert Plant, Elton John and its original composer Pete Shelley. The B-side was the original Buzzcocks' recording.

2006
CHRIS JAGGER – *ACT OF FAITH*
UK: SPV 78572 (CD album).
Gilmour played guitar on 'It's Amazing (What People Throw Away)' and 'Junkman'.

LIVE PERFORMANCE

ABOUT FACE - EUROPEAN TOUR 1984
Gilmour assembled an impressive band for his first solo tour comprising Gregg Dechart (keyboards), Mickey Feat (bass guitar), Jodi Linscott (percussion), Mick Ralphs (guitar and vocals), Raphael 'Raff' Ravenscroft (saxophone) and Chris Slade (drums).

Friday 30 March
TV SHOW
Tyne Tees Television Studios, Newcastle-upon-Tyne, England
Gilmour previewed his world tour on the live music programme *The Tube*, performing two tracks, 'Until We Sleep' and 'Blue Light'. It was broadcast on Channel 4 TV at 5.30pm.

Saturday 31 March
CONCERT
National Stadium, Dublin, Republic of Ireland
The tour was an uncomplicated presentation in comparison with Waters' full-scale assault of the same year. Gilmour preferred a very simple stage set and lighting, concentrating on the musicianship rather than the spectacle.
Set list at this show and all shows to 1 May unless otherwise noted: 'Until We Sleep' / 'All Lovers Are Deranged' / 'Love On The Air' / 'Mihalis' / 'There's No Way Out Of Here' / 'Run Like Hell' / 'Out Of The Blue' / 'Let's Get Metaphysical' / 'Cruise' / 'Short And Sweet' / 'You Know I'm Right' / 'Blue Light' / 'Murder' / 'Near The End' / encore: 'Comfortably Numb'. 'I Can't Breathe Anymore' was performed as an additional encore at some shows.

Monday 2 April
CONCERT
Whitla Hall, Belfast, Northern Ireland

Thursday 5 April
CONCERT
Grote Zaal, Muziekcentrum Vredenburg, Utrecht,
The Netherlands

Friday 6 April
CONCERT
Auditorium Q, Campus Etterbeek, Vreij Universität
Brussel, Brussels, Belgium

Sunday 8 April
CONCERT
Hall A, Parc des Expositions, Nancy, France

Monday 9 April
CONCERT
Hall Tivoli, Strasbourg, France

Tuesday 10 & Wednesday 11 April
CONCERTS
Le Zénith, Parc de Villette, Paris, France
The show of 10 April was recorded by RTL Radio and
the following tracks were later broadcast: 'Run Like
Hell', 'Out Of The Blue', 'Cruise', 'Blue Light', 'Near The
End' and 'Comfortably Numb'.

Thursday 12 April
CONCERT
Salle Albert Thomas, Bourse du Travail, Lyon,
France

Friday 13 April
CONCERT
Kongress-saal, Kongresshaus, Zurich, Switzerland

Saturday 14 April
CONCERT
Circus Krone, Munich, West Germany

Sunday 15 April
CONCERT
Alte Oper, Frankfurt, West Germany

Monday 16 April
CONCERT
Musensaal, Mannheim, West Germany

Wednesday 18 April
CONCERT
Saal 1, Internationales Congress Centrum, West
Berlin, West Germany

Thursday 19 April
CONCERT
Saal 1, Congress Centrum Hamburg, Hamburg,
West Germany

Saturday 21 April
CONCERT
Philipshalle, Düsseldorf, West Germany

Tuesday 24 April
CONCERT
Johanneshovs Isstadion, Stockholm, Sweden

Wednesday 25 April
CONCERT
Falconer Centret, Copenhagen, Denmark

Saturday 28, Sunday 29 & Monday 30 April
CONCERTS
Hammersmith Odeon, Hammersmith, London,
England

Set list at all three shows: 'Until We Sleep' / 'All
Lovers Are Deranged' / 'Love On The Air' / 'Mihalis' /
'There's No Way Out Of Here' / 'Run Like Hell' / 'Out
Of The Blue' / 'Let's Get Metaphysical' / 'Cruise' /
'Short And Sweet' (with Roy Harper on vocals) / 'You
Know I'm Right' / 'Blue Light' / 'Murder' / 'Near The
End' / encore: 'Comfortably Numb' (with Nick Mason
on drums).
All three London concerts were recorded for MTV
and first broadcast on 26 May 1984. The show, which
was later released as a VHS video in the USA
included 'Until We Sleep', 'All Lovers Are Deranged',
'There's No Way Out Of Here', 'Short And Sweet', 'Run
Like Hell', 'Out Of The Blue', 'Blue Light', 'Murder' and
'Comfortably Numb'. The video footage was later
combined with behind-the-scenes material from the
European tour in an MTV documentary entitled
Beyond The Floyd, and broadcast at the earlier date
of 20 May 1984.
The concerts were also recorded by the Westwood
One radio network for their *In Concert* series and the
following tracks were broadcast in the USA on 2 May
1984: 'Money', 'Run Like Hell' and 'Comfortably
Numb'.
The Television Personalities supported Gilmour on the
first night and performed a version of 'See Emily Play'
in their set before revealing Syd Barrett's home
address to the audience. The band were instantly
dismissed from the remaining two London dates by
an infuriated Gilmour and the opening slot was
replaced by Billy Bragg who was and still is managed
by one of Pink Floyd's former managers, Peter
Jenner. Although Rick Wright attended the last
show, he did not perform.

Tuesday 1 May
CONCERT
Odeon, Birmingham, England
The last night of the tour.

ABOUT FACE – NORTH AMERICAN TOUR 1984

Gilmour's band for this show and the rest of the tour were Gregg Dechart (keyboards), Mickey Feat (bass guitar), Jodi Linscott (percussion), Mick Ralphs (guitar and vocals), Raphael 'Raff' Ravenscroft (saxophone) and Chris Slade (drums).

Set list at this show and all shows on this tour: 'Until We Sleep' / 'All Lovers Are Deranged' / 'Love On The Air' / 'Mihalis' / 'There's No Way Out Of Here' / 'Run Like Hell' / 'Out Of The Blue' / 'Let's Get Metaphysical' / 'Cruise' / 'Short And Sweet' / 'You Know I'm Right' / 'Blue Light' / 'Murder' / 'Near The End' / encore: 'Comfortably Numb'. 'I Can't Breathe Anymore' was performed as an additional encore at some shows.

Tuesday 8 May
CANCELLED CONCERT
Chicoutimi, Québec, Canada

Wednesday 9 May
CONCERT
Colisee de Québec, Québec City, Québec, Canada

Thursday 10 May
CANCELLED CONCERT
Rimouski, Québec, Canada

Thursday 10 & Friday 11 May
CONCERTS
The Forum, Montréal, Québec, Canada

Saturday 12 May
CONCERT
Civic Centre Theatre, Ottawa Civic Centre, Lansdowne Park, Ottawa, Ontario, Canada

Monday 14 & Tuesday 15 May
CONCERTS
Massey Hall, Toronto, Ontario, Canada

Wednesday 16 May
CONCERT
Shea's Buffalo Theatre, Buffalo, New York, USA

Thursday 17 May
CONCERT
Landmark Theatre, Syracuse, New York, USA

Friday 18 May
CONCERT
Mair Hall, Mid-Hudson Civic Center, Poughkeepsie, New York, USA

Sunday 20 May
CONCERT
Bushnell Auditorium, Hartford, Connecticut, USA

Tuesday 22, Wednesday 23 & Thursday 24 May
CONCERTS
Beacon Theatre, Manhattan, New York City, New York, USA

Friday 25 & Saturday 26 May
CONCERTS
The Orpheum Theatre, Boston, Massachusetts, USA

Sunday 27 May
CONCERT
Veterans Memorial Coliseum, New Haven, Connecticut, USA

Tuesday 29, Wednesday 30 & Thursday 31 May
CONCERTS
Tower Theatre, Philadelphia, Pennsylvania, USA

Friday 1 June
CONCERT
Daughters Of The American Revolution Constitution Hall, Washington, District of Columbia, USA

Sunday 3 June
CONCERT
Public Hall, Cleveland, Ohio, USA

Monday 4 June
CONCERT
Veterans Memorial Hall, Columbus, Ohio, USA

Wednesday 6 June
CONCERT
Pine Knob Music Theatre, Clarkston, Michigan, USA

Thursday 7 June
CONCERT
Cincinnati Gardens, Cincinnati, Ohio, USA

Friday 8 June
CONCERT
Chicago Pavilion, Chicago, Illinois, USA

Sunday 10 June
CONCERT
Kiel Opera House, St. Louis, Missouri, USA

Monday 11 June
CONCERT
Starlight Theatre, Kansas City, Missouri, USA

Wednesday 13 June
CONCERT
The Summit Sports Arena, Houston, Texas, USA

Thursday 14 June
CONCERT
Frank Erwin Center, University of Texas, Austin, Texas, USA

Friday 15 June
CONCERT
Majestic Theatre, San Antonio, Texas, USA

Saturday 16 June
CONCERT
Reunion Arena, Reunion Park, Dallas, Texas, USA

Tuesday 19 June
CONCERT
The Amphitheatre, Mesa, Arizona, USA

Wednesday 20 June
CONCERT
Open Air Theatre, San Diego State University, San Diego, California, USA

Thursday 21 & Friday 22 June
CONCERTS
Universal Amphitheatre, Universal City, Los Angeles, California, USA

Saturday 23 & Sunday 24 June
CONCERTS
Irvine Meadows Amphitheatre, Irvine, California, USA

Tuesday 26 & Wednesday 27 June
CONCERTS
Kabuki Theatre, San Francisco, California, USA

Thursday 28 June
CONCERT
California Exposition Amphitheater, California Exposition Fairgrounds, Sacramento, California, USA

Friday 29 June
CONCERT
Greek Theatre, University of California, Berkeley, California, USA

Thursday 5 July
CONCERT
Sunrise Music Theatre, Sunrise, Florida, USA

Sue Evans replaced Jodi Linscott at this show and all subsequent shows on the tour.

Friday 6 July
CONCERT
Civic Centre Arena, Lakeland, Florida, USA

Sunday 8 July
CONCERT
Garden State Arts Center, Holmdel, New Jersey, USA

Wednesday 11 July
CONCERT
Syria Mosque Theater, Pittsburgh, Pennslyvania, USA

Thursday 12 July
CONCERT
Stabler Arena, Lehigh University, Allentown, Pennsylvania, USA
This show was recorded by the Westwood One radio network In Concert series and the following tracks were broadcast in the USA on 31 August 1984: 'Until We Sleep' / 'All Lovers Are Deranged' / 'Money' / 'Love On The Air' / 'Short And Sweet' / 'You Know I'm Right' / 'Run Like Hell' / 'Blue Light' / 'Murder' / 'Comfortably Numb'.

Friday 13 July
CONCERT
Jones Beach Theatre, Wantagh, Long Island, New York, USA

Saturday 14 July
CONCERT
Merriweather Post Pavilion, Columbia, Maryland, USA

Sunday 15 July
CONCERT
Saratoga Performing Arts Center, Saratoga Springs, New York, USA

Monday 16 July
CONCERT
NYC Convention Pier, Manhattan, New York City, New York, USA
The last night of the tour.

MELTDOWN
Gilmour performed a unique solo 'Unplugged' style show as part of the South Bank Centre's annual Meltdown festival, at the invitation of this year's curator Robert Wyatt. Held over a period of a week the festival included performances by Tricky, The Residents, Baaba Maal and Elvis Costello among many others. This show as well as those at the same venue in 2002 were filmed and recorded for the David Gilmour – In Concert DVD.

Friday 22 June 2001
CONCERT
Meltdown, Royal Festival Hall, South Bank, London, England
Supported by Sparklehorse.

Set list: 'Shine On You Crazy Diamond, Parts 1-5' / 'Terrapin' (Syd Barrett) / 'Fat Old Sun' / 'Coming Back To Life' / 'High Hopes' / 'Je Crois Entendre Encore' (from the opera *Les Pecheurs de Perle* by George Bizet) / 'Smile' (a new composition) / 'Wish You Were Here' / 'Comfortably Numb' / 'The Dimming Of The Day' (Richard Thompson) / 'Shine On You Crazy Diamond, Parts 6-9' / encore: 'A Great Day For Freedom' / 'Hushabye Mountain' (from the film *Chitty Chitty Bang Bang*).
Gilmour was supplemented on stage by Dick Parry (saxophone on 'Shine On You Crazy Diamond'), Michael Kamen (piano, oboe), Chucho Merchan (bass), Neil MacColl (guitars), Nick France (drums, percussion), Caroline Dale (cello), Robert Wyatt (additional vocals on 'Comfortably Numb' from side of stage) and Chris Ballin, Pete Brown, Sam Brown, Margot Buchanan, Michelle Carol, Claudia Fontaine, Michelle John-Douglas, Carol Kenyon and Aitch McRobbie (backing vocals).

DAVID GILMOUR - IN CONCERT
Following the success of his Meltdown show, Gilmour arranged a series of three more shows in London and two in Paris. His band comprised Dick Parry (saxophone on both parts of 'Shine On You Crazy Diamond' and 'Breakthrough'); Michael Kamen (piano, oboe); Chucho Merchan (bass); Neil MacColl (guitars); Nick France (drums, percussion); Caroline Dale (cello); Rick Wright (keyboards and vocals on 'Breakthrough' and piano on 'Wish You Were Here' and 'Comfortably Numb'); Robert Wyatt (additional vocals on 'Comfortably Numb' on 16 January from side of stage); Sir Bob Geldof (additional vocals on 'Comfortably Numb' on 17 January); Kate Bush (additional vocals on 'Comfortably Numb' on 18 January); Chris Ballin, Pete Brown, Sam Brown, Margot Buchanan, Claudia Fontaine, Michelle John-Douglas, Sonia Jones, Carol Kenyon, David Laudat, Durga McBroom, Aitch McRobbie and Beverli Skeete (backing vocals).

Wednesday 16, Thursday 17 & Friday 18 January 2002
CONCERTS
Royal Festival Hall, South Bank, London, England
Set list for all shows in London and Paris: 'Shine On You Crazy Diamond, Parts 1-5' / 'Fat Old Sun' / 'Coming Back To Life' / 'Dominoes' (Syd Barrett) / 'High Hopes' / 'High Hopes' (backing vocals chorus) / 'Je Crois Entendre Encore' (from the opera *Les Pecheurs de Perle* by George Bizet) / 'Smile' / 'Breakthrough' (Richard Wright) / 'Wish You Were Here' / 'Comfortably Numb' / 'The Dimming Of The Day' (Richard Thompson) / 'Shine On You Crazy Diamond, Parts 6-9' / encore: 'A Great Day For Freedom' / 'Hushabye Mountain' (from the film *Chitty Chitty Bang Bang*).
The shows on 16 and 17 January were supported by

Ghostland (featuring Caroline Dale on cello with the London Metropolitan Orchestra) and on 18 January by Trashmonk (featuring Nick Laird-Clowes). All three shows were filmed and recorded for the *David Gilmour – In Concert* DVD.

Wednesday 23 & Thursday 24 January 2002
CONCERTS
Palace de Congrès de Paris, Paris, France

DAVID GILMOUR - ON AN ISLAND TOUR 2006
Gilmour's band for the tour comprised Jon Carin (keyboards), Steve DiStanislao (drums), Phil Manzanera (guitar), Dick Parry (saxophone), Guy Pratt (bass guitar) and Richard Wright (keyboards).

Saturday 4 March
RADIO SHOW
BBC Broadcasting House, Portland Place, London, England
Gilmour effectively launched his tour on this date performing 'Smile' and 'On An Island' with Phil Manzanera as part of a live interview on the *Jonanthan Ross Show*. It was broadcast on BBC Radio 2 at 10.00am.

Monday 6 March
PRIVATE PARTY
Porchester Hall, Bayswater, London, England
Set list: 'Castellorizon' / 'On An Island' / 'The Blue' / 'Take A Breath' / ''Red Sky At Night'' / 'This Heaven' / 'Then I Close My Eyes' / 'Smile' / 'A Pocketful Of Stones' / 'Where We Start' // 'Wish You Were Here' / 'Dominoes' / encore: 'Happy Birthday' song.
A Who's Who of celebrity guests were invited to attend David Gilmour's 60th birthday party and were treated to some musical entertainment by Gilmour and his band.

Tuesday 7 March
RADIO SHOW
Mermaid Theatre, Puddle Dock, Blackfriars, London, England
Set list: 'Castellorizon' / 'On An Island' / 'The Blue' / 'Take A Breath' / 'Smile' / 'This Heaven' / 'Shine On You Crazy Diamond, Parts 1-5' / 'Wearing The Inside Out' // 'High Hopes' / 'Comfortably Numb' / 'On An Island' (second take) / 'The Blue' (second take) / finale: 'Happy Birthday' song.
This show was staged by BBC Radio 2 for recording and filming with the audience largely made up of competition winners. An hour-long edit of the show comprising 'Castellorizon', 'On An Island', 'The Blue', 'Take A Breath', 'Smile', 'Shine On You Crazy Diamond, Parts 1-5', 'Wearing The Inside Out' and 'Comfortably Numb' was broadcast simultaneously on BBC Radio 2 and could be viewed on the BBC Radio 2 website on 11 March at 9.30pm and was archived until 18 March

2006. Various other edits were shown and repeated on numerous broadcast channels worldwide.

The complete edited show was also screened with additional footage, including 'High Hopes' live, the promo film for 'On An Island' as well as interview footage as part of a nationwide cinema presentation across 100 selected US cinemas under the banner *Big Screen Concerts* on 16 May 2006.

Additionally, in what was the BBC's first ever interactive TV production, a 30-minute edit of the concert was made available via BBC Interactive TV between 11 and 14 March 2006 featuring 'On An Island', 'Shine On You Crazy Diamond, Parts 1-5' and 'Comfortably Numb'.

Friday 10 March
CONCERT
Konzerthaus, Dortmund, Germany
Set list: 'Castellorizon' / 'On An Island' / 'The Blue' / 'Red Sky At Night' / 'This Heaven' / 'Then I Close My Eyes' / 'Smile' / 'Take A Breath' / 'A Pocketful Of Stones' / 'Where We Start' // 'Shine On You Crazy Diamond, Parts 1-5' / 'Wot's Uh... The Deal' / 'Wearing The Inside Out' / 'Breathe' / 'Time' / 'Breathe (reprise)' / 'Dominoes' / 'High Hopes' / 'Echoes' / encore: 'Wish You Were Here' / 'Comfortably Numb'.

Saturday 11 March
CONCERT
Saal 1, Congress Centrum Hamburg, Hamburg, Germany
Set list: 'Castellorizon' / 'On An Island' / 'The Blue' / 'Red Sky At Night' / 'This Heaven' / 'Then I Close My Eyes' / 'Smile' / 'Take A Breath' / 'A Pocketful Of Stones' / 'Where We Start' // 'Shine On You Crazy Diamond, Parts 1-5' / 'Wot's Uh... The Deal' / 'Wearing The Inside Out' / 'Breathe' / 'Time' / 'Breathe (reprise)' / 'Dominoes' / 'High Hopes' / 'Echoes' / encore: 'Wish You Were Here' / 'Comfortably Numb'.

Wednesday 15 March
CONCERT
Le Grand Rex, Paris, France
Set list: 'Castellorizon' / 'On An Island' / 'The Blue' / 'Red Sky At Night' / 'This Heaven' / 'Then I Close My Eyes' / 'Smile' / 'Take A Breath' / 'A Pocketful Of Stones' / 'Where We Start' // 'Shine On You Crazy Diamond, Parts 1-5' / 'Wot's Uh... The Deal' / 'Wearing The Inside Out' / 'Breathe' / 'Time' / 'Breathe (reprise)' / 'Dominoes' / 'High Hopes' / 'Echoes' / encore: 'Wish You Were Here' / 'Comfortably Numb'.

Thursday 16 March
CONCERT
L'Olympia, Paris, France
Set list: 'Castellorizon' / 'On An Island' / 'The Blue' / 'The Great Gig In The Sky' (with guest Sam Brown) / 'Red Sky At Night' / 'This Heaven' / 'Then I Close My Eyes' / 'Smile' / 'Take A Breath' / 'A Pocketful Of Stones' / 'Where We Start' // 'Shine On You Crazy Diamond, Parts 1-5' / 'Wot's Uh... The Deal' / 'Wearing The Inside Out' / 'Fat Old Sun' / 'Breathe' / 'Time' / 'Breathe (reprise)' / 'High Hopes' / 'Echoes' / encore: 'Wish You Were Here' / 'Comfortably Numb'.

Saturday 18 March
CONCERT
Alte Oper, Frankfurt, Germany
Set list: 'Castellorizon' / 'On An Island' / 'The Blue' / 'Red Sky At Night' / 'This Heaven' / 'Then I Close My Eyes' / 'Smile' / 'Take A Breath' / 'A Pocketful Of Stones' / 'Where We Start' // 'Shine On You Crazy Diamond, Parts 1-5' / 'Wot's Uh... The Deal' / 'Wearing The Inside Out' / 'Fat Old Sun' / 'Breathe' / 'Time' / 'Breathe (reprise)' / 'High Hopes' / 'Echoes' / encore: 'Wish You Were Here' / 'Comfortably Numb'.

Sunday 19 March
CONCERT
Heineken Music Hall, Amsterdam, Netherlands
Set list: 'Castellorizon' / 'On An Island' / 'The Blue' / 'Red Sky At Night' / 'This Heaven' / 'Then I Close My Eyes' / 'Smile' / 'Take A Breath' / 'A Pocketful Of Stones' / 'Where We Start' // 'Shine On You Crazy Diamond, Parts 1-5' / 'Wot's Uh... The Deal' / 'Wearing The Inside Out' / 'Dominoes' / 'Breathe' / 'Time' / 'Breathe (reprise)' / 'High Hopes' / 'Echoes' / encore: 'Wish You Were Here' / 'Comfortably Numb'.

Monday 20 March
CONCERT
Heineken Music Hall, Amsterdam, Netherlands
Set list: 'Castellorizon' / 'On An Island' / 'The Blue' / 'Red Sky At Night' / 'This Heaven' / 'Then I Close My Eyes' / 'Take A Breath' / 'Smile' / 'A Pocketful Of Stones' / 'Where We Start' // 'Shine On You Crazy Diamond, Parts 1-5' / 'Wot's Uh... The Deal' / 'Fat Old Sun' / 'Coming Back To Life' / 'Breathe' / 'Time' / 'Breathe (reprise)' / 'High Hopes' / 'Echoes' / encore: 'Wish You Were Here' / 'Comfortably Numb'.

Friday 24 March
CONCERT
Teatro Degli Arcimboldi, Milan, Italy
Set list: 'Castellorizon' / 'On An Island' / 'The Blue' / 'Red Sky At Night' / 'This Heaven' / 'Then I Close My Eyes' / 'Take A Breath' / 'Smile' / 'A Pocketful Of Stones' / 'Where We Start' / 'Shine On You Crazy Diamond, Parts 1-5' / 'Wot's Uh... The Deal' / 'Wearing The Inside Out' / 'Coming Back To Life' / 'Breathe' / 'Time' / 'Breathe (reprise)' / 'High Hopes' / 'Echoes' / encore: 'Wish You Were Here' / 'Comfortably Numb'.

Saturday 25 March
CONCERT
Teatro Degli Arcimboldi, Milan, Italy
Set list: 'Castellorizon' / 'On An Island' / 'The Blue' / 'Red Sky At Night' / 'This Heaven' / 'Then I Close My Eyes' / 'Take A Breath' / 'Smile' / 'A Pocketful Of Stones' / 'Where We Start' // 'Shine On You Crazy Diamond, Parts 1-5' / 'Wot's Uh... The Deal' / 'Wearing The Inside Out' / 'Fat Old Sun' / 'Breathe' / 'Time' / 'Breathe (reprise)' / 'High Hopes' / 'Echoes' / encore: 'Wish You Were Here' / 'Comfortably Numb'.

Sunday 26 March
CONCERT
Sala Santa Cecilia, Auditorium Parco della Musica, Rome, Italy
Set list: 'Castellorizon' / 'On An Island' / 'The Blue' / 'Red Sky At Night' / 'This Heaven' / 'Then I Close My Eyes' / 'Take A Breath' / 'Smile' / 'A Pocketful Of Stones' / 'Where We Start' // 'Shine On You Crazy Diamond, Parts 1-5' / 'Wearing The Inside Out' / 'Dominoes' / 'Fat Old Sun' / 'Breathe' / 'Time' / 'Breathe (reprise)' / 'High Hopes' / 'Echoes' / encore: 'Wish You Were Here' / 'Comfortably Numb'.

Tuesday 4 April
CONCERT
Radio City Music Hall, Manhattan, New York City, New York, USA
Set list: 'Castellorizon' / 'This Heaven' / 'Smile' / 'Red Sky At Night' / 'Take A Breath' / 'Then I Close My Eyes' / 'On An Island' (with guests David Crosby and Graham Nash) / 'The Blue' (with guests David Crosby and Graham Nash) / 'A Pocketful Of Stones' / 'Where We Start' / 'Shine On You Crazy Diamond, Parts 1-5' (with guests David Crosby and Graham Nash) / 'Wearing The Inside Out' / 'Dominoes' / 'Fat Old Sun' / 'Breathe' / 'Time' / 'Breathe (reprise)' / 'High Hopes' / 'Echoes' / encore: 'Wish You Were Here' / 'Find The Cost Of Freedom' (with guests David Crosby and Graham Nash) / 'Comfortably Numb'.

Wednesday 5 April
CONCERT
Radio City Music Hall, Manhattan, New York City, New York, USA
Set list: 'Castellorizon' / 'This Heaven' / 'Smile' / 'Red Sky At Night' / 'Take A Breath' / 'Then I Close My Eyes' / 'On An Island' (with guests David Crosby and Graham Nash) / 'The Blue' (with guest vocals David Crosby and Graham Nash) / 'A Pocketful Of Stones' / 'Where We Start' / 'Shine On You Crazy Diamond, Parts 1-5' (with guest vocals David Crosby and Graham Nash) / 'Wot's Uh... The Deal' / 'Wearing The Inside Out' / 'Coming Back To Life' / 'Breathe' / 'Time' / 'Breathe (reprise)' / 'High Hopes' / 'Echoes' / encore: 'Wish You Were Here' / 'Find The Cost Of Freedom' (with guest vocals David Crosby and Graham Nash) / 'Comfortably Numb'.

Friday 7 April
RADIO SHOW
Studio Z, Sony Studios, Manhattan, New York City, New York, USA
This was essentially an intimate interview and performance with Gilmour accompanied by Phil Manzanera in which they performed 'Smile' and 'Where We Start' arranged by the XM Internet Radio broadcasting group as part of their *Artist Confidential* series to an exclusive audience of no less than 30 people – mostly record company executives, friends and family. It was broadcast from 5 June.

Friday 7 April
RADIO SHOW
AOL Studios, Rockefeller Center, Manhattan, New York City, New York, USA
Set list: 'On An Island' / 'This Heaven' / 'Take A Breath' / 'Smile' / 'High Hopes' / 'Comfortably Numb'. This was a live studio concert recorded exclusively for the AOL Internet provider and was available for viewing in 5.1 surround sound for a limited period from 21 April 2006.

Sunday 9 April
CONCERT
Massey Hall, Toronto, Ontario, Canada
Set list: 'Castellorizon' / 'On An Island' / 'The Blue' / 'Red Sky At Night' / 'This Heaven' / 'Then I Close My Eyes' / 'Take A Breath' / 'Smile' / 'A Pocketful Of Stones' / 'Where We Start' // 'Shine On You Crazy Diamond, Parts 1-5' / 'Wot's Uh... The Deal' / 'Wearing The Inside Out' / 'Fat Old Sun' / 'Breathe' / 'Time' / 'Breathe (reprise)' / 'High Hopes' / 'Echoes' / encore: 'Wish You Were Here' / 'Comfortably Numb'.

Monday 10 April
CONCERT
Massey Hall, Toronto, Ontario, Canada
Set list: 'Castellorizon' / 'On An Island' / 'The Blue' / 'Red Sky At Night' / 'This Heaven' / 'Then I Close My Eyes' / 'Take A Breath' / 'Smile' / 'A Pocketful Of Stones' / 'Where We Start' // 'Shine On You Crazy Diamond, Parts 1-5' / 'Wearing The Inside Out' / 'Dominoes' / 'Coming Back To Life' / 'Breathe' / 'Time' / 'Breathe (reprise)' / 'High Hopes' / 'Echoes' / encore: 'Wish You Were Here' / 'Comfortably Numb'.

Wednesday 12 April
CONCERT
Rosemont Theatre, Rosemont, Chicago, Illinois, USA
Set list: 'Castellorizon' / 'On An Island' / 'Red Sky At Night' / 'The Blue' / 'Then I Close My Eyes' / 'This Heaven' / 'Smile' / 'Take A Breath' / 'A Pocketful Of Stones' / 'Where We Start' // 'Shine On You Crazy Diamond, Parts 1-5' / 'Wot's Uh... The Deal' / 'Wearing The Inside Out' / 'Fat Old Sun' / 'Breathe' / 'Time' / 'Breathe (reprise)' / 'High Hopes' / 'Echoes' / encore: 'Wish You Were Here' / 'Comfortably Numb'.

Thursday 13 April
CONCERT
Rosemont Theatre, Rosemont, Chicago, Illinois, USA
Set list: 'Castellorizon' / 'On An Island' / 'The Blue' / 'Red Sky At Night' / 'This Heaven' / 'Then I Close My Eyes' / 'Smile' / 'Take A Breath' / 'A Pocketful Of Stones' / 'Where We Start' // 'Shine On You Crazy Diamond, Parts 1-5' / 'Wot's Uh... The Deal' / 'Dominoes' / 'Coming Back To Life' / 'Breathe' / 'Time' / 'Breathe (reprise)' / 'High Hopes' / 'Echoes' / encore: 'Wish You Were Here' / 'Comfortably Numb'.

Sunday 16 April
CONCERT
Paramount Theatre Of The Arts, Oakland, California, USA
Set List: 'Breathe' / 'Time' / 'Breathe (reprise)' / 'Castellorizon' / 'On An Island' / 'The Blue' / 'Red Sky At Night' / 'This Heaven' / 'Then I Close My Eyes' / 'Smile' / 'Take A Breath' / 'A Pocketful Of Stones' / 'Where We Start' // 'Shine On You Crazy Diamond, Parts 1-5' / 'Wot's Uh... The Deal' / 'Dominoes' / 'Coming Back To Life' / 'High Hopes' / 'Echoes' / encore: 'Wish You Were Here' / 'Comfortably Numb'.

Monday 17 April
CONCERT
Paramount Theatre Of The Arts, Oakland, California, USA
Set list: 'Breathe' / 'Time' / 'Breathe (reprise)' / 'Castellorizon' / 'On An Island' / 'The Blue' / 'Red Sky At Night' / 'This Heaven' / 'Then I Close My Eyes' / 'Smile' / 'Take A Breath' / 'A Pocketful Of Stones' / 'Where We Start' // 'Shine On You Crazy Diamond, Parts 1-5' / 'Wearing The Inside Out' / 'Fat Old Sun' / 'Arnold Layne' / 'Coming Back To Life' / 'High Hopes' / 'Echoes' / encore: 'Wish You Were Here' / 'Comfortably Numb'.

Wednesday 19 April
CONCERT
Kodak Theatre, Hollywood & Highland Center, Hollywood, Los Angeles, California, USA
Set list: 'Breathe' / 'Time' / 'Breathe (reprise)' / 'Castellorizon' / 'On An Island' (with guest vocals David Crosby and Graham Nash) / 'The Blue' / 'Red Sky At Night' / 'This Heaven' / 'Then I Close My Eyes' / 'Smile' / 'Take A Breath' / 'A Pocketful Of Stones' / 'Where We Start' // 'Shine On You Crazy Diamond, Parts 1-5' (with guest vocals David Crosby and Graham Nash) / 'Wearing The Inside Out' / 'Fat Old Sun' / 'Arnold Layne' / 'Coming Back To Life' / 'High Hopes' / 'Echoes' / encore: 'Wish You Were Here' / 'Find The Cost Of Freedom' (with guest vocals David Crosby and Graham Nash) / 'Comfortably Numb'.

Thursday 20 April
TV SHOW
NBC Studios, Burbank, Los Angeles, California, USA

Gilmour made a live appearance on *The Tonight Show with Jay Leno* in an outdoor setting at the NBC studios to a small audience and performed a shortened version of 'On An Island' with David Crosby and Graham Nash. The band also performed 'Wish You Were Here' over the closing credits.

Thursday 20 April
CONCERT
Gibson Amphitheater, Universal City, Los Angeles, California, USA
Set list: 'Breathe' / 'Time' / 'Breathe (reprise)' / 'Castellorizon' / 'On An Island' (with guest vocals David Crosby and Graham Nash) / 'The Blue' / 'Red Sky At Night' / 'This Heaven' / 'Then I Close My Eyes' / 'Smile' / 'Take A Breath' / 'A Pocketful Of Stones' / 'Where We Start' // 'Shine On You Crazy Diamond, Parts 1-5' (with guest vocals David Crosby and Graham Nash) / 'Wot's Uh... The Deal' / 'Fat Old Sun' / 'Arnold Layne' / 'Coming Back To Life' / 'High Hopes' / 'Echoes' / encore: 'Wish You Were Here' / 'Find The Cost Of Freedom' (with guest vocals David Crosby and Graham Nash) / 'Comfortably Numb'.

Tuesday 23 May
TV SHOW
BBC Television Centre, White City, London, England
Gilmour made a live appearance on *Later With Jools Holland* performing 'Take A Breath', 'On An Island' and 'Arnold Layne'. Also appearing on the show were David Crosby and Graham Nash who lent backing vocals to 'On An Island'. It was broadcast on BBC2 TV on 26 May at 11.35pm.

Friday 26 May
CONCERT
Bridgewater Hall, Manchester, England
Set list: 'Breathe' / 'Time' / 'Breathe (reprise)' / 'Castellorizon' / 'On An Island' (with guest vocals David Crosby and Graham Nash) / 'The Blue' (with guest vocals David Crosby and Graham Nash) / 'Red Sky At Night' / 'This Heaven' / 'Then I Close My Eyes' / 'Smile' / 'Take A Breath' / 'A Pocketful Of Stones' / 'Where We Start' // 'Shine On You Crazy Diamond, Parts 1-5' (with guest vocals David Crosby and Graham Nash) / 'Wearing The Inside Out' / 'Fat Old Sun' / 'Arnold Layne' / 'Coming Back To Life' / 'High Hopes' / 'Echoes' / encore: 'Wish You Were Here' / 'Find The Cost Of Freedom' (with guest vocals David Crosby and Graham Nash) / 'Comfortably Numb'.

Saturday 27 May
CONCERT
Clyde Auditorium, Scottish Exhibition & Conference Centre, Glasgow, Scotland
Set list: 'Breathe' / 'Time' / 'Breathe (reprise)' / 'Castellorizon' / 'On An Island' (with guest vocals David Crosby) / 'The Blue' (with guest vocals David Crosby) / 'Red Sky At Night' / 'This Heaven' / 'Then I

Close My Eyes' / 'Smile' / 'Take A Breath' / 'A Pocketful Of Stones' / 'Where We Start' // 'Shine On You Crazy Diamond, Parts 1-5' (with guest vocals David Crosby) / 'Wearing The Inside Out' / 'Fat Old Sun' / 'Coming Back To Life' / 'High Hopes' / 'Echoes' / encore: 'Wish You Were Here' / 'Arnold Layne' / 'Comfortably Numb'.

Gilmour was interviewed by the STV (part of the ITV network) programme *Scotland Today* prior to the show and along with a clip of 'On An Island' from the show. It was broadcast on STV on 30 May at 2.32pm and archived on the station website.

Monday 29 May
CONCERT
Royal Albert Hall, Kensington, London, England
Set list: 'Breathe' / 'Time' / 'Breathe (reprise)' / 'Castellorizon' / 'On An Island' (with guest vocals David Crosby) / 'The Blue' (with guest vocals David Crosby and Graham Nash) / 'Red Sky At Night' / 'This Heaven' / 'Then I Close My Eyes' (with guest trumpet Robert Wyatt) / 'Smile' / 'Take A Breath' / 'A Pocketful Of Stones' / 'Where We Start' // 'Shine On You Crazy Diamond, Parts 1-5' (with guest vocals David Crosby and Graham Nash) / 'Wot's Uh... The Deal' / 'Wearing The Inside Out' / 'Coming Back To Life' / 'High Hopes' / 'Echoes' / encore: 'Wish You Were Here' / 'Find The Cost Of Freedom' (with guest vocals David Crosby and Graham Nash) / 'Arnold

Layne' (with guest vocals David Bowie) 'Comfortably Numb' (with guest vocals David Bowie).

Tuesday 30 May
CONCERT
Royal Albert Hall, Kensington, London, England
Set list: 'Breathe' / 'Time' / 'Breathe (reprise)' / 'Castellorizon' / 'On An Island' (with guest vocals David Crosby and Graham Nash) / 'The Blue' (with guest vocals David Crosby and Graham Nash) / 'Red Sky At Night' / 'This Heaven' / 'Then I Close My Eyes' (with guest trumpet Robert Wyatt) / 'Smile' / 'Take A Breath' / 'A Pocketful Of Stones' / 'Where We Start' // 'Shine On You Crazy Diamond, Parts 1-5' (with guest vocals David Crosby and Graham Nash) / 'Fat Old Sun' / 'Arnold Layne' / 'Coming Back To Life' / 'High Hopes' / 'The Great Gig In The Sky' (with guest vocals Mica Paris) / 'Echoes' / encore: 'Wish You Were Here' / 'Find The Cost Of Freedom' (with guest vocals David Crosby and Graham Nash) / 'Comfortably Numb'.

Wednesday 31 May
CONCERT
Royal Albert Hall, Kensington, London, England
The last night of the tour.
Set list: 'Breathe' / 'Time' / 'Breathe (reprise)' / 'Castellorizon' / 'On An Island' (with guest vocals David Crosby and Graham Nash) / 'The Blue' (with guest vocals David Crosby and Graham Nash) / 'Red Sky At Night' / 'This Heaven' / 'Then I Close My Eyes' (with guest trumpet Robert Wyatt) / 'Smile' / 'Take A Breath' / 'A Pocketful Of Stones' / 'Where We Start' // 'Shine On You Crazy Diamond, Parts 1-5' (with guest vocals David Crosby and Graham Nash) / 'Fat Old Sun' / 'Dominoes' / 'Arnold Layne' / 'Coming Back To Life' / 'High Hopes' / 'The Great Gig In The Sky' (with guest vocals Mica Paris) / 'Echoes' / encore: 'Wish You Were Here' (with guest drums Nick Mason) / 'Find The Cost Of Freedom' (with guest vocals David Crosby and Graham Nash) / 'Comfortably Numb' (with guest drums Nick Mason).

Thursday 27 July
CONCERT
Burg Clam, Klam, near Linz, Austria
Set list: 'Breathe' / 'Time' / 'Breathe (reprise)' / 'Castellorizon' / 'On An Island' / 'The Blue' / 'Red Sky At Night' / 'This Heaven' / 'Then I Close My Eyes' / 'Smile' / 'Take A Breath' / 'A Pocketful Of Stones' / 'Where We Start' // 'Shine On You Crazy Diamond, Parts 1-5' / 'Astronomy Dominé' / 'Dark Globe' / 'Fat Old Sun' / 'Coming Back To Life' / 'High Hopes' / 'Echoes' / encore: 'Wish You Were Here' / 'Comfortably Numb'.

Saturday 29 July
CONCERT
Königsplatz, Munich, Germany

Set list: 'Breathe' / 'Time' / 'Breathe (reprise)' / 'Castellorizon' / 'On An Island' / 'The Blue' / 'Red Sky At Night' / 'This Heaven' / 'Then I Close My Eyes' / 'Smile' / 'Take A Breath' / 'A Pocketful Of Stones' / 'Where We Start' // 'Shine On You Crazy Diamond, Parts 1-5' / 'Astronomy Dominé' / 'Dark Globe' / 'Fat Old Sun' / 'Coming Back To Life' / 'High Hopes' / 'Echoes' / encore: 'Wish You Were Here' / 'Comfortably Numb'.

Monday 31 July
CONCERT
Théâtre Antique, Vienne, France
Set list: 'Breathe' / 'Time' / 'Breathe (reprise)' / 'Castellorizon' / 'On An Island' / 'The Blue' / 'Red Sky At Night' / 'This Heaven' / 'Then I Close My Eyes' / 'Smile' / 'Take A Breath' / 'A Pocketful Of Stones' / 'Where We Start' // 'Shine On You Crazy Diamond, Parts 1-5' / 'Wot's Uh... The Deal' / 'Fat Old Sun' / 'Arnold Layne' / 'Coming Back To Life' / 'High Hopes' / 'Echoes' / encore: 'Wish You Were Here' / 'Comfortably Numb'.

Wednesday 2 August
CONCERT
Piazza Di Santa Croce, Florence, Italy
Set list: 'Breathe' / 'Time' / 'Breathe (reprise)' / 'Castellorizon' / 'On An Island' / 'The Blue' / 'Red Sky At Night' / 'This Heaven' / 'Then I Close My Eyes' / 'Smile' / 'Take A Breath' / 'A Pocketful Of Stones' / 'Where We Start' // 'Shine On You Crazy Diamond, Parts 1-5' / 'Wearing The Inside Out' / 'Astronomy Dominé' / 'Fat Old Sun' / 'Coming Back To Life' / 'High Hopes' / 'Echoes' / encore: 'Wish You Were Here' / 'Comfortably Numb'.

Friday 11 August
CONCERTS
Piazza San Marco, Venice, Italy
Both shows in Venice were rescheduled from 3 & 4 August due to a structural defect with the staging.
Set list: 'Breathe' / 'Time' / 'Breathe (reprise)' / 'Castellorizon' / 'On An Island' / 'The Blue' / 'Red Sky At Night' / 'This Heaven' / 'Then I Close My Eyes' / 'Smile' / 'Take A Breath' / 'A Pocketful Of Stones' / 'Where We Start' // 'Shine On You Crazy Diamond, Parts 1-5' / 'Astronomy Dominé' / 'Wot's Uh... The Deal' / 'Fat Old Sun' / 'On The Turning Away' / 'High Hopes' / 'Echoes' / encore: 'Wish You Were Here' / 'Comfortably Numb'.

Saturday 12 August
CONCERTS
Piazza San Marco, Venice, Italy
Set list: 'Breathe' / 'Time' / 'Breathe (reprise)' / 'Castellorizon' / 'On An Island' / 'The Blue' / 'Red Sky At Night' / 'This Heaven' / 'Then I Close My Eyes' / 'Smile' / 'Take A Breath' / 'A Pocketful Of Stones' / 'Where We Start' // 'Shine On You Crazy Diamond,

Parts 1-5' / 'Wot's Uh... The Deal' / 'Arnold Layne' / 'Dark Globe' / 'Fat Old Sun' / 'On The Turning Away' / 'High Hopes' / 'Echoes' / encore: 'Wish You Were Here' / 'Comfortably Numb'.

Saturday 26 August
CONCERT
Przestrzeń Wolności [Spread Freedom], Stocznia Gdańska [Gdansk Shipyards], Gdansk, Poland
The last night of the tour.
Set list: 'Breathe' / 'Time' / 'Breathe (reprise)' / 'Castellorizon' / 'On An Island' / 'The Blue' / 'Red Sky At Night' / 'This Heaven' / 'Then I Close My Eyes' / 'Smile' / 'Take A Breath' / 'A Pocketful Of Stones' / 'Where We Start' // 'Shine On You Crazy Diamond, Parts 1-5' / 'Wot's Uh... The Deal' / 'Astronomy Dominé' / 'Fat Old Sun' / 'High Hopes' / 'Echoes' / encore: 'Wish You Were Here' / 'A Great Day For Freedom' / 'Comfortably Numb'.
Zbigniew Preisner, composer of the orchestrations for the *On An Island* album, conducted a 38-piece orchestra for the show which was attended by over 100,000 people and was staged to mark the 26th anniversary of the Solidarity trade union movement at the invitation of the President and founder of Solidarity, Lech Walesa. Gilmour attended a press conference the day before the show accompanied by the Mayor of Gdansk, Pawel Adamowicz, and the chairman and vice-chairman of Fundacja Gdanska, Stanislaw Plakwicz and Ryszard Bongowski.

Tuesday 29 August
TV SHOW
Studio One, EMI Studios, Abbey Road, St.John's Wood, London, England
Gilmour and his touring band performed 'On An Island', 'Take A Breath', 'Smile' and 'Astronomy Dominé' live in an afternoon session with a small invited audience for the Channel 4 TV series *Live From Abbey Road*. Only the first three tracks were used for transmission. It was first broadcast on More4 on 2 March 2007 at 11.00pm.

OTHER LIVE APPEARANCES

Spring/Summer 1973
PRIVATE PARTY
London, England
Gilmour played guitar with Unicorn on a cover of Neil Young's 'Heart Of Gold' at the wedding reception of mutual friend, Ricky Hopper. Their meeting here led to Gilmour's future involvement with the band.

Wednesday 28 November 1973
RADIO SHOW
BBC Langham 1 Studios, West End, London, England
Gilmour played guitar with Unicorn for this live recording session for BBC Radio One. It was

broadcast on *Sounds Of The 70's: Bob Harris* on 10 December 1973 at 10.00pm.

Saturday 31 August 1974
CONCERT
Hyde Park, London, England
Gilmour played guitar with the Roy Harper Band at one of the last Hyde Park free concerts organised by Blackhill. The event started at midday and featured Roger McGuinn, Julie Felix, Toots & The Maytals, Chilli Willi & The Red Hot Peppers and Kokomo.

Sunday 10 November 1974
CONCERT
Newcastle Polytechnic, Newcastle-upon-Tyne, England
Gilmour shared lead guitar with Tim Renwick and Richard Wright played keyboards at this Sutherland Brothers & Quiver show.

Monday 23 December 1974
CONCERT
The Marquee, Wardour Street, Soho, London, England
Gilmour played guitar at this Sutherland Brothers & Quiver show, supported by Unicorn.

Tuesday 3 October 1978
TV SHOW
Studio 2, EMI Abbey Road Studios, St. John's Wood, London, England
Gilmour played guitar as part of a supergroup calling itself Rockestra formed by Paul McCartney for the purpose of recording the songs 'Rockestra Theme' and 'So Glad To See You Here' for his forthcoming album *Back To The Egg*. The featured musicians included Speedy Acquaye (percussion), Tony Ashton (keyboards), John Bonham (drums), Gary Brooker (piano), Tony Carr (percussion), Howie Casey (horns), Ray Cooper (percussion), Tony Dorsey (horns), Steve Holly (drums), Steve Howard (drums), John Paul Jones (bass guitar, piano), Kenny Jones (drums), Laurence Juber (guitar), Denny Laine (guitar), Ronnie Lane (bass), Hank Marvin (guitar), Linda McCartney (keyboards), Maurice Pert (percussion), Thaddeus Richard (horns), Bruce Thomas (horns), Pete Townshend (guitar). McCartney arranged for the session to be professionally filmed for future use and in 1980 edited the footage to produce a 40-minute programme. The film remains unreleased, but a 15-minute excerpt was screened at the *Back To The Egg* launch party held at Abbey Road on 11 June 1979.

Tuesday 20 November 1984
CONCERT
The Guitar Greats, Capitol Theatre, Passiac, New Jersey, USA
As part of this all-star event sponsored by MTV, Gilmour performed 'You Know I'm Right' and

'Murder'. He was later joined by yet more musicians for a blues number and a rendition of 'Johnny B. Goode' with Chuck Leavell (keyboards), Kenny Aaronson (drums), La Bamba, Stanley Harrison, Ed Manion, Mike Spengler and Steven Groppen (horns), Johnny Winter, Link Wray, Dave Edmunds and Neal Schon (guitars).

Saturday 13 July 1985
CONCERT
Live Aid, Wembley Stadium, Wembley, England
Gilmour was the only member of Pink Floyd to appear at this landmark event, playing guitar with Bryan Ferry's band, which consisted of Neil Hubbard (guitars), Chester Kamen (guitars), Jimmy Maelen (percussion), Andy Newmark (drums), Marcus Miller (bass), Jon Carin (keyboards) and Michelle Cobbs, Ednah Holt and Fonzi Thornton (backing vocals). The set comprised: 'Sensation', 'Boys And Girls', 'Slave To Love' and 'Jealous Guy'. Gilmour also participated in the grand finale, 'Do They Know It's Christmas?'. The event was broadcast live on global TV and finally received a DVD video release in 2004 (UK: Warner 2564618952). 'Slave To Love' appeared on the Bryan Ferry and Roxy Music VHS video *Total Recall* (UK: Virgin Music Video VVD649).

Friday 10 October 1985
TV SHOW
Tyne Tees Television Studios, Newcastle-upon-Tyne, England
Gilmour played guitar with Pete Townshend's Deep End, on the live music programme *The Tube*, in a band which Townshend had formed to raise money for the Double O charity, in aid of victims of drug abuse. The Deep End band comprised John 'Rabbit' Bundrick (keyboards), Simon Philips (drums), Jodi Linscott (percussion), Pete Hope-Evans (harmonica), Chucho Merchan (bass guitar), Ian Ellis, Gina Foster, Coral Gordon, Billy Nicholls, Chris Staines, (backing vocals) and The Kick Horns - comprising Simon Clarke, Roddy Lorimer, Dave Plews, Tim Sanders and Peter Thoms (brass). Deep End performed 'Give Blood', 'Face The Face' and 'Second Hand Love' - all from Townshend's album *White City*. It was broadcast on Channel 4 TV at 5.30pm.

Friday 1 & Saturday 2 November 1985
CONCERTS
The Academy, Brixton, London, England
Gilmour played guitar with Deep End at these two shows in London (a third show was booked but poor ticket sales forced its cancellation). Set list: 'Mary-Anne With The Shaky Hand' / 'Won't Get Fooled Again' / 'A Little Is Enough' / 'Second Hand Love' / 'That's Alright Mama' / 'Behind Blue Eyes' / 'The Shout' / 'Harlem Shuffle' / 'Barefootin'' / 'After The Fire' / 'Love On The Air' / 'Midnight Lover' / 'Blue Light' / 'I Put A Spell On You' / 'I'm The One' / 'Magic

ABOVE: PERFORMING WITH DEEP END AT BRIXTON ACADEMY AND BELOW AT MIDEM.

Fire' / 'Slit Skirts' / 'Blue Light' / 'I Put A Spell On You' / 'Hiding Out' / 'The Sea Refuses No River' / 'Face The Face' / 'Pinball Wizard' / 'Little Is Enough' / 'Rough Boys' / 'Night Train'.

The show was co-promoted by Germany's WDR TV *Rockpalast* music programme and segments of the show were later broadcast across several European TV networks.

Sunday 9 February 1986
CONCERT
Colombian Volcano Appeal, **Royal Albert Hall, Kensington, London, England**

At the request of Deep End musician Chucho Merchan, Gilmour assembled a band to perform at this fund-raising concert. The 'house band' line-up comprised Sam Brown and Paul Carrack (vocals), Simon Philips (drums), Mick Ralphs (guitar), Jodi Linscott (percussion), Chucho Merchan (bass guitar) and John 'Rabbit' Bundrick (keyboards). Gilmour performed 'Blue Light', 'Run Like Hell', 'Out Of The Blue' and 'Comfortably Numb'.

The show also featured performances by Pete Townshend with Emma Townshend and Peter Hope-Evans, Annie Lennox, Jaki Graham, Chrissie Hynde with Robbie McIntosh, The Communards, Working Week and the London School of Samba.

Recorded highlights were later released on VHS video as *The Colombian Volcano Concert* (UK: Hendring Video HEN2086). Highlights were also broadcast on the Channel 4 programme *The Late Shift* on 20 July 1988 at 11.15pm. Numerous American radio networks have also broadcast highlights of the concert.

Bus' / 'Save It For Later' / 'Eyesight To The Blind' / 'Walkin'' / 'Stop Hurting People' / 'The Sea Refuses No River' / 'Boogie Stop Shuffle' / 'Face The Face' / 'Pinball Wizard' / 'Give Blood' / 'Night Train'. (The show of 2 November also included 'Driftin' Blues' after 'I'm The One').

Film of the band's rehearsals, including a segment of 'Give Blood', was broadcast in the UK as part of an ITV *South Bank Show* documentary on Pete Townshend. A VHS video of the full 87-minute concert was released in 1986 (UK: Virgin Music Video VVD318).

In addition, the USA's *King Biscuit Flower Hour* radio network broadcast the second show in two parts on 19 January ('Magic Bus' / 'Won't Get Fooled Again' / 'A Little Is Enough' / 'Stop Hurting People' /'Blue Light' / 'After The Fire' / 'Eyesight To The Blind' / 'That's Alright Mama' / 'Harlem Shuffle' / 'Face The Face') and 26 January 1986 ('Behind Blue Eyes' / 'Love On The Air' / 'Midnight Lover' / 'Mary-Anne With The Shaky Hand' / 'Save It For Later' / 'The Sea Refuses No River' / 'I Put A Spell On You' / 'I'm The One' / 'Pinball Wizard' / 'Give Blood') and repeated highlights on the Westwood One *Superstars In Concert* radio network series between 9 and 11 June

1989 ('Mary-Anne With The Shaky Hand' / 'Won't Get Fooled Again' / 'Harlem Shuffle' / 'Barefootin'' / 'Behind Blue Eyes' / 'Second Hand Love' / 'Save It For Later' / 'Driftin' Blues' / 'Magic Bus' / 'That's Alright Mama' / 'Love On The Air' / 'The Sea Refuses No River' / 'Pinball Wizard' / 'Give Blood' / 'Night Train'). A further radio show on the DIR network broadcast 'I'm The One', 'Save It For Later', 'Pinball Wizard' and 'Magic Bus' on 27 November 1986 as part of a *Thanksgiving Super Concert* special that also included highlights of the *Columbian Volcano Appeal* concert of 29 January 1986.

Wednesday 29 January 1986
CONCERT
Gala du MIDEM, **Grand Auditorium, Palais des Festivals, Cannes, France**

Gilmour played guitar with Deep End at their final performance held to coincide with the international record industry's annual trade show, MIDEM. Set list: 'Won't Get Fooled Again' / 'Second Hand Love' / 'Give Blood' / 'Behind Blue Eyes' / 'After The

Sunday 15 February 1987
CONCERT
The London Jam, **Town & Country Club, Kentish Town, London, England**

Gilmour played guitar at this fund-raiser organised by *Guitar* magazine on behalf of the Childline charity alongside many other musicians including Albert Lee, James Burton, Geoff Whitehorn, Seymour Duncan, Tony Muschamp, Robbie Gladwell, Esmond Selwyn, Phil Hilborne, Andy Powell and Neil Murray.

Saturday 28 & Sunday 29 March 1987
CONCERTS
The Secret Policeman's Third Ball, The Palladium, Soho, London, England
Gilmour played guitar for Kate Bush in a band comprising Tony Franklin (bass), Stuart Elliot (drums) and Kevin McAlea (keyboards) for renditions of 'Running Up That Hill' and 'Let It Be' for Amnesty International's occasional fund-raiser. The all-star line up for the finale of 'I Shall Be Released' included Gilmour on bass, and, on the second night, Nick Mason on drums. Highlights of the event including 'Running Up That Hill', were released on VHS video (UK: Virgin Music Video VVD 270) and on CD (UK: Virgin CDV 2458).

Saturday 12 December 1987
TV SHOW
NBC TV Studios, RCA Building, Manhattan, New York City, New York, USA
Gilmour made a live appearance on *Saturday Night Live* performing 'Ah, Robertson It's You' with the studio house band. It was broadcast on NBC Network TV at 11.30pm.

Thursday 18 August 1988
CONCERT
Les Paul Tribute Concert, Majestic Theater, Brooklyn Academy of Music, Brooklyn, New York City, New York, USA
Gilmour played guitar on 'How High The Moon' at this commemoration gala for guitar guru Les Paul alongside Tony Levin (bass) and Jan Hammer (keyboards) among others. Additional sets were performed by BB King, The Stray Cats and Eddie Van Halen. The all-star finale was a rendition of 'Knee Deep In The Blues' and 'Blue Suede Shoes'. A VHS video of the concert entitled, *Les Paul - He Changed The Music* was released the following year (UK: Magnum MMGV 023).

Thursday 27 April 1989
CONCERT
The Red Balloon Ball, Dinosaur Room, Natural History Museum, Kensington, London, England
Gilmour played guitar on 'A Whiter Shade of Pale' alongside Mark Knopfler, Gary Brooker, Chris Rea, Gary Moore and Sam Brown at this fund-raising concert for The Lung Foundation charity. The track was recorded and broadcast the following day in the UK on BBC Radio One's *Friday Rock Show* at 10.00pm.

Monday 18 September 1989
CONCERT
Hysteria 2, Sadlers Wells Theatre, Islington, London, England
Gilmour played guitar with Jools Holland (piano) and Eddie Reader (vocals) at this AIDS charity benefit,

playing guitar on 'My Girl'. The event was hosted by comedian Lenny Henry and a VHS video of the event, *Hysteria 2 - The Second Coming* (UK: Palace PVC 2173A), was later released.

Saturday 30 September 1989
CONCERT
Mitchell O'Brien's New York Deli, Soho, London, England
Gilmour played guitar at this Louise Goffin concert billed as part of the annual *Soho Jazz Festival* with Neil Conte on drums.

Wednesday 11 October 1989
CONCERT
NSPCC Benefit, Barbican Arts Centre, Barbican, London, England
Gilmour performed at this National Society for the Prevention of Cruelty to Children benefit concert.

Wednesday 15 November 1989
PRESS LAUNCH
Metropolis Studios, Chiswick, London, England
Gilmour played guitar on 'Smoke On The Water' at the media launch of the Rock Aid Armenia single. Other musicians who performed the song alongside him included Richie Blackmore, Tony Iommi, Alex Lifeson, Brian May, Bryan Adams, Bruce Dickinson, Ian Gillan, Paul Rodgers, Chris Squire, Keith Emerson, Geoff Downes and Roger Taylor.

Saturday 31 March 1990
CONCERT
Shaw Theatre, Euston, London, England
Gilmour played guitar at this second of two solo shows by John Martyn, playing on 'The Apprentice', 'John Wayne' and 'One World'. A VHS video of the performance, *John Martyn - The Apprentice Tour*, was released in the UK later that year (UK: Virgin Music Video VVD725) and a DVD release *John Martyn: The Apprentice In Concert* (UK: PBZ14) was released in 2006. A CD album, *John Martyn Live* (UK: Permanent PERM CD33) captured the whole show. Gilmour and Martyn were also interviewed at this show for the Channel 4 music programme *Rock Steady*, which was broadcast on 1 May 1990 at 10.30pm.

Monday 19 April 1990
TV SHOW
BBC Television Centre, White City, London, England
Gilmour appeared with Ralph McTell, Mark Knopfler, Lemmy, Gary Moore and Mark King in a pre-recorded edition of the comedy show *French And Saunders*. The sketch illustrated the pitfalls of learning to play guitar without tablature. Gilmour, pretending to be defeated by the riff from 'Another Brick', complained that there were no 'little pictures that show you where to put your fingers'. It was broadcast on BBC2 TV at 9.00pm.

Thursday 6 December 1990
CONCERT
The Red Balloon Ball, Alexandra Palace, Muswell Hill, London, England
Gilmour performed with Jools Holland, Ian Paice and Justin Hayward at this Lung Foundation charity concert.

Friday 1 February 1991
CONCERT
Rock-a-Baby, Empire Theatre, Hackney, London, England
Gilmour played guitar at this charity performance as part of the all-star band on the second of a three-day event (31 January to 2 February 1991) that also featured Paul Young and Paul Carrack (vocals), Andy Fairweather-Low (guitars), Guy Pratt (bass guitar) and Andy Newmark (drums). The set included 'Wish You Were Here' and 'Comfortably Numb'. Support was provided by the group Five Easy Pieces.

Sunday 24 March 1991
CONCERT
Bloomsbury Theatre, Bloomsbury, London, England
Gilmour played guitar during this Dream Academy concert.

Sunday 30 June 1991
CONCERT
Hysteria 3, The Palladium, London, England
Gilmour played guitar with the Jools Holland Band on 'Together Again,' which also featured vocals by Sam Brown at this charity fund-raiser. The all-star finale, featuring Gilmour, was led by Elton John. A CD of highlights, *The Best Of Hysteria 3*, (UK: EMI CDP 7980212), and a VHS video (UK: PMI MVN 9913183) was later released.

Friday 13 December 1991
TV SHOW
Central Independent TV Studios, Nottingham, England
Gilmour and Jools Holland were installed as musical directors for the recording of *Amnesty Internationals Big 3-0*, a commemorative broadcast featuring Gilmour and Holland performing 'On The Turning Away' with Tim Renwick (guitars), Jon Carin (keyboards), Pino Palladino (bass), Jodi Linscott (percussion) and Sam Brown (vocals). Gilmour also joined Tom Jones to play 'Kiss' and 'I Can't Turn You Loose,' played lead guitar on Seal's rendition of 'Hey Joe'; performed 'Hard To Handle' and 'What's Going On' with Andrew Strong of *The Commitments*, and played bass guitar with Spinal Tap on 'Big Bottom'. It was broadcast on the ITV network on 28 December at 10.40pm. A VHS video of the show was later released (UK: Video Collection VC6198).

June 1992
CONCERT
Stars Ball, Cafe Royal, Soho, London, England
Gilmour joined Nick Mason and Eric Stewart on stage to raise money for The Anthony Nolan Research Centre.

Saturday 6 June 1992
TV SHOW
Channel 4 TV, London, England
Gilmour appeared in a pre-recorded edition of the Jools Holland series *Mister Roadrunner* in which Holland goes biking on a Vincent Rapide across Tennessee and Mississippi in search of 'The Lost Chord,' stopping off at suitable locations en-route, with appropriate musical interludes one of which was provided by Mica Paris singing 'I Put A Spell On You' with a band comprising David Gilmour (guitar), Jools Holland (piano), Matt Irving (keyboards), Gilson Lavis (drums) and Pino Palladino (bass guitar). Other musical celebrities he encountered included George Harrison, Robert Palmer, Rufus Thomas and Yvonne Fair. It was broadcast on Channel 4 TV at 9.00pm.

Saturday 13 June 1992
TV SHOW
ITV TV Studios, South Bank, London, England
Gilmour played guitar with Tom Jones in a live audience edition of his six part series *The Right Time*, performing 'Purple Rain' with Tom Jones and musicians Tim Renwick (guitar), Gary Wallis (drums) and Jodi Linscott (percussion). It was broadcast on the ITV network at 10.15pm.

Monday 22 June 1992
CONCERT
Town & Country Club, Kentish Town, London, England
Gilmour played guitar during this Tom Jones concert.

Sunday 11 October 1992
CONCERT
Chelsea Arts Ball, Royal Albert Hall, Kensington, London, England
At this high-society AIDS fund-raiser Gilmour joined the house band: Guy Pratt (bass), Jon Carin (keyboards), Jodi Linscott (percussion), Tim Renwick (guitars), Gary Wallis (drums) and Sam Brown (vocals) and guest musicians Nick Mason, Rick Wright, Tom Jones, Hugh Cornwell, Mica Paris, Elvis Costello and Sam Moore. The set list comprised: 'River Deep Mountain High' / 'The Sun Ain't Gonna Shine Anymore' / 'Golden Brown' / 'Stone Free' / 'I Put A Spell On You' / 'Can't Stand Up For Falling Down' / 'Another Brick In The Wall, Part 2' / 'Wish You Were Here' / 'Comfortably Numb' / 'Superstition' / 'Knock On Wood' / 'Kiss'.

Saturday 7 November 1992
TV SHOW
The Astoria, Soho, London, England
Gilmour played guitar with Jools Holland in a live audience edition of his series *The Happening*, performing 'Such A Night', 'Wide-Eyed And Legless' and 'Movin' On' with Andy Fairweather-Low (guitar/vocals). It was broadcast on Channel 4 TV at 12.35am.

Friday 4 December 1992
CONCERT
Festival Ecomundo, América de Cali Stadium, Cali, Colombia, South America
Gilmour played guitar at this benefit show organized as part of the Ecomundo ecology conference with Roger Daltrey (vocals), Phil Manzanera (guitar) and Chucha Merchan (bass). Also appearing were Kool & The Gang, Kronos, Rata Blanca and Dagoberto Pedraja Cepero.

Sunday 6 February 1994
CONCERT
Bop For Bosnia, Studio One, BBC Television Centre, White City, London, England
Gilmour played guitar on this invitation only fund-raiser (the show was not recorded for broadcast) organised by Chris Jagger that also featured a band comprising Dave Stewart (keyboards), Leo Sayer (vocals), Simon Kirke (percussion), Jon Newey (drums) and Ben Waters (piano). As well as performing material mainly from Jagger's album *Atcha* they performed several blues numbers.

Thursday 6 July 1995
CONCERT
Tango For Tibet, The Pagoda, Battersea Park, London, England
Gilmour performed at this fundraiser, which also featured Leo Sayer and the Chris Jagger Band to celebrate the 60th birthday of the Dalai Lama of Tibet.

Saturday 23 March 1996
PRIVATE PARTY
Fulham Town Hall, Fulham, London, England
David Gilmour's 50th birthday party. Entertainment was provided by The Bootleg Beatles and The Australian Pink Floyd, who were joined on stage by Richard Wright and Guy Pratt for a rousing rendition of 'Comfortably Numb'. The band then handed over their instruments to David Gilmour, Richard Wright, Guy Pratt, Tim Renwick, Gary Wallis and Claudia Fontaine who treated the gathered guests to renditions of 'Money', 'What Do You Want From Me' and various other jams.

Saturday 29 June 1996
CONCERT
The Prince's Trust Concert, Hyde Park, London, England
Gilmour played guitar on 'The Dirty Jobs' and 'Love Reign O'er Me' on The Who's reworked version of *Quadrophenia* for the Prince's Trust all-day concert, which also featured guest appearances by Phil Daniels (Narration), Trevor McDonald (Newscaster), Ade Edmundson (Bell Boy; later with shotgun and scooter), Gary Glitter (Rocker) and Stephen Fry (Hotel Manager). The event also featured sets by Bob Dylan and Ron Wood, Eric Clapton and Alanis Morissette.

Saturday 20 July 1996
CONCERT
A Day For Tibet, Alexandra Palace, Muswell Hill, London, England
Gilmour performed at a concert benefit for the Dalai Lama of Tibet at a benefit concert, which also featured Sinead O'Connor, Andy Summers and The Chris Jagger Band. Gilmour performed with the latter and also gave a surprise solo acoustic rendition of Syd Barrett's 'Terrapin' followed by the more familiar 'On The Turning Away', 'Wish You Were Here' and 'Coming Back To Life' with Chucho Merchan (bass) and other supporting musicians.

Wednesday 31 December 1997
TV SHOW
BBC Television Centre, White City, London, England
Gilmour played guitar with BB King on 'Eyesight For The Blind' as part of the live broadcast of *Later With Jools Holland: 5th Annual Hootenanny*, that also featured Jools Holland and his Rhythm & Blues Orchestra, 1st Battalion Welsh Guards, Shaun Ryder, Blur, Bentley Rhythm Ace and Fun Lovin' Criminals. It was broadcast on BBC2 TV at 11.55pm. (Please refer to 23 November 2003 entry for DVD release information.)

Saturday 2 May 1998
CONCERT
Lavender Trust Concert, Institute of Contemporary Arts, The Mall, London, England
Gilmour performed a short set at this event, for the launch of the Lavender Trust charity that included 'The Dimming Of The Day', 'Forever Young' and 'Wish You Were Here'. The event also featured a set by former Eurythmics duo Dave Stewart and Annie Lennox, in their first public appearance together since the band split in the Eightees.

Sunday 6 September 1998
CONCERT
Studio 2, EMI Abbey Road Studios, St. John's Wood, London, England
Gilmour performed with The Pretty Things at an invitation only reunion concert to perform their album

S.F. Sorrow with the following line-up: Phil May (lead vocals, percussion), Dick Taylor (lead guitar, vocals), John Povey (keyboards, vocals, percussion, sitar), Wally Waller (bass, vocals), Skip Allen (drums, percussion), Arthur Brown (narration) and Gilmour on guitar on the tracks marked *. The set list comprised: 'S.F. Sorrow Is Born' / 'Bracelets Of Fingers' / 'She Says Good Morning' * / 'Private Sorrow' / 'Balloon Burning' / 'Death' / 'Baron Saturday' / 'The Journey' / 'I See You' * / 'Well Of Destiny' * / 'Trust' * / 'Old Man Going' * / 'Loneliest Person'. The concert was also filmed and broadcast live over the Internet. A limited edition CD entitled The Pretty Things: Resurrection. Died 1968 Born 1998 At Abbey Road (UK: Snapper 160042) was released in January 1999 and a double CD of the original SF Sorrow album and Resurrection (UK: Snapper Recall SMDCD415) was released on 21 April 2003. A DVD entitled The Pretty Things: SF Sorrow At Abbey Road (UK: Snapper SMADVD004) was released on 28 September 2003 and re-released in 2005 (UK: Snapper SDVD512).

Saturday 18 September 1999
CONCERT
PETA Awards Show, Paramount Studios, Hollywood, Los Angeles, California, USA
Gilmour played guitar in Paul McCartney's band, which also featured Ian Paice (drums), Mick Green (guitar) and Pete Wingfield (piano) at a benefit concert for The People For The Ethical Treatment of Animals (PETA) that was later broadcast in edited form on the US television channel Video Hits 1 (VH1) on 16 October 1999. The performance was part of PETA's Part of the Century and Humanitarian Awards in an evening that also featured performances by the B-52s, Sarah McLachlan and Chrissie Hynde with comedy from Ellen De Generes and Margaret Cho. McCartney co-hosted the evening with Alec Baldwin, Jamie Lee Curtis and Woody Harrelson.

Tuesday 2 November 1999
TV SHOW
BBC Television Centre, White City, London, England
Gilmour played guitar in Paul McCartney's band, which also featured Ian Paice (drums), Mick Green (guitar) and Pete Wingfield (piano) in a pre-recorded edition of the music programme *Later With Jools Holland*. It was broadcast on BBC1 TV on 6 November 1999 at 11.25pm. The set list comprised: 'Honey Hush' / 'Brown Eyed Handsome Man' / 'No Other Baby' / '(Let's Have A) Party'.

Thursday 2 December 1999
TV SHOW
BBC Television Centre, White City, London, England
Gilmour played guitar in Paul McCartney's band, which also featured Ian Paice (drums), Mick Green (guitar) and Pete Wingfield (piano) in a pre-recorded edition of a *Michael Parkinson* TV special subtitled

'Parkinson Meets Paul McCartney' (returning a long-forgotten favour to appear on his show following Parkinson's appearance on his *Band On The Run* album sleeve). Although the full band did not perform on all of the songs the set list comprised: 'Honey Hush' / 'Twenty Flight Rock' / 'Mary's Song' / 'Yesterday' / 'The Long And Winding Road' / 'The New York Song (Chase My Blues Away)' / 'The Cabaret Song' / 'Suicide' / 'All Shook Up'. It was broadcast on BBC1 TV on Friday 3 December at 9.30pm.

Tuesday 14 December 1999
CONCERT
Cavern Club, Liverpool, England
Gilmour played guitar in Paul McCartney's band, which also featured Iain Paice (drums), Chris Hall (accordion), Mick Green (guitar) and Pete Wingfield (piano). The set list comprised: 'Honey Hush' / 'Blue Jean Bop' / 'Brown Eyed Handsome Man' / 'Fabulous' / 'What It Is' / 'Lonesome Town' / 'Twenty Flight Rock' / 'No Other Baby' / 'Try Not To Cry' / 'Shake A Hand' / 'All Shook Up' / 'I Saw Her Standing There' / '(Let's Have A) Party'. The show was broadcast live over the Internet as well as BBC Radio One and was also broadcast on BBC1 TV the following evening. US radio networks and PBS TV also broadcast the show over the weekend of 20 – 23 January 2000. It was subsequently released as a DVD video with interview footage and promo videos for 'Brown Eyed Handsome Man' and 'No Other Baby' and packaged with a complete audio CD of the show (UK: BMG IX0384MPUKD).

Friday 29 June 2001
CONCERT
A Tribute To Leiber And Stoller, The Apollo, Hammersmith, London, England
Gilmour performed alongside a huge cast of guest musicians as part of a tribute concert to songwriters Jerry Leiber and Mike Stoller in aid of Nordoff Robbins Music Therapy. Guests featured included Ben E. King, Bob Geldof, Chris Rea, Edwin Starr, Elkie Brooks, Heather Small, Jim Capaldi, Jonathan Wilkes, Keith Emerson, Leo Sayer, Meatloaf, Michael Patto, Paul Carrack, Ruby Turner, Sam Brown, Steve Harley and Tom Jones. Gilmour's main contribution to the show was a rendition of Elvis's 'Don't', which by all accounts, was one of the high spots of the show. The show has since been released on a 120-minute VHS video (UK: Direct Video Distribution IX13563DUKV) and DVD video (UK: Direct Video Distribution IX13563DUKD) featuring Gilmour's segments.

Monday 17 September 2001
MEMORIAL SERVICE
Memorial Service for Douglas Adams, St. Martin-in-the-Fields Church, Trafalgar Square, London, England

Gilmour performed a solo rendition of 'Wish You Were Here' at the memorial service for Douglas Adams. He was a close friend of Gilmour's, who is best remembered as the author of *The Hitchhikers Guide To The Galaxy*. The service was also seen as a BBC webcast.

Friday 19 October 2001
CONCERT
Mind Your Head (A Sonic Trip On The South Bank), Royal Festival Hall, South Bank, London, England
As part of the four events running across two weeks, *Mind Your Head* brought psychedelia and strangeness to an otherwise straight-laced auditorium. Performers over the period included Hawkwind supported by Add N To (X), Gong with The Orb supported by Acid Mothers Temple and Faust supported by Gary Lucas. The final concert of the season saw The Pretty Things performing their rock-opera *S.F. Sorrow* for the very first time to a public audience with a support slot from The Soft Boys. Gilmour played guitar with The Pretty Things and also played with The Soft Boys on their encore, 'Astronomy Dominé'.
The Pretty Things set list ran as follows with Phil May (lead vocals, percussion), Dick Taylor (lead guitar, vocals), John Povey (keyboards, vocals, percussion, sitar), Wally Waller (bass, vocals), Skip Allen (drums, percussion), Frank Holland (guitar, vocals), Mark St. John (percussion, drums, vocals), Arthur Brown (narration) and Gilmour (on guitar on the tracks marked *). The set list comprised: 'S.F. Sorrow Is Born' / 'Bracelets Of Fingers' / 'She Says Good Morning' * / 'Private Sorrow' / 'Balloon Burning' / 'Death' / 'Baron Saturday' / 'The Journey' / 'I See You' * / 'Well Of Destiny' * / 'Trust' * / 'Old Man Going' * / 'Loneliest Person'. The encore comprised of Arthur Brown performing his hit 'Fire' (complete with flaming helmet) followed by The Pretty Things, Arthur Brown and Gilmour performing 'Rosalyn' and 'Route 66'.

Wednesday 14 November 2001
CONCERT
The Gala Lunch, Hilton Hotel, Park Lane, London, England
Gilmour performed with other celebrity guests at this benefit event.

Wednesday 21 November 2001
TV SHOW
BBC Television Centre, White City, London, England
Gilmour performed 'I Put A Spell On You' with Mica Paris and Jools Holland in a pre-recorded edition *Later With Jools Holland* that also featured performances by other artists that were guests on Holland's recently released all-star album *Small World Big Band*. It was broadcast on BBC2 TV on 23 November at 11.35pm and an audio broadcast was aired on the *Jools Holland Show* on BBC Radio 2 on

10 December at 9.00pm.
A compilation of highlights from the Jools Holland year-end shows spanning 1997 to 2003 was released on a single DVD collection (UK: Warner Vision International 2564611879) entitled *Later with Jools Holland Hootenanny*, on 1 December 2003, which included this performance as well as his performance with BB King on 31 December 1997.

Sunday 10 February 2002
CONCERT
When Love Speaks, The Old Vic Theatre, Lambeth, London, England
Gilmour performed a short set at this event that also featured sets by Des'Ree, Michael Kamen and Annie Lennox and Dave Stewart, in support of the launch of a fund-raising multi-artist world music album of the same title (which Gilmour did not appear on).

Friday 21 June 2002
CONCERT
An Evening of Beatles Music, Cowdray House, Midhurst, England
Gilmour appeared with Ringo Starr, Mike Rutherford, Roger Taylor, Lulu, Bob Geldof, Paul Carrack, Donovan, Gary Brooker, Kenny Jones, Damon Hill and Mike Sanchez and his band, plus other special guests and compered by Chris Tarrant, performing at this exclusive fundraiser for the benefit of the White Lotus School, Ladakh and the Tibet House Trust. Gilmour was seen playing guitar on 'Please Please Me', 'I Want To Hold Your Hand', 'Love Me Do' and 'Across The Universe' among others.

Friday 27 September 2002
RADIO SHOW
BBC Broadcasting House, Portland Place, London, England
Gilmour performed 'Fat Old Sun' and 'Smile', with Melvoin Duffy on slide guitar, as part of a live interview on the *Johnnie Walker Show* broadcast on BBC Radio 2 at 5.00pm.

Friday 11 April 2003
RADIO SHOW
BBC Broadcasting House, Portland Place, London, England
Gilmour was interviewed by Sue Lawley for the long-running radio show *Desert Island Discs* during which he selected as follows: 'Waterloo Sunset' by The Kinks; 'Ballad In Plain D' by Bob Dylan; 'I'm Still Here' by Tom Waits; 'Dancing In The Street' by Martha and the Vandellas; 'Anthem' by Leonard Cohen; 'A Man Needs A Maid' by Neil Young; 'For Free' by Joni Mitchell and 'Rudi With A Flashlight' by The Lemonheads. Asked what three items (record, book and luxury item) he would take on a desert island he selected 'Dancing In The Street' by Martha and the Vandellas as his record, an English translation of the Koran as his book and an acoustic Martin D35 guitar as his luxury. It was broadcast on BBC Radio 4 at 9.00am.

Sunday 4 May 2003
CONCERT
Dave Douglas – Freak In, Queen Elizabeth Hall, South Bank, London, England
Gilmour performed on guitar as part of the Dave Douglas band including Dave Douglas (trumpet), Jamie Saft (keyboards), Ikue Mori (electronic percussion), Seamus Blake (saxophone), Brad Jones (bass) and Derrek Phillip (drums).

Friday 7 November 2003
MEMORIAL SERVICE
Funeral Service for Steve O'Rourke, Chichester Cathedral, Chichester, England
In an extraordinary memorial to their manager, band mates Gilmour, Mason and Wright performed 'Fat Old Sun' at the funeral service. Additionally, Dick Parry played 'The Great Gig In The Sky' on saxophone as the gathered mourners followed the coffin into the Cathedral.

Saturday 22 November 2003
MEMORIAL SERVICE
Memorial Service for Michael Kamen, Dukes Hall, Royal Academy of Music, London, England
Gilmour performed a solo rendition of 'Wish You Were Here' at the memorial service for Michael Kamen who passed away on 18 November 2003. Those able to attend included several colleagues and friends with whom Michael had worked closely over the years. Annie Lennox performed one of Michael's favourite songs followed by a moving and characteristically humorous speech by Alan Rickman. Bryan Adams sang 'Everything I Do'.

Thursday 1 April 2004
CONCERT
Teenage Cancer Trust Concert, Royal Albert Hall, Kensington, London, England
Gilmour played guitar with Jools Holland's band at this show – part of an annual series of benefit concerts organised by The Who's Roger Daltrey. Guest performers this evening also included Mica Paris, Jeff Beck, Ronnie Wood, Tom Jones, Solomon Burke, Chrissie Hynde, Ruby Turner and John Cale.

Friday 24 September 2004
CONCERT
Miller Strat Pack, Wembley Arena, Wembley, England
Gilmour performed the Pink Floyd songs 'Marooned', 'Coming Back To Life' and 'Sorrow' and appeared in the all-star finale of 'Stay With Me' at this Nordoff-Robins Music Therapy event to celebrate the Fender Guitar. The event included appearances by Ronnie Wood, Joe Walsh, Brian May, Hank Marvin, Phil Manzanera, Mike Rutherford, Paul Carrack, The Crickets, Gary Moore and, for some bizarre reason, Jamie Cullum and Amy Winehouse. A DVD of highlights entitled *The Strat Pack Live In Concert* (UK: Eagle Rock EREDV464) including Gilmour's set was released in May 2005.

Friday 3 December 2004
CONCERT
A Tribute To The King, EMI Abbey Road Studios, St. John's Wood, London, England
Gilmour performed the song 'Don't' with Bill Wyman & The Rhythm Kings as part of this celebration of 50 years of Elvis and the birth of rock 'n' roll. Helmed by Scotty Moore, guest performers included Eric Clapton, Mark Knopfler, Ron Wood, Ringo Starr and Keith Richards. The show was released in October 2005 on DVD video (UK: Universal Island 9872949) featuring Gilmour's contribution.

nick mason

Nicholas Berkeley Mason was born in Edgbaston, Birmingham on 27 January 1944 to Bill and Sally Mason and has three sisters. His father was a filmmaker, relocating to Hampstead, north London in the late Forties.

After prep school he attended Frensham Heights, a private school near Farnham in Surrey and in 1962 enrolled to the Regent Street Polytechnic's Architectural School where he was class-mates with Roger Waters and Richard Wright. He is the only member of Pink Floyd to have been in every line-up and played on every recorded work since its inception in 1964.

Outside of Pink Floyd he has made no solo recordings in the strict sense of the term but has collaborated on two albums that were released under his name. He has, however, co-written and performed much soundtrack material for films and television advertisements and has acted as a producer and played on several albums by other artists.

A keen motoring enthusiast, Mason regularly takes part in the annual London to Brighton vintage car rally and regularly competes in various motor sport events in the UK and Europe. He is also proprietor of Ten Tenths, a company based in North London that supplies vintage motorcars to the film and television industry.

In recent years he renewed his friendship with Roger Waters and has appeared on stage with him on numerous occasions, most notably on his 2006 tour performing *The Dark Side Of The Moon* in its entirety. He also published the memoirs of his life in Pink Floyd in 2005 with an entertaining book entitled *Inside Out: A Personal History of Pink Floyd*.

DISCOGRAPHY

FICTITIOUS SPORTS

The first album that Mason worked on outside of Pink Floyd was essentially the work of jazz artist Carla Bley, composed and played keyboards on all the pieces, and co-produced the record with Mason.

Friday 1 May 1981
FICTITIOUS SPORTS
UK: EMI Harvest SHSP 4116 (vinyl album).
US: Columbia FC 37307 (vinyl album).
US: Sony Music Special Products A37307 (CD album released 2003).
Track list: 'Can't Get My Motor To Start' / 'I Was Wrong' / 'Siam' // 'Hot River' / 'Boo To You Too' / 'Do Ya? '/ 'Wervin'' / 'I'm A Mineralist'.
Additional musicians: Robert Wyatt and Karen Kraft (vocals), Chris Spedding (guitar), Steve Swallow (bass guitar), Gary Windo (woodwind instruments), Gary Valente (trombones), Michael Mantler (trumpets), Howard Johnson (tuba), Terry Adams (piano) and Carlos Ward, D. Sharpe, Vincent Chancey and Earl McIntyre (additional vocals).
Although the album was recorded in October 1979, it was not released until 1981, owing to contractual difficulties.
Recorded at Grog Kill Studio, Willow, New York by Michael Mantler, assisted by Nick Mason in October 1979. Mixed at Village Recorders and the Producer's Workshop, Los Angeles, USA by James Guthrie in December 1979 and May 1980.
Produced by Nick Mason and Carla Bley.
Artwork by Hipgnosis.
Highest chart position US No.170.

PROFILES

Mason's second 'solo' album was a joint collaboration with ex-10cc guitarist Rick Fenn. The pair had been introduced through a mutual friend, Eric Stewart, also of 10cc, when Mason was looking for someone to help him with some music for a TV advert. However, Stewart was preoccupied with other matters and suggested Fenn. The pair hit it off and eventually formed a production company, Bamboo Music, to supply music for films and commercials. *Profiles* was the first of their commercially available works and was recorded at Mason's Britannia Row studios and Fenn's Basement Studios.

Monday 19 August 1985
PROFILES
UK: EMI Harvest MAF 1 (vinyl album).
US: Columbia FC 40142 (vinyl album).
US: Columbia CK 40142 (CD album).
Track list: 'Malta' / 'Lie For A Lie' / 'Rhoda' / 'Profiles,

Parts 1 & 2' // 'Israel' / 'And The Address' / 'Mumbo Jumbo' / 'Zip Code' / 'Black Ice' / 'At The End Of The Day' / 'Profiles, Part 3'.
Additional musicians: Mel Collins (saxophone), Craig Pruess (emulator bass on 'Malta'), Maggie Reilly and David Gilmour (vocals on 'Lie For A Lie') and Aja Fenn (intro keyboards on 'Malta').
Recorded at Britannia Row Studios, London, England and Basement Studios, London, England.
Produced by Nick Mason and Rick Fenn. Engineered by Nick Griffiths (Britannia Row) and Rick Fenn (Basement).
The lyrics on 'Lie For A Lie' and 'Israel' were written by Danny Peyronel, who also sang on the latter.
Artwork cover design by Jeremy Pemberton.
Reissued:
US: Sony Music Special Products A40142 (CD album reissued, 2003).

Monday 23 September 1985
'Lie For A Lie' / 'And The Address'
UK: EMI Harvest HAR 5238 (7-inch single).
'Lie For A Lie' // 'And The Address' / 'Mumbo Jumbo'
UK: EMI Harvest 12 HAR 5238 (12-inch single).

FILMS & SOUNDTRACKS

The composing partnership of Mason and guitarist Rick Fenn led to several collaborations on film soundtracks and music for television commercials in the mid Eighties, including HMV, Rowenta, Rothman's and Barclay's Bank, although a great many more remain undocumented. Their film soundtracks include *White Of The Eye* (1987) and *Tank Malling* (1988). Others reportedly by Mason-Fenn include the TV films *Body Contact* and *Cresta Run*.
Mason and Fenn also wrote the soundtrack, including a reworking of their 'Lie For A Lie' (from *Profiles*) as well as a new recording of 'Sh-boom' with Eric Stewart on vocals, for *Life Could Be A Dream*. Directed by Mike Shakleton, this 26 minute film, also known as *One Of These Days*, is a semi-autobiographical account of Mason's motoring and professional career featuring material from his home archive as well as vintage Pink Floyd performances, including 'One Of These Days' from the film *Pink Floyd Live At Pompeii*. It was shown as part of Britannia Airways' in-flight film selection during 1985.

1987
WHITE OF THE EYE
Mason and Fenn composed the soundtrack to this cinematic film. It was released on VHS PAL video in 1986 (UK: Warner Home Video PEV37208).

RADIO SHOWS

1985
INNER-VIEW – *NICK MASON - PROFILES*
US: *Inner-View* (vinyl album). Show No.34-13; broadcast 1985.
Documentary includes music and interviews with Nick Mason.

COMPILATIONS

1985
MOST VALUABLE NEW PLAYERS
US: Columbia CAS 2181 (vinyl album).
Promotional compilation includes 'Lie For A Lie' and 'Israel'.

GUEST APPEARANCES & PRODUCTION
(UK Catalogue numbers and original format only).

1971
PRINCIPAL EDWARDS MAGIC THEATRE - *THE ASMOTO RUNNING BAND*
UK: Dandelion Records DAN 8002 (vinyl album).
Produced by Mason.

1971
PRINCIPAL EDWARDS MAGIC THEATRE - 'Stackwaddy' // 'The Way We Live' / 'Siren'
UK: Dandelion Records D 7001 (promotional 7-inch single).
Produced by Mason.

1974
PRINCIPAL EDWARDS MAGIC THEATRE - *ROUND ONE*
UK: Deram SML 1108 (vinyl album).
Produced by Mason.

1974
ROBERT WYATT - *ROCK BOTTOM*
UK: Virgin V2017 (vinyl album).
Produced by Mason.

1974
ROBERT WYATT - 'I'm A Believer' / 'Memories'
UK: Virgin VS114 (7-inch single).
Produced by Mason.

1975
ROBERT WYATT - *RUTH IS STRANGER THAN RICHARD*
UK: Virgin V2034 (vinyl album).
Produced by Mason.

1976
GONG - *SHAMAL*
UK: Virgin V2046 (vinyl album).
Produced by Mason.

1976
MICHAEL MANTLER - *THE HAPLESS CHILD AND OTHER STORIES*
UK: Watteau WATT 4 (vinyl album).
Engineered and mixed at Britannia Row studios by Mason, who also appears as an additional speaker.

1977
THE DAMNED - *MUSIC FOR PLEASURE*
UK: Stiff SEEZ 5 (vinyl album).
Produced by Mason at Britannia Row studios. Also the 7-inch singles 'Problem Child' / 'You Take My Money' (Stiff BUY18) and 'Don't Cry Wolf' / 'One Way Love' (Stiff BUY24).

1977
ROBERT WYATT - 'Yesterday Man' / 'Sonia'
UK: Virgin VS115 (7-inch single).
Produced by Mason.

1978
STEVE HILLAGE - *GREEN*
UK: Virgin V2098 (vinyl album).
Produced by Mason and Hillage. Mason played drums on 'Ley Lines To Glassdom'. Also on the 7-inch single 'Getting Better' / 'Palm Trees' (Virgin VS 212).

1983
MICHAEL MANTLER - *SOMETHING THERE*
UK: ECM Watteau WATT 13 (vinyl album).
Mason played drums on this album, which also features Carla Bley (piano), Mike Stern (guitar), Steve Swallow (bass guitar) and the London Symphony Orchestra conducted by Michael Gibbs.

1987
MICHAEL MANTLER - *MICHAEL MANTLER LIVE!*
UK: ECM Watteau WATT 18 (vinyl album).
Mason played drums on this album recorded at Mantler's concert held on 8 February 1987 in Frankfurt, Germany (see concerts listing below).

1996
GARY WINDO - *HIS MASTER'S BONES*
UK: Cuneiform Rune 89 (CD album).
Mason played drums on 'Letting Go' and 'Is This The Time?', recorded at Britannia Row in the spring and summer of 1976 on this compilation of Windo material, which is sometimes referred to as *The Steam Radio Tapes*, the remainder of which was recorded between 1971 and 1984.

2002
CHIMERA - *CHIMERA*
UK: Tenth Planet TP054 (vinyl album. Limited edition of 1,000 copies).
Mason played drums on 'The Grail' and produced most of the tracks on this compilation album of Chimera material originally recorded between 1969 and 1970.

2005
ROBERT WYATT - *ROBERT WYATT & FRIENDS IN CONCERT*
UK: Hannibal HNCD 1507 (CD album).
Mason played drums on this Robert Wyatt concert recorded on 8 September 1974 at the Theatre Royal, Drury Lane, London. Track list: 'Introduction: John Peel' / 'Dedicated To You But You Weren't Listening' / 'Memories' / 'Sea Song' / 'A Last Straw' / 'Little Red Riding Hood Hit The Road' / 'Alifie' / 'Alifib' / 'Mind Of A Child' / 'Instant Pussy' / 'Signed Curtain' / 'Calyx' / 'Little Red Robin Hood Hit The Road' / 'I'm A Believer'.

LIVE APPEARANCES

Sunday 8 September 1974
CONCERT
Theatre Royal, Drury Lane, London, England
With Twickenham (Robert Wyatt, Mike Oldfield, Fred Frith, Mongezi Feza, Gary Windo, Julie Tippet, Dave Stewart, Hugh Hopper, Laurie Allan and Ivor Cutler) and compere John Peel. Mason played drums as part of this one-off line-up. Set list: 'Dedicated To You But You Weren't Listening' / 'Opportunity Knocks' – 'Memories' / 'Sea Song' / 'A Last Straw' / 'Little Red Riding Hood Hit The Road' / 'Alfie' / 'Alifib' / 'The God Song' / 'Mind Of A Child' – 'Behind Blue Eyes' / 'Instant Pussy' – 'Signed Curtain' / 'Calyx' / 'First Verse' / 'Little Red Robin Hood' / 'I'm A Believer' / 'Laughing Policeman'. A recording of highlights of the concert was finally released in October 2005. (See discography for further information).

Friday 13 September 1974
TV SHOW
BBC Lime Grove Studios, Shepherd's Bush, London, England
Mason played drums for Robert Wyatt in a live TV studio recording session for *Top Of The Pops* in which his band performed 'I'm A Believer'. It was broadcast on BBC1 TV at 7.05pm.

Friday 11 October 1974
RADIO SHOWS
Studio 4, BBC Maida Vale Studios, Maida Vale, London, England
Mason played drums for Robert Wyatt in a combined recording session for BBC Radio 1 between 8.00pm and 11.30pm in which the band performed 'Alifib', 'Soup Song', 'Sea Song' and 'I'm A Believer'. It was

first broadcast on the *David Hamilton Show* on 14 October 1974 at 2.00pm and repeated on 4 November 1974 at 2.00pm and also broadcast on the *Radio One Club* on 21 October 1974 at 5.00pm and repeated on 28 October 1974 at 5.00pm.

Friday 28 November 1975
CONCERT
Maidstone College of Art, Maidstone, England
Mason played drums with Gary Windo's band that featured Pam Windo (piano), Richard Brunton (guitars) and Bill MacCormick (bass guitar).

Saturday 28, Sunday 29 & Monday 30 April 1984
CONCERTS
Hammersmith Odeon, Hammersmith, London, England
Mason played drums on 'Comfortably Numb' during this run of David Gilmour solo concerts.

Tuesday 1 May 1984
CONCERT
Sendesaal, Cologne, West Germany
Mason played drums in Michael Mantler and Carla Bley's 'Music For Six Piece Orchestra' concert.

Sunday 8 February 1987
CONCERT
1st International Art Rock Festival, **Kongresshalle, Frankfurt, West Germany**
Mason played drums on this 'Michael Mantler - Nick Mason Projekt' concert, formed for this one event which also featured Rick Fenn (guitars), Don Preston (synths), John Greaves (bass) and Jack Bruce (vocals). Highlights were broadcast on the German TV channel WDR3 on 31 May 1987 and released as a CD as *Michael Mantler Live!* (UK: ECM Records WATT 18). Set list: 'Alien (from Part 3)' / 'Slow Orchestra Piece No.6' / 'Slow Orchestra Piece No.3' / 'Slow Orchestra Piece No.8' / 'Alien (from Part 1)' / 'For Instance' / 'When I Run' / 'The Remembered Visit' / 'The Doubtful Guest' / 'The Hapless Child' / 'No Answer' / 'Preview' / 'Something There'.

Sunday 29 March 1987
CONCERTS
The Secret Policeman's Third Ball, **The Palladium, Soho, London, England**
Mason made a brief appearance on drums during the all-star line up for the finale of 'I Shall Be Released' at this occasional Amnesty International benefit that also featured Gilmour performing with Kate Bush.

June 1992
CONCERT
Stars Ball, **The Cafe Royal, Soho, London, England**
Mason played drums in the house band that also featured David Gilmour and Eric Stewart at this charity event to raise money for The Anthony Nolan

Research Centre.

Sunday 11 October 1992
CONCERT
Chelsea Arts Ball, **Royal Albert Hall, Kensington, London, England**
Mason played drums at this high-society fund-raiser on behalf of AIDS sufferers. Other musicians who performed included the house band - David Gilmour (vocals, guitars), Guy Pratt (bass), Jon Carin (keyboards), Jodi Linscott (percussion), Tim Renwick (guitars), Gary Wallis (drums) and Sam Brown (vocals) - and guest musicians Richard Wright, Tom Jones, Hugh Cornwell, Mica Paris, Elvis Costello and Sam Moore.

Friday 12 March 1999
TV SHOW
Riverside Studios, Hammersmith, London, England
Mason played drums with a band that comprised of Jools Holland (piano), Elvis Costello (vocals, guitar), Damon Hill (rhythm guitar) and All Saints (backing vocals) in the finale of a special BBC edition of *TFI Friday* performing 'Stand By Me' produced for the annual Comic Relief fundraising night. It was broadcast on BBC1 TV at 11.30pm.

Saturday 25 December 1999
RADIO SHOW
BBC Radio 4, Broadcasting House, London, England
Mason played drums and percussion with Kevin Powell on bass on the soundtrack to *Aladdin, The Chinese Laundry Boy*, a pantomime adaptation of the story of *Aladdin* that featured Terry Jones, Clive Anderson, Penelope Keith and Tony Robinson. It was broadcast on BBC Radio 4 at 11.00pm and repeated on 26 December at 7.15pm.

Wednesday 19 April 2000
CONCERT
Grand Prix Anniversary Ball, **Dorchester Hotel, Park Lane, London, England**
Mason played drums at this all-star concert hosted by Bernie Ecclestone to celebrate the 50th anniversary of the modern Formula One Championship and to raise money for the NSPCC. The first event in the World Championship, won by Giuseppe Farina driving an Alfa Romeo, took place at Silverstone in May 1950.

Thursday 22 June 2000
CONCERT
Rebuild The Roundhouse, **The Roundhouse, Chalk Farm, London, England**
Mason played drums at this private gala to raise funds to restore the Roundhouse as a concert venue and educational centre. The event featured performances from Hugh Cornwell (who performed a solo acoustic of 'Golden Brown'), Jools Holland and his

Rhythm & Blues Band (with Hugh on guitar with a rendition of The Doors' 'People Are Strange') and a version of 'Interstellar Overdrive' featuring Jools Holland, Hugh Cornwell and Nick Mason.

Wednesday 26 & Thursday 27 June 2002
CONCERTS
Wembley Arena, Wembley, England
Mason played drums on 'Set The Controls For The Heart of The Sun' at these Roger Waters shows. (See Roger Waters' entry for further details.)

Saturday 5 February 2005
CONCERT
Tsunami Appeal, **The Olympiad, Chippenham, England**
Mason played drums at this charity fundraiser as a member of Andy Scott's Sweet. Other acts on the bill included Iron The Cat, The Wurzels, The Specials, Chapter 13 and The Bersley Brothers.

Saturday 20 May 2006
CONCERT
Highclere Rocks, **Highclere Castle, Newbury, England**
Mason along with Roger Waters, Eric Clapton, Bryan Ferry, Roger Taylor, Roger Daltrey and Georgie Fame appeared as special guests of 'The Band Du Lac' featuring Gary Brooker (electric piano), Jodi Linscott (percussion), Mike Rutherford (guitars), Geoff Whitehorn (lead guitar) and Paul Carrack (vocals) in this benefit concert on behalf of the Countryside Alliance. Mason appeared with Roger Waters on 'Wish You Were Here' and 'Comfortably Numb' with the house band supplemented by Eric Clapton (acoustic guitar), Georgie Fame (keyboards) and Andy Fairweather-Low (guitars). Mason continued to play drums throughout the remainder of the show including a band rendition of 'A Whiter Shade Of Pale', Clapton's rendition of 'Cocaine', the closing song, Bob Marley's 'Get Up, Stand Up' and the encore of Bob Dylan's 'Rainy Day Women #12 & 35'.

ROGER WATERS – TOUR 2006
Mason played drums in Waters' band on selected dates on his solo tour during the *Dark Side Of The Moon* set as well as the encores alongside Graham Broad (drums), Jon Carin (keyboards), Andy Fairweather-Low (guitar, bass guitar and vocals), Dave Kilminster (guitar, vocals), Ian Ritchie (saxophone), Harry Waters (keyboards), Snowy White (guitar, vocals), Carol Kenyon, Katie Kissoon and PP Arnold (backing vocals). (See the Roger Waters section for tour dates, set lists and further information.)

BELOW: AS A KEEN AVIATOR MASON FLEW HIMSELF BETWEEN STOPS ON A PROMOTIONAL TOUR OF THE UK TO PUBLICISE THE *PROFILES* ALBUM.

roger waters

George Roger Waters was born in Great Bookham, Surrey on 6 September 1943. He was the youngest of three brothers to Eric Fletcher Waters, a second lieutenant in the Royal Fusiliers, and Mary Waters, a schoolteacher. Following the death of his father during the ill-fated Anzio campaign in Italy in January 1944, the family relocated to Cambridge. He was educated at the Cambridgeshire High School For Boys, which, judging from the bitter resentment in his later songwriting was not an altogether pleasant experience for him. He enrolled to the Regent Street Polytechnic's Architecture School in 1962 where he shared classes with both Nick Mason and Richard Wright and was instrumental in the formation of the precursor bands to Pink Floyd.

Both before and shortly after leaving Pink Floyd in 1985, Roger Waters attempted, with varying degrees of success, to emulate the band's extravagant stage shows in his own live concerts. Perhaps because the band has had a somewhat faceless image throughout its lifetime, the general public did not readily identify Waters the solo artist as being one of the prime movers of the band in its heyday. Consequently, they did not immediately take to his work with the same enthusiasm, despite some excellent achievements. However, the period between 1999 and 2002 saw a significant increase in his profile producing some fine material assisted by lengthy touring and has now found the deserved recognition that eluded him for so long.

Waters recently branched into the classical field of music and produced a critically acclaimed operatic work that he began in 1996 entitled *Ca Ira*. He wasted little time in capitalising on the success of his *Live 8* appearance with Pink Floyd by announcing tours of Europe and the US through the summer and autumn of 2006 by performing *The Dark Side Of The Moon* in its entirety. He is also working on a new rock album and rewriting *The Wall* for Broadway theatre production.

DISCOGRAPHY

THE BODY

Waters embarked on his first solo project outside of Pink Floyd in 1970, collaborating with the avant-garde performer-composer Ron Geesin on a bizarre experimental documentary film called *The Body*. It was not widely known until recently that the other members of Pink Floyd also appeared on the album – on the final track, 'Give Birth To A Smile' – for which they were paid as session musicians but remain uncredited. The film premiered in London on 29 October 1970, although it had limited cinematic distribution.

Friday 27 November 1970
THE BODY
UK: EMI Harvest SHSP 4008 (vinyl album).
US: Restless Retro 772395-2 (CD album, released Monday 22 October 1990).
Track list: 'Our Song' / 'Sea Shell And Stone' / 'Red Stuff Writhe' / 'A Gentle Breeze Blew Through Life' / 'Lick Your Partners' / 'Bridge Passage For Three Plastic Teeth' / 'Chain Of Life' / 'The Womb Bit' / 'Embryo Thought' / 'March Past Of The Embryo's' / 'More Than Seven Dwarfs In Penis-Land' / 'Dance Of The Red Corpuscles' // 'Body Transport'/ 'Hand Dance - Full Evening Dress' / 'Breathe' / 'Old Folks Ascension' / 'Bed-Time-Dream-Clime' / 'Piddle In Perspex' / 'Embryonic Womb Walk' / 'Mrs. Throat Goes Walking' / 'Sea Shell And Soft Stone' / 'Give Birth To A Smile'.
Recorded at EMI Studios Abbey Road, London, England.
Produced by Roger Waters and Ron Geesin.
Engineered by Brian Humphries.
Cover photo by Richard Rush Studio Inc.

THE PROS AND CONS OF HITCH-HIKING

Waters' first solo album is a concept piece with the original demos being recorded at the same time as *The Wall*. Through a series of dreams, it tells the story of a man struggling with a mid-life crisis in a motel room.
Gerald Scarfe's album sleeve depicting a naked female hitch-hiker was branded as sexist by many and a large number of sleeves as well as album and concert advertisements were censored in parts of Europe, USA and Japan.

Monday 16 April 1984
'5:01AM (The Pros And Cons Of Hitch-Hiking)' / '4:30AM (Apparently They Were Travelling Abroad)'
UK: EMI Harvest HAR 5228 (7-inch single).
US: Columbia 38-04455 (7-inch single released on Monday 9 April 1984).
'5:01AM (The Pros And Cons Of Hitch-Hiking)' / '5:01AM (The Pros And Cons Of Hitch-Hiking)'

US: Columbia 38-04455 (promotional 7-inch single).

5:01AM (The Pros And Cons Of Hitch-Hiking)'
// '4:30AM (Apparently They Were Travelling
Abroad) / 4:33AM (Running Shoes)'
UK: EMI Harvest 12 HAR 5228 (12-inch single).
US: Columbia 44 05002 (12-inch single).

'5:01AM (The Pros And Cons Of Hitch-Hiking)'
/ '5:01AM (The Pros And Cons Of Hitch-
Hiking)'
US: Columbia AS 1861 (promotional 12-inch single).

May 1984
SELECTION FROM THE PROS AND CONS OF
HITCH-HIKING
US: Columbia AS 1864 (12-inch single).
Track list: '4:30am (Apparently They Were Travelling Abroad)' / '4:33am (Running Shoes)' / '4:56am (For The First Time Today, Part 1)' // '4:41am (Sexual Revolution)' / '5:01am (The Pros And Cons Of Hitch-Hiking)' / '5:06am (Every Strangers Eyes)'.

Tuesday 8 May 1984
THE PROS AND CONS OF HITCH-HIKING
UK: EMI Harvest SHVL 24-0105-1 (vinyl album).
US: Columbia FC 39290 (vinyl album released on Monday 7 May 1984).
Track list: '4:30am (Apparently They Were Travelling Abroad)' / '4:33am (Running Shoes)' / '4:37am (Arabs With Knives And West German Skies)' / '4:39am (For The First Time Today, Part 2)' / '4:41am (Sexual Revolution)' / '4:47am (The Remains Of Our Love)' // '4:50am (Go Fishing)' / '4:56am (For The First Time Today, Part 1)' / '4:58am (Dunroamin, Duncarin, Dunlivin)' / '5:01am (The Pros And Cons Of Hitch-Hiking)' / '5:06am (Every Strangers Eyes)' / '5:11am (The Moment Of Clarity)'.
Additional musicians: Andy Bown (Hammond Organ and 12-string guitar), Ray Cooper (percussion), Eric Clapton (lead guitar), Michael Kamen (piano), Andy Newmark (drums), David Sanborn (saxophone), Raphael Ravenscroft, Kevin Flanigan and Vic Sullivan (horns), Madeline Bell, Doreen Chanter and Katie Kissoon (backing vocals). The National Philharmonic Orchestra was conducted and arranged by Michael Kamen.
Recorded at Olympic Studios, London, England; Eel Pie Studios, Twickenham, England and The Billiard Room, London, England between February and December 1983.
Produced by Roger Waters and Michael Kamen. Engineered by Andy Jackson.
Mastered by Doug Sax & Mike Reese at the Mastering Lab, Los Angeles, USA. Holophonics by Zuccarelli Labs Ltd.
Artwork concept by Roger Waters and executed by Gerald Scarfe and Artful Dodgers.
Highest chart position UK No.13, US No. 31.
Certified Gold in the US on 19 April 1995.
Reissued:

UK: EMI Harvest CDP 7460292 (CD album, 1989).
US: Columbia CK 39290 (CD album, 1987).

Monday 4 June 1984
'5:06AM (Every Strangers Eyes)' / '4:39AM
(For The First Time Today, Part 2)'
UK: EMI Harvest HAR 5230 (7-inch single).
US: Columbia 38-04566 (7-inch single released on Monday 11 June 1984).

'5:06AM (Every Strangers Eyes)' / '4:39AM
(For The First Time Today, Part 2)'
US: Columbia 38-04566 (promotional 7-inch single).

WHEN THE WIND BLOWS
Waters recorded the bulk of the soundtrack to the animated film of Raymond Briggs' cartoon strip book. A runaway success, it was a black comedy focusing on a retired couple living in the north of England during the cold war era and the resultant effect on their lives with the advent of a nuclear attack on the UK.

Monday 27 October 1986
WHEN THE WIND BLOWS
UK: Virgin V2406 (vinyl album).
US: Virgin 90599-1 (vinyl album, released on Monday 27 October 1987)
Track list: 'When The Wind Blows' (David Bowie) / 'Facts And Figures' (Hugh Cornwell) / 'The Brazilian' (Genesis) / 'What Have They Done?' (Squeeze) / 'The Shuffle' (Paul Hardcastle) // Roger Waters: 'The Russian Missile' / 'Towers Of Faith' / 'Hilda's Dream' / 'The American Bomber' / 'The Anderson Shelter' / 'The British Submarine' / 'The Attack' / 'The Fallout' / 'Hilda's Hair' / 'Folded Flags'.
Additional musicians: Paul Carrack (guest vocals on 'Folded Flags'), Mel Collins (saxophone), Nick Glenny-Smith (keyboards), John Gordon (bass guitar), Matt Irving (keyboards), Freddie KRC (drums), John Linnwood (Linn programming), Jay Stapley (electric guitar) and Clare Torry (vocals).
Roger Waters' tracks produced by Roger Waters and Nick Griffiths.
Roger Waters' tracks recorded at The Billiard Room, London, England. Engineered by Nick Griffiths.
Artwork illustrations by Raymond Briggs. Sleeve design by Assorted Images.

Monday 27 October 1986
WHEN THE WIND BLOWS
UK: CBS Fox 5156 (VHS PAL video).
US: International Video Entertainment 68599 (VHS NTSC video).
Reissued:
UK: Channel 4 C4DVD10007 (DVD PAL video, 2005).
The film also saw a very limited cinematic release and has also been shown on TV.

RADIO KAOS
Radio KAOS was another concept piece telling the complex story of Billy, an apparent 'vegetable', who accesses government defence computers to simulate a world-wide nuclear conflagration in order to convince the superpowers that they must discuss peace if global destruction is to be averted. Using a voice synthesiser, he communicates on air with a radio DJ, Jim Ladd, whose show becomes a vehicle for spreading his anti-war message.

Monday 11 May 1987
'Radio Waves' / 'Going To Live In L.A.'
UK: EMI EM6 (7-inch single).
US: Columbia 38-07180 (7-inch single released on Monday 8 June 1987).
'Radio Waves' / 'Radio Waves'
US: Columbia 38-07180 (promotional 7-inch single).
'Radio Waves' (single version) / 'Radio Waves'
(edit)
US: Columbia CS7 02745 (promotional 7-inch single).
'Radio Waves' (extended remix) // 'Going To
Live In L.A.' / 'Radio Waves' (7-inch version)
UK: EMI 12EM6 (12-inch single).
UK: EMI CDEM6 (CD single).
US: Columbia 44 06816 (12-inch single).
'Radio Waves' (7-inch version) / 'Radio Waves'
(album version)
US: Columbia CAS 2723 (promotional 12-inch single).
Highest chart position UK No.74.

Monday 8 June 1987
'Sunset Strip' / 'Money' (live)
UK: EMI EM20 (7-inch single).
US: Columbia 38-07364 (7-inch single).
'Sunset Strip' / 'Sunset Strip'
US: Columbia 38-07364 (promotional 7-inch single).

June 1987
RADIO KAOS
Banded promotional radio vinyl album in custom sleeve with no dialogue).
UK: EMI KAOSDJ1.
US: Columbia CAS 2722.

Track list: 'Radio Waves' / 'Who Needs Information' / 'Me Or Him' / 'The Powers That Be' // 'Sunset Strip' / 'Home' / 'Four Minutes' / 'The Tide Is Turning'.

Monday 15 June 1987
RADIO KAOS
UK: EMI KOAS1 (vinyl album).
UK: EMI CDKAOS1 (CD album).
US: Columbia FC 40795 (vinyl album, released Monday 15 June 1987).
US: Columbia CK 40795 (CD album).
Track list: 'Radio Waves' / 'Who Needs Information' / 'Me Or Him' / 'The Powers That Be' // 'Sunset Strip' / 'Home' / 'Four Minutes' / 'The Tide Is Turning'.
Additional musicians: Andy Fairweather-Low and Jay Stapley (guitars), Mel Collins (saxophones), Ian Ritchie (Fairlight programming, drum programming, piano, keyboards and tenor saxophone on 'Who Needs Information', 'Sunset Strip' and 'The Powers That Be'), Graham Broad (drums and percussion), John Linwood (drums on 'The Powers That Be'), Nick Glenny-Smith (DX7 and Emu on 'The Powers That Be'), Matt Irving (Hammond organ on 'The Powers That Be'), Paul Carrack (vocal on 'The Powers That Be'), Clare Torry (vocal on 'Home' and 'Four Minutes'), Suzanne Rhatigan - Main backing vocals on 'Radio Waves', 'Me Or Him', 'Sunset Strip' and 'The Tide Is Turning'), Madeline Bell, Vicki Brown, Doreen Chanter, Katie Kissoon & Steve Langer (backing vocals on 'Who Needs Information', 'The Powers That Be' and 'Radio Waves'), John Phirkell (trumpet on 'Who Needs Information', 'Sunset Strip' and 'The Powers That Be'), Peter Thoms (trombone on 'Who Needs Information', 'Sunset Strip' and 'The Powers That Be'), The Pontardoulais Male Voice Choir led by Noel Davis arranged by Eric Jones, Jim Ladd (as himself), Andy Quigley (The "Forgive me, Father" speech on 'Me Or Him'), Shelley Ladd (Monkey and Dog Lady), Jack Snyder (Guppy), Ron Weldy (I Don't Like Fish), JJ Jackson (Flounder), Jim Rogers (Doesn't like fish, marine fish), John Taylor (Shellfish Shrimp Crab Lobster), Stuart the spaniel (Uncle David's Great Dane, with the help of an AKAI 900 sampler and a DX7 to make him sound bigger), BBC master computer (Billy), Harry & India Waters (Children in the garden). Horns on 'Who Needs Information' and 'The Powers That Be' arranged by Ian Ritchie. Horns on 'Sunset Strip' arranged by Roger Waters.
Recorded at Skylight Suite, London, England (pre-production programming); The Billiard Room, London, England (October – December 1986) and Odyssey Studios, London, England (February – March 1987).
Produced by Roger Waters, Ian Ritchie and Nick Griffiths. Engineered by Chris Sheldon.
Artwork by Kate Hepburn and Pearce Marchbank.
Highest chart position UK No.25, US No. 50.

Monday November 2 1987
'Who Needs Information' / 'Molly's Song'
US: Columbia 38-07617 (7-inch single).
'Who Needs Information' / 'Who Needs Information'
US: Columbia 38-07617 (promotional 7-inch single).

Monday 16 November 1987
'The Tide Is Turning' / 'Money' (live)
UK: EMI EM37 (7-inch single).
'The Tide Is Turning' // 'Money' (live) / 'Get Back To Radio' (demo)
UK: EMI 12EM37 (12-inch single).
UK: EMI CDEM37 (CD single).
Highest chart position UK No.54.

Tuesday 31 May 1988
RADIO KAOS
UK: PMI MVS KAO5 (VHS PAL video).
US: CMV 49012 (VHS HTSC video, released on Monday 30 May 1988).
Track list: 'Radio Waves' / 'Sunset Strip' / 'Four Minutes' / 'The Tide Is Turning'.

THE WALL - LIVE IN BERLIN
This ambitious live project spawned a plethora of releases and promotional items documenting the concert.

September 1990
THE WALL – LIVE IN BERLIN
UK: Mercury Phonogram (promotional box set with CD, concert video and illustrated booklet).
US: Mercury 082730-0 (promotional box set with CD, concert video and illustrated booklet).

September 1990
PIECES FROM THE WALL
UK: Mercury Phonogram 878147-2 (promotional CD EP housed in a 9x6x2–inch sponge 'brick').
Track List: 'Another Brick In The Wall, Part 2' (edit) / 'Young Lust' (edit) / 'Run Like Hell' / 'In The Flesh'

Monday 10 September 1990
'Another Brick In The Wall, Part 2' / 'Run Like Hell'
UK: Mercury Phonogram MER 332 (7-inch single).
'Another Brick In The Wall, Part 2' // 'Run Like Hell' (Potsdamer Mix) / 'Another Brick In The Wall, Part 2' (full version)
UK: Mercury Phonogram MERX 332 (12-inch single).
UK: Mercury Phonogram MERCD 332 (CD single).

Monday 17 September 1990
THE WALL - LIVE IN BERLIN
UK: Mercury Phonogram 846611-2 (double CD album).
UK: Mercury Phonogram 846611-1 (double vinyl album).

US: Mercury 846611-2 (double CD album, released on Monday 10 September 1990).
US: Mercury 846611-1 (double vinyl album).
Track list: 'In The Flesh' / 'The Thin Ice' / 'Another Brick In The Wall, Part 1' / 'The Happiest Days Of Our Lives' / 'Another Brick In The Wall, Part 2' / 'Mother' / 'Goodbye Blue Sky' / 'Empty Spaces' / 'Young Lust' / 'One Of My Turns' / 'Don't Leave Me Now' / 'Another Brick In The Wall, Part 3' / 'Goodbye Cruel World' // 'Hey You' / 'Is There Anybody Out There?' / 'Nobody Home' / 'Vera' / 'Bring The Boys Back Home' / 'Comfortably Numb' / 'In The Flesh' / 'Run Like Hell' / 'Waiting For The Worms' / 'Stop' / 'The Trial' / 'The Tide Is Turning'.
Produced by Nick Griffiths and Roger Waters. Engineered by Nigel Jopson. Mixed by Nick Griffiths and Nigel Jopson. Orchestra recorded by Steven McGlaughlin.
Live recording facilities by Eurosound Mobile & Manor Mobile Studios. Mixed at Olympic Studios.
Artwork by Mark Norton / 4i Collaboration.
Highest chart position UK No.27, US No.56.
Reissued:
UK: Universal Mercury 0385962 (Hybrid SACD, 2003).
US: Mercury B0000753-26 (Hybrid SACD, 2003).

Monday 24 September 1990
THE WALL – LIVE IN BERLIN
The full-length concert film; track listing as album, above.
UK: Channel 5 Music Video CFM 2648 (VHS PAL video).
US: Polygram 082649-3 (VHS NTSC video, released on Monday 24 September 1990).
Certified Gold in the US on 8 January 1992.
Reissued:
UK: Universal Island 0384379 (DVD PAL video, 2003).
US: Universal Mercury B0000369-09 (DVD NTSC video re-issue of the full-length concert film on DVD; track listing as video, above. Also contains additional features including digitally re-mastered visuals and a 5.1 surround mix produced from the original concert multi-tracks by the original recording engineer Nick Griffiths. Complete with new artwork and exclusive liner notes, the DVD also includes a new 30-minute documentary entitled Behind The Wall, a selection of Gerald Scarfe's animation footage and Mark Fisher's set and character designs. As a special bonus feature, unreleased footage of Rupert Everett portraying Pink that was never used during the concert has also been added, 2003).
UK: Universal Island 9817605 (DVD PAL video & double CD album of the full-length concert film on DVD plus a double CD of the concert in 5.1 surround mix; track listing as album and video, above, 2004).

Monday 15 October 1990

'The Tide Is Turning' / 'Nobody Home'
UK: Mercury Phonogram MER 336 (7-inch single).

'The Tide Is Turning' (LP version) // 'Nobody Home' / 'The Tide Is Turning' (7-inch version)
UK: Mercury Phonogram MERX 336 (12-inch single).
UK: Mercury Phonogram MERCD 336 (CD single).

AMUSED TO DEATH

Waters third solo album, *Amused To Death*, is by far his most accomplished. In this work he continues to vent spleen over subjects dear to his heart. Foremost among these is the futility of warfare: the piece is dedicated to Private William Hubbard, a rifleman remembered by fellow soldier Alf Razzell, who relived the horror of the First World War trenches in a TV documentary and whose words Waters samples for the album. Waters' other bugbears in this work continue to be consumerism and market forces. His main asset was to secure Jeff Beck as his lead guitarist and Patrick Leonard as his producer but, as with all of his solo albums, this concept-based work is heavy going and best appreciated through headphones. The album was originally planned for release on EMI, but its extended production time, coupled with contractual difficulties and Waters' ongoing litigation against Pink Floyd, prompted a shift to Sony. Incidentally, at this time there were rumours of an original sleeve design by Gerald Scarfe, showing Waters' three former colleagues floating lifelessly in a cocktail glass which Scarfe has since denied.

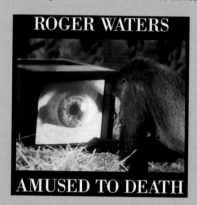

Monday 24 August 1992

'What God Wants, Part 1' (video edit) / 'What God Wants, Part 1' (album version)
UK: Columbia Sony 6581390 (7-inch single).
US: Columbia 38-74363 (7-inch single, released Monday 24 August 1992).

'What God Wants, Part 1' (video edit) / 'What God Wants, Part 1' (album version) / 'What God Wants, Part 3'
UK: Columbia Sony 6581395 (CD single).
UK: Columbia Sony 6581399 (limited CD box-set single with prints).

August 1992

AMUSED TO DEATH
Promotional box set containing the CD and cassette.
UK: Columbia Sony – no catalogue number.

Monday 7 September 1992

AMUSED TO DEATH
UK: Columbia Sony COL 4687612 (CD album).
US: Columbia CK 47127 (CD album, released on Monday 7 September 1992).
Track list: 'The Ballad Of Bill Hubbard' / 'What God Wants, Part 1' / 'Perfect Sense, Part 1' / 'Perfect Sense, Part 2' / 'The Bravery Of Being Out Of Range' / 'Late Home Tonight, Part 1' / 'Late Home Tonight, Part 2' / 'Too Much Rope' / 'What God Wants, Part 2' / 'What God Wants, Part 3' / 'Watching TV' / 'Three Wishes' / 'It's A Miracle' / 'Amused To Death'.
Additional musicians: Don Henley, Rita Coolage and PP Arnold (lead vocals), John Joyce, Jim Haas, N'Dea Davenport, Natalie Jackson, Lynn Fiddmont-Lindsay, Katie Kissoon and Doreen Chanter (backing vocals), Jeff Beck, Andy Fairweather-Low, Tim Pierce, Steve Lukather, B.J. Cole, Rick DiFonzo, Bruce Gaitsch and Geoff Whitehorn (guitars), James Johnson, John Pierce and Randy Jackson (bass guitars), John Patitucci (upright and electric bass), Graham Broad, Denny Fongheiser and Jeff Porcaro (drums), Luis Conte and Brian MacLeod (percussion), Patrick Leonard (keyboards and piano), John 'Rabbit' Bundrick (Hammond organ), Steve Sidwell (cornet), Guo Yi & The Peking Brothers (dulcimer, lute, zhen, oboe and bass), The National Philharmonic Orchestra was arranged and conducted by Michael Kamen and The London Welsh Chorale conducted by Kenneth Bowen.
Produced by Patrick Leonard and Roger Waters.
Engineered by Hayden Bendall, Jerry Jordan and Stephen McLaughlan.
Recorded at The Billiard Room, London, England; Olympic Studios, London, England; CTS Studios, London, England; Angel Studios, London, England; EMI Abbey Road Studios, London, England; Compass Point Studios, Nassau, Bahamas; Devonshire Studios, Los Angeles, USA; Ameraycan Studios, Los Angeles, USA; Evergreen Recording, Los Angeles, USA and Visual Studios, Los Angeles, USA.
Mixed at Devonshire Studios, Los Angeles, USA and Visual Studios, Los Angeles, USA. Mastered by Doug Sax & Ron Lewter at The Mastering Lab, Los Angeles, USA.
Artwork by Christopher Austopehuk, Mark Burdett and Paul M. Martin.
Highest chart position UK No.8, US No. 21.
Certified Silver in the UK in 1992.
Reissued:
US: Columbia CK 53196 (24 bit super bit-mapping 24 karat gold CD album, 2003).

Monday 23 November 1992

AMUSED TO DEATH
UK: Columbia Sony COL 4687610 (limited-edition double vinyl album set with 16-page booklet, released in early 1993 in response to lobbying by fans).

Monday 23 November 1992

AMUSED TO DEATH
UK: Video Collection SMV 49148-2 (VHS PAL video EP).
Track list: 'What God Wants, Part 1' / Roger Waters interview / 'What God Wants, Part 2'.

Monday 23 November 1992

'The Bravery Of Being Out Of Range' / 'What God Wants, Part 1' / 'Perfect Sensee, Part 1'
UK: Columbia Sony 6588192 (CD single).

ROGER WATERS - IN THE FLESH

Following the completion of his second US tour in the summer of 2000, Waters released a document of an entire live show on a double CD taken from a selection of performances from Phoenix (16 June), Las Vegas (17 June), Los Angeles (24 June) and Portland (27 June).

Monday 4 December 2000

ROGER WATERS - IN THE FLESH
UK: Columbia Sony 5011372 (double CD album).
US: Columbia C2K 85235 (double CD album, released on Monday 4 December 2000).
Track List: 'In The Flesh' / 'The Happiest Days Of Our Lives' / 'Another Brick In The Wall, Part 2' / 'Mother' / 'Get Your Filthy Hands Off My Desert' / 'Southampton Dock' / 'Pigs On The Wing, Part 1' / 'Dogs' / 'Welcome To The Machine' / 'Wish You Were Here' / 'Shine On You Crazy Diamond, Parts 1-8' / 'Set The Controls For The Heart Of The Sun' / 'Breathe' / 'Time' / 'Money' / '5:06 am (Every Stranger's Eyes)' / 'Perfect Sense, Parts 1 & 2' / 'The Bravery Of Being Out Of Range' / 'It's A Miracle' / 'Amused To Death' / 'Brain Damage' / 'Eclipse' / 'Comfortably Numb' / 'Each Small Candle'.
Produced and mixed by James Guthrie who recorded the concerts as a 48-track analogue recording before

ROGER WATERS

4

mixing it down to high resolution digital. Mastered by Doug Sax at Das Boot recording.
'Each Small Candle' is a new track part written by a South American who'd been a victim of torture. An Italian journalist, active in the initiative against torture in Northern Italy, had given Waters the short poem years ago. The poem lay in a drawer in Waters' studio until, during the crisis in Kosovo, he read a piece in *The Times* describing a Serbian soldier who saw an Albanian woman lying in a burned-out building. The soldier left his platoon to give aid to the woman, then rejoined his men and marched off. The image inspired Waters to set the short poem, 'Each Small Candle', to music and pen additional lyrics. Artwork cover design by Chris Hudson for Hudson Wright Limited; Photography by Neal Preston & Jimmy Ienner Jnr. The cover artwork depicts a cityscape scene in the background, (originally created by 4i for The Wall Live in Berlin show) the 'In the Flesh' tour pig logo in solid black beneath, crossed barbed wire in the foreground, (similar to the graphics projected during the tour for 'Each Small Candle') a lunar eclipse in the upper right corner and in the upper left are the words 'Roger Waters' in white block lettering with blue block lettering of in the flesh in lower case underneath. On the back cover is the track listing above the same 4i cityscape amongst which are silhouettes of the hitchhiker, (from The *Pros and Cons*) the monkey watching TV, (from *Amused To Death*), and the radio tower (from *Radio KAOS* even though no song from that album is on the CD or was played during this leg of the tour). In the foreground is white-feathered photo of Roger standing with his bass waving to fans. The inside 24 page booklet is filled with great photos from the tour and of course the album credits. It also contains a narrative by Roger Waters talking to Nick Sedgewick about the album, the tour, and the future. The discs themselves are picture discs of a lunar eclipse with titles and track listing.
Reissued:
US: Columbia C2S 85235 (SACD double CD album, 2001).

Monday 18 March 2002
ROGER WATERS - IN THE FLESH
UK: Columbia Sony 541859 (DVD PAL video).
US: Columbia Music Video 54185 (DVD NTSC video, released on Monday 17 December 2001).
DVD version of 'In The Flesh', featuring a Hi-Definition live concert video with 5.1 Dolby Digital and LPCM Stereo music mixes. Also contains additional features including a 30-minute behind-the-scenes documentary, band biographies, still photographs, projected images and lyrics.
Certified Gold in the US on 3 April 2002.

FLICKERING FLAME - THE SOLO YEARS VOLUME 1
Essentially this is a *Best Of* album featuring unreleased demos, released to coincide with the start of Waters European 'In The Flesh' tour.

Tuesday 7 May 2002
FLICKERING FLAME - THE SOLO YEARS VOLUME 1
UK: Columbia Sony 5079062 (CD album).
Track list: 'Knockin' On Heaven's Door' (a Bob Dylan cover) / 'Too Much Rope' (from *Amused To Death*) / 'Radio Waves' (from *Radio KAOS*) / 'Three Wishes' (from *Amused To Death*) / 'The Tide Is Turning' (from *Radio KAOS*) / 'What God Wants, Part 2' (from *Amused To Death*) / '5:06am (Every Strangers Eyes)' (from *The Pros And Cons Of Hitch-Hiking*) / 'Each Small Candle' (a new song) / '5:01am (The Pros And Cons Of Hitch-Hiking)' (from *The Pros And Cons Of Hitch-Hiking*) / 'Who Needs Information?' (from *Radio KAOS*) / 'Go Fishing' (from *The Pros And Cons Of Hitch-Hiking*) / 'Perfect Sense, Part 1' (from *Amused To Death*) / 'Perfect Sense, Part 2' (from *Amused To Death*) / 'Lost Boys Calling' (original demo) / 'Towers Of Faith' (from *When the Wind Blows* soundtrack) / 'Flickering Flame' (a new song, demo).

ROGER WATERS ÇA IRA - THERE IS HOPE - AN OPERA IN THREE ACTS
Waters embarked on his most curious project to date: that of a classical opera entitled *Ça Ira* (There Is Hope) based around the history and politics of the French Revolution, its title taken from a popular revolutionary song of the period. The album, produced by Roger Waters and Rick Wentworth, and engineered by Simon Rhodes at Abbey Road Studios, was the result of an exhaustive 12 year process that unfortunately saw the death of Waters' three project collaborators, Philippe Constantin and Etienne and Nadine Roda-Gil who originally conceived the project.

Monday 25 July 2005
SELECTIONS FROM ROGER WATERS ÇA IRA - AN OPERA IN THREE ACTS
US: Sony (promotional CD album, no catalogue number).
Track List: 'Honest Bird, Simple Bird' / 'I Want To Be King' / 'To Freeze In The Dead Of Night' / 'So To The Streets In The Pouring Rain' / 'My Dear Cousin Bourbon Of Spain' / 'To The Windward Isles' / 'The Last Night On Earth' / 'Liberty' / 'And In The Bushes Where They Survive'.
Produced by Roger Waters and Rick Wentworth. Recorded at Air Lyndhurst, London, England; EMI Abbey Road, London, England; Angel Studios, London, England; Whitfield Street Studios, London, England; Sony Studios, London, England; Sphere Studios, London, England; Guilliaume Tell, Paris, France and Mega Studios, Paris, France.

Monday 26 September 2005
ROGER WATERS ÇA IRA – THERE IS HOPE - AN OPERA IN THREE ACTS
UK: Sony BMG S2H60867 (double CD album with an enhanced CD that includes the complete sung lyrics viewable on a CD-ROM drive).
UK: Sony BMG S2H60867 (double enhanced CD album issued as a limited edition digipack including the full opera on two hybrid SACD's, plus a bonus *Making Of Ça Ira* PAL DVD and a 60-page four-colour booklet containing the libretto, cast credits, and original illustrations).
US: Sony Classical S2K 96439 (double CD album with an enhanced CD that includes the complete sung lyrics viewable on a CD-ROM drive, released on Monday 26 September 2005).
US: Sony Classical S2H 60867 (Double CD album issued as a limited edition digipack including the full opera on two hybrid SACD's, plus a bonus *Making Of Ça Ira* PAL DVD and a 60-page four-colour booklet containing the libretto, cast credits, and original illustrations).
A=Act, S=Scene. Track List: 'The Gathering Storm' / 'Overture' / A1S1: 'Garden In Vienna 1765' / A1S1: 'Madame Antoine' / A1S2: 'Kings, Sticks And Birds' / A1S2: 'Honest Bird, Simple Bird' / A1S2: 'I Want To

Be King' / A1S2: 'Let Us Break All The Shields' /
A1S3: 'Grievances Of The People' / A1S4: 'France In
Disarray' / A1S4: 'To Laugh Is To Know How To Live'
/ A1S4: 'Slavers, Landlords, Bigots At Your Door' /
A1S5: 'Fall Of The Bastille' / A1S5: 'To Freeze In The
Dead Of Night' / A1S5: 'So To The Streets In The
Pouring Rain' / A2S1: 'Dances And Marches' / A2S1:
'Now Hear Ye' / A2S1: 'Flushed With Wine' / A2S2:
'The Letter' / A2S2: 'My Dear Cousin Bourbon Of
Spain' / A2S2: 'The Ship Of State Is All At Sea' /
A2S3: 'Silver, Sugar And Indigo' / A2S3: 'To The
Windward Isles' / A2S4: 'Papal Edict' / A2S4: 'In
Paris There's A Rumble Under The Ground' // A3S1:
'The Fugitive King' / A3S1: 'But The Marquis Of Boulli
Has A Trump Card Up His Sleeve' / A3S1: 'To Take
Your Hat Off' / A3S1: 'The Echoes Never Fade From
That Fusillade' / A3S2: 'Commune De Paris' / A3S2:
'Vive La Commune De Paris' / A3S2: 'The National
Assembly Is Confused' / A3S3: 'The Execution Of
Louis Capet' / A3S3: 'Adieu Louis, For You It's Over' /
A3S4: 'Marie Antoinette – The Last Night On Earth' /
A3S4: 'Adieu My Good And Tender Sister' / A3S5:
'Liberty' / A3S5: 'And In The Bushes Where They
Survive'.

Ça Ira features orchestration and choral
arrangements by Rick Wentworth and Roger Waters.
The principal characters in the opera are brought to
life by the Welsh bass-baritone Bryn Terfel (as The
Ringmaster, The Troublemaker and Louis Capet - The
King of France); internationally acclaimed soprano
Ying Huang (as Marie Marianne - The Voice of
Liberty, Reason and the Republic, Marie Antoinette -
The Queen of France); American tenor Paul Groves (as
A Revolutionary Priest and A Military Officer); and
Senegalese 'one man orchestra' Ismael Lo (as a
Revolutionary Slave). Other parts were sung by Jamie
Bower (as Honest Bird - the young Revolutionary
Priest) and Helen Russill (as Madame Antoine - the
young Marie Antoinette).
Produced by Roger Waters and Rick Wentworth.

SOUNDTRACKS

1977
L'ART ET LA MACHINE
Waters reunited with Ron Geesin to produce the
soundtrack for this French made-for-TV film produced
by Adrian Maben. The music remains unreleased and
the film is very rarely shown.

1978
MAGRITTE
This biographical made-for-TV film of the surrealist
artist Rene Magritte was written and directed by
Adrian Maben with music by Bela Bartok and Roger
Waters. The film was released on VHS video (US: RM
Arts Home Video 8339011) in 1987 and DVD (US:
Image Entertainment ID9292RADVD) in 2001.

1984
THE HIT
The unreleased soundtrack to this cinematic film
featured a soundtrack by Paco de Lucia and Eric
Clapton. Waters made a small contribution to Eric
Clapton's piece. The film was released on VHS video
(US: Embassy Home Entertainment 7599).

1986
THE SAMARITANS
Waters re-recorded the Pink Floyd track 'Is There
Anybody Out There?' from *The Wall* for use in a
cinema advertisement for The Samaritans. A few
years' later parts of 'Welcome To The Machine' were
also used in another advertisement for this charitable
organisation.

1997
THE DYBBUK OF THE HOLY APPLE FIELD
Waters recorded a version of Bob Dylan's 'Knockin' On
Heaven's Door' for this Israeli cinematic film. To date
no soundtrack album has been officially released.

1999
LA LEGGENDA DEL PIANISTA SULL' OCEANO
(THE LEGEND OF THE PIANIST ON THE OCEAN)
Waters wrote the lyrics to the song 'Lost Boys Calling'
(sung by Waters with music by Ennio Morricone and
produced by Patrick Leonard) for this Italian
cinematic film scored primarily by Ennio Morricone.
The cinematic release in the UK and US was titled
The Legend Of 1900 and was released on DVD video
(US: Alliance Atlantis 3734) in 2001.

RADIO SHOWS

1984
INNER-VIEW – ROGER WATERS – PROS AND
CONS OF HITCH-HIKING
US: Inner-view (vinyl album). Show No.28-12,
broadcast 1984.
Documentary includes music and interviews with
Roger Waters.
Reissued:
Show No.32-3; broadcast 1985.

1987
IN CONCERT – ROGER WATERS
US: In Concert (double vinyl album). Show No.85-18;
broadcast 23 November 1987.
Roger Waters live at Colisee de Québec, Québec City
on 7 November 1987. Track list: 'Radio Waves' /
'Welcome To The Machine' / 'Money' / 'In The Flesh' /
'Have A Cigar' / 'Pigs (3 Different Ones)' / 'Wish You
Were Here' / 'Mother' / 'Get Your Filthy Hands Off My
Dessert' / 'Southampton Dock' / 'If' / 'The Powers
That Be' / 'Brain Damage' / 'Eclipse' / 'Another Brick
In The Wall, Part 1' / 'The Happiest Days Of Our Lives'
/ 'Another Brick In The Wall, Part 2'.

1992
OFF THE RECORD – ROGER WATERS
US: Westwood One (CD album). Show No.92-42;
broadcast 12 October 1992
Documentary includes music by and interviews with
Roger Waters.

1993
UP CLOSE – ROGER WATERS
US: Media America Radio (double CD album). Show
No.93-11; broadcast 24 February 1993 / Show 93-12;
broadcast 3 March 1993.
Documentary includes music by and interviews with
Roger Waters.

1994
SUPERSTAR CONCERT SERIES – PINK FLOYD
US: Westwood One (double CD album). Show No.94-
19; broadcast 2 May 1994.
Compilation of Pink Floyd and solo live recordings
including Pink Floyd at BBC Paris Theatre, London on
30 September 1971: 'One Of These Days' / 'Echoes' /
David Gilmour at Hammersmith Odeon, London on 30
April 1984: 'Money' / 'Run Like Hell' / 'Comfortably
Numb' / Roger Waters at Colisee de Québec, Québec
City on 7 November 1987: 'Wish You Were Here' /
'Another Brick In The Wall, Part 1' / 'The Happiest
Days Of Our Lives' / 'Another Brick In The Wall, Part 2'.

1995
SUPERSTAR CONCERT SERIES – PINK FLOYD /
ROGER WATERS
US: Westwood One (double CD album). Show No.95-
25; broadcast 12 June 1995.
Compilation of Pink Floyd and Roger Waters live
recordings including Pink Floyd at Knebworth Park on
30 June 1990: 'Shine On You Crazy Diamond, Parts 1-
5' / 'The Great Gig In The Sky' / 'Wish You Were Here'
/ 'Sorrow' / 'Money' / 'Comfortably Numb' / 'Run Like
Hell' / Roger Waters at Colisee de Québec, Québec City
on 7 November 1987: 'Another Brick In The Wall, Parts
1 & 2'.

2000
SFX RADIO NETWORK – ROGER WATERS – IN
THE FLESH
US: SFX Radio Network (double CD album). Broadcast
1-4 December 2000.
Documentary about *In The Flesh* includes music by and
interviews with Roger Waters.

2003
SUPERSTAR CONCERT SERIES – ROGER WATERS
/ DAVID GILMOUR
US: Westwood One (double CD album). Show No.03-15;
broadcast 12 April 2003.
Compilation of David Gilmour and Roger Waters live
recordings including David Gilmour at Lehigh
University, Allentown on 12 July 1984: 'Money' / 'Run

Like Hell' / 'Short And Sweet' / 'Comfortably Numb' / Roger Waters at Colisee de Québec, Québec City on 7 November 1987: 'Welcome To The Machine' / 'In The Flesh' / 'Have A Cigar' / 'Pigs (Three Different Ones)' / 'Another Brick In The Wall, Part 1' / 'The Happiest Days Of Our Lives' / 'Another Brick In The Wall, Part 2'.

COMPILATIONS

1992
SONY MUSIC HOLIDAY SAMPLER
US: Columbia / Sony TBJ 91 (promotional double CD album).
Compilation includes 'The Bravery Of Being Out Of Range'.

1992
SPREAD THE HITS
US: Navarre Records (promotional CD album).
Compilation includes 'What God Wants, Part 1'.

1992
COLUMBIA FALL FEAST
US: Columbia SCK 4827 (promotional CD album).
Compilation includes 'What God Wants, Part 1'.

1993
COLUMBIA RECORDS GRAMMY NOMINEE SAMPLER
US: Columbia CSK 5034 (promotional CD album).
Compilation includes 'What God Wants, Part 1'.

FREE DOWNLOADS
In August 2004 Waters made available two new compositions, 'Leaving Beirut' and 'To Kill The Child' available for download through his official site and that of other approved download sites. It was released as a Japanese-only, limited edition single in 2005 by Sony (SICP695).

GUEST APPEARANCES, PRODUCTION & COMPILATIONS
(UK Catalogue numbers and original format only)

1969
SYD BARRETT - 'Octopus' / 'No Good Trying'
UK: Harvest (HAR) 5009 (7-inch single).
Produced by Waters, Gilmour and others.

1970
SYD BARRETT - THE MADCAP LAUGHS
EMI Harvest SHVL 765 (vinyl album).
Produced by Waters, Gilmour and others

1997
ISMAEL LO - JAMMU AFRICA
Triloka Records 3145342332 (CD album).
Includes the song 'Without Blame' co-written by Waters, Ismael Lo and Etienne Roda-Gil.

1997
VARIOUS ARTISTS - WORLD MUSIC THAT SPEAKS TO THE SPIRIT
Triloka Records 3145346582 (CD album).
Label sampler that includes the song 'Without Blame' co-written by Waters, Ismael Lo and Etienne Roda-Gil.

1999
MARIANNE FAITHFULL - VAGABOND WAYS
Virgin / IT ITRCD1 (CD album).
Includes the track 'Incarceration Of A Flower Child', an unrecorded Roger Waters song from 1968, which oddly enough contains the identical opening refrain of 'Your Possible Pasts' from The Final Cut. Waters also plays Bass Synth on this track.

1999
HARVEST FESTIVAL
UK: EMI Harvest 724352119820 (CD album box set).
A 5 CD box set celebration of the Harvest Records catalogue including 'Breathe' from The Body by Waters and Geesin.

2000
VARIOUS ARTISTS - BAH HUMBUG!
Classic Rock CR23/14/00 (CD album).
A free cover mounted CD compilation issued with the December edition of Classic Rock magazine includes 'Wish You Were Here' from the live album Roger Waters In The Flesh.

2002
VARIOUS ARTISTS – ART SCHOOL DANCING
EMI Harvest 5387762 (CD album).
A Harvest label compilation that includes the track 'Our Song' from the album Music From The Body and also Syd Barrett's 'Love You'.

2006
VAN MORRISON AT THE MOVIE - SOUNDTRACKS
UK: EMI 3842242 (CD album).
Includes 'Comfortably Numb' (edit from The Wall Live In Berlin) from the film The Departed.

LIVE PERFORMANCE

THE PROS & CONS OF HITCH HIKING - EUROPEAN TOUR 1984
For his debut solo tour Waters assembled a band that consisted of many of the key players on the album, The Pros And Cons Of Hitch-Hiking, the big surprise being Eric Clapton (reportedly joining the tour against his management's advice). Also included were Mel Collins (saxophones), Michael Kamen (keyboards), Chris Stainton (keyboards and bass), Andy Newmark (drums), Tim Renwick (guitar and bass) and Doreen Chanter and Katie Kissoon (backing vocals).
The first half of the show featured a retrospective of

Waters' best-known Pink Floyd songs, complete with vintage films. The songs were performed well, but had been re-arranged and given an up-tempo feel, which in some cases didn't work at all well. Clapton, although a competent guitarist, was clearly no match for Gilmour's style on these numbers. The second half consisted of the entire The Pros And Cons Of Hitch-Hiking album. The stage production was very similar to Pink Floyd's 'The Wall' shows, using the same three-projector arrangement to project animation and film on to three screens spanning the full width of the back of the stage. To increase the visual depth, the second half of the show featured three gauze screens suspended in front of the projected images. Live-action film by Nicholas Roeg and animation by Gerald Scarfe were projected on to both the gauze and the screens behind them. One screen depicted the motel window; the second a lounge table and the third, a huge TV set. The sets were designed by Mark Fisher and Jonathan Park, who had worked extensively with Pink Floyd, and quadraphonic sound was also used. However, despite its ambition, Waters had underestimated the public response to him as a solo artist and poor attendances and in some cases outright cancellations marred the tour.

Saturday 16 & Sunday 17 June
CONCERTS
Johanneshovs Isstadion, Stockholm, Sweden
Set list at this show and all shows on the tour unless otherwise noted: 'Set The Controls For The Heart Of The Sun' / 'Money' / 'If' / 'Welcome To The Machine' / 'Have A Cigar' / 'Wish You Were Here' / 'Pigs On The Wing, Part 1' / 'In The Flesh' / 'Nobody Home' / 'Hey You' / 'The Gunners Dream' // The Pros And Cons Of Hitch-Hiking / encore: 'Brain Damage' / 'Eclipse'.

Tuesday 19 June
CONCERT
Sportpaleis Ahoy, Rotterdam, The Netherlands

Thursday 21 & Friday 22 June
CONCERTS
Earl's Court Exhibition Hall, Earl's Court, London, England
No encore was performed at the show on 21 June.

Tuesday 26 & Wednesday 27 June
CONCERTS
National Exhibition Centre Arena, Birmingham, England

Friday 29 June
CANCELLED CONCERT
Westfalenhalle, Dortmund, West Germany
Show cancelled due to poor ticket sales.

Sunday 1 July
CANCELLED CONCERT
Messehalle, Frankfurt, West Germany
Show cancelled due to poor ticket sales.

Sunday 1 July
CANCELLED CONCERT
Apollon Auditorium, Parc des Expositions, Nice, France
Show cancelled due to poor ticket sales.

Tuesday 3 July
CONCERT
Hallenstadion, Zurich, Switzerland

Friday 6 July
CONCERT
Palais Omnisports de Paris-Bercy, Paris, France
The last night of the tour.

THE PROS & CONS OF HITCH HIKING - NORTH AMERICAN TOUR 1984

Tuesday 17, Wednesday 18 July
CONCERTS
Hartford Civic Center, Hartford, Connecticut, USA
Set list at these shows and all the shows on the tour unless otherwise noted: 'Set The Controls For The Heart Of The Sun' / 'Money' / 'If' / 'Welcome To The Machine' / 'Have A Cigar' / 'Wish You Were Here' / 'Pigs On The Wing, Part 1' / 'In The Flesh' / 'Nobody Home' / 'Hey You' / 'The Gunners Dream' // *The Pros And Cons Of Hitch Hiking* / encore: 'Brain Damage' / 'Eclipse'.

Monday 20, Tuesday 21 & Wednesday 22 July
CONCERTS
Brendan Byrne Meadowlands Arena, Rutherford, New Jersey, USA

Friday 24 July
CONCERT
Spectrum Theater, Philadelphia, Pennsylvania, USA

Sunday 26 July
CONCERT
Rosemont Horizon, Rosemont, Chicago, Illinois, USA

Tuesday 28 & Wednesday 29 July
CONCERTS
Maple Leaf Gardens, Toronto, Ontario, Canada

Friday 31 July
CONCERT
The Forum, Montréal, Québec, Canada
The last night of the tour.

PROS & CONS PLUS SOME OLD PINK FLOYD STUFF – NORTH AMERICAN TOUR 1985

A second leg of the Pros And Cons Of Hitch-Hiking tour was booked for North America but this time Eric Clapton, Tim Renwick and Chris Stainton didn't participate and were replaced by Andy Fairweather-Low (guitar and bass) and Jay Stapley (guitar).

Tuesday 19 March
CONCERT
Joe Louis Arena, Detroit, Michigan, USA
Set list at this show and all shows on the tour unless otherwise noted: 'Set The Controls For The Heart Of the Sun' / 'Money' / 'If' / 'Welcome To The Machine' / 'Have A Cigar' / 'Wish You Were Here' / 'Pigs On the Wing, Part 1' / 'In The Flesh' / 'Nobody Home' / 'Hey You' / 'The Gunners Dream' // *The Pros And Cons Of Hitch-Hiking* / encore: 'Brain Damage' / 'Eclipse'.

Wednesday 20 March
CONCERT
The Coliseum, Richfield, Cleveland, Ohio, USA

Thursday 21 March
CONCERT
Buffalo Memorial Auditorium, Buffalo, New York, USA

Saturday 23 March
CONCERT
Maple Leaf Gardens, Toronto, Ontario, Canada

Tuesday 26, Wednesday 27 & Thursday 28 March
CONCERTS
Radio City Music Hall, Manhattan, New York City, New York, USA
The show of 28 March was broadcast live on the *Westwood One* radio network across the USA as a live simulcast with holophonic sound and was

later broadcast on BBC Radio 1's *Friday Rock Show* on 29 November 1985 at 10.00pm.

Friday 29 March
CONCERT
Spectrum Theater, Philadelphia, Pennsylvania, USA

Saturday 30 March
CONCERT
The Centrum, Worcester, Massachusetts, USA

Wednesday 3 April
CONCERT
Oakland Coliseum Arena, Oakland, California, USA

Thursday 4 April
CONCERT
The Forum, Inglewood, Los Angeles, California, USA

Saturday 6 April
CONCERT
Veterans Memorial Coliseum, Phoenix, Arizona, USA

Monday 8 April
CONCERT
The Summit Sports Arena, Houston, Texas, USA

Tuesday 9 April
CONCERT
Frank Erwin Center, University of Texas, Austin, Texas, USA

Thursday 11 April
CONCERT
The Omni Coliseum, Atlanta, Georgia, USA

Saturday 13 April
CONCERT
The Sportatorium, Hollywood, Florida, USA

Sunday 14 April
CONCERT
Civic Center Arena, Lakeland, Florida, USA
The last night of the tour.

RADIO KAOS - NORTH AMERICAN TOUR 1987

Waters' tour was launched at almost exactly the same time as his former band mates revived Pink Floyd. As a result, *Radio KAOS* often reached the same town within days of the Pink Floyd road show, although, as the media was at great pains to point out, Waters usually performed to considerably fewer people. For this tour The Bleeding Hearts Band comprised: Andy Fairweather-Low and Jay Stapley (guitars), Paul Carrack (keyboards), Graham Broad (drums),

Mel Collins (saxophone) and Doreen Chanter and Katie Kissoon (backing vocals). Jim Ladd played the part of the radio DJ.

Sponsored by the Canadian beer maker Moosehead, the show was a simpler production than *The Pros And Cons Of Hitch-Hiking*. Again the sets were designed by Fisher-Park, who used a circular screen on to which were back-projected films and animation, including some amusing adverts and sketches. A digital message board conveyed Billy's lines and a further innovation was a telephone booth in the audience with a line to the stage, allowing Waters to take fans' questions. As in Waters' previous shows, quadrophonic sound was also used.

Friday 14 August
CONCERT
Providence Civic Center, Providence, Rhode Island, USA
Set list at this show and all shows on the tour unless otherwise noted: Jim Ladd intro and audience telephone calls / Film advertisement for Club Nowhere / Audience telephone calls to Jim Ladd / 'Tempted' (Paul Carrack solo) / 'Radio Waves' / 'Welcome To The Machine' / 'Who Needs Information' / 'Money' / Film advertisement for The Bimbo School / Medley comprising: 'In The Flesh' – 'Have A Cigar' – 'Pigs (3 Different Ones)' – 'Wish You Were Here' / 'Mother' / 'Molly's Song' / 'Me Or Him' / 'The Powers That Be' // Film advertisement for Moosehead beer / Audience telephone calls to Roger Waters / Film advertisement for the Shredding Alternative / 'Going To Live In LA' / 'Sunset Strip' / Film sketch 'Fish Report With A Beat' / '5:01am (The Pros And Cons Of Hitch-Hiking)' / 'Get Your Filthy Hands Off My Desert' / 'Southampton Dock' / 1967 promotional film of 'Arnold Layne' / 'If' / '5:06am (Every Strangers Eyes)' / 'Not Now John' / 'Another Brick In The Wall, Part 1' / 'The Happiest Days Of Our Lives' / 'Another Brick In The Wall, Part 2' / 'Nobody Home' / 'Home' / 'Four Minutes' / 'The Tide Is Turning' / encore: 'Breathe' / 'Brain Damage' / 'Eclipse'.

Saturday 15 August
CONCERT
Hartford Civic Center, Hartford, Connecticut, USA

Monday 17 August
CONCERT
Kingswood Music Theatre, Toronto, Ontario, Canada

Wednesday 19 August
CONCERT
Blossom Music Center, Cuyahoga Falls, Ohio, USA

Thursday 20 August
CONCERT
Buffalo Memorial Auditorium, Buffalo, New York, USA

Saturday 22 August
CONCERT
Great Woods, Mansfield, Boston, Massachusetts, USA

Monday 24 August
CONCERT
Spectrum Theater, Philadelphia, Pennsylvania, USA

Wednesday 26 August
CONCERT
Madison Square Garden, Manhattan, New York City, New York, USA

Friday 28 August
CONCERT
Saratoga Performing Arts Center, Saratoga Springs, New York, USA

Sunday 30 August
CONCERT
Capitol Music Theatre, Landover, Maryland, USA

Monday 31 August
CANCELLED CONCERT
The Coliseum, Greensboro, North Carolina, USA
Show cancelled for unknown reasons.

Wednesday 2 September
CONCERT
The Omni Coliseum, Atlanta, Georgia, USA

Friday 4 September
CONCERT
Fox Theatre, St Louis, Missouri, USA

Saturday 5 September
CONCERT
Market Square Arena, Indianapolis, Indiana, USA

Sunday 6 September
CONCERT
Ohio Center, Columbus, Ohio, USA

Tuesday 8 September
CONCERT
Pine Knob Music Theatre, Clarkston, Michigan, USA

Wednesday 9 September
CONCERT
Poplar Creek Music Theater, Hoffman Estates, Chicago, Illinois, USA

Thursday 10 September
CONCERT
Metropolitan Center, Minneapolis, Minneapolis, USA

Saturday 12 September
CONCERT
McNichols Sports Arena, Denver, Colorado, USA

Monday 14 September
CONCERT
Frank Erwin Center, University of Texas, Austin, Texas, USA

Tuesday 15 September
CONCERT
Reunion Arena, Reunion Park, Dallas, Texas, USA

Thursday 17 September
CONCERT
Veterans Memorial Coliseum, Phoenix, Arizona, USA

Sunday 20 September
CONCERT
The Forum, Inglewood, Los Angeles, California, USA
Set list included an additional encore of 'Outside The Wall' with *The Wall* show backing vocalists John Joyce, Jim Haas and Joe Chemay.

Wednesday 23 September
CONCERT
Sports Arena, San Diego, California, USA

Saturday 26 September
CONCERT
Oakland Coliseum Arena, Oakland, California, USA

Monday 28 September
CONCERT
Seattle Center Arena, Seattle, Washington, USA

Tuesday 29 September
CONCERT
Expo Theatre, Vancouver, British Columbia, Canada
The last night of the tour.

RADIO KAOS - CANCELLED FAR EAST TOUR 1987

A tour of Australia and Japan was scheduled for October 1987 but was cancelled, reportedly due to poor ticket sales, including the following dates: NBC Arena, Honolulu, Hawaii, USA (3 October); Festival Hall, Brisbane, Australia (9 October 1987); Entertainment Centre, Melbourne, Australia (15 October); Entertainment Centre, Sydney, Australia (20 October); Entertainment Centre, Perth, Australia (24 October); Osaka, Japan (27 October); NHK Hall, Tokyo, Japan (28 & 29 October).

Waters and his colleagues spent the time working on a new album at the Compass Point recording studios in the Bahamas. The tour resumed in November with the same cast and set list.

RADIO KAOS - NORTH AMERICAN TOUR 1987

Set list at this show and all shows on the tour unless otherwise noted: Jim Ladd intro and audience telephone calls / Film advertisement for Club Nowhere / Audience telephone calls to Jim Ladd / 'Tempted' (Paul Carrack solo) / 'Radio Waves' / 'Welcome To The Machine' / 'Who Needs Information' / 'Money' / Film advertisement for The Bimbo School / Medley comprising: 'In The Flesh' – 'Have A Cigar' – 'Pigs (3 Different Ones)' – 'Wish You Were Here' / 'Mother' / 'Molly's Song' / 'Me Or Him' / 'The Powers That Be' // Film advertisement for Moosehead beer / Audience telephone calls to Roger Waters / Film advertisement for the Shredding Alternative / 'Going To Live In LA' / 'Sunset Strip' / Film sketch: 'Fish Report With A Beat' / '5.01am (The Pros And Cons Of Hitch-Hiking)' / 'Get Your Filthy Hands Off My Desert' / 'Southampton Dock' / 1967 promotional film of 'Arnold Layne' / 'If' / '5:06am (Every Strangers Eyes)' / 'Not Now John' / 'Another Brick In The Wall, Part 1' / 'The Happiest Days Of Our Lives' / 'Another Brick In The Wall, Part 2' / 'Nobody Home' / 'Home' / 'Four Minutes' / 'The Tide Is Turning' / encore: 'Breathe' / 'Brain Damage' / 'Eclipse'.

Tuesday 3 November
CONCERT
Cumberland County Convention Center, Portland, Maine, USA
This show was reportedly broadcast live via satellite to French radio.

Wednesday 4 November
CONCERT
Brendan Byrne Meadowlands Arena, East Rutherford, New Jersey, USA

Friday 6 November
CONCERT
The Forum, Montréal, Québec, Canada

Saturday 7 November
CONCERT
Colisee de Québec, Québec City, Québec, Canada
This show was recorded by the Westwood One radio network *In Concert* series and the following tracks were broadcast in the USA on 23 November 1987: 'Radio Waves' / 'Welcome To The Machine' / 'Money' / 'In The Flesh' / 'Have A Cigar' / 'Pigs (3 Different Ones)' / 'Wish You Were Here' / 'Mother' / 'Get Your Filthy Hands Off My Dessert' / 'Southampton Dock' / 'If' / 'The Powers That Be' / 'Brain Damage' / 'Eclipse' / 'Another Brick In The Wall, Part 1' / 'The Happiest Days Of Our Lives' / 'Another Brick In The Wall, Part 2'.

RIGHT: ROGER WATERS ON STAGE AT WEMBLEY ARENA, 21 NOVEMBER 1987.

Monday 9 November
CONCERT
The Civic Center, Ottawa, Ontario, Canada

Tuesday 10 November
CONCERT
Copps Coliseum, Hamilton, Ontario, Canada

Friday 13 November
CONCERT
Milwaukee Expo & Convention Centre & Arena, Milwaukee, Wisconsin, USA

Saturday 14 November
CONCERT
Arie Crown Theater, Chicago, Illinois, USA

Monday 16 November
CONCERT
The Centrum, Worcester, Massachusetts, USA
The last night of the tour.

RADIO KAOS – UK SHOWS 1987

Saturday 21 & Sunday 22 November
CONCERTS
Wembley Arena, Wembley, England
The show of 22 November was the last night of the tour.
Set list at both shows: Jim Ladd intro and audience telephone calls / Film advertisement for Club Nowhere / Audience telephone calls to Jim Ladd / 'Tempted' (Paul Carrack solo) / 'Radio Waves' / 'Welcome To The Machine' / 'Who Needs Information' / 'Money' / Film advertisement for The Bimbo School / Medley comprising: 'In The Flesh' – 'Have A Cigar' – 'Pigs (3 Different Ones)' – 'Wish You Were Here' / 'Mother' / 'Molly's Song' / 'Me Or Him' / 'The Powers That Be' // Film advertisement for Moosehead beer / Audience telephone calls to Roger Waters / Film advertisement for the Shredding Alternative / 'Going To Live In L.A.' / 'Sunset Strip' / Film sketch: 'Fish Report With A Beat' / '5:01am (The Pros And Cons

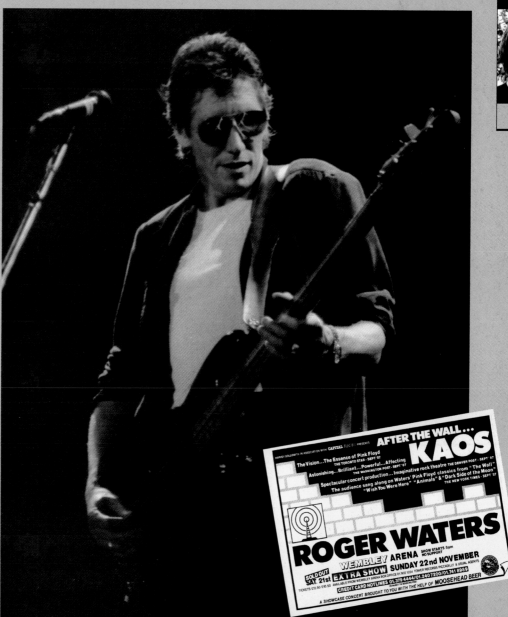

Of Hitch-Hiking)' / 'Get Your Filthy Hands Off My Desert' / 'Southampton Dock' / 1967 promotional film of 'Arnold Layne' / 'If' / '5:06am (Every Strangers Eyes)' / 'Not Now John' / 'Another Brick In The Wall, Part 1' / 'The Happiest Days Of Our Lives' / 'Another Brick In The Wall, Part 2' / 'Nobody Home' / 'Home' / 'Four Minutes' / 'The Tide Is Turning' / encore: 'Breathe' / 'Brain Damage' / 'Eclipse'.

Waters invited *Dark Side Of The Moon* vocalist Clare Torry to sing on 'The Great Gig In The Sky' on both nights. However, he was unsuccessful in his efforts to get the Pontardoulais Male Voice Choir to perform on stage at this and his earlier show at New York's Madison Square Gardens.

The first Wembley show was recorded and edited to make a 71-minute presentation for London's Capital Radio and broadcast on 17 April 1988. The tracks broadcast were: 'Radio Waves' / 'Welcome To The Machine' / 'Who Needs Information' / 'The Powers That Be' / 'Sunset Strip' / 'If' / 'Every Strangers Eyes' / 'Nobody Home' / 'Home' / 'Four Minutes' / 'The Tide Is Turning'.

THE WALL- LIVE IN BERLIN 1990

Possibly the most ambitious outdoor concert event ever staged and at the suggestion of rock merchandiser Mick Worwood, Waters agreed to perform a one-off production of *The Wall* in order to raise money for the Memorial Fund For Disaster Relief, a charity dedicated to raising five pounds (UK Sterling) for every life lost in the Second World War, for the relief of natural world catastrophes. It was founded by Leonard Cheshire VC OM DSO DFC, the highly decorated Second World War airman who devoted his post-war life to charitable organisations. There was much talk of staging the concert in other prime locations, but the collapse of the Communist Bloc made the former East Berlin an appropriate location. A 25 acre site formerly occupying the no man's land between East and West was cleared, in order to stage the show. As well as harbouring a vast amount of unexploded armaments from the War, the land had also contained Hitler's bunker. In this climate of unaccustomed reconciliation it took at least six months to establish which of the governments could give authority to stage the event.

The production, designed by Fisher-Park, incorporated a wall 82 feet high by 591 feet across, with a stage wide enough and strong enough to carry a marching band, military trucks and trailers, motorbikes and limousines as well as all the necessary mechanisms and scenery. Rehearsals began in Berlin two weeks before the show and there was a final dress rehearsal the night before. It was fortunate that this was filmed, because on the night of the show so many satellite TV stations were linked to the site that power failures occurred repeatedly throughout the performance. For this reason, many scenes were re-shot for the benefit of the video after the crowds had dispersed at the end of the concert.

An international array of guest musicians complemented Waters on stage, although his own Bleeding Hearts Band formed the core of his musical support: Graham Broad (drums), Snowy White and Rick Di Fonzo (guitars), Andy Fairweather-Low (guitar and bass), Nick Glennie-Smith and Peter Wood (keyboards), Joe Chemay, Jim Haas, Jim Farber and John Joyce (backing vocals).

Leonard Cheshire officially opened the show with the sounding of a First World War whistle.

Saturday 21 July 1990
CONCERT
The Wall - Live In Berlin, Potzdamer Platz, Berlin, Germany

Set list (with featured artist): 'In The Flesh' (The Scorpions) / 'The Thin Ice' (Ute Lemper as The Wife) / 'Another Brick In The Wall, Part 1 '(Garth Hudson, saxophone solo) / 'The Happiest Days Of Our Lives' (Joe Chemay, John Joyce, Jim Farber, Jim Haas, vocals) / 'Another Brick In The Wall, Part 2' (Cyndi Lauper, vocals; Rick Di Fonzo and Snowy White, guitars; Peter Wood, keyboards; Thomas Dolby as The Teacher) / 'Mother' (Sinead O'Connor, vocals with The Band) / 'Goodbye Blue Sky' (Joni Mitchell, vocals; James Galway, flute) / 'Empty Spaces' (Bryan Adams, vocals and guitar) / Young Lust (Bryan Adams, vocals and guitar) / 'One Of My Turns' (Jerry Hall as The Groupie) / 'Another Brick In The Wall, Part 3' / 'Goodbye Cruel World' // 'Hey You' (Paul Carrack, vocals) / 'Is There Anybody Out There?' (Snowy White and Rick Di Fonzo, classical guitars; Berliner Rundfunk Orchestra & Choir) / 'Nobody Home' (Snowy White, guitar) / 'Vera' (Berliner Rundfunk Orchestra & Choir) / 'Bring The Boys Back Home' (Berliner Rundfunk Orchestra & Choir) / 'Comfortably Numb '(Van Morrison, vocals; The Band; Rick Di Fonzo and Snowy White, guitar solos) / 'In The Flesh?' (Berliner Rundfunk Orchestra & Choir; Military Orchestra Of The Soviet Army (both to the end of the show) / 'Run Like Hell' / 'Waiting For The Worms' / 'Stop' / 'The Trial' (Tim Curry as The Prosecutor; Thomas Dolby as The Teacher; Ute Lemper as The Wife; Marianne Faithfull as The Mother; Albert Finney as The Judge) // encore: 'The Tide Is Turning' (all).

The estimated audience of over 250,000 (many of whom entered free after the collapse of the perimeter fence) must make it one of the biggest single concert attendances ever. But despite the sale of worldwide TV rights and the royalties later realised from the album and video sales, the production costs had spiralled out of control to such an extent that, by May 1992, only an estimated £100,000 had been raised for the Memorial Fund For Disaster Relief - a figure far short of the original target.

The renowned London auction house Christie's staged a dedicated sale, in aid of the Memorial Fund For Disaster Relief, of the stage props and costumes used by the Roger Waters production of his Berlin Wall concert on 21 September 1990. Also on sale, and viewed with interest by Gerald Scarfe, was a large quantity of animation cells from the original 1982 film.

ROGER WATERS IN THE FLESH - NORTH AMERICAN TOUR 1999

Roger Waters' tour of 1999 was a far more successful venture than previous tours and seemed at last to have found his own core audience and indeed many of the venues had to be scaled up to larger capacities. Roger's band for this tour comprised: Andy Fairweather-Low (guitars), Doyle Bramhall II (guitar/vocals), Snowy White (guitars), Graham Broad (drums), Jon Carin and Andy Wallace (keyboards), Katie Kissoon and PP Arnold (backing vocals).

Friday 23 July
CONCERT
Bruce Hall, Milwaukee Auditorium, Milwaukee, Wisconsin, USA

Set list at this show and all shows on the tour unless otherwise noted: 'In The Flesh' / 'The Thin Ice' / 'Another Brick In The Wall, Part 1' / 'Mother' / 'Get Your Filthy Hands Off My Desert' / 'Southampton Dock' / 'Pigs On The Wing, Part 1' / 'Dogs' / 'Welcome To The Machine' / 'Wish You Were Here' / 'Shine On You Crazy Diamond, Parts 1-4, 6, 7 & 1 (reprise)' // 'Breathe' / 'The Great Gig In The Sky' (keyboard introduction only) / 'Money' / '5:06am (Every Strangers Eyes)' / 'The Powers That Be' / 'What God Wants, Part 1' / 'Perfect Sense, Part 1' / 'Perfect Sense, Part 2' / 'It's A Miracle' / 'Amused To Death' / 'The Happiest Days Of Our Lives' / 'Another Brick In The Wall, Part 2' // encore: 'Brain Damage' / 'Eclipse' / 'Comfortably Numb'.

Saturday 24 July
CONCERT
Rosemont Theatre, Rosemont, Chicago, Illinois, USA

Sunday 25 July
CONCERT
New Pine Knob Music Theatre, Clarkston, Michigan, USA

Tuesday 27 July
CONCERT
Gund Arena, Cleveland, Ohio, USA
Show rescheduled from Nautica Stage, Cleveland, Ohio.

Friday 30 July
CONCERT
Agora du Vieux, Port de Québec, Québec City, Québec, Canada

Saturday 31 July
CONCERT
Molson Centre, Montréal, Québec, Canada
Set list at this show and all shows on the tour unless otherwise noted: 'In The Flesh' / 'The Thin Ice' / 'Another Brick In The Wall, Part 1' / 'The Happiest Days Of Our Lives' / 'Another Brick In The Wall, Part 2' / 'Mother' / 'Get Your Filthy Hands Off My Desert' / 'Southampton Dock' / 'Pigs On The Wing, Part 1' / 'Dogs' / 'Welcome To The Machine' / 'Wish You Were Here' / 'Shine On You Crazy Diamond, Parts 1-4, 6, 7 & 1 (reprise)' // 'Breathe' / 'The Great Gig In The Sky' (keyboard introduction only) / 'Money' / '5.06am (Every Strangers Eyes)' / 'The Powers That Be' / 'What God Wants, Part 1' / 'Perfect Sense, Part 1' / 'Perfect Sense, Part 2' / 'It's A Miracle' / 'Amused To Death' / encore: 'Brain Damage' / 'Eclipse' / 'Comfortably Numb'.

Sunday 1 August
CONCERT
Molson Amphitheatre, Toronto, Ontario, Canada

Wednesday 4 August
CONCERT
Tweeter Performing Arts Center, Mansfield, Boston, Massachusetts, USA

Friday 6 August
CONCERT
Garden State Arts Center Amphitheatre, Holmdel, New Jersey, USA

Saturday 7 August
CONCERT
Jones Beach Theatre, Wantagh, Long Island, New York, USA

Sunday 8 August
CONCERT
SNET Oakdale Theatre, Wallingford, Connecticut, USA

Tuesday 10 August
CONCERT
Pepsi Arena, Albany, New York, USA
Show rescheduled from Landmark Theatre, Syracuse, New York on 28 July.

Wednesday 11 August
CONCERT
Blockbuster-Sony Music Entertainment Center, Camden, New Jersey, USA

Friday 13 August
CONCERT
Montage Mountain Performing Arts Center, Scranton, Pennsylvania, USA
Heavy thunderstorms and rain forced a two-hour

break in the show during 'Another Brick In The Wall, Part 1'. The show resumed thereafter starting with 'Another Brick In The Wall, Part 1'.

Saturday 14 August
CONCERT
Darien Lake Performing Arts Center, Six Flags Theme Park, Darien Lake, New York, USA

Sunday 15 August
CONCERT
Jerome Schottenstein Center, Ohio State University, Columbus, Ohio, USA
Show rescheduled from Franklin County Veterans Memorial Auditorium, Columbus, Ohio.

Tuesday 17 August
CONCERT
Hershey Star Pavilion, Hershey, Pennsylvania, USA

Wednesday 18 August
CONCERT
Star Lake Amphitheatre, Burgettstown, Pittsburg, Pennsylvania, USA
Show rescheduled from IC Light Amphitheatre & Tent Stadium, Pittsburgh, Pennsylvania.

Friday 20 August
CONCERT
Baltimore Arena, Baltimore, Maryland, USA
Show rescheduled from Pier Six Concert Pavilion, Baltimore, Maryland.

Sunday 22 August
CONCERT
Lakewood Amphitheatre, Atlanta, Georgia, USA
Show rescheduled from Chastain Park Amphitheatre, Atlanta, Georgia.
Richard Wright and members of his family attended the show.

Tuesday 24 August
CONCERT
Deer Creek Music Center, Noblesville, Indianapolis, Indiana, USA

Wednesday 25 August
CONCERT
Van Andel Arena, Grand Rapids, Michigan, USA

Friday 27 August
CONCERT
Riverport Amphitheatre, Maryland Heights, St. Louis, Missouri, USA

Saturday 28 August
CONCERT
Kemper Arena, Kansas City, Missouri, USA
The last night of the tour.

Roger Waters performed a new song entitled 'Each Small Candle' as a second encore.

ROGER WATERS IN THE FLESH - NORTH AMERICAN TOUR 2000
Roger's band for this tour comprised: Andy Fairweather-Low (guitar, bass guitar, and vocals), Doyle Bramhall II (guitar, vocals), Snowy White (guitar, vocals), Graham Broad (drums), Jon Carin (keyboards, vocals), Andy Wallace (keyboards), Katie Kissoon and Susannah Melvoin (backing vocals). In addition, a different saxophone player joined the band on stage each night as follows: Mike MacArthur (2 June); Ed Calle (3 June); Wayne Jackson - trumpet and Andrew Love – saxophone (6 June); Tim Gordon (7 June); Shelley Carroll (10, 11 and 13 June); Don Menza (16, 17 & 19 June); Steve Tavaglione (21, 22 & 23 June); Norbert Stachel (25 & 27 June); Eric Walton (30 June & 1 July); Mark Harris (3 July); Steve Eisen (6 July); Mel Collins (8, 9, 11, 13, 15 & 16 July).
The shows at Phoenix, Las Vegas, Los Angeles and Portland were filmed and recorded for the *Roger Waters In The Flesh* live CD and DVD. Veteran broadcaster Jim Ladd made appropriate introductions at each of these shows to alert the fans to this fact.

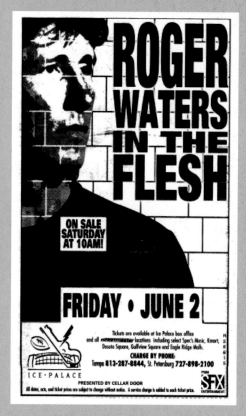

Friday 2 June
CONCERT
The Ice Palace, Tampa, Florida, USA
Set list at this show and all shows on the tour unless

otherwise noted: 'In The Flesh' / 'The Happiest Days Of Our Lives' / 'Another Brick In The Wall, Part 2' / 'Mother' / 'Get Your Filthy Hands Off My Desert' / 'Southampton Dock' / 'Pigs On The Wing, Part 1' / 'Dogs' / 'Welcome To The Machine' / 'Wish You Were Here' / 'Shine On You Crazy Diamond Parts 1-4, 6 & 7' // 'Set The Controls For The Heart Of The Sun' / 'Breathe' / 'Time' / 'Breathe (reprise)' / 'Money' / '5:06am (Every Strangers Eyes)' / 'What God Wants, Part 1' / 'Perfect Sense, Part 1' / 'Perfect Sense, Part 2' / 'The Bravery Of Being Out Of Range' / 'It's A Miracle' / 'Amused To Death' / 'Brain Damage' / 'Eclipse' // encore: 'Comfortably Numb' / 'Each Small Candle'.

Saturday 3 June
CONCERT
Mars Music Amphitheatre, South Florida Fairgrounds, West Palm Beach, Florida, USA
'What God Wants, Part 1' was dropped from the set at all subsequent shows.

Tuesday 6 June
CONCERT
AmSouth Amphitheatre, Antioch, Nashville, Tennessee, USA

Wednesday 7 June
CONCERT
Blockbuster Pavilion, Charlotte, North Carolina, USA

Thursday 8 June
CANCELLED CONCERT
New Orleans Arena, New Orleans, Louisiana, USA
For unknown reasons the show was cancelled before tickets were put on sale.

Saturday 10 June
CONCERT
Cynthia Woods Mitchell Pavilion, Woodlands, Houston, Texas, USA

Sunday 11 June
CONCERT
Starplex Amphitheatre, Dallas, Texas, USA

Tuesday 13 June
CONCERT
Alamodome, San Antonio, Texas, USA

Friday 16 June
CONCERT
America West Arena, Phoenix, Arizona, USA
This show was recorded for the *Roger Waters In The Flesh* live album.

Saturday 17 June
CONCERT
Grand Garden Arena, MGM Grand Casino, Las Vegas, Nevada, USA
This show was recorded for the *Roger Waters In The Flesh* live album.

Monday 19 Jun
CONCERT
Coors Amphitheatre, Chula Vista, San Diego, California, USA

Wednesday 21 & Thursday 22 June
CONCERTS
Universal Amphitheater, Universal City, Los Angeles, California, USA

Saturday 24 June
CONCERT
Irvine Meadows Amphitheater, Irvine, Los Angeles, California, USA
This show was recorded for the *Roger Waters In The Flesh* live album.

Sunday 25 June
CONCERT
Shoreline Amphitheater, Mountain View, near San Francisco, California, USA

Tuesday 27 June
CONCERT
Rose Garden Arena, Rose Quarter, Portland, Oregon, USA
This show was recorded for the *Roger Waters In The Flesh* live album.

Friday 30 June
CONCERT
The Gorge Amphitheater, George, Washington, USA
The show commenced with Roger Waters' private jet buzzing the audience at about 800 feet creating a spectacular introduction to 'In The Flesh'.

Saturday 1 July
CONCERT
Idaho Centre Arena, Nampa, Idaho, USA

Monday 3 July
CONCERT
Fiddlers Green Amphitheater, Englewood, Denver, Colorado, USA

Thursday 6 July
CONCERT
Target Center, Minneapolis, Minnesota, USA

Saturday 8 July
CONCERT
New World Music Theatre, Tinley Park, Chicago, Illinois, USA

Sunday 9 July
CONCERT
Pavilion Lawn, The Riverbend Music Center, Cincinnati, Ohio, USA

Tuesday 11 & Thursday 13 July
CONCERTS
Madison Square Garden, Manhattan, New York City, New York, USA

Saturday 15 July
CONCERT
Nissan Pavilion, Stone Ridge, Bristow, Virginia, USA

Sunday 16 July
CONCERT
Civic Center, Providence, Rhode Island, USA
The last night of the tour. This show was rescheduled from 11 July to make way for an additional New York show on the same date. This in turn forced a cancellation at Walnut Creek, Raleigh, North Carolina on 16 July.

ROGER WATERS IN THE FLESH - WORLD TOUR 2002

Waters most ambitious and successful tour to date saw him take his show to many new and unusual territories across the world. The tour, announced in person at a press conference at EMI Abbey Road Studios on 19 October 2001, was critically acclaimed by the media and fans alike and brought together some of his stronger solo material, some newly written as well as vintage Pink Floyd that was performed faithfully to the original recordings. Roger's band for this tour comprised: Andy Fairweather-Low (guitar, bass guitar and vocals), Snowy White (guitar, vocals), Chester Kamen (bass guitar, vocals), Harry Waters and Andy Wallace (keyboards), Graham Broad (drums), Norbert Stachel (saxophone, penny whistle), Katie Kissoon (backing vocals), PP Arnold (backing vocals), Linda Lewis (backing vocals).

Wednesday 27 February
CONCERT
Bellville Velodrome, Capetown, South Africa
Set list at this show and all shows on the tour unless otherwise noted: 'In The Flesh' / 'The Happiest Days Of Our Lives' / 'Another Brick In The Wall, Part 2' / 'Mother' / 'Get Your Filthy Hands Off My Desert' / 'Southampton Dock' / 'Pigs On The Wing, Part 1' / 'Dogs' / 'Shine On You Crazy Diamond, Parts 1-5' / 'Welcome To The Machine' / 'Wish You Were Here' / 'Shine On You Crazy Diamond, Parts 6-9' // 'Set The

Controls For The Heart Of The Sun' / 'Breathe' / 'Time' / 'Money' / '5:06am (Every Strangers Eyes)' / 'Perfect Sense, Part 1' / 'Perfect Sense, Part 2' / 'The Bravery Of Being Out Of Range' / 'It's A Miracle' / 'Amused To Death' / 'Brain Damage' / 'Eclipse' / 'Comfortably Numb' / encore: 'Flickering Flame'.

Friday 1 March
CONCERT
MTN Sun Dome, Northgate, Johannesburg, South Africa
Set list as 27 February except encore: 'Each Small Candle'.

Tuesday 5 March
CONCERT
Estadio Nacional, Santiago, Chile
Set list as 27 February except encore: 'Each Small Candle'.

Thursday 7 March
CONCERT
Estadio Velez Sarsfield, Buenos Aires, Argentina
Set list as 27 February except encore: 'Each Small Candle'.

Saturday 9 March
CONCERT
Sambódromo Carnaval, Praça da Apoteose, Rio de Janeiro, Brazil
Set list as 27 February except encore: 'Each Small Candle'. Roger Waters appeared as part of a season of events at this venue.

Tuesday 12 March
CONCERT
Estádio Olímpico, Porto Alegre, Brazil
Set list as 27 February except encore 15 March: 'Each Small Candle'.

Thursday 14 & Friday 15 March
CONCERTS
Estádio Do Pacaembu, São Paulo, Brazil
Set list as 27 February except encore 15 March: 'Each Small Candle'.

Sunday 17 March
CONCERT
Caracas Pop Festival, Valle Del Pop, Caracas, Venezuela
Set list as 27 February except encore: 'Each Small Candle' and 'Flickering Flame'. Roger Waters appeared as part of a season of events at this venue.

Tuesday 19 March
CONCERT
Foro Sol, Mexico City, Mexico

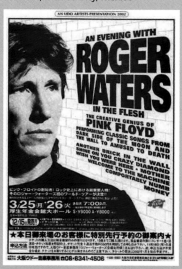

Monday 25 & Tuesday 26 March
CONCERTS
Kosei Nenkin Kaikan, Osaka, Japan

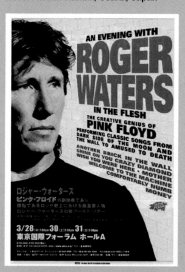

Thursday 28, Friday 30 & Saturday 31 March
CONCERTS
Hall A, Tokyo International Forum, Chiyoda-Ku, Tokyo, Japan

Tuesday 2 April
CONCERT
Chamsil Sports Field, Seoul, South Korea

Friday 5 & Saturday 6 April
CONCERTS
Newcastle Entertainment Centre, Newcastle Showgrounds, Sydney, New South Wales, Australia

Monday 8 April
CONCERT
Rod Laver Arena, Melbourne, Victoria, Australia

Wednesday 10 April
CONCERT
Impact Arena, Bangkok, Thailand

Saturday 13 April
CONCERT
Palace Grounds, Bangalore, India
Show rescheduled from 14 April. This also replaced a scheduled show at New Standard Engineering Grounds, Mumbai, India on 12 April.

Monday 15 April
CONCERT
Creek Golf and Yacht Club, Dubai Festival City, Dubai, United Arab Emirates

Wednesday 17 April
CONCERT
Beirut International Exhibition and Leisure Center, Beirut, Lebanon
The last night of the tour.

ROGER WATERS IN THE FLESH - EUROPEAN TOUR 2002

Saturday 4 & Sunday 5 May
CONCERTS
Sala Atlântico, Pavilhão Atlântico, Lisbon, Portugal
Set list at this show and all shows on the tour unless otherwise noted: 'In The Flesh' / 'The Happiest Days Of Our Lives' / 'Another Brick In The Wall, Part 2' / 'Mother' / 'Get Your Filthy Hands Off My Desert' / 'Southampton Dock' / 'Pigs On The Wing, Part 1' / 'Dogs' / 'Set The Controls For The Heart Of The Sun' / 'Shine On You Crazy Diamond, Parts 1-5' / 'Welcome To The Machine' / 'Wish You Were Here' / 'Shine On You Crazy Diamond, Parts 6-9' // 'Breathe' / 'Time' / 'Money' / '5:06am (Every Stranger's Eyes)' / 'Perfect Sense, Part 1' / 'Perfect Sense, Part 2' / 'The Bravery Of Being Out Of Range' / 'It's A Miracle' / 'Amused To Death' / 'Brain Damage' / 'Eclipse' / 'Comfortably Numb' / encore on 4 May and all shows onward: 'Flickering Flame', except encore on 5 May,

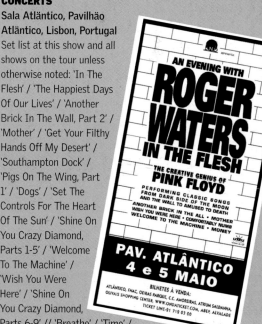

'Each Small Candle'.
Carol Kenyon replaced Linda Lewis as backing vocalist from this show onward.

Wednesday 8 May
CONCERT
Estádio Olímpico Palau Sant Jordi, Parque Monjuic, Barcelona, Spain

Friday 10 May
CONCERT
Fila Forum, Assago, Milan, Italy

Saturday 11 May
CONCERT
Hallenstadion, Zurich, Switzerland

Monday 13 May
CONCERT
Sportpaleis, Antwerp, Belgium

Wednesday 15 May
CONCERT
Sportpaleis Ahoy, Rotterdam, The Netherlands

Friday 17 May
CONCERT
Messe Halle, Erfurt, Germany

Saturday 18 May
CONCERT
Kölnarena, Cologne, Germany

Tuesday 20 May
CONCERT
Arena, Oberhausen, Germany

Wednesday 22 May
CONCERT
Preussag Arena, Hannover, Germany

Friday 24 May
CONCERT
Spektrum, Oslo, Norway

Saturday 25 May
CONCERT
Globe Arena, Stockholm, Sweden

Monday 27 May
CONCERT
New Arena, St. Petersburg, Russia

Wednesday 29 May
CONCERT
Olimpiski Arena, Moscow, Russia

Friday 31 May
CONCERT
Hartwall Arena, Helsinki, Finland

Sunday 2 June
CONCERT
Forum København, Copenhagen, Denmark

Tuesday 4 June
CONCERT
Olympiahalle, Munich, Germany

Wednesday 5 June
CONCERT
Festhalle, Frankfurt, Germany

Friday 7 June
CONCERT
Stadion Gwardii, Warsaw, Poland

Sunday 9 June
CONCERT
Velodrome, Berlin, Germany

Monday 10 June
CONCERT
Paegas Aréna, Prague, Czech Republic

Wednesday 12 June
CONCERT
Stadio Flamino, Rome, Italy
Show rescheduled from Curva Olympia, Rome, Italy.

Friday 14 June
CONCERT
Zipfer Zone, Festivalgelände, Wiesen, Austria

Saturday 15 June
CONCERT
Kisstadion, Budapest, Hungary

Monday 17 June
CONCERT
Schleyer-Halle, Stuttgart, Germany

Wednesday 19 June
CONCERT
Palais Omnisports de Paris-Bercy, Paris, France

Friday 21 June
CONCERT
National Exhibition Centre Arena, Birmingham, England

Saturday 22 June
CONCERT
Manchester Evening News Arena, Manchester, England

Monday 24 June
CONCERT
The Point, Dublin, Republic of Ireland

Wednesday 26 & Thursday 27 June
CONCERTS
Wembley Arena, Wembley, England
Nick Mason played drums on 'Set The Controls For The Heart Of The Sun' at both shows.

Saturday 29 June
CONCERT
Glastonbury Festival of Performing Arts, Pyramid Stage, Worthy Farm, Pilton, England
The final date of the tour was performed in front of some 70,000 festival-goers on the second day of Europe's largest performing arts event (28–30 June). Edited highlights were also screened on BBC2 TV on 29 June 2002.
Set list: 'In The Flesh' / 'The Happiest Days Of Our Lives' / 'Another Brick In The Wall, Part 2' / 'Mother' / 'Pigs On The Wing, Part 1' / 'Dogs' / 'Shine On You Crazy Diamond, Parts 1-5' / 'Wish You Were Here' / 'Shine On You Crazy Diamond, Parts 6-9' / 'Breathe' / 'Time' / 'Money' / 'Perfect Sense, Part 1' / 'Perfect Sense, Part 2' / 'It's A Miracle' / 'Amused To Death' / 'Brain Damage' / 'Eclipse' / 'Comfortably Numb' // encore: 'Flickering Flame'.

ÇA IRA LIVE PERFORMANCES

Wednesday 16 October 2002
CONCERT
Whip Craic, Royal Albert Hall, Kensington, London, England
The Royal Philharmonic Concert Orchestra, opening for Roger Waters' set at this concert, performed the 'Ça Ira Overture' live. (See concert listings for full show information.)

Saturday 1 May 2004
PLAYBACK CONCERT
Fort St. Angelo, Grand Harbour, Valetta, Malta
Recorded extracts from the opera were played back during the official celebrations to mark Malta's accession to the European Union accompanied by a huge lightshow and fireworks display. Titles included 'Ça Ira Overture', 'The Taking Of Bastille' and 'Silver, Sugar And Indigo' and mixed into one continuous piece of music by Gert Hoff.

Saturday 7 August 2004
CONCERT
Bridgehampton Chamber Music Festival, Bridgehampton Presbyterian Church, Bridgehampton, New York, USA
The Bridgehampton Chamber Orchestra performed 'Ça Ira Overture (The Gathering Storm)', 'The Letter' and 'Bastille' at this classical music event with music

arranged for Chamber Ensemble by Robert Sadin.

Monday 25 July 2005
PRESS RECEPTION
Florence Gould Hall, Manhattan, New York City,
New York, USA
Sony Music hosted a press reception during which a
video presentation of the opera was shown followed
by a question and answer session with Roger Waters.
Guests were also given an 8-track promotional CD of
the work in progress (see discography for further
information).

Thursday 17 & Friday 18 November 2005
CONCERTS
Sala Santa Cecilia, Auditorium Parco della Musica,
Rome, Italy
The live premiere of the *Ça Ira* opera, which Roger
Waters introduced. Rick Wentworth conducted 100
members of the Rome Symphony Orchestra, along
with an 80-strong choir that included many children.
Featured performers included tenor Paul Groves,
soprano Ying Huang and bass-baritone John Relyea.
A=Act, S=Scene. Set List: 'The Gathering Storm' /
'Overture' / A1S1: 'Garden In Vienna 1765' / A1S1:
'Madame Antoine' / A1S2: 'Kings, Sticks And Birds' /
A1S2: 'Honest Bird, Simple Bird' / A1S2: 'I Want To
Be King' / A1S2: 'Let Us Break All The Shields' /
A1S3: 'Grievances Of The People' / A1S4: 'France In
Disarray' / A1S4: 'To Laugh Is To Know How To Live'
/ A1S4: 'Slavers, Landlords, Bigots At Your Door' /
A1S5: 'Fall Of The Bastille' / A1S5: 'To Freeze In The
Dead Of Night' / A1S5: 'So To The Streets In The
Pouring Rain' / A2S1: 'Dances And Marches' / A2S1:
'Now Hear Ye' / A2S1: 'Flushed With Wine' / A2S2:
'The Letter' / A2S2: 'My Dear Cousin Bourbon Of
Spain' / A2S2: 'The Ship Of State Is All At Sea' /
A2S3: 'Silver, Sugar And Indigo' / A2S3: 'To The
Windward Isles' / A2S4: 'Papal Edict' / A2S4: 'In
Paris There's A Rumble Under The Ground' // A3S1:
'The Fugitive King' / A3S1: 'But The Marquis Of Boulli
Has A Trump Card Up His Sleeve' / A3S1: 'To Take
Your Hat Off' / A3S1: 'The Echoes Never Fade From
That Fusillade' / A3S2: 'Commune De Paris' / A3S2:
'Vive La Commune De Paris' / A3S2: 'The National
Assembly Is Confused' / A3S3: 'The Execution Of
Louis Capet' / A3S3: 'Adieu Louis, For You It's Over' /
A3S4: 'Marie Antoinette – The Last Night On Earth' /
A3S4: 'Adieu My Good And Tender Sister' / A3S5:
'Liberty' / A3S5: 'And In The Bushes Where They
Survive'.

Friday 25 August 2006
CONCERT
Międzynarodowe Targi Poznańskie [Poznań
International Fair Grounds], Poznań, Poland
Set list same as the shows in Rome, above. Show
moved from 6 & 7 July 2006 due to Waters' solo
tour commitments. This was a massive production,

featuring a large cast of costumed performers, sets
and props. Choirs sang on the surrounding terraces
and pavilions and projectors illuminated the
surrounding buildings and an abundance of
pyrotechnics highlighted key moments. A further
string of similar productions in other locations were
to be announced at the time of writing. A special
Polish edition *Ça Ira* CD was also made available for
sale at the concert.

**ROGER WATERS – EUROPEAN
SUMMER FESTIVAL TOUR 2006**
Roger's band for his European and US tours
comprised: Graham Broad (drums), Jon Carin
(keyboards), Andy Fairweather-Low (guitar, bass
guitar and vocals), Dave Kilminster (guitar, vocals),
Ian Ritchie (saxophone), Harry Waters (keyboards),
Snowy White (guitar, vocals), Carol Kenyon, Katie
Kissoon and PP Arnold (backing vocals). All shows are
Roger Waters solo shows except some multi-artist
festival dates, which are noted.

Friday 2 June
CONCERT
Rock In Rio Lisboa, World Stage, Parque da Bela
Vista, Lisbon, Portugal
Roger Waters headlined The World Stage on the first
day of this three-day multi-artist festival.
Set list: 'The Happiest Days Of Our Lives' / 'Another
Brick In The Wall, Part 2' / 'Mother' / 'Shine On You
Crazy Diamond, Parts 1-5' / 'Have A Cigar' / 'Wish
You Were Here' / 'Set The Controls For The Heart Of
The Sun' / 'The Gunners Dream' / 'Southampton Dock'
/ 'The Fletcher Memorial Home' / 'Perfect Sense,
Parts 1 & 2' / 'Leaving Beirut' / 'Sheep' // *The Dark
Side Of The Moon* // encore: 'In The Flesh' / 'Vera' /
'Bring The Boys Back Home' / 'Comfortably Numb'.
A proposed broadcast live on the AOL Internet
provider was cancelled at the very last minute due to
a contractual dispute.

Sunday 4 June
CONCERT
Arena di Verona, Verona, Italy
Set list: 'In The Flesh' / 'Mother' / 'Shine On You Crazy
Diamond, Parts 1-5' / 'Have A Cigar' / 'Wish You
Were Here' / 'Set The Controls For The Heart Of The
Sun' / 'The Gunners Dream' / 'Southampton Dock' /
'The Fletcher Memorial Home' / 'Perfect Sense, Parts
1 & 2' / 'Leaving Beirut' / 'Sheep' // *The Dark Side Of
The Moon* // encore: 'The Happiest Days Of Our Lives'
/ 'Another Brick In The Wall, Part 2' / 'Vera' / 'Bring
The Boys Back Home' / 'Comfortably Numb'.

Monday 5 June
CONCERT
Arena di Verona, Verona, Italy
Set list: 'In The Flesh' / 'Mother' / 'Shine On You Crazy

Diamond, Parts 1-5' / 'Leaving Beirut' / 'Have A Cigar'
/ 'Wish You Were Here' / 'Set The Controls For The
Heart Of The Sun' / 'The Gunners Dream' /
'Southampton Dock' / 'The Fletcher Memorial Home' /
'Perfect Sense, Parts 1 & 2' / 'Sheep' // *The Dark Side
Of The Moon* // encore: 'The Happiest Days Of Our
Lives' / 'Another Brick In The Wall, Part 2' / 'Vera' /
'Bring The Boys Back Home' / 'Comfortably Numb'.

Tuesday 6 June
CANCELLED CONCERT
Velodromo Paolo Borsellino, Palermo, Sicily, Italy
Concert cancelled for technical reasons.

Thursday 8 June
CONCERT
Kindl-Bühne Wuhlheide, Berlin, Germany
Set list at this show and all subsequent shows on the
tour unless otherwise noted: 'In The Flesh' / 'Mother'
/ 'Set The Controls For The Heart Of The Sun' / 'Shine
On You Crazy Diamond, Parts 1-5' / 'Have A Cigar' /
'Wish You Were Here' / 'Southampton Dock' / 'The
Fletcher Memorial Home' / 'Perfect Sense, Parts 1 &
2' / 'Leaving Beirut' / 'Sheep' // *The Dark Side Of The
Moon* // encore: 'The Happiest Days Of Our Lives' /
'Another Brick In The Wall, Part 2' / 'Vera' / 'Bring
The Boys Back Home' / 'Comfortably Numb'.

Saturday 10 June
CONCERT
Arrow Rock Festival, Main Stage, Lichtenvoorde,
The Netherlands
Roger Waters headlined the second day of this two-
day multi-artist festival.

Monday 12 June
CONCERT
Egilshöllin Arena, Reykjavík, Iceland
Nick Mason played drums on *The Dark Side Of The
Moon* and the encores at this show.

Wednesday 14 June
CONCERT
Norwegian Wood Festival, Hovedscene,
Frognerbadet, Oslo, Norway
Roger Waters appeared as part of a season of events
at this venue.

Friday 16 June
CONCERT
Stadio Olympico, Rome, Italy

Sunday 18 June
CONCERT
Terra Vibe Park, Malakassa, Athens, Greece

Tuesday 20 June
CONCERT
Kuruçeşme Arena, Istanbul, Turkey

Thursday 22 June
CONCERT
Latrun Monastery, Neve Shalom, Israel
Show moved from Ha-Yarkon Park, Tel Aviv, Israel
due to protests from Palestinian pressure groups.
Latrun Monastery is situated in a village of Israeli-
Palestinian co-existence. The show was broadcast live
on Israel's 88FM radio and Reshet Bet radio.

Saturday 24 June
CONCERT
Vasilyevsky Spusk, Moscow, Russia
Show moved from Red Square, Moscow, Russia due
to a clash with state ceremonies.

Monday 26 June
CONCERT
Viking Stadion, Jåttåvågen, Stavanger, Norway

Thursday 29 June
CONCERT
Live At The Marquee, **Showgrounds, Cork, Ireland**
Roger Waters appeared as part of a season of events
at this venue. Nick Mason played drums on *The Dark
Side Of The Moon* and the encores at this show.

Saturday 1 July
CONCERT
Hyde Park Calling, **Hyde Park, London, England**
Roger Waters headlined on the first day of this two-
day multi-artist festival. Nick Mason played drums on
The Dark Side Of The Moon and the encores at this
show.

Sunday 2 July
CONCERT
Roskilde Festival, **Orange Stage, Roskilde, Denmark**
Roger Waters headlined on the third day of this
three-day multi-artist festival (30 June – 2 July
2006).

Friday 7 July
CONCERT
Sportpaleis Ahoy, Rotterdam, The Netherlands

Saturday 8 July
CANCELLED CONCERT
Olimpiyskyi Stadium, Kiev, Ukraine
Show cancelled due to a contractual dispute.

Monday 10 July
CONCERT
**Loxol Car Park [formerly The Parade Grounds],
Pembroke, Malta**

RIGHT: ROGER WATERS PERFORMING IN HYDE PARK,
LONDON AND WITH NICK MASON AS SPECIAL GUEST.

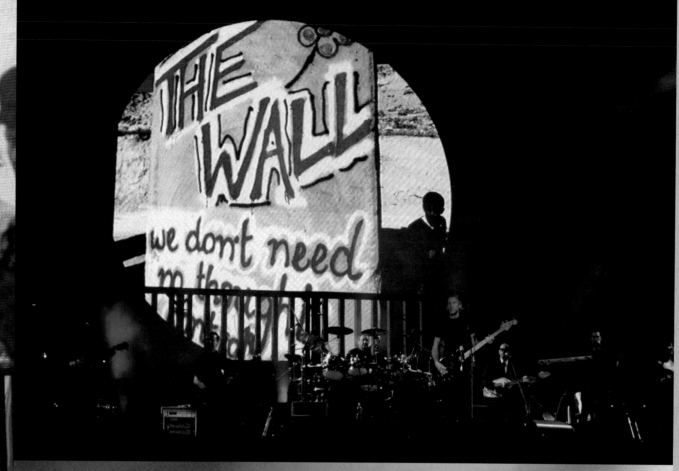

Wednesday 12 July
CONCERT
Summer Festival, Piazza Napoleone, Lucca, Italy
Roger Waters appeared as part of a season of events
at this venue. Nick Mason played drums on *The Dark
Side Of The Moon* set and encores at this show. The
show was broadcast live on the Italian RAI 1 radio
network.

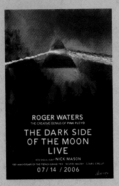

Friday 14 July
CONCERT
Circuit De Nevers-Magny Cours, Magny-Cours,
France
Supported by Laurent Voulzy. Nick Mason played
drums on *The Dark Side Of The Moon* set and encores
at this show.

Sunday 16 July
CONCERT
Moon & Stars Festival '06, Piazza Grande, Locarno,
Switzerland
The last night of the tour. Roger Waters appeared as
part of a season of events at this venue.

ROGER WATERS – US AUTUMN TOUR 2006
Roger's band and set list remained the same
throughout this tour.

Wednesday 6 September
CONCERT
PNC Bank Arts Center, Holmdel, New Jersey, USA

Friday 8 & Saturday 9 September
CONCERTS
Tweeter Performing Arts Center, Mansfield, Boston,
Massachusetts, USA

Tuesday 12 & Wednesday 13 September
CONCERTS
Madison Square Garden, Manhattan, New York
City, New York, USA
Nick Mason played drums on *The Dark Side Of The
Moon* set and the encores at these shows.

Friday 15 September
CONCERT
Nikon Jones Beach Theatre, Wantagh, Long Island,
New York, USA

Saturday 16 September
CONCERT
Tweeter Center, Camden, New Jersey, USA

Monday 18 September
CONCERT
Palace of Auburn Hills, Auburn Hills, Detroit,
Michigan, USA

Wednesday 20 September
CONCERT
Air Canada Centre, Toronto, Ontario, Canada

Thursday 21 September
CONCERT
Bell Centre, Montréal, Québec, Canada

Saturday 23 September
CONCERT
Nissan Center, Bristow, Virginia, USA

Sunday 24 September
CONCERT
Post Gazette Pavilion, Pittsburgh, Pennsylvania,
USA

Wednesday 27 September
CONCERT
Quicken Loans Arena, Cleveland, Ohio, USA

Friday 29 September
CONCERT
First Midwest Bank Amphitheatre, Chicago, Illinois,
USA

Saturday 30 September
CONCERT
Verizon Wireless Music Center, Noblesville, Indiana,
USA

Tuesday 3 October
CONCERT
Cricket Pavilion, Phoenix, Arizona, USA

Thursday 5, Friday 6 October & Sunday 8 October
CONCERTS
Hollywood Bowl, Hollywood, Los Angeles,
California, USA
Nick Mason played drums on *The Dark Side Of The
Moon* set and the encores at these shows.

Sunday 8 October
CANCELLED CONCERT
Theater Under The Stars, Hard Rock Hotel, Las
Vegas, Nevada, USA
This show was cancelled in order to accommodate an
extended run of shows at the Hollywood Bowl.

Tuesday 10 October
CONCERT
Shoreline Amphitheatre, Mountain View, near San
Francisco, California, USA

Thursday 12 October
CONCERT
Key Arena, Seattle, Washington, USA
The last night of the tour.

ROGER WATERS – 2007 TOUR

At the time of going to print Roger Waters had just
announced there would be up to 62 further dates
across the world for his continuing *Dark Side Of The
Moon* tour, although only the initial dates for
Australia and New Zealand had been publicised:

Thursday 25 January
CONCERT
Acer Arena, Olympic Park, Sydney, New South
Wales, Australia

Monday 29 January
CONCERT
North Harbour Stadium, Albany, Auckland, New
Zealand

Thursday 1 & Friday 2 February
CONCERTS
Rod Laver Arena, Melbourne & Olympic Park,
Melbourne, Victoria, Australia

Monday 5 February
CONCERT
Entertainment Centre, Boondall, Brisbane,
Queensland, Australia

Wednesday 7 February
CONCERT
Entertainment Centre, Hindmarsh, Adelaide, South
Australia, Australia

Friday 9 February
CONCERT
Members Equity Stadium, Perth, Western Australia,
Australia

OTHER LIVE APPEARANCES

Friday 5 December 1986
TV SHOW
BBC Television Centre, White City, London, England
Waters and Andy Fairweather-Low made a surprise
appearance in a special tribute to John Lennon in the
BBC2 documentary arts programme *Arena*
performing a pre-recorded rendition of 'Across The
Universe'. It was broadcast on BBC2 TV at 9.30pm.

18 October 1991
CONCERT
The Guitar Legends Festival, Auditorium Expo '92,
Seville, Spain.
Set list: 'In The Flesh' / 'The Happiest Days Of Our
Lives' / 'Another Brick In The Wall, Part 2' / 'What
God Wants' / 'Brain Damage' / 'Eclipse' /
'Comfortably Numb'.
This was an unusual event for Waters to take part in,
since he is not chiefly known as a guitarist. He
performed a set on the fourth of a five night festival
(15 - 19 October 1991) which featured Robert Cray,
Steve Cropper, B.B. King, Bo Diddley, Ricky Lee Jones,
John McLaughlin, George Benson, Joe Cocker, Bob
Dylan, Keith Richards, Jack Bruce, Steve Vai, Cozy
Powell, Paul Rodgers and others. Bruce Hornsby and
Robbie Robertson also performed on the night of
Waters' appearance.
Waters' backing band for his set included Snowy
White and Andy Fairweather-Low (guitars), Tony
Levin (bass), Pat Leonard and Peter Wood
(keyboards), Graham Broad (drums) and Doreen
Chanter and Katie Kissoon (backing vocals). Bruce
Hornsby played keyboards and vocals on 'Comfortably
Numb' and was included both on audio and DVD on
the box set retrospective *Bruce Hornsby:
Intersections 1985-2005* released in 2006.
Rehearsals took place at Nomis Studios in west
London on the two days before the event. Waters' set,
which featured a work in progress that would
become 'What God Wants' on the *Amused To Death*
album, was recorded for TV and broadcast on many
worldwide networks, including BBC2 in the UK.

Wednesday 1 April 1992
CONCERT
Walden Woods Benefit Concert, Universal
Amphitheatre, Universal City, Los Angeles,
California, USA.
Set list: 'In The Flesh' / 'The Happiest Days Of Our
Lives' / 'Another Brick In The Wall, Part 2' / 'Mother'
/ 'Comfortably Numb'.
Waters performed at a benefit concert in aid of the
preservation of Walden Woods in Massachusetts, at
the request of Don Henley. He was joined on stage by
Don Henley's band and additional sets were
performed by Neil Young and John Fogerty.

Monday 7 October 2002
CONCERT
Music To My Ears, Fleet Center, Boston,
Massachusetts, USA
Set list: 'Comfortably Numb' / 'Wish You Were Here' /
'Flickering Flame' / encore: 'This Train' / 'Everyday
People'.

Tuesday 8 October 2002
CONCERT
Music To My Ears, Madison Square Garden,
Manhattan, New York City, New York, USA
Set list: 'Wish You Were Here' / 'Flickering Flame' /
'Comfortably Numb' / encore: 'This Train' / 'Everyday
People'.
Waters appeared at the above two concerts dubbed
'Music To My Ears' that paid tribute to the highly
respected rock journalist and friend of Roger Waters,
Timothy White, who passed away suddenly on 27
June 2002. Other guests at these events included
Jimmy Buffett, Sheryl Crow, Don Henley, Billy Joel,
John Mellancamp, Sting, James Taylor and Brian
Wilson with the encore performed by all and sundry.
The 'house band', also backing Waters, featured Don
Henley (guest vocals), Steve Jordan (drums/music
director), Willie Weeks (bass guitar), Danny
Kortchmar and Waddy Wachtel (guitars), Ricky
Peterson (keyboards) and Norbert Stachel
(saxophones & horns).

Saturday 12 & Sunday 13 October 2002
CONCERTS
Royal Festival Hall, South Bank, London, England
Set List: 'What God Wants, Part 1' / 'What God
Wants, Part 3'.
Waters was one of number of guest performers on
two of three Jeff Beck concerts held at this venue.
Waters band comprised of those he had recently
toured with in addition to Beck's own backing band:
Andy Fairweather-Low (guitar), Tony Hymas (bass
guitar), Randy Hope-Taylor (guitar), Jennifer Batten
(guitar), Steve Barney (drums), Carol Kenyon, PP
Arnold and Katie Kissoon (backing vocals).

Wednesday 16 October 2002
CONCERT
Whip Craic, Royal Albert Hall, Kensington, London,
England
Set list: 'Ça Ira Overture' / 'Wish You Were Here' /
'Flickering Flame' / 'Comfortably Numb'.
Waters participated at this event held in support of
the Countryside Alliance; a body that was formed in
opposition to the Government's bill to ban fox hunting.
The show featured a programme of both music and
monologue. Waters performed with the Royal
Philharmonic Concert Orchestra throughout his set
and the RPCO opened with a five-minute overture
from his forthcoming *Ça Ira* opera. Waters' band
comprised of Andy Fairweather-Low and Snowy

White (guitars), Chester Kamen (bass guitar, vocals),
Andy Wallace and Harry Waters (keyboards), Graham
Broad (drums), Carol Kenyon, PP Arnold and Katie
Kissoon (backing vocals) and Ian Ritchie (penny
whistle).

Saturday 28 August 2004
CONCERT
Twelfth Annual Huggy Bears Invitational, Tony
Forstmann's, Cobb Road Estate, Hamptons, New
York, USA
Waters performed 'Comfortably Numb' and 'Mother'
on acoustic guitar at this Don Henley-led private fund-
raising event that also featured Stevie Nicks.

Saturday 15 January 2005
TV SHOW
NBC TV Studios, Manhattan, New York City, New
York, USA
Waters performed 'Wish You Were Here' on acoustic
guitar, with Eric Clapton, also on acoustic guitar, with
Katie Kissoon, PP Arnold and Carol Kenyon on
backing vocals in a pre-recorded session as part of
NBC TV's charity gala night *Tsunami Aid – A Concert
Of Hope*.

Saturday 20 May 2006
CONCERT
Highclere Rocks, Highclere Castle, Newbury,
England
Waters along with Nick Mason and Eric Clapton,
Bryan Ferry, Roger Taylor, Roger Daltrey and Georgie
Fame appeared as special guests of 'The Band Du Lac'
featuring Gary Brooker (electric piano), Jodi Linscott
(percussion), Mike Rutherford (guitars), Geoff
Whitehorn (lead guitar) and Paul Carrack (vocals) at
this benefit concert on behalf of the Countryside
Alliance. Waters performed 'Wish You Were Here'
and 'Comfortably Numb' with the house band
supplemented by Eric Clapton (acoustic guitar),
Georgie Fame (keyboards) and Andy Fairweather-Low
(guitars). Waters joined in on acoustic guitar for
Clapton's rendition of 'Cocaine' and rather
energetically hit a beer can with a drumstick
throughout the closing song, 'Get Up, Stand Up'.

richard wright

Richard William Wright was born in Hatch End, Middlesex on 28 July 1943 to Cedric and Bridie Wright. He was educated at Haberdasher's Aske's Grammar School, in Hampstead and in 1962 enrolled to the Regent Street Polytechnic where he met Roger Waters and Nick Mason. However, Wright was less suited to academia and briefly turned his attention to a course at the London College of Music before giving up on studies altogether, preferring to sail around the Greek islands - which seems to have been a lifelong passion - before finally settling into the role of keyboard player from the early incarnations of Pink Floyd onwards. His solo career has been less active outside of Pink Floyd than the other members of the band. However, Rick Wright has nevertheless made two solo albums, which included contributions from artists previously associated with Pink Floyd. He has also made an album as one half of the band Zee, the other member being Dave Harris, guitarist and vocalist of Fashion. Despite making a surprise appearance on David Gilmour's 2006 tour, he has rarely appeared on stage, even as a guest performer.

DISCOGRAPHY

WET DREAM

Richard Wright recorded his first solo album at the Super Bear Studios in France in record time, between 10 January and 14 February 1978.

Friday 22 September 1978
WET DREAM
UK: EMI Harvest SHVL 818 (vinyl album).
US: Columbia JC 35559 (vinyl album).
Track list: 'Mediterranean C' / 'Against The Odds' / 'Cat Cruise' / 'Summer Elegy' / 'Waves' / 'Holiday' / 'Mad Yannis Dance' / 'Drop In From The Top' / 'Pink's Song' / 'Funky Deux'.
Additional musicians: Mel Collins (saxophone), Reg Isadore (drums, guitars), Larry Steele (bass) and Snowy White (guitars).

Recorded at Super Bear Studios, Berre des Alpes, France between 10 January and 14 February 1978. Produced by Richard Wright. Engineered by John Etchells.

IDENTITY

Wright entered into a recording project with Dave Harris of New-Wave group, Fashion under the name Zee having been introduced by mutual friend Raphael Ravenscroft, the instigator of the project, who had just finished working with David Gilmour on his solo album. After several rehearsals and personnel changes, only Wright and Harris remained who wrote all of the music although the lyrics were all by Harris. It was recorded at the Rectory Studio in Cambridge and overdubbed and mixed at Utopia in London and composed and performed almost entirely on the Fairlight computer. It was regarded as too clinical by many Pink Floyd fans, who were expecting something more akin to Wright's first solo album. Wright, along with the vast majority of Pink Floyd fans, looks back on it as an experiment best forgotten.

Monday 12 March 1984
ZEE – 'Confusion' (edit) / 'Eyes Of A Gypsy'
UK: EMI Harvest HAR 5227 (7-inch single).
ZEE – 'Confusion' (extended version) / 'Eyes Of A Gypsy' (dub mix) / 'Confusion' (7-inch version)
UK: EMI Harvest 12 HAR 5227 (12-inch single).

Monday 9 April 1984
ZEE - IDENTITY
UK: EMI Harvest SHSP 2401018 (vinyl album).
Track list: 'Confusion' / 'Voices' / 'Private Person' / 'Strange Rhythm' / 'Cuts Like A Diamond' / 'By Touching' / 'How Do You Do It?' / 'Seems We Were Dreaming'.
The cassette release featured the additional track 'Eyes Of A Gypsy'.
Recorded at Rectory Studios, Cambridge, England and Utopia Studios, London, England.
Produced by Richard Wright and Dave Harris and co-produced by Tim Palmer.

BROKEN CHINA

Wright's third album, his second solo release, was in collaboration with Anthony Moore as sole lyricist. It was written and recorded at Wright's home studio in the south of France, David Gilmour's Astoria Studio near London and Whitfield Studios, London shortly after Pink Floyd's 'Division Bell' tour. While leaning towards a concept piece, it inevitably lacks the weight of a Pink Floyd album. Although Wright entertained the idea of taking the album on tour, sales were insufficient to justify the cost.

September 1996
BROKEN CHINA
UK: EMI CD EMDJ 1098 (promotional CD).
'Night Of A Thousand Furry Toys' / 'Breakthrough' /
'Satellite' / 'Along The Shoreline'.
BROKEN CHINA
UK: EMI CD RW 101 (promotional CD) and EMI 12
RW 101 (promotional 12-inch single).
'Runaway' (Lemonade Mix) / 'Runaway' (Leggit Dub) /
'Night Of A Thousand Furry Toys' (Inverted Gravy
Mix).
Track 1 remixed by The Orb; tracks 2 and 3 remixed
by William Orbit with Matt Ducasse.

September 1996
BROKEN CHINA
UK: EMI CD INT 105 (banded promotional interview
CD - no music).

Monday 7 October 1996
BROKEN CHINA
UK: EMI CD EMD 1098 (CD album).
US: Guardian Records 724385364525 (CD album).
Track list: 'Breaking Water' / 'Night Of A Thousand
Furry Toys' / 'Hidden Fear' / 'Runaway' / 'Unfair
Ground' / 'Satellite' / 'Woman Of Custom' / 'Interlude'
/ 'Black Cloud' / 'Far From The Harbour Wall' /
'Drowning' / 'Reaching For The Rail' / 'Blue Room In
Venice' / 'Sweet July' / 'Along The Shoreline' /
'Breakthrough'.
Additional musicians: Sian Beli (cello), Steve Bolton
(guitars), Manu Katche (drums), Dominic Miller
(guitars), Sinead O'Connor (vocals on 'Reaching For
The Rail' and 'Breakthrough'), Tim Renwick (guitars),
Maz Palladino (backing vocals), Pino Palladino (bass),
Kate St. John (oboe). David Gilmour played guitar on
'Breakthrough' during the sessions but his
performance did not appear on the album.
Recorded and composed at Studio Harmonie, Paris,
France. Overdubs at Whitfield Studios, London,
England, RAK Studios, London, England and Astoria
Studios, Hampton, England.
Produced by Richard Wright and Anthony Moore.
Engineered by Richard Wright and Anthony Moore.
Engineered and co-produced by Max Hayes, Jake
Davies and Graeme Stewart. Mastered by Doug Sax
and Ron Lewter at the Mastering Lab, Los Angeles,
USA.

SONGWRITING

1964
**ADAM, MIKE & TIM - 'Little Baby' / 'You're
The Reason Why'**
UK: Decca F12040 (7-inch single).
Wright wrote the B-side to this obscure single by
Liverpool trio Adam and Mike Sedgwick and Tim
Saunders.

2006
**HELEN BOULDING - 'I Don't Know What I Want
But I Know What I Need' / 'Hazel Eyes'**
UK: Main Spring MSEP003 (CD single).
Wright co-wrote the song 'Hazel Eyes' with Chris
Difford.

GUEST APPEARANCES
(UK Catalogue numbers and original format only)

1970
SYD BARRETT - BARRETT
UK: EMI Harvest SHSP 4007 (vinyl album).
Wright played keyboards on Barrett's second solo
album.

1990
BLUE PEARL - NAKED
UK: Big Life BLR LP4 (vinyl album).
Wright played keyboards on 'Alive'. Also on the same
track on the 12-inch single 'Alive' (Goa Mix) / 'Down
To You' (Massey Mix) / 'Alive' (Organapella Mix) (UK:
Big Life BLR T44) and the CD single 'Alive' (Edit) /
'Alive' (Goa Mix) / 'Down To You' (Massey Mix) (UK:
Big Life BLR D44).

2002
CHIMERA - CHIMERA
UK: Tenth Planet TP054 (vinyl album. Limited edition
of 1,000 copies).
Wright played keyboards on 'Lady With Bullets In Her
Hair' on this compilation album of Chimera material
originally recorded between 1969 and 1970.

LIVE APPEARANCES

Sunday 10 November 1974
CONCERT
Newcastle Polytechnic, Newcastle-upon-Tyne,
England
Wright played keyboards and David Gilmour shared
lead guitar with Tim Renwick at this Sutherland
Brothers & Quiver show.

Sunday 11 October 1992
CONCERT
Chelsea Arts Ball, Royal Albert Hall,
Kensington, London, England
Wright played keyboards at this high-
society AIDS fund-raiser. Other
musicians who performed included the
house band - David Gilmour (vocals,
guitars), Guy Pratt (bass), Jon Carin
(keyboards), Jodi Linscott (percussion),
Tim Renwick (guitars), Gary Wallis
(drums) and Sam Brown (vocals) - and
guest musicians Nick Mason, Tom
Jones, Hugh Cornwell, Mica Paris, Elvis
Costello and Sam Moore.

Saturday 23 March 1996
PRIVATE PARTY
Fulham Town Hall, Fulham, London, England
David Gilmour's 50th birthday party. Entertainment
was provided by The Bootleg Beatles and The
Australian Pink Floyd, who were joined on stage by
Richard Wright and Guy Pratt for a rousing rendition
of 'Comfortably Numb'. They then handed over their
instruments to David Gilmour, Richard Wright, Guy
Pratt, Tim Renwick, Gary Wallis and Claudia Fontaine
who treated the gathered guests to renditions of
'Money', 'What Do You Want From Me' and various
other jams.

Wednesday 16, Thursday 17 & Friday 18 January
2002
CONCERTS
Royal Festival Hall, South Bank, London, England
Wright played keyboards at these series of David
Gilmour solo shows including his own song
'Breakthrough' and also piano on 'Wish You Were
Here' and 'Comfortably Numb'.

Wednesday 23 & Thursday 24 January 2002
CONCERTS
Palace de Congrès de Paris, Paris, France
Wright played keyboards at these series of David
Gilmour solo shows including his own song
'Breakthrough' and also piano on 'Wish You Were
Here' and 'Comfortably Numb'.

DAVID GILMOUR - ON AN ISLAND TOUR 2006
Richard Wright played keyboards in Gilmour's band
for his solo tour alongside Jon Carin (keyboards),
Steve DiStanislao (drums), Phil Manzanera (guitar),
Dick Parry (saxophone) and Guy Pratt (bass guitar).
(See the David Gilmour section for tour dates, set lists
and further information.)

BELOW: ON STAGE AS PART OF DAVID GILMOUR'S BAND AT
THE ROYAL ALBERT HALL, MARCH 2006.

discography

This book gives catalogue information for original UK and US Pink Floyd and solo pressings. It does not include every variation of re-pressed discs, variations in label or sleeve design or specialist collectibles such as acetates and test pressings, unless they are significantly different to that of the originals. However, catalogue number changes, reissues and promotional items of special interest are included. Additionally there are a vast amount of Pink Floyd and solo radio-only shows, radio show compilations and even military pressings both on vinyl and CD that originate from the USA that are highly collectible but are just too many in number to accurately catalogue, although a few of notable interest are listed.

The release dates of the recordings are as accurate as can be expected, and it must be emphasised that much of this information comes from contemporary press reports and music industry trade publications, which are known to contain erroneous or contradictory details. Unfortunately, none of the dates could be completely verified by the record labels, as they do not retain this information on file.

For reader information, up until 1982 all records in the UK were released on a Friday. This changed to a Monday in order to benefit from a full week of sales to contribute to the weekly Sunday chart compilation. The only exception to this rule was if the Monday fell on a public holiday, in which case the release date moved to the next working day.

In the USA all albums up until 1984 were released on a Saturday and all singles were released on a Monday. With the merger of several major international record labels this was brought into line with the European standard release date of Monday for all formats.

Listed items are formatted as follows, although not all of these details appear for every item: original release date where known; the title of the recording; the name of the record company and the item's original catalogue number on release with format and other notations; the track list; the supporting musicians (note: additional musicians largely remain the same for all subsidiary single releases); the producer / director; recording studio; artwork designer and the highest chart placing and sales disc status.

The division between the two sides of a vinyl single is indicated by a single oblique (/); tracks on a vinyl album or CD is indicated by a single oblique (/) and the two sides of a vinyl album is indicated by a double oblique (//).

ORIGINAL RECORDS

Friday 10 March 1967
'Arnold Layne' / 'Candy And A Currant Bun'
UK: Columbia EMI DB 8156 (7-inch single. Promotional copies were issued with picture sleeves).
US: Tower 333 (7-inch single, released on Monday 24 April 1967. Also issued as a white label promotional single).
Produced by Joe Boyd.
Recorded at Sound Techniques Studios, London, England and EMI Studios Abbey Road, London, England.
Highest chart position UK No.20.

Friday 16 June 1967
'See Emily Play' / 'Scarecrow'
UK: Columbia EMI DB 8214 (7-inch single. Promotional copies were issued with picture sleeves).
US: Tower 356 (7-inch single, released on Monday 24 July 1967. Also issued as a white label promotional single).
Produced by Norman Smith.
Recorded at Sound Techniques Studios, London, England and EMI Studios Abbey Road, London, England.
Picture sleeve artwork by Syd Barrett.
Highest chart position UK No.6, US No. 134.
Reissued:
US: Tower 356 (7-inch white label promo single, released on Monday 22 July 1968).
The following text appears on the rear cover: "Everything is a matter of timing. This record was released almost one year ago in England and made Top 5. Tower released it here at the same time. No action. Now is the time to release See Emily Play. That's what we have been hearing from many of the country's top PD's and DJ's, as well as several music reviewers. We hope they're right. We're re-releasing the record. Will you play it?"

Friday 4 August 1967
THE PIPER AT THE GATES OF DAWN
UK: Columbia EMI SCX 6157 (stereo vinyl album).
UK: Columbia EMI SX 6157 (mono vinyl album).
Track list: 'Astronomy Dominé' / 'Lucifer Sam' / 'Matilda Mother' / 'Flaming' / 'Pow R Toc H' / 'Take Up Thy Stethoscope And Walk' // 'Interstellar Overdrive' / 'The Gnome' / 'Chapter 24' / 'Scarecrow' / 'Bike'.
Produced by Norman Smith. Recorded at EMI Studios Abbey Road, London, England. Engineered by Peter Brown. Front cover photo by Vic Singh. Rear cover illustration by Syd Barrett outlined from a group photo of the band taken by Colin Prime in Ruskin Park, Denmark Hill, London, England in July 1967.
Highest chart position UK No.6.
Certified Gold in the US on 11 March 1994.
Reissued:
UK: EMI Fame FA 3065 (stereo vinyl album, 1979).
UK: EMI CDP 7463842 (CD album, 1985).
UK: EMI CD EMD 1073 (digitally remastered stereo CD album with new artwork, 1994).
UK: EMI CD EMD 1110 (limited edition 30th anniversary digitally remastered mono CD album box set with a selection of art prints, 1997).
UK: EMI LP EMP 1110 (limited edition digitally remastered mono vinyl album with new artwork, 1997).
US: Capitol CDP 7463842 (CD album 1985).
US: Capitol CDP 7463844 (digitally remastered stereo CD album with new artwork, 1994).

Saturday 21 October 1967
PINK FLOYD
US: Tower ST5093 (stereo vinyl album).
US: Tower T5093 (mono vinyl album).
Track list: 'See Emily Play' / 'Pow R Toc H' / 'Take Up Thy Stethoscope And Walk' / 'Lucifer Sam' / 'Matilda Mother' //

'Scarecrow' / 'The Gnome' / 'Chapter 24' / 'Interstellar Overdrive'.
Highest chart position US No. 131.
The US edition of *Piper At The Gates Of Dawn* is notable by the completely different track listing to the original UK release: 'See Emily Play' has been inserted to the album and the tracks 'Astronomy Dominé, 'Flaming' and 'Bike' do not appear. Furthermore, the sleeve contains several misspellings: 'Pow R Toc H' is spelt 'Pow R Toch' and 'Take Up Thy Stethoscope And Walk' is spelt 'Take Up My Stethoscope And Walk'.

Monday 6 November 1967
'Flaming' / 'The Gnome'
US: Tower 378 (7-inch single. Also issued as a white label promotional single).

Friday 17 November 1967
'Apples And Oranges' / 'Paintbox'
UK: Columbia EMI DB8310 (7-inch single. Promotional copies were issued with picture sleeves).
Produced by Norman Smith.
Recorded at EMI Studios Abbey Road, London, England.

Friday 19 April 1968
'It Would Be So Nice' / 'Julia Dream'
UK: Columbia EMI DB8410 (7-inch single).
US: Tower 378 (7-inch single, released on Monday 3 June 1968. Also issued as a white label promotional single).
Produced by Norman Smith.
Recorded at EMI Studios Abbey Road, London, England.

Friday 28 June 1968
A SAUCERFUL OF SECRETS
UK: Columbia EMI SCX 6258 (stereo vinyl album).
UK: Columbia EMI SX 6258 (mono vinyl album).
US: Tower ST 5131 (stereo vinyl album, released on Saturday 27 July 1968).
Track list: 'Let There Be More Light' / 'Remember A Day' / 'Set The Controls For The Heart Of the Sun' / 'Corporal Clegg' // 'A Saucerful Of Secrets' / 'See-Saw' / 'Jugband Blues'.
Produced by Norman Smith.
Recorded at EMI Studios Abbey Road, London, England.
Artwork by Hipgnosis. Rear cover photo taken in Richmond Park, Surrey, England.
Highest chart position UK No.9.
Certified Gold in the US on 11 March 1994.
Reissued:
UK: EMI Fame FA 3163 (stereo vinyl album, 1979).
UK: EMI CDP 7463832 (CD album, 1985).
UK: EMI CDEMD 1063 (digitally remastered CD album with new artwork, 1994).
US: Capitol CDP 7463832 (CD album, 1987).
US: Capitol CDP 7463836 (digitally remastered CD album with new artwork, 1994).

Monday 19 August 1968
'Let There Be More Light' (edit) / 'Remember A Day' (edit)
US: Tower 440 (7-inch single. Also issued as a white label promotional single).

Friday 6 December 1968
'Point Me At The Sky' / 'Careful With That Axe, Eugene'
UK: Columbia EMI DB 8511 (7-inch single. Also issued a promotional green 'A' label single with a 'flying suit' photo postcard of the band).
Produced by Norman Smith.
Recorded at EMI Studios Abbey Road, London, England.

Friday 13 June 1969
MORE
UK: Columbia EMI SCX 6346 (vinyl album).
US: Tower ST 5169 (vinyl album, released on Saturday 9 August 1969).
Track list: 'Cirrus Minor' / 'The Nile Song' / 'Crying Song' / 'Up The Khyber' / 'Green Is The Colour' / 'Cymbaline' / 'Party Sequence' // 'Main Theme' / 'Ibiza Bar' / 'More Blues' / 'Quicksilver' / 'A Spanish Piece' / 'Dramatic Theme'.
Produced by Pink Floyd.
Recorded at Pye Recording Studios, London, England.
Highest chart position UK No.9, US No. 153 (1973 reissue).
Artwork by Hipgnosis.
Certified Gold in the US on 11 March 1994.
Reissued:
UK: EMI CDP 7463862 (CD album, 1985).
UK: EMI CDEMD 1084 (digitally remastered CD with new artwork, 1995).
US: Harvest SW 11198 (vinyl album, 1973).
US: Capitol SW 11198 (vinyl album, 1983).
US: Capitol CDP 7463862 (CD album, 1985).
US: Capitol CDP 74638623 (digitally remastered CD with new artwork, 1995).

Friday 7 November 1969
UMMAGUMMA
UK: EMI Harvest SHDW 1/2 (double vinyl album).
US: Harvest STBB 388 (double vinyl album, released on Saturday 8 November 1969).
Track list: 'Astronomy Dominé' / 'Careful With That Axe, Eugene' // 'Set The Controls For The Heart Of the Sun' / 'A Saucerful Of Secrets' // 'Sysyphus, Parts 1-4' / 'Grantchester Meadows' / 'Several Species Of Small Furry Animals Gathered Together In A Cave And Grooving With A Pict' // 'The Narrow Way, Parts 1-3' / 'The Grand Vizier's Garden Party, Part 1 – Entrance'; 'Part 2 – Entertainment'; 'Part 3 – Exit'.
Live tracks recorded at Mother's Club, Birmingham on 27 April 1969 and The College of Commerce, Manchester on 2 May 1969. Studio tracks recorded at EMI Studios Abbey Road, London, England.
Studio tracks produced by Norman Smith. Live tracks produced by Pink Floyd and Brian Humphries. Engineered by Peter Mew and Brian Humphries.

Artwork by Hipgnosis. Front cover photo taken at the Cambridge house of Storm Thorgerson's girlfriend, Libby January; Rear cover photo taken at Biggin Hill Aerodrome, Kent, England and the inside photo's at various locations in London with Gilmour's having been taken at the Elfin Tree, Hyde Park, London, England.

Highest chart position UK No.5, US No.74.

Certified Gold in the US on 28 February 1974 and Platinum on 11 March 1994.

Reissued:

UK: EMI CDP 74640452 (double CD album, 1985).

UK: EMI CDEMD 1074 (digitally remastered CD album with new artwork, packaging and poster, 1995).

US: Capitol SKBB 388 (double vinyl album, 1983).

US: Capitol CDPB 74640452 (double CD album, 1985).

US: Capitol CDP 74640428 (digitally remastered CD album with new artwork, packaging and poster, 1995).

Note: On the original vinyl release, 'The Narrow Way' and 'The Grand Vizier's Garden Party' were single tracks. On the remastered CD re-release, Part 1 of 'Sysyphus' was split into two tracks and labelled 'Part 1' and 'Part 2'. 'Part 2' on vinyl became 'Part 3' on CD, while 'Part 4' of the re-release consists of 'Part 3' and 'Part 4' ('Part 4' beginning with the large orchestral thud).

Friday 2 October 1970
ATOM HEART MOTHER

UK: EMI Harvest SHVL 781 (vinyl album).

US: Harvest SKAO 382 (vinyl album, released on Saturday 10 October 1970).

Track list: 'Atom Heart Mother' a) 'Father's Shout'; b) 'Breast Milky'; c) 'Mother Fore'; d) 'Funky Dung'; e) 'Mind Your Throats Please'; f) 'Remergence' // 'If' / 'Summer '68' / 'Fat Old Sun' / 'Alan's Psychedelic Breakfast' a) 'Rise And Shine'; b) 'Sunny Side Up'; c) 'Morning Glory'.

Produced by Pink Floyd. Executive producer Norman Smith.

Recorded at EMI Studios Abbey Road, London, England. Engineered by Peter Bown and Alan Parsons.

Artwork by Hipgnosis. Cow photos taken near Potters Bar, Hertfordshire.

Highest chart position UK No.1, US No.55.

Certified Gold in the US on 11 March 1994.

Reissued:

UK: EMI Harvest EMI Q4 SHVL 781 (quadraphonic vinyl album, 1973).

UK: EMI CDP 7463812 (CD album, 1985).

UK: EMI CDEMD 1072 (digitally remastered CD album with new artwork, 1994).

UK: EMI LP EMP 1112 (digitally remastered limited edition vinyl album with new artwork, 1997).

US: Harvest SMAS 382 (vinyl album, 1973).

US: Capitol SMAS 382 (vinyl album, 1983).

US: Mobile Fidelity Sound Lab MFSL 1-202 (Half-speed original master recording pressed on 200gsm Super Vinyl, 1994).

US: Capitol CDP 7463812 (CD album, 1985).

US: Mobile Fidelity Sound Lab UDCD 595 (MFSL Original Master Recording Gold Ultra Disc II CD album, 1994).

US: Capitol CDP 74638128 (digitally remastered CD album

with new artwork, 1994).

Friday 5 November 1971
MEDDLE

UK: EMI Harvest SHVL 795 (vinyl album).

US: Harvest SMAS 832 (vinyl album, released on Saturday 30 October 1971).

Track list: 'One Of These Days' / 'A Pillow Of Winds' / 'Fearless' / 'San Tropez' / 'Seamus' // 'Echoes'.

Produced by Pink Floyd.

Recorded EMI Studios Abbey Road, London, England; Morgan Sound Studios, London, England and Air Studios, London, England. Engineered by Peter Brown, John Leckie, Rob Black and Peter Quested.

Highest chart position UK No.3, US No.70.

Artwork by Hipgnosis.

Certified Gold in the US on 29 October 1973 and Multi-Platinum (2 times over) on 11 March 1994.

Reissued:

UK: EMI CDP 7460342 (CD album, 1985).

UK: EMI CDEMD 1061 (digitally remastered CD album with new artwork, 1994).

US: Capitol SMAS 832 (vinyl album, 1983).

US: Harvest CDP 7460342 (CD album, 1985).

US: Mobile Fidelity Sound Lab UDCD 518 (MFSL original master recording on a 24 carat gold Ultra Disc CD, 1989).

US: Mobile Fidelity Sound Lab MFSL 1190 (half-speed original master recording pressed on 118gsm vinyl, 1994).

US: Capitol CDP 74603423 (digitally remastered CD album with new artwork, 1994).

Monday 29 November 1971
'One Of These Days' / 'Fearless'

US: Capitol 3240 (7-inch single).

US: Capitol P 3240 (promotional 7-inch single).

Friday 2 June 1972
OBSCURED BY CLOUDS

UK: EMI Harvest SHSP 4020 (vinyl album).

US: Harvest ST 11078 (vinyl album, released on Saturday 17 June 1972).

Track list: 'Obscured By Clouds' / 'When You're In' / 'Burning Bridges' / 'The Gold It's In The...' / 'Mudmen' / 'Wot's... Uh The Deal' // 'Childhood's End' / 'Free Four' / 'Stay' / 'Absolutely Curtains'.

Produced by Pink Floyd.

Recorded at Strawberry Studios, Chateau d'Hérouville, France.

Artwork by Hipgnosis.

Highest chart position UK No.6.

Certified Silver in the UK on 1 January 1974.

Highest chart position US No.46.

Certified Gold in the US on 11 March 1994.

Reissued:

UK: EMI CDP 7463852 (CD album, 1985).

UK: EMI CDEMD 1083 (digitally remastered CD album with new artwork, 1995).

US: Harvest SW 11078 (vinyl album, 1975).

US: Capitol SW 11078 (vinyl album, 1983).

US: Capitol CDP 7463852 (CD album, 1995).
US: Capitol CDP 74638524 (digitally remastered CD album with new artwork, 1995).

Monday 10 July 1972
'Free Four' / 'Stay'
US: Capitol 3391 (7-inch single).
US: Capitol P 3391 (promotional 7-inch single).

Friday 23 March 1973
THE DARK SIDE OF THE MOON
UK: EMI Harvest SHVL 804 (vinyl album).
US: Harvest SMAS 11163 (vinyl album, released on Saturday 10 March 1973).
Original vinyl editions were issued with two posters and two stickers as inserts.
Track list: 'Speak To Me' / 'Breathe' / 'On The Run' / 'Time' / 'The Great Gig In The Sky' // 'Money' / 'Us And Them' / 'Any Colour You Like' / 'Brain Damage' / 'Eclipse'.
Additional musicians: Dick Parry (saxophones on 'Us and Them' and 'Money'), Clare Torry (vocals on 'Great Gig In The Sky'), Doris Troy, Leslie Duncan, Liza Strike, Barry St.John (backing vocals).
Recorded at EMI Studios Abbey Road, London, England.
Produced by Pink Floyd. Engineered by Alan Parsons. Mixed by Chris Thomas.
Artwork by Hipgnosis.
Highest chart position UK No.2.
Certified Silver in the UK on 1 June 1974; Gold on 14 June 1974; Platinum on 1 January 1976; Multi-Platinum (7 times over) on 1 May 1993 and Multi-Platinum (9 times over) on 15 April 2005.
Highest chart position US No.1.
Certified Gold in the US on 17 April 1973; Multi-Platinum (11 times over) on 16 February 1990; Multi-Platinum (12 times over) on 19 September 1991; Multi-Platinum (13 times over) on 7 March 1994 and Multi-Platinum (15 times over) on 4 June 1998.
Reissued:
UK: EMI Harvest Q4 SHVL 804 (quadraphonic vinyl album, 1975).
UK: EMI CDP 7460012 (CD album, 1985).
UK: EMI 78147923 (limited edition 20th anniversary remastered CD in a box set with new artwork and postcards, 1992).
UK: EMI 78147923 (promotional 20th anniversary remastered CD in a long-box with biographical notes printed on multi-coloured paper, postcard photo's, colour slides and the CD album, 1992).
UK: EMI CD EMD 1064 (digitally remastered CD album with new artwork, 1994).
UK: EMI 724385567315 (limited edition EMI 100 anniversary series pressed on 180 gram virgin vinyl, 1997).
UK: EMI EMD 1114 (limited edition digitally remastered vinyl album with new artwork, 1997).
UK: EMI 5821362 (30th Anniversary edition reissued on Hybrid SACD in 5.1 surround sound with new artwork, 2003).
UK: EMI 5821361 (limited edition 30th Anniversary digitally

remastered vinyl album with SACD artwork and poster insert, 2003).
US: Capitol SEAX 11902 (picture disc album, 1978).
US: Mobile Fidelity Sound Lab MFSL 1-017 (half-speed original master recording pressed on 100gsm vinyl, 1979).
US: Mobile Fidelity Sound Lab MFQR 1-017 (original master recording pressed on 200gsm Super Vinyl and issued in a box set and limited to 5,000 editions, 1981).
US: Capitol SMAS 11163 (vinyl album, 1983).
US: Capitol CDP 7460012 (CD album, 1985).
US: Mobile Fidelity Sound Lab UDCD 517 (MFSL original master recording on 24 carat gold Ultra Disc CD, 1988).
US: Mobile Fidelity Sound Lab UDCD 517 (re-issued MFSL original master recording 24 carat gold Ultra Disc II CD album , 1993).
US: Capitol CDP 78147923 (digitally remastered CD album with new artwork, 1994).
US: EMI / Capitol C21X-81479 (digitally remastered limited edition 20th anniversary CD album in a box set with new artwork and postcards, 1992).
US: Capitol CDP 724358213621 (30th Anniversary edition reissued on Hybrid SACD in 5.1 surround sound with new artwork, 2003).
The Dark Side Of The Moon is the second-best-selling album of all time, worldwide, and the 21st best-selling album of all time in the United States. It peaked at No.1 on The Billboard 200, and also reached No.1 on Billboard's Pop Catalog Chart on release. However, claims that the original album remained in the chart for 15 consecutive years is complete myth: In fact it debuted at No.95 on 17 March 1973 and climbed to No.1 on 7 April 1973 staying on the chart for 84 weeks until 19 October 1974. It appeared again on 12 April 1975 and stayed on the chart for 48 weeks until 6 March 1976 and stayed on chart for a record 11 years until 23 April 1988 – a grand total of 723 weeks. The 2003 Hybrid SACD issue reached No.1 on Billboard's *Pop Catalog Chart* and sold 800,000 SACDs in the US alone. Since it was first released, it has sold over 35 million copies worldwide as of 2004. In 2003 alone some 250,000 copies were bought, and as of 2004 it was selling over 8,000 copies a week. It is estimated that one in every 14 people in the US under the age of 50 owns a copy of the album.
On later CD pressings, many people believe a barely audible orchestral version of The Beatles' 'Ticket to Ride' can be heard after 'Eclipse'. Why this is so is unknown, but could possibly be the result of the re-use of recording tapes as was a common studio practice. The bootleg album *A Tree Full of Secrets* includes an amplified, enhanced version of this oddity.
Some more recent pressings of the album, starting with those included in the *Shine On* box set and the live version on *PULSE* have slightly different writing credits. These versions add Roger Waters' name to the writing credits for 'Speak to Me' and 'The Great Gig In The Sky', and Richard Wright's name to 'On the Run'. Following a high court ruling over the writing credits and royalties for 'The Great Gig In The Sky' all pressings after 2005 bear the credit Richard Wright/Clare Torry.
The 30th anniversary hybrid Super Audio CD (SACD) with a

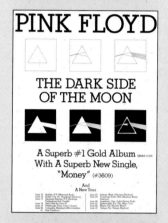

5.1 channel DSD surround mix was mastered from the original 16-track studio tapes. Some surprise was expressed when James Guthrie was called in to make the SACD mix, rather than the original LP engineer Alan Parsons, who was however called in to add a small crossfade between 'The Great Gig In The Sky' and 'Money'. The 30th anniversary edition won four Surround Music Awards in 2003.

Monday 7 May 1973
'Money' / 'Any Colour You Like'
US: Harvest 3609 (7-inch single).
Highest chart position US No.13.
Reissued:
US: Capitol Starline 6256 (7-inch single, 1981).

Monday 7 May 1973
'Money' / 'Money'
US: Harvest PRO 3609 (promotional 7-inch single).
Issued as two-sided white label promo that features an alternate mono mix of the song 'Money' with the word "bullshit" edited out. The stereo side still includes the word "bullshit" in the song. The promo itself was issued again after a short while with an insert that stated, "Please disregard the previous Pink Floyd promo single which you have received. This is the correct Pink Floyd promo single with the word bulls—t edited on both the mono and stereo sides. From the LP "The Dark Side of the Moon", a certified million seller, and #1 album in the country".

October 1973
'Time' / 'Breathe' // 'Us And Them' / 'Money'
US: Harvest PRO 6746/7 (promotional 7-inch EP single issued in a picture sleeve with mono mixes for radio play. Includes an edited version of the song 'Money' with the word "bullshit" edited out).

Monday 4 February 1974
'Time' / 'Us And Them'
US: Harvest 3832 (7-inch single).
'Us And Them' (mono) / 'Us And Them' (stereo)
US: Harvest PRO 6829 (promotional 7-inch single).

October 2000
'Money' (edit) / 'Time' (edit)
US: EMI Capitol 72438-58884 (jukebox 7-inch single).

March 2003
'Money'
UK: EMI CD EMDJ 620 (promotional CD single for the SACD release of *The Dark Side Of The Moon*).
US: Capitol CA 4280 (promotional CD single for the SACD release of *The Dark Side Of The Moon*).

Friday 12 September 1975
WISH YOU WERE HERE
UK: EMI Harvest SHVL 814 (vinyl album).
US: Columbia PC 33453 (vinyl album released on Saturday 13 September 1975).
Track list: 'Shine on You Crazy Diamond, Parts 1-5' /

'Welcome To The Machine' // 'Have A Cigar' / 'Wish You Were Here' / 'Shine On You Crazy Diamond, Parts 6-9'. Additional musicians: Dick Parry (saxophones on 'Shine on You Crazy Diamond'), Roy Harper (vocals on 'Have A Cigar'), Venetta Fields and Carlena Williams (backing vocals). Recorded at EMI Studios Abbey Road, London, England. Produced by Pink Floyd. Engineered by Brian Humphries. Artwork by Hipgnosis. Photos of the Hollywood stunt men Ronnie Rondell and Danny Rogers who feature in the burning handshake photos were taken at Warner Brothers Studios, Los Angeles, USA; the red veil against the trees was taken near Ely, Cambridgeshire, England; the faceless salesman was taken in the Yuma Desert, California, USA and the diver taken at Mono Lake, California, USA.
The first vinyl editions had a black shrink-wrap cover obscuring the sleeve artwork with a round 'Wish You Were Here' sticker on the front and an inserted 'Wish You Were Here' postcard.
Highest chart position UK No.1, US No.1.
Certified Silver and Gold in the UK on 1 August 1975.
Highest chart position US No.1. Certified Gold in the US on 17 April 1975; Multi-Platinum (3 times over) on 21 November 1986; Platinum on 21 November 1986; Multi-Platinum (4 times over) on 9 August 1989; Multi-Platinum (5 times over) on 2 May 1995 and Multi-Platinum (6 times over) on 16 May 1997.
Since it was first released, it has sold over 13 million copies worldwide as of 2004. In 2003 *Rolling Stone* named it No.209 of the 500 'Greatest Albums of All Time'. This happened twenty-eight years after the magazine initially panned the recording saying that, 'Passion is everything of which Pink Floyd is devoid.'
Reissued:
UK: EMI Harvest Q4 SHVL 814 (quadraphonic vinyl album, 1976).
UK: EMI Harvest SHVL 814 (A special vinyl album pressing for *Hi-Fi Today* magazine and available only by mail order. The cover has a sticker with the following text: "Supercut – Mastered and Pressed Exclusively for Readers of *Hi Fi Today* by Nimbus Records", 1980).
UK: EMI CDP 7460352 (CD album, 1985).
UK: EMI CD EMD 1062 (digitally remastered CD album with new artwork, 1994).
UK: EMI EMD 1115 (digitally remastered limited edition vinyl album with new artwork, 1997).
US: Columbia PCQ 33453 (quadraphonic vinyl album, 1976).
US: Columbia HC 33453 (Columbia Records Master Sound Half-Speed Master vinyl album, 1981).
US: Columbia CK 33453 (CD album, 1983).
US: Columbia CK 53753 (limited edition Master Sound Sony Records 20 Bit Super Bit Mapping 24-carat gold CD album issued in a special long box, 1994).
US: Columbia CK 64405 (limited edition Master Sound Sony Records 20 Bit Super Bit Mapping picture disc CD, 1997).
US: Columbia CK 68522 (Columbia Records 1997 Anniversary Edition CD album, 1997).
US: Capitol CDP 724382975021 (Capitol Records 2000 reissue CD album, 2000).

Friday 12 September 1975
WISH YOU WERE HERE
US: Columbia PC 33453 (promotional vinyl album release of *Wish You Were Here* for radio play. The disc is banded, with the songs separated with gaps).
Track list: 'Shine On You Crazy Diamond, Parts 1, 2 & 3' (7:35) / 'Shine On You Crazy Diamond, Parts 4 & 5' (5:50) / 'Welcome to the Machine' (7:33) // 'Have A Cigar' (5:25) / 'Wish You Were Here' (5:23) / 'Shine On You Crazy Diamond, Parts 6, 7, 8 & 9' (12:32).

November 1975
'Have A Cigar' (mono) / 'Have A Cigar' (stereo)
US: Columbia 3-10248 (promotional 7-inch single).
'Have A Cigar' / 'Welcome To The Machine'
US: Columbia 3-10248 (promotional 7-inch single).

October 2000
'Wish You Were Here' / 'Have A Cigar'
US: EMI Capitol 72438-58885 (jukebox 7-inch single).

Friday 21 January 1977
ANIMALS
UK: EMI Harvest SHVL 815 (vinyl album).
US: Columbia JC 34474 (vinyl album, released on Saturday 12 February 1977).
Track list: 'Pigs On The Wing, Part 1' / 'Dogs' // Pigs (3 Different Ones)' // 'Sheep' / 'Pigs On The Wing, Part 2'.
Recorded at Britannia Row Studios, London, England.
Produced by Pink Floyd. Engineered by Brian Humphries.
Artwork concept by Roger Waters and executed by Hipgnosis. Photos taken at Battersea Power Station, London.
Highest chart position UK No.2.
Certified Silver and Gold in the UK on 21 April 1977.
Highest chart position US No.3.
Certified Gold in the US on 12 February 1977; Platinum on 10 March 1977; Multi-Platinum (2 times over) on 26 October 1984; Multi-Platinum (3 times over) on 9 August 1989 and Multi-Platinum (4 times over) on 31 January 1995,
Reissued:
UK: EMI CDP 7461282 (CD album, 1985).
UK: EMI CD EMD 1060 (digitally remastered CD album with new artwork, 1994).
UK: EMI EMD 1116 (digitally remastered limited edition vinyl album with new artwork, 1997).
US: Columbia CK 34474 (CD album, 1987).
US: Columbia CK 68521 (Columbia Records 1997 Anniversary Edition CD album, 1997)
US: Capitol CDP 724382974826 (Capitol Records 2000 reissue CD album, 2000).

February 1977
ANIMALS
US: Columbia AP1 (promotional vinyl album of Animals for radio play).
The disc is banded, with the songs separated with gaps. The lyrics for 'Pigs (Three Different Ones)' have been changed to "you old hag" instead of "you fucked up old hag". Also issued with an orange cue sheet.

Track list: 'Pigs on the Wing, Part 1' (1:20) / 'Dogs' (edit, part 1) (5:10) / 'Dogs' (edit, part 2) (5:55), 'Dogs' (edit, part 3) (5:25) // 'Pigs (Three Different Ones)' (11:05) / 'Sheep' (edit, part 1) (4:25) / 'Sheep' (edit, part 2) (5:45).

Friday 23 November 1979
'Another Brick In The Wall, Part 2' / 'One Of My Turns'
UK: EMI Harvest HAR 5194 (7-inch single).
US: Columbia 1-11187 (7-inch single, released on Monday 7 January 1980).
Highest chart position UK No.1 (for 5 weeks).
Certified Silver and Gold in the UK on 1 December 1979 and Platinum on 1 January 1980.
Highest chart position US No.1 (for 4 weeks).
Certified Gold in the US on 24 March 1980 and Platinum on 25 September 2001.
Reissued:
US: Columbia 13-03118 (7-inch single, 1981).
'Another Brick In The Wall, Part 2' / 'Another Brick In The Wall, Part 2'
US: Columbia 1-11187 (promotional 7-inch single).

Friday 30 November 1979
THE WALL
UK: EMI Harvest SHVL 822 (double album).
US: Columbia PC2 36183 (double vinyl album, released on Saturday 8 December 1979).
Track list: 'In The Flesh?' / 'The Thin Ice' / 'Another Brick In The Wall, Part 1' / 'The Happiest Days Of Our Lives' / 'Another Brick In The Wall, Part 2' / 'Mother' // 'Goodbye Blue Sky' / 'Empty Spaces' / 'Young Lust' / 'One Of My Turns' / 'Don't Leave Me Now' / 'Another Brick In The Wall, Part 3' / 'Goodbye Cruel World' // 'Hey You' / 'Is There Anybody Out There?' / 'Nobody Home' / 'Vera' / 'Bring The Boys Back Home' / 'Comfortably Numb' // 'The Show Must Go On' / 'In The Flesh' / 'Run Like Hell' / 'Waiting For The Worms' / 'Stop' / 'The Trial' / 'Outside The Wall'.
Additional musicians: Ron de Blassi (nylon string guitar on 'Is There Anybody Out There?'), Joe Chemay, (backing vocals), Bob Ezrin (additional keyboards and orchestral arrangements), Stan Farber (backing vocals), James Guthrie (miscellaneous effects), Jim Haas (backing vocals), Bobby Hall (congas), Bruce Johnson (backing vocals), John Joyce (backing vocals), Freddie Mandell (additional Hammond organ), Frank Marocco (concertina on 'Outside The Wall'), Blue Ocean (snare drum on 'Bring The Boys Back Home'), Jeff Porcaro (additional drums on 'Mother'), Joe Porcaro (snare drum on 'Bring The Boys Back Home'), Lee Ritenour (additional guitars), Toni Tennille (backing vocals), Trevor Veitch (mandolin on 'Outside The Wall'), Larry Williams (clarinet on 'Outside The Wall'), Peter Woods (additional keyboards), Children of Islington Green Primary School (backing chorus on 'Another Brick In The Wall, Part 2'), Members of The New York City Opera (backing chorus on 'Bring The Boys Back Home'), The New York Philharmonic Orchestra conducted by Michael Kamen (orchestral arrangements).
Recorded at Britannia Row Studios, London, England; Super

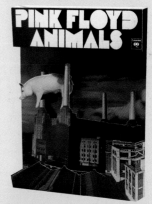

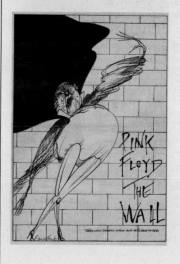

Bear Studios, Berre des Aples, France; Miravel Studios, Le Val, France; CBS Studios, New York City, New York, USA; Cherokee Recording Studios, Los Angeles, California, USA; The Village Recorder, Los Angeles, California, USA and Producers Workshop, Los Angeles, California, USA.
Produced by Bob Ezrin, David Gilmour and Roger Waters. Co-produced by James Guthrie. Engineered by James Guthrie, Nick Griffiths, Patrice Quef, Brian Chrstian, Rick Hart and John McClure.
Artwork concept by Roger Waters and executed by Gerald Scarfe.
The original sleeve offers no credits to any musicians except the words "Written by Roger Waters". Sleeves printed after 1980 list all of the members of Pink Floyd.
Highest chart position UK No.3.
Certified Silver and Gold in the UK on 1 December 1979 and Platinum on 12 December 1979.
Highest chart position US No.1 (for 15 weeks).
Certified Gold and Platinum in the US on 13 March 1980; Multi-Platinum (4 times over) on 26 October 1984; Multi-Platinum (7 times over) on 9 August 1989; Multi-Platinum (8 times over) on 28 May 1991; Multi-Platinum (10 times over) on 2 May 1995; Multi-Platinum (11 times over) on 16 May 1997; Multi-Platinum (22 times over) on 8 September 1997 and Multi-Platinum (23 times over) on 29 January 1999.
In 1980 the album was awarded a Grammy for the Best Engineered, Non Classical Album and sits in third place on the list of best-selling albums ever in the US.
Reissued:
UK: EMI CDS 7460368 (double CD album, 1985).
UK: EMI CD EMD 1111 (remastered CD album with new artwork, 1994).
UK: EMI EMD 1111 (digitally remastered limited edition vinyl album with new artwork, 1997).
US: Columbia H2C 46183 (Master Sound Half-Speed Master double vinyl album, 1981).
US: Harvest C2K 36183 (double CD album, 1983).
US: Mobile Fidelity Sound Lab UDCD 2-537 (original master recording 24 carat gold Ultra Disc CD album and issued in a limited edition long box with unique sleeve art, 1990).
US: Mobile Fidelity Sound Lab UDCD 2-537 (re-issued MFSL CD album in a regular slip case, 1991).
US: Columbia C2K 68519 (Columbia Records 1997 Anniversary Edition CD album, 1997).
US: Capitol CDP 724383124329 (Capitol Records 2000 reissue CD album, 2000).

December 1980
PINK FLOYD – OFF THE WALL
US: Columbia AS 736 (promotional vinyl album issued in a specially designed Gerald Scarfe 'Wall' sleeve).
Track list: 'Another Brick in the Wall, Part 2' / 'Goodbye Blue Sky' / 'Young Lust' / 'One of My Turns' // 'Hey You' / 'Nobody Home' / 'Comfortably Numb' / 'Run Like Hell'.

Monday 9 June 1980
'Run Like Hell' / 'Don't Leave Me Now'
US: Columbia 1-11265 (7-inch single).
Highest chart position US No.53.
'Run Like Hell' / 'Run Like Hell'
US: Columbia 1-11265 (promotional 7-inch single).
'Run Like Hell' / 'Don't Leave Me Now'
US: Columbia AS 777 (promotional 12-inch single).
'Run Like Hell' / 'Another Brick In The Wall, Part 2'
US: Columbia AS 783 (promotional 12-inch single).

Monday 23 June 1980
'Comfortably Numb' / 'Hey You'
US: Columbia 1-11311 (7-inch single).
'Comfortably Numb' (long version) / 'Comfortably Numb' (short version)
US: Columbia 1-11311 (promotional 7-inch single).

Monday 30 June 1980
'Run Like Hell' / 'Comfortably Numb'
US: Columbia 13-02165 (7-inch single).
Reissued:
US: Columbia Hall Of Fame 13-03118 (7-inch single, 1981).
US: Columbia Records Collectibles 13-03118 (7-inch single, 1984).

Monday 26 July 1982
'When The Tigers Broke Free' / 'Bring The Boys Back Home'
UK: EMI Harvest HAR 5222 (7-inch single issued in both a single and a six-panel fold out sleeve).
US: Columbia AS 1541 (promotional 12-inch single).
Highest chart position UK No.39.
'When The Tigers Broke Free' / 'When The Tigers Broke Free'
US: Columbia X18-03142 (7-inch single issued in a six-panel fold out sleeve).

Monday 21 March 1983
THE FINAL CUT
UK: EMI Harvest SHPF 1983 (vinyl album).
US: Columbia QC 38243 (vinyl album, released on Saturday 2 April 1983).
Track list: 'The Post War Dream' / 'Your Possible Pasts' / 'One Of The Few' / 'The Hero's Return' / 'The Gunner's Dream' / 'Paranoid Eyes' // 'Get Your Filthy Hands Off My Desert' / 'The Fletcher Memorial Home' / 'Southampton Dock' / 'The Final Cut' / 'Not Now John' / 'Two Suns In The Sunset'.
Additional musicians: Michael Kamen (piano, harmonium), Andy Bown (Hammond organ), Ray Cooper (percussion), Andy Newmark (drums on 'Two Suns In The Sunset'), Raphael Ravenscroft (tenor sax), uncredited female backing vocalists (although most likely to have been Katie Kissoon, Doreen Chanter and Madeline Bell) and the National Philharmonic conducted and arranged by Michael Kamen.
Recorded at Mayfair Studios, London, England; Olympic Studios, London, England; EMI Abbey Road Studios, London, England; Eel Pie Studios, London, England; Audio

International, London, England; RAK Studios, London, England; Hookend Studios, London, England and The Billiard Room Studios, London, England between July and December 1982.

Produced by Roger Waters, James Guthrie and Michael Kamen. Engineered by James Guthrie and Andy Jackson. Artwork concept by Roger Waters and executed by Artful Dodgers. The front cover shows a selection of British Second World War medal ribbons that would have been awarded to a member of the Royal Air Force: The Distinguished Flying Cross (White with diagonal purple stripes); The 1939-45 Star (Equal stripes of dark blue, red and light blue); The Africa Star (Sand with dark blue, red and light blue stripes); followed by The Defence Medal (Orange with wide green edges bearing narrow black stripes).

Highest chart position UK No.1.

Certified Silver and Gold in the UK on 24 March 1983.

Highest chart position US No.6.

Certified Gold and Platinum in the US on 23 May 1983 and Multi-Platinum (2 times over) on 31 January 1997.

Reissued:

UK: EMI CDP 7461292 (CD album, 1985).

UK: EMI CD EMD 1070 (digitally remastered edition with a bonus track, 'When the Tigers Broke Free' and new artwork, 2004).

US: CBS CK 38243 (CD album, 1985).

US: Columbia CK 68517 (Columbia Records 1997 Anniversary Edition CD album, 1997).

US: Capitol 724357673426 (digitally remastered edition with a bonus track, 'When the Tigers Broke Free' and new artwork, 2004).

April 1983
THE FINAL CUT
US: Columbia AS 1636 (promotional vinyl album for radio play. The disc is banded, with the songs separated with gaps).

Track list: 'The Post War Dream' / 'Your Possible Pasts' / 'One Of The Few' / 'The Hero's Return' / 'The Gunner's Dream' / 'Paranoid Eyes' // 'Get Your Filthy Hands Off My Desert' / 'The Fletcher Memorial Home' / 'Southampton Dock' / 'The Final Cut' / 'Not Now John' / 'Two Suns In The Sunset'.

May 1983
'Not Now John' (obscured version) / 'Not Now John' (obscured version)
US: Columbia AE7 1653 (promotional 7-inch single. The recording has the expletive edited out).

'Not Now John' (obscured version) / 'Not Now John' (obscured version)
US: Columbia 38-03905 (promotional 7-inch single. The recording has the expletive edited out).

May 1983
SELECTIONS FROM THE FINAL CUT
US: Columbia AS 1635 (promotional 12-inch single).
Track list: 'Your Possible Pasts' / 'The Final Cut'.

Tuesday 3 May 1983
'Not Now John' (single version) // 'The Hero's Return (Parts 1 & 2)' / 'Not Now John' (album version)
UK: EMI Harvest 12 HAR 5224 (12-inch single).
'Not Now John'/ 'The Hero's Return (Parts 1 & 2)'
UK: EMI Harvest HAR 5224 (7-inch single).
UK: EMI Harvest HAR DJ 5224 (promotional 7-inch single).
Highest chart position UK No.30.
The chorus on 'Not Now John' of "fuck all that" was overdubbed with "stuff all that" for the single release to ensure radio play.

August 1987
'Learning To Fly' (album version) / 'Learning To Fly' (edit)
US: Columbia CSK 2775 (promotional CD single).
'Learning To Fly' (edit) / 'Learning To Fly' (edit)
US: Columbia 38-03905 (promotional 7-inch single).
'Learning To Fly' (album version) / 'Learning To Fly' (edit)
US: Columbia CAS 2775 (promotional 12-inch single).

Monday 7 September 1987
A MOMENTARY LAPSE OF REASON
UK: EMI EMD 1003 (vinyl album).
UK: EMI CDP 7480682 (CD album).
US: Columbia OC 40599 (vinyl album, released on Tuesday 8 September 1987).
US: Columbia CK 40599 (CD album).
Track list: 'Signs Of Life' / 'Learning To Fly' / 'The Dogs Of War' / 'One Slip' / 'On The Turning Away' // 'Yet Another Movie' / 'Round And Around' / 'A New Machine, Part 1' / 'Terminal Frost' / 'A New Machine, Part 2' / 'Sorrow'.
Additional musicians: Bob Ezrin (keyboards, percussion, sequencers), Tony Levin (bass guitar, stick), Jim Keltner (drums), Steve Forman (percussion), Jon Carin (keyboards), Tom Scott (alto & soprano saxophone), Scott Page (tenor saxophone), Carmine Appice (drums), Pat Leonard (synthesizers), Bill Payne (Hammond organ), Michael Landau (guitar), John Halliwell (saxophone), Darlene Koldenhaven, Carmen Twillie, Phyllis St.James, Donnie Gerrard (backing vocals).
Recorded at The Astoria, Hampton, England; Britannia Row Studios, London, England; Mayfair Studios, London, England; Audio International Studios, London, England; A&M Studios, Los Angeles, USA; Village Recorder, Los Angeles, USA and Can Am Studios, Los Angeles, USA.
Produced by Bob Ezrin and David Gilmour. Engineered and mixed by Andrew Jackson. Additional re-mixing James Guthrie.
Artwork by Storm Thorgerson. The front cover shot was taken at Saunton Sands, Devon, England using 800 wrought iron hospital beds and won photographer Robert Dowling a gold award at the Association of Photographers Awards for his photo. The band portrait was by David Bailey.
Highest chart position UK No.3.
Certified Silver and Gold in the UK on 1 October 1987.
Highest chart position US No.3.
Certified Gold and Platinum in the US on 9 November 1987;

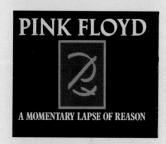

349

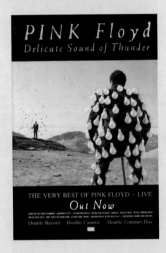

Multi-Platinum (2 times over) on 18 January 1988; Multi-Platinum (3 times over) on 10 March 1992 and Multi-Platinum (4 times over) on 16 August 2001.
Reissued:
UK: EMI EMDS 1003 (limited edition poster-pack vinyl album with a guaranteed ticket application for the upcoming UK concerts, 1988)
UK: EMI CD EMD 1003 (digitally remastered CD album with new artwork, 1994).
US: Columbia CK 68518 (Columbia Records 1997 Anniversary Edition CD album, 1997).

Monday 14 September 1987
'Learning To Fly' (edit) / 'Learning To Fly' (edit)
US: Columbia 38-07363 (7-inch single).
Highest chart position US No.70.

Monday 5 October 1987
'Learning To Fly' (edit) / 'One Slip' (edit)
UK: EMI EM 26 (promotional 7-inch pink vinyl single).
UK: EMI EM 26 (promotional 7-inch black vinyl single).

November 1987
'On The Turning Away'/ 'On The Turning Away'
US: Columbia 38-07660 (promotional 7-inch single).
'On The Turning Away' (7-inch edit) / 'On The Turning Away' (live)
US: Columbia CAS 2878 (promotional 12-inch single).

November 1987
A MOMENTARY LAPSE OF REASON OFFICIAL TOUR CD
US: Columbia CSK 1100 (promotional CD EP).
Track list: 'The Dogs Of War' (edit) / 'The Dogs Of War' / 'On The Turning Away'.

Monday 14 December 1987
'On The Turning Away' / 'Run Like Hell' (live)
UK: EMI EM 34 (7-inch single).
UK: EMI EMP 34 (limited 7-inch pink vinyl single).
UK: EMI EM DJ 34 (promotional 7-inch single).
US: Columbia 38-07660 (7-inch single released on Monday 23 November 1987).
'On The Turning Away' // 'Run Like Hell' (live) / 'On The Turning Away' (live)
UK: EMI 12 EM 34 (12-inch single).
UK: EMI 12 EMP 34 (limited 12-inch single in poster sleeve).
'Run Like Hell' (live) and 'On The Turning Away' (live) were recorded live in Atlanta on 5 November 1987.
Highest chart position UK No.55.

Monday 13 June 1988
'One Slip' / 'Terminal Frost'
UK: EMI EM52 (7-inch single).
UK: EMI EMG 52 (limited 7-inch pink vinyl single in gatefold sleeve).
'One Slip' // 'Terminal Frost' / 'The Dogs Of War' (live)
UK: EMI 12 EMP 52 (limited 12-inch single in poster sleeve).
Highest chart position UK No.50.

November 1988
DELICATE SOUND OF THUNDER
UK: EMI CD PINK 1 (promotional CD single).
Track list: 'Wish You Were Here' / 'Learning To Fly' / 'Run Like Hell'.
DELICATE SOUND OF THUNDER
UK: EMI 12 PF1 (promotional 12-inch single).
Track list: 'Another Brick In The Wall, Part 2' / 'One Of These Days' // 'Run Like Hell'.
DELICATE SOUND OF THUNDER
Columbia CSK 1375 (promotional CD EP).
Track list: 'Comfortably Numb' / 'Learning To Fly' / 'Time' / 'Another Brick In The Wall, Part 2'.

Monday 21 November 1988
DELICATE SOUND OF THUNDER
UK: EMI EQ 5009 (double vinyl album).
UK: EMI CDEQ 5009 (double CD).
US: Columbia PC2 44484 (double vinyl album released on Monday 21 November 1988).
US: Columbia C2K 44484 (double CD).
Track list: 'Shine On You Crazy Diamond, Parts 1-5' / 'Learning To Fly' / 'Yet Another Movie' / 'Round And Around' / 'Sorrow' / 'The Dogs Of War' / 'On The Turning Away' // 'One Of These Days' / 'Time' / 'Wish You Were Here' / 'Us And Them' (not on vinyl) / 'Money' (not on cassette) / 'Another Brick In The Wall, Part 2' / 'Comfortably Numb' / 'Run Like Hell'.
Recorded live at the Nassau Veterans Memorial Coliseum, New York, USA between 19 and 23 August 1988 by Remote Recording Services.
Produced by David Gilmour. Engineered by Buford Jones. Artwork by Storm Thorgerson.
Highest chart position UK No.11.
Certified Silver and Gold in the UK on 8 December 1988.
Highest chart position US No.11.
Certified Gold and Platinum in the US on 23 January 1989 and Multi-Platinum (3 times over) on 8 September 1987.

March 1994
'Keep Talking' (radio edit) / 'High Hopes' (radio edit)
UK: EMI CD EMDJ 342 (promotional CD single for *The Division Bell*).
'Keep Talking'
US: Columbia CSK 6007 (one-track promotional CD single for *The Division Bell*).

Monday 28 March 1994
THE DIVISION BELL
UK: EMI EMD 1055 (vinyl album).
UK: EMI CD EMD 1055 (CD album).
US: Columbia C 64200 (vinyl album - also issued on limited edition blue vinyl, released on Monday 4 April 1994).
US: Columbia CK 64200 (CD album).
Track list: 'Cluster One' / 'What Do You Want From Me' / 'Poles Apart' / 'Marooned' / 'A Great Day For Freedom' / 'Wearing The Inside Out' / 'Take It Back' / 'Coming Back To Life' / 'Keep Talking' / 'Lost For Words' / 'High Hopes'.
Note: The vinyl album is shorter than the CD version and the

following songs were edited in length to allow the album to fit onto an LP: 'Poles Apart', 'Marooned', 'Wearing The Inside Out', 'Coming Back To Life', 'Lost For Words' and 'High Hopes'.

Additional musicians: Jon Carin (programming, additional keyboards), Guy Pratt (bass), Gary Wallis (played & programmed percussion), Tim Renwick (guitars), Dick Parry (tenor saxophone), Bob Ezrin (keyboards, percussion), Sam Brown, Durga McBroom, Carol Kenyon, Jackie Sheridan and Rebecca Leigh-White (backing vocals). Orchestrations by Michael Kamen and Edward Shearmur and arranged by Michael Kamen.

Recorded at Britannia Row Studios, London England; The Astoria, Hampton, England; Metropolis Studios, London England and The Creek Recording Studios, London, England. Produced by David Gilmour and Bob Ezrin. Mixed by Chris Thomas and David Gilmour. Recording and Mixing by Andrew Jackson.

Artwork by Storm Thorgerson. Cover photos of the sculptures taken near Ely, Cambridgeshire.

Highest chart position UK No.1.

Certified Silver and Gold in the UK on 1 April 1994, Platinum on 1 May 1994 and Multi-Platinum (2 times over) on 1 October 1994.

Highest chart position US No.1.

Certified Gold and Multi-Platinum (2 times over) in the US on 6 June 1994 and Multi-Platinum (3 times over) on 29 January 1999.

April 1994
PINK FLOYD INTERVIEW

US: Columbia CSK 6060 (38 track promo CD album with interviews and music for *The Division Bell*).

Track list: 'Keep Talking' / Interviews / 'Take It Back'.

Printed on the inner cover is the text: 'What you are hearing on this CD is music from Pink Floyd's *THE DIVISION BELL* and an interview done in Southern California, March 26, 1994. It took place just prior to their US tour which sold nearly three million tickets across the country. *THE DIVISION BELL* is an album made up of songs about communication. The disc is an effort to provide you with the opportunity to have questions answered and to gain insight into Pink Floyd'. (Tracks 1 & 38) 'Taken from the Columbia release: *The Division Bell* 64200. Tracks 2-18 David Gilmour, Tracks 19-31 Nick Mason, Tracks 32-37 Richard Wright.

Monday 16 May 1994
'Take It Back' (edit) / 'Astronomy Dominé (live)

UK: EMI EM 309 (limited edition 7-inch red vinyl single).
US: Columbia 38-77493 (7-inch single released on Tuesday 31 May 1994).
'Astronomy Dominé' was recorded live in Miami on 30 March 1994.
Highest chart position US No.73.

'Take It Back'

UK: EMI CD EMDJ 309 (one-track promotional CD single for *The Division Bell*).
Highest chart position UK No.23.

'Take It Back' (edit) / 'Take It Back' (album version)

US: Columbia CSK 6069 (promotional CD single for *The Division Bell*).

June 1994
'Lost For Words' (clean version) / 'Lost For Words' (album version)

US: Columbia CSK 6228 (promotional CD single for *The Division Bell*).
The 'clean version' has the word 'fuck' bleeped out.

July 1994
'High Hopes'

US: Columbia CSK 6440 (promotional CD single for *The Division Bell*).

Monday 17 October 1994
'High Hopes' (radio edit) / 'Keep Talking' (radio edit)

UK: EMI EM 342 (limited 7-inch clear vinyl single with poster sleeve).

'High Hopes' (album version) / 'Keep Talking' (album version) / 'One Of These Days' (live)

UK: EMI CD EM 342 (CD single).
UK: EMI CD EMS 342 (limited CD single in digipak with postcards).
UK: EMI 12 EM 342 (12-inch one sided single in etched coloured vinyl with postcards).
Highest chart position UK No.26.

May 1995
'Coming Back To Life' (edit) / 'Coming Back To Life'

US: Columbia CSK 7096 (promotional CD single for *PULSE*).

May 1995
'What Do You Want From Me' (live)

US: Columbia CSK 7143 (promotional CD single for *PULSE*).

Monday 5 June 1995
PULSE

UK: EMI CD EMD 1078 (double CD album with hard-back booklet and flashing LED on spine).
US: Columbia C2K 67065 (double CD album with hard-back booklet and flashing LED on spine released on Monday 5 June 1995).
Track list: 'Shine On You Crazy Diamond, Parts 1-6' / 'Astronomy Dominé' / 'What Do You Want From Me' / 'Learning To Fly' / 'Keep Talking' / 'Coming Back To Life' / 'Hey You' / 'A Great Day For Freedom' / 'Sorrow' / 'High Hopes' / 'Another Brick In The Wall, Part 2' // *The Dark Side Of The Moon* / 'Wish You Were Here' / 'Comfortably Numb' / 'Run Like Hell'.
Recorded in Europe 1994 (see below for sources).
Produced by James Guthrie and David Gilmour. Recorded and mixed by James Guthrie.
Artwork by Storm Thorgerson.
Highest chart position UK No.1.
Certified Silver and Gold in the UK on 1 October 1995.
Highest chart position US No.1.

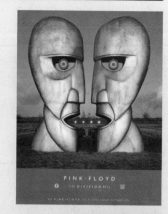

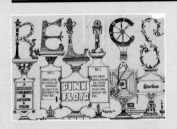

Certified Gold and Platinum in the US on 31 July 1995.
Reissued:
UK: EMI CD EMD 1078 (double CD album in slim case, 1995).
US: Columbia C2K 67064 (double CD album in slim case, 1995).

PULSE

UK: EMI TC EMD 1078 (double cassette album).
US: US: Columbia C2K 67065 (double cassette album).
Track list: 'Shine On You Crazy Diamond, Parts 1-6' / 'Astronomy Dominé' / 'What Do You Want From Me' / 'Learning To Fly' / 'Keep Talking' / 'Coming Back To Life' / 'Hey You' / 'A Great Day For Freedom' / 'Sorrow' / 'High Hopes' / 'Another Brick In The Wall, Part 2' / 'One Of These Days' // *The Dark Side Of The Moon* / 'Wish You Were Here' / 'Comfortably Numb' / 'Run Like Hell' / pre-concert sound effects.

PULSE

UK: EMI LP EMD 1078 (quadruple album box set with hard-back book).
Track list: 'Shine On You Crazy Diamond, Parts 1-6' / 'Astronomy Dominé' / 'What Do You Want From Me' / 'Learning To Fly' / 'Keep Talking' / 'Coming Back To Life' // 'Hey You' / 'A Great Day For Freedom' / 'Sorrow' / 'High Hopes' / 'Another Brick In The Wall, Part 2' / 'One Of These Days' // *The Dark Side of The Moon* ('Speak to Me' through to 'Money') // *The Dark Side Of The Moon* ('Us and Them' through to 'Eclipse') / 'Wish You Were Here' / 'Comfortably Numb' / 'Run Like Hell'.

PULSE – the recording sources:
'Shine On You Crazy Diamond, Parts 1-6' (London, 20 October) / 'Astronomy Dominé' (London, 15 October) / 'What Do You Want From Me' (Rome, 21 September) / 'Learning To Fly' (London, 14 October) / 'Keep Talking' (Hannover, 17 August) / 'Coming Back To Life' (Rome, 21 September) / 'Hey You' (London, 13 October, except last verse London, 15 October) / 'A Great Day For Freedom' (London, 19 October) / 'Sorrow' (Rome, 20 September) / 'High Hopes' (London, 20 October) / 'Another Brick In The Wall, Part 2' (London, 21 October) / 'One Of These Days' (London, 16 October, except ending London, 20 October) / 'Speak To Me' (London, 20 October) / 'Breathe' (London, 20 October) / 'On The Run' (London, 20 October) / 'Time' (Rome, 20 September except introduction Modena 17 September and explosion London, 15 October) / 'Breathe (reprise)' (Rome, 20 September except fade out London, 20 October) / 'The Great Gig In The Sky' (London, 20 October) / 'Money' (Modena, 17 September) / 'Us And Them' (London, 20 October except second and third chorus London, 19 October) / 'Any Colour You Like' (London, 23 October except fade out 19 October) / 'Brain Damage' (London, 19 October) / 'Eclipse' (London, 19 October) / 'Wish You Were Here' (Rome, 20 September) / 'Comfortably Numb' (London, 20 October) / 'Run Like Hell' (London, 15 October).

COLLECTIONS

Friday 14 May 1971
RELICS

UK: Starline EMI SRS 5071 (vinyl album).
US: Harvest SW 759 (vinyl album released on Saturday 17 July 1971).
Track list: 'Arnold Layne' / 'Interstellar Overdrive' / 'See Emily Play' / 'Remember A Day' / 'Paintbox' // 'Julia Dream' / 'Careful With That Axe, Eugene' / 'Cirrus Minor' / 'The Nile Song' / 'Biding My Time' / 'Bike'.
Tracks produced variously by Pink Floyd, Norman Smith and Joe Boyd.
Artwork by Nick Mason.
Highest chart position UK No.32, US No.153.
Reissued:
UK: EMI Music For Pleasure MFP 50397 (vinyl album, 1980).
UK: EMI CDEMD 1113 (digitally remastered CD album with new artwork, 1996).
UK: EMI EMD 1113 (digitally remastered vinyl album with new artwork, 1997).
US: Harvest SW 759 (vinyl album, 1975).
US: Capitol SN 16234 (vinyl album, 1983).
US: Capitol CDP 724383560325 (digitally remastered CD album with new artwork, 1996).

Friday 18 January 1974
A NICE PAIR

UK: EMI Harvest SHDW 403 (double vinyl album).
US: Harvest SABB 11257 (double vinyl album released on Saturday 8 December 1974).
A repackage of the albums *The Piper At The Gates Of Dawn* and *A Saucerful Of Secrets*.
Artwork by Hipgnosis. Original copies featured a photograph of the window of Dr. Phang's dental surgery, but because dentists were not allowed to advertise in the UK at that time, a re-print was made with this picture replaced by that of a gargling monk.
Highest chart position UK No.21.
Certified Silver in the UK on 1 May 1974 and Gold on 1 February 1975.
Highest chart position US No.36.
Certified Gold in the US on 11 March 1994.
Reissued:
US: Capitol SABB 11257 (re-issued double vinyl album, 1983).

April 1975
TOUR '75

US: EMI SPRO 8116/7 (promotional vinyl album issued in a plain white sleeve and a cover mounted print with the track listing).
Track list: 'The Gold It's In The...' / 'Wot's... Uh the Deal' / 'Free Four' / 'One Of These Days' // 'Fat Old Sun' / 'Astronomy Dominé' / 'Careful With That Axe, Eugene'.

Friday 6 July 1979
PINK FLOYD FIRST XI
UK: EMI Harvest PF11 (vinyl box set).
Limited edition of 1,000 pressings containing 11 albums in original sleeves:
The Piper At The Gates Of Dawn / _A Saucerful Of Secrets_ / _More_ / _Ummagumma_ / _Atom Heart Mother_ / _Relics_ / _Meddle_ / _Obscured By Clouds_ / _The Dark Side Of The Moon_ (issued as a picture disc) / _Wish You Were Here_ (issued as a picture disc) / _Animals_.

November 1981
'Money' (remix) / 'Another Brick In The Wall, Part 2'
US: Columbia AS 1334 (promotional 12-inch single on pink vinyl taken from _A Collection Of Great Dance Songs_).

Monday 23 November 1981
A COLLECTION OF GREAT DANCE SONGS
UK: EMI Harvest SHVL 822 (vinyl album)
US: Columbia TC 37680 (vinyl album released on Saturday 21 November 1981).
Track list: 'One Of These Days' / 'Money' (re-recorded version) / 'Sheep' // 'Shine On You Crazy Diamond, Parts 1-9' / 'Wish You Were Here' / 'Another Brick In The Wall, Part 2'.
Produced by Pink Floyd, except the re-recorded version of 'Money' produced by David Gilmour and recorded at New Roydonia Studios, London, England.
Artwork by Hipgnosis.
Highest chart position UK No.37.
Certified Silver and Gold in the UK on 24 November 1981.
Highest chart position US No.31.
Certified Gold in the US on 29 January 1982; Platinum on 6 July 1989 and Multi-Platinum (2 times over) on 16 August 2001.
Reissued:
UK: EMI Fame EMI FA 3144 (vinyl album, 1983).
UK: EMI CDP 7 90732 2 (CD album, 1985).
US: Columbia HC 47680 (CBS Master Sound Half-Speed Master vinyl album, 1981).
US: Columbia FC 37680 (vinyl album, 1983).
US: Columbia CK 37680 (CD album, 1985).
US: Columbia CK 68520 (Columbia 1997 anniversary edition CD album, 1997).
US: Capitol CDP 72435262452 (Capitol Records 2000 edition CD album, 2000).

November 1981
'Money' (re-recorded version)
UK: EMI Harvest HAR 5217 (promotional one-sided pink vinyl 7-inch single taken from _A Collection Of Great Dance Songs_).
'Money' (re-recorded version) / 'Let There Be More Light' was scheduled as a 12-inch single for release on Monday 7 December 1981 but was never pressed.

Saturday 18 June 1983
WORKS
US: Capitol ST 12276 (vinyl album).
Track list: 'One of These Days' / 'Arnold Layne' / 'Fearless' /

'Brain Damage' / 'Eclipse' / 'Set the Controls for the Heart of the Sun' // 'See Emily Play' / 'Several Species of Small Furry Animals Gathered Together In A Cave And Grooving With a Pict' / 'Free Four' / 'The Embryo'.
Highest chart position US No.68.
Reissued:
US: Capitol CDP 7464782 (CD album, 1987).

June 1988
PINK FLOYD IN EUROPE 1988
UK: EMI PSLP 1016 (promotional 12-inch EP).
Track list: 'Money' / 'Shine On You Crazy Diamond, Parts 1-5' / 'Another Brick in The Wall, Part 2' / 'One Slip' / 'On The Turning Away' / 'Learning To Fly'.

Monday 2 November 1992
SHINE ON
UK: EMI PFBOX 1 (CD box set).
Nine CD box set with postcards and a hard-back book containing the albums: _A Saucerful Of Secrets_ (EMI CDS 78056423) / _Meddle_ (EMI CDS 78056522) / _The Dark Side Of The Moon_ (EMI CDS 78056621 / _Wish You Were Here_ (EMI CDS 78056720 / _Animals_ (EMI CDS 78056829 / _The Wall_ (Part 1) (EMI CDS 78056928 / _The Wall_ (Part 2) (EMI CDS 78057024) / _A Momentary Lapse Of Reason_ (EMI CDS 78057123 / Bonus CD: _The Early Singles_ (EMI CDS 78057222) (containing: 'Arnold Layne' / 'Candy And A Currant Bun' / 'See Emily Play' / 'Scarecrow' / 'Apples And Oranges' / 'Paintbox' / 'It Would Be So Nice' / 'Julia Dream' / 'Point Me At The Sky' / 'Careful With That Axe, Eugene'.
US: Columbia CXK 53180 S1 (CD box set released on Monday 2 November 1992).
Nine CD box set with postcards and a hard-back book containing the albums: _A Saucerful Of Secrets_ (CK 53182) / _Meddle_ (CK 53183) / _The Dark Side Of The Moon_ (CK 53184) / _Wish You Were Here_ (CK 53185) / _Animals_ (CK 53186) / _The Wall, Part 1_ (CK 53187) / _The Wall, Part 2_ (CK 53188) / _A Momentary Lapse Of Reason_ (CK 53189) / Bonus CD: _The Early Singles_ (CK 53181) containing: 'Arnold Layne' / 'Candy And A Currant Bun' / 'See Emily Play' / 'Scarecrow' / 'Apples And Oranges' / 'Paintbox' / 'It Would Be So Nice' / 'Julia Dream' / 'Point Me At The Sky' / 'Careful With That Axe, Eugene'.
Artwork by Hipgnosis.
Certified Gold in the US on 2 April 1993 and Platinum on 8 October 1996.

November 1992
SELECTED TRACKS FROM SHINE ON
UK: EMI SHINE 1 (promotional CD album).
US: Columbia CSK 4848 (promotional CD album).
Track list: 'See Emily Play' / 'Set The Controls For The Heart Of The Sun' / 'One Of These Days' / 'Money' / 'Shine On You Crazy Diamond' (radio edit) / 'Dogs' / 'Comfortably Numb' / 'Another Brick In The Wall, Part 2' / 'One Slip'.

November 1992
A CD FULL OF SECRETS
US: Westwood One Volume 10 (promotional CD issued by the Westwood One radio network).
Track list: 'Candy And A Currant Bun' / 'See Emily Play' / 'Flaming' / 'Apples And Oranges' / 'Paintbox' / 'It Would Be So Nice' / 'Julia Dream' / 'Point Me At The Sky' / 'Heart Beat, Pig Meat' / 'Crumbling Land' / 'Come In Number 51, Your Time Is Up' / 'Biding My Time' / 'Money' / 'When The Tigers Broke Free' / 'Not Now John' / 'Terminal Frost' / 'Run Like Hell'.

Monday 5 April 1993
PINK FLOYD GIFT SET
US: Capitol C2-91340 (CD box set).
A four CD budget box set that includes the albums *Atom Heart Mother, Meddle, Obscured By Clouds,* and *The Dark Side of the Moon. The Dark Side of the Moon* CD is the 1992 remastered version.

Monday 4 August 1997
THE FIRST THREE SINGLES
UK: EMI CD EMD 1117 (CD album).
A mini-album housed in a gatefold card sleeve was issued at the same time as the 30th anniversary edition of *Piper At The Gates Of Dawn* CD and in some cases given way as a free bonus CD. It contains the original A and B side mono mixes of the first three singles ('Arnold Layne' / 'Candy And A Currant Bun' / 'See Emily Play' / 'Scarecrow' / 'Apples And Oranges' / 'Paintbox') and its front and back cover features reproduced sleeves of the original 7-inch singles.

Monday 18 August 1997
1997 VINYL COLLECTION
UK: EMI 724385989315 (vinyl album box set).
A limited edition vinyl box set with 180 gram vinyl pressings including *Piper At The Gates Of Dawn, Atom Heart Mother, The Dark Side Of The Moon* (issued as a picture disc), *Wish You Were Here* (issued as a picture disc), *Animals, The Wall* and *Relics.* Each album has a gatefold sleeve with new artwork designed by Storm Thorgerson with a sticker in the middle of the front sleeve and a catalogue insert.
All above albums made available individually as follows:
Piper At The Gates Of Dawn (EMI LP EMP 1110), *Atom Heart Mother* (EMI LP EMP 1112), *Relics* (EMI LP EMP 1113), *The Dark Side Of The Moon* (EMI LP EMP 1114. Issued as a picture disc), *Wish You Were Here* (EMI LP EMP 1115. Issued as a picture disc), *Animals* (EMI LP EMP 1116), *The Wall* (EMI LP EMP 1111).

February 2000
'Young Lust' (live)
US: Columbia 62055 (promotonal one-track CD single for *Is There Anybody Out There? The Wall Live: Pink Floyd 1980-81*).

February 2000
IS THERE ANYBODY OUT THERE? THE WALL LIVE: PINK FLOYD 1980-81
US: Columbia CSK 12680 (promotional CD EP).
Track list: 'In The Flesh' / 'Another Brick In The Wall, Part 2' / 'Goodbye Blue Sky'.

27 March 2000
IS THERE ANYBODY OUT THERE? THE WALL LIVE: PINK FLOYD 1980-81
UK: EMI 5235622 (limited edition double CD album housed in a slipcase and presented with a detailed booklet with interviews from all band members and supporting hands).
US: Columbia C2K 62055 (also as a limited edition double CD album in long box slipcase and booklet released on Monday 17 April 2000).
Produced and mixed by James Guthrie.
Recorded live at Earls Court, London, England on 7, 8, 9 August 1980 and 14, 15, 16 & 17 June 1981.
Additional musicians as per the live performances.
Track list: MC introductions (Gary Yudman) / 'In The Flesh' / 'The Thin Ice' / 'Another Brick In The Wall, Part 1' / 'The Happiest Days Of Our Lives' / 'Another Brick In The Wall, Part 2' / 'Mother' / 'Goodbye Blue Sky' / 'Empty Spaces' / 'What Shall We Do Now?' / 'Young Lust' / 'One Of My Turns' / 'Don't Leave Me Now' / 'Another Brick In The Wall, Part 3' / 'The Last Few Bricks' / 'Goodbye Cruel World' // 'Hey You' / 'Is There Anybody Out There?' / 'Nobody Home' / 'Vera' / 'Bring The Boys Back Home' / 'Comfortably Numb' / 'The Show Must Go On' / MC introductions (Gary Yudman) / 'In The Flesh' / 'Run Like Hell' / 'Waiting For The Worms' / 'Stop' / 'The Trial' / 'Outside The Wall'.
Artwork by Storm Thorgerson.
Highest chart position UK No.15.
Certified Silver in the UK on 7 April 2000.
Highest chart position US No.19.
Certified Gold and Platinum in the US on 22 May 2000.

February 2005
'Another Brick In The Wall, Part 2' / 'Another Brick In The Wall, Part 2'
US: Columbia CS751388 (promotional 7-inch single for *Is There Anybody Out There? The Wall Live: Pink Floyd 1980-81* issued on white vinyl).

Monday 5 November 2001
ECHOES – THE BEST OF PINK FLOYD
UK: EMI 5361112 (double CD album).
US: Capitol CDP 7243 5 36111 2 5 (double CD album released on Monday 5 November 2001).
Track List: 'Astronomy Dominé' / 'See Emily Play' / 'The Happiest Days Of Our Lives' / 'Another Brick In The Wall, Part 2' / 'Echoes' / 'Hey You' / 'Marooned' / 'The Great Gig In The Sky' / 'Set The Controls For The Heart Of The Sun' / 'Money' / 'Keep Talking' / 'Sheep' / 'Sorrow' / 'Shine On You Crazy Diamond, Parts 1-7' / 'Time' / 'The Fletcher Memorial Home' / 'Comfortably Numb' / 'When The Tigers Broke Free' / 'One Of These Days' / 'Us and Them' / 'Learning To Fly' / 'Arnold Layne' / 'Wish You Were Here' / 'Jugband Blues' /

'High Hopes' / 'Bike'.
Artwork by Storm Thorgerson.
Highest chart position UK No.2.
Certified Silver and Gold in the UK on 16 November 2001;
Platinum on 21 December 2001 and Multi-Platinum (2 times over) on 11 January 2002.
Highest chart position US No.1.
Certified Gold, Platinum and Double Platinum in the US on 6 December 2001 and Multi-Platinum (3 times over) on 8 January 2002.

November 2001
ECHOES – THE BEST OF PINK FLOYD – 6 TRACK SAMPLER
UK: EMI CD LRL 054 (promotional CD in custom card sleeve).
Track List: 'See Emily Play' / 'Money' / 'The Happiest Days Of Our Lives' / 'Another Brick In The Wall, Part 2' / 'Learning To Fly' / 'Wish You Were Here'.

November 2001
ECHOES – THE BEST OF PINK FLOYD – 8 TRACK SAMPLER
US: Capitol DPRO 708761599121 (promotional CD in custom card sleeve).
Track List: 'When The Tigers Broke Free' / 'Shine On You Crazy Diamond, Parts 1-7' / 'Wish You Were Here' / 'Another Brick In The Wall, Part 2' / 'Echoes' / 'Hey You' / 'Comfortably Numb' / 'Money'.

UNRELEASED ACETATES

February 1965
'Lucy Leave' / 'I'm A King Bee'
UK: Bev Productions (7-inch acetate single).
This refers to an Emidisc acetate and a surviving copy was discovered in the late 1980's. Whilst it clearly is a recording of Pink Floyd - Barrett's distinctive lead vocal and guitar is evident - it also shows a band performing a very straight up R&B style.

November 1970
PINK FLOYD LIVE AT MONTREUX CASINO
UK: EMI Disc Acetate (double acetate album).
Track list: 'Astronomy Dominé '// 'More Blues' // 'The Embryo' // 'Just Another 12-bar' * / Interview with David Gilmour (conducted in French). This refers to a set of two genuine white-label Emidisc acetates that found their way onto the collectors market in the late 1980's entitled "Pink Floyd Live At Montreux Casino" and contain recordings culled from Pink Floyd's shows at the Casino de Montreux, Montreux, Switzerland on 21 & 22 November 1970. However, it is likely these would have been intended as promotional tools, not for commercial release and given the fact that the interview piece is conducted in French, would have only been for the French language market.
* 'Just Another 12-bar' is a title given on the acetate label and is simply an improvised blues instrumental.

FILMS & SOUNDTRACKS

Friday 19 July 1968
TONITE LET'S ALL MAKE LOVE IN LONDON
UK: Instant INLP 002 (vinyl album).
Track list: 'Interstellar Overdrive' (Pink Floyd) / 'Changing Of The Guard' (Marquess Of Kensington) / 'Night Time Girl' (Twice As Much) / Interview with a "Dolly Bird" / 'Out Of Time' (Chris Farlowe) / Interview with Edna O'Brien / 'Interstellar Overdrive' (Pink Floyd) / Interview with Andrew 'Loog' Oldham / 'Winter Is Blue' (Vashti) / Interview with Andrew 'Loog' Oldham) / 'Winter Is Blue' (Vashti) / Interview with Mick Jagger / Interview with Julie Christie / Interview with Michael Caine / 'Paint It Black' (Chris Farlowe) / Interview with Alan Aldridge / Interview with David Hockney / 'Here Comes The Nice' (The Small Faces) / Interview with Lee Marvin) / 'Interstellar Overdrive' (Pink Floyd) / 'Tonite Let's All Make Love In London' (Alan Ginsberg).
Pink Floyd tracks produced by Joe Boyd.
Recorded at Sound Techniques Studios, London, England. The original film soundtrack album, featuring 'Interstellar Overdrive' was recorded on 11 and 12 January 1967. The release date given here is that of the New York cinema opening of the film, as no exact date for a UK record release can be found. It is generally accepted this opening occurred shortly after the release of 'A Saucerful Of Secrets' although the film had been previewed at the *5th New York Film Festival*, Philharmonic Hall, Lincoln Center, New York City, New York, USA as early as 26 September 1967.
Reissued:
UK: See For Miles SEEG 258 (vinyl album 1990. See For Miles Records re-issued the Instant album with expanded packaging and an additional Pink Floyd track, recorded at the same session, entitled 'Nick's Boogie').
US: Sony Music Special Products AK 47893 (CD album 1991).

December 1993
TONITE LET'S ALL MAKE LOVE IN LONDON - MINI PROMOTION ALBUM SAMPLER
UK: See For Miles SEA 4CD (CD EP, 1991).
Track list: 'Interstellar Overdrive' (Pink Floyd) / 'Nick's Boogie' (Pink Floyd) / Interview with David Hockney / Interview with Lee Marvin.
Contrary to popular belief this is not an industry promo only EP, but a stock item in order to carry the Pink Floyd material. However, contractual problems prevented the original CD EP containing Pink Floyd material only and therefore interview segments from the soundtrack album had to be inserted as well.

Monday 27 March 2000
PINK FLOYD LONDON 66-67
UK: See For Miles SFMDP3 (CD EP).
Contractual problems resolved, See For Miles released this EP with the Pink Floyd material only and was accompanied by a colour booklet of stills from the band's recording session.

Monday 11 July 2005
PINK FLOYD LONDON 1966-1967
Pucka PUC66 (Digitally remastered CD mini album).
Track List: 'Interstellar Overdrive' (full length version) /
'Nick's Boogie' / 'Interstellar Overdrive' (full length video for
Mac/PC) / Interview footage with Mick Jagger, David
Hockney, Michael Caine, Julie Christie, and an overview by
the director, Peter Whitehead.

Monday 2 October 1995
PINK FLOYD LONDON 66-67
UK: See For Miles PFVP1 (VHS PAL video).
US: See For Miles PFVN1 (VHS NTSC video).
Directed by Peter Whitehead.
Live footage of the above session and of Pink Floyd's
appearance at UFO on 13 January 1967 also appears on this
video.
Reissued:
UK: See For Miles PFVP1 (VHS PAL video reissued with new
artwork, 1995).
UK: Snapper SMADVD 049 (DVD PAL video, remastered
soundtrack with bonus interviews, 2005).

Thursday 26 September 1968
THE COMMITTEE
US: Music Video Distribution (DVD NTSC video, 2006).
Directed by Peter Sykes.
Music Produced by Peter Sykes and Pink Floyd.
Recorded at 3 Belsize Square, London, England.
This bizarre film, made in 1968 (The date given here is the
cinematic premiere at the Cameo Poly Cinema, Regent
Street, London, England), features an improvised
instrumental score by Pink Floyd. The film itself is in black
and white, and runs for 55 minutes and the DVD includes an
interview by Oscar winning director Jon Blair with Max
Steuer (the film's writer and producer) and Peter Sykes
(director) that lasts for 50 minutes and a CD of the song
'The Committee', by Paul Jones and Max Steuer arranged by
Tim Whitehead for the Homemade Orchestra, plus two
tracks from earlier Homemade Orchestra CD's.

Monday 4 August 1969
MORE
US: Warner Home Video 35156 (VHS NTSC video, 1991).
Directed by Barbet Schroeder.
The home video release of the feature film (the date given is
its cinematic premiere at the *7th New York Film Festival*,
Alice Tulley Hall, Lincoln Center, New York City, New York,
USA), features some significant differences to the album
release, including on the actual soundtrack different mixes of
'Main Theme', 'Ibiza Bar', 'Party Sequence', 'Quicksilver',
'More Blues' and 'Up The Khyber'. 'Cymbaline' has alternate
lyrics and the tracks known as 'Hollywood' and 'Seabirds' are
unique to the film.
Reissued:
US: Home Vision Cinema MOR 070 (VHS NTSC video,
2000).
US: Home Vision Entertainment MOR 070 (DVD NTSC video,
2005).

Saturday 25 October 1969
EUROPEAN MUSIC REVOLUTION
Directed by Gérome Laperrousaz.
Also known as *Music Power*, this was a documentary film of
the *Actuel Festival*, Mont de l'Enclus, Amougies, Belgium
held between 24 and 28 October 1969 and featuring Pink
Floyd performing 'Green Is The Colour' and 'Careful With
That Axe, Eugene' on the 25 October. The film remains
unreleased on video but was shown on the French cinema
circuit throughout the summer of 1970.

Wednesday 18 March 1970
ZABRISKIE POINT
UK: MGM/UA MV 600196 (VHS PAL video, 1984).
US: MGM/UA MB 600196 (VHS NTSC video, 1984).
Directed by Michaelangelo Antonioni.
The home video release of the feature film. The date given
here is the cinematic premiere at The Coronet Theater,
Manhattan, New York City, New York, USA.

1970
ZABRISKIE POINT - RADIO SPOTS
MGM KAL 043 (promotional 7-inch one-sided EP single,
1970).
Contains four radio spots of 60 seconds, two at 30 seconds
and one at 10 seconds for the movie 'Zabriskie Point'. All
four spots include segments of the Pink Floyd song 'Come in
Number 51, Your Time Is Up'.

Friday 29 May 1970
ZABRISKIE POINT
UK: MGM 2315 002 (vinyl album).
US: MGM Records SE 4668ST (vinyl album, released on
Saturday 11 April 1970).
Track list: 'Heart Beat, Pig Meat' (Pink Floyd) / 'Brother
Mary' (The Kaleidoscope) / 'The Grateful Dead' (Dark Star) /
'Crumbling Land' (Pink Floyd) / 'Tennessee Waltz' (Patti
Page) / 'Sugar Babe' (The Youngbloods) / 'Love Scene'
(Jerry Garcia) / 'I Wish I Was A Single Girl Again' (Roscoe
Holcomb) / 'Mickey's Tune' (The Kaleidoscope) / 'Dance Of
Death' (John Fahey) / 'Come In Number 51, Your Time Is Up'
(Pink Floyd).
Pink Floyd tracks produced by Michaelangelo Antonioni and
Pink Floyd.
Pink Floyd tracks recorded at Technicolor Sound Studios,
Rome, Italy.
Reissued:
UK: MGM 2354 040 (vinyl album, 1973).
UK: EMI GO 2029 (vinyl album, 1990).
UK: CBS Hollywood Collection CBS 70279 (vinyl album,
1993).
US: MCA Classical Soundtracks MCA 25032 (vinyl album,
1986).
US: Columbia 70279 (vinyl album, 1987).
US: CBS 52417 (CD album, 1987).
US: Sony Music Special Products AK 52417 (CD album,
1992).
US: 4 Men With Beards 4M123 (vinyl album, 2004).

Monday 20 October 1997
ZABRISKIE POINT
UK: EMI Premier Soundtracks 823364 (double CD album).
US: Rhino Movie Music R272462 (double CD album).
The original soundtrack to the Antonioni feature film
reissued as a remastered double CD with previously
unreleased tracks including Jerry Garcia's 'Love Scene
Improvisations 1, 2, 3 & 4' and Pink Floyd's 'Country Song',
'Unknown Song', 'Love Scene, Version 6' and 'Love Scene,
Version 4'.

Sunday 28 June 1970
STAMPING GROUND
UK: Music World Video GEMTV-474 (VHS PAL Video
released as *Psychomania!*, 1984).
US: VCX Films (VHS NTSC video released as *Stamping
Ground*, 1979).
Track list: 'Zero She Flies' (Al Stewart) / 'Mardi Gras Day'
(Dr. John The Night Tripper) / 'Drowned In Wine' (Family) /
'Pavilions Of Sun' (T. Rex) / 'Human Condition' (Canned Heat)
/ 'So Sad' (Canned Heat) / 'White Rabbit' (Jefferson
Airplane) / 'Saturday Afternoon' (Jefferson Airplane) /
'Ballad of You And Me & Pooneil' (Jefferson Airplane) / 'Big
Bird' (Flock) / 'Open Up Your Hearts' (It's A Beautiful Day) /
'Wasted Union Blues' (It's A Beautiful Day) / 'Freedom Is A
Constant Struggle' (Country Joe & The Fish) / 'Old Blue'
(The Byrds) / 'Savor-Jingo–Gumbo' (Santana) / 'Set The
Controls For The Heart Of The Sun' (Pink Floyd) / 'A
Saucerful Of Secrets' (Pink Floyd).
A compilation of classic footage featuring an array of bands
and featuring clips of Pink Floyd performing 'Set The
Controls For The Heart Of The Sun' and 'A Saucerful Of
Secrets' live at the Holland Pop Festival on 28 June 1970
and taken from the *Stamping Ground* film which received a
cinematic release throughout Europe in the early 1970's.
Reissued:
UK: Synergie Logistics MMGV067 (VHS PAL video, 1994)
UK: Magnum Music (DVD PAL video released as
Psychomania – The Best Of Psychedelic Rock, 2003).
US: Good Times 8046 (VHS NTSC video released as
Stamping Ground, 1987).
US: Substance 21928 (VHS NTSC video released as
Stamping Ground, 1998).

1974
***STAMPING GROUND* - RADIO SPOT
ANNOUNCEMENTS**
US: Atlas Films ER 7302 (promotional 7-inch EP single,
1974).
A one-sided promotional single containing three radio
promos, of 60 seconds, 30 seconds, and 10 seconds, for the
film *Stamping Ground* that features Pink Floyd performing
'Set The Controls For The Heart Of The Sun' and 'A
Saucerful of Secrets' live at the Holland Pop Festival on 28
June 1970.

1974
***STAMPING GROUND* - RADIO SPOT
ANNOUNCEMENTS**
US: Fine Films F3 (promotional 7-inch EP single, 1974).
A one-sided promotional single that includes two radio
promos, of 30 seconds and 10 seconds for the film
Stamping Ground.

Thursday 29 June 1972
SOUND OF THE CITY 1964-1973
UK: Telstar TVE1003 (VHS PAL video released as
Superstars In Concert, 1989).
Directed by Peter Clifton.
The edited home video release of the feature film (the date
given is the recording date of Pink Floyd's segment from
their performance at The Dome, Brighton, England),
originally shot as a 104-minute documentary by Peter
Clifton of various artists performing live in London between
the two years and interspersed with interviews. Clips of this
material occasionally appear on television and other
compilation videos, more recently 'Careful With That Axe,
Eugene', which has appeared on a 'various artists' video,
Superstars In Concert (UK: Telstar Video Entertainment TVE
1003).

Tuesday 29 August 1972
LA VALLEE/OBSCURED BY CLOUDS
US: Warner Home Video 35149 (VHS NTSC video, 1991).
Directed by Barbet Schroeder.
The home video release of the feature film (the date given
here is the cinematic premiere at the *Venice International
Film Festival*, Venice, Italy) contains a different version on
the actual soundtrack of the song 'Free Four', with different
lyrics to the album release and the ending of 'Absolutely
Curtains', which is sung by the cast.
Reissued:
US: Home Vision Entertainment VAL020 (VHS NTSC video,
2001).

Saturday 2 September 1972
PINK FLOYD LIVE AT POMPEII
UK: Polygram (VHS PAL video, 1983).
US: Vestron Music Video MA1008 (VHS NTSC video, 1983).
Track list: 'Echoes' (Part 1) / 'Careful With That Axe, Eugene'
/ 'One Of These Days I'm Going To Cut You Into Little
Pieces' / 'Set The Controls For The Heart Of The Sun' /
'Mademoiselle Knobs' / 'Echoes' (Part 2).
Directed by Adrian Maben.
Music produced by Adrian Maben and Pink Floyd.
Recorded at the Roman Arena, Pompeii, Italy and Studio
Europasinor, Paris, France.
The home video release of the feature film (The date given
here is the cinematic premiere at the *26th Edinburgh Film
Festival*, Cameo Cinema, Tollcross, Edinburgh, Scotland).
Reissued:
UK: Channel 5 CFV 10422 (VHS PAL video, 1985).

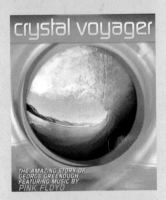

Monday 20 June 1994
PINK FLOYD LIVE AT POMPEII
UK: Polygram 0807303 (VHS PAL video).
US: Polygram Music Video Enterprises 0807313 (VHS NTSC video).
Track list: 'Echoes' (Part 1) / 'Careful With That Axe, Eugene' / 'A Saucerful of Secrets' / 'Us And Them' (studio session) / 'One Of These Days I'm Going To Cut You Into Little Pieces' / 'Set The Controls For The Heart Of The Sun' / 'Brain Damage' (studio session) / 'Mademoiselle Knobs' / 'Echoes' (Part 2).

Monday 20 October 2003
PINK FLOYD LIVE AT POMPEII
UK: Universal Pictures Video 1407652 (DVD PAL video, 2003).
US: Hip O Records B000131509 (DVD NTSC video, 2003).
Track list: 'Echoes' (Part 1) / 'Careful With That Axe, Eugene' / 'A Saucerful of Secrets' / 'Us And Them' (studio session) / 'One Of These Days I'm Going To Cut You Into Little Pieces' / 'Set The Controls For The Heart Of The Sun' / 'Brain Damage' (studio session) / 'Mademoiselle Knobs' / 'Echoes' (Part 2).
A remastered and fully repackaged edition containing the full concert film in stereo only plus a 20-minute interview with Adrian Maben along with an option to run the original concert film, a photo gallery, album graphics, lyrics, 'odds 'n' sods' and a map and history of Pompeii. Unfortunately, despite the original sound masters being in the custody of Adrian Maben, the band were not supportive of this release and Universal felt that a 5.1 mix could not be satisfactorily produced. Original radio and TV adverts were also to be included but copyright clearances could not be obtained in time for the release.

1974
PINK FLOYD LIVE AT POMPEII - RADIO SPOT ANNOUNCEMENTS
April Fool Films AF Floyd 1 (promotional 7-inch EP single).
A radio promo only EP containing twelve radio ads for the film, *Pink Floyd-Live at Pompeii*. Side 1 contains four 60-second spots, and two 30-second spots. Side 2 contains five 60-second spots, and one 30-second spot.

Wednesday 5 December 1973
CRYSTAL VOYAGER
UK: Blue Dolphin BDVD2003 (DVD PAL video, 2003).
UK: BDV2011 (VHS PAL video, 2003).
US: Wizard Video 012 (VHS NTSC video, 1980).
Directed by David Elfick.
The home video release of the feature film (the date given here is the cinematic premiere at the Sydney Opera House, Sydney, Australia), which is essentially a journey through the eyes of American ex-pat surfer George Greenough, taking the camera and you on a vibrant trip into the rolling, crashing ocean. Set to the music of Pink Floyd's 'Echoes' it is regarded as a sight and sound spectacular. A classic movie in surfing circles, *Crystal Voyager* was one of Australia's most successful surf movies, achieving 6-month run in

London's West End and also winning composer Phil Judd an award for Best Original Music Score.

Sunday 23 May 1982
PINK FLOYD THE WALL
UK: MGM/UA MB 400268 (VHS PAL video, 1983).
US: MGM/UA MV 400268 (VHS NTSC video, 1983).
Directed by Alan Parker.
The home video release of the feature film (the date given here is the cinematic premiere at the *35th Festival International Du Film*, Palais des Festivals, Cannes, France), *The Wall*. It had additional and altered music recorded after the original album release both in London, New York and Los Angeles resulting in following musicians being used for those parts: Andy Bown (bass guitar), Bob Geldof (vocals), Tim Renwick (additional guitars), Toni Tennille (backing vocals), Pontardulais Male Voice Choir led by Noel Davis (backing chorus). Significant changes to the film soundtrack included 'Bring The Boys Back Home' (extended), 'Hey You' (omitted), 'In The Flesh?' (with Bob Geldof lead vocals), Mother (re-recorded), 'Outside The Wall' (re-recorded'), 'Run Like Hell' (shortened), 'The Show Must Go On' (omitted), 'Stop' (re-recorded), 'What Shall We Do Now?' (a new track) and 'Empty Spaces' (a new track).
Reissued:
UK: Channel 5 CFV 08762 (VHS PAL video, 1989).
UK: Universal 501982 (VHS PAL video, 2000).
UK: Universal 501989 (Deluxe DVD NTSC remastered in 5.1 surround sound from a hi-definition film transfer with additional material including the previously unreleased 'Hey You' scene, *The Other Side Of The Wall* documentary film, and a retrospective with new interviews by Roger Waters, Alan Parker, Gerald Scarfe, Peter Biziou, Alan Marshall and James Guthrie. A special edition of the DVD included four collectible film- cards that feature Gerald Scarfe drawings from the film, 2002).
US: MGM/UA M400268 (VHS NTSC video, 1989).
US: MGM/UA M204694 (VHS NTSC video deluxe letter box edition, 1991).
US: Columbia Music Video CV50198 (VHS NTSC video, 2000).
US: Columbia Music Video CVD50210 (Deluxe DVD NTSC remastered in 5.1 surround sound from a hi-definition film transfer with additional material including the previously unreleased 'Hey You' scene, *The Other Side Of The Wall* documentary film, and a retrospective with new interviews by Roger Waters, Alan Parker, Gerald Scarfe, Peter Biziou, Alan Marshall and James Guthrie. A special edition of the DVD included four collectible cards that feature Gerald Scarfe drawings from the film, 2002).
US: Columbia Music Video CVD 58163 (NTSC DVD video, 2004).
US: Columbia Music Video CVD 58163 (NTSC DVD video 25th anniversary limited edition digipak with new artwork and a replica cinema poster. Otherwise is identical to the above, 2004).

Monday 25 April 1983
THE FINAL CUT
UK: Video Music Collection PM0010 (VHS PAL video EP).
Track list: 'The Gunners Dream' / 'Not Now John' / 'The Fletcher Memorial Home' / 'The Final Cut'.
Although not officially released on video in the US, the film was broadcast on MTV around the time of release in the UK.

Monday 12 June 1989
DELICATE SOUND OF THUNDER
UK: PMI MVN 9911863 (VHS PAL video).
US: Columbia Music Video 24V 49019 (VHS NTSC video, released on Monday 12 June 1989).
Directed by Wayne Isham.
Track list: 'Shine On You Crazy Diamond, Parts 1-5' / 'Signs Of Life' / 'Learning To Fly' / 'Sorrow' / 'The Dogs Of War' / 'On The Turning Away' / 'One Of These Days' / 'Time' / 'On The Run' / 'The Great Gig In The Sky' / 'Wish You Were Here' / 'Us And Them' / 'Comfortably Numb' / 'One Slip' / 'Run Like Hell' / 'Shine On You Crazy Diamond' (reprise for end credits).
Certified Gold, Platinum and Multi-Platinum (1.5 times over) in the US on 5 February 1990 and Multi-Platinum (2 times over) on 26 March 1991.

Monday 13 April 1992
LA CARRERA PANAMERICANA
UK: PMI MVN 9913453 (VHS PAL video).
US: Sony Music Video 19V 49128 (VHS NTSC video, released on Monday 1 June 1992).
Directed by Ian McArthur.
Track list: 'Run Like Hell' / 'Pan Am Shuffle' / 'Yet Another Movie' / 'Sorrow' / 'Signs Of Life' / 'Country Theme' / 'Mexico '78' / 'Big Theme' / 'Run Like Hell' / 'One Slip' / 'Small Theme' / 'Pan Am Shuffle' / 'Carrera Slow Blues'.
A documentary of the pan-American car-rally that Gilmour, Mason and their manager Steve O'Rourke participated.
Extracts of Pink Floyd's most recent music was used with some new passages recorded at The Astoria Studios, Hampton, England and EMI Studios Abbey Road, London, England and produced by David Gilmour.
Reissued:
UK: Video Collection International MC2134 (VHS PAL video, 1997).

Monday 12 June 1995
PULSE. EARLS COURT LONDON 20.10.94
UK: PMI MVD 4914363 (VHS PAL video).
US: Columbia Music Video 24V50121 (VHS NTSC video, released on Monday 12 June 1995).
Directed by David Mallet.
Track list: 'Shine On You Crazy Diamond, Parts 1-5 & 7' / 'Learning To Fly' / 'High Hopes' / 'Take It Back' / 'Coming Back To Life' / 'Sorrow' / 'Keep Talking' / 'Another Brick In The Wall, Part 2' / 'One Of These Days' / *The Dark Side Of The Moon* / 'Wish You Were Here' / 'Comfortably Numb' / 'Run Like Hell'.
Certified Gold and Platinum in the US on 14 August 1995 and Multi-Platinum (2 times over) on 1 November 1996.

Tuesday 26 August 2003
CLASSIC ALBUMS - THE MAKING OF DARK SIDE OF THE MOON
UK: Eagle Vision EREDV329 (DVD PAL video).
An official release of the 40 minute BBC TV *Classic Albums* series first broadcast on BBC1 TV on 11 May 2003 and expanded to an 84 minute DVD with newly recorded interviews with Waters, Gilmour, Mason and Wright, with previously unseen and unheard material including early demos of tracks and the band performing 'On The Run' live in 1972.

Monday 24 March 2003
THE PINK FLOYD & SYD BARRETT STORY
UK: Direct Video Distribution DVDUK009D (DVD PAL video).
UK: Direct Video Distribution DVDUK010V (VHS PAL video).
Directed by John Edginton.
An officially sanctioned documentary focussing on Pink Floyd's formative years. Includes newly recorded Roger Waters and David Gilmour interviews; Robyn Hitchcock performing 'Dominoes' and 'It Is Obvious'; Graham Coxon performing 'Love You' and a biography of Syd Barrett. The documentary was first broadcast on BBC2 TV on 24 November 2001.
Reissued:
UK: Direct Video Distribution DVDSD002D (double DVD PAL video, 2006).
An expanded and repackaged version of the above documentary: Disc 1 includes *The Pink Floyd & Syd Barrett Story* and a newly recorded Roger Waters interview. Disc 2 includes newly recorded interviews with David Gilmour, Richard Wright, Nick Mason and Robyn Hitchcock. Bonus material includes Syd Barrett's 'Love You' performed by Graham Coxon, Quiz, Tour of Abbey Road, Biographies, Discographies and a Pink Floyd time-line.

Monday 10 July 2006
PULSE
UK: EMI 4194369 (DVD PAL video).
USA: Sony 1C2D54171 (DVD NTSC video).
Directed by David Mallet.
Track list (Disc 1): Concert Part One: 'Shine On You Crazy Diamond, Parts 1-5 & 7' / 'Learning To Fly' / 'High Hopes' / 'Take It Back' / 'Coming Back To Life' / 'Sorrow' / 'Keep Talking' / 'Another Brick In The Wall, Part 2' / 'One Of These Days' / Screen Films: 'Shine On You Crazy Diamond' / 'High Hopes' / 'Learning To Fly' / Bootlegging The Bootleggers: 'What Do You Want From Me' / 'On The Turning Away' / 'Poles Apart' / 'Marooned' / Film: *PULSE* TV advert / Tour Stuff: Maps / Itinerary / Stage Plans / Videos: 'Learning To Fly' / 'Take It Back'.
Track list (Disc 2): Concert Part Two: *The Dark Side Of The Moon* / 'Wish You Were Here' / 'Comfortably Numb' / 'Run Like Hell' / Screen Films: 'Speak To Me' (graphic) / 'On The Run' / 'Time' (1994) / 'The Great Gig In The Sky' (wave) / 'Money' (1987) / 'Us And Them' (1987) / 'Brain Damage' / 'Eclipse' / Alternate Screen Films: 'Time' (Ian Eames 1974 film) / 'Money' (1994 alien) / 'Speak To Me' (1987) / 'The Great Gig In The Sky' (animation) / 'Us And Them' (1994) /

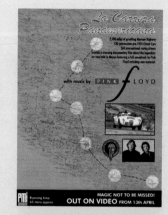

Behind The Scenes Footage: Say Goodbye To Life As We Know It / Photo Gallery / Rock And Roll Hall Of Fame Induction Ceremony, USA 1996: 'Wish You Were Here' (with Billy Corgan) / Cover Art / Additional Credits.

RADIO SHOWS

Pink Floyd have been the subject of numerous radio programmes all over the world and in some cases these have been packaged as pre-recorded, ready for broadcast shows that are syndicated to partner radio stations. In particular the BBC in the UK has for many years produced through its Transcription Services department both vinyl and taped radio shows – very often direct transcripts of radio shows such as *Top Gear* or *Sounds Of The Seventies* - for worldwide syndication. Similarly there are several independent radio production companies operating in the US that have produced both vinyl and CD programmes that are complete and ready for broadcast. Whilst many of these take the form of various artist radio shows, often with interviews and documentary pieces, some are very specifically Pink Floyd or solo member only shows that contain both music and interviews. Some of the more significant releases are listed here as well as in the solo discography sections.

1970
BBC - POP SPECTACULAR - FEATURING PINK FLOYD IN CONCERT
UK: BBC Transcription Services BBC 133525/26 (vinyl album).
Concert broadcast edited from Pink Floyd's Peel Sunday Concert at the Paris Theatre, London on 16 July 1970 with DJ John Peel: 'The Embryo' / 'Green Is The Colour' / 'Careful With That Axe, Eugene' // 'Atom Heart Mother'.

1971
BBC - PICK OF THE POPS - JOHN PEEL IN CONCERT WITH PINK FLOYD
UK: BBC Transcription Services BBC 129476/78 (vinyl album).
Concert broadcast edited from Pink Floyd's *Sounds Of The Seventies* BBC session at the Paris Theatre, London on 30 September 1971 with DJ John Peel: 'Fat Old Sun' / 'One Of These Days' // 'Echoes'.

1978
INNER-VIEW - PINK FLOYD
US: Innerview (double vinyl album).
Show No.13-1 & 13-2; broadcast 1978.
Documentary includes music and interviews with members of Pink Floyd.

1980
INNER-VIEW - PINK FLOYD SPECIAL
US: Innerview (quadruple vinyl album box set).
Show No.13-1, 13-2, 13-3 & 13-4; broadcast 1980.
Documentary includes music and interviews with members of Pink Floyd.

1980
INNER-VIEW - PINK FLOYD
US: Innerview (double vinyl album).
Show No.17-6 & 17-7; broadcast 1980.
Documentary includes music and interviews with members of Pink Floyd.

1981
TM SPECIAL PROJECTS – GUITAR – A ROCK EPISODE
US: TM Special Projects (vinyl album).
Show Hour No.14; broadcast 1981.
One album from a multi-disc radio show featuring Syd Barrett & David Gilmour: 'The Guitars Of Pink Floyd'. Track list: 'Welcome To The Machine' / 'Arnold Layne' / 'Free Four' / 'Money' / 'Breathe' / 'Time' / 'Breathe' (reprise) / 'Have A Cigar' / 'Another Brick In The Wall, Part 2' / 'Shine On You Crazy Diamond'.

1981
3RD ANNUAL ROCK RADIO AWARDS
US: DIR Broadcasting Corporation (vinyl album).
Show No.RRA-3; broadcast 7 March 1981.
Documentary includes music of Pink Floyd: 'Money' / 'Us And Them' / 'Another Brick In The Wall, Part 2' / 'Another Brick In The Wall, Part 1' / 'The Happiest Days Of Our Lives' / 'Run Like Hell'.

1982
INNER-VIEW - PINK FLOYD – THE MAKING OF THE WALL MOVIE
US: Innerview (vinyl album).
Show No.22-2; broadcast 1982.
Documentary includes music and interviews with Gerald Scarfe, Bob Geldof, Alan Parker and members of Pink Floyd.

1983
RKO RADIO NETWORKS – ROYALTY OF ROCK – PINK FLOYD
US: RKO Radio Networks (vinyl album).
Broadcast 1983.
Documentary includes music and interviews with members of Pink Floyd.

1983
INNER-VIEW - PINK FLOYD – THE FINAL CUT
US: Innerview (double vinyl album).
Show No.24-8 & 24-9; broadcast 1983.
Documentary includes music and interviews with members of Pink Floyd.

1984
THE SOURCE – PINK FLOYD / DAVID GILMOUR PROFILE
US: NBC Radio Young Adult Network (triple vinyl album set).
Show No.84-12; broadcast 6 April, 7 April & 8 April 1984.
Documentary includes music and interviews with members of Pink Floyd.

1984

ROLLING STONE CONTINUOS HISTORY OF ROCK & ROLL - PINK FLOYD - PAST, PRESENT & FUTURE
US: ABC Rock Radio Network / (double vinyl album).
Show No.140, volume 3; broadcast 10 June 1984.
Documentary includes music and interviews with members of Pink Floyd.

1984

THE SOURCE - SHADES OF PINK - THE LEGEND OF PINK FLOYD
US: NBC Radio Young Adult Network (six vinyl album set).
Show No.84-34; broadcast 31 August, 1 September & 2 September 1984.
Documentary includes music and interviews with members of Pink Floyd.

1987

UP CLOSE - PINK FLOYD
US: MCA Radio (CD album).
Broadcast 5 May 1987.
Documentary includes music and interviews with members of Pink Floyd.

1987

UP CLOSE - PINK FLOYD
US: MCA Radio (double CD album).
Broadcast 23 & 29 December 1987.
Documentary includes music and interviews with members of Pink Floyd.

1988

IN THE STUDIO - PINK FLOYD - THE DARK SIDE OF THE MOON
US: In The Studio (CD album).
Show No.7; broadcast 8 August 1988.
Documentary includes music and interviews with members of Pink Floyd.
Reissued:
US: In The Studio (CD album).
Show No.7; broadcast 12 March 1990.

1988

NBC RADIO - THE LEGEND OF PINK FLOYD (PARTS 1 & 2)
US: NBC Radio Entertainment (quadruple vinyl album set).
Part 1 broadcast 15-21 August 1988; Part 2 broadcast 22-28 August 1988.
Documentary includes music and interviews with members of Pink Floyd.

1988

UP CLOSE - PINK FLOYD
US: MCA Radio (double CD album).
Broadcast 1 & 7 October 1988.
Documentary includes music and interviews with members of Pink Floyd.

1989

UP CLOSE - PINK FLOYD
US: MCA Radio (double CD album).
Broadcast 18 & 24 January 1989.
Documentary includes music and interviews with members of Pink Floyd.

1989

MASTERS OF ROCK - PINK FLOYD
UK: Capital Radio Ventures (CD album).
Broadcast 13 & 26 March 1989.
Documentary includes music of Pink Floyd: 'Another Brick In The Wall, Part 2 '/ 'Arnold Layne' / 'Money' / 'Time' / 'Wish You Were Here' / 'Comfortably Numb' / 'On The Turning Away' / 'Shine On You Crazy Diamond, Parts 1-5'.

1989

IN THE STUDIO - PINK FLOYD - THE WALL PARTS 1 & 2
US: In The Studio (double CD album).
Show No.55 & 56; broadcast 10 & 17 July 1989.
Documentary includes music and interviews with members of Pink Floyd.
Reissued:
US: In The Studio (double CD album).
Show No.107 & 108; broadcast 9 & 16 July 1990.
US: In The Studio (double CD album).
Show No.333 & 334; broadcast 7 & 14 November 1994.
US: In The Studio (double CD album).
Show No.594 & 595; broadcast 8 & 15 November 1999.
US: In The Studio (double CD album).
Show No.856 & 857; broadcast 15 & 22 November 2004.

1990

THE SOURCE - CLASSIC CD'S - PINK FLOYD - THE DARK SIDE OF THE MOON
US: The Source / NBC Radio (double CD album).
Show No.90; broadcast 30 April 1990.
Documentary includes music and interviews with members of Pink Floyd.

1991

GLOBAL SATELLITE NETWORK - WISH YOU WERE HERE - THE PINK FLOYD STORY
US: Global Satellite Network (triple CD album).
Broadcast 28 November, 5 December & 12 December 1991.
Documentary includes music and interviews with members of Pink Floyd.

1992

WESTWOOD ONE - PINK FLOYD - 25TH ANNIVERSARY
US: Westwood One (six CD album set).
Show No. 92-21; broadcast 23 May 1992.
Documentary includes music and interviews with members of Pink Floyd.

1992

SUPERSTAR CONCERT SERIES – PINK FLOYD AT KNEBWORTH

US: Westwood One (double CD album).
Show No.92-23; broadcast 6 June 1992.
Pink Floyd live at Knebworth on 30 June 1990. Track list: 'Shine On You Crazy Diamond, Parts 1-5' / 'The Great Gig In The Sky' / 'Wish You Were Here' / 'Sorrow' / 'Money' / 'Comfortably Numb' / 'Run Like Hell'.

1992

IN THE STUDIO – PINK FLOYD – BOX SET PARTS 1 & 2

US: In The Studio (double CD album).
Show No.234 & 235; broadcast 14 & 21 December 1992).
Documentary includes music and interviews with members of Pink Floyd.
Reissued:
US: In The Studio (double CD album).
Show No.306 & 307; broadcast 2 & 9 May 1994.
US: In The Studio (double CD album).
Show No.414 & 415; broadcast 27 May & 3 June 1996.

1993

SUPERSTAR CONCERT SERIES – PINK FLOYD

US: Westwood One (double CD album).
Show No.93-39; broadcast 20 September 1993.
A compilation of Pink Floyd's BBC sessions in London on 16 July 1970 & 30 September 1971. Track list: 'The Embryo' / 'Green Is The Colour' / 'Careful With That Axe, Eugene' / 'If' / 'Atom Heart Mother' (edited) / 'One of These Days' / 'Echoes'.
Reissued:
US: Westwood One (double CD album).
Show No.97-31; broadcast 28 July 1997.
US: Westwood One (double CD album).
Show No.98-10; broadcast 2 March 1998.
US: Westwood One (double CD album).
Show No.01-17; broadcast 28 April 2001.
US: Westwood One (double CD album).
Show No.02-16; broadcast 27 April 2002.

1994

SUPERSTAR CONCERT SERIES – PINK FLOYD

US: Westwood One (double CD album).
Show No.94-19; broadcast 2 May 1994.
Compilation of Pink Floyd and solo live recordings including Pink Floyd at BBC Paris Theatre, London on 30 September 1971: 'One Of These Days' / 'Echoes' / David Gilmour at Hammersmith Odeon, London on 30 April 1984: 'Money' / 'Run Like Hell' / 'Comfortably Numb' / Roger Waters at Colisee de Québec, Québec City on 7 November 1987: 'Wish You Were Here' / 'Another Brick In the Wall, Part 1' / 'The Happiest Days Of Our Lives' / 'Another Brick In The Wall, Part 2'.

1994

WESTWOOD ONE – PINK FLOYD – THE SHOW GOES ON

US: Westwood One (three CD album set).

Show No. 94-27; broadcast 1-4 July 1994).
Documentary includes music and interviews with members of Pink Floyd.

1994

IN THE STUDIO – PINK FLOYD - THE DIVISION BELL

US: In The Studio (double CD album).
Show No.339 & 340; broadcast 19 & 26 December 1994.
Documentary includes music and interviews with members of Pink Floyd.
Reissued:
US: In The Studio (double CD album).
Show No.577 & 578; broadcast 12 & 19 July 1999.

1995

SUPERSTAR CONCERT SERIES – PINK FLOYD / ROGER WATERS

US: Westwood One (double CD album).
Show No.95-25; broadcast 12 June 1995.
Compilation of Pink Floyd and Roger Waters live recordings including Pink Floyd at Knebworth Park on 30 June 1990: 'Shine On You Crazy Diamond, Parts 1-5' / 'The Great Gig In The Sky' / 'Wish You Were Here' / 'Sorrow' / 'Money' 'Comfortably Numb' / 'Run Like Hell' / Roger Waters at Colisee de Québec, Québec City on 7 November 1987: 'Another Brick In The Wall, Parts 1 and 2'.

1995

UP CLOSE – PINK FLOYD

US: Media America Radio (four CD album set).
Show No.95-32; broadcast 31 July 1995 / 95-33; broadcast 7 August 1995 / 95-34; broadcast 14 August 1995 / 95-36; broadcast 21 August 1995.
Documentary includes music and interviews with members of Pink Floyd.

1995

WESTWOOD ONE – PINK FLOYD - ECHOES

US: Westwood One (six CD album set).
Show 95-36; broadcast 1-4 September 1995.
Documentary includes music and interviews with members of Pink Floyd.
Reissued:
US: XM Radio Deep Tracks - Pink Floyd – Echoes (six CD album set).
Show broadcast 5, 12, 19, 26 March and 2, 9 April 2006.

1995

IN THE STUDIO – PINK FLOYD - WISH YOU WERE HERE

US: In The Studio (CD album).
Show No.378; broadcast 18 September 1995.
Documentary includes music and interviews with members of Pink Floyd.
Reissued:
US: In The Studio (CD album).
Show No.564; broadcast 12 April 1999.
US: In The Studio (CD album).
Show No.639; broadcast 18 September 2000.

1996

OFF THE RECORD – CLASSIC
US: Westwood One (CD album).
Show No.96-41; broadcast 7 October 1996.
Documentary includes music and interviews with members
of Pink Floyd.

1997

OFF THE RECORD – CLASSIC
US: Westwood One (CD album).
Show No.97-13; broadcast 24 March 1997.
Documentary includes music and interviews with members
of Pink Floyd.

1997

OFF THE RECORD – CLASSIC
US: Westwood One (CD album).
Show No.97-40; broadcast 26 September 1997.
Documentary includes music and interviews with members
of Pink Floyd.

1998

**IN THE STUDIO – PINK FLOYD - THE DARK SIDE OF
THE MOON**
US: In The Studio (CD album).
Show No.248; broadcast 16 March 1998.
Documentary includes music and interviews with members
of Pink Floyd.
Reissued:
US: In The Studio (CD album).
Show No.508, broadcast 16 March 1998.
US: In The Studio (CD album).
Show No.770; broadcast 24 March 2003.

1998

OFF THE RECORD – CLASSIC
US: Westwood One (CD album).
Show No.98-28; broadcast 6 July 1998.
Documentary includes music and interviews with members
of Pink Floyd.

1998

**ABC RADIO TODAY – THE DARK SIDE OF THE MOON
25TH ANNIVERSARY SPECIAL**
US: ABC Radio Today Entertainment (CD album).
Broadcast 31 October 1998.
Documentary includes music and interviews with members
of Pink Floyd.

1999

OFF THE RECORD – CLASSIC
US: Westwood One (CD album).
Show No.99-07; broadcast 13 February 1999.
Documentary includes music and interviews with members
of Pink Floyd.

1999

GLOBAL SATELLITE NETWORK – PINK FLOYD
US: Global Satellite Network (double CD album).

Broadcast 24 April & 1 May 1999.
Documentary hosted by Jim Ladd includes music and
interviews with members of Pink Floyd.

2000

OFF THE RECORD – CLASSIC
US: Westwood One (CD album).
Show No.00-10; broadcast 28 February 2000.
Documentary includes music and interviews with members
of Pink Floyd.

2000

**SFX RADIO NETWORK – PINK FLOYD – IS THERE
ANYBODY OUT THERE? THE WALL LIVE 1980-81**
US: SFX Radio Network (double CD album).
Broadcast 7 April & 14 April 2000.
Documentary hosted by Jim Ladd includes music and
interviews with members of Pink Floyd.

2000

UP CLOSE – PINK FLOYD
US: Media America Radio (three CD album set).
Show No.00-24; broadcast 5 June 2000 / 00-25; broadcast
12 June 2000 / 00-26; broadcast 19 June 2000.
Documentary includes music and interviews with members
of Pink Floyd.

2000

**SFX RADIO NETWORK – PINK FLOYD – WISH YOU
WERE HERE - 25TH ANNIVERSAY SPECIAL**
US: SFX Radio Network (double CD album).
Broadcast 30 October 2000.
Documentary hosted by Alan Parsons includes music and
interviews with members of Pink Floyd.

2001

UP CLOSE – PINK FLOYD
US: Media America Radio (three CD album set).
Show No. 01-07; broadcast 12 February 2001 / 01-08;
broadcast 19 February 2001 / 01-09; broadcast 26
February 2001.
Documentary includes music and interviews with members
of Pink Floyd.

2001

OFF THE RECORD – CLASSIC
US: Westwood One (CD album).
Show No.01-44; broadcast 3 November 2001.
Documentary includes music and interviews with members
of Pink Floyd.

2002

IN THE STUDIO – PINK FLOYD - ANIMALS
US: In The Studio (CD album).
Show No.715 broadcast 4 March 2002).
Documentary includes music and interviews with members
of Pink Floyd.

2002

IN THE STUDIO – PINK FLOYD – A MOMENTARY LAPSE OF REASON

US: In The Studio (CD album).
Show No.745; broadcast 16 September 2002.
Documentary includes music and interviews with members of Pink Floyd.

2003

ROCKLINE – 30TH ANNIVERSARY TRIBUTE TO THE DARK SIDE OF THE MOON

US: Rockline (double CD album).
Broadcast 26 March 2003.
Documentary includes music and interviews with members of Pink Floyd.

2004

OFF THE RECORD – CLASSIC

US: Westwood One (CD album).
Show No.04-09; broadcast 28 August 2004.
Documentary includes music and interviews with members of Pink Floyd.

2004

OFF THE RECORD – CLASSIC

US: Westwood One (CD album).
Show No.04-48; broadcast 27 November 2004.
Documentary includes music and interviews with members of Pink Floyd.

2004

ROCKLINE –25TH ANNIVERSARY TRIBUTE TO THE WALL

US: Rockline (double CD album).
Broadcast 1 December 2004.
Documentary includes music and interviews with members of Pink Floyd.
Reissued:
US: Rockline (double CD album).
Broadcast 22 February 2006.

2005

OFF THE RECORD – CLASSIC

US: Westwood One (CD album).
Show No.05-22; broadcast 9 April 2005.
Documentary includes music and interviews with members of Pink Floyd.

COMPILATIONS

Pink Floyd tracks are rarely found on compilation albums, due in part to their fiercely protective policy of not being seen to cheapen their recorded works and in part to their suitability for mainstream compilation albums. The following is a list of compilations, including some promotional records, which may be incomplete.

1967

TOWER DEMONSTRATION ALBUM FOR SEPTEMBER

US: Tower PRO 4409 (vinyl album).
Promotional compilation includes 'See Emily Play' and 'The Scarecrow'.

1969

UNDERGROUND

US: Tower ST 5168 (vinyl album).
Compilation includes 'See Emily Play' and 'A Saucerful Of Secrets'.

1970

PICNIC - A BREATH OF FRESH AIR

UK: Harvest SHSS 1/2 (double vinyl album).
Compilation of Harvest Records repertoire includes the previously unreleased 'Embryo'. Also includes 'Terrapin' by Syd Barrett.

1970

LISTEN IN GOOD HEALTH - SONGS OF CELEBRATION AND DECAY

US: Capitol SPRO 5003 (vinyl album).
Promotional compilation subtitled, "A musical appraisal of man in harmony and conflict with his environment". Includes 'Several Species Of Small Fury Animals Gathered Together In A Cave And Grooving With A Pict'.

1970

THE NEW SPIRIT OF CAPITOL

US: Capitol SNP 6 (vinyl album).
Promotional sampler includes 'Astronomy Dominé' from *Ummagumma*.

1973

A VOICE TO REMEMBER

UK: EMI EMSP 75 (vinyl album box set).
Compilation subtitled 'The Sounds Of 75 Years On EMI Records 1898-1973' includes the 'On the Run' and a 64-page booklet on the history of EMI Records.

1973

KCBQ 1170

US: Capitol Records SPRO 6743 (vinyl album).
Promotional compilation for KCBQ FM radio includes 'Money'.

1973

KFRC

US: Capitol Records SPRO 6743 (vinyl album).
Promotional compilation for KFRC 610 AM radio includes 'Money'.

1973

93 KHJ

US: Capitol Records SPRO 6743 (vinyl album).
Promotional compilation for 93 KHJ AM radio includes 'Money'.

1973

KNDE

US: Capitol Records SPRO 6743 (vinyl album).
Promotional compilation for KNDE 147 AM radio includes 'Money'.

1973

A SAMPLER FOR SINGLES ONLY

US: Capitol Records SPRO 6744 (vinyl album).
Promotional compilation includes 'Money'.

1973

STAR BRITE

US: Capitol Records SPRO 104 (vinyl album).
Promotional compilation includes 'Money'.

1973

SONG & DANCE

US: Capitol Records SPRO 6849/6850 (double vinyl album).
Promotional compilation includes 'Us And Them'.

1974

SPECTRUM USA DIALOGUE '74

US: L-37/38 (vinyl album).
Promotional compilation for the Marine Corps Reserve includes 'Us And Them'.

1975

THE HEAVYWEIGHTS

US: Columbia A2S 174 (vinyl album).
Promotional compilation includes 'Have A Cigar'.

1975

QUADRAPHONIC GALA

US: Columbia Records ASQ 109 (vinyl album).
Compilation in SQ quadraphonic includes 'Money'.

1975

NEW QUADRAPHONIC GALA

US: Columbia Records ASQ 205 (vinyl album).
Compilation in SQ quadraphonic includes 'Have A Cigar'

1977

SUPERTRACKS

UK: Vertigo Sport 1 (vinyl album).
Compilation with proceeds to The Sports Aid Foundation includes 'Money'.

1978

A HARVEST SAMPLER

US: Harvest Records SPRO 8795 (vinyl album).
Promotional compilation includes 'Point Me At The Sky'.

1979

THE SUMMIT

UK: K-Tel NE1067 (vinyl album).
Compilation with proceeds to the Year Of The Child charity includes 'Welcome To The Machine'.

1980

HAVE A COKE AND A SMILE

US: Coca-Cola Records ARD 1952 (vinyl album).
Promotional compilation includes 'Another Brick In The Wall, Part 2'.

1980

HIT LINE '80!

US: Columbia A2S 890 (double vinyl album).
Promotional compilation includes 'Another Brick In The Wall, Part 2'.

1980

NICE PRICE

US: CBS Records AS 2129 (vinyl album).
Promotional in-store compilation includes 'Another Brick In The Wall, Part 2'.

1980

THE PITMAN SAMPLER

US: Columbia Records P 15663 (vinyl album).
Promotional compilation includes 'Another Brick In The Wall, Part 2'.

1983

MUSICLAND IN STORE SAMPLER

US: CBS Records AS 1656 (vinyl album).
Promotional in-store compilation for Musicland Record Stores includes 'The Final Cut'.

1985

FILMTRACKS

UK: Filmtracks Decca YEAR1 (double vinyl album).
Compilation includes 'Another Brick In The Wall, Part 2'.

1986

ROCK LEGENDS

UK: Telstar STAR 2290 (vinyl album).
Compilation includes 'Money'.

1989

THE MARQUEE - 30 LEGENDARY YEARS

UK: Polydor MQTV 1 (double vinyl album and CD).
Compilation celebrating 30 years of the infamous Marquee Club in London includes 'Another Brick In The Wall, Part 2' - a song they never performed at this venue.

1989

THE 80'S - THE ALBUM OF THE DECADE

UK: EMI EMTVD 48 (double vinyl album) / EMI EMTVCD 48 (double CD album).
Compilation includes 'Another Brick In The Wall, Part 2'.

1989

THE MOST BEAUTIFUL LOVE SONGS - PROGRESSIVE ROCK 1

US: Ace Music International AMI 500362 (CD album).
Compilation includes 'Wish You Were Here'.

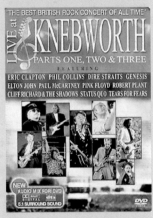

1989

GOLD AND PLATINUM: VOLUME 5
US: Realm Records 1P 7898 (vinyl album).
Compilation includes 'Learning To Fly'.

1990

ROCK 'N' ROLL - THE GREATEST YEARS - 1966
US: Strand Home Video 9549221533 (VHS NTSC video).
Compilation includes 'See Emily Play' taken from Belgian TV
in February 1968.

1990

ROCK GOES TO THE MOVIES
US: CBS Special Products AK46806 (CD album).
Compilation includes 'Crumbling Land', 'Heart Beat Pig Meat'
and 'Come In Number 51 Your Time Is Up' from the
Zabriskie Point soundtrack.

1990

KNEBWORTH - THE EVENT
UK: Polydor 843 921-1 (double vinyl album).
UK: Polydor 843 921-2 (double CD album).
US: Polydor 847 042-1 (double vinyl album).
US: Polydor 847 042-2 (double CD album).
Compilation of highlights of the concert held at Knebworth
on 30 June 1990 featuring 'Comfortably Numb' and 'Run
Like Hell'.

1990

KNEBWORTH - THE EVENT - PART 2
UK: Castle Music Pictures CMP 6008 (VHS PAL video).
US: Image Entertainment ID3474CA (VHS NTSC video).
US: Image Entertainment ID3950CDDVD (DVD NTSC
video).
Compilation of highlights of the concert held at Knebworth
on 30 June 1990 featuring 'Comfortably Numb' and 'Run
Like Hell'.
Reissued:
UK: Int. Licensing and Copyright Ltd EREDV273 (DVD PAL
video, 2002) as *Live At Knebworth Parts 1, 2 and 3*.
US: Eagle Eye Media EE19015 (DVD NTSC video, 2002) as
Live At Knebworth Parts 1, 2 and 3.

1990

**ROCK 'N' ROLL - THE GREATEST YEARS - 1967 -
VOLUME 2**
UK: Video Collection Int. Ltd. (VHS PAL video).
Compilation includes 'See Emily Play' taken from Belgian TV
in February 1968.

1990

ROCK 'N' ROLL - THE GREATEST YEARS - 1979
UK: Video Collection Int. Ltd. MC2091 (VHS PAL video).
Compilation includes the promotional video for 'Another
Brick In The Wall, Part 2'.

1991

FLASHBACK – ROCK CLASSICS OF THE 70'S
US: Realm Records 1P 8075 (vinyl album).
US: Realm Records 8075 (CD album).
Compilation includes 'Money'.

1991

GOLD & PLATINUM VOLUME 5
US: Realm Records ICD 7898 (CD album).
Compilation includes 'Money'.

1992

ROCK GOES TO THE MOVIES / IN DREAMS
US: Sony Music Special Products A22837 (CD album).
Promotional compilation includes 'Crumbling Land' and
'Come In Number 51 Your Time Is Up'.

1992

CENTURY 21'S GOLD DISC 3
US: Century 21 Programming Inc. (CD album).
Promotional compilation includes 'Money'.

1992

CAPITOL RECORDS 50TH ANNIVERSARY 1942-1992
US: Capitol DPRO 79387 (CD album).
Promotional compilation includes 'Money'.

1992

CAPITOL RECORDS 50TH ANNIVERSARY
US: Capitol DPRO 79244 (eight CD box set).
Promotional compilation includes 'Money'.

1992

ROCKIN' THE TOWER
US: Capitol DPRO 79247 (CD album).
Promotional compilation includes 'Money'.

1992

**THE CATALOG – CAPITOL RECORDS FIFTIETH
ANNIVERSARY 1942-1992**
US: Capitol DPRO 79387 (CD album).
Promotional compilation includes 'Money'.

1992

THE CLASSIC ROCK BOX
US: Polydor 3145159132 (CD album).
Promotional compilation for WNEW FM radio includes
'Comfortably Numb'.

1993

EMI – CAPITOL ENTERTAINMENT PROPERTIES
US: Capitol Records (CD album).
Promotional compilation includes 'Money'.

1993

THE RS500 SUPER AUDIO CD SAMPLER
US: Sony Records (CD album).
Promotional Super Audio CD sampler includes 'Money'.

1994

COLUMBIA RECORDS GRAMMY NOMINEES

US: Columbia CSK 5802 (CD album).
Promotional compilation includes 'Learning To Fly'.

1995

IN TUNE WITH THE WORLD

US: EMI TEM1 (CD album).
Promotional compilation includes 'Take It Back'.

1995

FLASHBACK! ROCK CLASSICS OF THE 70'S

US: Columbia (CD album).
Compilation includes 'Money'.

1997

THESE DREAMS – ROCK CLASSICS

US: Capitol 70876-12110-2-3 (CD album).
Promotional compilation includes 'Money'.

1997

NO MUSIC NO LIFE

US: Tower Records (CD album).
Promotional compilation for Tower Records customers includes 'Money'.

1999

HARVEST FESTIVAL

UK: EMI Harvest 724352119820 (five CD album box set).
Compilation box set celebrating the Harvest Records catalogue includes 'Money'.

1999

SONY MUSIC 100 YEARS: SOUNDTRACK FOR A CENTURY

US: Sony Music (26 CD album box set).
Compilation box set with hardback book that chronicles the history of Sony Music includes 'Learning To Fly'.

1999

TRAIN KEPT A ROLLIN'

US: Columbia J2K 65797 (double CD album).
Compilation includes 'Learning To Fly'.

1999

HEARTS OF GOLD – THE CLASSIC ROCK COLLECTION

US: Foundation Records 96647 (CD album).
Compilation includes 'Learning To Fly'.

2002

CAPITOL RECORDS 60TH ANNIVERSARY

US: Capitol (six CD album box set).
Promotional compilation box set includes 'Time'.

2005

THE BEST ALBUM TRACKS... EVER

UK: Virgin VTDCD714 (triple CD album).
Compilation includes 'Great Gig In The Sky'.

2005

JOHN PEEL – A TRIBUTE

UK: WSM WSMCD226 (double CD album).
Compilation includes 'Set The Controls For The Heart Of The Sun'.
Subtitled 'And This One Fades In Quietly...' is a collection of many of John Peel's favourite tracks, including those by his hero Lonnie Donegan, his favourite band The Fall and his all-time favourite song, 'Teenage Kicks' by The Undertones. A preceding single to promote the album, a cover of The Buzzcocks 'Ever Fallen In Love (With Someone You Shouldn't've)' features Gilmour among many other guest players.

2005

LIVE 8

UK: EMI ANGELDVD1 (quadruple DVD PAL set).
US: Capitol 09463419829 (quadruple DVD NTSC set).
Compilation covering the London *Live 8* concert held on 2 July 2005 includes 'Breathe', 'Wish You Were Here' and 'Comfortably Numb'. Also features a studio rehearsal session of 'Wish You Were Here'.

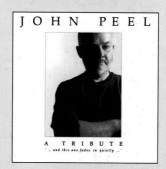

Thanks

For a work of this magnitude a huge debt of thanks is owed to a great many people who have generously provided contacts, personal recollections, and items of memorabilia, photos and research material, however large or small. Their assistance is gratefully acknowledged in my book *Pink Floyd: In The Flesh*, which forms the backbone of this volume, and my thanks are extended once again: Richard Allen, Nigel Applin, Lesley A. Ashby, Janice Bagwell, D. Bainborough, Rosemary Barbieri, John Baxter, Phil Beckett, Charles Beterams, Sandra J. Blickern, David Boderke, Tony Breen, Mrs. Jill Briggs, John Brisbrowne, Danny Burgess, Alastair Cameron, Rory Campbell, Mrs. E. Carmichael, Barry Christian, Mr. G. Cook, Ken Cook, Tony Crabtree, Tom Croson, Alan Cross, Eric Cuthbertson, John Delany, Chris Dennis, Mrs. Madeline Digby, Rupert Diggens, Steve Edwards, Jean-Manuel Esnault, Alan Felters, Evelyne Fenet, Vic Fledt, Ron Fleischer, M. Fletcher, Dave Ford, Lynn Gardiner, Will Garfit, Ron Geesin, Ian Gomeche, Elizabeth Gray, Peter R.F. Gunn, Peter Hearn, Malcolm Henderson, Kevin Hewick, Doug Hext, Doug Hinman, Christopher Hjort, Mr. J. Hopwood, Dave Howells, Trevor Jeffs, Chris Job, Matt Johns, Peter Johnson, Vic King, Peter Koks, Alain Lachaud, Richard Lawrence, John Lawson, Peter Levett, R.C. Lind, Alastair MacLean, John Mansfield, Dick Maunders, Steve Millard, Robert Morse, Gary Murphy, Keith Noble, Sheilagh Noble, Sara O'Brien, Yoshiko Ogiso, Rosina Osborn, David Parker, John Parkin, Mark Paytress, Kevin Peake, Lynda Pearce, John Phillips, John Phillpott, Darren Powter, Albert Prior, Noel Redding, Larry Reddington, John Revill, Mick Robshaw, Jon Rosenberg, Veronique Rothwell, Marc Skobac, Dave Scott, Ray Shepperd, Iain Smith, William Smythe, Henk Snoek, Mark Solomans, Fraser Speirs, Raymond Steeg, Ron Stewart, Ken Szymanek, A. Taylor, Caroline Taylor, Greg Taylor, Elliot Tayman, Stanford Thompson, Bruce Tippen, Peter Towner, John Tozer, Ivor Trueman, Chris Varney, Fred Vintner, Lindsay Wainwright, Ken Waterson, R.J. Webber, Clive Welham, Martin Wicker-Kempton, Brian Wilcock, Lindsay Williams, Tony Williams, Brain Wilson MP, Irene Winsby, A.L. Woodward and Jim Young. My sincere apologies are extended to anyone who has been inadvertently missed.

I would like to give thanks to those who have been especially helpful in providing valuable information and material for this particular book: Charles Beterams, Chris Job, Matt Johns, Chris Leith, Ed Paule, Danilo Steffanina, Phil Waters, Simon Wimpenny; Andy Neill who was also kind enough to proof read my manuscript but was also a source of constant support and advice in seeing this project to fruition; Jeff Walden at the BBC Written Archives Centre for his help and assistance in allowing me to use their facilities to research all of Pink Floyd's BBC TV and Radio sessions; Claude Mussou at the Institute National De Audiovisual, Paris, France for his assistance with the research of Pink Floyd's TV appearances in France and Sonita Cox and Jackie Bishop at the EMI Archives Trust for their assistance in helping me research some (but not all) of Pink Floyd's studio sessions.

Lastly, I would like to give a special mention to Laurence Bradbury at Bradbury and Williams who has made a terrific job of the design work and also to Steve Lam at ImageScanhouse for the reprographic work and arranging the print of the first edition.

Bibliography and Recommended Reading

The following publications may be of further interest to the reader and in some cases proved useful research tools for this book.

Crazy Diamond. Syd Barrett & The Dawn Of Pink Floyd
Mike Watkinson & Pete Anderson, Omnibus 1991.

The Dark Side Of The Moon. The Making Of The Pink Floyd Masterpiece
John Harris. 4th Estate, 2005

Inside Out – A Personal History of Pink Floyd
Nick Mason. Weidenfeld & Nicolson, 2004

Le Livre du Pink Floyd
Alain Dister, Jacques Leblanc, Udo Woehrle. Albin Michel/Rock & Folk, 1978

Lost In The Woods – Syd Barrett And The Early Pink Floyd
Julian Palacios. Boxtree, 1998.

The Pink Floyd Encyclopedia
Vernon Fitch. Collectors Guide Publishing, 2005

Pink Floyd: A Visual Documentary
Barry Miles. Omnibus Press, 1980

Random Precision – Recording The Music of Syd Barrett 1965-1974
David Parker. Cherry Red, 2001.

A Saucerful Of Secrets – The Pink Floyd Odyssey
Nicholas Schaffner. Harmony, 1991.

33 1/3 - The Piper At The Gates Of Dawn
David Cavanagh. Continuum, 2003.

Web Sites

There a great many Pink Floyd fan sites and chat rooms that could be listed here, but as a source of up to date news and features on the band and its former members I can thoroughly recommend the following web sites:

Brain Damage: www.brain-damage.co.uk

A Fleeting Glimpse: www.pinkfloydz.com

Pulse & Spirit: www.pulse-and-spirit.com

Updates

The author welcomes correspondence in connection with this book in order to present new information or corrections for future updated versions. Information on concert dates not listed here, first hand accounts, set lists, memorabilia and unpublished photographs are gratefully received.

Please write to:
Glenn Povey
Mind Head Publishing
PO Box 1224
Bovingdon
Herts HP1 9GJ
England

glenn@mindheadpublishing.co.uk
www.mindheadpublishing.co.uk